CANADIAN STATE TRIALS
VOLUME III

POLITICAL TRIALS AND SECURITY MEASURES,
1840–1914

PATRONS OF THE SOCIETY

Blake, Cassels & Graydon LLP

Gowlings

McCarthy Tétrault LLP

Osler, Hoskin & Harcourt LLP

Paliare Roland Rosenberg Rothstein LLP

Torkin Manes Cohen Arbus LLP

Torys LLP

WeirFoulds LLP

The Osgoode Society is supported by a grant from
The Law Foundation of Ontario.

The Law Foundation of Ontario
Building a better foundation for justice in Ontario

The Society also thanks The Law Society of Upper Canada
for its continuing support.

Canadian State Trials

VOLUME III

Political Trials and Security Measures, 1840–1914

Edited by
BARRY WRIGHT and SUSAN BINNIE

Published for The Osgoode Society for Canadian Legal History by
University of Toronto Press
Toronto Buffalo London

© Osgoode Society for Canadian Legal History 2009
www.utppublishing.com
www.osgoodesociety.ca
Printed in Canada

ISBN 978-1-4426-4015-3

Printed on acid-free, 100% post-consumer recycled paper
with vegetable-based inks.

Library and Archives Canada Cataloguing in Publication

Canadian state trials / edited by F. Murray Greenwood and Barry Wright.

Includes bibliographical references and index.
Contents: v. 1. Law, politics and security measures, 1608–1837 – v. 2. Rebellion
and invasion in the Canadas, 1837–1839 – v. 3. Political trials and security
measures, 1840–1914 / edited by Barry Wright and Susan Binnie.
ISBN-10: 0-8020-0913-1 (v. 1 : bound). – ISBN-10: 0-8020-7893-1 (v. 1 : pbk.). –
ISBN-10: 0-8020-3748-8 (v. 2 : bound). – ISBN-13: 978-1-4426-4015-3 (v. 3 : bound).

1. Political crimes and offenses – Canada – History.   I. Greenwood, F. Murray
(Frank Murray), 1935–   II. Wright, Barry, 1957–   III. Binnie, Susan W.S. (Susan
Wendy Strickland), 1941–   IV. Osgoode Society for Canadian Legal History

KE226.P6C351996   345.71′009   C969-311354

This book has been published with the help of a grant from the Canadian
Federation for the Humanities and Social Sciences, through the Aid to Scholarly
Publications Program, using funds provided by the Social Sciences and
Humanities Research Council of Canada.

University of Toronto Press acknowledges the financial assistance to its
publishing program of the Canada Council for the Arts and the
Ontario Arts Council.

University of Toronto Press acknowledges the financial support for its
publishing activities of the Government of Canada through the
Book Publishing Industry Development Program (BPIDP).

Contents

Contents vii

Foreword

THE OSGOODE SOCIETY
FOR CANADIAN LEGAL HISTORY

The Osgoode Society has published two previous volumes of its *Canadian State Trials* series, and this third volume takes the topic forward in time, starting in the 1840s and going to the First World War. It examines a range of political trials as traditionally defined, including those arising from the Fenian invasions of the 1860s and the later North-West rebellions. The volume also expands the definition of state trials to include studies on the early development of secret policing and the evolution of the legal regulation of riot and public order. We are very grateful to the editors, who have assembled a team of experts from across the country in a variety of fields and produced a comprehensive and fascinating set of studies of the use of law to control political dissent and public disorder.

The purpose of the Osgoode Society for Canadian Legal History is to encourage research and writing in the history of Canadian law. The Society, which was incorporated in 1979 and is registered as a charity, was founded at the initiative of the Honourable R. Roy McMurtry, formerly attorney general for Ontario and chief justice of the province, and officials of the Law Society of Upper Canada. The Society seeks to stimulate the study of legal history in Canada by supporting researchers, collecting oral histories, and publishing volumes that contribute to legal-historical scholarship in Canada. It has published seventy-eight books on the courts, the judiciary, and the legal profession, as well as on the history of crime and punishment, women and law, law and economy, the legal treatment of ethnic minorities, and famous cases and significant trials in all areas of the law.

Current directors of the Osgoode Society for Canadian Legal History are Robert Armstrong, Christopher Bentley, Kenneth Binks, Patrick Brode, Brian Bucknall, David Chernos, Kirby Chown, J. Douglas Ewart, Martin Friedland, John Honsberger, Horace Krever, C. Ian Kyer, Virginia MacLean, Patricia McMahon, Roy McMurtry, W.A. Derry Millar, Jim Phillips, Paul Reinhardt, Joel Richler, William Ross, Paul Schabas, Robert Sharpe, James Spence, Richard Tinsley, and Michael Tulloch.

The annual report and information about membership may be obtained by writing to the Osgoode Society for Canadian Legal History, Osgoode Hall, 130 Queen Street West, Toronto, Ontario, M5H 2N6. Telephone: 416-947-3321. E-mail: mmacfarl@lsuc.on.ca. Website: www.osgoodesociety.ca.

R. Roy McMurtry
President

Jim Phillips
Editor-in-Chief

Acknowledgments

This book is the third in the *Canadian State Trials* series. It follows the late Murray Greenwood's vision of a comprehensive and contextualized study of the historical record of political trials and state-security measures in British North America and Canada, inspired in part by the Cobbett-Howells series of *English State Trials*. Barry Wright, after working with Murray Greenwood on the first and second volumes in the series, sought to continue the project and was joined by Susan Binnie as co-editor in 2004. As editors, we are pleased that our collaborative working partnership, reflecting an equitable effort, has led to this volume covering the period 1840–1914.

An important task as we confronted this period was to view changes in security laws and measures in relation to political developments that included responsible government, increasing self-government, the emergence of the Dominion of Canada, and the accelerated colonization of the North-West. Institutional and technological developments as well as social, cultural, and economic change associated with industrialization also had a significant impact. It was a tumultuous era in Canadian history. Security measures, used in the face of real and perceived threats, showed continuity in reliance on legal responses rooted in an earlier era but also demonstrated significant transformations. The shifts in approaches to security matters proved intriguing and posed interesting analytical challenges for the editors and the contributors.

This volume reflects a truly collaborative undertaking on a broader front, and the editors wish to recognize the scholarship, patience, and hard work of the authors to whom we remain deeply indebted. We are especially appreciative of their efforts as we refined underlying themes and issues. Through their contributions in this and other ways they have helped to shape the volume into a whole beyond the sum of its individual parts.

The project has received continuing enthusiastic support from the Osgoode Society for Canadian Legal History, first under the late editor-in-chief, Peter Oliver, who saw it take form. His worthy successor, Jim Phillips, has offered unflagging support together with insightful comments and sound advice on an early version of this manuscript. Marilyn MacFarlane has continued in her role as a highly effective coordinator and reassuring administrative adviser. The field of Canadian legal history is fortunate to be the beneficiary of such a dedicated organization.

The anonymous readers for the Osgoode Society, the University of Toronto Press, and the Humanities and Social Sciences Federation of Canada produced detailed assessments that demonstrated a thorough grasp of the field and of key issues. We are grateful for their constructive comments which have undoubtedly strengthened the manuscript. Len Husband again coordinated the project for the University of Toronto Press, and we wish to express our gratitude to him and to Wayne Herrington and the entire production team. We were delighted when Curtis Fahey agreed to copy edit this volume, notwithstanding his encounters with the scholarly and stylistic anarchy of previous volume manuscripts in the series, and his editorial expertise and good judgment resulted in numerous improvements to the final text. Michael Bunn's expertise in producing an index in short order again provides easy access to the content of the volume. The volume has been published with the help of a grant from the Canadian Federation for the Humanities and Social Sciences, through the Aid to Scholarly Publications Program, using funds provided by the Social Sciences and Humanities Research Council of Canada.

Finally, Barry Wright would like to acknowledge the collegiality and intellectual engagement experienced during visits to the School of Law, University of Queensland, as well as the unqualified support and unending patience of his family, Meredith, Edward, and William, as this volume took shape. Susan Binnie wishes to thank the members of her immediate family for their continuing support but considers that naming them all might be excessive.

Contributors

Bob Beal is an independent historian who specializes in law, First Nations, and western Canada. He is co-author, with Rod Macleod, of *Prairie Fire: The 1885 North-West Rebellion*. He is currently working on a study of legal and constitutional developments in western Canada and the history of North American Indian treaties.

Susan Binnie was the research coordinator for the Law Society of Upper Canada Archives, has taught legal history at York University and the University of Ottawa, and is editor with Louis Knafla of *Law, Society and the State: Essays in Modern Legal History*.

Desmond H. Brown, adjunct professor of history, University of Alberta, is author of several articles on treason and sedition in Canada, *The Genesis of the Canadian Criminal Code of 1892*, and *The Birth of a Criminal Code*.

R. Blake Brown is assistant professor of history at St Mary's University and author of *A Trying Question: The Jury in Nineteenth-Century Canada*.

J.M. Bumsted, FRSC, is recently retired from the University of Manitoba and is author of numerous books including *Louis Riel v. Canada: The Making of a Rebel*.

Judi Cumming served at Library and Archives Canada as chief of the

Social and Cultural Archives, the Public Archives Service, and the Standards Office of the Manuscript Division. She has published in *Archivaria* and *The Archivist* and contributed to *Framing Our Past: Canadian Women's History in the Twentieth Century.*

Donald Fyson is professor, Département d'histoire, Université Laval, co-director of the Centre interuniversitaire d'études québécoises, and author of *Magistrates, Police, and People: Everyday Criminal Justice in Quebec and Lower Canada, 1764–1837.*

Gregory S. Kealey, FRSC, FRHistS, is provost and vice-president research at the University of New Brunswick.

Louis A. Knafla is emeritus professor of history and director of Socio-Legal Studies, University of Calgary. Recent publications are on lawyers and the Alberta legal profession (*Just Works*) and the early history of the Alberta Supreme Court (*The Alberta Supreme Court at 100*). He is currently editing a work entitled 'Native Title in Australia, Canada and New Zealand.'

Gilles Lesage is executive director of the Société historique de Saint-Boniface which manages the Centre du patrimoine, the archives documenting the francophone and Métis communities of Manitoba.

Kirk Niergarth teaches in the Canadian Studies Department at Trent University.

Andrew Parnaby is associate professor in the Department of History at the University of Cape Breton.

Ian Ross Robertson, professor emeritus of history, University of Toronto at Scarborough, is author of *The Tenant League of Prince Edward Island, 1864–1867: Leasehold Tenure in the New World* and *Sir Andrew Macphail: The Life and Legacy of a Canadian Man of Letters.*

Eric Tucker, professor, Osgoode Hall Law School, York University, is author of *Administering Danger in the Workplace* and co-author of *Labour before the Law* and *Self-Employed Workers Organize.*

Bill Waiser, SOM, FRSC, professor, Department of History, University of

Saskatchewan, is the author of twelve books, including (with Blair Stone-child) *Loyal till Death: Indians and the North-West Rebellion*, which was a finalist for the 1997 governor general's literary prize in non-fiction.

David A. Wilson is professor of history and Celtic studies at the University of Toronto and a fellow of the Royal Historical Society. He has written and edited nine books on Irish, American, and Canadian history, including *Thomas D'Arcy McGee: Volume 1 – Passion, Reason, and Politics, 1825–1857*.

Barry Wright is professor of law and criminology at Carleton University and co-edited the previous volumes of this series.

Abbreviations

AM	Archives of Manitoba
AO	Archives of Ontario
BAnQ	Bibliothèque et Archives nationales du Québec
BL	British Library
CHR	*Canadian Historical Review*
CIHM	Canadian Institute for Historical Microreproductions (see also Early Canadiana Online at Canadiana.org)
CO	Colonial Office
CSP	Canada, *Sessional Papers*
CSPC	Consolidated Statutes of the Province of Canada
CST 1, 2	F. Murray Greenwood and Barry Wright eds., *Canadian State Trials, Volume I: Law, Politics, and Security Measures, 1609–1837* (Toronto: Osgoode Society for Canadian Legal History / University of Toronto Press 1996); *Canadian State Trials Volume II: Rebellion and Invasion in the Canadas, 1837–1839* (Toronto: Osgoode Society for Canadian Legal History / University of Toronto Press 2002)
DCB	*Dictionary of Canadian Biography* (online at www.biographi.ca)
DNB	*Dictionary of National Biography*
GA	Glenbow Archives
HBCA	Hudson's Bay Company Archives
JLAPC	*Journals of the Legislative Assembly of the Province of Canada*

LAC	Library and Archives Canada (formerly NAC – National Archives of Canada)
NA	[United States] National Archives
NAI	National Archives of Ireland
NAUK	National Archives of the United Kingdom (formerly PRO – Public Record Office)
PAA	Provincial Archives of Alberta
PANS	Public Archives of Nova Scotia
PARO	Public Archives and Record Office of Prince Edward Island
RSC	Revised Statutes of Canada
SAB	Saskatchewan Archives Board
SC	Statutes of Canada
SCCP	[PEI] Supreme Court Papers
SO	Statutes of Ontario
SPC	Statutes of the Province of Canada
SPEI	Statutes of Prince Edward Island
SUC	Statutes of Upper Canada
UCR	*Upper Canada Reports*

CANADIAN STATE TRIALS
VOLUME III

POLITICAL TRIALS AND SECURITY MEASURES,
1840–1914

Introduction:
From State Trials to National-
Security Measures

SUSAN BINNIE and BARRY WRIGHT

This third volume in the *Canadian State Trials* series examines the legal regulation of security threats in Canada[1] from the mid-nineteenth to the early twentieth century. It follows chronologically from the two predecessor volumes: the first in the series, *Law, Politics, and Security Measures, 1608–1837*, surveyed trials for political offences and related proceedings in New France and British North America, while the second, *Rebellion and Invasion in the Canadas, 1837–1839*, focused on legal responses to the rebellions in Upper and Lower Canada. This volume is directed to a subsequent but equally tumultuous period of Canadian history, a time when governments confronted external invasions, internal rebellions, and new forms of collective disorder. This was the period during which Canada was transformed politically from a number of dependent British North American colonies into a self-governing Dominion. Confederation and geographical growth meant new responsibilities for territorial integrity and external and internal security. Subsequent developments and economic transformation contributed to new political challenges and concerns and the emergence of new approaches to what became understood as 'national security.'

The volume includes the traditional content of 'state trials' in the form of trials for treason and related political offences, but it ventures onto new ground by taking into account legal and related institutional developments associated with the creation of a modern post-colonial federal state. The restructured and more liberal political order that emerged in the wake of the Canadian rebellions, and expanded at the time of confederation, was by no means monolithic. The nature and functions of the state were affected by the shift in status from a colonial to federal system as well as by modernizing factors. There were new divisions of responsibility between the Dominion, provincial governments, and Westminster, and although the federal state became the dominant political actor in relation to security issues, it could not act in isolation. It was also a fledging state, a fragile union that required further cementing in the view of anxious federal governments. Continuing external and internal security threats and sectarian conflict, growing rural and urban tensions, and a developing labour movement presented formidable challenges. Older political offences were supplemented by pre-emptive and less visible security measures, supported by new police and security-intelligence institutions. These changes require us to revisit and expand the definitions of terms we employed in previous volumes.

DEFINITION OF TERMS AND HISTORIOGRAPHICAL CONSIDERATIONS

In its overall approach, the current volume follows the general model of its predecessors. The objective of the series is to provide a comprehensive examination of the Canadian historical record of trials for offences that were thought to threaten the safety of the state, as well as other legal responses to perceived threats to the internal or external security of the state. Studies of political trials and related measures raise difficult questions with respect to scope and the proposed range and reach of topics, as well as criteria for inclusion of cases, questions that are further complicated by changing official views of security threats and new legal responses.

The introduction to Volume I surveyed the English state trials collections, reports of political trials that appeared after the conflicts and the return to stability in seventeenth-century England. The genre was epitomised by Howells' series, initiated by William Cobbett and edited by Thomas Howell and his son from 1809 to 1826.[2] The English state trials series were so-named because they examined *public* criminal prosecutions by the crown, usually for offences such as treason and sedition, in an era when most criminal offences were privately prosecuted. Howells' and many other series were informed by eighteenth- and early-nineteenth-century libertarian Whig understandings of the implications of the constitutional compromises of the late seventeenth century. These included the impact of the 'Glorious Revolution' of 1689 and the 1701 Act of Settlement on the balance between parliamentary supremacy, crown prerogative, and judicial powers, and related matters such as the right to face all criminal charges in public trials before a jury, no prior restraint on the independent press, and protection of judicial independence by having office held according to good behaviour determined by Parliament rather than royal pleasure. The Habeas Corpus Act, 1679 was understood to prohibit indefinite detention (beyond the common law writ), and the Treason Act, 1696 introduced the right to defence counsel and other procedural protections. The study of such state prosecutions, and the struggles against them, were seen to illuminate the extent of political and legal rights in the British constitution.

The claims associated with the British constitution resonated in British colonial settings, especially during conflicts with local administrations in the period before the development of responsible government. Despite the diversities within colonial British North America, a common theme in previous volumes of this series was the manner in which the actions of executively dominated colonial governments, and in particular partisan resort to the criminal law to fend off challenges to the authority of local elites, evoked references to the British constitution and to the rule of law. The courts were a key pre-confederation political battleground in the struggles for more accountable and representative government. The rich record of treason and sedition trials and related legal processes examined in the first two volumes suggests that these cases represented more than exceptional suspensions of legal conventions under the extreme conditions of security crises. The cases, particularly those successfully defended, reflected the scope of liberties to be enjoyed by all British subjects and demonstrated the pressures on colonial states to conform to formal constitutional and legal claims.

The sheer number of such proceedings in British North America examined in previous volumes defies their easy dismissal as exceptional cases. But, on the other hand, a critical reductionism that presents such cases as straightforward illustrations of legal manipulation by political elites fails to engage with the complexity of our subject. Colonial governments and the groups that dominated them had too little solidarity, local support, and autonomy from the imperial centre to use the law in this fashion. Perhaps more important, the law itself could not be blatantly manipulated. As E.P. Thompson argued, in order for the law to legitimize the exercise of authority effectively, governments must take into account popular expectations about justice and formal claims concerning the rule of law. Law that obviously fails to conform or confounds deeply held public expectations has little credibility and diminishes or undermines the legitimacy of governments that seek to use it.[3] We have seen in previous volumes, and there are further examples in this one, that the constraint produced by such expectations, the effective 'check' of engaged public opinion, limited the law's repressive potential. We have seen, as well, that successful defences were more than symbolic gestures of law's impartiality. Prosecutorial failures clearly embarrassed and frustrated colonial governments.

Prosecutions for treason and sedition were the usual means of controlling civilian activities considered threats to state security in eighteenth- and early-nineteenth-century Britain and British North America. The development of both offences from the period examined in the first two volumes of *Canadian State Trials* is examined at length by Desmond H. Brown and Barry Wright in the final chapter of this volume and discussed briefly below in relation to applications of these laws as described in other chapters. There were other measures available. One was the suspension of habeas corpus to counter perceived threats by way of emergency legislation that temporarily overrode the 1679 act and authorized indefinite detention of suspected persons. As we have seen in previous volumes, this expedient was resorted to in Quebec at the end of the eighteenth century and in Upper Canada in 1814 and 1838,[4] while in this volume David Wilson's chapter examines use of the same practice in response to the Fenian crisis. Another measure was military intervention, by way of martial law and the court martial of civilians, an expedient used in serious crises when governments lacked confidence in the regular administration of justice or were unable to enact legislative expedients. This response is also examined at length in Volume I of *Canadian State Trials*, and in our second volume we see how British intervention in Ireland following the 1798 rebellion informed responses to the 1837–8 Canadian rebellions.[5]

As noted in the second volume of *Canadian State Trials*, the broad choice between expedient military interventions and more credible but unwieldy regular trials preoccupied governments during the Canadian crisis of 1837–9, when over 350 persons were tried for treason and related capital offences in regular trials and courts martial. In Upper Canada, regular trial proceedings continued well past the end of the rebellion, reflecting a compliant legislature and confidence in local juries, until the autumn of 1838, when raids from the U.S. frontier were seen to justify the partial suspension of civil authority. The crisis was more intense in Lower Canada, where martial law, the replacement of the legislature by a Special Council, and the suspension of habeas corpus followed the 1837 rebellion, and the trial of civilians by court martial came after the 1838 outbreak. While there is no displacement of regular justice on a comparable scale in the period examined in this volume, the Irish experience was an important context for the Fenian movement and there are numerous references here to militia interventions and the resort to military aid to the civil power in response to Fenian raids, insurrection in the North-West Territories (present-day Manitoba, Saskatchewan, and Alberta), and collective disorders.[6]

The experience of the 1837–8 rebellions also helped to precipitate the transformation of the colonial state.[7] The crisis not only opened the way for political change in the form of the union of Upper and Lower Canada and the development of responsible government, but it also led to wider institutional and cultural changes, as noted by historians such as Phillip Buckner, Allan Greer, Ian Radforth, Brian Young, and Bruce Curtis.[8] The more liberal and accountable order that emerged saw the development of new means of managing sources of potential disorder and political, economic, and social conflict. Refined executive powers and legal strategies reached more deeply into society, supported by new institutions that, over time, resulted in a more fully policed social order. There was a concurrent reduction in colonial expedients such as irregularities in the administration of justice typical of former administrations. These changes, combined with increased popular engagement with, and participation in, public affairs, and widening availability of effective defence counsel, made heavy-handed prosecutions for treason and sedition risky for governments, except in response to extreme crises.

As we see in the period covered in this volume, while treason and related offences continued to be resorted to (notably as responses to the 1866 Fenian invasions and the 1885 North-West rebellion), more refined security measures and means of enforcement were developed. These enabled the new federal state not only to better manage perceived security threats, as supposed sources of disorder were more readily identified, but to take pre-emptive action against them. Special security operations, consisting of a security branch and secret political policing, were developed in significant part to monitor unlawful activity and collect and assess intelligence about potential security threats. The overall effect was to reduce reliance on the prosecution of the classic political offences in the courts. At the same time, the development of professional policing facilitated the wider enforcement of unlawful assembly and riot laws and supported new measures to address collective unrest where it occurred, such as in relation to political meetings, public riots, sectarian violence, or strikes organized by emerging labour organizations. Although a considerable proportion of collective disorders constituted forms of protest, as demonstrated in the chapters that examine rioting against an unjust system of land ownership or in support of pay demands of working men,[9] this did not necessarily evoke security responses. However, from the mid-nineteenth century, disorders became increasingly unacceptable to governments and their most influential supporters.

Economic change fuelled concerns about collective disorder. Population increase, territorial expansion, industrial growth, and technological change were continuing features of the period and led to extraordinary social and economic transformations. Daily life altered fundamentally and many residents of the four founding colonies born before 1840 must have been astounded by their first experiences of train transportation or electrical and mechanical power or, more generally, by their encounters with urban growth, manufacturing, and new public institutions. These developments contributed to a new emphasis on public order, an emphasis supported by a growing middle class which placed an increasing value on order and civility. Disorder in general became viewed as a threat to middle-class goals and a direct threat to the developing economic order. Restoration of order to serve middle-class aspirations and the developing economy was increasingly seen as a state responsibility and governments assumed wider responsibilities for social conditions, especially in urban settings, and for economic progress.

Other developments in security measures were associated with confederation and the assumption of new responsibilities for external security, assertion of sovereignty over the North-West, and the coordination of internal security among the provinces. Both national defence and criminal law powers were allocated to the new federal government and its legislative authority under the British North America Act, 1867[10] (hereafter BNA Act), and the increased level of self-government accorded the Dominion meant more autonomy from the United Kingdom and increased responsibility for security issues.

Ottawa's exercise of its new responsibility for Native affairs and emerging economic-development priorities in the west clashed with Native and Métis traditions and interests and gave rise to unrest and new security concerns, as examined in Part Three of this volume. Louis Riel led resistance against annexation of the Red River area by Canada, which had purchased the North-West from the Hudson's Bay Company. Suppression of the rebellion in 1870 and Riel's exile did not resolve matters and, from the mid-1870s, disaffection intensified, boiling over into wider rebellion in 1885. This was met by treason prosecutions which included legal innovations introduced by the British government in 1848 in response to perceived revolutionary threats and renewed insurrection in Ireland.

As a result of such developments, our criteria for the parameters of the State Trials series require some expansion. The term 'state trials' is important in terms of the provenance of this series but there are limitations in its use as a means of describing the administration of security laws after the mid-nineteenth century. Trials that traditionally come under this rubric remain at the centre of our inquiry but cease to be the singular focus. Quite apart from the shift during this time to public prosecutorial authority, the traditional definition of a 'state trial' as confined to offences against the state, principally treason and sedition, is too narrow, even in the broader conception offered in the Howells' series (which included politically inspired riot and murder, parliamentary privilege proceedings, suspension of habeas corpus, and the resort to court-martial proceedings against civilians). A definition of 'state trials' for the later nineteenth century necessarily encompasses a wider range of legal responses and a more expansive view of the state and its repertoire of interventions for real, officially perceived, and potential threats to internal or external security. It stops well short, however, of attempting to confront all the complex interactions of law and politics.[11]

Such a definition admittedly remains imprecise. As we move in this volume to later nineteenth-century trials for political offences and examine a wider range of legal responses to actual and apprehended threats, we enter a territory that might be termed, in Bishop Berkeley's words, a 'slippery slope' of security threats. Terms such as 'state security' or 'national security' do not have clear and evident meanings. In a recent review of national-security concepts in Canadian law, Craig Forcese has noted that at least thirty-three current federal statutes use the term 'national security' (or equivalent phrases such as 'the security of the Canadian state'). But the term is rarely defined and 'lacks a precise meaning even in the public policy literature.' As Lorne Sossin similarly notes, the problem with these expressions 'is not their indeterminacy *per se* ... but, rather that their meaning may change with the political currents of the day.'[12] From a legal-historical perspective, shifting notions of 'state security' appear to be an inescapable fact of historical life. The identification of what constitutes a threat, or is perceived to constitute a threat to the security of the state, is situation-specific and changes over time with the political context. A series such as this reflects such complexities and our approach is thus more dependent on time period and historical setting than on fixed definition or editorial perspective.

The volume, then, takes up the challenge of examining the continued application of the laws and the legal proceedings that were the focus of our previous volumes (and of the English state trials series) and explores new security-related legal developments. This challenge also requires us to situate the project within modern scholarly contexts that have influenced the study of our subject matter.[13] While two series of English state trials and supplementary materials covering the period 1163–1858 have recently become available in electronic format, the study of such proceedings fell out of academic fashion for much of the twentieth century, influenced in part by shifts in scholarly disciplines: in political science, from 'historical institutionalism' to empirical studies of political behaviour; in historical scholarship, from political history to social and cultural histories; and, in legal scholarship, a narrowing professionalized focus on technical doctrine and vocation training.[14] Otto Kirchheimer's comparative work on modern political trials and national-security measures represents one of several exceptions to the main trend.[15] Relatively recent developments in historical and legal scholarship, and new concerns about legal and political responses to terrorism, have renewed interest and scholarly debate in our area.[16]

These definitional and historiographical considerations do not imply a fundamental change in orientation from earlier volumes in the *Canadian State Trials* series but rather a broadening of focus to account for the new complexities that emerged in the period. All of the chapters in this collection, as in the previous two volumes, can be said to focus on legal responses to 'incidents where governments perceive, or profess to perceive, fundamental threats to the state's internal or external security.' But the security issues that concerned authorities changed over time, some assuming forms in the nineteenth century that have a clear continuity and resonance in relation to issues current in the twenty-first century. In sum, the suggestion in Volume I that later volumes in this series would need to include issues falling 'outside the traditional concept of state trials' and situations that lie 'beyond the confines of the trial of security offences in the criminal courts' is a useful one that has been taken up and applied in this volume.

COLONIAL LEGACIES AND NEW CHALLENGES: SECURITY THEMES AND THE LAW, 1840–1914

There were numerous officially perceived threats to security in Canada during the 1840–1914 period. Issues relating to territorial integrity, at the forefront of government concerns during the War of 1812 and the Patriot raids of 1838, came to predominate again in the 1860s with the Fenian[17] invasions from the United States. These continued with the unification of the four former colonies and the expansion of Canada across the continent between 1867 and 1873 as the Dominion assumed increased responsibilities for the frontier with the United States and for its own North-West. New internal security concerns developed as the federal government attempted to assert sovereignty and its development priorities in the west, and conflict was fuelled by Ottawa's failure to respond to Métis, First Nations, and white settler grievances. Economic change, notably industrialization and urbanization, also led to conflicts and collective disturbances, which likewise evoked security concerns.

.The powers of the new federal government were considerable in relation to security matters and included control over substantive criminal law and criminal procedure under the BNA Act. During the confederation debates, John A. Macdonald, soon to be the first federal justice minister as well as prime minister, drew a direct connection between defence and criminal law powers, arguing that the coordination of both under proposed federal jurisdiction was essential to the Dominion's security and stability. Macdonald urged avoidance of the U.S. federal model which he, and many others, believed had contributed to the then-raging U.S. civil war by creating a decentralized federation with state rights over matters such as criminal law.[18] There was broad support for Macdonald's position on criminal law jurisdiction. No opposition is recorded in the records of the confederation debates and it is one of the few matters that remained unchanged in successive constitutional drafts.[19] However, this support involved more than avoiding replication of the perceived dysfunctional U.S. federation.

Experience in Canada during the previous fifty years included two major security crises (the War of 1812 and the 1838 Patriot raids), both of which involved invasions from the United States that sought to exploit internal disaffection and foment insurrection. The American Patriot raids in the aftermath of the Canadian rebellions had been a formative experience for Macdonald as a young defence counsel, and, as we see in this volume, he later orchestrated the Fenian prosecutions in the 1860s as attorney general for Canada West. After 1867, he moved quickly to assert the new federal government's jurisdiction over criminal law. It is thus not surprising that Ottawa, supported by the BNA Act, acquired wide powers around national security beyond jurisdiction over defence. This contrasts with the United States, where treason narrowly defined was the only federal criminal offence authorized originally under its constitution, and with the later Australian federal constitution, where national-security laws had to be developed under incidental powers. While federal powers over criminal law under section 91 overlapped somewhat with provincial jurisdiction over the administration of justice under section 92, the federal government was responsible for senior judicial appointments and the new federal Department of Justice monitored provincial application of the law, directly supervised territorial jurisdictions, and directly handled matters related to national security.[20] Residual powers, including those related to emergencies, came under Ottawa's jurisdiction over 'peace, order and good government.' The federal powers over these matters in addition to defence supported a coordinated approach to national-security laws and their administration.

The ongoing anxieties about external security, highlighted by the Fenian border raids during the confederation period, were soon overlaid by new security concerns in the North-West, beginning with the 1870 rebellion. The Dominion government became preoccupied with asserting sovereignty over, and developing, the vast North-West Territories, as the influence of the Hudson Bay Company declined, European settlement and American incursions increased, and the British government's obligations to indigenous groups were passed on to Ottawa.[21] Dealing with insurgency in the west was not a simple matter, as signalled by the difficulties in responding to the rebellion of 1870 and the eventual decision to prosecute Ambroise Lépine for the murder of Thomas Scott in 1874.[22] Ottawa's initiatives operated at a number of levels. A national economic policy (the 'National Policy' proposed in 1872 and adopted in the form of raised tariffs in 1879) was intended to create a Canadian market, cement an alliance between government and business, encourage western settlement, and protect Canadian farmers. Institutions such as the North-West Mounted Police and the Department of Indian Affairs were designed to better assert the rule of law on the frontier and to manage the conflicts arising out of attempts to promote a more compliant citizenry. Should crisis erupt again, as it did in 1885, Ottawa's military and national-security-related criminal law powers could be rapidly deployed.

At the same time, economic development, marked by industrialization, increasing urbanization, and public-works initiatives, gave rise to frequent outbreaks of collective disorder and these, added to more traditional sources of disturbances including sectarian or ethnic rivalries, created security concerns. Certain periods were characterized by distinct increases in the levels of disorder. This was true for urban areas such as Montreal and Toronto in the 1870s, a period of economic downturn and unemployment. Local policing became the normal resort in instances of disorder, and the expansion of municipal police forces and their professionalization made this more feasible. But disorder remained an endemic problem in many parts of Canada, and rural areas were not immune to sectarian violence or other patterns of conflict. Many disturbances were viewed as outstripping local police resources. In these instances, the only major alternative open to local authorities was to call on the armed militia. This nation-wide system of volunteers had been developed to respond to security threats, primarily in anticipation of invasion or insurrection.[23] However, deployment of militia became a regular response to threats of large-scale disturbances, including organized strikes.

Although the Dominion of Canada emerged as a largely self-governing state that, as set out in the preamble to the BNA Act, acquired all the relevant modern provisions of the British constitution, there were still colonial remnants in the administration of justice. While federally appointed judges held security of tenure (according to good behaviour determined by Parliament rather than royal pleasure), and responsible cabinet government promoted the separation of powers, concerns about judicial independence, an endemic problem in earlier colonial jurisdictions, were not fully laid to rest. Judges were active in many of the political controversies of the period. For example, as Brown and Wright note in the final chapter, Judge James Gowan played an active role in the consolidation of Dominion criminal law and its eventual codification.[24] Federally appointed territorial magistrates continued to hold office according to royal pleasure. As the chapter by Bob Beal and Barry Wright suggests, questions about independence loom large over Hugh Richardson's conduct of the 1885 rebellion trials.[25] Also, the crown's widely exercised prerogative powers over prosecutions continued, as colonial practices were confirmed with the creation of the Department of Justice and the passage of the Criminal Code of 1892.[26] In particular, for residents of the North-West Territories and the First Nations, London's imperial role had been transferred to Ottawa.[27] Obvious remnants of colonial administration of justice were preserved in the special procedures set out for the territories. Cases proceeded on informations rather than indictments, a crown prerogative widely resorted to in colonial settings that circumvented public pre-trial review, such as grand jury proceedings, and were heard by six rather than twelve trial jurors and magistrates who held office according to royal pleasure.[28] As we see in this volume, this abbreviated form of frontier justice had an enormous impact on the outcomes of trials held in the wake of the 1885 North-West rebellion.

Volume I of this series outlined the basic English legal doctrines of treason, sedition, and habeas corpus along with the complex issues of the colonial reception of English laws and their local adaptations and administration. Volume II described the elaboration of these laws by way of emergency legislation and executive orders during the 1837–8 crisis and the balance struck between legal and military responses. In this volume, the final chapter, focusing on the 1892 Canadian Criminal Code, examines in detail the background and the modernization of these doctrines as well as new ones introduced in the nineteenth century. The main legal developments will therefore be summarized only briefly here.

The most serious offence in Canadian law was still high treason, based on the 1352 Statute of Treasons,[29] recalling the repressive Tudor and Stuart state trials and the horrific traditional punishment in which the condemned suffered several symbolic deaths. One of the three main categories of high treason under the 1352 statute was levying war (armed insurrection), which was applied to Louis Riel in 1885 and threatened against his leading associates. The Treason Act, 1696,[30] part of the late-seventeenth-century constitutional compromises noted earlier, introduced important procedural protections for the accused. These included the right to defence counsel (not available in English felony cases until 1836), advanced notice of details of the indictment and jury panel, and the requirement that the government provide two witnesses for each treason alleged. The 1696 act deterred wide application of treason law, although the restrictions could be circumvented by judicial constructions and temporary emergency legislation.[31] Britain's Treason Act, 1795 broadened treason law to deal with activities and advocacy associated with French revolutionary and Napoleonic intrigues.[32] It was renewed several times and eventually replaced by the Treason-Felony Act, 1848,[33] a permanent non-capital version of treason that included constructions aimed to overcome the reluctance of juries to convict for high treason. Neither the Treason Act, 1795 nor the Treason-Felony Act, 1848 applied in the British North American colonies, but the latter was adopted by the Dominion of Canada in 1868, and its applications in 1885 are examined in the chapters by Bob Beal and Barry Wright and Bill Waiser.[34] However, the 1696 act did not did not apply in the North-West Territories, depriving the accused of significant procedural protections when prosecuted for offences under the 1352 act, a significant exception as explained in the chapters by Beal and Wright and J.M. Bumsted.[35]

The British reforms to treason law from the late eighteenth century reflected attempts to renew the offence to account for changes in the nature of the state and the doctrine of allegiance. John Barrell brilliantly deconstructs the contradictions around attempts to apply pre-modern law to modern republican political movements in the context of George III's madness and the French Revolution, requiring a conceptual shift from actions that aimed to kill the sovereign to a figurative imagining of the king's death.[36] Allegiance had previously been personal and the sovereign embodied the state.[37] The emerging complexity of government coincided with the transition from a presumed personal duty of loyalty, deference to authority, and perpetual allegiance to an increasingly Lockean notion that governments are delegated agents of the people and allegiance to the abstract state could be legitimately withdrawn.

It is hardly surprising that the doctrine of natural allegiance, a traditional extension of allegiance where British birth was held to prevail over subsequent naturalization, came under increasing doubt in the wake of the American Revolution. The only viable extension of liability for treason became local allegiance, where residency of non-British subjects placed them under the temporary protection of the crown. However, local allegiance was not useful in the context of Canada's long, easily crossed border with the United States. With natural allegiance in doubt for those who happened to be of British birth, and a finding of local allegiance elusive, it was difficult to hold armed raiders liable to prosecution for treason. At the same time, armed foreign invaders from countries at peace with Britain who levied war against her dominions did not clearly come under martial law, normally authorized only in wartime or when a crisis was so severe that civil authority could no longer function. The Fenian raiders from the United States, who aimed to take Canada in exchange for Irish independence, fell in this legal lacuna.[38] As we see in this volume, the 1885 crisis was addressed by prosecutions for high treason and treason-felony but the Fenian invasions were handled by a third, serious, and uniquely Canadian political offence, that of lawless aggression, originating in 1838 Upper Canadian legislation and known after the mid-1860s as the 'Fenian Act.'[39] After the 1866 trials, the Fenian movement remained the focus of attention of the political police within the new federal security branches, developed under Macdonald by Gilbert McMicken and Frederick Ermatinger.[40]

Sedition prosecutions became less frequent after the mid-nineteenth century and the law faced possible demise as a viable modern security measure. The common law offence of seditious libel, widely applied in Britain and later in colonial settings as a means to control the press after the emergence of the late-seventeenth-century constitutional convention prohibiting prior restraint, clashed with the growing Lockean notion that criticism of authority was a right. Prosecutions were increasingly frustrated by jury acquittals by the second quarter of the nineteenth century in Britain and British North America. The vindication of the jury's freedom of verdict under Fox's Libel Act, 1792 set the stage for developing public tolerance of criticism of authority, and the offence was further limited by the acceptance of the defence of truth under Lord Campbell's Libel Act, 1843.[41] The gap was filled in part by increasing resort to laws related to breaches of the peace which were becoming more effectively policed,[42] but, rather than being repealed, sedition was renewed by legislation as explained in the Brown and Wright chapter. Although the offence was narrowed to advocacy of governmental change by force or unlawful means when included in the 1892 Canadian Criminal Code, the requisite intent and actions that flowed from advocacy remained vague. The code also included separate new 'official secrets' measures, derived from late-nineteenth-century U.K. laws, which were to become another means of limiting expression and public access to government deliberations.[43]

Offences related to breaches of the peace were elaborated in Canada from the second quarter of the nineteenth century onward, as explained in greater detail by Brown and Wright in this volume. Traditionally, the authorities had relied on a wide range of offences against the public peace such as riot, unlawful assembly, and assault. However, riot – the most serious offence in the category – could be prosecuted under the British statute of 1715 as a felony (where that statute had been received) or under common law as a misdemeanour. But prosecutions for riot as a capital felony in this period were rare or non-existent. The legal definition of riot was so vague that it covered both private and public purposes as well as small or large gatherings. In practice, some incidents legally classifiable as riots might not be of concern to local authorities (unless they included large numbers or appeared likely to result in serious violence) and disturbances that served as direct protest on a large scale might still fail to draw a response from the central state. Applications of such laws to maintain the public peace are discussed in chapters by Ian Robertson, Donald Fyson, Susan Binnie, and Eric Tucker, who examine their administration in the settings of Prince Edward Island and Quebec and in relation to labour protests. Threats of collective violence were also addressed by new Canadian laws dealing with labour, public works, and Aboriginal populations, including some borrowed from English law and occasionally from Irish or imperial laws enacted for Ireland. The development of professionalized policing and related institutions of crime prevention, notably security branches capable of systematic surveillance and intelligence gathering and assessment, also helped to refine state responses to collective disorder.

In sum, the legal developments underscore a shift in government responses to real and perceived security threats from a reactive mode, relying on prosecutions for the traditional political offences, to more pre-emptive legal interventions which were supported by institutional developments in policing and security operations. We also see the introduction of delegated law making and administration intended to fine-tune measures that were insulated from regular legislative and judicial scrutiny.[44]

OVERVIEW OF CHAPTERS

The volume is divided into four main subject areas. The sections on the Fenians and the North-West rebellions of 1870 and 1885 deal with the most obvious security crises during the period and the proceedings resulting from each fall within the traditional parameters of state trials. The sections on managing collective disorder and securing the Dominion reflect newer trends, including changing identification of state-security threats and developments in security laws and their administration. As with Volume I of the series, the span of time covered necessitated a difficult process of editorial selection that resulted in the decision to focus on the topics examined here. Some security-related incidents and proceedings during the period have been omitted, for instance events during the U.S. Civil War such as the temporary suspension of habeas corpus in Nova Scotia, the Confederate attempts to free prisoners on Lake Erie, and the raid at St Alban's, Vermont, and the extradition proceedings that followed. However, the Fenian raids examined in this volume are a reflection, in part, of this American crisis.[45] Other major topics, such as the Rebellion Losses riots in the 1840s, are referred to in passing. Topics that might warrant separate chapters, including Patrick Whelan's 1868 trial for the assassination of D'Arcy McGee and the Asian-exclusion measures of the late nineteenth and early twentieth centuries, appear as prominent themes in the chapters by David Wilson and by Andrew Parnaby and Greg Kealey with Kirk Niergarth.

Part One of the volume examines the external and internal security crises provoked by Fenian invasions, Fenian agitation within Canada, and political assassination. The risk of invasion was a preoccupation for the Province of Canada and the threat continued to alarm Macdonald's government after confederation. The crisis developed in the post-Civil War period because elements among U.S. Fenians – primarily organized to effect the transformation of Ireland into a republic – saw British North America as a suitable target. Two factors underlay their hostility: Canada was a surrogate for the United Kingdom; and Canada, like the United Kingdom, was regarded as having favoured the South during the American Civil War. While Washington may not have condoned Fenian invasion plans, there was little official intervention until plans turned into fact and the Battle of Ridgeway ensued in 1866 on Canadian territory. Continuing fears of Fenianism were stoked by McGee's assassination in Ottawa.[46] It was against this background that the arrests and trials of Fenian invaders and Canadian Fenian supporters took place.

Blake Brown's chapter focuses on the Fenian trials, both in Canada West after the Battle of Ridgeway and in Canada East after the attempted invasion from Vermont. His study illuminates the complex legal issues underlying trials of the invaders and of Canadian supporters of Fenianism in 1866 and early 1867, including the status and retroactive effect of the Fenian acts. It also highlights the contradictory political considerations behind the trials. John A. Macdonald, as attorney general of the Province of Canada, was closely involved in shaping the trials and in settling prosecution approaches. Politically, while there was strong demand within Canada for conviction of the invaders, a key issue in the context of American/Canadian/British relations was concern on the part of British officials not to offend U.S. political feeling in dealing with American-Irish prisoners. The situation led to a range of legal complications, including a review of the legislation under which Fenian prisoners were charged, Colonial Office interventions, the subsequent commutations of capital sentences, and the eventual release of prisoners part way through their terms of imprisonment.

David Wilson's contribution looks at the complex legal and political issues arising in the wake of the assassination of D'Arcy McGee. Habeas corpus had been suspended in the Province of Canada in response to the 1866 invasions and Wilson analyses the extension of this policy by the Dominion of Canada and the use of arrest and detention without trial against Fenian supporters from the spring of 1868. The government's use of emergency powers and Whelan's trial for the murder of McGee were closely supervised by Macdonald. Investigation and arrests were extended to Fenian supporters already known to have no direct connection to the murder. At the same time, Wilson emphasizes the careful use of the detention process, which he sees as orchestrated largely at Macdonald's behest, in an effort to strike a balance between national-security concerns and the risk of political alienation of the Irish Catholic vote vital to the Tory Party.

Part Two of the volume turns to problems of collective disorder, a recurrent issue for authorities at different levels of government through the period. Disorder is described in situations of riots and strikes in all four chapters in this section. But disorder arose for many different reasons, often reflecting rational protest on the part of those involved. How then to analyse disorders or the patterns of responses by the authorities at different levels of the state? As Donald Fyson points out in his chapter on Quebec, there is a substantial body of Canadian scholarship that examines particular incidents of collective violence, ranging from crowd violence growing out of political issues or sectarian rivalries to incidents occurring during labour strikes or as resistance to state interventions. What is less developed in the academic literature is any attempt to examine state responses in a systematic way. The issue becomes how to examine official responses when manifestations of disorder were deemed to require state interventions. In very broad terms, the four authors approach interventions in two distinct ways: Robertson and Tucker consider disorders arising from particular situations and the resulting forms of state responses; and Fyson and Binnie consider certain kinds of responses and ask when and why such methods were adopted.

The chapter by Ian Robertson takes the first approach by looking at legal and military responses to the actions of protestors against the land-tenancy system in operation in Prince Edward Island. He examines the situation in 1864–5 in detail as members of the local Tenant League, organized to resist the refusal of the landlord class to sell land to sitting tenants, embarked on a 'rent strike.' The initial responses of the authorities were fairly cautious. Was the league 'an illegal combination,' as some owners or senior politicians argued? Were supporters of the league publishing seditious material? And, if so, would juries convict members or supporters of the league? Later, as the effects of the rent strike were felt and supporters harassed local officials attempting to carry out their functions – including the serving of writs – the government stepped in. A demand for British troops to be sent from Halifax was granted. The soldiers, in turn, became the subjects of a campaign conducted by the Tenant League to encourage desertion. Although a substantial number of league members were eventually indicted for riot or for lesser offences, no one was convicted of riot and only a few on lesser charges. Robertson argues that the league's illegal campaign assisted the beginnings of the collapse of the old system of land tenure as landlords gave way and sold out their land to tenants or to the government of PEI. The situation also highlights the limits of legal and even military responses in light of local support for the militant strategy of tenant farmers.

The chapter by Donald Fyson focuses on the uses of riot law in Quebec in relation to public disorder, particularly in urban settings. His research, primarily in the district of Quebec but also across the province including the District of Montreal, examines arrests and prosecutions for riot between 1840 and 1892. Prosecutions at the beginning of the period were high. However, Fyson finds that no accused were indicted for the capital offence of felony riot and prosecutions for other forms of riot fell off sharply across the province, although not uniformly, during the period. Analysis of the reasons for such patterns of police and court activity leads him to investigate alternatives to prosecution for riot and the reasons for their adoption. Fyson suggests that those responsible for public order, especially the local police, had priorities and preferences for modes of prosecution which may have led them to use categories of offences other than riot and also to rely on newly available procedural possibilities.

The chapter by Susan Binnie focuses on minor criminal legislation used to impose prohibition on railway labourers building the Pacific Railway in the late 1870s and 1880s and to prosecute liquor-related offences. There were marked differences between the approach by the state to potential disorder among railway labourers and other situations of unrest or protest. Prohibition was applied to railway construction by the federal cabinet by administrative fiat as a pre-emptive measure often before any evidence of serious disorder was established. The approach was relatively unique in Canadian criminal law in the post-confederation decades, and it suggests the significance that the state – in the persons of the federal parliamentarians who enacted the statute (and amended and re-amended it so as to make it harsher) and the Conservative ministers who ordered its application – attached to the construction of a railway that had essential political significance for their country and for their political party.

Eric Tucker's chapter on street railway strikes also looks at the repressive possibilities and limits (notably what he has described as the 'social zone of toleration') of official responses to collective disorder. Unlike Robertson, Tucker analyses a number of distinct labour incidents in different settings, as opposed to one, albeit major, organized campaign. The seventeen incidents of Canadian street railway strikes or lockouts examined between 1886 and 1914 were not independent events; labour organizers were fully aware of workers' gains or failures in negotiations with employers elsewhere. Governments and employers were also aware how responses to disorder had worked in other settings. Tucker shows the high levels of initial public support for most incidents of labour action, and he focuses on particular circumstances which allowed local officials to apply coercive measures to deal with disorder resulting from labour protests. Reliance on the militia or special constables to quell disorder was common. Private security forces, including armed strike-breakers, were also allowed. Governments colluded with, or turned a blind eye to, this encroachment on their monopoly of the legitimate use of force.

Both the Tucker and the Binnie chapters illuminate some of the changing patterns of state-security issues during the later nineteenth century. Together they show how maintaining public order was deemed essential in certain situations, specifically in some cities during street rail-way strikes and in remote areas during construction of a national railway. As a result, we can suggest that not only had the focus of state concerns around public order begun to broaden to include major labour disputes in key economic areas but also that an underlying shift was occurring towards a greater emphasis on the need for economic order. While the maintenance of order remained a major concern for the Canadian state, certain forms of collective disorder, such as those related to sectarian clashes and elections or other local political issues, either declined in frequency or were managed better by way of new forms of regulation, improved policing, and changing notions of appropriate social conduct. But collective social disorder was treated harshly when the incidence and scale affected the economic order. The economy was a new aspect of national security, an increasingly prominent one, in effect becoming a preoccupation of Canadian governments especially in the wake of the Winnipeg General Strike.

Part Three of the volume turns to government reactions to the crises of 1870 and 1885 and marks the first study of security issues in western Canada in this series. Métis grievances resulted in a rebellion in 1870 which in turn led to the trial of Ambroise Lépine in 1874 for the murder of Thomas Scott, a trial that Louis Knafla describes as a surrogate political trial and 'a rehearsal' for the trial of Louis Riel. Knafla's examination of Lépine's trial illuminates the complexities of substantive law and procedure in the North-West in this period. Although many of the legal uncertainties of the Lépine trial had been settled by 1885, the government reacted far more harshly to the later and wider rebellion, initiated by the Métis but also fuelled by First Nations and settler grievances.

The 1885 North-West rebellion is the largest security crisis examined in this volume, generating a complex array of over 130 cases. Bob Beal and Barry Wright analyse Ottawa's overall prosecution strategy and examine two series of less prominent cases, namely a form of 'summary justice' applied to Riel's leading Métis associates, who pleaded guilty to treason-felony under the threat of high treason charges, and the trials of the so-called 'white rebels,' designed to deter settler unrest and demonstrate that the prosecutions were even-handed. The chapter introduces legal issues and concerns about the competence of the bench and defence counsel that are further demonstrated in the following chapters by J.M. Bumsted and Bill Waiser.

Unlike the cases examined by Beal and Wright, Riel's is the most studied treason trial in Canadian history. As Bumsted points out, Macdonald's government was determined to make an example of Riel and fully exploited its legal options, including the availability of the 1352 Statute of Treasons as well as procedural expedients existing in the territories. Riel was naive in thinking that surrendering to the law would provide him with a platform for voicing the grievances of the Métis. Bumsted assesses the existing scholarship and sets out a detailed analysis of particular legal aspects of the trial. He concludes that, among a number of questions about the fairness and legality of the trial, the shortcomings of Riel's defence counsel were a principal reason for the failure of justice. Riel was not well served by the decision to focus on the defence of insanity following the collapse of initial defence objections to the court's jurisdiction, a position that reflected Riel's lawyers' lack of preparation in facing unexpected charges of high treason. More attention to treason law, and to Riel's own wishes – including his desire to speak to the failure of the government to respond to Métis problems – could well have raised serious doubts about his guilt in the minds of one or more jurors.

While Riel's trial has dominated analysis of the 1885 crisis, no group involved in the resistance suffered as heavily as First Nations prisoners whom, as Waiser shows, were often wrongly accused and then tried summarily in Regina and Battleford in 1885. Waiser's research on the involvement of Aboriginal leadership in the rebellion leads him to conclude that, while some warriors attacked settlers, most were restrained by leaders who remained loyal to the queen. In addition, certain bands were forced by the Métis to move to Batoche and thus appeared to join the uprising. Waiser's scrutiny of communications between local Dominion officials and members of the government in Ottawa during the military operations after the rebellion shows that deliberate decisions were made to treat First Nations people with harsh exemplary justice without applying the counterbalancing measure of mercy, informed by political considerations, that was extended to the other participants. Native chiefs who were present but took no active part in the rebellion were charged with treason-felony. Little accommodation was made in court for those put on trial. Defences were poorly conducted and many of the Native accused did not have defence counsel. Judge Hugh Richardson in Regina and Judge Charles Rouleau in Battleford nonetheless imposed harsh sentences, including death for those implicated in murder.

Part Four, the final section of the volume, deals with the modernization of Canada's national-security laws and with their enforcement. A number of chapters, particularly those that concern the management of collective disorder, highlight the impact of institutional changes on the administration of security-related laws. The chapter by Andrew Parnaby and Gregory Kealey with Kirk Niergarth focuses on this matter by examining the political police first formed by Macdonald in 1864, its elaboration after confederation, and the operations it conducted up to the Great War. Anti-colonial movements were a primary target, from the work of a network of informants tracking the activities of Fenians in Canada and the United States in the 1860s (introduced earlier in Wilson's chapter) to the role of the security branch in monitoring immigration from the Indian subcontinent and the surveillance of immigrants in the early twentieth century. The significance of a national network of security agents and the coordination of a Canadian network with intelligence operations in other countries are assessed. The increased reliance on regular and secret policing within national and international networks had a significant impact on security responses and the place of classic state trials. Other themes in this chapter include the impact of attitudes of official racism (which contradicted British claims of justice) and the growing prominence of global migration as a national-security concern.

Brown and Wright survey the origins of Canada's national-security laws and their nineteenth-century development and modernization as background to a comprehensive review of the security provisions of the 1892 Canadian Criminal Code. This examination draws together the multiple facets of legal development referred to in previous chapters and places the first codification of criminal law by a self-governing British jurisdiction within a broader setting. The context includes nineteenth-century English criminal law reform, colonial Canadian and Dominion criminal law consolidations, and codifications elsewhere in the British empire. The imposed British colonial criminal law codifications (derived from Thomas Macaulay's Indian Penal Code and Robert Wright's Jamaica Code) and the first codes from the self-governing jurisdictions (Canada, New Zealand, and Queensland) were prompted in part by local public-order crises and can be understood as modern legal rationalizations designed to make the rule of law more effective in culturally diverse frontier settings.[47] Brown and Wright argue that the 1885 North-West crisis, a challenge to Ottawa's sovereignty, authority, and development agenda, helped to make the large legislative project of codification a political priority in Canada. Security provisions formed a prominent part of the 1892 code which pulled together diverse laws into a coherent, comprehensive, and formidable array of national-security laws.

The volume, like the previous two, closes with brief archival essays and supporting illustrative primary documents and compendia. As we have noted, John A. Macdonald was a key figure in many of the events examined here, from the 1866 Fenian prosecutions to the 1885 crisis and the drafting of the 1892 Canadian Criminal Code. Judi Cumming overviews the Macdonald Papers at Library and Archives Canada and highlights research strategies relevant to state trials and national-security issues.[48] Riel's trial is the most famous and contentious case of treason in Canadian history, one that has generated an enormous literature, and Gilles Lesage's survey of key relevant archival holdings provides a primary navigation aid.[49] Both essays furnish starting points for further research on many of the issues examined in this volume. As with the previous volumes in the series, one of our main objectives is to stimulate additional interest and debate about these formative experiences in Canadian law and politics.

The period 1840–1914 was one of extraordinary change in the Canadian state and in Canada's cultures. The tensions between plural identities and the common obligations of conformity to the dominant order, between an increasingly liberal polity that emphasized the rule of law and the repressive reflexes of the sovereign state, are reflected in the security crises and manifestations of protest and disorder examined in this volume. The classic state trials do not disappear but their prominence and the handling of political prosecutions changed as the result of new legal options and increased reliance on regular and secret policing. The emergence of the modern post-colonial federal Canadian state is marked by continuities and change, as reflected in the incidents and legal responses analysed in the following chapters.

NOTES

1 The term Canada is used here broadly to include the North American colonies before 1867.
2 Published in thirty-three volumes. The genre emerged in the early eighteenth century and declined in the late nineteenth century with the British

government-sponsored and sanitized 'new' state trials series and the misnamed American state trials collections. The editors of the first two volumes in this series, Murray Greenwood and Barry Wright, took Howells' series as their starting point. See F. Murray Greenwood and Barry Wright, 'Introduction: State Trials, the Rule of Law, and Executive Powers in Early Canada,' *CST 1*, 3–51, and nn.11 and 13 below.

3 See E.P. Thompson, *Whigs and Hunters: The Origins of the Black Act* (Harmondsworth, U.K.: Penguin 1977); 'The Moral Economy of the English Crowd,' *Past and Present* 50 (1971): 76–136. Also, D. Hay, P. Linebaugh, et al., eds., *Albion's Fatal Tree: Crime and Society in Eighteenth Century England* (London: Penguin 1977).

4 An imperial suspending act was passed in 1777 as a response to the American Revolution and its use in Nova Scotia is examined by Ernest A. Clarke and Jim Phillips, 'Rebellion and Repression in Nova Scotia in the Era of the American Revolution,' *CST 1*, 184–5. On suspension of habeas corpus in Quebec during this period, see Jean-Marie Fecteau and Douglas Hay, 'Government by Will and Pleasure instead of Law: Military Justice and the Legal System in Quebec, 1775–83,' ibid., 146–56. On the same practice in Lower Canada from 1794 to 1813, see F. Murray Greenwood, 'Judges and Treason Law in Lower Canada, England, and the United States during the French Revolution, 1794–1800,' ibid., 267, and Jean-Marie Feacteau, F. Murray Greenwood, and Jean-Pierre Wallot, 'Sir James Craig's Reign of Terror and Its Impact on Emergency Powers in Lower Canada,' ibid., 333–5, 344–8; and, for suspension in Upper Canada from 1812 to 1814, see Paul Romney and Barry Wright, 'State Trials and Security Proceedings in Upper Canada during the War of 1812,' ibid., 381, 385. For the 1837–8 rebellions, see Rainer Baehre, 'Trying the Rebels: Emergency Legislation and the Colonial Executive's Overall Legal Strategy in the Upper Canadian Rebellion,' *CST 2*, 44; and Steven Watt, 'State Trial by Legislature: The Special Council of Lower Canada, 1838-41,' ibid., 258–61.

5 See Fecteau and Hay, 'Government by Will and Pleasure,' and Douglas Hay, 'Civilians Tried by Military Courts: Quebec, 1759–64,' *CST 1*, 114–28. The option was also considered during the War of 1812 (Romney and Wright, 'State Trials and Security Proceedings,' ibid.) and was widely embraced during the 1837–8 crisis, as discussed in three essays in *CST 2*: Barry Wright, 'The Kingston and London Courts Martial,' 130–59; Jean-Marie Fecteau, 'This Ultimate Resource: Martial Law and State Repression in Lower Canada, 1837–8,' 207–47; and F. Murray Greenwood, 'The General Court Martial at Montreal, 1838–9: Operation and the Irish Comparison,' 279–324.

6 On the later suspension of regular legal processes and resort to military jus-

tice in other nineteenth-century British colonial jurisdictions, see R.W. Kostal, *A Jurisprudence of Power: Victorian Empire and the Rule of Law* (Oxford: Oxford University Press 2005).

7 While the resort to military justice produced the largest proportion of convictions, executions, and transported convicts in 1838, as Jean-Marie Fecteau ('This Ultimate Resource') argues, the suspension of the regular courts undermined the notion of legitimate justice. The continuation of regular government and legal processes is an important measure of the stability of the state; military interventions characterize states in crisis. On British debates about the rule of law sparked by other nineteenth-century colonial crises, see Kostal, *Jurisprudence of Power*, and Nasser Hussain, *The Jurisprudence of Emergency: Colonialism and the Rule of Law* (Ann Arbor: University of Michigan Press 2003). As Brown and Wright argue in this volume, codification can be understood in part as an attempt, in the wake of the 1885 crisis, to reconstitute and better legitimize authority through emphasis on the rule of law.

8 While the emergence of professional policing and the penitentiary, as well as criminal law consolidation, pre-date the rebellions, institutional and administrative transformations accelerated in the wake of the crisis, as did efforts to reconstitute the relation of subjects to the state. See Brian Young, 'Positive Law, Positive State: Class Realignment and the Transformation of Lower Canada,' in Allan Greer and Ian Radforth, eds., *Colonial Leviathan: State Formation in Mid-Nineteenth-Century Canada* (Toronto: University of Toronto Press 1992), 50; also, Greer and Radforth, 'Introduction,' Greer, 'The Birth of Police in Canada,' 17, and Radforth, 'Sydenham and Utilitarian Reform,' 64, in the same volume. Also: Bruce Curtis, *The Politics of Population: State Formation, Statistics, and the Census of Canada, 1840–1875* (Toronto: University of Toronto Press 2001); P. Corrigan and D. Sayer, *The Great Arch: English State Formation as Cultural Revolution* (Oxford: Blackwell 1985).

9 See the chapters in this volume by Ian Ross Robertson and Eric Tucker.

10 Constitution Act, 1867 (U.K.) 30&31 Vic. c.3.

11 Greenwood and Wright anticipated that later volumes would include new security legislation and means of enforcement extending beyond the trial of classic political offences, but that issues not directly related to national security, such as partisanship in the administration of the law, or politics in the more diffuse sense of the assertion of authority, interests, and social ordering which arguably takes place in the routine business of the courts, would fall outside the series' scope: see 'Introduction,' *CST 1*.

12 Forcese's focus on judicial review of 'government invocations of "national security"' is useful for demonstrating the executive powers accorded to the Canadian government under the heading of security. See Craig Forcese,

'Through a Glass Darkly: The Role and Review of "National Security" Concepts in Canadian Law,' *Alberta Law Review* 43 (2006): 963–1000, 964. Sossin is cited at 980.

13 The editors, when commencing the *Canadian State Trials* series, recognized that a more contextual approach was required than that used in Howells' series, in order to deal with the fragmentary colonial records and to consider a wider range of official records. They also concluded that the political events leading to legal responses, the policies informing their administration, and some sense of the impact and experience of the proceedings needed illumination, aims that could not be met by a selection of trial proceedings left largely to speak for themselves. Instead of presenting compilations of trial records annotated with lengthy editorial comment, as is the case with Howells' series, the editors collected interpretative essays supported by selected illustrative primary documents. They also emphasized attention to the standards of the period and comparative examples.

14 State Trials series may be reaching new audiences given the electronic publication of the *State Trials, 1163–1858* series in 2001. Compiled from Howells' series and a series edited by Macdonell, with other material added, the version includes more than one thousand trials. See Thomas P. Gallanis, 'Adversarial Culture, Adversarial Doctrine: Cross-Examination and Leading Questions in *The State Trials on CD-ROM*,' *Journal of Legal History* 24 (2003): 86–96.

15 Otto Kirchheimer rejected the prevailing Cold War view that dismissed political trials as an exclusive preoccupation of undemocratic regimes. He distinguished between show trials, which involve minimal risk to governments, and political trials, which do not. He further divided political trials into those involving the prosecution of classic political offences (treason and sedition trials that diminish in frequency with recognition of the legitimacy of organized political opposition and criticism of government), substitute political trials (where criminal charges for more routine offences are brought to discredit political opposition), and trials involving crimes committed for political purposes. See Kirchheimer's *Political Justice: The Use of Legal Procedure for Political Ends* (Princeton, N.J.: Princeton University Press 1961), 46–64, as well as Judith N. Shklar, *Legalism: Law, Morals, and Political Trials* (Cambridge, Mass.: Harvard University Press 1964, 1986). Kirchheimer's typology was further developed by T.L. Becker in T.L. Becker, ed., *Political Trials* (New York: Bobbs-Merrill 1971). During this period, the myopia of political scientists, preoccupied with the 'end of ideology debate,' was also criticized by Nathan Hakman ('Political Trials in the Legal Order: A Political Scientist's Perspective,' *Journal of Public Law* 21 [1973]: 73–176). The general neglect of the area

continued in the United States, with some notable exceptions (Austin T. Turk, *Political Criminality: The Defiance and Defence of Authority* [Beverly Hills, Calif.: Sage 1982]; Ron Christenson, *Political Trials: Gordian Knots in the Law* [Oxford: Transaction 1986]); while elsewhere, from the late 1970s, new scholarship was prompted by responses to terrorism arising out of the Northern Ireland conflicts. More recently, the proliferation of new national-security measures in response to terrorist attacks in the United States, Britain, Spain, and other countries has sparked new interest in the subject among political and legal theorists and critical re-examination of the tensions between the rule of law and emergency measures, and between civil liberties and public safety. See, for example, Victor Ramraj, ed., *Emergencies and the Limits of Legality* (Cambridge: Cambridge University Press 2008).

16 Recent historical scholarship, influenced by concepts such as 'modern state formation' (e.g., Corrigan and Sayer, *The Great Arch*) and the 'emerging public sphere (e.g., Jurgen Habermas, *The Structural Transformation of the Public Sphere: An Inquiry into a Category of Bourgeoise Society*, trans. T. Burger [Cambridge, Mass.: MIT Press 1992]), has resulted in critical reassessments of late-eighteenth- and nineteenth-century institutional developments in response to the challenges of the growing popular engagement with politics and the development of modern civic identity and citizenship. Historians such as Christopher Bayly (*The Birth of the Modern World, 1780–1914: Global Connections and Comparisons* [London: Basil Blackwell 2004]) have renewed interest in imperial networks and nineteenth-century developments in relation to the mapping, surveying, and assessment of colonial governance. There has been a parallel growth in legal history. These recent scholarly trends have sparked debate with postmodernist scholars. For a discussion of the implications of Michel Foucault's suggestion that scholars must 'eschew Leviathan' in the study of modern power, see in particular Mitchell Dean, *Critical and Effective Histories: Foucault's Methods and Historical Sociology* (London: Routledge 1994). On the relationship of this debate to the historical study of political trials and security measures, see B. Wright, 'Quiescent Leviathan? Citizenship and National Security in Late Modernity,' *Journal of Law and Society* 25 (1998): 213–36.

17 The Fenians, or Irish Republican Brotherhood, were a nineteenth-century revolutionary organization prominent in the United States and directed at the overthrow of the British government in Ireland. See the chapters by Blake Brown and David Wilson in this volume.

18 Peter B. Waite, ed., *The Confederation Debates in the Province of Canada*, 2nd ed. (Montreal and Kingston: McGill-Queens's University Press 2006), 24–5. See also *Parliamentary Debates on Confederation* (Quebec: Hunter Rose 1865), 508, 576–7.

19 For more details, see the Brown and Wright chapter in this volume. See also D.H. Brown, *The Genesis of the Canadian Criminal Code of 1892* (Toronto: Osgoode Society for Canadian Legal History / University of Toronto Press 1989), 59–60.

20 See generally J.G. Snell and Frederick Vaughan, *The Supreme Court of Canada: History of the Institution* (Toronto: Osgoode Society for Canadian Legal History / University of Toronto Press 1985); Jonathan Swainger, *The Canadian Department of Justice and the Completion of Confederation, 1867–1878* (Vancouver: UBC Press 2000).

21 There were clear parallels here, as one of our reviewers has pointed out, between Canada's treatment of its Native peoples in the North-West and the Colonial Office's treatment of native labour in the African colonies and elsewhere (admittedly in the latter case in terms of labour legislation). In each instance, the central power either failed to become well informed on local situations or neglected to deal with situations that cried out for better treatment of indigenous peoples. See M.K. Banton, 'The Colonial Office, 1820–1955: Constantly the Subject of Small Struggles,' in D. Hay and Paul Craven, eds., *Masters, Servants, and Magistrates in Britain and the Empire, 1562–1955* (Chapel Hill: University of North Carolina Press 2004).

22 See the chapter by Louis Knafla in this volume.

23 The volunteer militia was relied upon by the British and was effectively a substitute for a regular Canadian army after the British Army left Canada in 1871. Efforts were made by governments to professionalize militia troops over the period covered in this volume.

24 See the chapter by Brown and Wright in this volume. Once the Supreme Court of Canada was created, the federal government could take reference cases directly to it for advisory opinions, a power not found in federations such as the United States or Australia (see Snell and Vaughan, *Supreme Court of Canada*). The resort to extrajudicial opinions in the pre-confederation period had often compromised judicial independence on security matters, as we have seen in *CST 1* and *CST 2*.

25 See the chapters by Beal and Wright, Bumsted, and Waiser in this volume.

26 See Philip C. Stenning, *Appearing for the Crown: A Legal and Historical Review of Criminal Prosecutorial Authority in Canada* (Cowansville, Que.: Yvon Blais/ Brown 1986); Swainger, *Department of Justice.*

27 Again, possible parallels occur between the operation of Dominion government in the North-West and the Colonial Office in some British colonies in Africa. See Banton, 'The Colonial Office, 1822–1955.'

28 See the chapter by Beal and Wright in this volume.

29 25 Ed. 3 st.5 c.2.

30 7&8 Wm. 3 c.3.
31 See detailed discussion of these matters, along with attempts to bypass the protections by emergency legislation, in *CST 1* and *CST 2*.
32 36 Geo. III c.7 (GB).
33 11&12 Vic. c.12 (U.K.). See the chapter by Brown and Wright in this volume for more details.
34 31 Vic. c.69. See Supporting Documents in this volume.
35 Neither the 1352 nor the 1696 act was explicitly transferred by the Dominion government under the North-West Territories Act (43 Vic. c.25), but the former applied as the result of Rupert's Land reception in 1670. See also Brown and Wright in this volume and D.H. Brown, 'The Meaning of Treason in 1885,' *Saskatchewan History* 28 (1975): 65–73.
36 John Barrell, *Imagining the King's Death: Figurative Treason, Fantasies of Regicide, 1793–1796* (Oxford: Oxford University Press 2000).
37 Iain Pears captures the original conception superbly, as expressed in the words of Dr John Wallis (who worked in intelligence for both Cromwell and Charles II): 'Strike only one small blow at the heart, and the effect is catastrophic. And the living beating heart of the Kingdom was the King. One man indeed could bring all to ruin where an entire army would be ineffective.' See *An Instance of the Fingerpost* (London: Vintage Random House 1998), 434.
38 See F. Murray Greenwood, 'The Prince Affair: "Gallant Colonel" or "The Windsor Butcher"?' *CST 2*, 160–87, and further discussion of these matters in the Brown and Wright chapter in this volume. The prosecution of regular criminal offences, as a surrogate for the prosecution of political offences, was another possibility, one that was exploited in the murder trial of Lépine examined in the Knafla chapter in this volume.
39 31 Vic. c.14. See Supporting Documents.
40 See the chapters by Brown, Wilson, and Parnaby and Kealey with Niergarth in this volume. The Fenian Act was contemplated for prosecuting Riel but there were concerns about aggravating relations with the United States after the earlier Fenian cases. See Beal and Wright in this collection and Jeremy Ravi Mumford, 'Why Was Louis Riel, a United States Citizen, Hanged as a Canadian Traitor in 1885?' *Canadian Historical Review* 88 (2007): 237–62.
41 32 Geo. III c.60; 6&7 Vic. c.86. See the chapter by Brown and Wright in this volume, as well as three essays in *CST 1*: Barry Wright, 'The Gourlay Affair: Seditious Libel and the Sedition Act in Upper Canada, 1818–19,' 487–504; Paul Romney, 'Upper Canada in the 1820s: Criminal Prosecution and the Case of Francis Collins,' 505–21; and Barry Cahill 'R. v Howe (1835) for Seditious Libel: A Tale of Twelve Magistrates,' 547–75. For the decline of seditious libel prosecutions in the colonial context, see Barry Wright, 'Libel and the Colonial

Administration of Justice in Upper Canada and New South Wales c.1825–30,'
in H. Foster, B.L. Berger, and A.R. Buck, eds., *The Grand Experiment: Law and
Legal Culture in British Settler Societies* (Vancouver: Osgoode Society for Canadian Legal History / UBC Press 2008).

42 See Michael Lobban, 'From Seditious Libel to Unlawful Assembly: Peterloo
and the Changing Face of Political Crime,' *Oxford Journal of Legal Studies* 10
(1990): 307–52.

43 See the Brown and Wright chapter in this volume for more details.

44 Some of the new laws and procedures anticipate the emergency executive-
enabling War Measures Act. Fine-tuned security-related orders, including
the suspension of habeas corpus (indefinite detention), were no longer under
direct legislative and judicial oversight, thus avoiding the controversies and
risks of reactive trials for the classic political offences. See the Binnie and
Brown and Wright chapters in this volume for more details.

45 Canada had harboured Confederate soldiers, and Confederate attempts to
free prisoners held on Lake Erie and the raid on St Albans were both initiated
out of Canada in 1864. These events reinforced the impression that Canada
sympathized with the South in the Civil War. Many of the Fenian raiders
were demobilized Union soldiers, and it was this aspect of what was essentially an American crisis that had the most direct impact on the security
concerns of British North America and Canada. The Guibord affair in Quebec
and the anti-confederation movement in Nova Scotia are other unexamined
topics. These events threatened the unity of the new federation but the legal
proceedings that flowed from them fall outside our focus on security or surrogate security-related proceedings.

46 D'Arcy McGee (1825–68) was a leading Irish Canadian politician, a father
of confederation, an outstanding orator, and a Conservative member of the
House of Commons. See David A. Wilson, *Thomas D'Arcy McGee: Passion, Reason and Politics 1825–1857* (Montreal and Kingston: McGill-Queen's University
Press2008), and Wilson's chapter in this volume.

47 See the Brown and Wright chapter in this volume. The parallels between the
British imperial and British self-governing-jurisdiction codifications of the
nineteenth century are further explored in Barry Wright, 'Criminal Law Codification and Imperial Projects: The Self Governing Jurisdiction Codes of the
1890's,' *Legal History* 12 (2008): 19–49.

48 Inclusion of an essay on Macdonald reflects his wide influence on matters
examined throughout this volume but is not intended to stress the role of
individual agency in history. Since Donald Creighton's comprehensive and
magisterial study of Macdonald fifty years ago, particularism has arguably
tended to obscure larger political narratives, debate over which has been

sparked by Richard Gwyn's recent biography of Macdonald, *John A: The Man Who Made Us: The Life and Times of John A. Macdonald Volume 1* (Toronto: Random House 2007).

49 There are numerous general documentary collections on Riel and the North-West rebellions, as noted by Gilles Lesage in this volume. On Riel's treason trial specifically, see Desmond Morton's edition of *The Queen v. Louis Riel* (Toronto: University of Toronto Press 1974).

PART ONE

Fenians

1

'Stars and Shamrocks Will Be Sown': The Fenian State Trials, 1866–7

R. BLAKE BROWN

In early June 1866 the Fenians launched two raids across the American border into the United Province of Canada to initiate their long-threatened invasion of British North America. The attack proved unsuccessful and its leaders slipped back to the United States. Canadian forces captured a substantial number of Fenian fighters, and in late 1866 and early 1867 these Fenian prisoners faced trial in Toronto and in Sweetsburg, Lower Canada. Twenty-five defendants were found guilty of capital charges, but not a single Fenian was put to death and by 1872 every Fenian prisoner in Kingston Penitentiary had been set free.

This relatively lenient treatment accords with Kenneth McNaught's broad assessment of Canadian political trials[1] but stands in stark contrast to the experience of defendants in most state-security crises in nineteenth-century British North America. For example, in the trials following the 1837–8 rebellions in Upper and Lower Canada, Canadian officials vigorously pursued legal proceedings against a number of rebels and executed numerous defendants. Regular trials were suspended immediately in Lower Canada, and eventually in Upper Canada, because of concerns that juries could not be trusted to convict.[2] Following the 1885 North-West rebellion, the Dominion government hanged Louis Riel and eight Aboriginal warriors in a demonstration of the severity of Canadian law.[3] The unusually gentle treatment of the Fenians thus begs for an explanation.

The two leading historians of the Fenians in Canada have both studied the prosecutions. W.S. Neidhardt focuses on their diplomatic importance and argues that the lenient treatment of the Fenian defendants resulted from Britain's desire to protect its relationship with the United States.[4] Hereward Senior portrays the criminal law as posing little real threat to the captured Fenians, suggesting that all of those involved felt sure that those convicted would be released quickly.[5] Senoir and Neidhardt, however, pay little attention to the details of the prosecutorial processes, nor do they enquire into what efforts were made at different levels of government to influence the processes adopted for the trials.

A complex web of local and international conditions explains the mild treatment of the Fenians. These conditions included the need of both Britain and the British North American colonies/Canada during and after the Civil War to smooth the frayed relationship with the United States. The Union leadership believed that Britain favoured the Confederacy, a sense strengthened by the October 1864 raid launched on St Albans, Vermont, by a group of Confederate soldiers operating clandestinely in British North America. The raid angered authorities in Washington, as did the decision that the soldiers, who had been arrested upon their return to Canada, would not be extradited to the United States.[6] A desire to avoid antagonizing Irish Americans, who might decide if provoked to join the Fenian movement and launch future attacks on Canada, further motivated mild treatment. The Irish diaspora of the 1840s had created new nodes of Irish Catholic power and dissatisfaction that were beyond the reach of the British government. The Fenian raiders were based in a relatively safe haven (the fractured United States) and held deep-seated grievances rooted in a long history of persecution at the hands of the English and their Protestant Irish allies and in a sense of dislocation from their homeland.[7] British and Canadian officials realized that a future attack could be prevented only by a public-relations program centred on the trial and punishment of the Fenians that demonstrated fairness and firmness while avoiding creating martyrs for the Fenian cause. Canadian and British officials also treated the Fenians relatively mildly because of the continued efforts to attract the Irish to a hegemonic 'British' identity.[8] While Fenians in the United States were beyond the physical reach of the British government, the ideology of Britishness, the perceived benefits of which could be shown through a strict adherence to the tenets of 'British Justice,' was meant to mitigate Irish dissatisfaction and draw the Irish within the orbit of existing state structures in British North America and the United Kingdom.[9] Finally, the desire of colonial politicians, in particular John A. Macdonald, to avoid alienating Irish Canadian voters shaped the legal response.

In explaining the handling of the Fenian prisoners, this chapter briefly discusses the development of the Fenian movement and the 1866 raids. It then addresses the fair but firm treatment of the Fenians, starting with the pre-trial decision regarding how to prosecute. Next, the trials themselves are considered, beginning with the Fenian prosecutions in Toronto in October and November 1866 and the resulting appellate decisions. Attention then shifts to the trials in Sweetsburg, prosecuted under legislation that had been recently extended to apply to Lower Canada. Developments return to Toronto in January 1867, when the third group of Fenian trials took place. The form and strategy of the prosecutions, the various legal manoeuvres of the defendants, jury-selection issues, and the interplay between the appellate decisions and subsequent trials are all explored. Finally, the punishment of the Fenian convicts is examined.

THE FENIANS AND THE FENIAN ATTACKS OF 1866

Following the bloody Irish rebellion in 1798, the British Parliament passed the Act of Union, which formally combined all of England and Ireland in 1801. Resistance to this formal bond soon began in earnest. Daniel O'Connell led a movement for Catholic 'emancipation' – that is, the removal of restrictions on Roman Catholics, including the ban on Catholics from serving in Parliament – a goal that was achieved in 1829. During the 1830s and 1840s, O'Connell hoped to negotiate a repeal of the Act of Union. More radical elements, the so-called 'Young Ireland' movement, attempted a revolt in 1848, though it failed to garner widespread support. The 1848 Treason-Felony Act, later adopted by the Dominion of Canada in 1885, was one of the major legal responses to these events.[10]

One of the members of the failed 1848 uprising, John O'Mahony, escaped to the United States, where around 1857 he established the Fenian Brotherhood, the members of which bound their allegiance to the Irish republic and swore to take up arms against England. The Fenians were an underground movement in Ireland aided with funds collected by O'Mahony in the United States, where, by the 1860s, the Irish constituted a growing politicized minority. The large body of Irish resident in North America affected Canadian, American, and British politics. By the end of 1865, 100,000 Irish Americans, many of whom were experienced Civil War soldiers, joined Fenian military clubs. Internal divisions within the Fenian movement led to the creation of two factions, one led by O'Mahony that pursued an uprising in Ireland, and the other led by William Roberts that focused on capturing British North America in the hope of exchanging it for Ireland's freedom. The chapters in this volume by David Wilson and by Andrew Parnaby and Gregory Kealey with Kirk Niergarth explore the intelligence operations deployed against the movement.

Michael Murphy, the leader of a small group of Canadian Fenians, supported the O'Mahony wing, which in April 1866 launched a minor raid across the New Brunswick frontier when it became apparent there would be no successful Fenian uprising in Ireland. Murphy was sent a telegram telling him to attack, but government officials intercepted the telegram and arrested Murphy at the railway station in Cornwall (in eastern Upper Canada) on 9 April 1866, along with six of his companions. The government also arrested several other Toronto Fenians and sent them to Cornwall.[11] William Roberts's Fenian group launched an attack from Buffalo across the Niagara frontier on the night of 31 May. This force of approximately 800 Fenians commanded by Lieutenant-Colonel ('General') John O'Neill, a former Union cavalry commander, secured boats and crossed the Niagara River. O'Neill's force encamped initially near his landing place at Thomas Newbiggin's farm. O'Neill then defeated a group of Canadian militiamen on 2 June at the Battle of Ridgeway, killing ten Canadians and injuring thirty-eight others. The United States government took no major steps to prevent the initial attack, in part because of continuing anger over Britain's support for the southern Confederacy, though American authorities subsequently interrupted Fenian supply lines across the Niagara River and arrested Fenian reinforcements attempting to cross into Canada. Poorly organized, wracked by desertions, and without new supplies, the Fenians withdrew on the night of 2–3 June back across the American border, where O'Neill and his remaining troops surrendered their arms to waiting American authorities, but not before a number of Fenian troops were captured in Canada. By 4 June, sixty-five alleged Fenians found themselves in the Toronto gaol.[12]

Approximately 1,000 Fenians under Brigadier-General Samuel B. Spears crossed from near Franklin, Vermont, into Quebec on 7 June. The main body of the Fenian infantry never moved more than a mile into Canadian territory. Most of the Fenians remained in Quebec for only forty-eight hours. Spears ordered his soldiers back across the border when he received news of approaching Canadian and British soldiers. Approximately 200 Fenians nevertheless lingered around Pigeon Hill, where they were attacked and dispersed on 9 June. Sixteen of these Fenians were captured and would be put on trial.[13]

FRAMING THE FENIAN TRIALS

The captured Fenians presented an immediate legal problem for Canadian officials: Should they be prosecuted and, if so, how? The vast majority were Irish-born and had lived for various lengths of time in the United States. Should they be tried as British subjects or as Americans, and what charges should be laid?

To try the prisoners captured in Upper Canada, the Province of Canada had at its disposal the Upper Canada Lawless Aggressions Act, a controversial piece of legislation with a complicated legislative history.[14] The act, further examined by Desmond Brown and Barry Wright in this volume and first passed in 1838, sought to avoid perceived limitations of treason law in light of British North America's large, easily crossed border with the United States – limitations that became acutely apparent with the border raids in the wake of the 1837–8 rebellions.[15] High treason required that an alleged offender owe allegiance to the British crown, while captured soldiers of a foreign state at war with Britain who invaded British territory were treated as prisoners of war according to international law. The Lawless Aggressions Act extended liability to deal with foreigners from a country at peace with Britain who attacked the colony. They could be tried for the felony of 'lawless aggression' by either a regular court or a court martial. Americans were culpable under the original statute if they joined with British subjects who were traitorously in arms and then continued in arms. The phrase 'in arms' had a particular meaning in this context: to be in arms did not necessarily require carrying arms oneself but only being associated with those who did. The act provided that those convicted could be sentenced to death 'or such other punishment as shall be awarded by the court.'[16]

Filling a perceived lacuna in the law, the Lawless Aggressions Act could be administered without the procedural safeguards available in cases of treason. The British Treason Act of 1696, and a subsequent amendment in 1708, offered defendants special procedural safeguards: two or more witnesses to an act of treason, the right to have counsel make a full defence and subpoena witnesses, and the right to a copy of the indictment, lists of crown witnesses, and the jury panel before trial.[17] Many of these safeguards were unavailable in ordinary felony proceedings, including those for lawless aggression, until later in the nineteenth century. Foreigners could also be tried by a court martial without juries. The Lawless Aggressions Act provided as well that British subjects who allied themselves with invaders could be tried for either high treason before the regular courts or for lawless aggression before a court martial.

Upper Canada repealed the 1838 act in 1840, before re-enacting it with alterations later that same year that made it easier to prosecute defendants. The new act dropped the 1838 provision that foreign raiders had to join themselves to British traitors to be tried. It instead made it an offence for foreigners to be merely 'in arms' in Upper Canada, with or without the company of traitorous subjects. It also made it a capital offence for foreigners to commit any act of hostility in Upper Canada, to enter Upper Canada intending to levy war, or to enter the colony intending to commit a capital felony.[18]

The Fenian raids led the Province of Canada to amend the law again in 1866 (see this volume's Supporting Documents). On 8 June a new statute extended the lawless-aggression provisions to Lower Canada. It allowed foreign citizens or subjects taken in arms in Lower Canada to be tried by either courts martial or by the regular courts, and provided that British subjects levying war with foreigners (or aiding them) could be tried by courts martial.[19] A subsequent statute, passed in August 1866, permitted the regular courts of Lower Canada to try British subjects or foreign citizens for any offence committed under the June statute. The August act made this provision retroactive, providing that 'every subject of Her Majesty and every citizen or subject of any foreign state or country who has at any time heretofore offended or may at any time hereafter offend' might be tried by the regular courts.[20] In August the legislature also passed a similar piece of legislation for Upper Canada allowing British subjects, as well as foreigners, to be tried for lawless aggression (not just treason) in the regular courts for acts committed earlier.[21]

When first passed in 1838, the lawless-aggression legislation was controversial, and British authorities seriously considered disallowing the act, in part because it permitted courts martial when regular courts might have been as easily employed.[22] For officials in British North America, however, the legislation would prove convenient in trying the Fenian prisoners. As we shall see, it allowed the government to prosecute the Fenians who had taken residence in the United States as either British subjects or foreign citizens (or both). As well, prosecutions under the statute did not need to comply with the procedural safeguards required under British treason law. The legislation would be employed to such an extent to try the Fenians that it became widely known as the Fenian Act.

A number of Upper Canadian newspapers expressed the hope that the captured Fenians would face the full weight of the law.[23] The Fenian Brotherhood reacted by threatening those involved in the trials. John A. Macdonald heard warnings that the Fenian leadership in Buffalo talked brazenly of murdering the judge and jurors involved in the Fenian trials, as well as reports that the Fenians intended to launch an attack to free prisoners from the Toronto gaol.[24] One of the prosecutors, Robert Harrison, also received threatening letters in November 1866. A letter from New York warned that Harrison's 'last hour approaches! As true as there is a God in Heaven you shall die and that speedily. This is no idle threat but a deep-laid plan and will be carried out to the letter. So be prepared for death – companionship of the devil and the joys of hell. For every drop of Fenian blood you spill rivers will flow in revenge. Die, thou shalt, hard-hearted ruffian, villainous tyrant.'[25] Such threats reflect the emotion the cases stirred among supporters of the Fenians, and thus how important it would be for the trial to help defuse, rather than accentuate, tensions.

Despite the heated rhetoric, Canadian officials generally pursued a moderate course in dealing with the alleged Fenians. This approach was, in part, motivated by the desire to avoid antagonizing Fenians in Upper Canada, where a province-wide network of Fenian lodges provided entertainment, companionship, and self-protection to its members, many of whom continued to face discrimination as Irish Catholic immigrants.[26] Canadian officials knew that a fair but firm approach to the prisoners would help prevent angering these local Fenians.

British officials also consistently encouraged a cautious approach to the trials to prevent a further degeneration of relations with the United States, while making sure to avoid the appearance that Washington was shaping British and Canadian decisions.[27] Britain's envoy to Washington, Sir Frederick Bruce, wrote to the governor general of British North America, Lord Monck, at the end of June to warn him about 'the state of opinion here' and to suggest that the 'future tranquility of Canada and her relations with the United States' depended on the treatment of the Fenian prisoners.[28] Monck, who supported a lenient approach, was particularly well suited to dealing with the Fenian issue. He had been governor general since 1861 and had become skilled in dealing with the United States. Born in County Tipperary and a member of the Irish bar, Monck also benefited from his knowledge of the law and of Irish affairs. He believed in the idea of the polyethnic state and saw Ireland as an integral part of Britain. In the debates over how to proceed against the Fenians, he would demonstrate this knowledge, experience, and world view, as well as his reputation for shrewdness and common sense.[29]

In the discussions of how to prosecute, Canadian, and especially British, authorities expressed concern over both the possibility of using court-martial procedures and the retroactive application of the legislation. Monck knew of the earlier concerns of the British law officers regarding the court-martial provisions of the 1838 Lawless Aggressions Act, having contacted Macdonald about the questionable legality of the legislation after Michael Murphy had been arrested in Cornwall in April.[30] He thus sent to England a copy of the legislation extending the Lawless Aggressions Act's provisions to Lower Canada within days of its passage.[31] The British secretary of state for the colonies, Edward Cardwell, stressed moderation in responding to the Fenians. Cardwell, a Liberal lawyer, had served as secretary of state since 1864, although he lost this position when the Conservatives formed a government in 1866. He had some experience with Irish affairs, having served as the chief secretary for Ireland from 1859 to 1861.[32] Cardwell told Monck that he would rely on his 'discretion for the use you will make of these extensive powers.' He expressed his hope that Monck would have recourse, 'in every case in which it may be possible to do so, to the ordinary tribunals for the punishment of offenders.' Cardwell, like many other officials, was keen to ensure that the Fenians would appear before juries – a traditional symbol of British justice – rather than have their cases decided by courts martial. Cardwell also believed that the failure of the Fenian raids would enable Monck to deal with the prisoners 'with deliberate consideration of the various reasons which should affect your treatment of them, and without incurring any appearance of precipitation or undue severity.'[33]

The Earl of Carnarvon (Henry Howard Molyneux) succeeded Cardwell as secretary of state in 1866, and he continued to press Canadian officials to employ a temperate policy towards the Fenian prisoners. Carnarvon, unlike Monck and Cardwell, lacked legal training and expertise in Irish affairs. Yet, as a 'moralizing imperialist,'[34] Carnarvon believed firmly that the empire could not be ruled arbitrarily. For him, the law had to be applied fairly regardless of the circumstances, and his interventions in the Fenian trials seemed motivated by a belief that the Irish could be ruled without resort to coercive laws. In July, Carnarvon noted the 'exceptional character' of the lawless-aggression legislation, while expressing, like Cardwell, his hope that no recourse would be made to courts martial. Carnarvon took pains to juxtapose the condition of Upper Canada in 1838 with its situation in 1866. While the state of affairs in 1838 was 'in many respects a very critical one,' in 1866, owing to the loyalty of Canadians and the helpfulness of the America government, attacks from the United States had been 'baffled and no immediate danger appears to threaten the peace of the Province.' The British government therefore expressed its desire that the prisoners should be tried 'with all deliberation and should not be deprived of any advantages which can be claimed under the ordinary forms of law.' Monck agreed, replying that the summary method by which the prisoners were brought to trial was initially thought necessary given the fear of further Fenian attacks, but that the utter failure of the invasion had made it apparent that ordinary tribunals could deal with the prisoners.[35]

Carnarvon also expressed concerns with the *appearance* of fairness in the trials. He was particularly worried that prosecutors might attempt to apply provisions of the new legislation retroactively. He discussed the 8 June legislation that applied the Lawless Aggressions Act to the Fenian prisoners captured in Lower Canada, following the 7 June attack, telling Monck that the provisions relating to Lower Canada were 'a matter of substantial importance,' since 'a man might apparently be punished as a felon for an act which was not a felony when it was committed.' Such a law was 'liable to serious objection, even as regards her Majesty's subjects; and its application to foreigners would be inconsistent with recognized principles of international law.' Carnarvon thus gave explicit instructions that the legislation should not be used in cases where it would have 'a retrospective operation.'[36]

After receiving Carnarvon's dispatch, Monck expressed another concern to the attorney general of Upper Canada, John A. Macdonald, regarding the possible retrospective application of the legislation. Monck focused on the provisions that allowed British subjects to be tried by a regular court, instead of by court martial, for violation of the lawless-aggression legislation that had occurred before 15 August. Monck said it was plain that the recently passed legislation did not affect the status of foreigners, and he hoped that all of the Fenians would plead as foreigners since then 'there would be no difficulty in dealing with them.' He believed, however, that the revised act had 'a retrospective operation if applied to a British subject' since it had allowed British subjects to be tried for lawless aggression by a regular court, not just by a court martial.[37]

In response to Carnarvon's concern about retroactivity, Attorney General Macdonald and the attorney general of Lower Canada, George-Étienne Cartier, prepared a report on the legislation. Macdonald was especially familiar with the Upper Canada Lawless Aggressions Act, having served as a defence lawyer in 1838 for those charged under the legislation. Macdonald and Cartier detailed the legislative history of the provisions that had begun as the Lawless Aggressions Act, and concluded that the relevant law of Upper Canada had been in continuous operation since 1840. The attorneys general did acknowledge, as Monck had claimed, that the legislation affecting Upper Canada had been altered slightly since the alleged Fenian attack, so that British subjects could be tried by a regular court for lawless aggression, though they contended that this was accept-able because it benefited those accused. As for the legislation applying to prisoners in Lower Canada, Macdonald and Cartier stated that they only intended to try parties who committed hostile acts since 8 June, the date the Lower Canada legislation received royal assent.[38]

Carnarvon's concerns frustrated Macdonald. On 9 October, he wrote to Robert Harrison, telling him that 'I have, until today, been a good deal em-barrassed about the Fenian trials.' He was irritated especially by Carnar-von: 'Lord Carnarvon at first objected to our Acts of last session, in fact he did not understand them, and I thought, at one time, that we would have been obliged to postpone the trials until a special assize sometime during the winter.'[39] The trials nevertheless proceeded, as Monck told Macdon-ald to prosecute so long as there was no retrospective aspect that would violate Carnarvon's dispatch. He also told Macdonald that he assumed that juries would hear the cases.[40] A few days later, however, Macdonald asked Harrison to prosecute the American prisoners first because of the continued confusion stemming from the interventions of Carnarvon and Monck. 'The fact is,' wrote Macdonald, 'we have received rather obscure instructions from Lord Carnarvon, and Lord Monck seems to think, at present, that under those instructions, British subjects must be tried for high treason, and not under the Act of last Session for felony.'[41]

Macdonald tried to convince Monck of the necessity of trying British subjects using regular trials under the legislation passed after the raids. He argued that, unless he could use the new statutes, the order to employ juries would force him to prosecute any one deemed to be a British sub-ject for treason. On 13 October, Macdonald warned Monck that 'a person accused of Treason can only be convicted on the oath of two lawful wit-nesses, unless on voluntary confession, and there are certain provisions as to serving him with lists of the witnesses and panel of jury etc, etc, which are not required in mere felonies.' This was especially problematic, said Macdonald, because there 'will be great difficulty in identifying the prisoners generally, and it will be almost impossible to get the evidence of two witnesses against the British subjects if tried for Treason.' Since 'it would never do to let them go scot free and only convict citizens of the United States,' Macdonald argued that the British subjects should be tried by juries as provided under the August statutes.[42] Macdonald's argu-ments to Monck thus played on Monck's fears that the prisoners would either go free, because of the procedural protections of treason law, or be prosecuted by courts martial, an option that officials in England had for-bidden. Macdonald apparently convinced Monck, who told Carnarvon that the retroactive legislative amendments allowing British subjects to be tried by regular courts for lawless aggression should be used, for if the 'prisoners, being British subjects, be not tried under the Acts of the last session, they must either be liberated without trial, tried by court-martial, or tried for high treason,' and all of these options involved 'very serious difficulties.'[43] It was thus decided to move forward carefully with prosecutions, while paying attention to avoid the perception that these statutes were being applied retroactively.

This concern with avoiding prosecutions for treason also played a role in the handling of the convicts captured in Cornwall in April. The prisoners were to be tried at the autumn assizes in Cornwall, but Murphy and five others escaped and fled to the United States on the night of 1 September. This was a great embarrassment, though Macdonald had not supported the initial decision to capture Murphy, believing that he should have been observed so that more evidence could have been collected. After the escape, Macdonald inquired whether the three remaining prisoners could be tried for aiding invaders. This would be the best course, Macdonald believed, since it would avoid the more complex procedural rights of defendants when charged with treason. By the end of October, the three Fenians remaining had been transferred to Toronto, though none would ultimately be tried.[44]

TORONTO FENIAN TRIALS I (OCTOBER–NOVEMBER 1866)

The Fenian prosecutions occurred in three batches. In October and November 1866, the first group of Fenians faced trial in Toronto. In December, the Sweetsburg trials took place, and in January 1867 another batch of alleged Fenians faced juries in Toronto. The Fenian trials in both Toronto and Sweetsburg were handled with a considerable amount of procedural fairness. In the Toronto trials, the crown employed several leading lawyers to prosecute the defendants. Robert Harrison conducted many of the trials. Born in Montreal to parents from northern Ireland, Harrison was always proud of his ethnic heritage and was a devout Anglican. He was also a long-time friend of Macdonald, with whom he shared an affinity for Conservative politics. After joining the bar in 1855, he served as the chief clerk of the Crown Law Department and then built a reputation as a brilliant advocate in both civil and criminal matters, though he continued to serve often as a counsel for the crown. Peter Oliver suggests that Harrison's 'measured courtroom language' in the Fenian trials, 'and his failure to resort to the histrionics he so often deployed before juries,' suggests that he 'sympathized to some extent' with the Fenian prisoners, regarding them 'more as dupes than as evil-minded marauders.'[45] John Hillyard Cameron also represented the crown. Like Harrison, Cameron was a talented lawyer, an Anglican, and a Conservative. Unlike Harrison, Cameron had a history of holding antagonistic views of Roman Catholics, having served as a grand master of the Orange Order from 1859 to 1870. There is no evidence, however, that Cameron allowed his anti-Catholic views to affect his actions during the trials, and Lord Monck, in fact, asked Cameron to mute Orange anger that might emerge from the Fenian trials. A third crown counsel in the Toronto trials was James Cockburn. Like Harrison and Cameron, Cockburn was an Anglican and a Conservative, and, though he lacked their legal talents, he became solicitor general for Upper Canada in 1864. John McNab, the York County crown attorney, was also a prominent participant.[46]

Several able lawyers arrayed themselves against the crown. The United States government paid the legal expenses of the American prisoners because most of the alleged Fenians were destitute.[47] Kenneth Mckenzie took the lead in the courtroom for the vast majority of the defendants. Mckenzie would prove to be a tough opponent for the crown. Born in Scotland, Mckenzie had served as the judge of the County Court of the United Counties of Frontenac, Lennox and Addington from 1853 until 1865, when he resigned and resumed his private practice, developing a reputation as an especially skilled criminal lawyer. During the Fenian trials, he frequently challenged jurors believed to be biased, and objected strenuously to any perceived error or sign of partiality by the bench. Another active lawyer for many defendants was Matthew Crooks Cameron, who attacked the legality of the June and August legislation. Cameron was a Conservative and a member of the Legislative Assembly of the Province of Canada who had built a strong reputation as a skilful advocate in both criminal and civil cases. Also representing the defence was James Doyle, while the government of the United States paid another attorney to observe the trials. In a few instances, particular defendants chose to have other lawyers represent them.[48]

The crown conducted the trials with a keen eye to creating the appearance of complete impartiality, although this was not Robert Harrison's initial goal. His diary suggests that he personally had found the Fenian raid very unsettling. Upon news of the 1 June attack, he claimed never to have seen Toronto so excited. He purchased a revolver, went on night patrol, and wrote that there was in Toronto a 'universal determination to face danger in any share and put down the foe.'[49] Harrison's fears perhaps led him initially to cast away any concern with the perceived fairness of the trials. On 22 June, he encouraged John A. Macdonald to try the Fenians by courts martial, as 'any other mode of trial' would 'be attended with great risk and expense.'[50] Despite Harrison's early plea for courts martial, Macdonald, armed with instructions from Monck and Carnarvon, carefully shaped the legal proceedings at the Toronto trials. Harrison recorded a two-hour meeting on 4 September with Macdonald and Solicitor General James Cockburn at the Queen's Hotel in Toronto to discuss the Fenian cases.[51] In early October, Macdonald encouraged Harrison to prosecute one or two of the leaders separately, then group the remaining defendants to save expense. Macdonald also told Harrison not to discharge any of the prisoners; rather, he recommended that Harrison 'go before the Grand Jury and get the Bills ignored as to those against whom there is no evidence that affords a reasonable chance of conviction.'[52]

The desire to ensure that the Fenian trials appeared fair but firm permeated the general approach taken by the judge presiding over the Toronto trials in October and November, John Wilson. Nicknamed 'Honest John Wilson,' he had been an able lawyer and a Conservative politician before his appointment to the Court of Common Pleas in 1863. Wilson, like Harrison, received death threats because of his involvement in the Fenian trials,[53] but he remained intent on conducting the trials fairly (although his anger at the Fenian movement would eventually seep through). For example, Wilson allowed a number of the defendants to delay their trials to permit witnesses, many of whom had to travel from the United States, to arrive and give evidence.[54] Wilson sounded most impartial in his 8 October charge to the grand jurors who would determine whether there was sufficient evidence for the prisoners' cases to go before a trial jury. He began by providing a history of the Fenian movement. He talked romantically about the Irish diaspora, noting, for example, that Irish emigrants 'retained with deep devotion the memory of her music, her song and her scenery, and have cherished with intense feeling the undefined belief that Ireland had been wronged, and that the blight of the wrong still rests upon her.' Instead of lashing out at the Fenians in his charge, Wilson took aim at the United States, where he said an attitude existed that no other country had a worthy political system: 'The native-born citizen of the United States seems earnestly impressed with the belief that the American type of a republican government is the very best,' and that 'he seems to take it for granted that rational liberty can be enjoyed under no other, and that all nations would eagerly adopt it if they had the opportunity of shaking off the governments which oppress them.'[55] Wilson said that the American government should have denounced the attacks (which it had not because politicians in the United States were appealing to the Irish vote in the 1866 congressional elections by defending the actions of the Fenian raiders).[56]

Wilson believed that most of the prisoners were simply reckless, and he cautioned jurors not to let their personal anger over the raid shape their decisions. The accused were 'chiefly of that young, reckless, unthinking class.' Most joined 'this nefarious enterprise with the approbation of those to whom they naturally looked up, as a cause worthy of true manhood, the prosecution of which would yield, at least, excitement, and its consummation applause and renown. These considerations and others which they suggest will, I hope, tone down your minds to judicial calmness in the investigation now to come before you.'[57] Wilson also made sure to point out that Canadian authorities had chosen to prosecute the defendants using ordinary British trials, not courts martial, since 'our agricultural and commercial people' would have been 'shocked when they reflected upon it, that men should have suffered death upon the sentence of a court-martial.'[58]

The crown chose to prosecute first the three prisoners thought to be the most important: Robert Blosse Lynch, John McMahon, and David F. Lumsden. According to Cameron, the 'Crown selected the men who were represented to them as being the leaders and inciters of the men in custody.' The crown would later proceed 'against those who were the mere dupes of the leaders.'[59] Considerable fanfare accompanied the first prosecutions. When Lynch's trial opened on 24 October, the sheriff attempted to keep the courtroom from becoming overcrowded, but he had little success, as hundreds of people tried to witness the proceedings.[60]

As Macdonald had recommended to Harrison on 12 October, the first three defendants were all charged as Americans to avoid any problems raised by the use of ordinary courts to try British subjects for lawless aggression as allowed under the August legislation. Robert Lynch's trial was representative of many that would follow in Toronto. Lynch was a middle-aged man said to be from Louisville, Kentucky, who allegedly served as a 'colonel' in the Fenian army. The indictment charged that Lynch had entered Canada with the intent to levy war, that he had been 'unlawfully and feloniously in arms' against the queen, and that he had attacked British subjects with the intent to levy war. Like every Fenian trial, Lynch's case began with jury selection, and, as in many of the trials, the lawyers made extensive use of their right to challenge jurors.[61]

John Hillyard Cameron, in addressing the jury for the prosecution, crafted a message meant both for the jurors and for the public who would read his words in the press. His address contained little law; rather, he appealed to the jurors' sense of patriotism, and, through the newspapers, tried to dissuade the Irish from supporting further attacks. He said that the case was of the utmost importance to the future of Canada since it had 'a direct bearing upon the question as to whether we shall be allowed to pursue in quiet our peaceful avocations henceforth and for all time to come.' Cameron discussed the history and necessity of the Fenian Act, promising that it would be employed only in special circumstances. He also emphasized British North America's close ties to the United States and asserted that the Fenians had only 'imaginary ills or grievances.' Cameron complimented the Irish Catholics of Upper Canada, noting proudly that the Fenians 'speedily found how mistaken they were in their belief that they would be joined by a large number of our people.' Employing the trope of 'British Justice' to good effect, he told the jurors that Lynch would be tried 'by that British justice and in presence of that impartial British tribunal which he and many others like him have so often regarded with contempt.' As a result, Lynch 'may feel sure of a fair and impartial trial according to the just forms of British law.'[62] Cameron's message was clear: the crown would seek justice, not vengeance.

Several aspects of the crown's strategy in the Lynch trial were repeated with more or less success in subsequent cases. First, the crown produced a witness who provided evidence of the damage and injury caused by the Fenians. In the Lynch case, and others, this took the form of a veteran of the Battle of Ridgeway. In addition, in the Lynch trial, as in the other Fenian prosecutions, the crown provided evidence that the prisoner was an American (if the prisoner was indicted solely as an American). To prove Lynch's American citizenship, the crown introduced into evidence a seized letter in which Lynch said that he was an American working as a newspaper reporter during the Fenian raids.

A frequent problem for the crown was how to tie the accused to the events in question, rather than show that he was simply present in Upper Canada at the time of the attacks. Eyewitness identifications were thus key to the success of many of the prosecutions. To demonstrate that Lynch had been an active participant, Cameron attempted to show that Lynch had been called 'colonel,' that he had given orders, and that he had been seen armed with a sword.[63] Thomas Newbiggin said that he had been directed to Lynch when he attempted to regain possession of his family's horses, which the Fenians had commandeered for their operations. In addition, Thomas Ryall, a Fenian who had turned queen's evidence, served as a second eyewitness.[64]

While the prosecution strategy with Lynch was typical, his defence was representative of the weak defence strategy that some Fenians had to employ. The rank and file of the Fenian movement consisted of poor, urban, and unmarried Irish American immigrants. Though defended by counsel during their trials, such men were often unable to provide much in the way of evidence that would either exonerate them or cast them in a sympathetic light. Fenians with employment and family ties were better able to produce witnesses who offered alibis or sympathetic character evidence concerning the defendant's good work habits or committed family life.[65] In other trials, 'character' witnesses told of defendants' propensity for drink as a way of excusing their intemperate actions during the Fenian raid.[66]

Despite his alleged high position in the Fenian movement, Lynch lacked alibi or character evidence. Instead, he had to rely on the evidence provided by his co-accuseds. For example, John McMahon, who would be the next person tried, claimed that he saw Lynch at Fort Erie taking notes for a Louisville newspaper. He also suggested that there was a man from Indianapolis with the Fenians who looked similar to Lynch. David Lumsden provided similar evidence, as did Daniel Whalen and several other prisoners.[67] This kind of testimony, not surprisingly, was not given much weight since jurors undoubtedly knew that the prisoners could collude to give such evidence for each other. As well, none of the alleged Fenians who faced upcoming trials would of course admit their own involvement, meaning that each had to offer a story about why they were innocently in Upper Canada during the Fenian attack. The crown's lawyers made mincemeat of such witnesses. For example, after Whalen gave evidence for Lynch, John Hillyard Cameron launched a very effective cross-examination. Cameron asked why Whalen was in Upper Canada. 'I was seduced to come over on Friday morning,' Whalen replied. This elicited laughter from the spectators in the courtroom. Whalen also admitted that he had 'met with an accident' on 2 June. Cameron chortled, 'An accident, eh! what kind of accident?' Whalen paused, then admitted that 'I was shot in the neck with a Minie ball' at Ridgeway. Cameron mocked him: 'A good many accidents of that kind happened to the Fenians at Ridgeway, I believe,'[68] causing more laughter. Cameron eventually suggested that Lynch's lawyer should consider the difficult position in which he was placing the witnesses, since they risked implicating themselves in the Fenian raid.

In his closing statement for the defence, Richard Martin demonstrated a faith in the fairness of the trial. He acknowledged 'the very great urbanity and fairness with which this trial has been conducted by the gentlemen in charge of the prosecution,'[69] a statement that government officials concerned with the appearance of fairness were glad to hear. Martin then argued that the crown could show no evidence that Lynch had harmed anyone, while emphasizing Lynch's story that he was a reporter. Martin used the trope of 'British Justice' for the defence; he told the jury that 'I am confident every one of you wishes to do British justice towards the prisoner,' and he urged them to prove 'to the world that no Canadian jury can be brought to yield to prejudice.'[70] Martin's closing was also representative of many of the other Fenian trials, in that he claimed that the exculpatory evidence needed by the defence could have been provided had the Canadian government allowed the defence to call the Fenian leadership resident in the United States to testify that Lynch had not been involved in the raid.

In charging the jury, Justice Wilson again gave a measured analysis of the evidence, though one weighted to achieve a conviction. He provided a very expansive reading of the Fenian Act, a reading that would be used in all of the cases in Toronto. He said that, if Lynch was in Upper Canada to aid and comfort the Fenians in any way whatsoever, then he was guilty under the statute. Even if he came as a spiritual adviser or doctor, 'or in any capacity which would give them encouragement and assistance, even although he did not bear arms,' then the law made 'no distinction between him or any other who merely assisted about the camp, and those who actually bore arms and committed acts of hostility.'[71] The jury deliberated for an hour and a half before returning with a guilty verdict.

Sentencing followed immediately after the jury's decision, and statements by Lynch and Wilson indicated both the success at making the trial seem fair and the fact that Wilson held some strong personal views about the Fenian raid that he had suppressed in his charge to the jury. Wilson asked Lynch whether he had anything to say before sentencing. Lynch again claimed his innocence before complimenting the proceedings. 'I must say I think I have been fairly dealt with,' said Lynch, who believed that the crown had 'acted very fairly towards me.' Wilson did not reciprocate Lynch's compliment in sentencing. Instead, he said that the jury's verdict allowed him to finally speak freely. He then launched into an attack on the Fenian movement and Lynch's role in it. 'You alleged that the iron heel of the Saxon was pressed on the neck of the Celt hundreds of years ago,' said Wilson, 'and that your object was to free your land from that oppression. If you had reflected you would have seen that you began to do this by attempting to inflict upon us the very injuries under which you complained your native land was suffering.'[72] Wilson sentenced Lynch to hang.

The prosecutions of the other two prominent prisoners – McMahon and Lumsden – repeated many aspects of Lynch's trial. McMahon, who would also be convicted and sentenced to death, was a Roman Catholic priest from Anderson, Indiana. Described as a quiet-looking man with several ugly scars on his face, McMahon was about forty-five years old and dressed in the garb of the Catholic clergy during his trial.[73]

An important difference between the Lynch and McMahon trials was that McMahon's counsel attempted to attack the propriety of the Fenian Act. Defence lawyer Matthew Crooks Cameron issued a series of objections that threatened to undermine the perceived legitimacy of the trials. Cameron was an experienced lawyer, and he used his knowledge to full effect in attacking the legality of the crown's case. For example, when Harrison began calling witnesses, Cameron objected on the ground that the defendant had not been told the identity of the witnesses prior to trial. He argued that the Fenian Act had created a crime analogous to treason, and thus the defendant had a right to be warned of the crown's witnesses. In response, Harrison asserted that the defendant was not charged with treason but with a statutory felony. Justice Wilson agreed with Harrison, but Cameron nevertheless objected to every subsequent witness on the same ground.[74]

The crown's case against McMahon suggested that he had come to aid the raiders by caring for wounded Fenians and burying the dead. Cameron decided to call no witnesses for the defence; he seemed to believe that the jury would acquit his client because of the lack of evidence that he had carried arms during the raid. He argued that McMahon had simply done his duty as a Christian clergyman. John Hillyard Cameron closed for the prosecution. He asserted that the crown had to show only that McMahon had the intent to levy war; it did not need to show that McMahon had carried arms. McMahon's position in the clergy served as a sign of approval for the actions of the average Fenians. Justice Wilson agreed with the crown's interpretation of the law, although the question of what acts were needed to establish culpability would later be taken up on appeal.[75]

The proceedings against McMahon raised another potentially troubling issue for the legitimacy of the Fenian trials: jury selection. In the trial of McMahon, Matthew Crooks Cameron suggested in his closing statement that none of the jurors were Catholic, and he urged the jurors to prevent religious intolerance from affecting their verdict.[76] His comment suggested that the officials responsible for selecting jurors had removed potential

Catholic jurors from the jury pool or that the prosecution had challenged Catholics and prevented them from joining the jury. Evidence presented at subsequent trials indicates that juries were not consistently packed with Protestants in the Fenian trials, and that Cameron's charge, if true, most likely stemmed from the prosecution's use of challenges.

Jury selection had long been a controversial issue in Upper Canada, especially in political trials. After numerous failed reform efforts dating back to the aftermath of the War of 1812, in 1850 Upper Canada created a new method of selecting jurors meant to avoid allegations of jury packing. The 1850 jury act established perhaps the most complex method of jury selection in the common law world at mid-century. To prevent jury packing, the new act used a series of balloting procedures, instituted a number of checks on officials, and required detailed record keeping of the selection process.[77] The Fenian trials tested the ability of the 1850s jury legislation to prevent packing. For their part, the Irish in Upper Canada had complained about packed juries well before the Fenian trials. In the mid-1860s, for example, the *Irish Canadian* and the *Canadian Freeman* frequently charged that officials ensured that the jury lists of Upper Canada contained few Irish Catholics.[78] Upper Canada's Irish Catholic citizens were also exposed to, and drew from, the long history of complaints of packed juries in Ireland.[79] The Fenian trials resulted in yet more complaints about the jury system. The *Irish Canadian* commented on the composition of the jury panel for the Toronto trials, alleging in late November that there was not a single Catholic on the panel. 'Are the United Counties of York and Peel so barren in Catholic yeoman that there could not be found within their wide domain a solitary person professing that religion intelligent enough to serve as a juror?'[80] The *Canadian Freeman* also told its readers 'how carefully the Irish element appears to have been eliminated from the jury panel.'[81]

Despite these claims, defendants adduced little evidence that officials had packed juries in the Fenian trials. Several defendants issued array challenges in an attempt to have the entire panel of jurors quashed, though in no case could the defendants prove their allegations of jury irregularities. Such array challenges were a frequent tactic in state trials in Ireland, where they were used to object to genuine cases of jury packing, to delay trial, or to cast aspersions on the fairness of a trial.[82] On 13 November, for example, Mckenzie challenged the array of assembled jurors. Justice Wilson refused the challenge on the ground that insufficient cause had been shown to support it. Mckenzie also challenged the array in the trial of John Quinn. Justice Wilson appointed two triers to weigh the validity of the challenge. They held the array valid and the trial went ahead.[83] In a later Fenian trial, Justice Joseph Curran Morrison tried to smooth complaints about jury selection. In the trial of James Burke, he said that the sheriff had informed him that the juries 'had been selected for these Assizes without reference to nationality or religion, and at a time when the selectors could not know that the jurymen would be called to serve on these trials.'[84] The most important evidence countering the claim that the panel called for the Fenian trials lacked Catholics comes from the trial of David Lumsden, in which defence lawyer Matthew Crooks Cameron noted that Lumsden's jury had both Catholics and Protestants.[85] Lumsden's trial thus suggests that Catholics had been included in the panel of potential jurors, and hints that the ability of the prosecution to challenge individual jurors might have allowed for the formation of all-Protestant juries in other cases.

It therefore appears that the jury-selection system introduced in 1850 had limited the packing of juries with virulent partisans. The use of ballot boxes ensured that the jury panel could not be carefully stacked with the strongest anti-Fenians.[86] Defendants who felt that they faced a packed jury also benefited from their ability to request 'mixed' juries of six Americans and six Canadians. Aliens traditionally possessed a right under English law to have a jury composed half of aliens and half of English citizens called a jury *de medietate linguae* (or 'of half tongue').[87] In the Fenian trials, several defendants asked for, and were allowed, mixed juries, though at times the court was unable to locate six Americans able to serve.[88] The care taken around the jury was perhaps the most important element in creating a wide perception of impartiality, and stood in some contrast to the legal responses in Ireland in the late 1840s.[89]

The third prominent defendant was David F. Lumsden, an Episcopal minister, described as tall and genteel looking. The accusations against Lumsden were similar to those levelled against McMahon. The York County crown attorney, John McNab, argued that although Lumsden had never carried a gun, he had walked with the invaders, was at Newbiggin's farm, counselled Fenian officers, and exercised a certain amount of control by representing himself as someone with authority.[90]

Despite the similarity to McMahon's case, a jury acquitted Lumsden, possibly because, as an Episcopalian, he was not a typical Fenian, and certainly because he was able to mount a more vigorous defence using character witnesses. This defence included having Mrs Lumsden, a 'young and lady-like person' who was 'buried in grief and anxiety,'[91] appear in court in support of her husband. Others in attendance included

Bishop Arthur Cleveland Coxe of Buffalo, several American gentlemen, and clergy from Toronto. Lumsden claimed not to have supported the Fenians; rather, he had pretended to be a Roman Catholic priest during the raid to help the wounded. He also claimed to be a reporter for the New York *Herald*. The defence offered a series of upstanding witnesses to give evidence. For example, James Fuller, a physician from Syracuse, said that Lumsden had in the past claimed to be against Fenianism.[92] George Morgan Hill said that he had known Lumsden for twenty years and that Lumsden was a Scot. Bishop Coxe, the bishop of the Episcopal Church in the western diocese of New York, gave evidence that Lumsden had been disciplined professionally because of intemperance, and that Lumsden could no longer serve in the clergy. This, he suggested, had led Lumsden to go to Fort Erie to start his life over, not to help the Fenians. Other defence witnesses confirmed Lumsden's propensity to drink. The story that thus emerged was a sad tale of a Protestant clergyman who had been bedevilled by his own intemperance and who had been caught up in the Fenian cause while looking to restart his life. In his address to the jury, Matthew Crooks Cameron asked the jurors to think of Lumsden's wife and children and to extend the mercy of British justice: 'There are his wife and helpless children who at this moment are resting in dreadful suspense, anxiously thinking of what a British jury may do in reference to the husband and father who has chosen to assume the position of an American citizen – thinking that in a British court of justice he will receive that fair trial which it has been our boast to give every man charged with crime.'[93] The jury acquitted.

With the prominent men tried, proceedings switched to prosecuting the 'dupes.' Several defendants indicted as Americans were found guilty. William Slavin was found guilty after crown witnesses claimed to have seen him with a Fenian rifle. A jury convicted William Hayden when witnesses identified him as riding around on horseback with a Fenian rifle and threatening people to extort money. The crown also convicted Daniel Whalen as an American. The crown demonstrated that Whalen had been a Fenian soldier who had been injured at the Battle of Ridgeway. A jury also found John Quinn guilty based upon evidence that he had stood guard over a captured house.[94]

The crown secured indictments against several defendants as both American and British subjects. In these cases, defendants faced six indictments, three as British subjects and three nearly identical indictments as Americans.[95] This crown strategy was designed to avoid the situation that occurred in the trial of Patrick McGrath on 8 November. The crown had indicted McGrath as an American and had offered evidence that he had stood guard over a captured soldier of the Royal Canadian Rifles. Crown evidence then indicated that McGrath was from Galway, Ireland, and had not taken American citizenship. This led to his acquittal, but he was then immediately reindicted, this time as a British subject, despite the strong objections of defence counsel that McGrath could not be tried a second time for the same alleged crime.[96] After his conviction in January 1867, McGrath appealed, but, as we shall see, the judiciary skirted around the propriety of trying him twice.

Indicting defendants as both British subjects and American citizens avoided the appearance of 'retrying' Irish-born Fenians who might (or might not) have become American citizens, but it was a controversial strategy because it potentially undermined the appearance of fairness by glossing over the difficult question of allegiance. Kenneth Mckenzie strongly objected to defendants facing two sets of indictments and argued that the crown had to elect whether to prosecute defendants as British subjects or American citizens, but for the crown it had the clear benefit of preventing defendants from seeking an acquittal by clouding their citizenship before juries. Whether this was an appropriate strategy for the crown was subsequently taken up on appeal. In the meantime, one prisoner, Thomas School, was convicted after being charged with six counts.[97]

Juries acquitted a number of defendants against whom the crown could offer only weak evidence of their involvement in the raid. These included Benjamin Parry, a sixteen-year-old American citizen, who claimed to be visiting his uncle and who had thrown down a weapon after being asked to hold it by a Fenian. Daniel Drummond, also charged as an American, had been found with a loaded revolver, but there was no proof that he was associated with the Fenians. Indicted as both a British and an American subject, William Duggan was acquitted on all charges. A married railway labourer who had lived in Fort Erie since 1862, Duggan had been dragged from his bed on 20 June, although officials possessed no evidence that he had aided the Fenian attack. The crown also lacked enough evidence to secure a conviction against Patrick Donohue, an American citizen who had crossed into Upper Canada on 3 June and been arrested with no guns at a tavern in Fort Erie where, under the influence of drink, he had lamented that the Fenians had been beaten back across the American border.[98] In addition, grand juries failed to find true bills against several other alleged Fenians. As a result, on 17 November, Robert Harrison and John Hillyard Cameron helped make arrangements to send thirty-nine prisoners to the United States by special train. The trip was kept secret and an armed guard accompanied the prisoners. On reaching the American border, the *Globe* reported that the prisoners gave three cheers for the sheriff, the 'governor' of the goal, and the gaol officials generally.[99]

The first set of Fenian trials had thus ended with the conviction of seven men. Although all of those convicted were sentenced to hang, the decision to commute the death sentences was made in secret almost immediately. Monck wrote to Carnarvon on 3 November that it was the 'unanimous opinion of my Council that the sentence of death in these cases should not be carried into effect,'[100] but that he would await Carnarvon's instructions. Carnarvon responded by recommending that the sentences of Lynch and McMahon be commuted to twenty years' imprisonment. In making this recommendation, Carnarvon expressed his hope that this lesser punishment would be of 'sufficient severity to warn others of the still graver consequences to which they will inevitably render themselves liable by a repetition of such insane and criminal proceedings.'[101] In early December, Monck delayed the hangings until 13 March 1867, and on 3 January all of the Fenians prisoners convicted in October and November had their sentences reduced to twenty years' hard labour at the Kingston Penitentiary.[102]

Overall, the government believed that the trials had gone relatively smoothly, appearing both fair and firm. Attempts to undermine the legitimacy of the proceedings by attacking jury selection and the propriety of the Fenian Act had achieved little. Lord Carnarvon was especially pleased with the conduct of the prosecutions. After reading transcripts of the Toronto trials, he expressed his belief that 'not the faintest shadow of an imputation can, in the opinion of any reasonable person, rest upon the perfect fairness of the proceedings or the justice of the verdict,' for 'every privilege that could be conceded to the prisoners appears to have been allowed.' Even Lynch had 'bore witness to the fairness and impartiality with which his case was tried.'[103]

THE CONVICTS APPEAL

While Carnarvon was pleased, several of the defendants launched appeals of their guilty verdicts. In late November, Kenneth Mckenzie argued appeals on behalf of John McMahon, Robert Lynch, Thomas School, and William Slavin. Mckenzie recognized that the Upper Canadian judiciary would do its best to uphold the convictions. In a confidential letter to the American consul in Toronto, David Thurston, Mckenzie expressed his frustration that it appeared 'as clear as light at noon-day' that the judges were 'determined to uphold the convictions of these unfortunate men if they possibly can do so in the face of the law.'[104] All of the appeals were unsuccessful, and the judiciary's decisions cleared away legal questions that had arisen in the trials that had risked clouding the legitimacy of the Upper Canada proceedings.

John McMahon's appeal rested on a number of grounds that could be grouped into two broad complaints, each of which was disposed of by the chief justice of the Upper Canada Court of Queen's Bench, William Henry Draper.[105] Draper had past experience in dealing with border raiders and political rebels. After the failure of the 1837 rebellion, Draper had organized many of the prosecutions that took place over the next two years, including many that were tried under the Lawless Aggressions Act.[106] Mckenzie's first argument focused on whether the crown had demonstrated that McMahon was a citizen of the United States, as claimed in the indictment. According to the defence, McMahon was a British-born subject who could not relieve himself of the obligations, or protections, of his native allegiance. After surveying the authorities, Draper, however, concluded that a 'natural born subject may, by his own voluntary acts, deprive himself of the exercise of rights which in that capacity he might otherwise claim.' Thus, a person 'may be by birth a British subject, and by naturalization an American citizen.'[107] Draper further suggested that McMahon's complaint was moot anyway, since if he had been deemed a British subject he would have been tried for substantially the same felony.

A second broad argument on appeal queried whether there was evidence of McMahon's intent to levy war. Draper considered the evidence at trial and concluded that it had been sufficient for the judge to send the case to the jury. Draper dismissed the defence suggestion that McMahon should get a new trial because he had been unarmed and had come to minister to wounded or dying Fenians. Draper said that, even if McMahon had been unarmed, 'he would, being so joined to and part of the body, be guilty of their acts of hostility, and of their intent, and so guilty of the felony created by the statute.'[108] Wilson had thus been right to tell the jury that McMahon, by coming to Canada to counsel and encourage the Fenians, was as guilty as if he had carried a rifle.

Justice John Hagarty applied similar reasoning to similar issues in disposing of Robert Lynch's appeal. Hagarty was Irish by birth and had been an active member of the Irish Canadian community, including serving as president of the St Patrick's Society in 1846, but his roots did not lead him to favour the Fenians' position.[109] Mckenzie had again argued the question of citizenship, and Hagarty, like Draper in the *McMahon* case, noted that the defendant could have been tried just as easily as a British subject on near identical charges. As well, Hagarty asserted that there was direct proof that a body of invaders had come from the United States, and 'prima facie we think they might be reasonably assumed to be citizens or subjects thereof.'[110] These assertions undermined the ability of other alleged Fenians to argue that they were British subjects who had been wrongly indicted as American citizens.[111] Hagarty also dismissed Lynch's claim that he had been working as a newspaper reporter for the Louisville *Courier* and thus had not been 'in arms' against Her Majesty. Just as ministering to the Fenians created culpability, so did serving as a journalist to record their accomplishments, concluded Hagarty: 'If a number of men band themselves together for an unlawful purpose, and in pursuit of their common object commit murder, it is right that the Court should pointedly refuse to accept the proposition that a full share of responsibility for their acts does not extend to the surgeon who accompanies them to dress their wounds, to the clergyman who attends to offer spiritual consolation, or to the reporter who volunteers to witness and record their achievements. The presence of any one, in any character, aiding and abetting or encouraging the prosecution of the unlawful design, must involve a share in the common guilt.'[112] Hagarty's decision, like Draper's, prevented alleged Fenians in subsequent trials from attempting to explain their place in Canada during the Fenian raids as related to some professional activity.

The third appeal case, *R. v. School*, settled in the crown's favour whether a defendant could face two sets of indictments, one that charged the defendant as a British subject and one charging the defendant as an American. Justice Joseph Curran Morrison wrote for the court in *School*. Born in Ireland, Morrison immigrated to Upper Canada in 1830 and joined the bar in 1839. He acted as a prosecutor in a number of prominent murder trials before his appointment to the bench in 1862, and his judgments tended to focus on achieving just results rather than always offering sound reasoning.[113] Morrison identified several English authorities to establish the crown's right to employ two sets of indictments. Moreover, it was, in his view, 'the usual practice, when it is uncertain whether the evidence will support the charges as laid, to insert several counts in an indictment.' Morrison also emphasized the similarity of the counts. 'The question of his being a British subject or a citizen of a foreign state,' reasoned Morrison, 'could not have embarrassed him in his defence, for ... if he was prepared to meet the one set of counts, he was prepared to meet the other.'[114]

The final case appealed from the first set of Toronto Fenian trials was *R. v. Slavin*, in which Justice Adam Wilson of the Upper Canada Court of Common Pleas refused to grant a new trial.[115] Wilson was born in Scotland, had immigrated to Upper Canada in 1830, and had served as solicitor general before his appointment to the bench in 1863.[116] He disposed of several grounds of appeal argued by Mckenzie, including that the crown had failed to show that Slavin had the intent to levy war or had carried arms. Slavin had apparently entered Upper Canada on his own, had spent some time with the Fenians, and had briefly carried a rifle (which he said he had found). He claimed, however, not to have actually been a Fenian, and there was no evidence that he had participated in any fighting (he was captured before the Battle of Ridgeway). In Mckenzie's opinion, the 'evidence upon which Slavin was convicted was very slight.'[117] On the issue of intent, Wilson dismissed Mckenzie's claim that intent had to be gleaned from an overt act of hostility or a written or stated declaration. Rather, Wilson reasoned that the Battle of Ridgeway could be taken as evidence of Slavin's intent: 'Whenever a joint participation in an enterprise is shown, any act done in furtherance of the common design is evidence against all who were at any time concerned in it.' Therefore, 'the fighting which took place on the day the prisoner was arrested, and after his arrest, was some evidence that such fighting was contemplated by the parties while the prisoner was with them before his arrest.' As had been decided in McMahon's and Lynch's cases, it was also held unnecessary for the defendant to have fired a gun to be 'in arms.'[118] The judgment in *Slavin* thus, like those in the other appeals, laid out principles that gave little assistance to the alleged Fenians who would be tried later at Sweetsburg and Toronto.

SWEETSBURG FENIAN TRIALS (DECEMBER 1866)

The trials of the sixteen prisoners captured at Pigeon Hill, Lower Canada, began in December, just after the appeal decisions had been handed down in Upper Canada. The issue of retroactive legislation had even more significance in the Sweetsburg trials than in the Toronto proceedings. Lord Carnarvon's order not to apply legislation retroactively was especially problematic in Lower Canada, which had not possessed legislation similar to the Lawless Aggressions Act when the Fenian troubles arose.[119] As a result, the prisoners in Lower Canada could be tried only for acts they committed after 8 June.

A smaller cast of lawyers worked for the crown and for the defendants. Thomas Kennedy Ramsay served as the crown prosecutor. A Scot by birth, Ramsay immigrated in 1847 to Lower Canada, where he became a lawyer and developed an excellent professional reputation. From 1864 to 1868 he served as the crown attorney at Montreal, the post in which he prosecuted the Fenian convicts. Bernard Devlin led the defence. Son of a rich landowner in Ireland, Devlin had immigrated in 1844 to Lower Canada, where he worked as a journalist, then as a lawyer. He developed a large practice, particularly in the area of criminal law. He was active in debates over Irish affairs, serving as president of the Montreal St Patrick's Society and even calling for the repeal of the Act of Union in 1848. He also served for fifteen years as an officer in the militia, and during the Fenian raid into Lower Canada he commanded the 1st regiment of the Prince of Wales Rifles.[120] Despite his role in dispersing the Fenian attacks, William Roberts claimed that the American Fenians had retained Devlin at a cost of 2,500 dollars to defend the prisoners in Lower Canada. James O'Halloran assisted Devlin in several of the trials. Born in the County of Cork, Ireland, O'Halloran represented Missisquoi in the Legislative Assembly in the 1860s. As in the Toronto trials, the American government sent a representative to watch the legal proceedings.[121]

Judge Francis Godschall Johnson heard the cases in Sweetsburg. Although born in England, Johnson was fluently bilingual in French and English, and during the 1840s he had developed a reputation as an exceptional criminal law lawyer. Johnson became the crown prosecutor for the District of Montreal in 1858, then a judge of the Superior Court for the District of Bedford in June 1865, the position in which he heard the Fenian cases in Sweetsburg.[122]

Proceedings opened on 3 December with considerably less fanfare than the Toronto Fenian trials. A correspondent for the Toronto *Globe* suggested that the crowd that came for the opening of the court was no bigger than for an ordinary sitting.[123] Johnson, like Wilson in Toronto, delivered a fairly impartial charge. He informed the jurors that the sixteen alleged Fenians were accused of very serious crimes. The defendants' actions were made worse, said Johnson, because of the peaceful state of affairs between the United States and British North America. They were 'an outrage upon our neighbours and upon ourselves.' Johnson warned the jurors, however, to avoid letting anger over the raid affect their decisions, suggesting that the trials must proceed 'upon known public rules of law existing for the protection of all alike.'[124]

The grand jury found true bills against fourteen of the sixteen defendants. Seven prisoners faced charges as American citizens, and seven as

British subjects. No defendant was initially charged as both a British subject and an American citizen. Each American defendant faced two counts, one for entering Lower Canada with intent to levy war against Her Majesty, and one for being and continuing in arms against Her Majesty. The indictments against the British subjects were for joining persons who had entered Lower Canada with intent to levy war; entering Lower Canada with subjects of a foreign state at peace with Her Majesty with intent to levy war; and levying war in company with citizens of a foreign state at peace with Britain.[125]

Devlin launched several objections to the proceedings before the trials began, including that the act used to prosecute the prisoners was a retroactive law, having received assent on 8 June. Ramsay met with Governor General Monck, who was headed to England, and then announced that the desire to avoid any appearance of retroactive legislation meant he would withdraw the charges against the American prisoners, since those indictments had accused the defendants of acts committed on 7 June. The crown, however, refused to release the Americans, saying that they would face other charges. On 13 December, the crown sought new true bills against the Americans. This time, a more diverse set of charges were offered. The grand jury found true bills against George Crawford as a foreign citizen and as a British subject for being in arms against Her Majesty. He also faced a larceny charge. The crown indicted Gustave Merrill for being a foreign citizen in arms, and for theft, and charged Terence McDonald for robbery and for assault with intent to rape. Three other defendants would be tried for being foreign citizens in arms against Her Majesty.[126]

The trouble with the indictments against American citizens would prove indicative of the crown's difficulties in securing convictions at Sweetsburg. The first trial, however, did result in a conviction. Thomas Madden was indicted as a British subject. About twenty-five years of age, Madden, among all the prisoners, was considered to have committed the most serious crimes. According to Lieutenant-General Sir John Michel, the commander of military forces in British North America who was the British administrator of the government during Monck's absence between December 1866 and June 1867, Madden's case was more serious than Lynch's or McMahon's since he had been captured with arms in his hands, and because he (or people he was with) had fired on those trying to arrest him.[127]

Jury composition would prove contentious in the trials in Lower Canada, just as it had in Toronto. Complaints about jury selection were frequent in Lower Canada in the mid-nineteenth century, and reforms created procedures for creating juries distinctive from those used in Upper Canada.[128] At the time of the Fenian trials in Lower Canada, the sheriff made lists of eligible jurors, and the panels of jurors to be called to court were drawn by ballot.[129] In Madden's case, Devlin attempted to challenge the panels of grand jurors and petit jurors, but with no success. In doing so, he charged, among other things, that neither the grand jury nor the petty jury had a single English-speaking Catholic member. Judge Johnson took this allegation seriously and delayed the trial to consider it, though he ultimately decided that the stated reasons for the challenge either were not specific enough or were disproved by his own examination of the jury books and jury lists.[130]

The crown then called a series of witnesses who gave evidence describing the raid as a means of establishing that the Fenians had levied war, though none of this first group identified Madden as a participant. The crown followed with witnesses who gave testimony that Madden had been armed and had resisted arrest, and was shot as a result, and that others had referred to him as 'captain.' The defence asked the jurors not to punish such a minor figure in the raid, nor to find him guilty for his actions on 9 June using a law passed on 8 June. The jury quickly reached a verdict of guilty, and Judge Johnson sentenced Madden to hang in February 1867.[131] Only two other defendants were convicted under the Lower Canada Fenian Act. Thomas Smith was an eighteen-year-old from Boston who had been captured after throwing away his rifle. The first jury hearing his case could not agree, but a second found him guilty. Michael Crowley received a conviction for being a British subject who had joined himself with those who entered Lower Canada to levy war against the queen.[132]

The crown failed to secure convictions against several defendants. A jury refused to convict Terence McDonald, who claimed to have been born in Scotland and to have served in the United States army. Cornelius Owens was discharged when the crown abandoned its case because of a lack of evidence for events that occurred after the passage of the legislation. Witnesses said that James Reardon had been assigned to protect a house and its occupants, though he had placed his gun in the house's shed. The crown witness said Reardon had protected the house well. Judge Johnson concluded that the crown had failed to make a case that Reardon was 'in arms' against the queen, and thus directed the jury to find him not guilty. Edward Gilgan, eighteen years old and from Massachusetts, was acquitted, as was Gustine Morrill, another teenager who was accused of being a bystander in a party of Fenians who had robbed a man. Judge Johnson also directed the acquittal of Edward Carroll and George Howard, both indicted as British subjects, because the crown lacked sufficient evidence for juries to consider their cases.[133]

There was little chance that the three men convicted of capital charges would be hanged. In light of the commutations given to the first group of Fenians tried in Toronto, Sir John Michel told Carnarvon on 27 December that he would not put the Sweetsburg convicts to death until he received further instructions. Michel also made sure to point out that 'on grounds of public policy it is my opinion that none of the convicts should suffer the extreme penalty of the law.'[134] Despite saying that he would await further instructions, Michel wrote to Carnarvon on 4 January to inform him that a decision had been made to commute the sentences of the Lower Canadian Fenians to twenty years' imprisonment, a move that Carnarvon subsequently approved. The three prisoners convicted in Lower Canada were transferred from the Bedford gaol to Kingston Penitentiary, in part because the Bedford gaol was only fifteen miles from the American border and therefore a tempting target for jailbreak attempts.[135]

TORONTO FENIAN TRIALS II (JANUARY 1867)

The Fenian trials in Toronto restarted on 11 January 1867. Justice Joseph Curran Morrison, who had written the appeal decision in *R. v. School*, presided. None of the defendants were as prominent as McMahon or Lynch, and most of the trials took much less time to complete, in part because the appeal judgments had settled several issues contentious in the earlier cases. Mckenzie nevertheless continued to put forward a rigorous defence. For example, he challenged a number of jurors and again suggested that the jury panel had been packed against the defendants, an issue that had not been settled on appeal. Defendants indicted as Americans again asked for, and were allowed, mixed juries, though at times the court was unable to locate six Americans able to serve.[136] Mckenzie also employed several new strategies. For instance, he attempted to undermine the credibility of John Metcalfe, a turnkey at the Toronto gaol who frequently gave evidence for the crown. Metcalfe had taken statements from prisoners in the gaol, which he then reported on the witness stand.[137] The crown relied heavily on Metcalfe, and Mckenzie began to cross-examine him fiercely about his method of collecting evidence. Mckenzie attacked Metcalfe by asking if he had told defendants that their statements would be used in court, and forced Metcalfe to admit to being accompanied in the jail by soldiers, leading Mckenzie to argue that prisoners had been intimidated into giving incriminating testimony.[138]

In all, fifteen more Fenians were found guilty under the Fenian Act, all of whom received death sentences. At least twelve others were acquitted or discharged for lack of evidence.[139] The acquitted defendants had often been brought to trial on weak evidence. John Smith, for example, had been found hiding in a hayloft armed only with some mediocre poetry:

> There is a Fenian band in America,
> Who are preparing now.
> We will strike a blow for freedom
> That will lay Old England low,
> With the assistance of the United States,
> To the world it will be seen
> That stars and shamrocks will be sown
> On Erin's ground of green.[140]

The trial of George J. Matthews was another weak case for the crown. Matthews had not actually taken part in the June raid but had been captured in Thorold in September by the governor general's bodyguard. Matthews had stopped a member of the bodyguard and proudly informed him that the Fenians were going to attack and that he could do Fenian drills (he asked for a gun to demonstrate; the perplexed bodyguard instead provided him with a stick). A crown witness claimed that he might have seen Matthews during the June raid, but the jury apparently concluded that Matthews was just an unstable character with a propensity to drink, and they acquitted him without leaving the jury box.[141]

Mckenzie once again complimented the court on its handling of the cases. At the conclusion of the assize, he spoke for the rest of the defence lawyers in expressing their 'appreciation of the very courteous way in which these trials have been conducted, from beginning to end,' and stated their appreciation for the 'very fair and impartial manner in which your Lordship has discharged your duties as presiding Judge.'[142] Mckenzie nevertheless appealed two cases, but failed to secure any new trials. The appeal of Owen Kennedy's conviction revolved around jury selection. On 23 November, the sheriff for the United Counties of York and Peel received the usual precept for the return of juries for the upcoming January assize in Toronto. On 1 January 1867, the United Counties of York and Peel divided into separate counties. The sheriff returned a panel of petit jurors containing the names of fifty-four jurors from what would become York County, and thirty from Peel County. After the division of the counties, however, only the jurors from York County attended, meaning that the sheriff had returned a panel of fifty-four jurors, rather than the eighty-four that had been ordered. A mixed jury of Americans and Canadians tried Kennedy, the six Canadian jurors coming from the fifty-four returned York jurors.[143] On appeal, Chief Justice Draper acknowledged the importance of the complaint and admitted that 'in strictness the panel should have been drafted from the jury list of York alone,' but he ruled that a provision of the jury act held that no failure to follow the statute could be grounds for quashing a decision. Thus, 'by the express words of the statute,' the error was 'no ground for impeaching the verdict.'[144]

Patrick McGrath also appealed his conviction. The crown had first tried McGrath as an American citizen in November 1866, when he was acquitted. He had been immediately reindicted as a British subject, then convicted in January.[145] In March the Court of Queen's Bench considered whether the guilty verdict in McGrath's case should be quashed. The defence pleaded *autrefois acquit* – that is, that McGrath had previously been acquitted of the same offence, on substantially the same evidence, and that therefore he could not be tried a second time. Mckenzie had initially stated that he had 'every confidence that, if the law has its due effect, he will succeed on this plea.'[146] Chief Justice Draper, however, held that the substance of the charges levied against American citizens and British subjects were *not* the same: 'The offence against the acts committed by a British subject, requires proof, not only of the *status* as such subject, but also of the joining with foreigners in the commission of it. The same evidence, irrespective of national *status*, which will convict a foreigner, would not convict the subject; a man indicted under this act as a foreigner is entitled, on proof of his being a subject, to an acquittal, because as against the subject additional averments and proofs are necessary.'[147] In Draper's view, a 'comparison of the two indictments brings to view variances which are substantial, not mere differences of time, *place or* quantity.'[148] Draper's judgment narrowed the grounds for prosecuting British subjects by requiring that evidence be produced that they had allied themselves with foreigners crossing the border to levy war. The ruling, however, had little impact on the fate of the Fenian prisoners, since all of the British subjects had presumably allied themselves to the Irish American raiders. His appeal judgment nevertheless stood in contrast to many comments made by the other Upper Canadian judges who claimed that the indictments used against British subjects and American citizens were all but identical.[149]

This led Mckenzie to rail privately against the judiciary. He said that he was 'much disappointed, as, notwithstanding the elaborate judgment delivered by the Court my reason is not convinced of its soundness.'[150]

'THE PAINS OF MARTYRDOM':
PUNISHMENT, COMMUTATION, AND RELEASE

The punishment and eventual release of the convicted Fenians provides a further illustration of how the justice system was meant to appear fair but firm. All of the death sentences were commuted to lengthy twenty-year terms of imprisonment. In a letter to Lord Lisgar in 1870, Macdonald hinted that he believed that the threat of such long prison terms could dissuade future Fenian aggression. He noted that General O'Neill and several other Fenian leaders had briefly been imprisoned in the United States before being released. Macdonald believed that their 'imprisonment, short as it has been, will be sufficient to crown them as martyrs in the eyes of their countrymen' but would not 'satisfy the injuries inflicted upon the people of Canada.' The American pardons would encourage future aggression in the future. 'If these people are taught, by the action of the American Government that a conviction is to be followed by a minimal punishment,' Macdonald reasoned, 'and that they can gain all the glory of martyrs without suffering the pains of martyrdom, the incentive to continued agitation and conspiracy will be irresistible.'[151] Presumably Macdonald believed that twenty-year jail terms sufficed as a disincentive to joining the Fenian cause.

These long prison terms had several other benefits for the government. If no further Fenian attacks took place, the prisoners could be released early. On the other hand, if there were threats of additional attacks, the prisoners could be kept in prison and used as examples of the possible punishment new prisoners would face for joining the Fenian cause. Macdonald discussed in private correspondence this consideration in January 1872. He claimed that the government had intended to release the Fenians gradually. Unfortunately for the inmates, 'that bad man General O'Neill re-commenced his Fenian movements on the Manitoba Frontier.' As a result, the Fenian prisoners at Kingston found out that 'their leaders in the United States are their worst enemies,' for had 'it not been for the latter they would have been released long ago.' Macdonald concluded that it was impossible to release Fenian prisoners in eastern Canada while the nation faced Fenian attacks in the west, even though he considered them 'more misguided than criminal.'[152]

A concern with making martyrs also ensured that the inmates received good treatment at Kingston Penitentiary. Kingston had three wardens in the period it held the Fenians: Donald Aeneas Macdonnell, who retired in 1869; James Ferres, a short-term replacement who died in 1870; and John Creighton. Both Ferres and Creighton took a humane approach to operating the prison, loosening harsh rules and providing inmates with a handful of new comforts.[153] Most of the Fenians admitted that they were treated well. In July 1871 the *Irish Canadian* reported on the release of Fenian prisoners, noting that Owen Kennedy of Cincinnati had been discharged, that he 'speaks feelingly of the kind treatment of Mr. Warden Creighton, to serve whom, he assured us, the Fenian prisoners would risk life and limb,' and that there could be 'no doubt that, under Mr. Creighton's considerate and judicious management, things have improved vastly in the Kingston Penitentiary.'[154] Soon after his release, Patrick McGrath thanked Creighton 'from the bottom of my heart for your kindness to me and my companions.'[155] Daniel Quinn wrote to Creighton as soon as arrived in Louisville. He wanted to express his gratitude 'for the kindness and the sympathy you have shown to us in prison. You are the first man that even came into prison that showed any kindness to us.'[156]

There were some exceptions to these statements of good treatment. John Quinn charged that he had been beaten by an Orange prison official.[157] Robert Lynch also complained about his treatment. According to an American official who visited Kingston Penitentiary, Lynch said that he was 'not treated as political prisoners are treated in Great Britain, and other Foreign Countries; that he is compelled to do hard labor for each and every day ten hours (Sunday excepted) and to wear convict uniform, the same as the commonest felon in the prison – there being no distinction made between political and other prisoners.' The official, however, reported that he was 'well satisfied that the Warden is a humane man, and would do for the prisoner Lynch all he could consistently to make his confinement as bearable as possible.'[158] As well, despite Lynch's complaints, Lynch wrote to Warden Creighton after his release to tell him that it was 'indeed a happy day for us when you became Warden of the Kingston Penitentiary.'[159]

For Canadian authorities, this good treatment also apparently had the benefit of dividing Fenian sympathizers. The pro-Fenian newspaper the *Irish Canadian* often charged that the inmates received poor treatment. In 1869, however, the editor of the *Irish Canadian*, Patrick Boyle, and F.B. McNamee of the Montreal St Patrick Society made a surprise visit to the penitentiary. They discovered that the inmates were in fact in good condition and had few complaints. After publishing this finding, they soon found themselves under attack by Fenian supporters. McNamee wrote to Macdonald about his visit to Kingston, asking Macdonald to shorten the prisoners' terms of imprisonment. He admitted some personal interest in the prisoners' release. 'You are probably aware that some time ago I went to the Penitentiary in order to judge for myself whether certain reports of ill-treatment of Fenian prisoners that had appeared were true or false,' offered McNamee, and that 'finding that they were false I at once published my knowledge and conviction to that effect, which brought upon me the anger of the Fenian Press of the United States, and also that of not a few of my countrymen in Canada.' McNamee thus suggested that two sick Fenians be released before they died to engender goodwill.[160] Macdonald took pride in having split the views of Irish Catholics on the prisoners. He wrote in December 1869 that Boyle and McNamee were under attack from Fenian supporters 'for the only honest act they ever did in their lives.'[161]

The government began receiving petitions for the release of the prisoners almost immediately. For the government, these pleas for pardons had the benefit of forcing Irish Canadians to plead their loyalty. For example, the Catholic bishop of Toronto, John Joseph Lynch, wrote in October 1869 to John A. Macdonald on behalf of the Catholics 'of this portion of Ontario' to ask for the release of the prisoners. According to Lynch, it would be 'a gracious act and a highly appreciated tribute to the liberal and loyal people of the Dominion' to 'give an order for the speedy release of those prisoners.' Lynch noted that he was quietly calling attention to the fate of the prisoners. There 'might have been meetings held and petitions forwarded from all parts of the country, which might have somewhat embarrassed the authorities'; however, the 'strong and quiet modes have succeeded best with us in keeping our people peaceful and loyal, though much excited by the strong events then transpiring at home and abroad.'[162]

At least one informal call for a pardon seems to have freed an innocent person. John O'Connor had been convicted on evidence that he had carried dispatches for General O'Neill.[163] A petition from O'Connor laid out a case for a pardon. It suggested that the 'only evidence against him was that of a witness named Raney, who swore that he saw him on Friday the first day of June carrying despatches' from General O'Neil, but that Raney 'would not swear that it was impossible for him to be mistaken.' O'Connor further expressed his concern that his alibi witnesses from Buffalo had not been believed because they were Americans.[164] The sheriff of Toronto wrote that O'Connor had conducted himself in a respectful manner while in gaol and had never expressed any disloyal sentiments.[165] Inhabitants of Wellington County prepared another petition, in which they claimed to have known O'Connor and his family for many years and that 'his conduct has always been most steady and exemplary, and his loyalty, until charged of the crime of which he is convicted, undoubted.' The petitioners wrote that they 'cannot but think, from the nature of the evidence, that some mistake has been made, and that he is guiltless of the offence charged.'[166] The trial judge, Justice Morrison, admitted that the jury could have gone either way in the O'Connor case, even suggesting that he was slightly dissatisfied with the verdict.[167] The government responded by pardoning O'Connor in April 1867.[168]

In deciding whether and when to release the Fenian convicts, Macdonald considered several issues, in addition to whether there were threats of more Fenian attacks or heartfelt appeals for pardons. Macdonald was often motivated by local political considerations. In a letter to J.G. Moylan, for example, he suggested that freeing Fenians would please Catholic voters. He noted that he might be criticized for pardons, but that he would not regret releasing the convicts because 'it will do one no harm, on the contrary I think it will prove to the Roman Catholics of Ontario that I have consulted their feelings in a matter.'[169]

In the end, none of the Fenian prisoners served more than a quarter of their prison terms. John McMahon received a pardon on 22 July 1869. The government then released William Slavin on 30 May 1870 and Robert Lynch on 6 April 1871, after considerable lobbying on Lynch's behalf.[170] The last Fenian prisoner at Kingston, Daniel Whalen, left the penitentiary in July 1872.

CONCLUSION

Decisions regarding how to try and punish the Fenians were influenced by the various goals of British officials, Canadian politicians, judges, lawyers, and prison staff. To different degrees, all wanted the response to the Fenian raids to appear firm but fair. Players in the drama, however, often had different audiences in mind in crafting the lesson to be taken from the trials. British officials, for example, issued directions requiring that those accused should benefit from scrupulous attention to the procedural norms of 'British Justice' as a means of placating antagonistic Americans and the Irish. For others, including John A. Macdonald, the desire to convict the Fenians led them to undercut the appearance of fairness, through, for instance, the attempts to make legislation retroactive, to gloss over the tricky legal issue of allegiance, and to re-prosecute prisoners. However, even when legal rules and procedures were bent to achieve prosecutions, officials and politicians remained intent on creating an image of the trials as fair and 'just' according to the tenets of 'British Justice.' Macdonald and his Canadian contemporaries wanted to try the Fenians in such a way that Irish Canadians felt the justice system had treated their countrymen fairly, to please British officials, and to develop better relations with the United States. Jury trials thus *had* to be used, and officials wrung their hands over the retrospective application of the Fenian Act. The law also had to be merciful. Commuting of the death sentences and the eventual pardon of the Fenian prisoners, as well as their treatment in prison, made the application of the law seem fair and kind. The use of oppressive punishment was not a viable option to stamp out the Fenian cause. The Irish diaspora of the mid-nineteenth century meant that the Fenian movement and its leaders would remain outside the formal reach of British justice. The Fenians could not be fought head on by the legal system. Rather, the ideology of 'British Justice,' as expressed through mercy and justice, had to create a message that could combat the Fenian threat at home *and* abroad. [171]

NOTES

Thanks to Philip Girard, Krista Kesselring, Cynthia Neville, John Reid, and the editors of this volume for their valuable comments. Special thanks to Peter Vronsky, who shared with me his research on the Fenian trials from the United States National Archives. Also, thanks to Bob Beal, who offered input on the early design of this article. Earlier versions of this article were presented at the 2006 Annual Meeting of the Canadian Historical Association and the Dalhousie University Legal History Reading Group.

1 Kenneth McNaught, 'Political Trials and the Canadian Political Tradition,' *University of Toronto Law Journal* 24 (1974): 149–69.
2 Beverley Boissery, *A Deep Sense of Wrong: The Treason Trials and Transportation to New South Wales of Lower Canadian Rebels after the 1838 Rebellion* (Toronto: Osgoode Society for Canadian Legal History / University of Toronto Press 1995); Rainer Baehre, 'Trying the Rebels: Emergency Legislation and the Colonial Executive's Overall Legal Strategy in the Upper Canadian Rebellion,' in *CST 2*, 41–61; Barry Wright, 'The Kingston and London Courts Martial,' in ibid., 130–59; F. Murray Greenwood, 'The Prince Affair: "Gallant Colonel" or

"The Windsor Butcher"?' in ibid., 160–87; Jean-Marie Fecteau, '"This Ultimate Resource": Martial Law and State Repression in Lower Canada, 1837–38,' in ibid., 207–47; F. Murray Greenwood, 'The General Court Martial at Montreal, 1838-9: Operation and the Irish Comparison,' in ibid., 279–324.

3 Bob Beal and Rod Macleod, *Prairie Fire: The 1885 North-West Rebellion* (Edmonton: Hurtig 1984); Louis Thomas, 'A Judicial Murder – The Trial of Louis Riel,' in Howard Palmer, ed., *The Settlement of the West* (Calgary: University of Calgary 1977), 37–59; Thomas Flanagan, 'The Riel Trial Revisited: Criminal Procedure and the Law in 1885,' *Saskatchewan History* 36 (1981): 57–73.

4 W.S. Neidhardt, 'The Fenian Trials in the Province of Canada, 1866–7: A Case Study of Law and Politics in Action,' *Ontario History* 66 (1974): 23–36; W.S. Neidhardt, *Fenianism in North America* (University Park: Pennsylvania State University Press 1975), 99–108.

5 Hereward Senior, *The Fenians and Canada* (Toronto: Macmillan 1978), 109–11.

6 Robin W. Winks, *The Civil War Years: Canada and the United States* (Lanham, Md.: University Press of America 1988), 295–336; Dennis K. Wilson, *Justice under Pressure: The Saint Albans Raid and Its Aftermath* (Lanham, Md.: University Press of America 1992).

7 A full description of the persecution suffered by the Irish is beyond the scope of this article, but a partial list of the long-term motivations for the Fenians includes the English conquest and colonization of Ireland over several centuries, the expropriation of land for Protestant settlers, and the limitations placed on Irish Catholics serving in the Irish, and then British, parliaments.

8 Paul Ward, *Britishness since 1870* (New York: Routledge 2004); Peter Gray, ed., *Victoria's Ireland?: Irishness and Britishness, 1837–1901* (Dublin: Four Courts Press 2004); Norman Davies, *The Isles: A History* (New York: Oxford 1999). On Irish Catholic integration in Toronto, see Mark G. McGowan, 'The De-greening of the Irish: Toronto's Irish Catholic Press, Imperialism, and the Forging of a New Identity, 1887–1914,' Canadian Historical Association *Historical Papers* 24 (1989): 118–45.

9 On the importance of the idea of 'British Justice,' see Greg Marquis, 'Doing Justice to "British Justice": Law, Ideology and Canadian Historiography,' in W.W. Pue and Barry Wright, eds., *Canadian Perspectives on Law and Society: Issues in Legal History* (Ottawa: Carleton University Press 1988), 43–69; Philip Girard, 'British Justice, English Law, and Canadian Legal Culture,' in Philip Buckner, ed., *Canada and the British Empire* (Oxford: Oxford University Press 2008), 259–77.

10 *Treason Felony Act*, 11, 12 Vic. c.12. (U.K.) On the Young Ireland movement, see D. George Boyce, *Nationalism in Ireland* (Baltimore: John Hopkins University Press 1982), 154–91; Richard P. Davis, *The Young Ireland Movement*

(Dublin: Gill and Macmillan 1988); Robert Sloan, *William Smith O'Brien and the Young Ireland Rebellion of 1848* (Dublin: Four Courts 2000).

11 Senior, *The Fenians and Canada*, 90; C.P. Stacey, 'A Fenian Interlude: The Story of Michael Murphy,' *CHR* 15 (1934): 133–54; W.S. Neidhardt, 'Michael Murphy,' *DCB*, 9: 587–9.

12 Lord Monck to Edward Cardwell, 4 June 1866, in *Correspondence respecting the Recent Fenian Aggressions upon Canada* (London: Harrison and Sons 1867), 2.

13 Hereward Senior, *The Last Invasion of Canada: The Fenian Raids, 1866–1870* (Toronto: Dundurn Press 1991), 109–29.

14 Lawless Aggressions Act, SUC 1838 c.3. See also the Supporting Documents section of this volume for 1866 and 1867 amendments.

15 F. Murray Greenwood and Barry Wright, 'Introduction: Rebellion, Invasion, and the Crisis of the Colonial State in the Canadas, 1837–9,' in Greenwood and Wright, eds., *CST 2*, 27.

16 Lawless Aggressions Act, SUC 1838 c.3 s.1.

17 F. Murray Greenwood and Barry Wright, 'Introduction: State Trials, the Rule of Law, and Executive Powers in Early Canada,' in *CST 1*, 24–7; Alexander H. Shapiro, 'Political Theory and the Growth of Defensive Safeguards in Criminal Procedure: The Origins of the Treason Trials Act of 1696,' *Law and History Review* 11 (1993): 215.

18 An Act to Alter and Amend an Act ...Intitled, "An Act to Protect the Inhabitants of this Provinces from Subjects of Foreign Countries at Peace with Her Majesty," SUC 1840 c.12.

19 An Act to Protect the Inhabitants of Lower Canada against Lawless Aggressions from Subjects of Foreign Countries at Peace with Her Majesty, SC 1866 c.2.

20 An Act to Amend the Act of the Present Session, Intitled: An Act to Protect the Inhabitants of Lower Canada against Lawless Aggressions from Subjects of Foreign Countries at Peace with Her Majesty, SC 1866 c.3.

21 An Act to Amend the Ninety-Eighth Chapter of the Consolidated Statutes for Upper Canada, SC 1866 c.4.

22 Greenwood, 'The Prince Affair,' 161–7.

23 Neidhardt, 'The Fenian Trials in the Province of Canada, 1866–7,' 25.

24 E. Tupper to G. McMicken, 31 Aug. 1866, LAC, MG 26A, vol. 238, 104699; E. Tupper to G. McMicken, 24 Sept. 1866, LAC, MG 26A, vol. 238, 104891–3; E. Tupper to G. McMicken, 4 Dec. 1866, LAC, MG 26A, vol. 238, 105296–7.

25 Peter Oliver, ed., *The Conventional Man: The Diaries of Ontario Chief Justice Robert A. Harrison, 1856–1878* (Toronto: Osgoode Society for Canadian Legal History / University of Toronto Press 2003), 286. These death threats led authorities to post a sentry outside Harrison's home.

26 George Sheppard, '"God Save the Green": Fenianism and Fellowship in Victorian Ontario,' *Histoire Social-Social History* 20 (1987): 129–44; Scott See, '"An Unprecedented Influx": Nativism and Irish Famine Immigration to Canada,' *American Review of Canadian Studies* 30 (2000): 429–53; Michael Cottrell, 'Green and Orange in Mid-Nineteenth Century Toronto: The Guy Fawkes' Day Episode of 1864,' *Canadian Journal of Irish Studies* 19 (1993): 12–21; Hereward Senior, *Orangeism: The Canadian Phase* (Toronto: McGraw Hill-Ryerson 1972).

27 Allen P. Stouffer, 'Canadian-American Relations in the Shadow of the Civil War,' *Dalhousie Review* 57 (1977): 332–46.

28 Sir Frederick Bruce to Lord Monck, 30 June 1866, LAC, RG 7, G21, vol. 403, file: 7792, Part II: Fenian Convicts.

29 W.L. Morton, 'Lord Monck and Nationality in Ireland and Canada,' *Studia Hibernica* 13 (1973): 77–99; Jacques Monet, 'Charles Stanley Monck,' *DCB*, 12: 749–51; T.B. Browning, 'Monck, Charles Stanley, fourth Viscount Monck of Ballytrammon (1819–1894),' rev. Jacques Monet, *Oxford Dictionary of National Biography* (Oxford: Oxford University Press 2004), http://www.oxforddnb.com.ezproxy.library.dal.ca/view/article/18937 (accessed 29 Aug. 2007); Elisabeth Batt, *Monck, Governor General, 1861–1868* (Toronto: McClelland and Stewart 1976).

30 Lord Monck to John A. Macdonald, May 1866, LAC, MG 26A, vol. 74, 28858–9.

31 Lord Monck to Edward Cardwell, 11 June 1866, in *Correspondence respecting the Recent Fenian Aggressions*, 4–6.

32 Brian Bond, 'Cardwell, Edward, First Viscount Cardwell (1813–1886),' *Oxford Dictionary of National Biography*, http://www.oxforddnb.com/view/article/4620 (accessed 23 Aug. 2007).

33 Edward Cardwell to Lord Monck, 30 June 1866, in *Correspondence respecting the Recent Fenian Aggressions*, 78, 79.

34 R.W. Kostal, *A Jurisprudence of Power: Victorian Empire and the Rule of Law* (Oxford: Oxford University Press 2005), 474. Also see Peter Gordon, 'Herbert, Henry Howard Molyneux, Fourth Earl of Carnarvon (1831–1890),' *Oxford Dictionary of National Biography*, http://www.oxforddnb.com.ezproxy.library.dal.ca/view/article/13035 (accessed 9 June 2006).

35 Lord Carnarvon to Lord Monck, 7 July 1866, in *Correspondence respecting the Recent Fenian Aggressions*, 79; Lord Monck to Lord Carnarvon, 21 July 1866, in ibid., 33.

36 Lord Carnarvon to Lord Monck, 13 Sept.1866, in ibid., 81.

37 Lord Monck to John A. Macdonald, 4 Oct.1866, LAC, MG 26A, vol. 58, 23574–5.

38 Bob Beal, 'Attacking the State: The Levying War Charge in Canadian Treason

Law,' MA thesis, University of Alberta 1994, 81; Wright, 'The Kingston and London Courts Martial,' 134–6, 139–42; Lord Monck to Lord Carnarvon, 6 Oct. 1866, in *Correspondence respecting the Recent Fenian Aggressions*, 35–6.

39 John A. Macdonald to R.A. Harrison, 9 Oct. 1866, LAC, MG 26A, vol. 513, pt. 2, 285.

40 Lord Monck to John A. Macdonald, 9 Oct. 1866, LAC, MG 26A, vol. 58, 23584; Lord Monck to John A. Macdonald, 9 Oct. 1866, LAC, MG 26A, vol. 58, 23586.

41 John A. Macdonald to Robert A. Harrison, 12 Oct. 1866, LAC, MG 26A, vol. 513, pt. 2, 319.

42 John A. Macdonald to Lord Monck, 13 Oct. 1866, LAC, MG 26A, vol. 513, pt. 2, 328.

43 Lord Monck to Lord Carnarvon, 18 Oct. 1866, in *Correspondence respecting the Recent Fenian Aggressions*, 37. Also see Lord Monck to John A. Macdonald, 15 Oct. 1866, LAC, MG 26A, vol. 74, 28995–9002.

44 C.P. Stacey, 'A Fenian Interlude: The Story of Michael Murphy,' *CHR* 15 (1934): 133–54; Neidhardt, 'Michael Murphy,' 587–9; John A. Macdonald to S.H. Strong, 2 Oct. 1866, LAC, MG 26A, vol. 513, pt. 1, 210; John A. Macdonald to Robert A. Harrison, 13 Oct. 1866, LAC, MG 26A, vol. 513, pt. 2, 325; 'Fenian Prisoners at Cornwall,' Toronto *Globe*, 30 Oct. 1866, 2. Macdonald's position was ironic since as a young defence counsel he had argued that defendants were arbitrarily deprived of the same rights at the Kingston courts martial in 1838. Wright, 'The Kingston and London Courts Martial,' 140.

45 Oliver, *The Conventional Man*, 79.

46 Ibid., 11, 44; Carole B. Stelmack, 'Robert Alexander Harrison,' *DCB*, 10: 336–7; Donald Swainson, 'John Hillyard Cameron,' *DCB*, 10: 122–3; Donald Swainson, 'James Cockburn,' *DCB*, 11: 195–7; Donald Swainson, '"Forgotten Men" Revisited – Some Notes on the Career of Hon. James Cockburn, a Deservedly Neglected Father of Confederation,' *Ontario History* 72 (1980): 230–42. The other two other members of Harrison's legal firm, the brothers John and James Paterson, also did work for the trials.

47 David Thurston to William H. Seward, 10 Oct. 1866; David Thurston to William H. Seward, 22 Oct. 1866; and David Thurston to William H. Seward, 25 Oct. 1866, NA, RG 59, Records of the Department of State, Despatches from U.S. Consuls in Toronto, Canada, 1864–1906 (National Archives Microfilm Publication T491, roll 1); 'The Fenian Prisoners in Toronto,' New York *Times*, 21 Oct. 1866, 1.

48 *The Canadian Biographical Dictionary and Portrait Gallery of Eminent and Self-Made Men, Ontario Volume* (Toronto: American Biographical Publishing Company 1880), 444–6; A. Margaret Evans, 'Sir Matthew Crooks Cameron,'

DCB, 11: 143–6; Richard Martin defended Robert Lynch, Patrick McCurrie represented John O'Connor, F. Fenton defended William Orr, and D.B. Read advocated on behalf of Francis King.

49 Oliver, *The Conventional Man*, 275.

50 R.A. Harrison to John A. Macdonald, 22 June 1866, LAC, MG 26A, vol. 58, 23210.

51 Oliver, *The Conventional Man*, 282.

52 John A. Macdonald to R.A. Harrison, 9 Oct. 1866, LAC, MG 26A, vol. 513, pt. 2, 285. As noted in the volume Introduction, although grand jury deliberations were closed to the public, they nonetheless contributed to the openness and accountability of pre-trial proceedings. Grand juries could check heavy-handed state prosecutions but could also reflect a public mood of vengeance. Macdonald was mindful of the public image of the proceedings (e.g., the appearance of restraint) as well as the importance of successful prosecutions.

53 Colin Read, 'John Wilson,' *DCB*, 9: 843–4.

54 See Kenneth Mckenzie to David Thurston, 1 Nov. 1866, NA, RG 59, T491, roll 1; 'Fall Assizes,' Toronto *Globe*, 1 Nov. 1866, 2; 'County Assizes,' Toronto *Globe*, 29 Jan. 1867, 1.

55 George R. Gregg and E.P. Roden, *Trials of the Fenian Prisoners at Toronto, Who Were Captured at Fort Erie, C.W., in June, 1866* (Toronto, 1867), 4, 5.

56 W.S. Neidhardt, 'The American Government and the Fenian Brotherhood: A Study in Mutual Political Opportunism,' *Ontario History* 64, no.1 (1972): 27–44.

57 Gregg and Roden, *Trials of the Fenian Prisoners at Toronto*, 6.

58 Ibid., 7.

59 Ibid., 174.

60 'The Fenian Trials,' Toronto *Globe*, 25 Oct. 1866, 2.

61 Gregg and Roden, *Trials of the Fenian Prisoners at Toronto*, 9, 11, 14; 'The Fenian Trials,' Toronto *Globe*, 25 Oct. 1866, 2.

62 Gregg and Roden, *Trials of the Fenian Prisoners at Toronto*, 15, 20, 24, 25.

63 The problem of identification led Macdonald to encourage Harrison to determine whether volunteer soldiers could identify the alleged Fenians. John A. Macdonald to L. McCallum, 11 July 1866, LAC, MG 26A, vol. 512, pt. 2, 407. Robert Harrison also identified this problem, and advocated using spies placed in the gaol with the prisoners in Toronto to secure the necessary information. He expressed no qualms about the idea, telling Gilbert McMicken that the 'end in such a case justifies the means,' since if 'men at present confined in the Toronto gaol really took part with the murderers who invaded Canada and their connection can be by any means satisfactorily established no stone must be left unturned.' Robert A. Harrison to Gilbert McMicken,

12 June 1866, LAC, MG 26A, vol. 237, 104101. Authorities also placed a man in the Toronto jail to copy the incoming and outgoing correspondence to and from the prisoners. A.P. Davis to G. McMicken, 11 Sept. 1866, LAC, MG 26A, vol. 238, 104770–1.

64 Gregg and Roden, *Trials of the Fenian Prisoners at Toronto*, 31. The testimony of Ryall was controversial. John Joseph Lynch, the bishop of Toronto, wrote to Macdonald on Lynch's behalf. Noting that the jury had relied on the testimony of Ryall, Bishop Lynch pointed out that Ryall had a notorious character and he warned Macdonald of the importance of protecting the trials' appearance of fairness. 'I know that governments of some countries have used base means to convict political offenders by any and every expediency,' suggested Bishop Lynch, who reminded Macdonald that the 'eyes of America and Europe are upon us. The proceedings of our courts will form a page in our Canadian History; therefore, let us so act, that no stain may fall on it from the mouth of a perjured villain, who was even encouraged by law officers of the Crown.' John Joseph Lynch to John A. Macdonald, 29 Oct. 1866, LAC, MG 26A, vol. 58, 23634–9.

65 See, for example, the trial of Benjamin Parry. 'The Fenian Trials,' Toronto *Globe*, 6 Nov. 1866, 2.

66 See, for example, 'The Fenian Trials,' *Toronto Globe*, 15 Nov. 1866, 1; 'The Fenian Trials,' Toronto *Globe*, 16 Nov. 1866, 2.

67 Gregg and Roden, *Trials of the Fenian Prisoners at Toronto*, 47–8. For another example of this strategy, see 'The Fenian Trials,' Toronto *Globe*, 15 Nov. 1866, 1.

68 Gregg and Roden, *Trials of the Fenian Prisoners at Toronto*, 48.

69 Ibid., 53. On the other hand, the defence argued in the trial of John Quinn that the proceedings were unfair because more time was needed to put on a proper defence. 'The Fenian Trials,' Toronto *Globe*, 15 Nov. 1866, 1.

70 Gregg and Roden, *Trials of the Fenian Prisoners at Toronto*, 60.

71 Ibid., 76. For Wilson's own summary of his charge to the jury, see Benchbooks of John Wilson, AO, RG 22–390–15, box 115, envelope 3, 154.

72 Gregg and Roden, *Trials of the Fenian Prisoners at Toronto*, 80, 81.

73 On McMahon, see Joseph A. King, 'The Fenian Invasion of Canada and John McMahon: Priest, Saint or Charlatan?' *Éire-Ireland* 23, no. 4 (1998): 32–51.

74 Gregg and Roden, *Trials of the Fenian Prisoners at Toronto*, 87.

75 Ibid., 113–14, 120.

76 Ibid., 104.

77 An Act for the Consolidation and Amendment of the Laws relative to Jurors, Juries and Inquests in That Part of This Province Called Upper Canada, SC 1850 c.55. Ontario made several amendments to the 1850 jury act during the

1850s, but the basic jury-selection scheme remained the same. For detailed discussion of jury legislation in Upper Canada, see R. Blake Brown, 'The Jury, Politics, and the State in British North America: Reforms to Jury Systems in Nova Scotia and Upper Canada, 1825–1867,' PhD thesis, Dalhousie University 2005.

78 See, for example, 'Tampering with Jury Lists,' *Irish Canadian*, 20 July 1864, 4; 'The Fenian Excitement,' *Canadian Freeman* (2nd ed.), 17 Nov. 1864, 2.

79 For discussions of jury packing in Ireland, see John F. McEldowney, 'The Case of *The Queen* v. *McKenna* (1869) and Jury Packing in Ireland,' *Irish Jurist* 12 (1977): 339; John D. Jackson, Katie Quinn, and Tom O'Malley, 'The Jury System in Contemporary Ireland: In the Shadow of a Troubled Past,' in Neil Vidmar, ed., *World Jury Systems* (Oxford: Oxford University Press 2000), 284–8; Neal Garnham, *The Courts, Crime and the Criminal Law in Ireland, 1692–1760* (Dublin: Irish Academic Press 1996), 133–45; David Johnson, 'Trial by Jury in Ireland, 1860–1914,' *Journal of Legal History*, 17 (1996): 270–93. For examples of the Irish press reporting on jury packing in Ireland, see, for example, 'News from Home,' *Irish Canadian*, 13 Dec. 1865, 4; 'The Fenian Movement in Ireland,' *Irish Canadian*, 27 Dec. 1865, 2; 'The Fenian Movement in Ireland,' *Irish Canadian*, 3 Jan. 1866, 3; 'News from Home,' *Irish Canadian*, 17 Jan. 1866, 9; *Irish Canadian*, 24 Jan. 1866, 4; 'Black Sheep,' *Irish Canadian*, 24 Jan. 1866, 5; 'News from Home,' *Irish Canadian*, 28 Feb. 1866, 6; 'Prosecuting the Press,' *Irish Canadian*, 12 Feb. 1868, 2; 'The Monaghan Jury Panel,' *Irish Canadian*, 31 March 1869, 4–5; 'An Irish Judge on the Jury System,' *Irish Canadian*, 6 April 1870, 2.

80 'Lynch and McMahon,' *Irish Canadian*, 2 Nov. 1866, 9.

81 'The Fenian Trials,' *Canadian Freeman* (2nd ed.), 29 Nov. 1866, 2.

82 R. Blake Brown, '"Delusion, A Mockery, and a Snare": Challenges to the Array and Jury Selection in England and Ireland, 1800–1850,' *Canadian Journal of History* 39 (2004): 1–26.

83 Gregg and Roden, *Trials of the Fenian Prisoners at Toronto*, 192. A copy of the challenge in Quinn's case may be found in ibid., 191–2. Also see 'The Fenian Trials,' Toronto *Globe*, 14 Nov. 1866, 1.

84 'The Fenian Trials,' Toronto *Globe*, 15 Jan. 1867, 2.

85 Gregg and Roden, *Trials of the Fenian Prisoners at Toronto*, 166.

86 The petit jury panel for the January trials of alleged Fenians in Toronto has survived. It indicates that the eighty-four jurors on the panel were properly drawn from all areas. York County Crown Attorney Fenian Trials Papers, AO, RG 22–5889, Petit Jury Panel, County Assizes, 10 Jan. 1867.

87 On juries *de medietate linguae*, see Marianne Constable, *The Law of the Other:*

The Mixed Jury and Changing Conceptions of Citizenship, Law, and Knowledge
(Chicago: University of Chicago Press 1994).

88 'Fenian Trials,' St Catharines *Constitutional*, 17 Jan. 1866, 2; 'The Fenian Trials,'
Toronto *Globe*, 17 Jan. 1867, 2; 'The Fenian Trials,' Toronto *Globe*, 19 Jan. 1867,
2; 'Fenian Trials,' Toronto *Globe*, 22 Jan. 1867, 2; 'Fenian Trials,' Toronto
Globe, 23 Jan. 1867, 1; 'Fenian Trials,' Toronto *Globe*, 28 Jan. 1867, 1; *Regina v.
Kennedy* (1867), 26 *Upper Canada Queen's Bench* (*UCQB*), 326; 'The Fenian Convicts,' Perth *Courier*, 8 Feb. 1867, 1. Mckenzie eventually questioned this strategy since he believed that many of American jurors were former Confederate
soldiers who were opposed to the Fenians out of their belief that the Fenians
had been part of the Union army that had ravaged the Confederacy. Kenneth
Mckenzie to David Thurston, 19 Jan. 1867, and Kenneth Mckenzie to David
Thurston, 22 Jan. 1867, NA, RG 59, T491, roll 2.

89 R. Blake Brown, '"Delusion, A Mockery, and a Snare,"' 1–26. R.W. Kostal
suggests, however, that there is little evidence that British authorities packed
juries against Fenians in Dublin in the mid-1860s. R.W. Kostal, 'Rebels in the
Dock: The Prosecution of the Dublin Fenians, 1865–6,' *Éire-Ireland* 34, no. 2
(1999): 79–80.

90 Gregg and Roden, *Trials of the Fenian Prisoners at Toronto*, 140–1. For a description of Lumsden's trial, also see 'The Fenian Trials,' Toronto *Globe*, 5 Nov.
1866, 2–3.

91 Gregg and Roden, *Trials of the Fenian Prisoners at Toronto*, 139.

92 The crown objected to the admissibility of these past statements and Wilson
agreed, although of course Cameron had managed to get them before the
jury.

93 Gregg and Roden, *Trials of the Fenian Prisoners at Toronto*, 168.

94 'The Fenian Trials,' Toronto *Globe*, 8 Nov. 1866, 1–2; 'The Fenian Trials,'
Toronto *Globe*, 12 Nov. 1866, 1; 'The Fenian Trials,' Toronto *Globe*, 15 Nov.
1866, 1.

95 John A. Macdonald had quickly recognized the importance of the citizenship
question, though in June he still had 'no doubt that most of the Irishmen born
will desire to claim American citizenship.' John A. Macdonald to W.S. Prince,
16 June 1866, LAC, MG 26A, vol. 512, pt. 2, 316.

96 'The Fenian Trials,' Toronto *Globe*, 9 Nov. 1866, 1.

97 'The Fenian Trials,' Toronto *Globe*, 13 Nov. 1866, 2; 'The Fenian Trials,'
Toronto *Globe*, 16 Nov. 1866, 2.

98 'The Fenian Trials,' Toronto *Globe*, 6 Nov. 1866, 2; 'The Fenian Trials,'
Toronto *Globe*, 10 Nov. 1866, 2; 'The Fenian Trials,' Toronto *Globe*, 13 Nov.
1866, 2; 'The Fenian Trials,' Toronto *Globe*, 16 Nov. 1866, 2.

99 'The Fenian Prisoners,' Toronto *Globe*, 19 Nov. 1866, 2; Oliver, *The Conventional Man*, 286.

100 Lord Monck to Lord Carnarvon, 3 Nov. 1866, in *Correspondence respecting the Recent Fenian Aggressions*, 37.

101 Lord Carnarvon to Lord Monck, 24 Nov.1866, in ibid., 83.

102 'The Condemned Fenians Respited,' Toronto *Globe*, 8 Dec. 1866, 2; Neidhardt, 'The Fenian Trials in the Province of Canada,' 34; LAC, RG 5, C1, vol. 869, no. 87.

103 Lord Carnarvon to Lord Monck, 24 Nov.1866, in *Correspondence respecting the Recent Fenian Aggressions*, 82.

104 Kenneth Mckenzie to David Thurston, 26 Nov. 1866, NA, RG 59, T491, roll 1.

105 For a detailed description of the grounds of appeal, see 'The Fenian Convictions,' Toronto *Globe*, 26 Nov. 1866, 2.

106 George Metcalf, 'William Henry Draper,' *DCB*, 10: 254.

107 *R. v. McMahon* (1866), 26 *UCR*, 195 at 200, 201. The full appeal judgments may also be found in 'The Condemned Fenians,' Toronto *Globe*, 4 Dec. 1866, 2.

108 *R. v. McMahon* (1866), 26 *UCR* 195 at 204.

109 Graham Parker, 'Sir John Hawkins Hagarty.' *DCB*, 12: 399–400.

110 *R. v. Lynch* (1866), 26 *UCR* 208 at 211.

111 Justice Morrison drew upon Hagarty's reasoning on this point in *R. v. Slavin*, in which he held that the defendants 'may be reasonably assumed to be citizens' of the United States. *R. v. Slavin* (1866), 26 *UCR* 212 at 214.

112 *R. v. Lynch* (1866), 26 *UCR* 208 at 210–11.

113 'Joseph Curran Morrison,' *DCB*, 11: 617–19.

114 *R. v. School* (1866), 26 *UCR* 212 at 216.

115 *R. v. Slavin* (1866), 17 *UCCP* 205.

116 Graham Parker, 'Sir Adam Wilson,' *DCB*, 12: 1107–9.

117 Kenneth Mckenzie to David Thurston, 8 Nov. 1866, NA, RG 59, T491, roll 1.

118 *R. v. Slavin* (1866), 17 *UCCP* 205 at 210.

119 Lord Carnarvon to Lord Monck, 24 Nov. 1866, in *Correspondence respecting the Recent Fenian Aggressions*, 83.

120 Jean-Charles Bonenfant, 'Thomas Kennedy Ramsay,' *DCB*, 11: 721–2; Jean-Charles Bonenfant, 'Bernard Devlin,' *DCB*, 10: 229–30.

121 'Fenian Trials at Sweetsburg,' Toronto *Globe*, 5 Dec. 1866, 2; 'The Fenian Senate,' Toronto *Globe*, 12 Dec. 1866, 2.

122 Clinton O. White, 'Sir Francis Godschall Johnson,' *DCB*, 12: 476–8.

123 'Fenian Trials at Sweetsburg,' Toronto *Globe*, 4 Dec. 1866, 2. In December 1866 Alexander Campbell, a Kingston lawyer, told Macdonald that the 'trials at Sweetsburgh drag along' and that Fenianism was '"dull and not in de-

mand.'" Alexander Campbell to John A. Macdonald, 28 Dec. 1866, LAC, MG 26A, vol. 194, 80758.

124 'Fenian Trials at Sweetsburg,' Toronto *Globe*, 4 Dec. 1866, 2.

125 'Latest from Sweetsburg,' Toronto *Globe*, 7 Dec. 1866, 2.

126 'Latest from Sweetsburg,' Toronto *Globe*, 11 Dec. 1866, 2; 'Latest from Sweetsburg,' Toronto *Globe*, 12 Dec. 1866, 2; 'Latest from Sweetsburg,' Toronto *Globe*, 13 Dec. 1866, 2; 'Latest from Sweetsburg,' Toronto *Globe*, 14 Dec. 1866, 2.

127 J. Michel to Lord Carnarvon, 27 Dec. 1866, in *Correspondence respecting the Recent Fenian Aggressions*, 65.

128 For a sampling of such complaints, see Brown, 'The Jury, Politics, and the State in British North America'; Donald Fyson, 'Jurys, participation civique et représentation au Québec et au Bas-Canada: les grands jurys du district de Montréal (1764–1832),' *Revue d'histoire de l'Amérique française* 55 (2001): 85–120.

129 An Act respecting Jurors and Juries, SC 1864 c.41.

130 Prosecutors and defendants also issued a number of challenges to individual jurors in the Sweetsburg trials: 'Second Despatch,' Toronto *Globe*, 19 Dec. 1866, 2; 'Latest from Sweetsburg,' Toronto *Globe*, 20 Dec. 1866, 2; 'Latest from Sweetsburg,' Toronto *Globe*, 22 Dec. 1866, 2; 'Latest from Sweetsburg,' Toronto *Globe*, 28 Dec. 1866, 2.

131 'Latest from Sweetsburg,' Toronto *Globe*, 20 Dec. 1866, 2; 'Latest from Sweetsburg,' Toronto *Globe*, 21 Dec. 1866, 3; 'Latest from Sweetsburg,' Toronto *Globe*, 22 Dec. 1866, 2.

132 'Latest from Sweetsburg,' Toronto *Globe*, 22 Dec. 1866, 2; 'Latest from Sweetsburg,' Toronto *Globe*, 24 Dec. 1866, 2; 'Latest from Sweetsburg,' Toronto *Globe*, 27 Dec. 1866, 2; 'Latest from Sweetsburg,' Toronto *Globe*, 28 Dec. 1866, 2. In addition, George Crawford pled guilty to the charge of receiving stolen goods and was sentenced to three months. 'Latest from Sweetsburg,' Toronto *Globe*, 29 Dec. 1866, 2.

133 'Latest from Sweetsburg,' Toronto *Globe*, 24 Dec. 1866, 2; 'Latest from Sweetsburg,' Toronto *Globe*, 25 Dec. 1866, 2–3; 'Latest from Sweetsburg,' Toronto *Globe*, 27 Dec. 1866, 2; 'Latest from Sweetsburg,' Toronto *Globe*, 28 Dec. 1866, 2.

134 Sir J. Michel to Lord Carnarvon, 27 Dec. 1866, in *Correspondence respecting the Recent Fenian Aggressions*, 66.

135 Sir J. Michel to Lord Carnarvon, 4 Jan. 1867, in ibid., 73; Lord Carnarvon to Sir J. Michel, 2 Feb. 1867, in ibid., 84; 'Arrival of the Fenian Prisoners from Sweetsburg,' Toronto *Globe*, 12 Jan. 1867, 1.

136 'The Fenian Trials,' Toronto *Globe*, 17 Jan. 1867, 1–2; 'The Fenian Trials,'

Toronto *Globe*, 19 Jan. 1867, 2; 'Fenian Trials,' Toronto *Globe*, 22 Jan. 1867, 2; 'Fenian Trials,' Toronto *Globe*, 23 Jan. 1867, 1; 'Fenian Trials,' Toronto *Globe*, 28 Jan. 1867, 1.

137 See, for example, 'Fenian Trials Resumed,' Toronto *Globe*, 12 Jan. 1867, 2.

138 'The Fenian Trials,' Toronto *Globe*, 14 Jan. 1867, 1.

139 A full summary of the result of all of the trials can be found in 'The Fenian Prisoners,' Toronto *Globe*, 1 Feb. 1867, 2. Also see Robert A. Harrison to John Stuart, 8 Feb. 1867, LAC, RG 5, C1, vol. 869, no. 87; Robert A. Harrison to James Cockburn, 14 Feb. 1867, LAC, RG 5, C1, vol. 869, no. 87.

140 'Fenian Trials Resumed,' Toronto *Globe*, 12 Jan. 1867, 2.

141 'Fenian Trials,' Toronto *Globe*, 22 Jan. 1867, 2.

142 'The Fenian Trials,' Toronto *Globe*, 31 Jan. 1867, 2.

143 'Fenian Prisoners,' Toronto *Globe*, 11 Feb. 1867, 2.

144 *Regina v. Kennedy* (1867), 26 UCQB 326 at 331.

145 'The Fenian Trials,' Toronto *Globe*, 14 Jan. 1867, 1.

146 Kenneth Mckenzie to David Thurston, 15 Jan. 1867, NA, RG 59, T491, roll 2.

147 Gregg and Roden, *Trials of the Fenian Prisoners at Toronto*, 221.

148 Ibid.

149 Draper's decision did not sit well with Justice William Buell Richards, who in May 1867 wrote to the provincial secretary that there were 'strong doubts as to the propriety of proceeding against the prisoner on the second indictment charging him with an offence strongly resembling in substance that for which he had been tried and acquitted on the previous indictment.' William Richards to provincial secretary, 13 May 1867, LAC, RG 5, C1, vol. 869, no. 87.

150 Kenneth Mckenzie to David Thurston, 4 March 1867, NA, RG 59, T491, roll 2.

151 John A. Macdonald to Lord Lisgar (Sir J. Young), 11 Oct. 1870, LAC, MG 26A, vol. 517, pt. 2, 304, 305.

152 John A. Macdonald to W.J. Keilty, 5 Jan. 1872, LAC, RG 26A, vol. 520, pt.1, 45, 46.

153 Peter Oliver, *'Terror to Evil-Doers': Prisons and Punishments in Nineteenth-Century Ontario* (Toronto: Osgoode Society for Canadian Legal History / University of Toronto Press 1998), 309–10; H. Pearson Gundy, 'John Creighton,' *DCB*, 11: 216–17.

154 'Another Fenian Released,' *Irish Canadian*, 17 July 1871.

155 Patrick McGrath to John Creighton (n.d.), LAC, MG 29, E12, John Creighton Papers.

156 Daniel Quinn to John Creighton, 5 Nov. 1871, ibid.

157 'The Last of the Fenian Prisoners – A Letter from Kingston – Five Years in a Cell' (n.p., n.d.), ibid.

158 Consul S.B.[?] House[?] to William Seward, 13 June 1868, LAC, RG 7, G21, vol. 403, file: 7792, Part II: Fenian Convicts.

159 R.B. Lynch to John Creighton, 23 Oct. 1871, LAC, MG 29, E12, John Creighton Papers.

160 F.B. McNamee to John A. Macdonald, 14 Feb. 1870, LAC, MG 26A, vol. 60, 24639.

161 John A. Macdonald to J.G. Moylan, 15 Dec. 1869, LAC, MG 26A, vol. 516, pt. 4, 744.

162 J.J. Lynch to John A. Macdonald, 4 Oct. 1869, LAC, MG 26A, vol. 60, 24505–6. Petitioners from Victoria County called for the release of John McMahon using religious appeals. They said that McMahon's apparent ill-health in prison was 'painful to a large body of Her Majesty's loyal subjects of this Province who are Roman Catholic to witness a Priest of their Church undergoing penal servitude.' His release would disprove the idea that 'there was one law for the Protestant and another law for the Roman Catholic.' Petition of inhabitants of the Town of Lindsay and Township of Ops, County of Victoria, Canada, 1 Aug. 1867, LAC, RG 7, G21, vol. 403, file: 7792, Part II: Fenian Convicts.

163 'The Fenian Trials,' Toronto *Globe*, 16 Jan. 1867, 1

164 Petition of John O'Connor, n.d., LAC, RG 5, C1, vol. 869, no. 87.

165 Letter of Frederick William Jarvis, 6 Feb. 1867, LAC, RG 5, C1, vol. 869, no. 87.

166 Petition from inhabitants of the County of Wellington, n.d., LAC, RG 5, C1, vol. 869, no. 87.

167 Letter of Joseph Curran Morrison, 22 March 1867, LAC, RG 5, C1, vol. 869, no. 87.

168 On the other hand, another early appeal for the release of a prisoner had less success. The trial jury in Owen Kennedy's case wrote a petition appealing for the release of Kennedy so that he could return to his father. LAC, RG 5, C1, vol. 869, no. 87.

169 John A. Macdonald to J.G. Moylan, 15 Dec. 1869, LAC, MG 26A, vol. 516, pt. 4, 745. When Macdonald was less interested in obliging appeals to free Fenians, he claimed that he had no power in the matter. In January 1870 he explained to the Reverend Daniel O'Connell that the decision regarding whether to release prisoners rested with the governor general and, ultimately, the imperial government. Macdonald wrote that 'this Fenian excitement will die away by and by' and then 'perhaps the Imperial Government may

feel themselves at liberty to extend Her Majesty's clemency to those remaining in prison.' John A. Macdonald to Rev. Daniel O'Connell, 21 Jan. 1870, LAC, MG 26A, vol. 516, pt. 4, 937–8.

170 See, for example, Petition of inhabitants of the Town of Lindsay and Township of Ops, 1 Aug. 1867.

171 On the role of mercy and justice in the eighteenth-century English criminal justice system, see Douglas Hay, 'Property, Authority and the Criminal Law,' in D. Hay et al., eds., *Albion's Fatal Tree: Crime and Society in Eighteenth-Century England* (London: Allen and Unwin 1975), 17–63.

2

The D'Arcy McGee Affair and the Suspension of Habeas Corpus

DAVID A. WILSON

In November 1867 John A. Macdonald, in his dual role as prime minister and minister of justice, announced during the first session of the Dominion Parliament that his government intended to renew the suspension of the Habeas Corpus Act. Habeas corpus had been suspended eighteen months earlier, in the wake of the Fenian invasion of the Niagara peninsula and the Battle of Ridgeway in June 1866. But that legislation was to expire at the end of 1867 and had applied only to the pre-confederation Province of Canada. Given the continuing Fenian threat, Macdonald argued, the suspension of habeas corpus should be extended and expanded throughout the Dominion. The new act would be substantially the same as the old, he explained; the only difference was that prisoners would now be held for a month rather than two weeks without charges, 'in order to give time to procure evidence.'[1]

Behind Macdonald's position was a desire not to repeat the mistakes of the past. Despite the activities of Canada's revamped secret police force under Gilbert McMicken in Canada West and William Ermatinger in Canada East, the Fenian invasion of June 1866 had taken the government completely by surprise.[2] In part, it was the familiar story of too much information; it was difficult to sort out fact from fantasy, and the failed Fenian attempt to invade New Brunswick from Eastport the previous April had lulled the government into a false sense of security. Writing to Lord Kimberley only a week before Ridgeway, D'Arcy McGee reported that 'the prospect of a Fenian invasion of Canada has gradually worn away to almost nothing. The promptitude of our Volunteers – the report that a few gunboats were coming out to patrol our inland waters – and the virulence of the schism among the New York ringleaders – saved us.' McGee went on to argue that 'the absurd fiasco at Eastport was a real gain to us, inasmuch as it first established the fact, and made it evident all over the Fenian circles, that the U.S. government would *not* connive, at any breach of the neutrality laws.'[3] All this seemed logical enough. But subsequent events demonstrated that such logic was not only inadequate; it was actually a source of vulnerability. Henceforth, the government would err on the side of caution.

The need for caution was only underlined by the aftermath of Ridgeway. Far from undermining Fenianism, the failed invasion attempt of 1866 became a source of inspiration for Irish revolutionaries on both sides of the Atlantic.[4] The Fenian retreat was less important than the fact that Irish soldiers, wearing green uniforms and fighting under the banner of the Irish Republican Army, had defeated the forces of the crown in open battle. Even the constitutional nationalist *Nation* newspaper in Dublin exulted that 'for the first time in well nigh seventy years the red flag of England has gone down before the Irish green.'[5] Within Fenian circles, there was a brief mood of euphoria, followed by anger at the trials and sentences of the Fenian prisoners; in particular, the fact that a Catholic priest, Father John McMahon, had been sentenced to death while a Protestant minister, David Lumsden, had been found not guilty became a lightning rod for republican outrage.[6] Sensing the potential for a massive Fenian backlash, and recognizing the power of Irish American republicanism, the British minister to the United States, Frederick Bruce, urged a policy of leniency; partly because of British pressure, the Canadian government decided not to execute any prisoners.[7]

In making his case for the renewal of the Habeas Corpus Suspension Act, Macdonald argued that the Fenian Brotherhood remained a 'widely extended organization' which had recently been responsible for violence in England and which was still a significant force in Ireland. Closer to home, he argued, the Canadian government had 'distinct evidence of increasing activity' on the border; Fenian arms were being stockpiled near the frontier, and the threat of another invasion remained very real. It was thus essential that renewed steps be taken for the apprehension and trial of 'foreign aggressors.' 'The object of the bill,' Macdonald declared, 'was to prevent parties from making undue raids upon our territory.' To strengthen his position, Macdonald also pointed out that the existing suspension of habeas corpus had not been 'harshly or improperly used.' In this, he was substantially correct; any concerns that the legislation would lead to an abuse of power had not materialized, and Macdonald had authorized a circular to magistrates warning them against 'hasty and ill-judged arrests' of suspected Fenians.[8]

The presentation of Fenianism as an external threat, together with the government's benign track record, meant that the bill generated very little any controversy. One critical voice was the Halifax *Morning Chronicle*, which condemned the legislation as an 'outrageous measure' that had no relevance to Nova Scotia and that was yet another deleterious consequence of confederation.[9] It is also probable that the pro-Fenian *Irish Canadian* opposed the measure, but there are no extant copies for 1867. All in all, the suspension of habeas corpus generated no public protests, no sense of panic, and no manifestations of popular anti-Fenianism; instead, it was treated as part of the humdrum business of Parliament. The *Globe* mentioned it briefly in a column entitled 'NOTHING TO DO,' the main theme of which was that Parliament had no serious or important matters to discuss.[10] Even this was more than appeared in other leading Canadian newspapers, which made no editorial comment at all.[11]

The principal exception was Timothy Warren Anglin's Saint John *Morning Freeman*, which initially reacted with scepticism. 'Some suspect,' wrote Anglin, 'that this proceeding is but a preparation for a military measure which neither the House would pass in its calmer moments, nor the people would submit to unless under the influence of alarm and excitement.'[12] Born in Clonakilty, County Cork, in 1822, Anglin had supported the extreme revolutionary wing of the Irish republican movement in 1848 – a fact that he successfully concealed after his immigration to New Brunswick the following year.[13] As a journalist and politician in New Brunswick, he emerged as a leading Irish Canadian opponent of D'Arcy McGee, attacking both McGee's pro-confederation and anti-Fenian position – although his hostility to confederation did not stop him from becoming a member of Parliament in 1867 and retaining his seat until 1882. Anglin's attitude to Fenianism was one of studied ambivalence; while he repudiated the Canadian invasion strategy, he sympathized with the goal of Irish independence.[14]

And yet even Anglin felt obliged to accept Macdonald's statement about Fenian activities on the frontier as having 'some foundation in fact, absurd as it seems to be.' In the brief parliamentary debate on the bill, Anglin suggested that the power to suspend habeas corpus should be 'held in abeyance' until an emergency actually arose. He quickly backed down, however, after being assured that the legislation was not merely a precautionary measure but was justified by a present threat; in the event of a sudden raid, Macdonald argued, the invaders could make their escape before the suspension of habeas corpus came into effect. The only other MP to question the legislation was Antoine-Aimé Dorion, the Montreal lawyer and leader of the Rouge party who later became the federal minister of justice under Alexander Mackenzie. Dorion 'did not think the circumstances at present required the suspension of the Act,' but he decided to give the government the benefit of the doubt and took consolation from the fact that the earlier legislation had not been abused. Dorion, like Anglin, wound up voting for the bill, which passed unanimously.[15]

The justification for the bill, it is clear, was framed in terms of external circumstances and government trustworthiness. As it turned out, however, the legislation would be applied solely against real or suspected internal Fenians, amid charges that the Conservatives were using the suspension of habeas corpus as a political weapon to bolster their own position and discredit their Irish Catholic Liberal enemies.

COUNTER-INTELLIGENCE

There is no doubt that the government was genuinely concerned about the prospect of another Fenian invasion attempt. The incursion into the Niagara peninsula had been organized by the Senate Wing of the Fenian Brotherhood, which had broken from the leadership of John O'Mahony and which continued to command considerable support. Drawing on a variety of secret sources, the Canadian government knew that the Senate Wing intended to complete the unfinished business of 1866; it seemed only a matter of when. Six months after Ridgeway, when the Fenians were still in a state of disarray, the Dublin Metropolitan Police agent in New York, 'D. Thomas' (a thinly disguised alias for Thomas Doyle), reported that the Fenians were planning another raid in Canada in the spring or summer of 1867.[16] More information about Fenian activities came from Charles Carroll Tevis, the former adjutant-general of the Fenian army. Having been blamed for the breakdown of the invasion, court martialled, and ousted from the Fenian Brotherhood, Tevis was now out for revenge – as well as £100 a month from the British government.[17]

The hub of British counter-intelligence was the British Consulate in New York, where the Nova Scotia-born Edward Archibald spent long evenings closeted with numerous Fenian informers whose reports he transmitted to the authorities in Britain and Canada. His 'principal and most reliable informant,' according to his daughter, was Rudolph Fitzpatrick, the assistant secretary at war in the Senate Wing.[18] Reporting from the Fenian convention in Troy in May 1867, Fitzpatrick revealed that the Fenians had sent 'about 2000 stand of arms' to Ogdensburg in upstate New York and were bringing cannons into Buffalo. But the main invasion force would come through Rouses Point in New York and St Albans in Vermont and march into Quebec along the Richelieu River.[19] The timing remained unclear, but Fitzpatrick's information that William Roberts, the leader of the Senate Wing, was leaving for France meant that there would not be an invasion before August.[20]

As in 1865–6, the key question for the British and Canadian governments concerned the accuracy of these reports. 'Some allowance must be made for *exaggeration*,' commented Pierrepont Edwards, the vice-consul in New York.[21] But how much allowance? Other evidence from New York indicated that the Fenians lacked the funds to launch another invasion during 1867 and were engaging in rhetorical overcompensation for organizational weakness. Besides, there had been so many stories about impending attacks that rumour fatigue was beginning to set in; Canadian politicians, McGee warned Macdonald as early as December 1866, were becoming too sceptical for their own good.[22] Precisely because of the plethora of information emanating from Fenian sources, the task of steering between alarmism and complacency proved particularly challenging.

There was good reason to believe that by the autumn of 1867 the Fenians were on the move. In September, Edward Archibald learned about the secret proceedings of the Fenian convention in Cleveland. According to his source – possibly Rudolph Fitzpatrick – plans were under way to attack Canada in March 1868.[23] This was corroborated by Gilbert McMicken's spies, who reported that re-energized Fenian circles were raising funds for a spring attack and that arms were being brought to the frontier.[24] In October, McMicken sent two of his best detectives to upstate New York, where they provided detailed information about the build-up of arms in Potsdam, Watertown, and Ogdensburg.[25] Shortly after receiving these reports, Macdonald announced his decision to renew suspension of habeas corpus.

And yet Macdonald's public statements that suspension was a prudent reaction to a foreign threat told only half the story. He deliberately omitted the role of revolutionary Irish Canadian nationalists in the Fenian strategy and the potential conjunction of external invasion with internal subversion. Informers in the United States provided no shortage of material on the subject. In January 1867, for example, Tevis revealed that 'a young man named Shields, a lawyer, of good education and address and with no appearance of being an Irishman,' had been sent to Montreal to coordinate plans for the next invasion; this probably referred to D.R. Shiel, a leading New York Fenian.[26] Writing from the Fenian convention at Troy in May, Rudolph Fitzpatrick reported that the Fenians were planning to send guns into Canada, and added that General John O'Neill, the Fenian hero of Ridgeway, was planning 'to go through Canada and reconnoitre.'[27] 'I find that Emissaries are being sent from the Fenian Head Quarters here to Canada,' wrote Archibald in August, 'that efforts are being made to organise Fenian circles there, & procure contributions towards the advancement of the cause.'[28] Among those contributions were $4,000 that had been received from the Fenian organization in Quebec City.[29]

One of the main Fenian objectives in Canada was to win the support of Irish soldiers serving in the British army. Similar efforts had been made in Britain and Ireland, and there was some substance in the fear expressed by Lady Monck, the governor general's wife, that British regiments were importing large numbers of Fenians into Canada.[30] The key, from the Fenian perspective, was to bring non-commissioned officers into the organization – and Archibald's informer at the Cleveland convention told him that this was already happening. 'The sum of 20,000 dollars has been voted by the Cleveland Convention for the purpose of drawing the Irish soldiers of the Queen's Service in Canada from their allegiance, and inducing them to join the organization,' he wrote. 'A number of trustworthy Agents have already been sent to Canada for this purpose, and I have myself read letters from non commissioned officers of the Army serving in Canada who are actually engaged in spreading disaffection among their comrades.' When the next invasion occurred, it was expected that Fenians in the Royal Artillery would spike the cannons, while Fenians in other regiments would spike the guns of loyal soldiers.[31]

Outside the army, Canadian Fenianism remained a potent force, despite its minority status. Within an Irish Catholic Canadian ethnic population of around 260,000, it is extremely unlikely that there were more than three thousand Fenians – and many of these were aligned with the faction that focused on Ireland rather than on invading Canada.[32] But the lines were fluid, and personal loyalties sometimes counted for more than strategic differences.[33] Beyond the sworn members were an undeterminable number of fellow travellers, and beyond them were many constitutional nationalists who had ambivalent feelings about the Fenians, believing that their hearts were in the right place even if their methods were misguided. Newspapers such as Patrick Boyle's *Irish Canadian* and Patrick

Meehan's New York-based *Irish American* disseminated Fenian ideas, and the Fenian presence could be found throughout Irish Catholic Canadian communities. In the context of American Fenian invasion plans, coteries of Canadian Fenians could easily assume an importance out of all proportion to their numbers.

Acutely aware of this, the Canadian government employed a wide range of intelligence sources to penetrate domestic Fenianism and to probe its links with the Senate Wing in the United States. Individual politicians and businessmen established their own networks of informers, and sometimes offered to serve as spies. The Catholic MP Richard Scott, for example, tried unsuccessfully to infiltrate the Fenian headquarters in New York; he was followed by the Montreal contractor James Goodwin, who passed himself off as a Canadian millionaire and potential donor and managed to meet the upper echelons of the organization.[34] Gilbert McMicken's secret police force continued to monitor Fenian activities on both sides of the border, and city police forces engaged in surveillance activities. The Montreal Water Police, under the magistrate Charles Coursol, had been established with the express purpose of assessing and countering the domestic Fenian threat.[35] In Toronto, the police chief William Prince kept a close eye on the Hibernian Benevolent Society, which functioned as a Fenian front organization, while in Ottawa the police magistrate Martin O'Gara was at the centre of counter-Fenian intelligence – which he later leaked to some of the city's leading Irish nationalists.[36]

From these sources, together with the intelligence reaching British diplomats in the United States, a reasonably coherent picture began to emerge: a militant Fenian minority in Canada was planning to support the next invasion not only by suborning soldiers and spiking guns but also by cutting communication lines, burning public buildings, and creating as much chaos as possible. Only two weeks before Macdonald renewed the suspension of habeas corpus, he received information that the Fenians in Hamilton, Toronto, Kingston, and Montreal had 1,500 rifles and revolvers hidden in private homes and were ready to take on the local police forces.[37] This was almost certainly another example of exaggeration, but the government was sufficiently concerned to put McMicken's detectives on the case. No arms were ever found, and McMicken probably discounted the story. But he remained convinced that there was a serious internal threat, which would be triggered by invasion. Summing up the situation in January 1868, he told Macdonald that the Fenians 'have *now* in *Canada* some of their organizing agents at work preparing their friends here for the contemplated movement in the spring – Montreal should be well looked after. If anywhere in Canada they are strong there and my opinion is that when a movement is made in Canada the Fenians in Montreal will as their first act of co-operation attempt to creat [sic] distrust there and retain the troops from going to the front by destruction of Property fire raising &c – this also may be expected in Ottawa and Toronto.'[38]

Since Macdonald had known of such plans well before the renewed suspension of habeas corpus, an obvious question arises: Why did he keep quiet about the danger within? There were probably two reasons for his silence. First, any public statement about the revolutionary intentions of some Canadian Fenians could easily have produced an anti-Catholic backlash, with heightened Protestant suspicions that Irish Canadian Catholics were untrustworthy, devious, or disloyal. Such a backlash would have intensified ethno-religious divisions within the country and produced an atmosphere in which Fenianism could flourish – the last thing that he wanted. And second, Macdonald had worked long and hard to cultivate the Irish Catholic vote, and he did not want to jeopardize that support with general pronouncements about a Canadian Fenian conspiracy. On the grounds of both prudence and political advantage, it made sense for Macdonald to focus on external invasion and say nothing about internal subversion.

ASSASSINATION

The combined external and internal threat persisted throughout the winter of 1867–8. There were rumours that a 'large number of Fenians' were planning to cross the St Lawrence when it froze and liberate the prisoners in the Kingston Penitentiary.[39] In Montreal, the Water Police received information that a joint party of Canadian and American Fenians was planning to burn down the city's principal stores, the fire stations, and the Grand Trunk buildings on Christmas Eve; two weeks later, McGee informed Macdonald that there were 'many suspicious strangers' in the city.[40] Macdonald immediately contacted Ermatinger, who confirmed McGee's report and instructed the police 'to watch their proceedings, to guard Public buildings, and the residences of private individuals.'[41]

Against this background, the government received new information that appeared to confirm earlier reports from the Cleveland convention that the next attack on Canada was scheduled for March 1868. According to 'James Rooney,' an informer who contacted the British consul in Boston, Irish revolutionaries in Montreal were bringing arms and ammunition from Vermont into Canada and planning to launch an insurrection on 17 March, using the St Patrick's Day celebrations as a cover.[42] The information was specific; Rooney supplied the British consul in Boston, Francis Lousada, with the names and sometimes the addresses of the Montreal Fenians with whom he worked in Vermont, and the Canadian government was sufficiently alarmed to keep the men under close surveillance.[43] One of the suspects, Nicholas Hart, ran a grocery store and sold illegal liquor to soldiers, 'which looks rather suspicious,' as Charles Coursol put it; two others were described by Chief Constable John McLoughlin as 'wild characters.'[44] Meanwhile, one of Ermatinger's detectives stationed on the frontier telegraphed that 'arms are coming to St. Albans daily.'[45] On St Patrick's Day, the military was put on full alert, and the apprehended insurrection failed to materialize. It remained unclear, however, whether the show of military force had deterred the Fenians or whether Rooney had been retailing false information. As might be expected, Rooney favoured the former explanation, while Ermatinger believed that this was yet another example of exaggeration; for his part, McMicken dismissed the reports as 'entirely baseless.'[46]

Whatever the case, the existence of a revolutionary Fenian underground in Montreal, with connections to Quebec, Ottawa, and Toronto, was something upon which all the counter-intelligence authorities in Canada could agree. And within this underground, no single figure was hated more than D'Arcy McGee. For McGee had once been a republican himself and had sat on the revolutionary council that was behind the Rising of 1848. But the failure of the Rising made him revert to constitutional nationalism, and his experiences as an exile in the United States eventually pushed him northward to Canada, where he moved through the Reform Party to become the country's leading Irish Catholic Liberal-Conservative politician.[47] Here, from the Fenian perspective, was the archetypal traitor, the man who had sold out his republican principles in the quest for power and prestige and was now North America's most outspoken opponent of revolutionary Irish nationalism.[48] In 1848 McGee had denounced government spies as 'fiends, whose element is falsehood and whose trade is perjury,' and had strongly attacked the British government's suspension of habeas corpus.[49] Now, the boot was on the other foot. He argued in the summer of 1867 that the suspension of habeas corpus was a regrettable but necessary response to Fenianism in Canada, and especially in Montreal.[50] Returning to the subject in November, McGee pointed out in Parliament that a recent meeting of the St Patrick's Society in Montreal had displayed the names of prominent Fenians on the walls, and he advised 'his friend the Minister of Justice to consider the matter seriously, before allowing the period for the suspension of the *Habeas Corpus* Act to expire.'[51]

Unlike Macdonald, McGee had no hesitation about acknowledging the existence of internal Canadian Fenianism; through a strategy of confrontation and polarization, he hoped to cut through Irish Catholic Canadian ambivalence about revolutionary Irish nationalism and leave the Fenians in an isolated and marginalized position. After Ridgeway, he argued that the authorities should set an example by hanging some of the leading Fenian prisoners and sentencing the rest to hard labour on projects that were needed for the defence of Canada.[52] During a speech in Montreal, after McGee was hissed for saying that the prisoners who had been found guilty deserved the death sentence, he told his enemies that he had 'evidences of your criminal folly, and I could have put some of you where you would not hiss or hear much; but you were not worth prosecuting – you may be worth watching, and there are those among yourselves, I can tell you, as there were among the Toronto Fenians, who are keeping a good account of all your ingoings and outcomings.'[53]

The nature of that evidence became clear during McGee's hard-fought election campaign against the Fenian-backed Bernard Devlin in August and September 1867. To discredit his opponent, McGee divulged information about Montreal's Fenian movement that could have come only from moles within the organization.[54] Among other things, he named the leading Fenians in the city and reported that two of them, Francis Bernard McNamee and John Carroll, had met an emissary from the United States who was on a reconnaissance mission in Canada.[55] In striking contrast to his earlier views, McGee had been more than willing to embrace spies and informers in his battle against Fenianism; it was essential, he wrote, to break with 'the hereditary Irish fear of the nickname "informer"' and expose the revolutionaries within.[56]

These revelations, and the sources on which they were based, unleashed a storm of criticism. At one election meeting, when Bernard Devlin described McGee as 'a foul informer, a corrupt witness, a knave and hypocrite' who should be 'hooted out of society,' there were cries of 'He's dead' from the crowd.[57] Among the Montreal Irish who were incensed by McGee's position was a tailor and former soldier, Patrick James Whelan, who repeatedly said that McGee was a traitor who deserved to be shot. Alec Turner, an Englishman who lodged at Whelan's house in Montreal, recalled that after one of McGee's anti-Fenian speeches, Whelan threatened to 'blow McGee's bloody brains out' and spent the night outside McGee's house, lying in wait.[58]

McGee had been receiving death threats since at least 1864 and was frequently accompanied by police bodyguards during his public engagements in Montreal.[59] His repeated attacks on revolutionary nationalism, his attitude to the Fenian prisoners in 1866, and his exposure of Montreal Fenianism in 1867 all made him a marked man. By the beginning of 1868, McMicken's and Ermatinger's detectives were picking up stories that some Fenians wanted to kill him in revenge for the execution of the so-called 'Manchester Martyrs' in Britain, three Fenians who had been found guilty of murdering a policeman.[60] On New Year's night 1868, there may well have been an attempt to assassinate McGee at his Montreal home; shortly afterwards, Ermatinger told Macdonald that McGee's life was in danger and that two of his detectives had been detailed to patrol his residence each night. ('The city police,' he added, 'cannot be depended on.'[61]) In February, McGee thanked Macdonald for warning him about his 'public safety,' and promised to be careful.[62]

Six weeks later, on the night of 6–7 April 1868, McGee was shot in the back of the head while walking to his boarding house from the House of Commons. Although his assassination was not altogether surprising, the shock reverberated around the country, amid outraged editorials, grief-stricken sermons, and anguished correspondence. Less apparent, but no less real, was the sense of exultation within Fenian circles on both sides of the border; the traitor McGee, it was said, had brought it on himself, and had finally got what he deserved.[63] While many Fenians celebrated his death and drank toasts to the man who shot McGee, Macdonald's government immediately swung into action; it would attempt not only to track down the assassin and any accomplices but also to break the Fenian movement in Canada. And the Habeas Corpus Suspension Act provided it with a ready-made weapon.

PATRICK JAMES WHELAN

Within twenty-four hours of McGee's death, the police believed that they had their man. Following a tip-off, they went to Michael Starrs's Ottawa Hotel and questioned Patrick James Whelan. In his room they found a loaded gun with burnt powder, 'as if the revolver had been but recently discharged.' There were several copies of the 7 March issue of the *Irish American*, suggesting that Whelan was a Canadian distributor of the newspaper. The police also found a green silk badge of the Toronto Hibernian Benevolent Society, established in 1858, with the sunburst and phoenix – Fenian symbols of an organization with a large Fenian membership. There was also a membership card of the Montreal St Patrick's Society, which the Fenians had effectively taken over by 1867.[64] Whelan, it quickly became clear, had the motive, means, and opportunity to have assassinated McGee. There was no need to resort to the Habeas Corpus Suspension Act to collect further evidence. Whelan was charged with murder, taken to the Ottawa jail, tried for murder in September 1868, found guilty, and hanged in February 1869.

The question of Whelan's political allegiance was not explicitly addressed during the trial, although the prosecuting attorney, James O'Reilly, an Irish Catholic Queen's Counsel from Kingston, did try to connect Whelan with the Fenian *Irish American*.[65] When the defence objected, however, he withdrew this line of inquiry and did not return to it. Nevertheless, Whelan's trial was unmistakably political, and was inseparable from the broader issue of Fenianism in the Canada and the United States. Particularly striking, in this context, was the fact that during one day of the week-long trial, John A. Macdonald and his wife sat next to the judge during the proceedings. The ostensible reason for this was simply that the courtroom was crowded and that the judge found a seat for him on the bench. But, as T.P. Slattery points out, this was clearly a breach of the constitutional principle that the executive should not interfere, or give the slightest appearance of interfering, in judicial proceedings; partly on these grounds, Slattery contends that there should have been a retrial. Remarkably, however, Macdonald's presence on the bench did not elicit any controversy at the time; it received only passing mention in the press, and even the letters and editorials in the *Irish Canadian*, where one would have expected an angry reaction, were silent on the subject. The argument that Macdonald's presence on the bench could have prejudiced the jury against Whelan was made only in retrospect.[66]

Although the question of Whelan's guilt remains controversial, there is no doubt that he was a Fenian sympathizer, and it is highly likely that he was a sworn member of the Fenian Brotherhood.[67] During the winter of 1865–6, when the Fenians were trying to infiltrate the army, he assumed the pseudonym Sullivan (his mother's maiden name) and was 'in company with a man who was tampering with the soldiers'; he was arrested, but the charges were eventually dropped for lack of corroborating evidence.[68] Three witnesses (one of whom was Alec Turner, his former lodger) came forward to say that, during the McGee-Devlin election contest in 1867, Whelan described McGee as a traitor to Ireland who ought to be shot, and McGee's half-brother, John Joseph, identified Whelan as one of two men who behaved suspiciously at McGee's house on New Year's

Day 1868.[69] It is also worth noting that two separate sources in the United States identified Patrick James Whelan as not simply a marginal figure in Canadian Fenianism but as one of the active supporters of the Fenian plan to invade Canada. After the assassination, an informer in the service of Edward Archibald identified Whelan as 'the Delegate from Canada to the Cleveland Convention' in September 1867, at which the Fenians discussed their invasion plans.[70] And 'James Rooney' told Francis Lousada in Boston that 'I know and had seen this man Whelan several times in New York and had herd [sic] him express his wish to dispatch some of her Majesty's Subjects and friends in Canada. You remember I mentioned his name sometimes long before the murder.'[71] The accuracy of this information cannot be confirmed, and these ex post facto sources should be treated with great scepticism; still, it is intriguing that 'Rooney' reminded the British consul that he had spoken about Whelan before McGee's assassination. These spy reports were not used in the trial; it was important to ensure that covers were not blown.

Beyond this, it soon became clear that Whelan was part of a wider familial and social network of revolutionary Irish nationalists. His brother, Joseph, had run a Fenian pub in Dublin. Like Patrick James, he had been arrested on charges of suborning soldiers; he had also participated in the Fenian rising of 1867, joining the attack on the police barracks at Tallaght. Found guilty of treason, he spent almost a year in prison before being released on condition that he leave for America.[72] Within Canada, Patrick James Whelan inhabited a male Irish Catholic subculture of Fenians and Fenian sympathizers, centred on places such as Kate Scanlan's tavern in Montreal. One of his closest friends was Patrick Doody, who was rumoured to have been the 'head centre' of the Fenians in Canada.[73]

ARRESTS

If Whelan had pulled the trigger – and the government was convinced that he had – the next question was whether he had acted alone. Macdonald initially believed that McGee's murder was 'a deliberate decision of the Fenian Organization' and that Whelan was acting on orders from New York.[74] This is understandable; the Fenians in Ireland, under the leadership of Thomas Kelly, had their own assassination circle, and it seemed reasonable to assume that American Fenians felt the same way.[75] However, the reports from spies and informers in New York immediately indicated otherwise. One of McMicken's moles reported that, although the Fenian leaders had 'no sympathy' for McGee, 'they repudiate any idea of the organization having anything to do with it.' Similarly, Archibald's sources informed him that 'O'Neill repudiates that outrage & probably does so sincerely.'[76]

Yet the possibility remained that the assassination had been planned and carried out by a group of Canadian Fenians, acting on their own initiative. Detective Edward O'Neill informed Macdonald of his belief that Whelan was part of a Fenian conspiracy that emanated from Kate Scanlan's tavern in Montreal.[77] Macdonald convinced himself that there was wider Canadian involvement, drawing in Fenians from Quebec City and Ottawa.[78] McGee's murder, he wrote, was 'not the act of one individual only, but the result of a conspiracy, and it is to be more than feared that many of the conspirators are now at large.' This was a major reason why he wanted a special commission and an early trial; the conspirators, he told Ontario premier Sandfield Macdonald on 4 May, 'will spare no pains to tamper with & intimidate the witnesses, or if need be, induce them to leave the Country. There is quite evidence enough already of intimidation and tampering, and in my opinion a postponement of the trial until Autumn will render all attempt to convict the guilty parties nugatory.'[79] One can see his point; three weeks later, Alec Turner, a key witnesses for the prosecution, was beaten up outside the Ottawa Hotel, and William Graham, another prosecution witness, received a threatening letter.[80] But Sandfield Macdonald, in his capacity as attorney general of Ontario, believed that the 'ordinary course' of justice must prevail, and insisted that the trial of Whelan and any other suspects must occur during the autumn assizes.[81]

Between McGee's assassination and Whelan's trial in September 1868, some twenty-five people were arrested under the suspension of habeas corpus, not counting those who were temporarily held as witnesses.[82] John A. Macdonald and James O'Reilly, the key figures in the investigation of Canadian Fenianism, conducted their inquiries against the background of continuing rumours about American Fenian reconnaissance missions in Canada, attempts to subvert the army, and more Fenian military preparations.[83] At the end of April, McMicken recommended that the Ottawa police should be issued with revolvers and that the 'Parliamentary and Departmental Buildings' should be protected against 'the sudden introduction of explosive preparations.'[84] The climate of fear was intensified when news reached Canada that an Irishman had shot and wounded Prince Alfred, the Duke of Edinburgh, in Australia.[85] In this light, and in the light of calls in the Orange press for vigorous repressive measures, what is striking about the arrests is their relatively limited number; Macdonald and O'Reilly sifted the evidence, acted according to their own estimation of specific cases, and refused to be driven by a generalized sense of panic.

The first man to be arrested was one of Whelan's closest friends, John Doyle. Whelan and Doyle had known each other in Montreal, where they supported Devlin during the recent election campaign; there were reports that Doyle, like Whelan, had been 'very violent in his expressions against Mr. McGee.'[86] In November 1867 Doyle moved to Ottawa and became a waiter at the Russell House. The two men were regular drinking companions and had spent some time together on the night of the murder; the authorities suspected that Doyle had acted as Whelan's accomplice.[87] Another of Whelan's Ottawa friends, Ralph Slattery, was arrested shortly afterwards. A schoolteacher whom the *Globe*'s reporter described as 'a very suspicious looking character,' Slattery had featured in intelligence reports as being involved in the Fenian plans to invade Canada.[88] Also caught in the net was William Mitchell, a cabinet maker who had moved into Starrs's Ottawa Hotel – where Whelan lodged – on the night of the murder. But there were no other grounds of suspicion, and he was released after two weeks in jail.[89]

From here, the focus shifted to Montreal. Bridget Whelan, the wife of Patrick James, was arrested on 9 April; she was released the following day, after her house was searched and nothing was found.[90] A week later, the government cracked down on the city's Fenian movement, arresting seven suspects, most of whom had close connections with Whelan. One of the prisoners was Henry Murphy, a prominent Montreal Fenian who had been the secretary of Bernard Devlin's election committee.[91] The weekend before McGee's assassination, Murphy had been in New York, closeted with the Fenian executive for a five-hour meeting. The authorities also had a roll of Fenian names in Murphy's handwriting; this was probably linked with fund-raising activities. According to the *Globe*'s reporter, the names included Patrick Doody, Michael Enright, and Thomas Murphy, who were among those arrested in Montreal.[92]

Doody had recently returned to Montreal after spending the winter in New Orleans; he suffered from asthma and had been advised by his doctor to avoid the Canadian winter.[93] Enright and Murphy were carters and had been Whelan's drinking companions at Kate Scanlan's tavern; Enright had also joined Whelan on an earlier threatening visit to McGee's house, during the 1867 election campaign.[94] Another regular at Scanlan's was James Kinsella; he had moved to Ottawa around the same time as Whelan and Doyle, and, like Doyle, he worked as a waiter at the Russell

House. Arrested at his father's house in Montreal, Kinsella had been in the Parliamentary Gallery with Whelan immediately before the assassination, and had reportedly held 'consultations with suspected parties' since his return to Montreal two days later.[95]

The two other men arrested in Montreal, Felix Callahan and John Curran, had long been in the government's sights. Callahan, a printer, was an active member of the city's St Patrick's Society and was among those named by McGee in his exposé of Fenianism the previous year; arrested on information supplied by Detective William Donohoe, he was thought to be the secretary of Doody's Fenian circle.[96] Curran was a pork dealer who had recently visited Rouses Point in New York, where the Fenians were preparing for the next invasion.[97] Two years earlier, Callahan and Curran had been part of a Fenian plot to raise an Irish company in Montreal, ostensibly to protect Canada, but actually to assist the invaders; whether or not the government knew of this, however, remains an open question.[98]

In targeting these men, the government was attempting not only to pry open a possible conspiracy behind McGee's assassination but also to disrupt the Fenian organization in Montreal; the Habeas Corpus Suspension Act provided the government with a powerful means to undermine Fenianism covertly, without the risks of acquittal that accompanied trials. Equally striking, however, is who was *not* arrested. None of the men named by 'James Rooney' was rounded up, and neither were most of the people whom McGee had publicly identified as Fenians in 1867 – not even the contractor Francis Bernard McNamee, who founded the first Fenian circle in the city. McNamee may have become an informer; some of his friends believed that he had been supplying information to George-Étienne Cartier and McGee.[99] If this was the case, the government would have left him at large to learn more about the assassination, and would also have had detailed information about the activities of Callahan and Curran. But if McNamee was indeed an informer, one wonders why many of his Fenian colleagues remained undisturbed. It is possible that some of Montreal's Fenians left town, that the government was worried about exposing informers by arresting more people, or that the other Fenians were deemed to be non-threatening. Whatever the case, the fact that only seven men were arrested in the leading Fenian city in Canada indicates that the Habeas Corpus Suspension Act was being used in a highly focused manner.

Meanwhile, in Ottawa, the government turned its attention to three prominent Irish nationalists in the city, each of whom was linked to

Whelan – Peter Eagleson, Michael Starrs, and Patrick Buckley. Eagleson, a merchant tailor, was Whelan's employer and had nominated him as assistant marshall in the Ottawa St Patrick's Day procession earlier in the year.[100] According to one reporter, Eagleson and his brother Patrick were well known 'for their extreme opinions on the question of Irish grievances.'[101] But it was not simply Eagleson's views and his connection with Whelan that led to his arrest. The government had intercepted a letter that Eagleson had sent to Fenian headquarters in New York, naming the Ottawa delegate for a Fenian convention – although which convention remains unknown.[102] If Eagleson was up to his neck in Fenianism, the evidence against Starrs was thin. As an organizer of the St Patrick's Day procession, Starrs had supported the election of Whelan as assistant marshall; his Ottawa Hotel was not only the place where Whelan boarded but also a social centre for the city's Irish nationalists.[103] Buckley was also part of this scene. The owner of a livery stable, he had been the chief marshall at the St Patrick's Day procession; he also worked as a doorkeeper at the House of Commons and had been engaged in conversation with Whelan on the night of the murder.[104] All three men were arrested during the third week of April.

Also arrested in Ottawa were Richard Quinn and Reuben Lawrence, both of whom had been with Whelan and Kinsella in the Parliamentary Gallery on the night of the murder. According to Edward Storr, a messenger in the House of Commons, all four of them had behaved suspiciously; Whelan and one of the others, he said, had made threatening gestures during McGee's speech.[105] Like Whelan, Lawrence had been a marshall at the St Patrick's Day procession in Ottawa; the *Globe* reported that 'his brother is a notorious Fenian at Cleveland, Ohio, and was violent towards Canadians during the raid in June, 1866.'[106] Quinn was a member of Ottawa's St Patrick's Society and a reader of the *Irish People*, the newspaper of the anti-invasion Fenian faction in New York.[107] The government quickly concluded that neither of them had anything to do with the murder, and they were both released within two days.

The next wave of arrests occurred in early May and had more to do with the government's general counter-offensive against Canadian Fenianism than with McGee's assassination. To weaken the link between American and Canadian Fenianism, the government had already announced that it would prosecute any newspaper dealers who sold American Fenian newspapers in Canada; now, it directed its attention to the pro-Fenian Toronto newspaper, the *Irish Canadian*.[108] On 4 May, in conjunction with the Toronto police force, McMicken moved against the newspaper's publishers, Patrick Boyle and his brother-in-law Edward Hynes. Also arrested were John Nolan, a moulder who served as the secretary of the Hibernian Benevolent Society, and Owen Cosgrove, an innkeeper. According to the warrants of commitment, they were part of a movement that had 'the purpose of making hostile incursions into Canada,' and had made contact with Fenian emissaries who were planning the next invasion.[109]

In Patrick Boyle's case, the government was not only aiming at his newspaper; it was also acting on information that Boyle had participated in Fenian fund-raising activities and had sold Fenian bonds the previous year. Among the purchasers was John Nolan.[110] Nolan's brother, Patrick, was a member of McMicken's secret police force and had supplied valuable information to the government about the Fenian circles within the Hibernian Benevolent Society.[111] Owen Cosgrove's tavern, the Coachman's Arms, was a well-known meeting place for the city's Irish nationalists and would become a frequent target for Orange crowds over the next decade.[112] For his part, Hynes seems to have been arrested solely on the strength of his connection with the *Irish Canadian*.

At the same time that these arrests were being made, McMicken's men focused on the Fenian organization in Guelph, described by the *Globe* as 'the central point for Fenian operations in Ontario.'[113] The key figure was Peter Mahon, a farmer and town councillor, who had been under surveillance since March 1868 and who had a strong following in the 'Little Ireland' district of Aberfoyle and Puslinch.[114] According to McMicken, Mahon had attended the Cleveland convention in September 1867, using the pseudonym McNamara; subsequent information indicated that Mahon had close connections with one John Turner from Guelph, who described himself as the 'Centre of the Ontario Fenian Brotherhood,' and with the Fenian colonel John Hoy from Buffalo, who had participated in the 1866 invasion and had recently visited the area under the pseudonym of Tyrell.[115] The correspondence among Mahon, Turner, and Hoy implicated two men who shared the name John Murphy. One of them, an eighteen-year-old, had apparently been involved in attempts to extend the Fenian organization into London; the other was a baggageman who worked for the Grand Trunk Railway. Turner managed to elude the authorities. But Mahon and the eighteen-year-old John Murphy were arrested on 4 May; the baggageman joined them in Guelph jail two days later.[116] These arrests, like the ones in Toronto, were aimed at Irish Canadians who actively supported the next Fenian invasion; there was no connection at all with McGee's murder.

But the next arrest, back in Montreal, was a different matter. In May, a detective with the Great Western Railway, Reuben Wade, came forward with the remarkable story that he had heard Whelan and four other men plotting McGee's death. Wade had been staying at Michael Duggan's tavern in Montreal over Christmas. Amid discussions among the men about McGee's treachery, the recent election, and the delegates for a Fenian convention, Wade claimed to have caught snatches of conversation about McGee's impending assassination, with Whelan acting as the hit man. If Wade was to be believed, Michael Duggan's brother John, a law clerk who was indentured with Bernard Devlin, was one of the people planning the assassination; Wade also said that Ralph Slattery was among the conspirators.[117] George Brown of the *Globe* was sceptical, remarking that the 'reported disclosures ... seem rather mythical.'[118] Given Wade's later behaviour – he wrote increasingly paranoid and conspiratorial letters to Macdonald in the winter of 1868–9 – it seems that Brown had a point.[119] But in the aftermath of the assassination, the government felt that it could not afford to ignore Wade's information, and placed Michael Duggan under arrest.

Two other men were arrested in May. One of them, John Lyons, was the Ottawa agent for the *Irish Canadian* and a member of the city's St Patrick's Society. His grocery store was a Fenian meeting place, and there were reports that he had recently been 'in communication with the leading Fenians in Ogdensburg'; here, it seemed, was someone connected with both Whelan and the American Fenians.[120] The other was a sailor and crimp named James Ward in Quebec City; after a brief investigation, the authorities concluded that he had been set up by a rival gang. He was a Protestant from the north of Ireland, and 'one of the greatest villains I ever met with,' according to George Irvine, the Quebec solicitor general. 'As he makes a great deal of money by his business,' Irvine concluded, 'I should think it on the whole improbable that he would meddle with political crimes ... But you may be quite satisfied that his imprisonment ... has not been a public loss.'[121] Shortly afterwards, he was released.

PERSONAL COSTS

There is much evidence, then, to indicate that the suspension of habeas corpus was applied selectively against individuals whom the government had good reason to suspect of Fenianism. The pattern of releases tends to confirm this assessment; people who were arrested on precautionary grounds were generally not incarcerated for long. Bridget Whelan was set free after one day; Richard Quinn and Reuben Lawrence, who had been with Whelan in the Parliamentary Gallery, were released two days after their arrest; William Mitchell, who had been in the wrong place at the wrong time, was let out after two weeks; James Ward was not detained much longer, and Michael Starrs was in prison for just over a month.[122] In Toronto, pressure from the Catholic community and the *Globe* resulted in the release of Edward Hynes some three weeks after his arrest, and Owen Cosgrove was set free at much the same time.[123] John Nolan was jailed for over two months before the city's leading Liberal-Conservative Catholics convinced Macdonald of his innocence.[124]

In contrast, men who were closely connected with Whelan or were regarded as significant Fenian figures spent several months in prison and were not released until after Whelan's trial in September. Even here, though, there were exceptions. After Patrick Boyle was released on a technicality in late July 1868, the government decided not to re-arrest him.[125] John Lyons was released on bail during the summer, and promptly continued his efforts to organize the Fenians on the Kemptville-Ogdensburg border.[126] And James O'Reilly argued in July that Peter Mahon and the two Murphys from Guelph could be 'admitted to bail, great care & concern being taken that it be of the most substantial Character.'[127]

Nevertheless, for those who were caught in the net, the personal costs were high – sometimes very high indeed. For all they knew, they could spend years in prison without being tried, and uncertainty quickly bred anxiety. When the *Globe*'s reporter visited the Ottawa jail towards the end of May, Michael Enright 'remarked that under the *Habeas Corpus* Suspension Act they could be kept there until they were grey.'[128] His fellow prisoner Patrick Buckley, who insisted that he was as 'innocent as the child unborn,' cracked under the pressure. When, in September, he learned that he would be tried as an accessory to McGee's murder, he broke down and wept. By the time of his trial, in April 1869, he 'had the appearance of having undergone considerable suffering,' and there were reports that he had 'become insane since his incarceration.' The case against him was so weak that the judge quickly threw it out; there was not a shred of evidence that he was involved in McGee's murder.[129] Still worse was the fate of Patrick Doody, who was almost certainly a Fenian but who had no connection with the assassination. Never in good health, he contracted tuberculosis in prison and died in January 1869. His friends erected a nine-foot monument to him in the Côte-des-Neiges cemetery, asserting that he died 'from the effects of cruel and bad treatment while confined in Ottawa prison for seven months on suspicion of Fenianism,' and calling him 'the first martyr in Canada to Ireland's rights and liberties.'[130]

Although these were extreme cases, and although the Ottawa prison was actually 'one of the model gaols of the Dominion,' the other prisoners suffered consequences beyond the loss of liberty.[131] Peter Eagleson's business was ruined, and he went bankrupt in June 1868; 'this is a serious matter,' commented the *Globe*, 'and the Government ought to be able to show sufficient reasons for their course of action.'[132] Equally serious, for those prisoners with families, was the fact that they were no longer able to provide for their wives and children. From Guelph jail, the baggageman John Murphy wrote that 'my wife, with my two young children of three and one year old, have been left without any means of support, and I have been kept out of my situation, and have no means of supplying bread to my family.'[133] The same point was made by Peter Mahon, who was kept in solitary confinement in the basement of the Guelph jail and whose health rapidly deteriorated as a result.[134] 'I am a farmer,' he wrote to Lord Monck, 'and your excellency will conceive the irreparable loss I have already sustained by not being permitted to attend to the farm when sowing should be done, and that which I am every day sustaining in consequence of my absence, such losses may seem trifling to men of state, but they are important to a poor man.'[135]

Not surprisingly, given these circumstances, the prisoners in the Ottawa jail told the *Globe*'s correspondent that they wanted early trials, rather than waiting for the autumn assizes.[136] It was a similar story in Guelph, although getting the message heard proved more difficult. 'I am a political prisoner,' declared Mahon in a letter to the Guelph *Evening Mercury* that was never published.[137] 'I do not desire to extenuate myself in the least,' he told Lord Monck; 'I leave that to the Trial which will sooner or later take place, and for which I am as ancious as the athourities can possiably be, I wish a thourough investigation, I owe it to myself, and also to those whose confidence in me has been somewhat shaken in concequence of the charge against me, but I think my right indefeasable to be accorded the same priveledges as others charged with a similar offences when it cannot in any way that I can see prejudice the ends of justice.'[138] In July, the *Globe* published a letter from the baggageman John Murphy, in which he called for 'an opportunity of proving my innocence' and described his situation as 'a disgrace to a free country, and a violation of the liberty of the subject, most arbitrary and most unjust.'[139]

REACTIONS

As the initial shock of McGee's assassination wore off, and as the arrests under the Habeas Corpus Suspension Act continued into May 1868, these voices from within the prisons began to find echoes outside. After the Toronto and Guelph arrests, George Brown began to fear that the government was caving in to popular demands for stronger action against suspected Fenians, and noted the emergence of a 'vague and uneasy feeling in the minds of our Roman Catholic fellow-citizens.' If the prisoners were kept in jail for months, he added, 'the effect will be to create a sympathy for them, and through them for the cause which they are held to represent.' The government's actions could become counterproductive, and actually increase Irish Catholic disaffection; unless just cause was shown for the arrests, he predicted in early May, 'we shall have plenty of Irishmen persuading themselves that they are as much ill-used here as ever they were in Ireland.'[140]

Not only did Brown have good grounds for concern; as the undeclared leader of the opposition to the government, he was also using the situation for political advantage. Over the next few weeks, he increasingly contended that the suspension of habeas corpus was characterized by mistakes, manipulation, and misuse. The early release of Edward Hynes, argued Brown, only demonstrated that the government should never have arrested him in the first place.[141] Even more disturbing, from Brown's perspective, was the case of John Nolan. In July, the Toronto *Leader* claimed that Nolan's release had been secured through the influence of James Moylan, the editor of the Catholic *Canadian Freeman* and a close ally of Macdonald.[142] This could mean only one of two things, Brown concluded: either the government had arrested an innocent man, or it had released a guilty man and endangered the state simply to boost Moylan's political influence among Irish Catholics. Either way, the picture was hardly reassuring; 'Lettres de Cachet Revived,' ran one of the *Globe*'s headlines on the subject.[143] Nor was the news from Montreal much better. In June, Andrew Cullen, a detective who had damning evidence against Whelan, was shot after arresting a burglar in the city. Cullen recovered, but it transpired that he had arrested the man under the Habeas Corpus Suspension Act – a clear case of abuse of process, according to the presiding judge.[144]

The real Fenian danger, Brown was convinced, came from the United States, and not within Canada. One of the things that struck him about the men arrested in Canada was their low social status. 'There is not a man of position, wealth, or ability among them – not a single one that any person would ever have thought of looking upon as a leader of his countrymen in his neighbourhood,' he wrote. 'When such men are the leaders, the following – if there is such a thing – must be in the last degree contemptible.'[145] Leaving aside Brown's class bias, it was indeed the case that most of the prisoners were artisans and tradesmen, with a sprinkling of labourers at one end and small-scale entrepreneurs at the other – although there is no inherent reason why this should have made them less formidable in the event of a Fenian invasion. But Brown also noted that Canadian Fenians had done nothing during the 1866 raid, and believed that they would remain quiet provided that any future attack was quickly repulsed.[146] Rather than focusing on a largely imaginary internal threat, he argued, the government should move its troops up to the frontier as a deterrent to the American Fenians.[147]

Among those who agreed with Brown was the Liberal politician and temperance advocate Malcolm Cameron. In his view, the government was using Fenian fear tactics to conduct a campaign of 'political persecution' against its Irish Catholic opponents; the idea behind the suspension of habeas corpus, he wrote, was to root out the 'radical Irish' in Ottawa so that 'the rank and file would be tractable as of yore.' It was no wonder, he continued, that 'a feeling of insecurity and dismay' permeated the Catholic Irish in Canada – a feeling that was also expressed in a letter to the *Globe* lamenting that Irish Catholic Canadians in general were being tarred with the brush of Fenianism.[148]

But the strongest endorsement of Brown's position came, not surprisingly, from Patrick Boyle's *Irish Canadian*, which resumed publication after a three-month hiatus in August 1868, with the headline 'STILL WE LIVE!' 'Let our countrymen, in future,' wrote Boyle, 'remember that, when Orange ascendancy and Tory bigotry and fanaticism shrieked in May last for there [sic] wholesale imprisonment under the provisions of the suspended habeas corpus, *the Globe was the only journal in the Dominion which dared to throw its protecting shield between them and tyranny.*' Thanking not only Brown but other members of the Reform Party in Toronto for their sympathy and support, Boyle argued that the government had behaved in a cruel, barbarous, and inhuman fashion, setting the 'perjured scoundrel' against the 'unfortunate victim,' suppressing Irish Catholic freedom of speech and assembly, and inflicting great hardship on innocent men. 'Is it good policy, is it statesmanlike,' he asked, 'to be periodically suspending the Constitution, and levelling arbitrary power against a certain section of the community?'[149]

Even more incensed by the government's actions was the *Irish Canadian*'s Montreal correspondent, probably W.B. Linehan, who claimed that the arrests were reproducing on Canadian soil the same kind of oppression that the Irish had experienced at home. It would not be true to say that Linehan, if he was indeed the writer, had been radicalized by the arrests, since his radicalism long predated 1868. But there was no mistaking his anger. *'The first use men made of freedom is to avenge themselves on those who are slow to grant it,'* he wrote, making the statement twice more in case anyone had missed the point. And he left little doubt about the form that such revenge would take. At a time when Nova Scotia was on the point of rebellion against confederation, and when a Fenian army was gathering on the Canadian frontier, he argued, the government had created an Irish enemy within – and 'One enemy within is worse than a hundred outside.' 'To be sure,' he conceded, 'very few have been arrested; but those arrests, being wanton, and the foul and voluminous abuse of our people are regarded as insults, and have created a positive distrust in the Government.'[150]

The same note was struck by John Lawrence Power O'Hanly, one of Ottawa's leading Irish nationalists, who responded to the government's arrests with a mixture of hyperbole, hysteria, and paranoia. Writing in May 1868 to John Hearn, a kindred spirit in Quebec City, O'Hanly declared that 'a large portion of this community' wanted a 'sectarian war of extermination' against Irish Catholics. Whelan's 'guilt and condemnation now seem predetermined,' he wrote, and 'every Irish Catholic in this country, who is not a slave or a hypocrite, stands in the shadow of a prison, if not a gibbet.' Men such as Peter Eagleson and Michael Starrs had been arrested simply because they knew Whelan, he asserted, and were assumed to be guilty by association. With the suspension of habeas corpus, O'Hanly concluded, no Irish Catholic was safe: 'The universal themes are: 'Hang ninety nine out of every hundred of the "bloody Irish papists"; and it is pretty safe to conclude that the right one will be of the number: "string them up first, and try them afterwards"; &c. &c.; and the tone of the press is strictly in keeping with this sanguinary disposition.' 'Should my suspicions be verified,' he added, 'the life of any Irish Catholic put on trial is not worth a *sous*.'[151]

CONSEQUENCES

Such language may have been over the top, but it is a good gauge of the fear and anger that gripped Irish Canadian nationalists during the popular backlash after McGee's assassination. There is some evidence to suggest that the operation of the Habeas Corpus Suspension Act, together with Whelan's trial, did indeed create more Irish Catholic sympathy for the prisoners, as George Brown had feared. When James O'Reilly was asked why he had rejected all the Catholic jurors for Whelan's trial, he referred to the 'well-known sympathy on the part of many Roman Catholics in this neighbourhood with Whelan.'[152] And after Whelan was hanged in February 1869, the government refused to give him a public burial, fearing that his funeral would become the occasion of a Fenian demonstration in Montreal.[153] At the same time, hard-line Fenians became even more alienated from the Canadian government; the Montreal correspondent who informed the *Irish American* in April 1868 that Canadian repression must be answered by an American invasion was far from alone.[154]

How much weight did the other criticisms of the government carry? It is true that innocent men were caught in the net. Michael Starrs and Edward Hynes clearly fell into this category, as did Patrick Buckley, who became a prime suspect in the murder of a man whom he described as his best friend.[155] It is also true that Detective Andrew Cullen used the Habeas Corpus Suspension Act against a common criminal, and there is substance in the charge that the Conservatives tried to make political capital from the release of John Nolan in Toronto. Against this, Starrs, Hynes, and Nolan were not kept in prison for long, and Cullen's action appears to have been an isolated case that was quickly rectified. On balance, the government used the suspension of habeas corpus with moderation and restraint; not surprisingly, there was more alarmism from the potential victims of the suspension than there was from the government itself.

The most striking testimony to the government's restraint, ironically, came from O'Hanly himself. In the course of his heated letter to John Hearn, he admitted that Macdonald had 'acted with moderation' and deserved 'great commendation for the manner in which he has throughout resisted the pressure brought to bear on him on the side of persecution.'[156] Equally interesting was O'Hanly's reaction to Macdonald's presence next to the judge at Whelan's trial. Far from believing that the prime minister had compromised the proceedings, O'Hanly argued that Macdonald's attendance at the trial had enabled him to see 'how the cat jumped,' after which he 'humanely shut down and muzzled the thirst for blood.'[157] Similarly, O'Hanly believed that O'Reilly had resisted the clamour for widespread arrests – something that also earned O'Reilly a good deal of criticism from the other side of the political spectrum, on the grounds that an Irish Catholic was being soft on his co-religious countrymen.[158]

The other key question concerns the impact of the Habeas Corpus Suspension Act on Fenianism in Canada. If it is true that many Irish Catholics sympathized with the prisoners, and that the arrests produced a hardening of Fenian attitudes, it was also the case that Canadian Fenians found themselves in an increasingly isolated position. Politicians such as Bernard Devlin in Montreal, who had drawn heavily on Fenian support in his campaign against McGee, now pulled back from the movement. When, in September 1868, a group of Montreal Fenians planned a meeting in support of the prisoners, Devlin condemned it as a 'most mischievous and objectionable undertaking.' In response, his former Fenian supporters denounced him as a traitor and turncoat, and refused to accept his donation to the relief fund for the prisoners' families. Other Irish Canadian leaders, such as Anglin, also put as much distance as possible between themselves and the Fenians.[159] Any future attempt by the Fenians to work through a broad Irish nationalist front was not going to succeed.

The arrests also had the more direct effect of temporarily disrupting Fenian circles in Montreal, Ottawa, Toronto, and Guelph; it is reasonable to assume, too, that some Fenians left the country and that others were scared away from the movement. After Whelan had been found guilty, and in the absence of evidence for a conspiracy to murder McGee, O'Reilly felt confident enough to admit to bail those who had been arrested largely on the strength of their connection with the condemned man – Thomas Murphy, Michael Enright, Peter Eagleson, Patrick Buckley, James Kinsella, and John Doyle.[160] Henry Murphy had seen the error of his ways and broken with the Fenian movement, according to O'Reilly: 'I am satisfied from a conversation I have had with him,' he wrote, 'that there is no danger of his again connecting himself with Fenianism.'[161] The last to be released were the prominent Fenians from Montreal and Ottawa – Felix Callahan, Ralph Slattery, and Patrick Doody – along with Michael Duggan. 'Fenianism is dead in the United States, and the prompt action of our Government in making arrests last Spring has effectually stamped it out in this Country,' O'Reilly told Macdonald, in justifying his position. 'It's now perfectly harmless and no longer to be feared.'[162]

In fact, he was quite wrong; the history of Fenianism is full of premature obituaries, and this is one of them. The Fenian Brotherhood in the United States continued to raise money, materiel, and men for the next invasion of Canada, and by the summer of 1870 it was ready for action. Within Canada, the Fenians regrouped and resumed their earlier plans to assist the invaders; as well as advancing the broader strategic goals of the Fenian leadership, the anticipated attack was expected to provide revenge for the repression of 1868. The Habeas Corpus Suspension Act did not provide the means to defeat Canadian Fenianism. What really finished off the Fenians in Canada was the abject failure of John O'Neill's second invasion attempt at the Battle of Eccles Hill in June 1870. The rapid dispersal of O'Neill's troops completely and comprehensively discredited the invasion strategy and pre-empted any internal rising of the remaining Canadian Fenians. Henceforth, Irish nationalists in Canada would direct their attention to Ireland and cease to threaten the state in which they lived.[163]

In this sense, it was George Brown who got it right: the best way to defeat Fenianism in Canada was not through suspending civil liberties but through ensuring an immediate and decisive victory against the invading army and thus removing the hope upon which so much of Canadian Fenianism was based.

NOTES

1 Toronto *Globe*, 20 Nov. 1867; House of Commons, *Debates*, 1867–8, 29 Nov. 1867, 158. See this volume's Supporting Documents for the 1866 and 1867 legislation. See also D.A. Cameron Harvey, *The Law of Habeas Corpus in Canada* (Toronto: Butterworths 1974), 2, 192–6. Habeas corpus suspensions were one of the primary responses (along with the prosecution of political offences) to real or perceived security threats, enabling governments to detain suspects for extended periods or indefinitely without charges or trial. The Habeas Corpus Act, 1679 (31 Ch.II c.2) was distinct from the common law writ and required the passage of temporary emergency legislation to support such detention. See F. Murray Greenwood and Barry Wright, 'Introduction: State Trials, the Rule of Law, and Executive Powers in Early Canada,' *CST 1*, 31–3; *CST 2*; and R.J. Sharpe, *The Law of Habeas Corpus*, 2nd ed. (Oxford: Clarendon Press 1989). For examples of habeas corpus suspensions in British North America, see *CST 1* and *CST 2*.

2 The chapter by Andrew Parnaby and Gregory Kealey with Kirk Niergarth in this volume examines Dominion intelligence operations in detail. For a rather harsh assessment of the intelligence service in Canada West, see Jeff Keshen, 'Cloak and Dagger: Canada West's Secret Police, 1864–1867,' *Ontario History* 79, no. 4 (1987): 353–81.

3 Thomas D'Arcy McGee to Lord Kimberley, 25 May 1866, Kimberley Papers, Bodleian Library, Oxford, 4047, f.76. On the 'absurd fiasco at Eastport,' when American Fenians attempted to invade Campobello Island, see Robert L. Dallison, *Turning Back the Fenians: New Brunswick's Last Colonial Campaign* (Fredericton: Goose Lane Editions 2006). The Fenian organizational structure was based on a series of circles, grouped around a 'head centre.'

4 See, for example, Peter M. Toner, 'The Rise of Irish Nationalism in Canada, 1858–1884,' PhD thesis, University College, Galway, 1974.

5 *Nation*, 16 June 1866.

6 See R. Blake Brown's chapter in this volume.

7 Frederick Bruce to Lord Clarendon, 18 June 1866, Fenian A Files, NAI, A165; Bruce to Lord Stanley, 10 Nov. 1866, ibid., A214; Bruce to Stanley, 28 May 1867, ibid., A270. See also Brian Jenkins, *Fenians and Anglo-American Relations during Reconstruction* (Ithaca, N.Y.: Cornell University Press 1969), 160–74. Lord Stanley succeeded Lord Clarendon as foreign secretary on 28 June 1866, when the Earl of Derby's Conservative government came to power.

8 House of Commons, *Debates*, 29 Nov. 1867, 158; Crown Law Department of Upper Canada Circular, LAC, RG 13, A2, vol. 15, file 667.

9 Halifax *Morning Chronicle*, 2 Dec. 1867.

10 *Globe*, 30 Nov. 1867.

11 This complacent attitude towards the potential threat to liberties posed by such security measures fits a wider pattern in Canadian history; see, for example, F. Murray Greenwood, 'The Drafting and Passage of the War Measures Act: Object Lessons in the Need for Vigilance,' in W. Wesley Pue and Barry Wright, eds., *Canadian Perspectives on Law and Society: Issues in Legal History* (Ottawa: Carleton University Press 1988), 291.

12 Saint John *Morning Freeman*, 29 Nov. 1867.

13 Timothy Warren Anglin to Joseph Brenan, 3 July 1848, James Fintan Lalor Papers, NLI, MS 340, f.1. He also concealed the fact from his biographer, William M. Baker; see Baker, *Timothy Warren Anglin 1822–96: Irish Catholic Canadian* (Toronto: University of Toronto Press 1977).

14 Willam M. Baker, 'Turning the Spit: Timothy Warren Anglin and the Roasting of D'Arcy McGee,' Canadian Historical Association *Historical Papers* (1974): 135–55; Baker, *Timothy Warren Anglin*, 119–32.

15 House of Commons, *Debates*, 29 Nov. 1867, 158. On Dorion's career, see Jean-Claude Soulard, 'Antoine-Aimé Dorion,' *DCB*, http://www.biographica.ca.

16 'D. Thomas' to J.S. Wood, 13 Nov. 1866, Fenian A Files, NAI, A206. It is not clear, however, whether this information actually reached the Canadian government.

17 Christy Campbell, *Fenian Fire: The British Government Plot to Assassinate Queen Victoria* (London: HarperCollins 2003), 74; Bruce to Stanley, 8 Jan. 1867, Fenian A Files, NAI, A250.

18 Edith J. Archibald, *Life and Letters of Sir Edward Mortimer Archibald, K.C.M.G., C.B.: A Memoir of Fifty Years of Service* (Toronto: George N. Morang 1924), 169–70.

19 Pierrepont Edwards to Thomas Larcom, 4 June 1867, Fenian A Files, NAI, A273; Edwards to John Godley, 3 June 1867, Fenian A Files, NAI, A277; Edwards to Stanley, 13 June 1867, Fenian A Files, NAI, A279.

20 Edwards to Stanley, 13 June 1867, Fenian A Files, NAI, A279.

21 Edwards to Godley, 3 June 1867, Fenian A Files, NAI, A273; see also Archibald, *Life and Letters*, 168, for Archibald's difficulty in sorting out fact from fiction.

22 McGee to John A. Macdonald, 19 Dec. 1866, Macdonald Papers, LAC, MG 26A, vol. 231, ff.99993-4.

23 Archibald to Stanley, 1 Oct. 1867, Fenian A Files, NAI, A291.

24 Gilbert McMicken to Macdonald, 3 Oct. 1867, Macdonald Papers, vol. 239, f.106237; McMicken to Macdonald, 21 Oct. 1867, Macdonald Papers, vol. 239, ff.106262-3.

25 McMicken to Macdonald, 29 Oct. 1867, Macdonald Papers, vol. 239, ff.106269–70; McMicken to Macdonald, October 1867, Macdonald Papers, vol. 239, f.106275; McMicken to Macdonald, 9 Nov. 1867, Macdonald Papers, vol. 239, ff.106288–91.

26 Charles Carroll Tevis to Frederick Bruce, 7 Jan. 1867, Fenian A Files, NAI, A250.

27 Pierrepont Edwards to John Godley, 3 June 1867, Fenian A Files, NAI, A277.

28 Archibald to Stanley, 20 Aug. 1867, Fenian A Files, NAI, A285.

29 Edwards to Stanley, 13 June 1867, Fenian A Files, NAI, A279.

30 'Journal of Lady Monck, June 20–June 28, 1867,' in W.L. Morton, ed., *Monck Letters and Journals 1863–1868* (Toronto: McClelland and Stewart 1970), 320–1.

31 Archibald to Stanley, 1 Oct. 1867, Fenian A Files, NAI, A291.

32 Even George Sheppard, who exaggerates the Fenian numbers in Toronto and the size of rural Fenian lodges, concludes that there were only 1,690 Fenians in Canada West. See Sheppard, '"God Save the Green": Fenianism and Fellowship in Victorian Toronto,' *Histoire-Sociale / Social History* 20 (May 1987): 133. The estimate of 260,000 Canadians of Irish Catholic ethnicity is extrapolated from Donald Harman Akenson, *Being Had: Historians, Evidence, and the Irish in North America* (Port Credit, Ont.: P.D. Meany 1985), 84, 88.

33 See, for example, F.B. McNamee to Mr Christian, 26 March 1866, Thomas Sweeny Papers, New York Public Library.

34 J.L.P. O'Hanly, Untitled Memoir, Folder VI, 'Status of Irish Catholics,' J.L.P. O'Hanley [sic] Papers, LAC, MG 29, B11.

35 On the activities of the Montreal Water Police, see LAC, RG 13, A-2, vol. 17, file 36 (1868).

36 On William Prince, see Peter Vronsky, 'History of the Toronto Police, 1859–1866,' http://www.russianbooks.org/crime/cph5a.htm, and William S. Prince to McGee, 19 March 1866, Chief Constables Correspondence, City of Toronto Archives, Toronto. On O'Gara, see O'Hanly, Untitled Memoir.

37 – to Macdonald, 5 Nov. 1867, Macdonald Papers, vol. 239, ff.106280–2.

38 McMicken to Macdonald, 27 Jan. 1868, Macdonald Papers, vol. 239, f.106403.

39 Wilkins to Ford, 21 Dec. 1867, Fenian A Files, NAI, A311.

40 John McLoughlin to Charles Coursol, 28 Dec. 1867, LAC, RG 13, A2, vol. 17, file 36 (1868); McGee to Macdonald, 11 Jan. 1868, Macdonald Papers, vol. 59, ff.23938.

41 Ermatinger to Macdonald, 10 Jan. 1868, Macdonald Papers, vol. 240, f.106291.

42 'James Rooney' to Francis Lousada, 4 Feb. 1868, NAUK, FO.5/1343, f.101; Lousada to Stanley, 6 Feb. 1868, ibid., f.103; 'Rooney' to Lousada, 14 March 1868, ibid., ff.231–2. The identity of 'Rooney' remains a mystery, but his information appears to have been accurate; some of the Canadian Fenians whom he named match anti-McGee Irishmen in Montreal, and he was also able to provide Lousada with the key to the cipher used in the Fenian headquarters in New York; see Lousada to Stanley, 26 March 1868, ibid., f.276.

43 Lousada to Stanley, 3 March 1868, NAUK, FO.5/1343, ff.167–9; see also 'Rooney' to Lousada, 4 Feb. 1868, NAUK, FO.5/1343, f.101, and 'Rooney's Diary,' 5 March 1868, NAUK, FO.5/1343, ff.194–5.

44 Coursol to Macdonald, 17 Feb. 1868, Macdonald Papers, vol. 240, ff.106458–9; John McLoughlin to Coursol, 18 March 1868, Macdonald Papers, vol. 240, f.106572.

45 A. Sewell to Ermatinger, 13 March 1868, Macdonald Papers, vol. 240, f.106549.

46 'Rooney' to Lousada, 24 March 1868, NAUK, FO.5/1343, f.278; Lousada to Stanley, 26 March 1868, ibid., f.276; Ermatinger to Macdonald, 26 March 1868, Macdonald Papers, vol. 240, f.106619; McMicken to Macdonald, 30 March 1868, f.106653.

47 For a slightly fuller account of McGee's Irish and American background, see David A. Wilson, *Thomas D'Arcy McGee, Volume I: Passion, Reason and Politics 1825–57* (Montreal and Kingston: McGill-Queen's University Press 2008).

48 For some examples of Fenian invective against McGee, see *Irish Canadian*, 30 March 1864, 13 April 1864, 28 June 1865, 12 July 1865, 15 Nov. 1865, 22 Nov. 1865, 30 May 1866.

49 *Nation*, 8 April 1848; Warrant for the Arrest of Thomas Darcy [sic] McGee, 28 July 1848, NLI, MS 7910.

50 McGee, 'Account of the Attempts to Establish Fenianism,' Montreal *Gazette*, 22 Aug. 1867.

51 *Globe*, 15 Nov. 1867. One of the principal speakers at that meeting had been Timothy Warren Anglin; see St Patrick's Society Minute Book, 2 Dec. 1867, Concordia University Archives, St Patrick's Society of Montreal Fonds, PO 26, and Saint John *Morning Freeman*, 12 Nov. 1867.

52 McGee to Kimberley, Kimberley Papers, 4049, ff.39–40.

53 *Globe*, 1 Dec. 1866. McGee went on to argue for clemency, remarking that 'the spirit of our times is opposed to the infliction of capital punishment'; see *Globe*, 2 Dec. 1866.

54 McGee, 'Account of the Attempts to Establish Fenianism,' Montreal *Gazette*, 17 Aug., 20 Aug., 22 Aug. 1867.

55 McGee, 'Account of the Attempts to Establish Fenianism in Montreal,' Montreal *Gazette*, 20 Aug., 22 Aug. 1867. McGee also named O.J. Devlin (Bernard's brother), J. Walsh, Daniel Lyons, W.B. Linehan, J.J. O'Mara, and John McGrath as prominent Fenians in the city. The accuracy of McGee's information was confirmed in a court case fifteen years later, when Francis Bernard McNamee sued John Patrick Whelan, his rival for control of the St Patrick's Society, for libel; see Montreal *Herald*, 27 Sept., 28 Sept., 29 Sept., 3 Oct. 1882.

56 McGee, 'An Account of the Attempts to Establish Fenianism in Montreal,' Montreal *Gazette*, 20 Aug. 1867.

57 Montreal *Herald*, 9 Aug. 1867.

58 *The Trial of Patrick J. Whelan* (Ottawa: Desbarats 1868), 33.

59 Montreal *Gazette*, 19 April 1864; *Irish Canadian*, 24 Jan. 1866.

60 See, for example, R. Wright to Macdonald, 10 April 1868, Macdonald Papers, MG 26A, vol. 341, ff.155929–30.

61 *Trial of Patrick J. Whelan*, 26–7, 31–2, 33–6; Ermatinger to Macdonald, 10 Jan. 1868, Macdonald Papers, vol. 240, f.106291.

62 McGee to Macdonald, 25 Feb. 1868, Charles A. Murphy Papers, LAC, MG 27, III, B8, ff.21583–4.

63 For Fenian celebrations of McGee's assassination, see H.C. Moore to George-Étienne Cartier, 20 April 1868, Macdonald Papers, vol. 59, f.24039; W. Lambert to Gilbert McMicken, 7 May 1868, Macdonald Papers, vol. 240, ff.106830–1; Rev. E.P. Roche to Bishop Horan, 15 April 1868, Bishop Edward John Horan Papers, Archives of the Archdiocese of Kingston, Ontario, DC18 C18/19; MacNeil Clarke to Macdonald, 8 April 1868, Macdonald Papers, vol. 184, f.76978; Statement of John Claire, 16 April 1868, Macdonald Papers, vol. 184, f.76970.

64 *Globe*, 10 April 1868; *Trial of Patrick J. Whelan*, 30.

65 *Canadian Freeman*, 17 Sept. 1868; the *Freeman*'s report mistakenly refers to the *Irish American* as the *Irish Canadian* – a revealing slip.

66 See, for example, T.P. Slattery, *'They Got to Find Mee Guilty Yet'* (Toronto: Doubleday 1972), 216, 352. Slattery further argued that the administration of justice was vitiated by an error of law in the jury selection and by the fact that the trial judge also participated in the appeals that arose from the case; see ibid., 288–98, 352.

67 See David A. Wilson, 'Was Patrick James Whelan a Fenian and Did He Assas-

sinate Thomas D'Arcy McGee?' in David A. Wilson, ed., *Irish Nationalism in Canada* (Montreal and Kingston: McGill-Queen's University Press, forthcoming).

68 *Globe*, 10 April 1868. It was very difficult to convict Fenians for suborning soldiers, since two witnesses were required; this had long been a complaint of the military authorities in Britain.

69 *Trial of Patrick J. Whelan*, 26, 31–3.

70 Archibald to Stanley, 9 April 1868, NAUK, FO.5/1343, f.342.

71 Rooney to Lousada, 7 May 1868, NAUK, FO.5/1343, f.377.

72 *Globe*, 25 April 1868; 'Dublin Special Commission, April, 1867,' NAI, Fenian Briefs, box 9, no. 6(a), ff.4, 58, 161–2; Fenian Photographs, NAI, box 4, f.506/811; 'Dublin – Special Commission, April 1867: Alphabetical List of Prisoners Arrested for Complicity in the Fenian Conspiracy,' and 'Lists of Warrants Issued, Arrests, Discharges, 1868,' NAI, Fenian Arrests and Discharges, 1866–9.

73 *Globe*, 18 April 1868.

74 Macdonald to David Morrison, 11 April 1868, Macdonald Papers, vol. 514, ff.644–5.

75 [Robert Anderson], 'Fenianism, Historical Sketch,' NAI, Fenian Police Reports, 1857–1883, box 4; Archibald, 'Despatch,' 30 Nov. 1866, ibid.; Barry Kennerk, 'Fenianism and Assassination: Its Influences, Objects and Methodologies (1858–1868),' paper delivered at Irish Fenianism conference, University of Ulster and Queen's University Belfast, 2008.

76 McMicken to Macdonald, 14 April 1868, Macdonald Papers, vol. 240, ff.106735–7; 'Abstract of Information in Letters Dated from Chicago, Il. on 23rd & 26th April 1868,' NAUK, FO.5/1343, f.405.

77 E.J. O'Neill to Macdonald, 13 April 1868, Macdonald Papers, vol. 184, ff. 76961–3.

78 Macdonald and James O'Reilly both suspected that a prominent 'Quebec gentleman,' possibly John Hearn or John O'Farrell (who was one of Whelan's defence lawyers), had a hand in the murder; see James O'Reilly to Macdonald, 10 Feb. 1869, Macdonald Papers, vol. 184, f.77023.

79 Macdonald to Sandfield Macdonald, 4 May 1868, Macdonald Papers, vol. 514, ff.702–3.

80 Ottawa *Times*, 27 May 1868; *Globe*, 28 May 1868.

81 Sandfield Macdonald to John A. Macdonald, Macdonald Papers, vol. 230, f.99446.

82 T.P. Slattery contends that, within a week of the assassination, seventy people were arrested under the suspension of habeas corpus, but he provides no evidence for his assertion. See Slattery, *'They Got to Find Mee Guilty Yet'*, 36.

83 McMicken to Macdonald, 14 April 1868, Macdonald Papers, vol. 240,

ff.106735–7; H.N. Hemans to Lord Monck, 22 June 1868, LAC, RG 13, A-2, vol. 20, file 726.

84 McMicken, Memorandum, 30 April 1868, LAC, RG 13, A-2, vol. 20, file 508.

85 *Globe*, 27 April 1868.

86 *Globe*, 9 April 1868.

87 Slattery, *'They Got to Find Mee Guilty Yet'*, 30–1, 114, 368; *Trial of Patrick J. Whelan*, 34.

88 *Globe*, 8 April 1868; Slattery, *'They Got to Find Mee Guilty Yet'*, 35.

89 *Globe*, 25 April 1868.

90 Slattery, *'They Got to Find Mee Guilty Yet'*, 35.

91 *Globe*, 17 April 1868, 29 May 1868. Edward Archibald identified Henry Murphy as 'one of the principal Fenians in Montreal'; see Archibald to Stanley, 9 April 1868, NAUK, FO 5/1343, ff.339–40.

92 *Globe*, 18 April 1868; Archibald to Stanley, 9 April 1868, NA, FO.5/1343, f.340.

93 Slattery, *'They Got to Find Mee Guilty Yet'*, 36, 363.

94 E.J. O'Neill to Macdonald, 13 April 1868, Macdonald Papers, vol. 184, ff.76961–3; *Irish Canadian*, 22 April 1868; *Trial of Patrick J. Whelan*, 33.

95 *Globe*, 17 April 1869; Guelph *Evening Mercury*, 17 April 1868.

96 St Patrick's Society Minute Book, 7 Nov. 1864; McGee, 'Account of the Attempts,' Montreal *Gazette*, 22 Aug. 1867; 'Information and Complaint of William Donohoe of the City of Montreal Police against Felix Callaghan at present of the City of Ottawa, Printer,' 17 April 1868, Macdonald Papers, vol. 184, f.76972; *Canadian Freeman*, 23 April 1868.

97 *Globe*, 18 April 1868; *Canadian Freeman*, 23 April 1868.

98 F.B. McNamee to Mr Christian, 26 March 1866, New York Public Library, Thomas Sweeny Papers; *Irish Canadian*, 18 April 1866.

99 See, for example, William Mansfield to Mr Christian, 9 April 1866, Sweeny Papers.

100 *Canadian Freeman*, 23 April 1868.

101 *Canadian Freeman*, 9 April 1868.

102 J.L.P. O'Hanly, Untitled Memoir.

103 *Canadian Freeman*, 23 April 1868; Francis Ritchie to McMicken, 12 Sept. 1868, Macdonald Papers, vol. 241, ff.107506–7.

104 *Canadian Freeman*, 23 April 1868; Guelph *Evening Mercury*, 11 April, 21 April 1868; *Globe*, 17 April 1869.

105 *Globe*, 21 April 1868; *Trial of Patrick J. Whelan*, 21–2.

106 *Trial of Patrick J. Whelan*, 59; *Globe*, 24 April 1868.

107 *Irish Canadian*, 23 Sept. 1868.

108 *Globe*, 4 May 1868.

109 *Globe*, 6 May 1868; Warrants of Commitment, LAC, RG 13, A-2, vol. 20, file 584.

110 Charles Clarke to McMicken, 10 May 1867, Macdonald Papers, vol. 239, ff.105922–6.

111 Keshen, 'Cloak and Dagger,' 365; Gregory S. Kealey, 'The Empire Strikes Back: The Nineteenth-Century Origins of the Canadian Secret Service,' Canadian Historical Association *Journal* 10 (1999): 11–12; Nolan to McMicken, 31 Dec. 1865, Macdonald Papers, vol. 236, ff.103131–4.

112 Brian Clarke, 'Religious Riot as Pastime: Orange Young Britons, Parades, and Public Life in Victorian Toronto,' in David A. Wilson, ed., *The Orange Order in Canada* (Dublin, 2007), 115–16, 118–19.

113 *Globe*, 6 May 1868.

114 McMicken to Macdonald, 4 March 1868, Macdonald Papers, vol. 240, f.106497; McMicken to Macdonald, 16 March 1868, Macdonald Papers, vol. 240, ff.106553–5.

115 McMicken to Macdonald, 14 April 1868, Macdonald Papers, vol. 240, ff.106735–7; O'Reilly to Macdonald, 27 July 1868, LAC, RG 13, A-2, vol. 20, file 585.

116 O'Reilly to Macdonald, 27 July 1868, LAC, RG 13, A-2, vol. 20, file 585; *Globe*, 6 May 1868; Guelph *Evening Mercury*, 6 May, 7 May 1868.

117 *Canadian Freeman*, 17 Sept. 1868; *Globe*, 14 May 1868.

118 *Globe*, 15 May 1868.

119 Wade to Macdonald, 23 Dec. 1868, Macdonald Papers, vol. 341, ff.156222–3; Wade to Macdonald, 1 March 1869, Macdonald Papers, vol. 342, ff.156344–7.

120 *Irish Canadian*, 23 Sept. 1868; Francis Ritchie to McMicken, 21 Sept. 1868, Macdonald Papers, vol. 241, ff.107529–31; *Globe*, 19 May 1868.

121 Warrant of Commitment for James Ward, 2 June 1868; Deposition of William Thompson, 2 June 1868; George Irvine to [Colonel] Bernard, 18 June 1868, LAC, RG 13, A-2, vol. 20, file 585.

122 Slattery, *'They Got to Find Mee Guilty Yet'*, 35; *Globe*, 25 April, 27 April, 19 May 1868.

123 *Globe*, 9 May, 13 May, 25 May 1868; Montreal *Gazette*, 26 May 1868.

124 *Globe*, 22 July 1868; *Canadian Freeman*, 23 July 1868.

125 *Globe*, 28 July 1868.

126 Francis Ritchie to McMicken, 13 Aug. 1868, Macdonald Papers, vol. 241, ff.107337–9. Ritchie refers to 'Patrick' Lyons, the 'noted Fenian sympathizer' who had been arrested after McGee's assassination and let out on bail. Since the only Lyons who fits this description is John, I assume that either Ritchie mistook the first name or John Lyons was calling himself Patrick.

127 O'Reilly to Macdonald, 27 July 1868, LAC, RG 13, A-2, vol. 20, file 585.

128 *Globe*, 29 May 1868.

129 *Globe*, 29 May 1868; Guelph *Evening Mercury*, 14 Sept. 1868; *Globe*, 17 April 1869.

130 Slattery, *'They Got to Find Mee Guilty Yet'*, 388.

131 *Globe*, 29 May 1868.

132 *Globe*, 9 June 1868; see also *Globe*, 17 Sept. 1868.

133 *Globe*, 17 July 1868.

134 Guelph *Evening Mercury*, 7 May, 18 May 1868.

135 Mahon to Lord Monck, 9 June 1868, LAC, RG 13, A-2, vol. 20, file 585.

136 *Globe*, 29 May 1868.

137 Mahon to McLagan [sic] and Innes, 24 May 1868, LAC, RG 13, A-2, vol. 20, file 585.

138 Mahon to Lord Monck, 9 June 1868, LAC, RG 13, A-2, vol. 20, file 585. The original orthography has been retained.

139 *Globe*, 17 July 1868.

140 *Globe*, 8 May 1868.

141 *Globe*, 9 May, 13 May 1868.

142 Toronto *Leader*, 21 July 1868.

143 *Globe*, 23 July 1868; see also *Globe*, 22 July 1868.

144 *Globe*, 10 June, 24 July 1868.

145 *Globe*, 13 May 1868.

146 *Globe*, 13 May 1868.

147 See, for example, *Globe*, 29 May, 12 June, 15 June 1868.

148 *Globe*, 17 Aug. 1868; O'Hanly, Untitled Memoir ; *Globe*, 18 May 1868.

149 *Irish Canadian*, 5 Aug. 1868.

150 *Irish Canadian*, 13 Aug. 1868. On Linehan, see David A. Wilson, 'The Fenians in Montreal, 1862–68: Invasion, and Assassination,' *Éire-Ireland*, 38, nos. 3–4 (2003): 115–17, 123–4.

151 O'Hanly to John Hearn, 4 May 1868, O'Hanley [sic] Papers. See also 'An Irish Nationalist' [O'Hanly], 'Home Rule; or, Truth Stranger than Fiction,' Ottawa *Citizen*, 25 June 1886.

152 *Globe*, 8 Sept. 1868.

153 Macdonald to O'Reilly, 12 Feb. 1869, Murphy Papers, f.14246.

154 *Irish American*, 25 April 1868.

155 Guelph *Evening Mercury*, 14 Sept. 1868.

156 O'Hanly to John Hearn, 4 May 1868, O'Hanley [sic] Papers.

157 O'Hanly, Untitled Memoir.

158 O'Hanly to John Hearn, 4 May 1868, O'Hanley [sic] Papers; Reuben Wade to Macdonald, 1 March 1869, Macdonald Papers, vol. 342, ff.156344–7.

159 Montreal *Herald*, 1 Sept., 2 Sept., 3 Sept., 5 Sept., 9 Sept. 1868.

160 O'Reilly to Macdonald, 17 Sept. 1868, 'Papers re. Parties Charged with Fenianism in Ottawa,' LAC, RG 13, A-2, vol. 20, file 510.
161 O'Reilly to Colonel Bernard, 28 Oct. 1868, ibid.
162 O'Reilly to Macdonald, 18 Nov. 1868, ibid.
163 Peter M. Toner, '"The Green Ghost": Canada's Fenians and the Raids,' *Éire-Ireland* 16, no. 4 (1981): 44–7; see also D.C. Lyne and Peter M. Toner, 'Fenianism in Canada, 1874–1884,' *Studia Hibernica* 12 (1972): 27–76.

PART TWO

Managing Collective Disorder

3

The Tenant League and the Law, 1864–7

IAN ROSS ROBERTSON

The British government distributed almost all the land on the future Prince Edward Island to individuals and small groups in 1767. The resulting sixty-seven townships of approximately 20,000 acres became known locally as 'lots' and were commonly identified by numbers, Lot 1 to Lot 67. That fateful decision, which left only one township, Lot 66, by far the smallest, as public land, marked the beginning of a century of leasehold tenure as the predominant means of land occupation on the Island. The 'land question' became a perennial source of political and social tension, and the law was an important means that the colonial authorities used in their attempts to contain the resistance of tenants and squatters to the exactions of the system. In the mid-1860s the Tenant League was a body that brought Island tenants and their sympathizers together in a 'direct action' movement willing to defy the law openly and without ambiguity. Even its enemies apparently accepted that, in a population numbering between 80,000 and 90,000, a realistic estimate of its membership was 11,000, a degree of support that was phenomenal.[1]

The demographic characteristics of Island society at the time are relevant to the history of the league. The pioneering historical geographer Andrew Hill Clark estimated that, by mid-century, close to one-half of the population traced its origin to Scotland, that about 10 per cent was Acadian, and that, of the remainder, more were English than Irish in ancestry.[2] In religion the colony was approximately 55 per cent Protestant, and, among the Protestants counted at the censuses of 1848, 1855, and 1861,

Presbyterians constituted a steady 58 per cent.[3] Among Roman Catholics, possibly one-half were Irish, but their Scottish co-religionists, by virtue of long establishment in the colony (dating back to the late eighteenth century), supplied most of the clergy. Although ethnic origins were undeniably important to Islanders' sense of self, the census of 1861 indicated that only 22.1 per cent were not native-born. Thus, their local roots were deep and well established. The same census revealed that almost 61 per cent of occupiers of land were either tenants or squatters, facts that created a sense of vulnerability.[4] Still more significantly, leasehold tenure was continuing to expand: since the previous census, in 1855, the number of leaseholders (although not their percentage among occupiers of land) had risen. The colony as a whole was overwhelmingly rural, with Charlottetown, the capital, being the only significant town and containing approximately 8 per cent of the population.[5] Moreover, its proportion did not appear to be growing; the chief clerk of the House of Assembly, in a brief introductory note to the 1861 census, noted that while the colony's population had increased 13 per cent since 1855, that of Charlottetown had risen by only 3 per cent.[6]

Since 1851 the Island had had responsible government, with an Executive Council directly answerable to the House of Assembly which, following the Franchise Act of 1853, was elected on virtually universal adult male suffrage.[7] From 1851 through 1859, with one brief interruption, the government had been Reform or Liberal. At the end of the 1850s, the Conservatives exploited religious tensions to come to office, uniting the Protestant majority against the Catholic minority and forming an all-Protestant administration; they repeated the strategy in 1863 and again succeeded. The Conservative government was closely linked to the economic and social elite, and the Island's class structure reflected the importance of the land question and shipbuilding. Most large landlords (or proprietors, as they were often called) were non-resident, but the land agents they hired were at the core of a tightly integrated local power structure centred in Charlottetown. The term 'Family Compact' was apt. As agents, the absentee landlords usually chose lawyers, local officials, merchants, or, possibly, resident landlords. In some cases the agents prospered to such an extent that eventually they bought out their employers. There was a long history of agents deriving more economic benefit from the properties they administered than did their principals, who were an ocean away.[8] Shipbuilding was particularly important for those of English origin, such as James Yeo, Sr, a Conservative executive councillor who was also a merchant, an agent, and eventually a landlord. Labouring in Yeo's shipyard might enable a tenant to pay his rent – perhaps to Yeo as an agent or as a landlord. In an era of open voting, such men could exercise enormous influence – so-called 'ledger influence' and 'rent roll influence' – at the polls.

Although many writers over a lengthy period alluded to the land question, and the Prince Edward Island-born man of letters Andrew Macphail even stated in 1914 that with respect to 'the relation between landlord and tenant ... nothing now remains to be said,' little of scholarly value that addressed the subject directly was written until the 1970s.[9] The Tenant League escaped serious examination for a particularly long time, perhaps because of its unconventionality. When historians and other writers mentioned it at all, they did so fleetingly, and sometimes simplistically and inaccurately. In 1996 a full-scale scholarly study of the Tenant League was published, which argued that it had been a success and that in Canadian history no other extra-parliamentary movement for radical change, willing to resort to civil disobedience, had been as successful as the league.[10] There has also been very little legal history written concerning the Island, and thus this chapter is a contribution to it, as well as to the history of Canadian state trials.[11]

INITIAL DEFIANCE

The Tenant League, from its founding in 1864, made no secret of its willingness to defy the law. The 'tenant's pledge' that members were to take was explicit in its requirements. They were 'to withhold the further liquidation of rent and arrears of rent; and ... to resist the distraint, coercion, ejection, seizure, and sale for rent and arrears of rent.'[12] In effect, without using the term, Tenant Leaguers were proposing a rent strike and, more seriously, preventing the execution of legal processes which might ensue from this refusal to pay.

To understand why the leaguers had decided upon this tactic, it is necessary to note the history of Island politics surrounding the land question over the previous several decades. Between the 1830s and 1864, the tenantry had witnessed the failures of a radical Escheat party/movement with its proposal of effective expropriation, a moderate Reform Party campaign with its incrementalist program, a royal commission to which leading landlords had originally assented, and a Tory government delegation sent to London to negotiate a compromise with the landlords.[13]

It was with this history in mind that seventy to eighty delegates and friends of the emerging tenant movement met in Charlottetown on 19 May 1864 and founded the Tenant Union of Prince Edward Island. The union – usually known to contemporaries (friends, foes, and uncommitted) as the Tenant League[14] – was to operate 'under the direction and guidance of a Central Committee' which would wield considerable authority. Each township was to have a local committee, which would decide upon 'a fair and reasonable price' to be offered to the proprietors for their lands. Any difficulties in this process, for example, over the price to be offered or the rejection by a proprietor of a fair price, were to be referred to the Central Committee. By resolving that 'any tenant who shall refuse to make a fair offer ... shall forfeit the sympathy and all the advantages of this Union,'[15] the convention made it clear that the new organization was not advocating expropriation without compensation, and thus had made a decisive break with the Escheat program. But delegates also left no doubt that they were serious about their determination to bring the leasehold system to an end, by publishing their 'tenant's pledge.' From the beginning, the members were absolutely clear about the fact that their proposed solution to the land question would involve defiance of the law and its enforcement officers.

The procedures that came into play when a proprietor or land agent took legal action against a tenant for non-payment of rent were central to the history of the league. When a tenant had failed to pay or had fallen into arrears, the landlord could bring a case against him; if the case was successful, the court would issue a writ of *fieri facias* to the plaintiff, who could then call upon the sheriff or his deputy to deliver it. The writ directed the sheriff 'to levy from the goods and chattels of the debtor a sum equal to the amount'[16] specified; once the sheriff had made the seizure, he was to sell the goods by auction. If the debtor – the tenant in this case – evaded the distraint, the next step was the more drastic action of a writ of *capias ad satisfaciendum*, which directed the arrest of the defendant who failed to satisfy a judgment against him for a sum of money.

These were the major legal weapons, short of eviction, used against tenants. If it was likely that assistance would be necessary, the sheriff or his deputy might enlist bailiffs or constables hired on a per diem basis. Given their position on the front line of law enforcement, these officers became the foci of strife as tension escalated.[17] Their failure to execute the writs of the court – if it should come to that – would raise the question of military aid to the civil power.

ATTITUDE OF THE AUTHORITIES

From the beginning of the Tenant League movement, at least some persons in positions of power noted the possible legal implications of the strategy the militants proposed, and where it might lead in terms of support for the civil power. Most notably, William Henry Pope, a central figure in Island public life, had expressed alarm and issued a public warning even before the founding convention. The editor of the *Islander* (the leading Conservative newspaper), an assemblyman, an executive councillor, and the colonial secretary in the government, Pope was also a lawyer trained at the Inner Temple, London.[18] Prior to the convention, there had been a series of at least twenty public meetings held across the Island expressing a sense of crisis over the land question. In an editorial published one week after the appearance of the notice advertising the convention, Pope focused on the determination avowed at some tenant meetings to resist the collection of rent 'legally,' a usage that suggested what might be termed a popular notion of legality.[19] This was something Pope rejected absolutely. He declared that 'there can be no *"legal"* resistance to the payment of rent, on the part of the tenants who hold lands under any proprietor.' After pointing out, step by step, the consequences of defying the law, he cautioned the tenants involved: 'Let no man be deceived in this matter. The law will be enforced even should it require the presence of a company of troops in every county in the Island.'[20]

The leap that Pope made from the failure to serve writs to calling in the army has to be understood in the context of the colony: it was widely recognized that the militia simply could not be relied upon to support state notions of legality in cases involving landlord-tenant relations. As the administrator, Chief Justice Robert Hodgson, substituting for the absent lieutenant governor, would explain to the British colonial secretary in the summer of 1865, 'the objections to calling out the militia in aid of the civil power under circumstances such as exist in this Colony will readily present themselves to you. To arm one portion of a community against another, is at all times, in my humble opinion, a proceeding of questionable propriety.' In his view, widespread sympathy for the tenantry meant that the militia was 'not ... available.'[21] There was also a quasi-military body on the Island known as the Volunteer Corps, organized during a war scare in 1861, but it had been possible to organize the Volunteers only by limiting their use to 'cases of actual invasion or appearance of an enemy in force on the coast of this Island,' effectively prohibiting their being called upon in cases of civil disorder.[22] Many members of the militia and the Volunteers would be tenants or former tenants themselves.

Yet legality, which was under challenge from the new tenant movement, was something that many, particularly beneficiaries of the established system, evidently took seriously. They certainly relied upon their conception of it in their initial responses to the emerging movement. Two proprietors, sisters who resided in Bath, England, complained to the Colonial Office of 'illegal combinations' after receiving an offer from 106 tenants to purchase, according to the method prescribed by the Tenant League, the lands they occupied.[23] The agent for Sir Samuel Cunard, the largest landholder, responded publicly to a petition of tenants declaring themselves to be leaguers by condemning the 'object' of the organization as 'unlawful and seditious,' and stating that he would not forward their petition to the landlord.[24]

In the summer of 1865, as examples of resistance to authorities increased dramatically, Hodgson wrote to the lieutenant governor of Nova Scotia, appealing for troops to assist Thomas W. Dodd, the sheriff of Queens County.[25] Dodd had reported that the disturbed condition in Queens, the most populous county and also the one with the highest proportion of tenants among land occupiers, had resulted in 'his utter inability to execute the process of the Supreme Court.' Explaining the disorder in his letter to Halifax, the administrator referred to the Tenant League, describing it as an 'illegal union.'[26] Later in the same month, the Island's lieutenant governor, George Dundas, then in Scotland, endorsed Hodgson's application for soldiers to support the civil power and called the league 'an illegal association.'[27] When Hodgson was back on the bench, addressing a grand jury on 9 January 1866 at the start of a term during which a number of league-related cases were to be dealt with, he alluded, without naming the organization, to 'a widespread and illegal combination amongst the tenantry to resist the payment of their rents.'[28]

During the summer of 1865, W.H. Pope had written in his editorial capacity that 'persons by assembling and associating under [the 'tenant's pledge'], thereby, in our humble opinion, commit an indictable offence, and render themselves liable to be indicted for a conspiracy to subvert the laws.'[29] This was quite different from arguing, as he had done around the time of the formation of the league, that adherence to the 'tenant's pledge' would lead leaguers to commit acts by which they would be breaking the law. In other words, Pope was in 1865 asserting that membership in the league was itself an offence; and he stuck to this opinion throughout the period of the league's prominence.[30]

But was the Tenant League in fact illegal? The issue came to a head when the government undertook a number of dismissals of minor officials associated with it. Some of the cases were relatively straightforward once the facts were established, although the government did encounter defiance on the part of those being dismissed.[31] Justices of the peace, commissioners for the recovery of small debts, and officers in the Volunteers all had roles in either the administration of justice or the defence of the crown, and an argument could be made that the 'tenant's pledge' had the potential of placing them in direct conflict with that commitment.

The situation of Alexander McNeill was more complex. He was a teacher and a founder of the league, indeed the secretary. On 27 July 1865 the Board of Education, consisting of government appointees, proposed to deprive teachers who supported the league of their salaries 'in future' and to remove them from the roll of licensed teachers.[32] In response to a letter from McNeill, who was owed £20 for services already performed, the board stated on 3 August that it 'could not ... be any longer responsible for the payment of his salary.'[33] It refused to authorize disbursement of the £20 without sanction of the Executive Council.

The Executive Council, for its part, seems to have doubted the legality of, in effect, dismissing teachers for Tenant League activism. Wary of making a misstep, the council referred the report of the board to Attorney General Edward Palmer (who was not a member of the council) for an opinion on the immediate issue of the board's power to withhold the salaries of teachers accused of association with the league.[34] Palmer, a member of the Island bar since 1830 and of the legislature since 1835, always a stickler for procedure, replied that such action would have to be taken under the rubric of 'gross misconduct or neglect of duty,' and that due process would have to be observed.[35] Eventually the council would authorize the payment to McNeill and ask Palmer, further, whether the board had been justified in withholding his salary.[36] The attorney general replied in the affirmative, but admitted that there was room for legal argument; in other words, there was the political risk of defeat over a legal challenge should the matter go before a judge.[37]

Beyond the Island bar, what contemporary legal opinion of an authoritative nature do we have regarding the legality of the Tenant League? On 12 October 1865 British Colonial Secretary Edward Cardwell, a practical and clear-headed man who had ample recent experience with contentious agrarian issues as the former chief secretary for Ireland (1859–61), and who had been trained as a lawyer, raised this question in an internal Colonial Office memorandum when he asked 'to see the actual proof that the society is illegal.'[38] The following day, Sir Frederic Rogers, permanent undersecretary of state for the colonies, and the person at the Colonial Office who was most learned in the law, replied. He had impressive scholarly credentials, for he had held a Vinerian Professorship of Law at Oxford.[39] In an unusually messy, stroked-through passage, he expressed doubt that the Tenant League was illegal in the sense of being 'punishable by Law.' Moreover, he added, 'I do not understand on what exact grounds it cd. [could] be so.' At the same time, he believed that the queen's representative was justified in dismissing servants of the queen – such as justices of the peace – who had continued to belong to the league after a proclamation by Dundas on 22 March 1865 denouncing it (although not by name) for its involvement in agreements to resist the payment of rent, given that such resistance led to breach of the peace.[40] In summary, although Rogers would not advise Cardwell to discourage the Island government from dismissing justices of the peace and others from office, neither was he persuaded that membership in the Tenant League could be construed as illegal. A memorandum by the chief clerk of the Colonial Office, T.F. Elliot, on 1 March 1866, possibly influenced by Rogers's memorandum, revealed that he too was uncertain whether the league was, properly speaking, an illegal organization.[41]

What could the Island government do to punish the leadership of the Tenant League through use of the law? John Ross, publisher of *Ross's Weekly*, the sole Island newspaper to support the league unequivocally, was one person against whom elements in the Island government seem to have been especially eager to take action. Writing to Cardwell on 25 August 1865, Dundas reported that he had repeatedly urged his 'Law Advisers' – the attorney general and the solicitor general – to prosecute Ross 'for the seditious advice which he was giving to the Tenantry, but they [the crown law officers] with every desire to proceed against him, assured me that it would be impossible to get a Jury to convict him.' The lieutenant governor portrayed both Liberals and Conservatives as having been sound from the outset concerning the illegitimacy of the league, and he made clear the local government's determination to take action against whomever it could through dismissals.[42]

Later that year, the Executive Council referred *Ross's Weekly* of 16 March to the crown law officers to determine whether prosecution of the publisher for sedition or libel was warranted, and, if it was, they directed them to 'adopt the most prompt and efficacious' measures. Sedition, of course, was a most serious offence, being, in theory, one step removed from the overt act of treason, that is, counselling or defending the use of force to change a regime; but one form of the offence, seditious libel, had been stretched to mean criticism of authorities which brought them into disrepute and caused discontent.[43] The issue of 16 March had included an article entitled 'The Tenant Union and the Courts of Law,' which characterized a sheriff or bailiff acting in certain circumstances as a 'raider.'[44]

The reply of Palmer and T. Heath Haviland, Jr, the solicitor general (and a member of the council),[45] as read to the Executive Council on 12 December, was that the article did create sufficient grounds for prosecuting Ross on a charge of libelling the administration of justice on the Island. They proceeded to recommend the best procedure for gaining a conviction, which involved delay. The recommendation was grounded in the assumption that pro-Tenant League sentiment still ran high among the general population from which both grand and trial jurors would be chosen; and they must have been aware that in Prince Edward Island there was *no* property qualification for either category of juror, which meant that both classes of jurors were drawn from the population at large with no screening mechanism to eliminate the hoi polloi.[46] The most prompt means of proceeding was not, in their view, the most efficacious.[47] When the crown did prefer a bill of indictment for libel against Ross in January 1866, the foreman of the Queens County grand jury, Benjamin Davies, a Charlottetown businessman who was a well-known and outspoken radical and who had served as an assemblyman many years earlier, wrote on it 'No Bill For Self and Fellows.'[48] The standard practice was to write simply either 'true bill' or 'no bill' when deciding whether a charge was going to go to trial; Davies, with his additional words, appeared to want to emphasize the point that the grand jury wanted this to go no further.

Curiously, the views of common Islanders were closer to British legal orthodoxy than were those of Hodgson and other members of the local elite. It was highly questionable whether any prosecutor could reasonably expect to convince a jury on Prince Edward Island, drawn as it would be from a political and social environment unfriendly to landlordism. Under the circumstances, prosecution of Tenant Leaguers for anything other than minor offences (such as assault) was a double-edged tool which involved a real risk of exposing in court the weakness of the government's position. Aware of this, the authorities, despite their strong anti-league sentiments, proceeded with caution. Members of the Island government and legal establishment apparently held the view that the league, its words, and its actions were illegal. But they were reluctant to let Islanders judge the issue, and the opinion of Rogers indicates that there were sound legal reasons to be wary of putting the matter to the test.

THE POSSE COMITATUS

As tension built over 1864–5 and as the local government was being placed in a defensive position, it responded by resort to the posse comitatus. The first indication that the government was considering its use came after a futile attempt on 10 March 1865 by James Curtis, the deputy sheriff of Queens County, to serve several writs in a part of eastern Queens long known for its acute hostility to the exactions of the leasehold system. Curtis encountered one obstruction after another, principally threats but also at least one attempt to block his path, and eventually he retreated as he noticed that more and more people seemed to be gathering with the purpose of stopping him. Back in Charlottetown, he reported that it would be 'useless' to undertake such missions in that area in future 'without being backed up with a strong force.'[49] The sheriff, John Morris, endorsed Curtis's assessment. Morris also stated on his own authority, in a letter to the premier, James C. Pope, the younger brother of W.H. Pope, that there were 'a large number' of Tenant Leaguers in Queens County 'whose real designs, I believe, are to resist the Laws, and to put the Sheriff and Constables at defiance.' Morris also reported that several magistrates (justices of the peace) and officers in the militia and the Volunteers were involved, at least to the extent of 'subscribing ... funds.'[50]

On 16 March the Executive Council decided to order that the sheriff 'be directed' (the verb is significant, given later obfuscation) to exercise his powers by calling out the posse comitatus.[51] This Latin term signified, literally, 'the power of the county,' and as a means of supporting the sheriff it enabled him to call upon the able-bodied male inhabitants of a county for assistance.[52] In the words of historians Sidney and Beatrice Webb: 'In the eye of the law the county was not ... an organisation of local self-government ... but ... a unit of obligation ... it was on the county itself, not on the individual officers, that rested the immemorial obligation of furnishing an armed force ... as the *posse comitatus*, to put down any resistance to the keeping of the peace ... From the standpoint of constitutional law the officers of the county were but instruments to secure the keeping of the King's peace, the due execution of the King's writs ... [etc.].'[53]

But the posse was a means of enforcement that would have been considered outmoded in most common law jurisdictions long before the emergence of the Tenant League. In a study of disturbances in England during the seventeenth and eighteenth centuries, historian Max Beloff noted that use of the posse rested on 'the legal doctrine of the responsibility of all citizens,' and that, where those disobeying the law had popular sympathy, 'the posse could not be relied upon for more than nominal obedience.' As evidence of the unreliability of such civil forces as the *posse* even as early as the period of the Stuart Restoration, Beloff cited 'the large number of instances in which military help was called for almost immediately on the outbreak of disorder.'[54]

The day after the council's instructions were conveyed to Sheriff Morris, a Tenant League demonstration was held in Charlottetown. This was the first time the league had made a public show of strength on the streets of the capital, which was also the traditional stronghold of political conservatism.[55] The sheriff estimated the demonstrators to number 500 or 600. All reports agreed that the procession was orderly, but Deputy Sheriff Curtis spotted and attempted to arrest Samuel Fletcher, a tenant against whom there was a writ outstanding. Fletcher was clearly a supporter of the league. He had signed at least two of its petitions, he was participating in a public rally of the league, and he was carrying a tin trumpet. In normal circumstances such a trumpet would be used at mealtime to summon those who were at work in the fields. But, as the Tenant League took shape, the trumpet had become the instrument of leaguer vigilance, the means by which supporters passed on the warning that suspicious persons – such as the sheriff, deputy sheriff, or constables – were approaching. It also summoned additional supporters to harass and impede physically the progress of the authorities. Part of the harassment was the din created by the blowing of many trumpets, horns, bugles, and conch shells, which could intimidate the officers and make their horses difficult to control.[56] The trumpet had therefore become an important symbol, and even a weapon.[57]

The justification for the attempt to arrest Fletcher was a writ for nonpayment of rent; according to an affidavit of debt sworn on 4 March, he was exactly two years in arrears. Thus, he was behaving as an orthodox member of the league by withholding his rent.[58] When Curtis made his move, Fletcher struck him in the face and attempted to escape. Others joined in attacking the deputy sheriff, and knocked him to the ground. Fletcher fled, despite the intervention of apothecary and Justice of the Peace Theophilus DesBrisay on Curtis's behalf. DesBrisay had a grip on Fletcher briefly, but 'the prisoner' swung his trumpet at him, 'which blow I narrowly escaped.' DesBrisay lost his footing and Fletcher 'escaped in double quick time up the street.'[59]

There is no evidence to suggest that Fletcher was a leader of the Tenant League. Yet, because of the events on 17 March, he became a celebrated figure and clearly the object of great concern for the local authorities. He symbolized, in Tenant League eyes, the ability of the ordinary leaguer to evade the grip of the clumsy and ineffective forces of the sheriff. Capturing him became a significant objective in the minds of government leaders and law-enforcement personnel precisely because of his symbolic importance. He personified successful defiance even in the centre of Charlottetown – in Sheriff Morris's words, 'when passing up the main Street nearly opposite the Police Station.'[60]

There ensued considerable manoeuvring within government and law-enforcement circles in Charlottetown. On 18 March, DesBrisay, who happened to be the father-in-law of W.H. Pope and himself a small-scale proprietor, provided Morris with a letter giving his account of the Curtis-Fletcher incident on the previous day and his own role in the attempted arrest. He also offered some advice: 'From what I witnessed on this occasion, and the apparent sympathy with these misguided men [the demonstrators],' he believed 'it would be perfectly useless for you [Morris] to look for assistance in the discharge of the duties of your office to the constitutional force of the County.' This was a reference to the posse comitatus. In DesBrisay's view, 'you must obtain a number of paid individuals from Charlottetown, as Special Constables, sworn to support and assist you.'[61]

This was an opinion Morris welcomed. In a covering letter written on the same day to Premier Pope, he commented on the events of the 17th and also on the instructions he had received to call out the posse comitatus. While acknowledging the propriety of such directions in a formal sense, he declared unequivocally that 'a party of Special Constables on whom confidence could be placed, and paid by the Government would answer a much better purpose.' He closed by stating that, if his advice and that of DesBrisay were rejected, he would follow instructions and call out the posse. But no one who read his letter could doubt that if he did so he would be acting against his better judgment – virtually under protest, in fact.[62]

The concern of Morris and DesBrisay seems to have been effective execution of whatever attempt might be made to capture Fletcher. They were clearly sceptical about using the posse, and with reason. In the only recorded Prince Edward Island case that could be viewed as a precedent and guide, involving the shooting of a horse from under a sheriff in Kings County in 1859, there had been two unsuccessful attempts to call out the posse. Ultimately, a special force of constables was organized at a cost of £137.[63]

But finding the best means of apprehending Fletcher did not appear to be the primary consideration of the Island government in deciding to order use of the posse comitatus. Its chief strategist was W.H. Pope, who was known for his ambition and ruthlessness. In addition, he was a brilliant, enigmatic man identified with an unpopular large-scale land transaction ('the Worrell Job'), visceral religious controversialism (despite reputedly lacking positive religious convictions of his own), and confederation, a cause that had little public support on the Island at the time. He had antagonized large numbers of fellow colonists, yet no one of discernment underestimated his talents or his determination. When he had been appointed colonial secretary for the Island in 1859, the leading Liberal journalist, Edward Whelan, had written that he had 'more cunning, more perseverance in the pursuit of his object, (no matter what it is,) and more real talent than any other man in his party.'[64] By the middle years of the 1860s, among knowledgeable political observers, his name connoted win-at-all-costs politics.

In the affair of the posse comitatus, Pope's cunning certainly emerges from the record, as do such qualities as vindictiveness. On 27 January 1865 he published an editorial in which he hinted at use of a posse and military force. In it, he was particularly scornful of those Charlottetown persons, such as tradesmen and merchants, who, although not believers in Tenant League principles, had subscribed funds to it out of 'expediency' in order to avoid their businesses being boycotted by leaguers. Pope warned that 'if the Sheriff should be interfered with in any district, he may call upon the inhabitants to assist him; and if they refuse, they will render themselves liable to fine and imprisonment.'[65] This was the first suggestion that the authorities might resort to the posse to deal with the league.

Virtually a dead letter in England, the posse comitatus was unlikely to be an effective force in Prince Edward Island in 1865. But apparently the fact that some Charlottetown residents gave financial support to the Tenant League had angered Pope deeply, and, after the thwarting of Curtis in eastern Queens on 10 March, he again referred in the *Islander* to the posse. He stated that those called upon by the sheriff must go, 'it matters not who they are,' and emphasized the responsibility of persons who had encouraged the league 'by their money and their countenance.'[66] Just exactly what he had in mind came into clearer focus on 24 March: 'Those who have encouraged the Tenant League in their unlawful designs, should be called upon to assist the Sheriff to overcome the evils which they have assisted to create. If some fifty or sixty persons shall be *weekly* called upon by the Sheriff, and required to proceed with him, to the neglect of their business, and at their own cost, and very great inconvenience, the country will very soon discover that the Tenant League is a much greater evil than they at first imagined.'[67] Involuntary participation in the posse, therefore, was to be an instrument of punishment for those who had gone along with the league.

When the Executive Council considered Sheriff Morris's letter of 18 March, along with DesBrisay's account of what had happened in Charlottetown on the previous day, it rejected their advice and ordered that Morris be directed to carry out the instructions he had already received – that is, to call out the posse comitatus. The council did authorize him to hire up to five special constables in addition to conscripting the posse, but clearly the constables were not to be a substitute.[68] Although the Conservative administration was bitterly factionalized, and had split over the issue of confederation only a few months earlier, no evidence of discord over use of the posse has emerged.[69]

Approximately 150 residents of Charlottetown set out as a posse comitatus under the reluctant leadership of Morris on 7 April, with the ostensible purpose of executing an arrest warrant against Fletcher at his home in Alberry Plains, some eighteen miles from the capital. Those called included Ross, the only newspaper publisher in Charlottetown who supported the league, and the veteran radical Davies. They failed in their task, and much of the local press treated the episode with derision.[70] It was not repeated, but the Island government remained eager to capture Fletcher, and subsequently made other efforts, much more discreet, to do so, always in vain. If one includes the original confrontation with Curtis in Charlottetown, there were five attempts within a year to arrest him. Eventually he departed for the United States, where he would die in 1870.[71]

Almost immediately after the conclusion of the expedition, blame began to be apportioned. Although the mastermind behind it was W.H. Pope, on 14 April, one week after the incident, his *Islander* newspaper more or less squirmed in embarrassment and said that the sheriff, not the Executive Council, was responsible for having called out the posse. Pope did not criticize the decision, but he did censure the sheriff for the manner in which he had executed his duty.

Pope went still further in his attempt to point the finger of responsibility elsewhere. In the same issue of the *Islander*, he published five letters in order to document the supposed necessity of using the posse. One crucial letter was missing from the *Islander*: Morris's of 18 March, in which he argued against use of the posse. Inclusion of that letter would have undermined Pope's claim that the sheriff had been responsible for choosing it as the means of pursuing Fletcher.[72] Clearly, Pope and the government had decided to make Morris the scapegoat for their insistence on use of the posse.[73] Pope even had the audacity to contrast unfavourably the efficacy of a posse of 150 with a body of five constables for the purpose of apprehending Fletcher – which had been precisely Morris's point in his now-suppressed letter of 18 March. Morris must have been pleased when his one-year term as sheriff expired a few weeks after the calling out of the posse.

THE TROOPS AND DESERTION

The posse had failed and would not be resorted to again. But the problem remained: the sheriff and his assistants could not perform their duty to execute the writs of the court. There had been no regular troops stationed on the Island since 1854, and this lack, combined with the impossibility of using the militia or the Volunteers, meant that there was no adequate local means for supporting the sheriff in the face of resistance. Consequently, the assistance of forces from the mainland would be required, and on 1 August 1865 Hodgson and the government led by James Pope appealed to Halifax for troops. On Thursday the 3rd of August in Halifax, Garrison Orders nos. 1 and 6 indicated that 135 members of the 16th Regiment of Foot were to leave for Charlottetown as soon as possible, supplied with sixty rounds of ammunition per man.[74]

Yet, once the soldiers were present, the local authorities were extremely reluctant to use them in active support of the sheriff. This created a complex tug-of-war between the Island government and the military leadership in Halifax who, almost from the beginning, were keen to get the troops back. Their concern revolved around the perennial problem of desertion. In addition to general considerations, the military authorities had specific concerns about leaving soldiers in Prince Edward Island. There had been a history of difficulty over desertion when troops had been on the Island previously,[75] and since the colony no longer had a barracks to house the men, controlling their movements promised to be especially difficult. From the perspective of Halifax, the men should be used for support of the Queens County sheriff as soon as possible, and once they had reasserted the authority of the civil power they should then be returned promptly to their permanent base.[76]

The viewpoint of the Island government was quite different. Premier Pope and his colleagues were anxious to reassert authority in the coun-

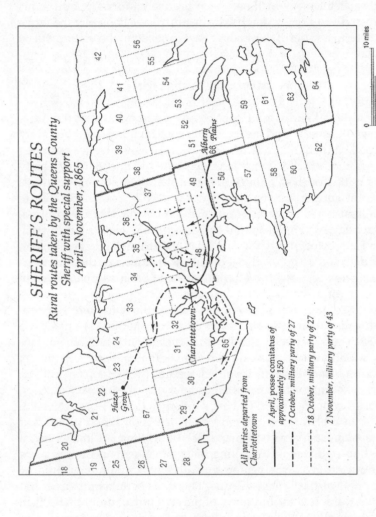

Sheriff's routes, 1865. From Ian Ross Robertson, *The Tenant League of Prince Edward Island, 1864–1867: Leasehold Tenure in the New World* (Toronto: University of Toronto Press 1996).

tryside without actually using the soldiers to accompany the sheriff and constables in person. There was a long-standing political taboo on the Island associated with collecting rent 'at the point of a bayonet.' This metaphor was probably borrowed from Irish experience, where it connoted a tenant refusing the demands of a landlord and using all possible obstructions until the sheriff arrived, thereby forcing the issue to the legal limit, causing the landlord maximum inconvenience, and facing significant legal costs himself. Adopting this course was a measure of resoluteness on the part of the tenant.[77] As most commonly employed in Prince Edward Island, the phrase had an entirely different meaning. It emphasized the harshness of the action the political authorities were taking in support of the landlord, and thus was an indication of heavy-handedness in enforcement.[78] Resort to 'the point of a bayonet' involved, for politicians, crossing a line beyond which the electoral consequences might be exceptionally negative.

Hodgson, in reporting to Downing Street about his appeal to Halifax for troops, expressed his belief that 'the presence of a regular military force in this Island will, in itself, have the effect of preventing further resistance to the Laws, and ... I have no reason to apprehend that there will be any necessity for bringing the troops into conflict with the people.'[79] His position was that knowledge of their proximity would deter resistance and allow the sheriff to proceed; he was making a sharp distinction between the 'deterrent' capacity of a military presence and the active employment of soldiers to support the civil power in the execution of legal processes. The deterrent function implied that the troops would be on the Island for an indefinite period – at least until the sheriff had time to set some precedents in executing writs successfully in disturbed parts of Queens. This would be a subtler use of the military than sending soldiers out with the sheriff, but could imply a much lengthier commitment. Hodgson and the Pope government appear to have agreed entirely on this matter.

The Tenant League, of course, had its own perspective. It was well aware of the history of military desertion on the Island, and its strategy appears to have been to promote as much desertion as possible in an effort to goad the military authorities in Halifax into withdrawing their men. There is no known surviving document in which league leaders declared this to be their policy, and in fact creation of such a written statement or record of intent would have been extraordinarily imprudent. If it fell into the wrong hands, it could be presented in a court as evidence of a conspiracy to violate the imperial statute which specified that it was a misdemeanour to make any attempt, direct or indirect, to persuade a soldier to desert.[80] But such an interpretation of league intentions is consistent with much contemporary commentary in local newspapers and with a critical reading of official correspondence. "'Bring your soldiers to the Island, and we will very soon induce the whole of them to desert," was the threat uttered by a Tenant Leaguer,' reported the *Islander* newspaper.[81] The league was also gambling that the Island government had no desire to use the troops against tenants because of the adverse political consequences that would follow. Desertion of soldiers in significant numbers, combined with non-use of the men to support the sheriff, would, leaguers hoped, create sufficient pressure from Halifax that London would order removal of the detachment – leaving the civil authorities alone to face non-compliant tenants and their supporters.

By 19 September 1865, there had been seventeen desertions. Only three deserters were ever captured. Although it is impossible to determine how many of these had actually been assisted by the Tenant League, it is clear from the record that the league went about promoting desertion audaciously. The best evidence on this point comes from the newspaper reports of the trials of two men convicted of attempting to induce desertion (both reproduced in the volume's Supporting Documents). On 3 November the *Islander* reported the case of Henry Green, a Charlottetown shopkeeper. At a hearing before T.H. Haviland, Sr, the mayor of Charlottetown,[82] and municipal councillor Theophilus DesBrisay, Green was convicted of trying on two separate occasions, more than two months apart, to persuade Private Peter Macgowan, the servant of the commanding officer, to desert. No date was given for his arrest or the hearing of his case, nor was it made precisely clear how he came to be arrested. But details that were published revealed a great deal.

The first attempt is noteworthy for having occurred a mere two days after arrival of the troops in Charlottetown. On 8 August, Green approached five soldiers, including two non-commissioned officers, who were drinking in a tavern:

After treating all the soldiers to drink, [Green] threw his purse on the table and said, according to the testimony of [Private] Macgory, 'that any man who wanted to desert he was the man to exchange the clothing. He was the very boy who would do it for him.' According to that of [Private] Lamb, Green threw his purse on the table and said, 'that if any man wished to change his clothing there was his purse at his command, and he, Green, would see them safe off the Island. Did not care what creed or profession they were, he would stand to them.' Macgrory stated that Green took out his purse and threw it on the table, saying 'there is plenty of money, and as long as the money lasted he would see any of them off the Island.' ... James Keenan, who was called on the part of the defendant, stated that he saw Green take out his purse and throw it on the table, saying 'that he did not care for creed or profession ... a man's principles was all he wanted.' All the witnesses agree in stating that Green was drunk.[83]

One of those Green approached on 8 August, Lance-Corporal George Mumby, age twenty-three, of Northampton, England, did desert, and was never apprehended.[84] Mayor Haviland noted, inter alia, the similarity between Keenan's account on behalf of the defendant and the testimony of three prosecution witnesses. He put little stock in the defence that Green was too intoxicated to know what he was saying or doing. 'The language made use of is connected and perfectly rational, and appears to be the result of a previous determination .... The proverb *In vino veritas* is not without an apt signification in the present case.'[85]

On 11 October, according to Private Macgowan, he met Green on the street between 5 and 6 p.m. Green was as direct as he had been previously, and 'asked him if there was any word of Private Moffit [sic][86] – one of the men who had deserted; to which he replied there was no word of him. Green then said there will not be, for it was I [who] put him away, and I buried his clothes [his uniform] by tying a stone to them to sink them. Green then said that if he, Macgowan, was willing to go, he, Green, would put him in the same way.' Several defence witnesses testified, but Haviland found their testimony to be either 'very curious' in terms of credibility, or irrelevant, or actually working against the defendant. Green received a sentence of six months' hard labour.[87]

The inescapable inference, if one credits the sworn testimony in the case of Green and that of the other person convicted,[88] is that the Tenant League worked hard and took significant risks to induce desertion. It especially targeted soldiers who had been drinking, and its approach was sophisticated, based on analysis and forethought about the need to create a supportive infrastructure in order to ensure success. The deserting soldier was in urgent need of civilian clothing and a place to go *to*; he almost certainly also needed money. Without a change of clothes, a British soldier 'stood out like a red thumb.'[89] This was in fact the intent of an army rule forbidding soldiers to own civilian clothing. Prevention of desertion was also the rationale for a long-standing tendency among officers to discourage any saving of money by the enlisted men; a deserting soldier without funds had less chance of success.[90] Tenant Leaguers offered a haven, civilian clothes, transportation, and money; and since American fishermen frequented the fishing ports of the Island in large numbers, the colony already provided the prospect of a link to the United States, from which deserters could not be extradited unless they had committed serious crimes. The appeal of the leaguers must have been tempting.

The desertions stopped by the latter part of September. But the Tenant League policy has to be considered a notable success in terms of tactics and execution. Of the 130 enlisted men who came to the Island, 17 deserted in the space of exactly six weeks, from 8 August to 19 September; the rate, if annualized, works out to well over 100 per cent, and even if subtraction is made for the three who were captured, the annualized rate was 93.6 per cent.[91] The key to explaining the high desertion rate during August and September 1865 in Prince Edward Island lies in the enticement and support the leaguers offered, which amounted to the opportunity to desert with a reasonable expectation of success.

The Tenant League strategy of promoting desertion did create a great deal of difficulty for the Island government and caused much friction between it and the military authorities in Halifax. In order to pacify the military, the local government resorted to unprecedented measures – such as purchase of civilian clothes for military search parties in order to reduce their visibility and hence increase their ability to travel undetected.[92] At the same time, the Tenant Leaguers continued their resistance to the civil forces of the sheriff. As a consequence, by early October the troops were being used to accompany the civil authorities.[93] There was no active resistance[94] on the part of Tenant Leaguers when troops were present, and the movement began to crumble. The league had been a body committed to direct action of a particular kind in pursuit of its land-reform agenda. The use of soldiers destroyed the credibility of its master-tactic, and consequently it withered. The soldiers remained on the Island until 27 June 1867, by which time the Tenant League no longer existed.

LEGAL OUTCOMES

After the collapse of resistance by the Tenant Leaguers, writs were successfully served, arrests were made, and trials were held. By the middle of October 1865, accused rioters had been listening to bailiffs and others giving sworn evidence against them before justices of the peace. At the end of that month and the beginning of November, they were bound over before the Supreme Court until the Hilary Term in January 1866.[95] So great was the sense of moment when the accused Tenant Leaguers met the Supreme Court to face charges of, in most instances, riot, assault, and conspiracy, that Whelan predicted 'it is likely to be the most important session that has occurred in this Island.'[96]

The first step in the proceedings involved the grand jury, and, by law, in Queens County the grand jurors for a term of the Supreme Court were chosen by ballot from a list of 100 qualified persons. The sheriff had the responsibility of drawing up the array or list of 100; he did so in the previous June or January and conveyed it to the prothonotary or chief clerk of the court, who conducted the ballot in open court. At least twenty grand jurors had to be summoned, and the maximum number was twenty-three. Once more than twelve had assembled, they could choose a foreman for the term. At least sixteen members had to be present in order to transact substantive business.[97] The twelve trial jurors were also selected by ballot, although from a different list, with 200 names. The work of the grand jury was complete once it had decided, by majority vote, whether the evidence warranted a trial; and, by common law, it acted in secret and heard evidence for only the crown.[98] In contrast, the trial jurors decided the guilt or innocence of indicted persons on the basis of evidence from both sides. They could convict only if they were unanimous.

On Tuesday the 9th of January the term commenced, with Chief Justice Hodgson and Assistant Judge James H. Peters presiding.[99] They constituted the entire Supreme Court of the colony. The chief justice delivered his charge to the grand jury of twenty-one members, beginning by focusing in some detail on the Tenant League campaign of rent resistance and expounding the nature of the alleged offences.[100] Given the content of Hodgson's charge to the grand jury, it appears, from historian Donald Fyson's explanation of the difference between 'misdemeanour' and 'felony' prosecutions for riot, that the crown was alleging a misdemeanour rather than a felony.[101] The grand jury met until the 20th; this was an uncommonly lengthy period, and Whelan believed that members had set a record in meeting so long.[102]

On 10 January, the grand jury began reporting the results of its deliberations. They added up to a mixture of 'true bills' against Tenant Leaguers and presentments against the authorities, particularly Deputy Sheriff Curtis, who was a focus of popular criticism. The presentments against the authorities constituted a turning of the tables which must have been disconcerting for them. In the midst of the deliberations, Whelan had commented that the grand jury included 'not a few gentlemen reputed as entertaining extreme views concerning the operations of the [Tenant] League'; he also noted the 'variety of sentiment.'[103]

Whelan was correct to draw attention to the wide range of opinion. Most conspicuously, Davies, the former Liberal assemblyman known to harbour radical views, was foreman. The fact that he was chosen foreman by other members suggested at least some support for his perspective.

Henry J. Callbeck, another grand juror, would be elected in 1867 to the House of Assembly, where he would be identified with a minority within the Liberal caucus who were strong sympathizers with the Tenant League tradition. Robert Mutch was associated with the league at its beginning, and would make a testimonial on behalf of a pro-league candidate at the election of 1867.[104] Other grand jurors included George W. DeBlois, a prominent land agent, Charles Wright, both land agent and proprietor, and William Swabey, a justice of the peace who had led the three expeditions of October and November 1865 that had provided military assistance for the sheriff. With Callbeck, Davies, DeBlois, Mutch, Swabey, and Wright on the grand jury, the debate over the various charges must have been intense.

On 16 January, before the Supreme Court, Joseph Hensley, a lawyer for nine persons accused of riot, assault, and conspiracy in the case of 'The Queen v. James Gorveatt et al.,' moved to challenge the array of the grand jury and to quash the indictment against his clients.[105] Hensley objected to the inclusion of Wright, land agent for the Cumberland estate, on the grand jury, for it was his pressing of claims for rent that had resulted in the confrontations leading to the bill of indictment against Gorveatt et al. on which the grand jury had to pass judgment. The lawyers on both sides argued the issue on 17 January. The court decided speedily. On 18 January, Judge Peters quashed the indictment and made a strong statement on the need for undoubted impartiality on the part of all grand jurors: 'The great object of the institution of the grand jury is to prevent persons being even called on to answer for alleged crimes without reasonable ground for accusation. It has been described by great jurists as the grand bulwark of civil liberty ... If individuals, who were actors on either side in transactions which form any material part of the subject matter of an accusation, could sit as jurors in deciding whether an accused should be subject to a public trial or not, the principal object of the institution might, in many cases, be defeated.'[106]

For most Tenant Leaguers facing Supreme Court proceedings in January 1866, this decision was the pivotal event. Afterwards, on the same day, Attorney General Palmer stated that he would enter a nolle prosequi – a stay of proceedings – in a similar case. In that instance, following Peters's reasoning, the presence of DeBlois, land agent for proprietor Laurence Sulivan, would invalidate the indictment against sixteen accused rioters on the Sulivan estate. Although in both cases the crown could have undertaken prosecution at a later date by taking bills of indictment to a new grand jury, this never happened. The cases were allowed to die slowly and quietly. On 26 June 1866 the defendants entered into recognizances to appear at the Hilary Term in 1867, but they were never called upon.[107]

There remained three indicted Tenant Leaguers – Charles Dickieson, Joseph Doucette, and Peter Gallant, all of whom qualified as rank and filers rather than formal leaders – to be dealt with. Over the next two days they were found guilty of 'common assault' for the so-called 'Battle of Curtisdale' (named for the nearby Curtisdale Hotel in Milton, Lot 32) on 18 July 1865 which had resulted in a broken arm for Curtis. They were acquitted of 'rescue,' an offence that referred to their successful attempt to reclaim by force distrained property (a horse and wagon) belonging to another tenant, who was absent when the bailiffs came with their writ.[108] Doucette, the man responsible for breaking Curtis's arm through a roundhouse blow with a fence post, was also found guilty of 'assault on constables' as a consequence of resisting violently a sheriff's party sent to arrest him at his home on 15 August.[109]

The court set 24 January 1866 for sentencing. Peters, rigorous in his regard for proper, untainted legal procedure, proved draconian when punishing Tenant Leaguers who had been convicted. For the July incident he sentenced Dickieson to eighteen months in jail and a £50 fine, and Doucette and Gallant each to one year of incarceration and a fine of £20; Doucette was given an additional year for his resistance in August. The sentences Peters gave the three Tenant Leaguers were undeniably severe when compared with others for comparable offences at the same time.[110] In an eloquent address on the importance of the rule of law, he assigned much weight to the degree of premeditation, the stalking of Curtis's party before the July affray, and the use of tin trumpets to summon assistance.[111]

Criticism of the sentencing, presented sometimes in coded ways, continued for months and even years, since Peters could be interpreted as having foiled the trial jury by ignoring its limited finding (assault) and treating the three as though they had been convicted of the greater offence (rescue). Indeed, in 1867 Davies would state in the House of Assembly that this is what Peters had done.[112] Peters's own words could be read as supporting this view, for, when addressing Dickieson, he said, 'In awarding punishment against offenders, I am bound to consider all the circumstances detailed in evidence,' and then made a remarkable declaration: 'As the attempt to rescue, which led to this assault, was fully proved, *the limited nature of the finding can make no material difference in the sentence* which it is now my painful duty to pass upon you.'[113] Over a period of

several months, the issue of clemency for the rioters became the main focus of public expressions of sympathy for the Tenant League cause. On 24
April a deputation waited on the lieutenant governor with a 5,275-name
petition pleading for release of the three prisoners. On 1 August 1866 they
were freed and their fines were remitted.

SIGNIFICANCE: LAW, POLITICS, AND SOCIETY

The law's role in public life has rarely been so visible in Prince Edward
Island as it was during the Tenant League years. The role of politics in
enforcement of the law is also evident, especially in the posse comitatus
incident. This was a continuance of a pattern that J.M. Bumsted notes in
the early history of the colony: 'The outstanding feature of early law was
the degree to which it was politicized, intimately connected to Island
personalities and politics.'[114] The law did not exist in a vacuum. Political
calculation undoubtedly played a role in the decisions made by government concerning the use of law in dealing with such Tenant Leaguers as
Alexander McNeill and also in the great reluctance of crown law officers
to take the publisher Ross and others to court. The authorities feared the
consequences in the countryside of losing in attempts to use the law to
punish the activists.

More generally, the party in office feared the political costs of appearing heavy-handed in dealing with the tenantry. The Island had responsible government, and the franchise was almost universal among adult
males, facts of enormous significance. An Irish member of the British
Parliament and the last leader of the parliamentary group of the defunct
Irish Tenant League, John Francis Maguire, who visited in the autumn
of 1866, hinted at this when he referred to the Island as having 'a system
of government based upon popular suffrage and amenable to popular
control.'[115] Prince Edward Islanders had their own House of Assembly,
which determined who sat in government offices in Charlottetown, and
those government members knew that they were electorally accountable
to the mass of Islanders.

The Tenant League was undoubtedly successful in hastening the end
of leasehold tenure in the colony. Two unprecedented sales by landlords,
Robert P. Haythorne (a resident) and the Reverend James F. Montgomery (an absentee), directly to groups of tenants occurred in the mid-1860s;
these were arranged according to the Tenant League prescription, and
leaguers were involved.[116] The tenacious resistance to the exactions of
leasehold tenure that the Tenant League represented apparently created

a sense of pessimism about the system among landlords. In the spring of 1865, Cunard and Sulivan, two absentee proprietors who owned, between them, one-fifth of the colony, informed the public that they would grant no more new leases and that all future agreements with settlers would be for the sale of land. This alteration in policy was momentous, virtually a recognition that the leasehold system of Prince Edward Island had no future. These changes – the decisions of Haythorne and Montgomery to sell and the shift in policy by Cunard and Sulivan – had occurred less than a year after the formation of the league, and they grew out of the increasingly confrontational atmosphere of which it was the product, embodiment, and stimulus.

The greatest achievement that can be credited to the league came on 1 July 1866: the Cunard family holdings, which included land in twenty townships, were sold to the local government for resale to the tenantry. The purchase of the huge Cunard estate, comprising more than 15 per cent of the Island's land mass, represented a decisive turning point in the struggle over leasehold tenure. A transformation had occurred. The terms of the debate would never again be the same. It was as though many of the supporters and beneficiaries of the old order knew that its days were numbered. There was at least one significant estate purchase by the Island government each year afterwards through 1871. The vendors tended to be resident proprietors with political connections. They included James Pope, T. Heath Haviland, Jr, and the Palmer family.[117] The falling of these dominoes was directly attributable to the willingness of the leaguers to defy the law with respect to their obligations under leasehold tenure. On 22 February 1871 Haviland declared in the Legislative Council that 'I considered it for the interest of the country, as well as my own, to get rid of the small quantity of land I held ... When proprietors are obliged to resort to the rigors of the law to obtain their rents, a bad feeling will of course arise.'[118]

Yet the Tenant League organization had disintegrated when faced with armed British regulars assisting the sheriff. The tenants' behaviour conformed to a pattern historian Eric Richards has discerned in cases of resistance during the Clearances in the Scottish Highlands: when the sheriff, after failing to do the job by ordinary means, showed up with a supporting military force, the people offered no opposition. 'The news of impending [military] intervention was usually enough of itself to lead to a collapse of resistance. Troops intervened on ten occasions but were never actually engaged in physical hostilities.'[119] There was a strong sense of limits to be observed. Richards quotes an estate factor as writing in 1853 that 'I am persuaded the people think they may do anything they please short of destroying life.'[120]

The Tenant League should be measured within the context of popular movements in Canadian and North American history. It is difficult to name another extra-parliamentary movement for radical change in Canadian history, willing to resort to civil disobedience, which was as successful as the league; and within North American history as a whole, only the African American desegregation movement of the 1950s and 1960s comes to mind.[121] In Canada this is a tradition that includes the Winnipeg General Strike of 1919, a demonstration of solidarity among the majority of the labouring population in that city which is unique in North American labour history for its combination of comprehensiveness and duration. Yet, despite the powerful display of support for a cause, the degree of its success is a matter on which there is a wide range of opinion among historians, much depending upon how long a temporal perspective one adopts.

Like the Winnipeg General Strike, the Tenant League had the support of an extraordinary proportion of the producing class in the society of which it was a part. This breadth of backing explains the intelligence system that assisted in warning the leaguers when the sheriff was on his way, a network that may have included sympathetic law clerks as a source of information on outgoing writs from the Supreme Court.[122] After the soldiers arrived on the Island, the depth of the league's support enabled it to work successfully to induce desertion, in the hope of provoking the Halifax authorities to withdraw the men. The real strength of the league was in that grassroots support, but there must also have been extensive coordination in order for it to spirit out of the colony as many soldiers as it did without being detected. The organizational capacity of the leadership would have been crucial in arranging the escapes of deserting soldiers from the colony; and again defiance of the law was integral to league strategy.

The history of the Tenant League has further significance within broader Canadian history in terms of resort to military aid for the civil power. The use of military assistance was a serious matter in this case, probably the most important, in terms of the challenge, between the rebellions of the 1830s in the Canadas and the disturbances in the west after confederation. This was not insurrection, yet it was defiance of the civil authorities on basic matters concerning the functioning of society and property relations under the British flag. Unlike situations where the military was used to deal with labour conflicts at Lachine in Lower Canada, election-related violence in Newfoundland, the Gavazzi riots in Quebec and Montreal, or disorderly lumberers in the Miramichi region of New Brunswick, the Tenant League episode was not provoked by the special circumstances of violent quarrelling over construction jobs, by a specific electoral contest, by an inflammatory public speaker, or by liquor.

Rent and arrears of rent were classified as legally collectible debts, and in the event of non-payment the landlord could eventually call upon the assistance of the law. Supporting those who failed to pay could lead, logically, to involvement in resisting the sheriff and his assistants. The 11,000 who had taken a pledge to refuse payment of rent or to support those who did so, as the case demanded, were by the summer and autumn of 1865 proving, in hundreds, ready to act on that pledge whenever they heard the blast of a tin trumpet. In the words of historian Charles Townshend regarding a parallel situation in Ireland, 'it was the derogation of law, the unenforceability of the royal writ, which constituted the gage which the government could not avoid picking up. The direct personal peril to land agents and process-servers meant, in abstract political terms, the breakdown of law and order.'[123] The challenge to civil authority on Prince Edward Island in 1865 was persistent, systematic, and fundamental, and it appeared to be escalating in audacity as well. The state could not ignore it.

NOTES

1 See Ian Ross Robertson, *The Tenant League of Prince Edward Island, 1864–1867: Leasehold Tenure in the New World* (Toronto: University of Toronto Press 1996), 86–7.

2 Andrew Hill Clark, *Three Centuries and the Island: A Historical Geography of Settlement and Agriculture in Prince Edward Island, Canada* (Toronto: University of Toronto Press 1959), 91; also see 88, on the problems involved in trying to be more precise.

3 Calculations based on *Censuses of Canada, 1665 to 1871*, IV, 174, 359; PEI, House of Assembly, *Journal*, 1856, app. D. There were four significant subgroupings of Presbyterians: Kirkmen, Secessionists, Free Churchmen, and McDonaldites.

4 The census listed three categories of occupiers of land (below, i–iii) who were not freeholders. I am including as 'tenants' the following: those classified as holding land (i) 'under lease or agreement for lease' (the latter meaning a *written* agreement to lease), and those holding (ii) 'by verbal agreement' (also known popularly as 'tenants at will'); and I am designating as 'squatters'

those listed in the census as (iii) 'occupants being neither freeholders nor tenants.' Of these three census categories, the first was by far the largest: 5,357 of 6,813, or 78.6 per cent. Calculations are based on corrected totals of the data in PEI, House of Assembly, *Journal*, 1862, app. A. For an attempt to quantify tenurial insecurity on Prince Edward Island in the 1860s, see Robertson, *The Tenant League*, map 2 on 21, app. 1 on 289; and on the significance of rent arrears for a sense of insecurity among tenants, see Robertson, *The Tenant League*, 22–3.

5 Calculation based on PEI, House of Assembly, *Journal*, 1862, app. A.

6 John Macneill to George Dundas, 10 Sept. 1861, in PEI, House of Assembly, *Journal*, 1862, app. A

7 For the history of the franchise on the Island during the colonial period, see John Garner, *The Franchise and Politics in British North America, 1755–1867* (Toronto: University of Toronto Press 1969), chapter 4; Garner summarizes the franchise as being held by 'all resident freeholders, leaseholders, and householders' (3). See Franchise Extension Act, SPEI 1853 c.9.

8 See, for example, J.M. Bumsted, 'Sir James Montgomery and Prince Edward Island, 1767–1803,' *Acadiensis* 7, no. 2 (1978): 76–102.

9 Andrew Macphail, 'The History of Prince Edward Island,' in Adam Shortt and Arthur G. Doughty, eds., *Canada and Its Provinces* (Toronto: Edinburgh University Press 1914), 305. On the historiography of the Prince Edward Island land question, Matthew G. Hatvany has published 'Tenant, Landlord and Historian: A Thematic Review of the "Polarization" Process in the Writing of 19th-Century Prince Edward Island History,' *Acadiensis* 27, no. 1 (1997): 109–32.

10 See Robertson, *The Tenant League*, 284–5; regarding the historiography, see ibid., 361–4.

11 For a brief but comprehensive survey, see J.M. Bumsted, 'The Legal Historiography of Prince Edward Island,' in Christopher English, ed., *Essays in the History of Canadian Law, Volume IX: Two Islands: Newfoundland and Prince Edward Island* (Toronto: Osgoode Society for Canadian Legal History / University of Toronto Press 2005), 39–45. Emphasizing the indifference displayed to the subject, Bumsted remarks that 'probably the best piece of legal history ever written about the province remains unpublished' (39). He is referring to Harry T. Holman's study of the Chancery Court in its early years. It is unavailable in any archive or library; information confirmed by H.T. Holman, 28 Nov. 2007. Since Bumsted's article went to press, several articles by Rusty Bittermann and Margaret E. McCallum, published in rapid succession, have added greatly to this limited body of work, but huge gaps remain. Only the most basic information on the court system is readily available, and there is,

for example, no study of justices of the peace – although there was local legislation defining their roles, we have no idea who they were, what they actually
did, how well they did it, and what their attitudes were. See Rusty Bittermann
and Margaret McCallum, 'When Private Rights Become Public Wrongs: Property and the State in Prince Edward Island in the 1830s,' in John McLaren,
A.R. Buck, and Nancy E. Wright, eds., *Despotic Dominion: Property Rights in
British Settler Societies* (Vancouver: UBC Press 2005), 144–68; Rusty Bittermann
and Margaret E. McCallum, 'The One That Got Away: Fishery Reserves in
Prince Edward Island,' *Dalhousie Law Journal* 28, no. 2 (2005): 385–408; Rusty
Bittermann and Margaret McCallum, 'Upholding the Land Legislation of a
"Communistic and Socialist Assembly": The Benefits of Confederation for
Prince Edward Island,' *CHR* 87, no. 1 (2006): 1–28; Margaret McCallum, 'Prob-
lems in Determining the Date of Reception in Prince Edward Island,' *Univer-
sity of New Brunswick Law Journal* 55 (2006): 3–10; Rusty Bittermann, 'Mi'kmaq
Land Claims and the Escheat Movement in Prince Edward Island,' *University
of New Brunswick Law Journal* 55 (2006): 172–6. Regarding the court system, see
Frank MacKinnon, *The Government of Prince Edward Island* (Toronto: University of Toronto Press 1951), 56–60; Jim Hornby, *In the Shadow of the Gallows:
Criminal Law and Capital Punishment in Prince Edward Island, 1769–1941* (Charlottetown: Institute of Island Studies 1998), 7–14; and J.M. Bumsted, 'Politics
and the Administration of Justice on Early Prince Edward Island, 1769–1805,'
in English, ed., *Essays in the History of Canadian Law, Volume IX*, 50–1, 53–5, 68.
On the JPs, see Justices of the Peace and Indictable Offences, SPEI 1856 c.22,
and Justices of the Peace and Summary Proceedings, SPEI 1856 c.23.

12 *Ross's Weekly* (Charlottetown), 26 May 1864.
13 There is a summary of this history of frustration of tenants' efforts in Robertson, *The Tenant League*, 24–40. For a scholarly study of the Escheat movement,
see Rusty Bittermann, *Rural Protest on Prince Edward Island: From British Colonization to the Escheat Movement* (Toronto: University of Toronto Press 2006).
14 For a possible explanation of why the organization chose the name 'Tenant
Union' when many people in the colony were already using the term 'Tenant
League' in referring to the movement as it took shape prior to 19 May 1864,
see Robertson, *The Tenant League*, 64.
15 *Ross's Weekly*, 26 May 1864.
16 John Burke, *Osborn's Concise Law Dictionary*, 6th ed. (London: Sweet and
Maxwell 1976), 146. In common parlance these writs were referred to, respectively, as *fi. fa.* and *ca. sa.*; and they did appear to be part of common parlance
in colonial Prince Edward Island, a reflection of their importance in the era of
leasehold tenure, the essential distinction being between the seizure of goods
and the seizure of the person.

17 More research is required to identify local peculiarities in the functions of these officials and overlaps in their duties. The relatively small population had been a factor in establishing a tradition of plural officeholding and also in developing variations from practices elsewhere. As D.G. Bell remarks, this small population resulted in lack of inferior-level courts, increasing the amount of petty business going to the Supreme Court, and the lack of general sessions on the Island meant 'apportion[ment] among its judiciary, governor-in-council, grand juries and Assembly [of] much local decision-making which, in other colonies, was performed by magistrates in their collective capacity.' Bell, 'Maritime Legal Institutions under the *Ancien Régime*, 1710–1850,' in DeLloyd J. Guth and W. Wesley Pue, eds., *Canada's Legal Inheritances* (Winnipeg: Canadian Legal History Project 2001), 115n.38. This observation is consistent with John A. Mathieson's comment more than a century ago that 'so completely did the supreme court dominate the judicial field ... that the other courts of justice were overshadowed by it and only emerged in the full light at a later day.' Mathieson, 'Bench and Bar,' in D.A. MacKinnon and A.B. Warburton, eds., *Past and Present in Prince Edward Island* (Charlottetown: B.F. Bowen 1906), 137.

18 See Ian Ross Robertson, 'William Henry Pope,' *DCB*, 10: 593–9. After reading law at the Inner Temple, Pope had articled with Edward Palmer in Charlottetown.

19 One must be careful, at least in the case of the Tenant League, not to push this too far, for the organization's rejection of the rule of law, as conventionally understood, was a means to attain an end, purchase, which was entirely legal; the league's program was not one of confiscation or seizures of land.

20 *Islander* (Charlottetown), 29 April 1864. Emphasis in original.

21 Robert Hodgson to Edward Cardwell, 2 Aug. 1865, printed in PEI, House of Assembly, *Journal*, 1866, app. G. Regarding Hodgson, see Ian Ross Robertson, 'Sir Robert Hodgson,' *DCB*, 10: 352–3. Hodgson, a native Islander and a graduate of King's College, Windsor, Nova Scotia, had studied law with Simon Bradstreet Robie and James W. Johnston in Halifax. In 1852 he had become the first Island-born chief justice. Commencing in 1859, on the Island the chief justice served as the representative of the crown when the lieutenant governor was on leave or when the position was vacant. Hodgson did so on three occasions, once for two years (during which time he asked to be named lieutenant governor!). Regarding the devolution of government, as it was known, see MacKinnon, *The Government of Prince Edward Island*, 88–92.

22 Volunteer Force Act, SPEI 1861 c.11 s.7. Compare that with the more inclusive definition of duties provided by new legislation in 1866, after the effective collapse of the Tenant League: 'by reason of war, invasion, civil commotion, or imminent danger' (Militia and Volunteer Forces Act, SPEI c.2 s.50). Issues

surrounding the possible uses of the Volunteers and who precisely was being armed had caused acrimonious debate in the House of Assembly in 1861; see Ian Ross Robertson, 'Religion, Politics, and Education in Prince Edward Island, from 1856 to 1877,' MA thesis, McGill University, 1968, 82–90.

23 Lady Louisa Wood and Maria Matilda Fanning to Cardwell, 31 Oct. 1864, Colonial Office (CO) 226/100, 612, microfilm, Library and Archives Canada (LAC).

24 George W. DeBlois to James Corley and eight others, 4 Feb. 1865, in *Protestant and Evangelical Witness* (Charlottetown), 11 Feb. 1865.

25 No soldiers had been stationed in Prince Edward Island since 1854; see Robertson, *The Tenant League*, 166, 206. Under the Office of Sheriff Act, SPEI 1860 c.41 s.1, Dodd would have been selected by the lieutenant governor in council (the government of the day) from a list of three nominees drawn up by the chief justice (Hodgson). The previous legislation had left the choice to the absolute discretion of the lieutenant governor in council – thereby politicizing the office to an extent that constituted a major break with earlier practice on the Island, as Katherine Dewar has noted in an unpublished research paper, '"Pricking for the Sheriff": The Office of the Sheriff in Pre- Confederation Prince Edward Island, 1769–1873' (2005), 12–13. See Office of Sheriff Act, SPEI 1855 c.7 s.2. Ms. Dewar has kindly allowed me access to her unpublished paper, and also to the following sheriff's manual in her possession, which was used on the Island in the nineteenth century and passed down from sheriff to sheriff (including her father) in the twentieth century: John Impey, *The Practice of the Office of Sheriff and Under-Sheriff; Shewing the Powers and Duties of Those Offices*, 6th ed. (London: J. and W.T. Clarke 1835).

26 Hodgson to Sir Richard Graves MacDonnell, 1 Aug. 1865, printed in PEI, House of Assembly, *Journal*, 1866, app. G. For a map showing where incidents of resistance occurred, which demonstrates the pre-eminent importance of Queens in this story, see Robertson, *The Tenant League*, map 3 on 46.

27 Dundas to Cardwell, 25 Aug. 1865, confidential, CO 226/101, 665. A former soldier and British MP, Dundas was not a lawyer; see Ian Ross Robertson, 'George Dundas,' *DCB*, 10: 264–5.

28 *Examiner* (Charlottetown), 15 Jan. 1866

29 *Islander*, 14 July 1865.

30 See *Islander*, 17 Aug. 1866.

31 See Robertson, *The Tenant League*, 153–4, 175–81.

32 Extract from the Minutes of the Board of Education (printed), 27 July 1865, acc. 2514/9, PARO.

33 J. Macneill, secretary of the Board of Education, to the clerk of the Executive Council, 5 Oct. 1865, acc. 2514/9, PARO.

34 PEI, Executive Council Minutes (microfilm), 7 Oct. 1865.

35 Palmer to Charles DesBrisay (clerk of the Executive Council), 16 Oct. 1865, acc. 2514/9, PARO. See Ian Ross Robertson, 'Edward Palmer,' *DCB*, 11: 664–70. He had studied law in Charlottetown in the office of his father, who had been a lawyer in Ireland. See H.T. Holman, 'James Bardin Palmer,' *DCB*, 6: 565–9.

36 PEI, Executive Council Minutes, 13 Nov. 1865.

37 Palmer to C. DesBrisay, 2 Dec. 1865, acc. 2514/9, PARO; PEI, Executive Council Minutes, 19 Dec. 1865.

38 Cardwell, memorandum dated 12 Aug. 1865, CO 226/101, 439. See E.D. Steele, *Irish Land and British Politics: Tenant-Right and Nationality 1865–1870* (Cambridge: Cambridge University Press 1974), 68–70; J.C. Brady, 'Legal Developments, 1801–79,' in W.E. Vaughan, ed., *A New History of Ireland, Vol. V: Ireland under the Union, I (1801–70)* (Oxford: Clarendon Press 1989), 457–63. Regarding Cardwell, see *DNB*, 3: 952–4.

39 *DNB*, 17: 120.

40 Sir Frederic Rogers, memorandum dated 13 Aug. 1865, CO 226/101, 440.

41 T.F. Elliot, memorandum dated 1 March 1866, CO 226/102, 29.

42 Dundas to Cardwell, 25 Aug. 1865, confidential, CO 226/101, 666–7.

43 On sedition law, see F. Murray Greenwood and Barry Wright, 'Introduction: State Trials, the Rule of Law, and Executive Powers in Early Canada,' *CST 1*, 27–31; and also, from the same volume, J.M. Bumsted, 'Liberty of the Press in Early Prince Edward Island, 1823–9,' 522; and Barry Cahill, '*R. v. Howe* (1835) for Seditious Libel: A Tale of Twelve Magistrates,' 547. For historical background on the offence of seditious libel, see the chapter by Desmond Brown and Barry Wright in this volume. Also note their comment on the more general issue of sedition prosecutions: 'The threat of jury acquittals, the long-term result of the Libel Act, 1792, became the most effective check on sedition prosecutions.'

44 The article does not seem to have survived. Its title is given here as it appears in 'The Queen *v.* John Ross,' Indictment for Libel, marked 'No Bill,' PEI, SCCP, 1866, PARO. The Executive Council cited a slightly different version of the title, namely, 'Courts of Law and Tenant Union'; PEI, Executive Council Minutes, 13 Nov. 1865.

45 Haviland had been educated in Belgium before studying law in the Charlottetown office of James H. Peters; see Andrew Robb, 'Thomas Heath Haviland [Jr],' *DCB*, 12: 415–18.

46 Whether there was a practice of using other means – such as a sheriff selecting 'the right men' – to bias juror selection is an aspect of Island legal history that has not been explored. No evidence of it has emerged in the Tenant League years.

47 PEI, Executive Council Minutes, 12 Dec. 1865. See Grand and Petit Jurors Act, SPEI 1861 c.10.

48 'The Queen *v.* John Ross,' Bill of Indictment, SCCP, 1866, PARO.

49 James Curtis to John Morris, 14 March 1865, acc. 2514/10, PARO.

50 Morris to James C. Pope, 15 March 1865, acc. 2514/10, PARO. The author of a modern study of the militia in colonial Prince Edward Island has written that 'many ... members probably belonged to the Tenant League as well.' David Webber, *A Thousand Young Men: The Colonial Volunteer Militia of Prince Edward Island 1775–1874* (Charlottetown: Prince Edward Island Museum and Heritage Foundation 1990), 101.

51 PEI, Executive Council Minutes, 16 March 1865. The actual letter sent to Morris added something to the command recorded in the Executive Council Minutes: he was to call out the posse *'in all cases* where resistance of this kind is offered' (emphasis added). C. DesBrisay to Morris, 17 March 1865, in *Islander*, 14 April 1865.

52 Burke, *Osborn's Concise Law Dictionary*, 6th ed., 256.

53 Sidney and Beatrice Webb, *The Parish and the County* (London: Frank Cass 1963 [1906]), 306–7.

54 Max Beloff, *Public Order and Popular Disturbances 1660–1714* (London: Frank Cass 1963 [1938]), 133, 139, 140. Also see 153; S. and B. Webb, *The Parish and the County*, 488–9n.4; F.C. Mather, *Public Order in the Age of the Chartists* (Manchester, U.K.: Manchester University Press 1959), 47, 80–1.

55 It was St Patrick's Day, but there was nothing particularly Irish about the demonstration and no surviving record suggests that anyone in the intensely nationality-conscious colony believed the date was a significant consideration in what happened.

56 Although at first glance the use of trumpets, horns, and the like is reminiscent of charivaris elsewhere, there was not a strong tradition of charivaris in the colony, and consequently the tactic is unlikely to have been drawn from it. There is one article on the subject, J.H. Fletcher, 'The Old Time Charivari,' *Prince Edward Island Magazine* 4, no. 9 (1902): 307–14. Although Fletcher was highly politicized, his account does not suggest that he thought there was any connection with, for example, the Tenant League. I thank folklorist and historian Georges Arsenault for this reference.

57 See Robertson, *The Tenant League*, 90–1, 99–102; CO 226/100, 338, 614.

58 'Louisa A. Lady Wood & other *v.* Samuel Fletcher,' Affidavit of Debt, 4 March 1865, PEI, SCCP, 1865, PARO.

59 Theophilus DesBrisay to Morris, 18 March 1865, acc. 2514/10, PARO.

60 Morris to J.C. Pope, 18 March 1865, acc. 2514/10, PARO.

61 T. DesBrisay to Morris, 18 March 1865, acc. 2514/10, PARO.

62 Morris to J.C. Pope, 18 March 1865, acc. 2514/10, PARO.

63 Dundas to Duke of Newcastle, 28 Nov. 1859, CO 226/91, 197–8; *Protestant*, 15 April 1865.

64 *Examiner*, 11 April 1859; also see Ian Ross Robertson, 'Party Politics and Religious Controversialism in Prince Edward Island from 1860 to 1863,' *Acadiensis* 7, no. 2 (1978): 36, 53–4.

65 *Islander*, 27 Jan. 1865.

66 *Islander*, 17 March 1865.

67 *Islander*, 24 March 1865. Emphasis added.

68 PEI, Executive Council Minutes, 21 March 1865. The Minutes, although correctly conveying the difference in opinion between the Executive Council and the sheriff, contain the statement that Morris had declared he would 'cheerfully' obey the instructions to call out the posse if his advice were rejected. The adverb is a gratuitous addition that is inconsistent with the tone of Morris's letter, and, although perhaps it may seem a small matter, this editorial work is of a piece with the 'damage control' operation the government mounted after the calling out of the posse comitatus. The sheriff would be made to appear the initiator.

69 The split over confederation had been tinged by a history of personal rivalries, which might have come into play again if there had been real division regarding use of the posse; they did resurface over other issues in subsequent years. See Robertson, 'Edward Palmer,' *DCB*, 11: 667–8.

70 No two accounts of the posse comitatus incident are identical. Even the number of marchers is uncertain, with 150 being more or less a median of the estimates; but in most instances the doubtful elements concern non-essentials. For detailed commentary on the sources, see Ian Ross Robertson, 'The *Posse Comitatus* Incident of 1865,' *The Island Magazine* 24 (fall-winter 1988): 10.

71 See Robertson, *The Tenant League*, 117–21.

72 Morris to J.C. Pope, 18 March 1865, acc. 2514/10, PARO. The five letters published in the *Islander*, 14 April 1865, are: Curtis to Morris, 14 March 1865; Morris to J.C. Pope, 15 March 1865; C. DesBrisay to Morris, 17 March 1865; T. DesBrisay to Morris, 18 March 1865; C. DesBrisay to Morris, 22 March 1865.

73 See, for example, Solicitor General and Executive Councillor T. Heath Haviland, Jr, in PEI, House of Assembly, *Debates*, 1866, 23, who hewed to the line that sole responsibility lay with the sheriff. Dewar notes that this was not the first time that an Island sheriff was 'sacrificed for political gain'; '"Pricking for the Sheriff,"' 30; see 27 for an example drawn from the Escheat agitation of the 1830s.

74 3 Aug. 1865, nos. 1 and 6, Garrison Orders, vol. 111, Headquarters Office Papers for Nova Scotia 1783–1907, Public Archives of Nova Scotia (PANS), Halifax.

75 See report of Captain J.D.G. Tulloch, n.d. [1850], War Office 1/563, 184–6, microfilm, LAC; PEI, House of Assembly, *Journal*, 1852, app. S; PEI, House of Assembly, *Journal*, 1853, app. J; PEI, House of Assembly, *Journal*, 1854, app. E; PEI, House of Assembly, *Journal*, 1855, app. F.

76 See Robertson, *The Tenant League*, 168.

77 See Paul Bew, *Land and the National Question in Ireland 1858–82* (Dublin: Gill and Macmillan 1978), 121–6, 155–61, 170–4, 221–3.

78 See, for example, *Examiner*, 23 Oct. 1865. For general reflections on similarities and differences between the Island's land issues in the Tenant League years and those of nineteenth-century Ireland and Scotland, see Robertson, *The Tenant League*, 5–8; for comparisons on such matters of detail as the use of notices to quit, see the page references in the index, 388, 394.

79 Hodgson to Cardwell, 2 Aug. 1865, printed in PEI, House of Assembly, *Journal*, 1866, app. G.

80 *Royal Gazette* (Charlottetown), 20 Sept. 1865, referred to 'the Imperial Act for punishing Mutiny and Desertion' (without giving a precise citation), which specified, among other things, that any person enticing or assisting a soldier to desert or concealing a deserter committed a misdemeanour; that any two justices of the peace could deal with the case; and that the maximum penalty would be six months' incarceration with or without hard labour. An Island statue, 50 Geo. III c.3, was also cited, adding a £20 penalty for harbouring or aiding and abetting deserters, and offering a £5 reward for apprehension of deserters.

81 *Islander*, 8 Sept. 1865.

82 The Mayor's Court, dealing with civil matters, and the Police Court, for criminal proceedings, had been established when the town was incorporated in 1855. See Charlottetown Incorporation Act, SPEI 1855 c.34 ss.23, 47, and Charlottetown Boundaries and Courts Act, SPEI 1856 c.18 ss.5, 7. The mayor and councillors were deemed to have the same jurisdiction, civil and criminal, within the city as justices of the peace had elsewhere in the colony. Regarding Haviland, who was not a lawyer but nonetheless had been assistant judge of the Supreme Court, a largely honorary position with no fixed salary, from 1824 to 1854, see Ian Ross Robertson, 'Thomas Heath Haviland [Sr],' *DCB*, 9: 375–7. He had held a multiplicity of offices and was at the centre of the Family Compact.

83 *Islander*, 3 Nov. 1865. The newspaper report spells the name of the soldier-witness Macgory / Macgrory inconsistently.

84 *Royal Gazette*, 30 Aug. 1865.

85 *Islander*, 3 Nov. 1865.

86 Thomas Moffatt, age twenty-five, a native of Ireland, had been reported as a deserter by 17 August; see *Royal Gazette*, 23 Aug. 1865. He was never captured.

87 *Islander*, 3 Nov. 1865.

88 Regarding the case of Donald McLeod, see Robertson, *The Tenant League*, 194–6.

89 The metaphor is that of the archivist Dr Brian Cuthbertson of PANS on 28 July 1981.

90 See Carol M. Whitfield, *Tommy Atkins: The British Soldier in Canada, 1759–1870* (Ottawa: National Historic Parks and Sites Branch, Parks Canada, Environment Canada, 1981), 59, 62; Peter Burroughs, 'Tackling Army Desertion in British North America,' *CHR* 61, no. 1 (1980): 51–4.

91 This success is especially apparent when one notes that the men were drawn from a military command where, in terms of its own history, the annual desertion rate had 'hit one of its low points' during the years 1861–4, fluctuating between 0.78 and 1.70 per cent. That rate was much lower than the contemporary rate in Canada where, during the same years, the rate had ranged from 3.85 to 8.35 per cent. Thus, by any realistic comparative yardstick, it would appear that the league was not dealing with a group of military men whom one might expect to be unusually prone to disaffection – just the reverse, in fact. See Whitfield, *Tommy Atkins*, app. C, 141; table 1, 143.

92 See Hodgson to Cardwell, 30 Aug. 1865, dispatch no. 71, printed in PEI, House of Assembly, *Journal*, 1866, app. G, app. Q. For rank-and-file soldiers, the irony of the situation must have been apparent. Ordinarily forbidden to possess civilian clothing in the interests of preventing desertion, now, for the purpose of pursuing deserters, they were provided with it free of charge and ordered to wear it! Regarding the measures taken to counteract desertion, see Robertson, *The Tenant League*, 170, 175, 193, 200–3.

93 For the routes taken by these expeditions, and also the route of the posse comitatus, see the map in this chapter.

94 For evidence of passive resistance, see Robertson, *The Tenant League*, 231, 233–4.

95 See Examination and Evidence of Andrew Cranston et al., 14 Oct. 1865, PEI, SCCP, 1865, PARO; PEI, Supreme Court Minutes, 31 Oct., 1 Nov. 1865, PARO; *Herald* (Charlottetown), 8 Nov. 1865.

96 *Examiner*, 15 Jan. 1866.

97 Grand and Petit Jurors Act, SPEI 1861 c.10 ss.5, 8.

98 Benjamin Davies in PEI, House of Assembly, *Debates*, 1867, 27.

99 See Ian Ross Robertson, 'James Horsfield Peters,' *DCB*, 12: 838–42. Peters, a native of New Brunswick and the son-in-law of Sir Samuel Cunard, had attended King's College, Fredericton, and had initially studied law under John Ambrose Street in Newcastle, New Brunswick, before putting in almost three years of further study in London, under both 'a Special Pleader in the Temple

and ... a Chancery Barrister.' On the bench since 1848, when he was appointed assistant judge in the Supreme Court and master of the rolls for the Court
of Chancery, he would hold both offices until 15 April 1891, shortly before
his death.

100 *Examiner*, 15 Jan. 1866.

101 This judgment is based on Donald Fyson's explanation that a misdemeanour
riot accusation involved specifying that three or more were involved, and
a felony riot accusation twelve or more. Hodgson stated in his explanation
of the alleged offence that a riot was a tumultuous meeting of three or more
persons assisting each other against any who opposed them in executing a
common purpose with violence, whether the purpose was itself lawful or
unlawful. See the chapter by Fyson in this volume.

102 *Examiner*, 22 Jan. 1866.

103 *Examiner*, 15 Jan. 1866.

104 See *Herald*, 6 Feb. 1867.

105 See Edward MacDonald, 'Joseph Hensley,' *DCB*, 12: 425–7. Born in England,
Hensley had trained in the law office of Hodgson and was his son-in-law.

106 See Francis L. Haszard and A. Bannerman Warburton, eds., *Reports of Cases
Determined in the Supreme Court, Court of Chancery, and Vice Admiralty Court
of Prince Edward Island .... [1850–1874]*, vol. 1 (Charlottetown: John Coombs
1885), 262–6. Peters also explained his view of the rationale for the secrecy of
the grand jury: 'Proceedings are conducted in secret, so that an accused or
suspected person may not, without reasonable proof of guilt, suffer the mor-
tification of a public trial.'

107 PEI, Supreme Court Minutes, 26 June 1866, PARO.

108 The term 'rescue' is used here in its legal meaning of 'forcibly taking back
goods which have been distrained and are being taken to the pound.' Such
action is known as 'pound-breach.' Burke, *Osborn's Concise Law Dictionary*,
6th ed., 290; also see 258. Regarding the Curtisdale incident, see Robertson,
The Tenant League, 147–52, and, for a further analysis of the main protagonists, Curtis and Dickieson, see ibid., 162–4.

109 For an account of the capture of Doucette, see Robertson, *The Tenant League*,
172–5.

110 See ibid., 252–3.

111 See report in *Islander*, 2 Feb. 1866.

112 PEI, House of Assembly, *Debates*, 1867, 27.

113 *Islander*, 2 Feb. 1866. Emphasis added.

114 Bumsted, 'Politics and the Administration of Justice,' 49–50.

115 John Francis Maguire, *The Irish in America* (New York: Arno Press 1969
[1868]), 29.

116 See Robertson, *The Tenant League*, 74–5, 80–2, 125–32, 273; map 9 on 260.

117 For a list, see PEI, House of Assembly, *Journal*, 1875, app. E.

118 PEI, Legislative Council, *Debates*, 1871, 21.

119 Eric Richards, 'How Tame Were the Highlanders during the Clearances?' *Scottish Studies* 17, no. 1 (1973): 40.

120 Cited in Eric Richards, *A History of the Highland Clearances, Volume One: Agrarian Transformation and the Evictions 1746–1886* (London: Croom Helm 1982), 446.

121 A point made to me by historian Kenneth McNaught on 30 May 1995. One other group in Canada willing to resort to calculated civil disobedience in order to thwart the authorities was the minority Sons of Freedom sect among the Doukhobors, a Russian-speaking religious group. But they cannot be classified as an extra-parliamentary movement seeking radical change. Their objectives involved resistance to state documentation of vital statistics, to state control over education of their children, etc. – and, apparently, simply demonstrating to affirm their right to be different; the conflict with authorities continued for decades. See the following by John McLaren: 'Creating "Slaves of Satan" or "New Canadians"?: The Law, Education, and the Socialization of Doukhobor Children, 1911–1935,' in Hamar Foster and McLaren, eds., *Essays in the History of Canadian Law, Volume VI: British Columbia and the Yukon* (Toronto: Osgoode Society for Canadian Legal History / University of Toronto Press 1995), 352–85; 'The Despicable Crime of Nudity: Law, the State, and Civil Protest among the Sons of Freedom Sect of Doukhobors, 1899–1935,' *Journal of the West* 38, no. 3 (1999): 27–33; 'The State, Child Snatching, and the Law: The Seizure and Indoctrination of Sons of Freedom Children in British Columbia, 1950–60,' in McLaren, Robert Menzies, and Dorothy E. Chunn, eds., *Regulating Lives: Historical Essays on the State, Society, the Individual, and the Law* (Vancouver: UBC Press 2002), 259–93.

122 See Robertson, *The Tenant League*, 214.

123 Charles Townshend, *Political Violence in Ireland: Government and Resistance since 1848* (Oxford: Clarendon Press 1983), 126.

4

The Trials and Tribulations of Riot Prosecutions: Collective Violence, State Authority, and Criminal Justice in Quebec, 1841–92

DONALD FYSON

Violence was endemic in post-rebellions Quebec.[1] British military force and colonial criminal justice had extinguished organized resistance in 1837–8, as examined in Volume II of *Canadian State Trials*, but large-scale collective violence continued in the decades that followed. Election violence persisted through to the 1870s; Protestant-Catholic tensions regularly culminated in violence; there were episodes of violent popular resistance to state measures such as school taxes or vaccination campaigns; sporadic labour violence accompanied industrialization; and popular forms of rough justice, such as the charivari, continued. These sorts of collective disturbances were evidently the most striking form of violence, but other forms of violence also spilled over into public: apart from the innumerable cases of more private violence, from common assaults through wife-beating and rape to murder itself, street fights, tavern brawls, assaults on constables and bailiffs, and the like all appeared regularly in police accounts, prison registers, and court documents and fed the local news sections of Quebec newspapers.[2]

Such violent incidents can tell us much about changes in social, political, and economic relations in nineteenth-century Quebec. These include the transition to industrial capitalism with the corresponding decline in autonomous labour; rapidly increasing urbanization, notably in Montreal (whose population exploded from about 40,000 in 1841 to about 220,000 in 1900) and, to a lesser extent, Quebec City (which increased from about 30,000 to about 65,000 inhabitants in the same period), with all the tensions that entailed; political struggles such as the fight for responsible government, the broader struggles between Reformers and Tories, and, later, the lop-sided contest between liberal, anti-clerical Rouges and conservative, Catholic Church-allied Bleus; ever-present tensions between francophones and anglophones and between Catholics and Protestants; and the continuing subordination of women in a patriarchal society, including their progressive exclusion from the public sphere.[3] But studying larger-scale collective violence can also inform us more specifically about the relationship between state and society and the place of law, especially if we take the state in its broadest sense, as the variegated collection of formalized and legitimated institutions and individuals exercising public authority, down to and including local and municipal administrations.

The decades from the 1840s onward have long been seen as a crucial period in state formation. The state, in Quebec as in British North America as a whole, became increasingly organized, extensive, and present in society, and the bases of the modern state were laid down. I have recently argued that this chronology needs to be revisited, notably to push back the roots of the development of the modern state to the earlier decades of the nineteenth century. But it is nonetheless clear that, with the growth and rationalization of government and judicial bureaucracies, police forces, municipal institutions, public education, and the like, the post-rebellions state was undeniably in a period of rapid expansion.[4]

One of the key aspects of the modern state, as implanted in nineteenth-century Quebec and elsewhere, was its claim to monopoly over the legitimate use of force.[5] At a very broad level, at least in theory, violence of any sort was thus a challenge to state authority. This extended to contemporary legal thought: long-standing legal doctrine held that most forms of physical violence, even common assaults, were construed at least in part as challenges to the state's guarantee of public order: 'against the peace of our said lady the Queen, her crown and dignity,' as indictments put it.[6] But violent challenges to state authority could also be more direct. Actions such as armed rebellions or attacks on state officials evidently struck at the heart of state authority; and other forms of collective violence, such as riots, even when not directed against the state itself, undermined the state's authority by demonstrating publicly its incapacity to guarantee peace and security. As a result, these forms of violence in particular might be expected to elicit a correspondingly vigorous response on the part of state authorities. Examining the ways in which the state responded to violence in general, and collective violence in particular, is thus one means of understanding its growing power and position within nineteenth-century Quebec society.

While we know a great deal about how those in power in Quebec used military force and political trials in response to the rebellions in the late 1830s,[7] the problem of state responses to violent challenges to its author- ity in the ensuing period has been only partially explored. Riots are a case in point. At a general level, there has been no broad examination of collective violence in nineteenth-century Quebec, other than as part of the general treatment of riots in Canada by Bryan Palmer.[8] There are nevertheless a number of focused studies. Some examine specific violent incidents, such as the burning of the Legislative Assembly building in Montreal in 1849 and the riots that followed, the 1850 riots that capped the anti-school-tax Guerre des Éteignoirs in the Quebec countryside, the anti-Protestant Gavazzi riots in Montreal and Quebec City in the early 1850s, and violent strikes by groups such as canal workers in the 1840s or Quebec City dockworkers in the late 1870s.[9] Others focus more gener- ally on specific aspects of collective violence and official responses, such as the charivari, election violence, or military aid to civil power.[10] From these, we can draw a general portrait of collective violence in Quebec (though there are still many incidents that await detailed study). We can note its presence in both urban and rural settings; the highly variegated reasons for collective violence (which make it difficult to fit the phenome- non into any simple explanatory framework); the overall decline in tradi- tional forms of collective violence such as labour riots, election violence, or charivaris; and the rise of newer forms such as violent strikes. These studies also provide us with a fairly good idea of the authorities' immedi- ate reaction to incidents of collective violence, including the use of both military and police throughout the period, and the overall inefficiency of official responses, especially in rural areas or in the face of large numbers of participants.

However, one aspect of state responses to collective violence in Quebec has been little studied: the judicial response after the fact of riot, notably the prosecution of rioters. There is thus no real equivalent of, for example, the work of Scott See on New Brunswick riots in the 1840s, where an ex- amination of the trials of rioters forms an integral part of the analysis.[11] And yet, as See and others have shown, riot trials are a key way to exam- ine the power, or lack of power, of the state in general, and the criminal justice system in particular, in the face of collective violence. Thus, on the one hand, the trials of rioters in England following the Gordon riots of 1780 or the Bristol riots of 1831 were showpieces of state power and exemplary punishment and, from the state's point of view, relatively success-ful. In the case of Orange-Catholic riots in New Brunswick and Ontario, on the other hand, political considerations, and notably the domination of the judiciary and juries by Protestants, meant that while Catholics were dealt with severely, Orangemen had little to fear from the courts, at least until mid-century.[12]

The analytical promise of examining the 'state trials' of rioters, along with the state of Quebec historiography and the evident impossibility of exploring either collective violence in general or all aspects of the state's response to violent challenges to its authority, leads me in this chapter to focus more specifically on the prosecution and trial of rioters in Quebec, from just after the rebellions to the end of the nineteenth century. While the chapter does attempt some coverage of Quebec as a whole, it concentrates on the judicial districts containing the two main cities, Montreal and Quebec City, and thus, largely, on responses to urban collective disorder. And, given the focus on law, courts, and trials, the period covered is bounded by two significant events in the history of riot law in Quebec: the adoption of riot provisions in the colonial Black Acts of 1841, and the parliamentary enactment of the Criminal Code in 1892.[13]

The chapter begins by examining the law relating to riot in Quebec between 1841 and 1892. It then attempts to provide a preliminary overview of the frequency of riot prosecutions in Quebec as a whole, based both on available official statistics and other sources. The text then turns to a more focused look at riot prosecutions in the judicial district of Quebec, which, as we will see, was the theatre of more such prosecutions than any other district. Finally, it explores alternatives to riot prosecutions as means of asserting state authority.

RIOT PROSECUTIONS: THE LEGAL CONTEXT

Riot, as Charles Tilly has pointed out, is a problematic term when applied to the study of collective violence as a social or political phenomenon, since it 'embodies a political judgment rather than an analytical distinction,' automatically assuming the perspective of those who condemned such violence. As Tilly puts it, rioters never referred to themselves as such.[14] When studying judicial responses to collective violence, however, the term is evidently essential, since the point is to examine how this specific type of prosecution was used to counter the broader phenomenon of collective violence.

To use the legal concept, one must first understand what, in law, constituted a riot. Superficially, the law of riot in Quebec between 1841 and 1892 was both simple and relatively stable. Throughout the period, the two basic English definitions of riot applied. First, there was what I will refer to as 'misdemeanour riot,' a common law offence wherein three or more people joined together to use violent means to effectuate a common but private purpose and thereby frightened others.[15] The notion of collective purpose was key: a group of people who suddenly began fighting each other, however large, did not constitute a riot. The range of incidents that could be covered was nevertheless still very wide, covering anything from three people violently assaulting another through to a crowd of thousands breaking into a prison so as to release prisoners; though under legal doctrine that seems to have prevailed in the eighteenth century, those who sought to effectuate general political change through collective violence were more properly charged with treason. In short, much like assault, misdemeanour riot was a highly extendable legal concept.

More serious than misdemeanour riot were the offences created by the 1715 Riot Act. Historians have concentrated largely on the immediate responses provided for under the act, notably the magistrates' infamous 'reading of the Riot Act' (actually the reading of the proclamation specified in the second section of the act), ordering the rioters to disperse within an hour, and the legal use of violence by authorities which could follow, up to and including armed troops firing on crowds who failed to disperse. But the Riot Act also created several new felonies. Most notable was what I will refer to here as 'felony rioting,' twelve or more rioters who remained together for an hour or more after the proclamation had been read. Other felonies created under the Riot Act included violently opposing the reading of the proclamation, and 'riotously demolishing,' where three or more people banded together to demolish churches, houses, and the like.[16]

These basic definitions of riot remained in effect in Quebec through to the 1892 Criminal Code and beyond. Canadian legislators do not appear to have seen them as problematic. Thus, the first Canadian federal statutes regarding rioting, passed in 1868 and 1869, apparently elicited no significant debate in the House of Commons. When legislative provisions regarding riots were consolidated and amended in 1887 in the Revised Statutes of Canada, there were no changes made between the initial provisions proposed by the commissioners and the final version adopted, again suggesting the uncontroversial nature of the initiative. And when the Criminal Code was adopted, there was no discussion at all of the sections defining and punishing rioting, in striking contrast to the lengthy debate concerning the rights and obligations of private citizens in the suppression of riots.[17] This silence makes it difficult to unpack the exact ideological underpinnings of the passing of these laws, which will have to await a more detailed examination of sources such as newspapers or the papers of the politicians involved.

But, despite the apparent stability and lack of discussion, there were nevertheless significant changes in two aspects of the law of riot: the definitions of the offences and the penalties attached. As far as misdemeanour riot was concerned, it was not until 1887 that the Revised Statutes of Canada established the first definition of the offence applicable to Canada as a whole and thus to Quebec. Until then, in Quebec at least, misdemeanour riot remained defined by English common law, with penalties (generally fine and/or imprisonment) at the discretion of the judge.[18] The 1887 definition, based on that in an earlier New Brunswick statute, followed the basic English definition but removed the notion of private purpose, potentially a significant modification given the legal doctrine concerning treason prosecutions of rioters who shared a more public goal. The Revised Statutes also established a maximum four-year punishment for misdemeanour rioting.[19] Finally, the 1892 Criminal Code, drawing on the never-enacted English draft code, slightly reworded the definition of misdemeanour rioting, established the maximum punishment at two years, and confirmed it as an indictable offence.[20] In sum, throughout the period, apart from the question of purpose and the fluctuating penalties, there was little substantive change in the law regarding misdemeanour rioting, which retained the very broad definition long established in England.

The situation of the felonies created by the Riot Act was more fluid. Until 1841, unlike Upper Canada, Lower Canada had no colonial statutory provisions regarding riot, so that the 1715 Riot Act continued in force unchanged. In 1841, however, a first significant modification was included in the so-called Black Acts that introduced parts of Peel's criminal law reform acts to the Province of Canada.[21] In a move that apparently put the emphasis on property damage rather than on breach of the public peace, riotously demolishing was included in the Malicious Injuries to Property Act as a non-capital felony, punishable by imprisonment up to life, with the range of buildings concerned being expanded from houses and churches to include manufactures and their machinery.[22] There was little change thereafter for the next quarter-century, but, from the mid-1860s, legislative action came more rapidly. Thus, in 1865, felony riot and opposing the proclamation were made non-capital, with the maximum punishment becoming life imprisonment.[23] In 1868 the federal Riots and Riotous Assemblies Act, though essentially repeating the provisions of the 1715 Riot Act, provided the first Canadian statutory definition of felony rioting applicable to Quebec (and may indeed have been passed in part because of the absence of such legislation in Quebec). In 1869 another federal statute, after restating and further expanding the provisions regarding riotously demolishing, added a new misdemeanour for rioters who damaged buildings, making them liable to imprisonment for up to seven years. In 1887 the Revised Statutes of Canada, while making no substantial changes to the law regarding felony rioting, nevertheless, on a more symbolic level, brought riotously demolishing and damaging back within the chapter dealing with riots, unlawful assemblies, and breaches of the peace rather than leaving the offence among property offences. Finally, the Criminal Code itself essentially reprised the 1887 provisions regarding felony riot, opposing the reading of the proclamation, and riotously demolishing or damaging; but it nevertheless halved to thirty minutes the period given for dispersal after the proclamation was read, and confirmed all four offences as indictable.[24]

Beyond these changes in the definition and punishment of rioting, there were also a substantial number of other legislative provisions which directly affected riot prosecutions in Quebec. First were the attempts to head off collective violence through prophylactic measures. Most notable were the successive statutes, from 1845 onward, directed at controlling collective labour violence on public works, which banned weapons and (later) alcohol sales on the works and provided for mounted police; or the federal Blake Act of 1878, regulating the carrying of offensive weapons, which was enacted in direct response to Orange-Catholic violence in Montreal.[25] While these did not lead to riot prosecutions as such, they demonstrate legislative concern with the problem of collective violence, as do other measures such as the mid-century provisions, following the 1853 Gavazzi riots, that sought to compel local authorities in Quebec City to respond more forcefully to riots by making the city corporation directly responsible for damage by rioters.[26] The legislature of the Province of Canada and, later, the province of Quebec also apparently sought to shift some of the responsibility for riot control to larger municipalities by empowering some of them in their charters to make by-laws against riots, which some at least followed up on. Thus, Quebec City's 1865 by-law on the preservation of peace and good order, in force through to the end of the nineteenth century and beyond, allowed the city's recorder to impose a $40 fine, or up to two months' imprisonment, on members of any tumultuous assembly (though whether this qualified as 'riot' legislation remains an open question), while Trois-Rivières passed an equivalent by-law in 1870 that referred even more specifically to riots.[27] Rioting was also covered in Quebec's municipal election laws, which gave returning officers the power to imprison rioters summarily.[28] In 1884 an amendment to the federal Indian Act, applicable in Quebec, made it a misdemeanour to incite Natives to riot.[29] Finally, on another level, there were also procedural changes that meant that riot charges could progressively be dealt with not by a full jury trial, as was historically the case, but summarily – a reflection of the broader rise of summary jurisdiction and decline of the jury trial in Canada.[30] Thus, offences prosecuted under the rioting provisions in municipal by-laws from mid-century onward could be dealt with summarily; and from 1869, the federal Speedy Trials Act meant that all riot cases could be dealt with expeditiously by magistrates sitting alone, if defendants so elected.[31]

In sum, legislative measures regarding riot prosecutions in nineteenth-century Quebec were far from simple and static. First, and most obviously, rioting evidently remained a concern for nineteenth-century legislators in Quebec and Canada, which is understandable given the persistence of such collective violence. Even at the very end of our period, the late 1880s and early 1890s, there was significant legislative activity. Second, while there was a general softening of the punishments attached to various types of riot, felony rioting in particular remained one of the more heavily punished offences in the criminal law. And finally, when charging and prosecuting rioters, authorities had the choice between a progressively broader range of offences, procedures, and penalties. With this variegated and apparently responsive legislative apparatus at their disposal, the question then becomes, what did the authorities and the criminal justice system in Quebec do in practice?

OVERALL TRENDS

If the legislative record suggests a continuing and perhaps even increasing activity with regard to riot, the judicial record in Quebec shows quite the opposite. Before 1841, charges for rioting were fairly frequent. In the district of Montreal in 1835, for example, in the Quarter Sessions alone, some 165 people were indicted for rioting of various sorts, with another dozen or so in the King's Bench; of these, a little under 60 per cent were from Montreal itself, with the rest from elsewhere in the district. This may have been exceptional, but having some fifty people per year accused of

Table 1: Individuals imprisoned (mainly pre-trial) for rioting or
riotously demolishing, Quebec, 1840–99

	District of Montreal	District of Quebec	Other districts**
1840–9	c.45–50*	55	no data
1850–9	c.40–45*	45	no data
1860–9	c.5–10*	24	103
1870–9	0	29	52
1880–9	0	7	32
1890–9	0	0	8

Figures are totals for each period.
*range based on a 20 per cent sample (see note 33)
**data incomplete

Table 2: Individuals accused of rioting or riotously
demolishing before the stipendiary magistrates of
Montreal and Quebec City, 1849–99

	Montreal	Quebec City
1849–54	37	83 (1850–4)
1860–9	3	163
1870–9	no data	77
1880–9	no data	22
1890–9	no data	5

Figures are totals for each period. The first period is
based on source availability.

riot, as was the case in the district of Quebec in 1835 (again, of whom
about half were from the city itself), was certainly not unusual.[32]

From the 1840s, however, the situation changed considerably, as shown
in tables 1 through 3. Any definitive quantitative analysis would, of
course, require a complete survey of Quebec's extensive judicial archives,
since there are no systematic and entirely reliable official statistics for the
period. But the tables, based both on extant published statistics and some
more limited forays into the sources, do give an idea of the general trend
across Quebec. They consider all rioting charges together, regardless of
the scale or nature of the incident, though, as we will see later, the charge
covered a very wide range of violent behaviours, not all of which fit easily into the notion of defiance of state authority. Figures given are totals
for each period.[33]

Table 3: Indictments for riot or riotously demolishing, 1860–99

	District of Montreal		District of Quebec		Other districts	Total for Quebec
	Queen's Bench	Quarter Sessions	Queen's Bench	Quarter Sessions	Queen's Bench	
1860–9	2	4	42	12	60	120
1870–9	0	0	32	0	18	50
1880–9	2	n/a	4	n/a	33	39
1890–9	0	n/a	0	n/a	4	4
Total	4	4	78	12	115	213

Figures are totals for each period. In the case of the district of Quebec and possibly others, they appear to refer to the number of people indicted rather than the number of indictments.

Overall, the story is simple: between 1841 and the end of the century, there was a steady decline in the number of people accused of rioting in Quebec. Superficially, this would seem no more than the reflection of the general decline of collective violence in Quebec (as elsewhere in British North America) from about the 1850s.[34] The decline in riot prosecutions would thus be a reflection of broader social trends. But, while this is partly true (evidently, with fewer riots, there were fewer occasions for prosecution), the geographical specificity of the decline of riot prosecutions suggests the need for a more complex explanation. In the district of Montreal, while there were still prosecutions for riot in the 1840s and 1850, the sources used to construct tables 1 through 3 show very few in the 1860s and almost none from the 1870s onward. This absence is confirmed in other sources, such as the annual federal criminal statistics from 1876 and the detailed arrest statistics for Montreal available from 1863 onward. In the district of Quebec, both the figures provided above and the more detailed examination of judicial records discussed below suggest that the decline came a couple of decades later: riot prosecutions were relatively common until the 1860s, more occasional but still regular through to the early 1880s, and essentially non-existent thereafter, with a single riot prosecution in 1892. Finally, elsewhere in the province, relatively frequent riot prosecutions seem to have continued through to the 1880s and then declined, though without disappearing completely.

This difference between Montreal and the other parts of Quebec was certainly not only a reflection of the relative levels of collective violence in these different places. From various sources, we can identify more than twenty instances of large-scale collective violence, such as major riots or violent strikes, in Montreal in the period between 1867 and 1892, including seven that involved calling out the army or militia and some very major incidents such as the Orange-Catholic riots of 1876–8 or the 1875 and 1885 anti-vaccination riots.[35] And in the last quarter of the nineteenth century, the rate of homicide charges, a rough indicator of violence levels, was significantly higher in the districts of Montreal and Quebec than elsewhere.[36] Furthermore, violent strikes of the sort that had previously led to prosecutions continued in Quebec as a whole in the 1890s.[37] Nor are the above figures simply artefacts of changing sources or judicial organization.[38] Clearly, something else was at play in the decline of riot prosecutions.

RIOT PROSECUTIONS IN THE DISTRICT OF QUEBEC

We will return later to the broader issue of the decline, but one thing is clear: the district of Quebec is more fertile ground than that of Montreal for studying riot prosecutions in post-rebellions Quebec.[39] Indeed, overall, the criminal justice system in Quebec City dealt with far more rioting charges in the period than did any other district. Drawing on most extant prison and court records, as well as a detailed examination of newspaper coverage of Queen's Bench trials and some more targeted newspaper consultation, I have been able to identify 109 instances of prosecutions for riot before the justice system in Quebec City between 1841 and 1892, involving about 700 accused.[40] These cases form the basis for the discussion that follows.

First, the overall course of riot prosecutions in the district of Quebec can be plotted more finely (Figure 1). The most important observation is, of course, the general downward trend already noted, but we can also distinguish two different periods: the first, from 1841 to 1857, when riot prosecutions were still quite common; and the second, from 1858 onward, when they became markedly less frequent (though with slight resurgences in the late 1860s and, again, in the late 1870s and early 1880s). As there was only one instance of a riot prosecution launched in the district of Quebec after 1882,[41] this means that the legislative reworking of the Canadian law of riot in 1887 and 1892 was almost entirely moot as far as Quebec City was concerned (as indeed it also was for the district of Montreal), at least in the period covered here. Equally remarkable is the huge variation in numbers of incidents and defendants from year to year. Even during the 1840s and 1850s, which were the heyday of riot prosecutions, there were years with only one or two prosecutions and a handful of de-

Figure 1: Riot prosecutions in the district of Quebec, 1841–92

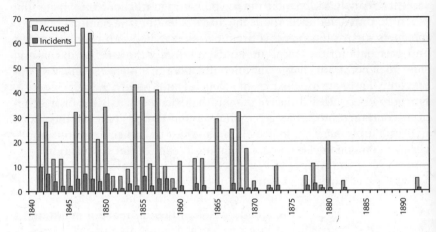

fendants, while other years had more than sixty defendants. The levels of prosecutions for riot were thus exceptional and unpredictable from year to year, unlike, for example, the consistent pattern of regular, everyday prosecutions for drunkenness, vagrancy, assault, or theft.

A closer examination reveals the very wide range of violent behaviours that prosecutors and courts fit under the legal heading of riot. Underscoring the broad legal definition of the offence, riot prosecutions covered incidents ranging from the 1849 riot and assault charge against Honoré Lachance, Charles Marquis, and Pierre Mauffette, notorious Quebec City rowdies, for forcing their way into a private dance, to the trials of the ship labourers involved in large-scale rioting in 1880. This leads us to a closer consideration of the nature of the charge. Social historians of rioting examining issues such as the causes of collective violence have often relied on the basic legal definitions in determining what constituted a riot.[42] But the historian examining rioting prosecutions from the perspective of state trials is faced with the more ambiguous task of separating out public and private issues, since a riot could involve one or the other. Under the common law, three people joining together to assault an enemy or ransack a private house could just as well be charged with rioting as a gang of ten attacking the police or a crowd of a hundred destroying a public building. The challenge to state authority was evidently less direct in the former cases than in the latter.

The easiest approach to this issue would, of course, be to focus only on large-scale riots, where public and state interests were very clearly at stake, both analytically and from the point of view of contemporaries. But where to draw the line? The legal shading in riot prosecutions between interpersonal violence and collective violence, between private interest and protection of the state, and hence between private prosecutions and state trials, was not clear even to contemporary observers. Thus, for example, when charging the Queen's Bench grand jury in 1859, Judge Jean-François-Joseph Duval declared that 'the calendar was clear of offences of a very aggravated character,' even though three people were charged with riot and assault.[43] However, as a collective breaking of the public peace guaranteed by the state, collective violence of any sort was still very much a state issue, especially in a period when the state was increasingly seeking to control such violence. This was in contrast to common assault cases, for example, which through the nineteenth century continued to be treated in part as civil matters to be prosecuted only on the initiative of the plaintiff.[44] In this respect, the notion of a continuum of collective violence, with entirely private motivations at one end and entirely public at the other, is perhaps the most theoretically prudent approach.[45]

At the same time, it is also useful to attempt to measure whether the scale of a riot and the degree of challenge to state authority made any difference in its judicial treatment. For this purpose, I have separated out 'major' riots – those that clearly involved twelve or more participants (and thus led, or could have led, to proceedings under the 1715 Riot Act and its Canadian successor) together with riots that directly attacked the interests of the state (as in attacks on government offices or significant collective resistance towards the police). Isolating these riot prosecutions also has the advantage that they are far better documented, as compared with less serious 'riots,' where circumstances are often unrecoverable from the sources. Using this distinction, among thirty-two major riots for which riot prosecutions were launched before the justice system in Quebec City, eight involved labour relations, eight concerned direct attacks on the state, six were related to party politics, five concerned popular justice (such as attacks on brothels or the repossession of disputed land), and two, religious tensions.[46] Riot prosecutions before the Quebec City courts, both major and minor, also concerned incidents both in the city itself (about three-fifths) and in the rural areas of the district, both before and after the judicial reorganization of the late 1850s. Riot prosecutions were thus directed at a wide range of violent collective behaviours, both in town and in country.

An examination of the people who were accused of major or minor riot, whatever its nature, is also instructive. First, and perhaps most strikingly, by far the largest group were francophones: about two-thirds in all over the entire period. Even for collective violence that took place in Quebec City itself between 1841 and 1857, when the city was barely 60 per cent francophone, about 60 per cent of those prosecuted for riot were also francophone. This strong francophone presence is surprising on a number of levels. It goes against many historiographical assumptions that identify anglophones in general, and the Irish in particular, as the principal sources of violence, especially in Quebec City itself.[47] And it is also in striking contrast to what one finds among other categories of offences, such as drunkenness, vagrancy, disorderly conduct, or prostitution, where francophones were very much in the minority: at the end of the 1840s, for example, they accounted for only about 20 per cent of those arrested for such offences by the municipal police. The weight of judicial repression of violent collective behaviour thus fell as much on the majority francophones as on more recent immigrants.

The social status of the accused ranged from notorious rowdies like the aforementioned Marquis, Lachance, and Maufette to the Reverend Antoine Lebel, curé of the parish of Saint-Gilles, indicted for riot and assault in 1845. However, the vast majority were members of the popular classes: labourers, artisans, and, in the countryside, farmers. Overall, what was being prosecuted was thus evidently not elite violence, though there were occasional instances of that as well. Finally, the accused were almost entirely men: among the 700-odd people accused of rioting in the district of Quebec, only five were women. Clearly, unlike prosecutions for vagrancy, drunkenness, or even theft and assault, where women were in the minority but nevertheless present, it was essentially men who were singled out for prosecution in cases of collective violence. This was true despite the fact that women were sometimes present and occasionally participated in the collective violence that led to these prosecutions.

If we turn to the legal proceedings, it is noteworthy that riot prosecutions in the district of Quebec were brought only under the common law charge of misdemeanour rioting or the Canadian statutory felony of riotously demolishing. Unlike in England, no one was ever charged with felony rioting under the 1715 Riot Act or, after 1869, the equivalent Canadian statute, even in what authorities considered the most serious cases. Thus, neither the Quebec City Gavazzi riots of 1853, nor the violent destruction of the Dorchester Bridge turnpike gate and toll house in 1860, nor a major anti-draft riot in Château-Richer in 1864 led to anything more than charges of misdemeanour rioting or riotously demolishing. Overall, among the prosecutions examined that went as far as a formal charge, just under a quarter were laid under the various statutory provisions against riotously demolishing, with the remainder being for misdemeanour riot. In practice the provisions of the 1715 Riot Act were used primarily as a justification for calling on aid to the civil power, and the statute was therefore referred to not in the prosecutions of rioters but in the inquests on those killed by troops during riots and (occasional) trials of officials and troops involved in violently suppressing riots, 'state trials' of a different sort.[48] The initial reasons for the avoidance of felony rioting charges are fairly obvious. Because it was a capital felony, it would have been difficult to secure jury convictions against rioters. But, even after this roadblock was obviated in 1865 when felony rioting was made non-capital, the charge was never used. Even in subsequent major anti-labour riot prosecutions, such as that launched against participants in the violent confrontations between rival groups of ship labourers in 1880, felony rioting, as severe as it might appear to be in the statute books, remained an entirely theoretical offence, at least in the district of Quebec. When rioters were charged with serious felonies, it was for specific offences such as murder or attempted murder (as was the case with some of the 1880 rioters).

At the same time, rioting charges were almost never subjected to the rapid forms of summary proceedings that increasingly became possible from mid-century onward, especially after 1869. Jail records suggest that no one was specifically charged with participating in a tumultuous assembly under Quebec City's municipal by-law, though a full exploration of the extensive Recorder's Court records will be needed to confirm this finding. Further, the provisions of the 1869 Speedy Trials Act seem almost never to have been applied to rioting cases in Quebec City. With the exception of one case in 1870 involving mariners riotously demolishing a Lévis shop, and the 1892 prosecutions of five men from Saint-Féréol for election rioting, which were brought before the stipendiary magistrate, all riot trials in Quebec City were held before a jury. As we will see, this did not mean that rioters were not proceeded against summarily, but it was not for rioting as such.

Finally, what of the outcome of riot prosecutions? Here, the picture is even more strikingly one of the feebleness of the criminal justice system in countering collective violence in this way. As Table 4 shows, of the 700-odd people accused of rioting, only 83 were found guilty, or just over 10 per cent. Among riot prosecutions for collective violence in the city, the conviction rate was even lower, at about 5 per cent over the entire period, which amounted to only 19 people. Put another way, of the 109 instances

Table 4: Judicial outcomes for people accused of rioting, 1841–92

	Pre-trial			Trial	
	No prosecution	Abandoned	No bill	Not guilty	Guilty
All incidents	20%	22%	29%	18%	12%
Major riots	20%	22%	31%	16%	12%
Quebec City	24%	26%	32%	14%	5%
Elsewhere	13%	15%	25%	26%	22%

of riot prosecutions, only 17 resulted in any convictions whatsoever; and in the city itself, only 8 of 63. The conviction rate for riot, indeed, was among the lowest for all types of prosecutions: it was in stark contrast to the very high conviction rates for summary prosecutions for drunkenness or disorderly conduct, substantially lower than the rate for assault, and lower even than that for rape, an offence where convictions were notoriously hard to secure.[49]

The reasons for this almost complete lack of success in what were supposed to be state trials of serious challenges to state authority are evidently complex. For one thing, the very length and complexity of full-scale riot prosecutions ensured that a process of attrition reduced the numbers of accused at every stage of the prosecution process, just as was the case in other prosecutions for serious crimes. In about a fifth of instances, no formal legal action was apparently taken beyond the initial complaint. In another fifth, the prosecution was abandoned or at least not brought to a judicial conclusion, notably in cases where a grand jury indicted an individual who was never then brought to trial. And, in a little under half of the cases, there was formal absolution: either a bill was thrown out by the grand jury or a not-guilty verdict was found by the trial jury. Overall, about three-quarters of those accused of rioting never came to trial, cases being abandoned or resolved at the pre-trial stage.

The diversity of the stages at which prosecutions were dropped suggests that the lack of success was not due to a single phenomenon, such as large numbers of people being accused of rioting by witnesses but never proceeded against. Nor were other obvious factors at play. The success of a riot prosecution was not related to the degree of seriousness of the collective violence involved, since there was little difference in outcomes between major riots and less serious incidents. As well, unlike in New Brunswick and Upper Canada, consistent political bias on the part of judges and juries was not a factor. There was never any absolute Orange or even Protestant domination of the judicial hierarchy in Quebec, nor of municipal officials or of police. And juries were generally mixed, composed of both anglophones and francophones.[50]

The lack of success also did not stem from jury reluctance to see harsh punishments imposed on rioters. Jurors need not fear sending an innocent man to the gallows (as they did in rape cases), since, as we saw, there were no prosecutions for felony rioting.[51] If we look at the punishments imposed on the few people who were convicted of rioting, they were on the whole relatively mild, with about 60 per cent involving a fine only and 40 per cent some form of imprisonment occasionally combined with a fine. The heaviest punishment imposed by the Quebec City courts for riot was three years in the provincial penitentiary, meted out in 1865 on Xavier Larochelle for riotous demolition, and again in 1878 on François Forrest *dit* Barrette, one of the construction workers involved in a large-scale riot in 1878. Other than these two, only four men received sentences of a year or more, with the remainder receiving a few months or less.[52] Here alone there was a more substantial difference between major and minor riot prosecutions: apart from a single large-scale anti-school-tax riot in Saint-Gervais in 1847 (which resulted in twenty-eight people being convicted and fined), all of the dozen accused convicted in major riots were imprisoned, while fines were more common in lesser riots. Still, given the lack of capital punishment and the relatively light sentences, Quebec City juries had little on their consciences if they did convict, especially since they evidently had no such qualms in scores of other cases involving theft, serious assaults, and the like where penitentiary sentences were common.

The lack of success did not stem either from a generalized lack of will on the part of Quebec City's crown prosecutors or judges. Overall, judicial and other sources allow us to identify close to sixty major incidents of collective violence in Quebec City and its surrounding district between 1841 and 1880.[53] In just under half of such cases, prosecutions were launched against those involved for rioting, with indictments laid in most of those; in another fifth, prosecutions were launched for other charges, such as murder, conspiracy, or assault; and in just under a third of cases there were either apparently no charges at all (just under a quarter of all major cases) or no proceedings were instituted after the initial complaint. Prosecutors in Quebec City, in contrast it appears to those in Montreal, were thus not loath to bring riot charges and, although often unable to do so, were quite a bit more successful than their counterparts in Toronto during the same period, where only eight of twenty-nine major riots led to trials.[54]

As for Quebec City judges, their general attitude towards rioting, and towards major incidents in particular, was clearly spelled out not only in the sentences they imposed on those convicted of major riots but also in their charges to grand and petty juries. Especially revealing is the 1868 grand jury charge by Chief Justice Duval, in the context of a major riot prosecution of eighteen largely francophone ship carpenters involved in a violent strike that included a murder and the calling out of the army. Though congratulating the jury on the general absence of crime in the district, Duval nevertheless pointed out one exception: 'these gatherings of men which of late threatened to disturb the peace of the city.' After recalling the law regarding lawful meetings, he drew a stark contrast with

those tumultuous and unlawful assemblies, so damaging to the best interests of society, led by a few unprincipled characters, who availed themselves of the ignorance and the bad passions of the many, regardless of the rights of their fellow-citizens, and determined to set all laws at defiance. Such men, leaders they were called, ought not to go unpunished. They ought to be taught the lesson inculcated in their youth – and which they seemed to have forgotten – that one of the first duties of a citizen and an honest man was to respect and obey the laws of his country. Such meetings could possibly effect no good. They were the creations of evil passions violently indulged, and must be put down by the strong arm of the law. Ever acting in entire disregard of the rights of others, neither life nor property was secure, when such assemblies were allowed to exist. The suffering they had caused the laboring classes of this city was apparent in the increase of pauperism and absolute want, while the death of an unfortunate father of a family – though not evidenced to justify a criminal prosecution for the awful crime of murder – still left the perpetrators answerable before a higher tribunal, that of their Maker, to whom they would have to answer for the shedding of human blood. Let those men reflect seriously on the crime they had commited [sic], and make such amends as were in their power to the victims of their cruel deeds.[55]

And more succinctly, referring in 1880 to the pending rioting indictment of the ship labourers, Judge F.G. Johnson declared that 'riot strikes at the life of society itself' in contrast to murder which struck at the life of a man.[56] And yet, in both these cases, as in many others, none of the rioters was convicted and no trial ever took place. In the 1868 ship carpenters' strike, after the accused were duly indicted by the grand jury on misdemeanour riot charges, their case was postponed and then eventually disappeared from the judicial record. In 1880 the grand jury threw out the indictments against the ship labourers.

Nor was it a question of prosecutions that lacked interest for the general public. Riot trials, especially after major riots, were widely reported in Quebec City newspapers, which remarked on the difficulties of convicting rioters and the apparently light sentences they received. As the *Morning Chronicle* observed in 1856, following what it saw as unusually severe sentences meted out by Judge Duval on two men convicted of theft, 'we have seen rioters, men of violence and shedders of blood repeatedly elude justice, or expiate their guilt by a brief imprisonment; while here, for an inferior offence, imprisonment for life is sternly assigned by an uncompromising judge. There should really be something like consistency observed in these matters.' The newspaper may well have been referring to the light sentence imposed the previous year by Chief Justice Louis-Hippolyte La Fontaine on John Hearn, the only Gavazzi rioter to be convicted (and even then, only of simple assault). At the time, commenting on the prosecution case, the newspaper had declared: 'The great mountain in labour has brought forth a very ridiculous mouse.'[57] Commentators also remarked more generally (but likely erroneously) on the propensity of Quebec City juries to acquit, even in the face of overwhelming evidence. As a Montreal newspaper declared in 1861, following a murder acquittal, 'the community can place no reliance whatever on Quebec juries, in criminal cases,' while the *Morning Chronicle* attributed this to a jury law that was insufficiently restrictive.[58]

So why this lack of success? Any close analysis of the reasons for the failure of riot prosecutions in general comes up against the problem of individual circumstances, which varied greatly between different cases. As we saw, riot prosecutions, though more frequent in Quebec City than elsewhere, were nevertheless exceptional events, so that only a detailed microhistorical analysis of each individual case would allow for a full exploration of the range of factors and reasons. Nevertheless, it is possible to make some tentative general observations.

A first problem for riot prosecutions was the very nature of jury trials. Until 1869, as noted, jury trial was de rigueur in riot cases, and, even after the Speedy Trials Act of 1869, virtually no one accused of riot chose otherwise. Trial thus most often implied waiting several months for the Quarter Sessions or even longer for the Queen's Bench (which sat only twice a year). The accused were almost never held in prison through to trial since the rioting charges were not capital; indeed, a number of prisoners jailed for rioting made successful habeas corpus applications and were released. And in a number of cases, both before and after indictment, the accused simply left Quebec City, often for the United States. This was the case not only for relatively recent immigrants such as the Irish, for many of whom mobility was a fact of life, but also for some accused from the relatively stable francophone majority, who might join the general nineteenth-century exodus to the industrialized zones of 'les États.'

As well, in jury trials, there were a large number of decision makers involved, many of whom may not necessarily have held the state's interests paramount. As indicated, riot prosecutions were dropped at many different stages of the proceedings and thus the decision to drop a prosecution might come from a wide range of individuals. They included plaintiffs who abandoned prosecutions; grand juries who threw out bills; crown prosecutors who either decided not to proceed or who ended proceedings by filing nolle prosequi; and trial juries who refused to convict. Prosecutions witnesses were also a problem. As Scott See found in New Brunswick, in collective-violence cases that often involved broader social tensions, prosecutions witnesses were reluctant to testify for fear of reprisals. The result was bills thrown out by the grand jury.[59]

There were also procedural difficulties, notably the right of defendants to continuances, which were often granted by judges over the objections of crown prosecutors. Even apparently stringent judges such as Duval condoned this practice. Thus, in the 1873 case of a half-dozen men accused of rioting and destroying a poll book during recent elections, Duval granted one of several motions for continuance on the grounds that 'the accused had positively sworn that the witnesses mentioned in their affidavit were absolutely necessary, and that they could not expect a fair trial unless these witnesses who were now in the States were examined, under circumstances the Court thought their application should be granted, as tardy justice was better than injustice.'[60] The case was duly continued and, after further continuances through to 1874, disappeared from the record. Delaying tactics were a favourite of defence counsel and were very often successful, as can be seen in a number of cases where the grand jury found a true bill against the accused but no trial was ever held.

The role of defence counsel was also significant. Many rioters, especially in major riots, were represented by skilled defence counsel who were able to exploit procedural and other tactics to full advantage. For example, the success of Quebec City's ship labourers at avoiding conviction for strike-related violence in the late 1870s and early 1880s may have had something to do with the fact that their Benevolent Society's main legal counsel, Richard Alleyn, was a professor of criminal law at Laval University and also Quebec City's main crown prosecutor at the time.[61] Still, even high-profile defence counsel were not always successful. Take the case of Marc-Aurèle Plamondon, a leading Rouge in Quebec City, the editor of the liberal newspaper *Le National*, a twice-failed parliamentary candidate and future Superior Court judge, and also a frequent (and usually successful) defence counsel in riot cases.[62] In 1865 Plamondon defended five men from the working-class Saint-Roch suburb (his political base) in two consecutive trials for having riotously destroyed the houses of Adélaïde Singelais (or Saint-Gelais) and Boniface Singelais (or Saint-Gelais). The judge in the case, Charles Mondelet, himself a noted liberal,[63] nevertheless came out strongly against the rioters. Mondelet set the tone at the beginning of the session by decrying the lawless spirit that he observed in Quebec City. In the first trial, although Plamondon called large numbers of witnesses to prove that his clients took no part in the demolition but were only spectators (a favoured tactic of defence counsel in riot cases but entirely contrary to the law of riot, since their mere presence among the rioters was sufficient), and although he also sought to discredit the victims by asserting their disreputable character (which was, of course, no legal argument but nevertheless a powerful argument for the jury), Mondelet summed up strongly against the defence. When the jury came back with a not-guilty verdict against all but one of the defendants, Mondelet refused to accept it and sent them back; when they refused to change their verdict, he declared that 'the responsibility of such a verdict, in so plain a case, rested with the jury and their consciences.' Mondelet had better luck with the second jury, which convicted all but one of the accused. In sentencing, Mondelet was able to bring the full weight of his disapproval to bear on the three prisoners: Xavier Larochelle was one of only two accused ever to be given a three-year sentence for rioting; the other two were sentenced to one and two years each.[64]

The jury's actions in the Larochelle case underline a final key reason for the lack of success of riot prosecutions. There was indeed, as contemporary commentators suggested, a seeming reluctance on the part of juries to convict even in the face of clear evidence, suggesting tolerance towards collective violence. This attitude seems to have extended to at least part of Quebec City's 'respectable' population, who tolerated riots and collective violence as long as they remained within accepted bounds and did not directly threaten the interests of Quebec City's elites. Brothel riots are a case in point. As a form of popular rough justice carried out against undesirables in the neighbourhood, they were treated ambiguously by local newspapers, at times condemned, at other times supported. As the Quebec *Gazette* said of one such riot in 1858, 'we believe the intentions of the persons engaged in the affair were anything but vicious or felonious, but on the contrary that they were prompted by feelings the most virtuous, honest and honorable, by a desire to save their sisters, daughters, wives, and friends, from being drawn in by the snares of these monsters in human shape. The law of England gives the privilege to a man to "abate a nuisance with his own hand."'[65] However, that toleration did not extend to attacks on brothels for less respectable motives: in 1861 five people involved in prostitution themselves, including one woman, were convicted and condemned to fifteen months' imprisonment for destroying a rival brothel.[66] Election violence, too, was tolerated. As the *Morning Chronicle* declared in 1857, regarding a recent municipal election riot in the Saint-Roch suburb of Quebec City, 'An election brawl! Who thinks anything of it? What more natural than a disturbance at the choice either of a civil or parliamentary representative? Brawls are to be witnessed wherever constitutional government flourishes; and in all probability they will continue to be witnessed till the end of the chapter.' The newspaper did condemn this particular riot as having 'far outstripped the bounds which custom has set up, and within which it permits men to sport themselves,' but only because the chief of police had been seriously wounded. Even violence directly against state-sanctioned authorities was tolerated. In 1860, when a grand jury threw out the charges against several people for riotously demolishing the Dorchester Bridge toll gate and toll house, the newspaper regretted the incapacity of the prosecution to prove its case. But it also expressed sympathy for the rioters, declaring that 'the cause which has led to such subversion of law, among a hitherto peaceable and law abiding people, may be found in the exorbitant and unjust tolls exacted on the turnpike roads in the neighborhood of this city.'[67] From the mid-century onward, such notions of acceptable collective violence were increasingly being called into question. The change followed particularly violent incidents, such as the 1853 Gavazzi riot in Montreal.[68] But a substratum of tolerance remained and informed both elite and official attitudes towards at least some forms of collective violence.

Perhaps the most egregious example of the difficulties facing riot prosecutions came not from Quebec City but from Montreal in the trials following the 1849 Rebellion Losses riots. These riots, the most infamous of political riots in post-rebellions, nineteenth-century urban Quebec, included the burning down of the Legislative Assembly and attacks on Governor General Lord Elgin and on the houses of Reform leaders such as Louis-Hyppolite La Fontaine. The riots were thus prime examples of the sort of conservative 'lawless law' common in the Canadas through to the 1840s.[69] After lengthy preliminary proceedings, the rioters accused of burning down Parliament were eventually brought to trial in October 1850. Much in the trial seemed to be in the prosecution's favour. The charge was of riotously demolishing, rather than felony riot or even treason, thus largely obviating the issue of jury reluctance to condemn for capital crimes. Unlike similar Upper Canadian cases, the judicial establishment was not firmly on the side of the conservative rioters. The crown prosecutor, Solicitor General Lewis Thomas Drummond, a staunch Reformer and one of the defence lawyers in the treason trials of the Patriotes in 1838, was highly motivated since the accused were all Tory sympathizers. One of the two judges, Thomas Cushing Aylwin, was a former Reform cabinet member who, like Drummond, had defended Patriotes during the 1838 trials, while the other, Jean-Roch Rolland, was apparently politically neutral. There was thus little of the Baconian spirit here. The actions of the accused were highly public and even flaunted at the time of the riot. And yet, from the crown's point of view, the entire trial was a failure. Many prosecution witnesses failed to appear before the grand jury, probably out of fear, and the jurors accordingly threw out bills against all but one defendant, Henry Jamieson. At the trial itself, several prosecution witnesses refused to identify Jamieson as having been at the riot though others definitely placed him there. Jamieson's lawyer, William Mack, himself one of the defendants who had just been cleared by the grand jury on the same charge, mounted a stirring, emotional defence that was remarkable in its disregard for both law and evidence. Among other points, he argued (quite erroneously as we saw) that Jamieson must be cleared if it could not be proved that he had actually helped destroy Parliament; that burning was not the equivalent of demolishing; and that it was utterly impossible for anyone to have recognized anyone else at the scene. He finished on a bathetic note regarding the possible penitentiary term that Jamieson risked: 'Do you comprehend all the refined cruelty of this novel invention due to the humanity of the nineteenth century? We have heard of the tortures of the Spanish Inquisition ... But it was for the nineteenth century to drag the soul to death, while the body is kept alive ... This is the soul destroying violence – this the punishment to which you are called upon to condemn him.' Despite a summing up strongly in favour of the prosecution by Judge Aylwin, the trial jury quickly found Jamieson not guilty. And thus ended the state's attempt to punish those who had so far challenged its authority as to burn down Parliament itself.[70]

ALTERNATIVES TO RIOT PROSECUTIONS

This rather dismal (from the point of view of the state) portrait of the lack of success of riot prosecutions in the district of Quebec, combined with the virtual absence of such prosecutions in Montreal from the 1860s, should not, however, lead us to suppose that the authorities were without resources to deal with those who, through collective violence, threatened the state's monopoly on violence. For there were alternatives, and it is these alternatives, I argue, that account both for the striking difference between Montreal and elsewhere and for the later decline in riot prosecutions in the district of Quebec.

One alternative came from the policing of riots, long recognized as a dominant form of response to rioting by authorities. Police and military intervention, and the bloodshed that sometimes followed, were often enough of a statement of the state's power to make formal judicial proceedings unnecessary. If no one was ever executed in Quebec following a conviction for felony rioting, there were nevertheless a handful of incidents in which rioters were shot by the military, the most famous being the Beauharnois Canal riot of 1843 (six dead) and the Montreal Gavazzi riot of 1853 (seven dead), and there was also one death in Quebec City during the 1878 construction workers' riot. These were capital punishments of a very direct sort. In most cases, however, the mere presence of the military was enough to forestall or stop a riot, or, failing that, to allow the police to make arrests. Overall, between 1841 and 1892, the military provided aid to the civil power in cases of actual or apprehended collective violence twenty-six times in Quebec City and twenty-seven times in Montreal. Further, with the strengthening of urban police forces in the second half of the nineteenth century, including the adoption of military training and tactics in Montreal at least, it became easier for police to control and disperse rioters. Perhaps tellingly, from the 1860s onward, while there were some seventeen military interventions in Quebec City, there were only seven in Montreal.[71]

The impact of policing actions can be seen by examining pre-trial arrest and imprisonment as a form of control and punishment. While it is difficult to compile a complete list of those arrested for rioting and then released, the coupling of newspaper accounts with prison records in the district of Quebec does suggest that the practice was common. As for pretrial imprisonment, though only 10 per cent of those accused of rioting in the district of Quebec were found guilty, about 20 per cent of all accused nevertheless underwent some form of imprisonment before trial. While this imprisonment was generally of short duration and subject to habeas corpus petitions, it nevertheless represented a very immediate form of punishment.

Another way of looking at the impact, quite literally, of this growing police presence is through charges for assaulting or resisting the police.

Figure 2: Arrests and prosecutions for assaulting or resisting police, Montreal, 1849–92[74]

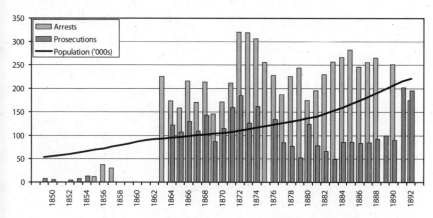

The new urban police forces were one of the principal, albeit imperfect, means by which the state sought to control the climate of collective violence. In Quebec City and Montreal, as in other large North American cities, professional policing emerged fully in the second half of the nineteenth century (though it had been in gestation since the early 1800s) and became one of the dominant instruments of social regulation.[72] As with riots, assaults on and resistance to the police were forms of violent resistance to this expanding state authority, and arguably an even more direct form than riots, many of which did not target state interests.

A full examination of prosecutions for assaulting or resisting the police lies beyond the scope of this chapter. However, a few preliminary observations are in order. First, as figures 2 and 3 suggest, in the 1840s such prosecutions were not much more common than those for riot, but, from about mid-century, they became far more frequent. Thus, in the 1840s in Quebec City, considerably more people were accused of riot than of assaulting the police; whereas in Montreal, between 1849 and 1854, the police magistrate dealt with thirty-seven people charged with assaulting the police, exactly the same number as those charged with rioting. In the 1850s, and by the late 1850s in particular, this had changed dramatically. In Montreal, from the 1860s to 1892, while riot prosecutions disappeared almost completely, there were generally between 150 and 300 arrests annually for various forms of resistance to the police. In Quebec City, the figure varied between 40 and 80 per year, with particular growth during

Figure 3: Arrests and prosecutions for assaulting or resisting police, Quebec City, 1842–90[75]

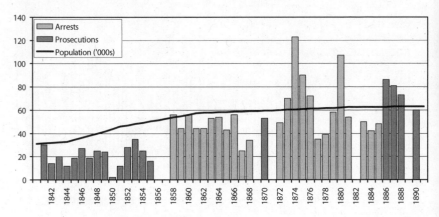

the 1860s and 1870s, exactly the decades when riot prosecutions began to diminish substantially. Assaults on the police were one of the offences specially singled out by the Montreal chief of police in his first published annual report in 1863. In the 1880 report, the chief of police even asserted that assaults on the police in Montreal were far more frequent than in other comparable cities such as Boston or Toronto.

Thus, just as riot prosecutions were diminishing, those for assaulting the police were becoming more common, in both Montreal and Quebec City. But this is not to suggest that there was a direct link between the two, with charges for assaulting police replacing rioting charges. Though this did occur on occasion, most charges for assaults on police were against single individuals rather than crowds; indeed, by the last decade of the nineteenth century, the charge of assaulting or resisting the police seems most often to have been simply an adjunct used against drunks or vagrants who refused to come along quietly when arrested.[73] But it does indicate the growing use of the police to control violent or potentially violent forms of resistance to state authority.

The most important factor in the increase in such prosecutions was the growth of summary proceedings. At one level there was effectively a form of summary punishment by the police themselves through their powers of arrest and temporary detention. In Montreal at least in the 1870s and 1880s, a significant proportion of those arrested for assaulting or resisting the police were not brought to court, since far more people were arrested than eventually charged. This suggests that many of those arrested were let off after undergoing the informal punishment of arrest and being taken to the station house. A more specific factor was an 1858 law extending the summary jurisdiction of recorders and police magistrates which allowed them to try assaults on police summarily on consent of the parties concerned.[76] Before 1858, assaults on the police had to be tried before a full jury, with all of the difficulties that that entailed. Small wonder that, much like riot trials, these prosecutions were not especially successful, even when they made it to court. In Quebec City between 1841 and 1857, fewer than 20 per cent of people against whom indictments were brought for assaulting constables or bailiffs were eventually found guilty, so it is not surprising that relatively few of these prosecutions were launched by police. However, all this changed after 1858. Given the choice between immediate trial and possible pre-trial imprisonment, most accused appear to have opted for summary trial, and, from 1858 onward, almost all such charges were dealt with summarily, with very few accused tried before courts with juries (the Quarter Sessions or Queen's Bench). The proceedings in these summary trials meant that they were state trials of a very different sort: generally without lawyers, certainly without juries, and hence with the balance of power stacked very heavily in favour of the state. And the effects on conviction rates were dramatic. Between 1870 and 1897, over 80 per cent of those brought before the courts for assaulting police in Quebec City were convicted, while in Montreal between 1876 and 1895 the rate was closer to 90 per cent.[77] The contrast between prosecutions for assaulting the police and those for riot is striking; and, while the rise of the first cannot directly explain the decline of the second, both can be explained in part by their relationship to summary justice.

This still, however, does not explain the difference in riot prosecutions between Montreal and Quebec City. We must thus turn to the judicial alternatives to a classic riot prosecution, namely, charging rioters with something other than rioting. In cases where people were actually killed or injured during a riot, this might take the form of charges for murder, attempted murder, wounding, and so forth. For example, in 1879, seven Quebec City men, all but one francophone, were charged with having been part of a crowd of ten or fifteen who invaded a family dance in a private house, insisting on joining in and, when opposed, assaulting the occupants. Newspaper coverage described the case as one of 'riotous assault' but the indictment laid was for inflicting grievous bodily harm, resulting in five defendants being found guilty while two others fled to the

United States. In such cases, the tone of the trials shifted as the focus was much more on the victim than on the riot. However, the results were not much different, with only a small proportion of the accused being convicted, and, overall, such charges appear to have been uncommon.

More often, however, rioters were charged with lesser offences: disturbing the peace, weapons charges, resisting the police, even vagrancy, all charges that were not necessarily related to collective violence but that could be used against rioters. Weapons charges are a case in point. Legislative provisions controlling weapons such as knives, iron knuckles, clubs, and firearms, as we saw, were often a direct response to collective violence and an attempt to control it or at least limit its potentially fatal effects by limiting weapons. Thus, as indicated, the 1878 Blake Act was passed in direct response to Orange-Irish confrontations in Montreal; it was proclaimed in force in Quebec City as of 1879. But local authorities did not need to wait for the Blake Act to begin cracking down on the carrying of dangerous weapons in public. Already from 1859, legislation explicitly prohibited the carrying of knives and other offensive weapons; between 1866 and 1876, Montreal's recorder summarily tried an average of five people per year for such weapons-related offences. In 1877, a year before the Blake Act, the federal government passed the Firearms Act, prohibiting the carrying of pistols, and the number charged with weapons offences in Montreal soared to forty, of whom thirty were tried summarily by the recorder, with the remainder sent on to Quarter Sessions for trial. In 1878 forty-seven were charged, all but two of whom were tried summarily by the recorder. Weapons-related charges were also relatively successful, with the key, as in cases of assaulting the police, being the summary nature of the proceedings, before recorders or police magistrates. Thus, in Quebec City, while the conviction rate for those tried before the recorder remains to be determined, more than 90 per cent of those tried for weapons offences before the judge of the sessions were found guilty, whereas in the handful of cases tried in Quarter Sessions, the conviction rate was below 40 per cent.[78]

Arrests and summary convictions of rioters for vagrancy and general disorderly conduct were even more significant. Although there were almost no riot prosecutions in Montreal in the 1870s and 1880s, a period of significant large-scale collective violence, this did not mean that authorities did not take action against those who participated in collective violence. Take the example of the 1875 anti-vaccination riots in Montreal, which involved hundreds of people stoning city hall and sacking the pharmacy of the public health officer. Two men, Alphonse Dupuis and

Zéphirin Poulin, were arrested by the police, and the next day they were summarily fined $20 by the recorder and jailed for a month. Newspaper coverage stated that they had been charged with having participated in the riot, but the formal charge against them in the prison register was for being loose, idle, and disorderly (the standard charge for disorderly conduct such as prostitution, drunkenness, or vagrancy).[79] A year later, during a minor Orange-Catholic riot in Montreal, the police arrested one of the men who had allegedly instigated the violence (by attacking Orangemen wearing orange lilies); again, he was charged not with rioting but with assault and illegally carrying pistols.[80] A year later, in 1877, during a major and violent dockworkers' strike in the city during which workers pelted police with stones, two of the strikers were arrested for inciting the strike but released by the recorder after a warning, while a third was arrested and fined for assaulting the police.[81] These were rapid, exemplary punishments of rioters without the need to wait for lengthy jury trials. Their very rapidity was meant as an example and a warning to other would-be rioters.

This speed and dispatch comes through clearly in the judicial response to the large-scale anti-vaccination riots in Montreal in 1885, which again included the stoning of city hall. Alphonse Marois and William Bélec were arrested and brought before the police magistrate almost immediately. They were charged not with rioting but with vagrancy, disorder, and breaking windows. As one newspaper noted, 'on aurait pu les poursuivre en vertu de la loi des émeutes mais les procédures auraient été trop longues.' They both pleaded guilty, hoping for clemency, and as a result, according to the newspaper, they were given 'only' four months imprisonment at hard labour – in other words, a sentence similar to that which they would have received if found guilty of misdemeanour rioting. Further, the police magistrate, Calixte-Aimé Dugas, declared that if this example did not suffice, future accused would be sent to the penitentiary. Under exactly which law he acted and threatened is unclear, since both federal and provincial vagrancy statutes provided for not more than two months' imprisonment and, even if breaking windows was considered property damage, it would be subject to speedy trial only by consent. But, from the state's point of view, that was the beauty of summary proceedings before police magistrates and recorders: their powers were so broad that they could very largely convict as they saw fit.[82]

Along with the increasing efficiency of the police, it was the practice of exemplary summary conviction of those involved in collective violence that, quite likely, accounts for the decline in classic riot prosecutions in

Montreal. After all, why bother with a lengthy and expensive jury trial, with little chance of success, when essentially the same punishment could be imposed summarily, the next day, by a magistrate, and serve as an immediate example? And here we return to the question posed at the end of the discussion of overall trends in riot prosecutions in Quebec: Why did such prosecutions decline in Montreal so much sooner than in the district of Quebec? The question should perhaps be turned around: not why did judicial authorities in Montreal stop launching riot prosecutions, but rather, why did classic riot prosecutions continue to be launched before the Quebec City courts, at least until the early 1880s? In the other judicial districts of Quebec, the relative absence of police and readily available summary courts may perhaps explain why the summary course was less rapidly adopted. But Quebec City had essentially the same structure of courts and police as Montreal, and thus the same capacity for police and summary court action. Indeed, there are examples of summary justice being used against rioters in Quebec City later in the period. In August 1887, for example, there was a riot involving a Catholic crowd opposed to a Salvation Army march. Four young men were later arrested, but, rather than being charged with riot, they were accused of assault and disorderly conduct and tried summarily before the recorder. Much to the outrage of the city's Catholic newspapers, the recorder convicted the men, sending the ringleader to jail for two months.[83]

For Quebec City at least, the persistence of riot prosecutions through to the early 1880s may be a question of legal culture more than anything else. Other research currently in progress suggests that the penal justice system in Quebec City became progressively more conservative and inward-looking over the second half of the nineteenth century. Quebec City was slower to adopt innovations than Montreal and its personnel were drawn increasingly from people trained in Quebec City itself. In other words, these were the perfect circumstances for the development of a closed judicial culture and one resistant to change. But without a great deal of further research in records, including the papers of the individuals who were attorneys general and local crown prosecutors, and a detailed reconstruction of the exchanges and relationships between colonial and federal law officers, local prosecutors, magistrates, and clerks of the courts, this remains only a hypothesis.[84]

CONCLUSION

This chapter has shown, for nineteenth-century Quebec, a decline in riot prosecutions at the same time as the rise of the police and the extension of summary justice. Despite continuing legislative interest in riot, prosecutorial practice on the ground meant that, by the end of the nineteenth century, classic riot prosecutions had all but vanished from the Quebec legal landscape. What could be a better metaphor for the formation of the modern state and the expansion of state control through the nineteenth century? After all, was not the nineteenth century the period of the rise of the regulatory state and of police power, with the corresponding decline of exemplary justice, of which large-scale riot trials were emblematic? In other words, was this not the transition from early modern judicial terror to the modern policeman's truncheon?[85]

And yet, as we have seen, though this overall portrait is accurate, things were not so simple. For one thing, classic riot prosecutions were never very successful as instruments of state terror – far less, for example, than the treason trials that followed the 1837–8 rebellions. Despite the shading between public and private interest, many riot prosecutions clearly qualified as state trials, given both the interests of the state in maintaining collective peace and the involvement of state prosecutors. But such formal proceedings often provided the state with only a feeble response to attacks on its authority. For a variety of reasons, from prosecutorial disinterest through procedural tactics to public tolerance, riot prosecutions rarely succeeded, at least in the ideal sense of leading to formal condemnation and punishment. And even when convictions could be secured, the punishments imposed were rarely severe; indeed, they were much less so than those for many of the more common serious crimes such as thefts or serious assaults.

Further, the influence of local legal institutions and cultures also muddied the waters. The striking differences between the fate of riot prosecutions in Montreal and in Quebec City, and the contrast between urban districts and those in rural Quebec, show how perilous it is to generalize about riot prosecutions specifically, and about state formation in general, even at the level of a single, relatively homogeneous society such as Quebec. The precocious decline of riot prosecutions in Montreal did not indicate that state officials were simply throwing up their hands in the face of collective violence. Instead, it demonstrated their adaptability and their willingness to use the new tools put at their disposal, notably the police and summary justice, quite a bit sooner than their counterparts in Quebec City or the more rural districts, where more conservative practices prevailed.

Riot prosecutions did not, of course, disappear completely in Quebec, even in the twentieth century. In the first few decades of the new century, there were still occasional riot trials, mainly in the rural districts but including some in Quebec City, such as the small number of summary trials that followed the 1918 anti-conscription riots and subsequent bloody military repression. But these were occasional events – so much so that riot did not even figure in the standardized and fairly extensive list of offences established for the compilation of judicial statistics by the Quebec government. It was the nineteenth century that was both the heyday of riot prosecutions and the period of their decline as one of the state's primary responses to violent challenges to its authority. From the mid-nineteenth century onward, with new and more efficient means to regulate violence in society, state officials progressively but definitively turned the page on the ancien régime.

NOTES

My thanks to Susan Binnie, Paul Craven, Jim Phillips, Jarrett Rudy, Barry Wright, and Brian Young, as well as the anonymous external evaluators, for their comments on earlier versions of this chapter.

1 In this chapter, for the sake of simplicity, I generally use Quebec to refer to Lower Canada, Canada East, and post-confederation Quebec.
2 There is no overview of violence in post-rebellions nineteenth-century Quebec. For collective violence, see nn.8–10. On interpersonal violence, studies have essentially been limited to domestic violence. See, for example, Kathryn Harvey, 'To Love, Honour and Obey: Wife-Battering in Working-Class Montreal, 1869–79,' *Urban History Review* 19, nos. 1–2 (1990): 128–41, and 'Amazons and Victims: Resisting Wife-Abuse in Working-Class Montreal, 1869–79,' Canadian Historical Association, *Journal* 2 (1991): 131–48; Joane Martel, 'Femme battue et mari batteur: une reconstruction médiatique dans La Presse au XIXe siècle,' *Criminologie* 27, no. 1 (1994): 117–34; and Sylvie Frigon, *L'homicide conjugal au féminin: d'hier à aujourd'hui* (Montreal: Éditions du Remue-ménage 2003).
3 In general, see John Dickinson and Brian Young, *A Short History of Quebec*, 3rd. ed. (Montreal and Kingston: McGill-Queen's University Press 2003), 106–97.
4 See, for example, the articles in Allan Greer and Ian Radforth, eds., *Colonial Leviathan: State Formation in Nineteenth-Century Canada* (Toronto: University of Toronto Press 1992), or again, Jean-Marie Fecteau, *La liberté du pauvre: sur la régulation du crime et de la pauvreté au XIXe siècle québécois* (Montreal: VLB 2004); for the argument concerning periodization, see Donald Fyson, *Magis-*

trates, Police, and People: Everyday Criminal Justice in Quebec and Lower Canada, 1764–1837 (Toronto: Osgoode Society for Canadian Legal History / University of Toronto Press 2006).

5 The literature is, of course, too vast to summarize here. For a historical perspective, see, for example, Wim Blockmans and Jean-Philippe Genet, eds., *The Origins of the Modern State in Europe* (Oxford: Clarendon Press 1995–2000).

6 W.C. Keele, *The Provincial Justice: or, Magistrate's Manual*, 2nd ed. (Toronto: H. and W. Rowsell 1843), 60. Of course, many forms of violence, such as everyday violence between men or violence against women, were in practice tolerated by police and by the criminal justice system, though even these came up regularly before the courts.

7 *CST 2.*

8 'Labour Protest and Organization in Nineteenth-Century Canada, 1820–1890,' *Labour / Le travail* 20 (1987): 61–83; 'The Changing Face of Labour Protest,' in R. Louis Gentilcore, ed., *Historical Atlas of Canada, Volume II: The Land Transformed 1800–1891* (Toronto: University of Toronto Press 1993), 57.

9 On 1849, Elinor Kyte Senior, *British Regulars in Montreal: An Imperial Garrison, 1832–1854* (Montreal and Kingston: McGill-Queen's University Press 1981), 78–108; Gaston Deschênes, ed., *Une capitale éphémère: Montréal et les événements tragiques de 1849* (Montreal: Septentrion 1999). On the Éteignoirs, Wendie Nelson, '"Rage against the Dying of the Light": Interpreting the Guerre des éteignoirs,' *CHR* 81, no. 4 (2000): 551–81. On the Gavazzi riots, Robert Sylvain, *Clerc, garibaldien, prédicant des deux mondes: Alessandro Gavazzi (1809–1889)* (Quebec: Centre pédagogique 1962), 2: 344–423; Senior, *British Regulars in Montreal*, 109–33; Vincent Breton, 'L'émeute Gavazzi: pouvoir et conflit religieux au Québec au milieu du 19e siècle,' MA thesis, Université du Québec à Montréal [UQAM] 2004. On canal workers, Ruth Elisabeth Bleasdale, 'Unskilled Labourers on the Public Works of Canada, 1840–1880,' PhD thesis, University of Western Ontario 1984; and Raymond Boily, *Les Irlandais et le canal de Lachine: La grève de 1843* (Ottawa: Lemeac 1980). On the Quebec dockworkers, Serge Courville, 'À l'heure de l'industrie,' and Robert Grace, 'La Quebec Ship Laborers' Benevolent Society,' in Serge Courville and Robert Gagnon, eds., *Atlas historique du Québec: Québec, ville et capitale* (Sainte-Foy: Presses de l'Université Laval 2001), 207–9; Peter C. Bischoff, 'La société de bienfaisance des journaliers de navires à Québec, 1855 à 1878,' *CHR* 84, no. 3 (2003): 321–53; Herman Van Ommen, 'Labour Riots in Quebec, 1857–1879,' *The Register* 1, nos. 1–2 (1980): 50–67.

10 René Hardy, 'Le charivari dans l'espace québécois,' in Serge Courville and Normand Séguin, eds., *Espace et culture / Space and Culture* (Sainte-Foy: Presses de l'Université Laval 1995), 175–86, and 'Le charivari: divulguer et sanction-

ner la vie privée?' in Manon Brunet and Serge Gagnon, eds., *Discours et pratiques de l'intime* (Quebec: Institut québécois de recherche sur la culture 1993), 47–69; Jean Hamelin and Marcel Hamelin, *Les moeurs électorales dans le Québec: de 1791 à nos jours* (Montreal: Éditions du Jour 1962), chapters 3–4; Jean Pariseau, 'Les mouvements sociaux, la violence et les interventions armées au Québec 1867–1967,' *Revue d'histoire de l'Amérique française* 37, no. 1 (1983): 67–79.

11 Scott W. See, *Riots in New Brunswick: Orange Nativism and Social Violence in the 1840s* (Toronto: University of Toronto Press 1993), 123–32, 139–41, 152–3, 171–5.

12 On the general incapacity or unwillingness of authorities to deal with Orange riots through to mid-century, see also, other than See's work, Gregory S. Kealey, 'The Orange Order in Toronto: Religious Riot and the Working Class,' in Kealey and P. Warrian, eds., *Essays in Canadian Working-Class History* (Toronto: McClelland and Stewart 1976), 13–34, and 'Orangemen and the Corporation: The Politics of Class in Toronto during the Union of the Canadas,' in Kealey, *Workers and Canadian History* (Montreal and Kingston: McGill-Queen's University Press 1995), 163–208; and Peter Way, 'Street Politics: Orangemen, Tories and the 1841 Election Riot in Toronto,' *British Journal of Canadian Studies* 6, no. 2 (1991): 275–303. On England in general, John Stevenson, *Popular Disturbances in England, 1700–1832*, 3rd. ed. (London: Longman 1996). On the Gordon riots and subsequent trials, George Rudé, 'The Gordon Riots: A Study of the Rioters and their Victims,' *Transactions of the Royal Historical Society*, 5th series, 6 (1956): 93–114; Nicholas Rogers, 'The Gordon Riots Revisited,' *Historical Papers*, 1988: 16–34; Uwe Böker, '"The People That the Maddest Times Were Ever Plagued With": English Justice and Fair Trials after the Gordon Riots (1780)?' *Erfurt Electronic Studies in English*, 2003, http://webdoc.sub.gwdg.de/edoc/ia/eese/artic23/boeker/5_2003.html. On the Bristol riot trials, Jeremy Caple, *The Bristol Riots of 1831 and Social Reform in Britain* (Lewiston, N.Y.: E. Mellen Press 1990).

13 The 1892 code came into force in mid-1893; 1892 has been adopted here as the final full year under the pre-code legislation.

14 Charles Tilly, *The Politics of Collective Violence* (Cambridge: Cambridge University Press 2003), 18–19. In the same vein, see J.M. Beattie, *Crime and the Courts in England, 1660–1800* (Princeton, N.J.: Princeton University Press 1986), 76.

15 If there was no actual violence, the offence was characterized either as an illegal assembly or as a rout.

16 For overviews of the English law as it applied to Quebec (hence, as it stood in 1774), Richard Burn, *The Justice of the Peace and Parish Officer*, 14th ed. (London: W. Strahan and M. Woodfall 1776), 4: 69–83; Jacques Crémazie, *Les lois*

criminelles anglaises ... (Quebec: Fréchette 1842), 46–8, 562–5; Keele, *The Provincial Justice*, 535–42. On the English situation, W. Nippel, 'Reading the Riot Act: The Discourse of Law Enforcement in Eighteenth Century England,' *History and Anthropology* 1 (1985): 401–26, and, in more general terms, Stevenson, *Popular Disturbances in England*. On Canadian riot law in general, with corresponding English precedents, Henri-Elzéar Taschereau, *The Criminal Code of the Dominion of Canada, As Amended in 1893* ... (Toronto: Carswell 1893), 52–63. Note that the provisions of the 1715 act providing for compensation by the inhabitants of the hundred did not apply in Quebec since no such entity existed, local administration being based on the Catholic parish. See Crémazie, *Les lois criminelles anglaises*, 564; Donald Fyson, 'La paroisse et l'administration étatique sous le Régime britannique (1764–1840),' in Serge Courville and Normand Séguin, eds., *Atlas historique du Québec: La paroisse* (Sainte-Foy: Presses de l'Université Laval 2001), 25–39.

17 On the 1868 and 1869 laws, discussed below, House of Commons, *Debates*, 1867–8 and 1869. On the RSC, this comes from a reading of the successive versions of the commissioners' reports. On the Criminal Code, Desmond H. Brown, ed., *The Birth of a Criminal Code: The Evolution of Canada's Justice System* (Toronto: University of Toronto Press 1995), 287–94.

18 There had nevertheless been at least one previous attempt at legislative definition, in William Badgley's failed criminal codification bills of 1850/1851, which proposed a rather unwieldy discussion cum definition of the offence: William Badgley, *An Act to Amend and Consolidate the Criminal Laws of this Province* (Toronto: Lovell and Gibson 1850), 42–9.

19 RSC 1887 c.147.

20 Criminal Code 1892 ss.79–80, 82.

21 The colonial Black Acts or Black Laws, 4&5 Vic. c.24–7, are named after their sponsor, Quebec City lawyer Henry Black. They are not to be confused with the earlier English statutes of the same name. On the colonial Black Acts, see Desmond H. Brown, *The Genesis of the Canadian Criminal Code of 1892* (Toronto: Osgoode Society for Canadian Legal History / University of Toronto Press 1989), 56–7. Unless otherwise noted, references to pre-confederation statutes are to those of the Province of Canada, while post-confederation statutes are those of the Dominion of Canada.

22 4&5 Vic. c.26 (1841) s.5.

23 29 Vic. c.13 (1865). Felony rioting had already been made non-capital in England in 1837 by 7 William IV and 1 Vic. c.91.

24 31 Vic. c.70 (1868); 32&33 Vic. c.22 (1869); Susan W.S. Binnie, 'Explorations in the Use of Criminal Law in Canada, 1867–1892,' PhD thesis, Carleton University 1991, 146, 315–17; RSC 1887 c.147; Criminal Code 1892 ss.83, 85–6. In

1868 it appears that the Commons initially intended to reduce the period giv-en for dispersing from one hour to fifteen minutes but were called back into line with English practice by the Senate (House of Commons, *Journals*, 1867–8, 383).

25 Binnie, 'Explorations in the Use of Criminal Law,' 163–374.

26 16 Vic. c.233 (1853), 19&20 Vic. c.5 (1856). This was necessary since the English provisions regarding responsibility of the hundred did not apply in Quebec (see n.16), a fact explicitly evoked during parliamentary debate around the adoption of the acts. Danielle Blais, ed., *Debates of the Legislative Assembly of United Canada Vol. XIII (1856)* (Montreal: Presses de l'École des haute etudes commerciales 1994), 1023–35.

27 18 Vic. c.162 (1855) s.8 ss.1 (Montreal); 20 Vic. c.131 (1857) s.74 (Saint-Hya-cinthe); Mathias Chouinard, *Règlements du Conseil de ville de la cité de Québec* (Quebec: L.-J. Demers, 01), 59–63; J.G.A. Frigon, *Règlements de la cité des Trois-Rivières* ... (Trois-Rivières: Constitutionnel 1871), 105.

28 18 Vic. c.100 (1855) s.27 ss.6, referred to in the index of the published law as 'Riots At Municipal Elections.' The equivalent laws on colonial and provincial elections, such as 6 Vic. c.1 (1842) s.25, referred more generally to breaches of the peace.

29 47 Vic. c.27 (1884) s.1.

30 See, notably, Nancy Kay Parker, 'Reaching a Verdict: The Changing Structure of Decision-Making in the Canadian Criminal Courts, 1867–1905,' PhD thesis, York University 1999, and, more specifically on Quebec, Martin Dufresne, 'La reforme de la justice pénale bas-canadienne: le cas des assauts communs à Québec,' *Revue d'histoire de l'Amérique française* 53, no. 2 (1999): 247–75.

31 On Speedy Trials, Parker, 'Reaching a Verdict,' 81–129, 147–51. In Montreal and Quebec City, the power was conferred on the judges of the sessions of the peace, and elsewhere, on district magistrates and sheriffs.

32 These figures are based on the data collected for Fyson, *Magistrates, Police, and People*.

33 For imprisonment, based on a 20 per cent sample of the Montreal prison population, 1840–99, kindly provided by Jean-Marie Fecteau of the Centre d'histoire des régulations sociales of UQAM; a systematic scan of the Quebec City prison registers, 1840–99; and incomplete prison returns for elsewhere in Quebec, available from 1860 onward within the annual series of judicial statistics published in the *Canada Gazette* and, later, *Gazette de Québec*. For appearances before stipendiary magistrates (called inspectors and superin-tendents of police to 1862 and then judges of the sessions of the peace), based on figures provided in *JLAPC*, 1854–5, appendix AAA (for 1849–54), and on the judicial statistics (from 1860 onward; from the 1870s, the reports from

the Montreal stipendiaries are too incomplete to be of use). Finally, for riot indictments, based again on the judicial statistics, which in this case are relatively complete for Quebec City, incomplete for Montreal in the 1880s and 1890s (with five and six years missing respectively for the Queen's Bench), and also likely incomplete for many of Quebec's other judicial districts; in this case, it is unclear whether officials reported the number of indictments (likely the case for Montreal) or the number of people indicted (almost certainly the case for Quebec City). Note that, from the 1880s, Quarter Sessions in both Quebec City and Montreal appear to have been largely replaced by summary and expeditious jurisdictions. Given the partial nature of many of the records, and especially the judicial statistics, the numbers presented here should be treated only as indicators of general trends; these latter are, however, confirmed by other sources, such as the federal criminal statistics published under varying names for the years 1876 onward (henceforth *Criminal Statistics*), or again, detailed arrest statistics for Montreal, available from 1863 onward in the chief of police's annual report (again, published under varying names). On the use of judicial and criminal statistics and on the nature of the statistical series, see Donald Fyson, 'The Judicial Prosecution of Crime in the Longue Durée: Quebec, 1712–1965,' in Jean-Marie Fecteau and Janice Harvey, eds., *La régulation sociale entre l'acteur et l'institution: Pour une problématique historique de l'interaction* (Quebec: Presses de l'Université du Québec 2005), 85–119.

34 Palmer identifies forty-nine riots in the 1840s, twenty-six in the 1850s, nineteen in the 1860s, and twelve for 1870–5 ('The Changing Face of Labour Protest,' 57).

35 Based largely on the incidents reported in Jean Pariseau, 'Forces armées et maintien de l'ordre au Canada, 1867–1967: un siècle d'aide au pouvoir civil,' PhD thesis, Université Paul Valéry III (Montpellier), 1981; Jean Hamelin et al., *Répertoire des grèves dans la province de Québec au XIXe siècle* (Montreal: HEC 1970); and Robert Rumilly, *Histoire de Montréal*, vol. 3 (Montreal: Fides 1972), along with a few other references, such as Binnie, 'Explorations in the Use of Criminal Law in Canada,' 290–303, 310–11, on the Orange-Catholic riots in Montreal, and Michael Bliss, *Plague: A Story of Smallpox in Montreal* (Toronto: HarperCollins 1991), chapter 8, on the 1885 anti-vaccination riots.

36 Based on the information provided in *Criminal Statistics*, the rate of homicide charges in Montreal was generally about one and a half to two times higher than that in Quebec City (apart from 1876–84, when Quebec City's rate was considerably higher) and three to five times higher than elsewhere in the province.

37 Hamelin et al., *Répertoire des grèves*; Douglas Cruikshank and Gregory Kealey,

'Strikes in Canada, 1891–1950,' in Kealey, ed., *Workers and Canadian History* (Montreal and Kingston: McGill-Queen's University Press 1995), 361, 364.

38 The late 1850s and early 1860s saw a significant reorganization of the colony's judicial system, with the division of Quebec into some twenty judicial districts and a corresponding reduction in the size and population of the districts of Montreal and Quebec. However, given the fact that at least half of those charged with rioting came from the cities themselves, the drop-off in rioting charges, especially in the district of Montreal, is far too sudden to be attributed to this alone and does nothing to explain the later decline in the district of Quebec.

39 Until the judicial reorganization of 1857, the district of Quebec, centred on Quebec City, was composed of most of the eastern half of the colony, with Quebec City accounting for perhaps 10 per cent of its population. Within a few years of the 1857 reorganization, the district was reduced to Quebec City and the surrounding rural counties; from then until the end of the period under consideration here, the city itself comprised a little under 40 per cent of the population.

40 The sources used to gather this information are as follows: BAnQ, Centre d'archives de Québec, E17 (Quebec City prison registers, 1841–99), TP9, S1, SS1, SSS1, and SSS11 (Queen's Bench dossiers, 1841–99, and registers, 1863–99), TL31, S1, SS1, SS11, and SS12 (Clerk of the Peace records, 1841–99, Quarter Sessions registers, 1841–78, and Police Court registers, 1857–99); and trial reports in the *Morning Chronicle* (which had by far the best coverage of such trials). Any unreferenced facts in the text concerning riot trials in Quebec City refer to information gathered in these sources. Queen's Bench dossiers were consulted fully until 1862, and selectively thereafter based on references in the registers and other sources. The only significant judicial series not fully exploited were the registers of the Quebec City Recorder's Court, which had no jurisdiction over riot cases as such; a small sampling of the registers around a few major riots revealed nothing significant, though, as we will see, much as was the case in Montreal, some rioters were arrested for disorderly conduct. The incoming correspondence files of the crown law officers, notably those in BAnQ, Centre d'archives de Québec, E17, might also perhaps provide further information on the conduct of certain prosecutions (the outgoing correspondence registers appear not to have survived); however, an examination of the files for 1868–70 and 1878–80, years during which there were major riots and riot prosecutions in Quebec City, revealed little of interest. Prosecutions have been defined in the broadest sense of formal complaints to the justice system and subsequent actions. The figures thus include a small number of complaints in which riots were complained of but specific individuals not identified.

41 There was another riot case tried before the Quebec King's Bench in 1887, but, since it had been initiated at Trois-Rivières and then transferred to Quebec City on a change of venue, it was excluded from the analysis.

42 For example, Palmer variously adopts the misdemeanour rioting (three people) and the felony rioting (twelve people) definition.

43 *Morning Chronicle*, 25 Jan. 1859.

44 My own ongoing examination of violence between men in nineteenth-century Quebec leads me to question the conclusions of Martin Dufresne regarding the public nature of assault cases ('La reforme de la justice pénale bas-canadienne'), as does the judicial treatment of cases of spousal abuse, examined by Kathryn Harvey ('To Love, Honour and Obey,' 'Amazons and Victims').

45 As suggested by Judy M. Torrance, *Public Violence in Canada, 1867–1982* (Montreal and Kingston: McGill-Queen's University Press 1986), 14–15.

46 In the remaining three cases, I have not yet been able to determine the exact circumstances.

47 On this view of the Irish in general, see Roger Swift, 'Heroes or Villains? The Irish, Crime, and Disorder in Victorian England,' *Albion* 29, no. 3 (1997): 399–421; for Quebec City, see John Hare, Marc Lafrance, and David-Thiery Ruddel, *Histoire de la ville de Québec 1608–1871* (Montreal: Boréal 1987), 195–6, or Gérald Gagnon, *Histoire du Service de police de la ville de Québec* (Sainte-Foy: Publications du Québec 1998), 41–2.

48 For example, the trials of soldiers and officials following the Gavazzi riots: Breton, 'L'émeute Gavazzi,' 53–5. These trials were rare; Pariseau notes only one instance in Quebec in the period 1867–92, the coroner's inquest following the death of rioters during the 1878 construction workers' riot in Quebec City (Pariseau, 'Forces armées et maintien de l'ordre,' APC 36, pp.14–15). They are not covered in this chapter because they form a quite different phenomenon that merits its own treatment, in conjunction with an examination of trials of police and other state violence in general. On police violence in Quebec City, see Louis Turcotte, 'Les conflits entre policiers et citoyens à Québec, 1870–1900,' MA thesis, Université Laval 2007.

49 In 1880 the conviction rate for drunkenness in Quebec was about 70 per cent, while for vagrancy it was almost 85 per cent (*Criminal Statistics*). These statistics may not have included people arrested and then discharged by the police, but, even counting those, conviction rates in Quebec City in the early 1860s were about 50 per cent. On assaults, see Dufresne, 'La reforme de la justice pénale bas-canadienne,' though he gives no specific statistics on conviction rates. Conviction rates for rape have yet to be calculated for post-rebellions Quebec; in the earlier part of the nineteenth century, they were just under 10 per cent, but another 15 per cent were convicted on reduced charges. Sandy

Ramos, "'A Most Detestable Crime'": Gender Identities and Sexual Violence in the District of Montreal, 1803–1843,' Canadian Historical Association, *Journal* 12 (2001): 29.

50 The practice of jury selection in post-rebellions Quebec has yet to be examined in any detail, though see François Rivet, 'La vision de l'ordre en milieu urbain chez les élites locales de Québec et Montréal: le discours des grands jurys, 1820–1860,' MA thesis, UQAM 2004, 22–5. From 1851, under 14&15 Vic. c.89, both grand and trial jurors were to be summoned in Montreal and Quebec City following the *de mediate* principle, with half francophones and half anglophones, and criminal defendants had the right to demand a jury *de mediate*, at least half of which was composed of jurors who spoke their language. In practice, even when the *de mediate* principle was not invoked, grand and trial juries in Quebec City at least tended to be mixed, though often not evenly divided between the two linguistic groups. It is difficult to evaluate the impact of jury composition on case results in Quebec City, especially for grand jury proceedings, which were entirely secret; for the few riot cases decided by trial juries, there were no hung juries and jurors generally came to a rapid decision.

51 On rape cases in Quebec, see Ramos, "'A Most Detestable Crime.'"

52 One person, Edmond Clavet, also found guilty in the 1878 construction worker riots, was never sentenced, since he had been sent to the penitentiary for life on an unrelated conviction for manslaughter.

53 This is based on the judicial sources listed in n.33, and also on Bryan Palmer, *Working-Class Experience: The Rise and Reconstitution of Canadian Labour, 1800–1980* (Toronto and Vancouver: Butterworth 1985), 300–20; Pariseau, 'Forces armées et maintien de l'ordre'; Hamelin et al., *Répertoire des grèves*; Jean-Marie Lebel, *Québec 1608–2008: les chroniques de la capitale* (Quebec: Presses de l'Université Laval 2008); and references gleaned from a wide variety of other primary and secondary sources. Evidently, the identification of major incidents is probably somewhat incomplete, notably for areas outside Quebec City, for which newspaper reporting was more scattered.

54 Kealey, 'Orangemen and the Corporation,' 165–6. The number of cases where there was no judicial action may actually be lower, given the possibility of people being arrested on other charges such as vagrancy or disorderly conduct.

55 *Morning Chronicle*, 25 Jan. 1868.

56 *Morning Chronicle*, 28 Oct. 1880.

57 *Morning Chronicle*, 29 Jan., 31 Jan. 1855, and 23 July 1856.

58 *Morning Chronicle*, 2 Aug. 1855, 8 Feb. 1858, and 10 July 1861.

59 See, *Riots in New Brunswick.*

60 *Morning Chronicle*, 30 Oct. 1873; see also 1 Feb. 1868.

61 Pierre-Georges Roy, *Les avocats de la région de Québec* (Lévis: Le Quotidien 1936), 3–4.

62 Andrée Désilets, 'Marc-Aurèle Plamondon,' *DCB*, 12: 930–1.

63 In later years, it was Mondelet who ordered the Catholic Church to bury the remains of Joseph Guibord, a member of the anti-church Institut canadien, in consecrated ground, setting off a political storm (Elizabeth Nish, 'Charles-Elzéar Mondelet,' *DCB*, 10: 526–8.

64 *Morning Chronicle*, 14 Feb., 15 Feb. 1865.

65 Quebec *Gazette*, 5 June 1852; on the same subject, see also Quebec *Mercury*, 16 Aug. 1864, and *Morning Chronicle*, 30 Aug. 1872.

66 *Morning Chronicle*, 13 Jan., 14 Jan. 1862; Quebec *Mercury*, 16 Jan. 1862.

67 *Morning Chronicle*, 6 July 1860.

68 Daniel Horner, 'A Barbarism of the Worst Kind: Negotiating Gender and Public Space in the Aftermath of Montreal's Gavazzi Riot,' MA thesis, York University 2004.

69 Carol Wilton, '"Lawless Law": Conservative Political Violence in Upper Canada, 1818–41,' *Law and History Review* 13, no. 1 (1995): 111–36.

70 The most complete descriptions of the trial itself are in the Montreal *Gazette* (30 Oct., 31 Oct. 1850) and the Montreal *Herald* (as published in the *Morning Chronicle*, 4 Nov., 6 Nov. 1850). The trial seems to have escaped the notice of many historians of the event, such as Deschênes and Senior. On Drummond, J.I. Little, 'Lewis Thomas Drummond,' *DCB*, 11: 281–3; on Aylwin, André Garon, 'Thomas Cushing Aylwin,' *DCB*, 10: 24; on Rolland, Claude Vachon, 'Jean-Roch Rolland,' *DCB*, 9: 682–3; and F. Murray Greenwood, 'The Montreal Court Martial, 1838–9: Legal and Constitutional Ramifications,' in *CST 2*, 327n.18.

71 On aid to civil power, Pariseau, 'Forces armées et maintien de l'ordre' (though his pre-confederation numbers may be incomplete), and Senior, *British Regulars in Montreal*. On riots and military drill in Montreal, Éric Giroux, 'Les policiers à Montréal: travail et portrait socio-culturel, 1865–1924,' MA thesis, UQAM 1996, 50–1, 98. On the rise of the police, see n.72.

72 On the police in Quebec City and Montreal after the rebellions, see Allan Greer, 'The Birth of the Police in Canada,' in Greer and Radforth, eds., *Colonial Leviathan*, 17–49; Michael McCulloch, 'Most Assuredly Perpetual Motion: Police and Policing in Quebec City, 1838–58,' *Urban History Review* 19, no. 1 (1990): 100–12; Martin Dufresne, 'La police, le droit pénal et le crime dans la première moitié du XIXe siècle: L'exemple de la ville de Québec,' *Revue juridique Thémis* 34, no. 2 (2000): 409–34; Gagnon, *Histoire du Service de police de la ville de Québec*; Jean Turmel, *Premières structures et évolution de la police de Montréal (1796–1909)* (Montreal: Service de la Police de Montréal 1971); Daniel

Dicaire, 'Police et société à Montréal au milieu du XIXe siècle,' MA thesis, UQAM 1999; Giroux, 'Les policiers à Montréal.' On the earlier professionalization of the police, see Fyson, *Magistrates, Police, and People*, chapter 4.

73 This is clear from Turcotte, 'Les conflits entre policiers et citoyens à Québec, 1870–1900,' and was also suggested by the clerk of Montreal's Recorder's Court in that court's annual report for 1898 (8–9).

74 Based on *JLAPC*, 1854–5, appendix AAA; *Le Pays*, 5 Feb. 1856 and 30 Jan. 1858; Montreal chief of police, Annual Reports, 1863–92 (excluding insulting the police); and Montreal Recorder's Court, Annual Reports, 1864–92. Prosecution data missing for 1875; arrest data missing for 1889 and 1891 and possibly incomplete for 1892. It remains to be seen whether, after 1858, substantial numbers of accused were judged summarily before Montreal's police magistrates; in Quebec City, between 1858 and 1891, the judge of the sessions apparently heard only twenty-two such cases, of which fifteen were assaults on bailiffs outside Quebec City.

75 Based largely on complaints and charges in BAnQ, Centre d'archives de Québec, TL31, S1, SS1; *JLAPC*, 1854–5, appendix AAA; police statistics in Archives de la Ville de Québec QC1-01\1370-01 to 04; and *Criminal Statistics*. Arrest statistics for 1872–84 are mostly for the year beginning that year. Prosecution statistics are given only in years where arrest statistics are not known. Some data on prosecutions drawn from Turcotte, 'Les conflits entre policiers et citoyens à Québec, 1870–1900.'

76 22 Vic. c.27 (1858) s.1.

77 On Quebec City, Turcotte, 'Les conflits entre policiers et citoyens à Québec,' 103; on Montreal, *Criminal Statistics* (sample years 1876, 1880, 1885, 1890, and 1895).

78 The relevant laws were 22 Vic. c.26 (1859), whose provisions were reprised in 32&33 Vic. c.20 (1868); 40 Vic. c.30 (1877); and 41 Vic. c.17 (1878). On the latter two, see Binnie, 'Explorations in the Use of Criminal Law,' 163–374.

79 *Minerve*, 11 Aug. 1875; *Morning Chronicle*, 12 Aug. 1875.

80 *Minerve*, 13–15 July 1876.

81 *Minerve*, 22–23 June 1877.

82 *La Patrie*, 29 Sept. 1885; 32&33 Vic. c.28 (1869); *Consolidated Statutes for Lower Canada*, 1861, c.102, s.1020. On the broad powers of police courts and the like and their relative disregard for legal niceties, see, for example, Gene Howard Homel, 'Denison's Law: Criminal Justice and the Police Court in Toronto, 1877–1921,' *Ontario History* 73, no. 3 (1981): 171–86.

83 *Morning Chronicle* and *Journal de Québec*, 25 Aug.-27 Sept. 1887. This was the prelude to a more important public-order case, *R v. Brice*, in which Quebec City's police chief, Léon-Philippe Vohl, launched a private prosecution in the

November 1887 Queen's Bench against the Salvation Army for nuisance and secured a jury conviction despite the judge's directions, only to see the verdict overturned on appeal. *Quebec Law Reports* 15 (1889): 147–64; William David Kenneth Kernaghan, 'Freedom of Religion in the Province of Quebec with Particular Reference to the Jews, Jehovah's Witnesses and Church-State Relations, 1930–1960,' PhD thesis, Duke University 1966, 196–9.

84 On growing judicial conservatism in Quebec City, see Donald Fyson, 'The Legal Profession and Penal Justice in Quebec City, 1856–1965: From Modernity to Anti-Modernity,' in Constance Backhouse and W. Wesley Pue, eds., *The Promise and Perils of Law: Lawyers in Canadian History* (Toronto: Irwin Law 2009), 141–57.

85 The postulate of the rise of the regulatory state and of police power is a classic in Quebec historiography, as elsewhere; for an overview of the position, see Fecteau, *La liberté du pauvre*.

86 The general observation is from a partial examination of criminal statistics for Quebec between 1900 and 1940 and would evidently require a more complete verification in the criminal records themselves. On the anti-conscription riots in Quebec City, see, among others, Jean Provencher, *Québec sous la loi des mesures de guerre 1918* (Trois-Rivières: Boréal Express 1971), and Pariseau, 'Forces armées et maintien de l'ordre,' APC 108.

87 This from the tables concerning the King's Bench and the district prisons in Quebec's annual series of judicial statistics in the 1920s.

5

Maintaining Order on the Pacific Railway: The Peace Preservation Act, 1869–85

SUSAN BINNIE

The newly elected federal government in 1878 faced responsibility for building a national railway across the country to the Pacific Ocean, the largest such project yet undertaken in Canada. The ruling Conservatives under Sir John A. Macdonald, concerned by the possibility of disorder among railway labourers, applied a system of prohibition of alcohol combined with the provision of criminal justice along the line of the railway (see Map 1). The government's approach relied on two statutes: the Peace Preservation Act, 1869[1] to apply prohibition (hereafter the Peace Act); and the Dominion Police Act, 1868[2] to deal with crime (hereafter the Police Act). Together the statutes allowed the federal state to appoint local officials to enforce prohibition and keep order among railway labourers.

The explanation for Ottawa's reliance on these statutes is that the goal of controlling labourers working on construction of a national railway had become a national-security issue for the Conservative government by the late 1870s. The railway was now so economically and politically significant to the state that the possibility of unrest or disorder[3] delaying construction had to be minimized. The government undertook legislative interventions through applications of the two statutes to facilitate the public policing of both private and publicly built sections of the railway.

The following account describes the context for the situation by discussing the construction of a national railway, the form and history of the two acts, and then the patterns of application of the statutes in the period. These considerations provide the background for three case studies of enforcement of prohibition analysed later in the chapter. The thesis is that the enforcement augured a shift in the focus of governments beyond traditional security matters and towards collective disorder relating to economic activity.

The federal Peace Act, 1869 could be used to apply prohibition 'to any place or places in Canada' where public works were in progress (s.1), but its use between 1878 and 1885 was restricted to the provision of prohibition along the line of construction of the Pacific Railway. No other public or private works received the same treatment but none held such significance for the government. Exceptionally, applications of the act relied on proclamation by cabinet order-in-council, with the result that liquor could be prohibited by state fiat. This 'discretionary exercise of executive measures' had previously characterized the imposition of martial law in British North America, an approach resorted to by common law jurisdictions in situations of serious threats to their security.[4] Reliance on proclamations of prohibition in railway-construction areas after 1869 therefore meant the same arbitrariness – absence of parliamentary involvement or opportunity for review by the courts – typical of proclamations of martial law. Thus, the method incorporated in the Peace Act not only echoed past emergency measures but foreshadowed federal security-related delegations of executive power, notably the War Measures Act.[5]

The Conservative government's use of the Peace Act and the Police Act along the Pacific Railway, beginning in 1878, directly reflected the importance of the project from the perspective of the state. With the railway seen as essential to the security and development of the Dominion, the two statutes together were expected to suppress the supply of liquor to labourers and help assure peaceful and efficient progress on construction of the line. The use of a power to apply prohibition in arbitrary fashion, exercised frequently by Macdonald's cabinet after 1878, suggests that politicians' notions of state security were shifting over the period of the late nineteenth century. Governments had begun to move beyond ideas about security that were bound up in events such as insurrection or invasion. Newer threats were perceived, in particular, issues related to economic security and public order. The government accordingly adopted the policy of reacting to the potential for disorder among railway 'navvies'[6] by proclaiming prohibition *in advance of* disorder. Applications of the two statutes became routine, a development that constitutes part of the evidence of a shift in the government's focus.

In conjunction with the policy of regular reliance on executive law-making powers to proclaim prohibition, the cabinet posted commissioners along the railway to enforce the law in the belief that this would assist companies and entrepreneurs in the management of labour. The officials

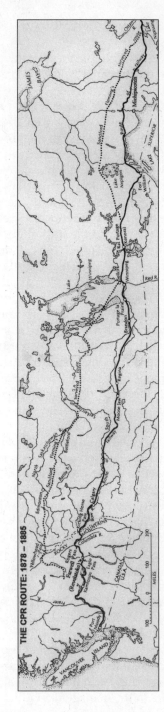

The CPR route, 1878–85. Map originally drawn by Courtney C. Bond. Excerpted from *The Last Spike: The Great Railway 1881–1885* by Pierre Berton. Copyright 1971 by Pierre Enterprises Ltd., 16–17. Reprinted by permission of Doubleday Canada.

were given the tasks of applying prohibition as well as the broader criminal law and of trying those accused of criminal offences. The system of federal appointments and the regimes of criminal justice resulting from proclamations have not been discussed at any length in Canadian scholarship, suggesting that little is known about the scale or consequences of the central state's actions in this regard.[7]

STATE SECURITY, THE PACIFIC RAILWAY, AND THE PEACE PRESERVATION ACT

Immediately after 1867, when Macdonald's Conservative Party formed a majority government, the newly established Dominion faced at least three broad and interrelated challenges: how to establish Canada as a national entity within a setting of continued colonial dependence; how to conduct relations with its powerful neighbour to the south; and how to maintain and extend the integrity of the new country's physical territory.[8] In practical terms, the predominant security problems faced by the federal government in the early years were threats of Fenian invasions from the United States, the possibility of Fenian-inspired insurrections within the country, and, in light of its powerful neighbour's ambitions, political uncertainty over control of the territories to the west.[9] As the chapters by David Wilson and by Andrew Parnaby and Gregory Kealey with Kirk Niergarth describe, intelligence operations relating to state security were still in their infancy. Prime Minister Macdonald continued to rely on a small security service of his own creation and to keep a close watch through his agents on issues such as threats of Fenian attacks.

By the time of confederation, many Canadians including Macdonald already considered a transnational railway essential to Canadian geopolitical and economic interests.[10] It would open up the North-West and confirm Canadian interests vis-à-vis the United States. The federal government's support for a national railway project was reinforced in 1873 as a result of a commitment made to British Columbia to build a line within ten years.[11] The Canadian state's growing reliance on the Peace Act and on federal policing for the railway must be seen in light of the 1873 commitment and the railway's significance for fundamental policy issues, including a protectionist 'National Policy' that Macdonald and his party eventually implemented in the late 1870s.[12]

When the government began to apply both statutes to construction of the Pacific line routinely in 1878, the threat of Fenianism had faded and the government's political concerns related more to the security and settlement of the west. The Pacific Railway was relevant not only to the National Policy, with its goals of increasing internal trade and, as Macdonald argued, eliminating Canadian dependence on U.S. railroads,[13] but also to the essential work (from the government's perspective) of populating the west through settling easterners and immigrants on the prairies. The movement of settlers to the Canadian prairies was to have the effect of increasing pressure on an already fragile political and economic situation. With the survival of the Métis and Native peoples threatened by the decline of the buffalo herds, the new intrusions worsened tensions between settlers and Aboriginal and Métis peoples.[14] The result was the 1885 crisis, discussed in this volume by Bob Beal and Barry Wright, J.M. Bumsted, and Bill Waiser.

A strong, pro-railway climate among Conservative politicians encouraged additional government funding for the railway, built after 1880 under the aegis of the Canadian Pacific Company (hereafter CPR).[15] In that decade, as costs of construction soared, the federal government's political support for the railway slowly transformed into a massive financial commitment, resulting in a symbiotic relationship between the government and the CPR. The level of financial support tied Tory political fortunes to the success of the railway project.[16] However, contributions towards the project could also be made in less direct ways. Proclamations of federal prohibition legislation to assist in control of railway labour, coupled with appointments of federal police commissioners to enforce criminal law on behalf of railway contractors, was one means at the government's disposal. As this chapter shows, Macdonald's ministers viewed the application of such a harsh and discriminatory prohibition statute as a suitable method for controlling labour and assisting the progress of construction. Macdonald remained deeply involved in matters relating to the construction of the Pacific Railway and he and members of his cabinet were well informed of developments along the line, including issues relating to liquor prohibition and to real and apprehended disorder among navvies.[17] Prohibition was regarded as useful because of the exceptionally large numbers of workers constructing the Pacific Railway and the apprehensions this raised over the likelihood of disorder.[18]

Problems with construction were unacceptable both to the government in Ottawa and to the privately owned CPR and its contractors, and, by the early 1880s, the prospect of labour disorder began to raise the spectre of delay and greater costs. The company, already dependent on its bankers and on state subsidies and now facing bankruptcy, could not afford incidents that might slow the progress of the project. For the government, the exercise of a criminal law power to proclaim prohibition demonstrated the state's commitment to building a transnational railway and its commitment to securing optimum conditions for contractors and for the CPR. Cabinet ministers and members of Parliament, contractors, local CPR managers, and officials of the company concurred in seeing application of prohibition legislation as a necessary measure along the Pacific line. Almost no support was voiced for permitting railway labourers the right to drink alcohol outside working hours.[19]

THE PEACE PRESERVATION ACT AND THE DOMINION POLICE ACT

The Peace Act, 1869 had been enacted as a minor piece of criminal legislation with specific application to public works. It contained two prohibitions: one on the sale or possession of alcohol on or near a public works; and the other on possession or carrying of weapons (see Supporting Documents).[20] 'Public works' were not defined and the act referred in several places to a 'Commissioner' without saying how such officials would be appointed. Within six years, the federal government amended the legislation twice. An 1870 amendment provided for prohibition *either* of alcohol *or* of weapons. (The weapons sections were never proclaimed after this date.) And the act was significantly broadened in 1875 to include 'private works.' The government could proclaim prohibition after this date on any public, provincial, municipal, or *private* work in Canada, except within cities.[21] So-called loopholes in the legislation were closed a decade later, giving a stronger hand to law-enforcement officials. An amending act of 1885 began innocuously by defining previously undefined terms in the Peace Act, including 'intoxicating liquor' and 'public work,' and then went on to say – presumably in an effort to silence provinces now opposing use of the statute – that 'all courts and magistrates shall take judicial notice of every such proclamation.' The amendment contained stringent provisions, including ones establishing the responsibility of employers for agents who sold alcohol illegally, providing for search warrants for searching boats, building, conveyances, and even dwelling houses, and automatic conviction for 'an owner, keeper or person in possession.'[22] In this form the Peace Act was subsequently included in the first Canadian Criminal Code of 1892 and applied to railway construction by federal governments into the twentieth century until repealed in 1950.[23]

The act had almost certainly been accepted by federal legislators in 1869 for use as a quasi-emergency measure, in keeping with the earlier use of two antecedent, pre-confederation statutes.[24] The assumption underlying the new legislation was that of a direct linkage between workers on public-works sites and serious disorder and unrest leading to riot, fighting, and possible deaths. The reasoning was grounded in recognition of events in Upper and Lower Canada when large-scale construction of canals was undertaken by immigrant Irish labourers.[25] Unrest and riots had been common occurrences during the 1830s and 1840s, with labourers resorting to violent methods to resist authority or to express complaints about adverse conditions. An initial Province of Canada act of 1845 had attempted to control rioting on canal construction by proclamations forbidding the carrying of weapons in stated areas; it also provided for a 'small mounted police force' to assist local magistrates.[26] A second statute of 1851 automatically prohibited the sale of liquor within three miles of any public work under construction[27] but provided no special enforcement measures.

The 1869 federal statute built directly on these Province of Canada statutes and on the experiences of 'troubles' on public works from the 1830s through the 1850s. The post-confederation legislation, however, provided a ban not only on the sale of alcohol but on its possession. In addition, the government now relied on a permanent and potentially cheaper system of resident commissioners to enforce prohibition for areas specified under a proclamation, rather than on a mounted police force.[28] The new legislation could be a useful tool in the event of problems of serious disorder among large workforces of labourers. The then current project of the Intercolonial Railway made the legislation relevant.[29]

But government policy concerning application of the statute changed within a decade. After the re-election of a Conservative government in 1878, proclamations of prohibition became a routine measure along sections of the Pacific Railway. In the new approach the statute was used in a pre-emptive fashion in order to protect the country's major railway construction project against labour disturbances. Prohibition was proclaimed regularly and commissioners appointed along lengthy sections of the railway whether or not serious labour disturbances had occurred. The Peace Act was declared in effect thirteen times between 1878 and 1885 from Ontario to British Columbia, and prohibition was in place at different times along most of the length of the railway across these two provinces and across Manitoba.[30] The two statutes were now employed to provide a technique for securing order on an economic project favoured and largely financed by the state.

Most commissioners of the peace, about twenty-two individuals, received appointments under both statutes during the period between 1878 and 1885. The use of dual appointments greatly strengthened the powers of federally appointed peace commissioners. They were able to act as local magistrates in Ontario, Manitoba, and British Columbia with 'all the powers and authority, rights and privileges by law appertaining to Police Magistrates of Cities, in the same Province,' so enforcing the criminal laws and other laws of the Dominion (s.4). Orders-in-council usually stated that police commissioners appointed might swear in a limited number of constables (s.2). The result was a series of regimes – consisting of a federal commissioner appointed under both acts and a few constables – along the Pacific Railway line, with all personnel under the direct control of federal ministers and civil servants in the departments of justice and of railways and canals in Ottawa.[31]

As stated, the Peace Act had the special feature of application by federal order-in-council which singled it out from typical criminal laws. Only one other criminal law statute enacted between 1867 and 1892 relied on an identical approach, namely, the Blake Act of 1878. This had been introduced by the Liberal[32] government of Alexander Mackenzie in response to fears of growing sectarian violence and urban disorder in the city of Montreal.[33] But the Blake Act – which prohibited the carrying of any of a large range of weapons without a licence – was proclaimed in force only three times, always for cities,[34] before a Conservative government allowed it to lapse in 1884.[35] In the examples of the Blake and the Peace acts, the standard federal approach of enactment of a general criminal law prohibition applicable throughout a jurisdiction was abandoned in favour of federal proclamations for local areas. The approach was taken directly from earlier Province of Canada legislation, since the 1845 act prohibiting weapons in the vicinity of public works had relied on executive proclamation. That in turn had drawn on the method used to impose martial law during the rebellion period,[36] which in turn seems likely to have drawn on the methods used by the British in suppressing the United Irishmen in Ireland in the last decade of the eighteenth century.[37] The approach is in itself suggestive of the status accorded by governments to the Peace Act and the Blake Act as security measures. The statutes shared the method of application of martial law by federal proclamation but lacked the requirement of exceptional wartime conditions. Nonetheless, the object underlying both statutes was to justify federal intervention into the local augmentation of the administration of justice including the appointment of extraordinary commissioners.[38]

The Peace Act as well as the Blake Act shared a second feature: they were proclaimed in restricted areas where the federal government *anticipated* violence. In effect, they replaced customary reliance on federal, provincial, or local authorities to respond to serious disorder or riot after the fact by bringing in armed force.[39] The federal government, in enacting the Peace Act, had recognized that the usual response to riot – reaction after the fact – could not be relied on in the inaccessible settings of new and remote public works. Admittedly, the enactment of the Blake Act was striking, given the reluctance of the federal government to intervene in most instances of urban violence, for example, during local strikes on street railways (as discussed in Eric Tucker's chapter). Even Montreal MPs who had pressed for legislation saw the act as stringent; one supporter and well-known lawyer, Bernard Devlin, considered Blake's bill as extreme as the suspension of habeas corpus.[40] The Conservatives had reintroduced the approach of relying on federal proclamations of local criminal law in 1869, but the succeeding Liberal government – in enacting the Blake Act – showed that it was not necessarily averse to putting criminal legislation into effect locally by executive decree if its perception was that situations warranted pre-emptive federal involvement.[41]

In summary, the Peace and Police acts as applied along the Pacific Railway represented a concern with state security in relation to social order, to be dealt with through direct and 'anticipatory' interventions by the federal state. Use of the Peace Act on public works sites after 1878 in conjunction with the Police Act helps to demonstrate (as does the Blake Act) the beginnings of a newer and more emphatically pre-emptive approach to perceived serious threats to the economic and social order.

THE STATUTES AS CRIMINAL LAW

The constitutional validity of the Peace Act appears not to have been questioned; there were no parliamentary debates on the issue of federal jurisdiction. But legislators were fully occupied in 1868 and 1869, dealing with a vast amount of legislation – including numerous criminal law bills – in efforts to unify the law of the four provinces forming the federation. The draft bill on its face was valid criminal law and provided for enforcement in an apparent re-enactment of earlier Province of Canada legislation. In effect, part of the act referred to the carrying of weapons by labourers at public works, and, although never used after 1875, those sections would have given some assurance to legislators that the act fell directly under the umbrella of the criminal law power of the federal Parliament. Equally, no questions were raised later about the right of Ontario and Quebec to continue pre-confederation Province of Canada legislation in the same field.[42]

In contrast, the Police Act was criticized by Liberal MP Edward Blake at the time of its introduction in 1868. In Blake's view as a leading constitutional lawyer, the act appeared to be a direct foray by the federal government into the local administration of justice.[43] Typically, Blake was more concerned about jurisdictional issues than his fellow MPs. Most in all likelihood would have assumed that a national police would be supported by the 'peace, order and good government' provisions of the British North America Act, 1867, s.91 (hereafter BNA Act). But Blake immediately introduced an amendment declaring the establishment of the police force to be beyond 'the competence of this Legislature,' belonging rather 'to the Legislature of the different Provinces.' His argument continued: 'Within the past few days he believed this House had passed several Acts, provisions of which were in violation of the Constitution. This might occasionally happen in spite of every precaution, but he considered they ought to avoid needlessly multiplying in such cases.'[44] Blake's amendment appeared to receive little support, suggesting that few MPs shared his concerns.[45]

Policing in common law countries had traditionally been a local responsibility.[46] At the time of confederation, policing appeared to fall directly under provincial powers for the administration of justice under the BNA Act, s.92(14). But the passage by the federal government of the Dominion Police Act, 1868 contradicted that assumption by permitting federal appointments of 'Commissioners of Police' anywhere in the country. The Police Act had been introduced partly as a legislative effort to rationalize several disparate police forces falling under federal control.[47] Under the rubric of the 'Dominion Police,' the government intended to bring together three existing forces, one responsible for the defence of the Parliament Buildings in Ottawa, another being the secret service run by Gilbert McMicken and William Ermatinger for John A. Macdonald,[48] and the third charged with the policing of the ports in Toronto and Montreal. Thus, the bill appeared designed to deal with extraordinary situations outside the framework of usual policing activities. The timing of its introduction, in May 1868, responded to public fears of Fenian invasions and political assassination. As described by Blake Brown in this volume, Fenian invasions in 1866 were followed by political trials in 1867 and 1868. The murder of Macdonald's cabinet minister, D'Arcy McGee, in April 1868 (described by David Wilson), assumed to be a Fenian crime, stoked fears of further assassinations. Despite Edward Blake's criticism of the federal assumption of policing powers, the Dominion bill received rapid passage in the month following McGee's death.[49]

The Police Act cannot, however, be seen only as an urgent reaction to political circumstances. It also reflected broader developments in policing, the early- to mid-nineteenth-century rationalization and professionalization of voluntary, unpaid, and untrained law-enforcement officials previously relied on in common law jurisdictions. In England, reform efforts had begun to achieve success in the 1820s.[50] In Canada they came later and, by confederation, the era of undisciplined, even corrupt, municipal police typical of the first half of the century was nearing its end.[51] Leading politicians in the Province of Canada in the 1850s had favoured improvements,[52] and Macdonald and other Canada West politicians such as Allan McNab and Sandfield Macdonald had continued to press for professional provincial policing. While the formation of the Dominion Police was in part an elaboration of Macdonald's earlier vision of professional policing, it also responded to his perception of the new federation's need for an elementary security service. In light of the continuing threats of Fenian invasions into Canada, Macdonald's desire to place his personal secret service on a firmer basis is not surprising.

By the time commissioners of the peace under the Peace Act were first appointed in 1878, the relevance of the Police Act to the railways must have been obvious to the federal government. Dominion police could be used to provide railway policing in conjunction with working as prohibition commissioners, since the legislation allowed for federal policing appointments anywhere in the country. There were advantages of cost and efficiency for the government in combining peace and policing appointments along the railway under the direction of the same federal politicians and bureaucrats. And, although use of the Police Act to appoint Dominion commissioners of police to specific locations within provinces might have been argued to overreach the federal criminal law power, this was not a concern in the period. The provinces could have claimed responsibility for policing under their exclusive powers under the BNA Act. But those affected, namely Ontario, Manitoba, and British Columbia, were unlikely in the late 1870s to have magistrates and police available to police remote areas of railway construction. There appear to have been no direct complaints from provinces, perhaps because the federal government either paid the costs of administering justice along proclaimed sections of railway lines or charged the costs to the subsidy for the Pacific Railway. Attacks on the federal policy did not begin until the 1880s, when the increasing strength of the provinces, their growing networks of local officials, and deteriorating relations with the federal state had already raised jurisdictional issues in other areas.

When more draconian Peace Act measures were debated and passed, in the spring and summer of 1885, the Senate and the Commons again failed to consider the constitutional status of the legislation. Adolphe Caron, minister of militia, who introduced the bill in the Commons at second reading, stated: 'This legislation, I take it, is much stricter than the criminal law, but we should go as far as possible, of course with due respect to the liberty of the subject, in our efforts to protect these public works against the evil effects resulting from the sale of intoxicants to the men who work upon them.'[53] Despite prolonged discussion of 'the rights of the subject' and mention of 'oppression,' opposition members refrained from asking which subsections of the BNA Act could be relied on to justify imposition of prohibition or federal appointments of agents to enforce criminal law within a province. Instead, they criticized a provision in the bill for holding a principal guilty when a servant committed an offence, and attacked the search provisions. The resulting debate included interventions by Macdonald, Blake, and David Mills but produced no changes to the bill.[54]

While it is understandable that constitutional questions did not arise in 1869, it is more puzzling that they were not raised in 1885. By then the province of Ontario under Premier Oliver Mowat had come into conflict with the federal government over the Peace Act and British Columbia was beginning to voice complaints.[55] It is possible that the timing of the 1885 debate on the amendment, a month after the end of the Riel rebellion in the west,[56] as well as increasing evidence of the failure of the government's National Policy, distracted parliamentarians from the constitutional status of the legislation. The suppression of the Riel rebellion shortly before second reading of the bill, and the clear evidence it presented of dissatisfaction in the west, may have discouraged questioning of federal constitutional powers in relation to railway building.[57]

More fundamentally, what the silence on constitutional questions in Parliament suggests is that parliamentarians of both parties were in broad agreement over the purposes and the effects of the Peace Act. The need for a response to potential disorder among railway labourers was sufficiently strong to allow passage of 'strict' amendments to the existing act in 1885. And prevention of disorder through prohibition was to remain classified under 'criminal law.' While the silence in parliamentary debate on the policy of reliance on federal officials to enforce criminal law within provinces is surprising from a modern perspective, the absence of constitutional discussion suggests that Macdonald, Blake, Mills, and many others saw the Peace Act (like the War Measures Act of the following century) as essential legislation in the interests of national security.

Later that year, over fifteen years after its passage, the constitutionality of the Peace Act was questioned publicly by none other than Sir Matthew Baillie Begbie, chief justice of British Columbia. He pointed out that Dominion appointees under the statute were not 'provincial officers,' their courts were not 'provincial courts,' and these situations were not consistent with arrangements under the BNA Act for the appointment of provincial officials (under s.92[4]) or for the administration of justice by the provinces (under s.92[14]).[58] He also suggested that the act was defective because it made no allowance for 'an express method of creation of a commissioner.'[59] However, Begbie was on weak ground, for he admitted that some of these considerations had already been rejected by the Supreme Court of Canada in a related case, *R. v. Thresher*.[60] His comments appear to have attracted little attention.[61]

PROCLAMATIONS OF THE STATUTES BY ORDER-IN-COUNCIL

Analyses of the Orders-in-Council

The processes of enforcement of the Peace Act – like other minor criminal legislation – cannot necessarily be assessed directly. Local records, given the settings of railway construction, were not usually preserved. Central government records are incomplete, scattered across different departments, but one complete source survives in the records of orders-in-council, the cabinet decisions required to implement the statute. Privy Council records provide details not only of proclamations under the Peace Act but of appointments under this act and the Police Act, together with lesser matters relating to both statutes. One limitation of this material is that the view of the operation of the prohibition system is one-sided; the perspective is that of civil servants and their political superiors. But detailed information exists in about eighty recorded instances of gazetted and proposed orders associated with justice on public works and the contents provide an outline of the structure of criminal justice created by the federal government for the railway.

Three approaches are used here to examine relevant orders for the period 1869 to 1885: their content is analysed to establish the range and frequency of types of directions included within them; the frequency of their use is investigated and linked to the political party in power in Ottawa; and, lastly, the geographical extent of regimes of prohibition is assessed in relation to the route of railway construction. The finding is, as stated, that the federal government issued proclamations of prohibition under the Peace Act seventeen times between 1869 and 1885. Fourteen concerned railways. Three were early post-confederation orders for the government project of a 'Red River Road' from Thunder Bay to the Red

River.[62] Thirteen of the fourteen orders for railways were proclamations for the Pacific Railway after the Conservative government regained office in 1878. The exception was an early order for the government-funded Intercolonial Railway.[63]

As the eighty proclaimed or draft orders-in-council varied greatly in terms of their subject matter, each order is broken down by content and the content items are divided into two groups. The first, termed 'major' content, includes directives proclaiming prohibition under the Peace Act or appointing commissioners under the Peace Act or the Police Act.[64] The second group includes 'minor' content such as the salaries or travel expenses of commissioners and other administrative matters.[65] Table 1 shows the classification of content and clarifies that proclamations of the statute constitute about 18 per cent of the total content of these orders.[66] Appointments of commissioners form a larger proportion – about 37 per cent – since officials were appointed under both statutes for each proclamation in force and appointees were likely to be transferred or replaced, requiring new orders-in-council. The breakdown in Table 1 establishes that processes for overseeing appointees and the system of justice on public works did not operate smoothly. Directives within orders were repeated and an order was often followed by a second clarifying the original.[67]

Table 1: Orders-in-councils and drafts, 1869–85

Content	No. of orders with this content[68]
Major proclamations and appointments or attempted proclamations	
Proclamation under Peace Act	17
Appointment of commissioner under Peace Act	22
Appointment of commissioner under Police Act	22
Minor proclamations	
Withdrawal or cancellation of Peace Act proclamations	7
Correction, amendment, error in issuing proclamations	5
Refusal to proclaim, dormant files. Drafts	7
Petition or application relating to Peace Act	4
Other appointments, transfer, withdrawal of appointments, retirement	10
Extension of commissioner's jurisdiction	2
Firing of commissioner	1
Salaries of commissioners, travel expenses, other payments	11
Authority to commissioners to appoint constables	7
Arrangements for jail, courtroom, etc	4
Contractors' costs for administration of justice	1

It seems remarkable that a session of the Privy Council should review all draft orders-in-council, however minor in content, before giving approval, but this appears to have been the case since a few proposed orders-in-council were rejected in cabinet. Further, on the assumption that signatories at least glanced at an order-in-council, the range of official signatures on different orders clarifies that most senior ministers sitting in council were aware of the workings of the Peace Act.[69]

Turning to the political party in power, Conservative and Liberal governments can be contrasted with respect to the number of orders-in-council proclaimed during their terms (see Table 2). When the years from 1869 to 1885 are divided into three periods, corresponding to Conservative and Liberal governments, the frequency of orders-in-council by political party demonstrates marked differences in relation to use of Dominion prohibition and police powers for transportation projects.

Table 2: Orders-in-council by political party in power, 1869–85[70]

| | | | Orders-in-council | |
Date	Political party in power	Recipients of major orders-in-council	Major	Minor
1869 1873	Conservatives	Government road and one government railway line	4	2
1873 1878	Liberals		0	1
1878 1885	Conservatives	Government and private construction of Pacific Railway	36	36

Macdonald's first government, from 1867 to 1873, issued proclamations of prohibition under the Peace Act four times but appointed no commissioners. Mackenzie's Liberal government of 1873 to 1878 never issued a proclamation. After Macdonald's return to power, proclamations were issued regularly, in all instances relating to the Pacific Railway and including appointments of officials. The Conservatives proclaimed prohibition on thirteen occasions in fewer than eight years,[71] and the cabinet made regular appointments of commissioners along the line of the railway in Ontario, Manitoba, and British Columbia. The total length of proclaimed railway line under the act amounted to about fifteen hundred miles.[72] Reliance on the legislation was part of Macdonald's policy towards the Pacific Railway between 1878 and 1880, even before the CPR took on the task of completing the railway.[73]

Why did the Liberal Party not use the Peace Act during its administration from 1873 to 1878? Alexander Mackenzie, as a deeply committed minister of public works as well as prime minister, was familiar with the statute and in favour of it.[74] The Liberal government's approach was probably a reflection in part of a downturn in railway construction in the 1870s and in part of Mackenzie's reluctance to expend yet more public funds on transportation infrastructure.[75] It is possible that the pause in private railway construction in the 1870s meant that fewer requests for proclamations were received.[76] However, some railway contractors were at work for the government in the period of Liberal government, both on the Intercolonial Railway and on the early stages of the Pacific Railway. Two requests from contractors for proclamations under the statute, one for the Pembina line during the first phase of the Pacific Railway and the other for a private works, were not acted upon. A third request, also from a contractor building the Pacific line, was in the process of being forwarded to the Privy Council by the Department of Justice in 1878 when the Liberal government was defeated.[77]

The third analysis establishes that prohibition was applied, pursuant to the Peace Act, to all sections of the Pacific Railway under construction in Ontario and British Columbia and to part of the line in Manitoba at some period between 1878 and 1885.[78] When the geographical limits of these proclamations are considered, together with the situation of permanent prohibition in the North-West Territories, the result is an almost complete regime of prohibition along the Pacific line during periods of construction, as set out in Table 3. Thus, the Canadian government had adopted a broad and unambiguous approach to railway construction; there was no suggestion of applying the Peace Act to restricted settings where exceptionally difficult labour situations existed. Instead, the administration imposed a blanket prohibition on liquor wherever construction occurred along the main line of the railway.

Appointments of Officials

Between 1878 and 1885, approximately twelve positions for commissioners of the peace and commissioners of police were filled for different periods of construction. Twenty-two different appointees held these posts owing to turnover when commissioners resigned or retired and were replaced by new appointees or when they were transferred to different locations. Thus Captain J.W. Brereton began work as a commissioner of the peace and of police at Cross Lake, Ontario (east of Kenora), in 1878

Table 3: Orders-in-council and sections of railway proclaimed, with distances and appointees, 1878–84*

Year o-in-c	Extent	Approximate Distance**	Number of appointees***
1878 #1066	Selkirk, Manitoba, east to Rat Portage (Kenora, Ontario)	130	1
1879 #1212	Rat Portage, Keewatin, east to Sunshine Creek, Ontario (seventy miles northwest of Thunder Bay)	250	2
1882 #139	Callendar, Ontario, west to Algoma Mills (north shore, Lake Huron) – the Algoma Branch line	175	
1882 #906	Port Moody to Savona's Ferry, British Columbia	210	1
1882 #2126	Prince Arthur's Landing east to River Pic (along North Shore of Lake Superior)	150	1
1883 2480	River Pic east to near Michipicoten (along north shore of Lake Superior)	110	1
1884 #1711	Sudbury to River Pic, including Algoma Branch	230	1
1884 #1174 #1980	Michipicoten Landing to line of CPR railway	50	1
1884 #985 #1233	From B.C. boundary westward, to near Craigellochie	150	3 NWMP
Total		1,455 miles	12

Notes:
   *This table covers the period of construction of the Pacific Railway and, within that period, only those proclamations identifying new sections of the railway for prohibition, with the result that the number of proclamations under the Peace Act is fewer than in the other two tables in the chapter.
   **Distances, based on current maps (or estimates for places no longer marked), are approximate.
   ***The figures for 'number of appointees' refer to the number of positions to which appointments were customarily made. The total number of appointees was much higher since many appointees stayed only for one or two construction seasons.

but was transferred to the interior of British Columbia in 1881. Only one commissioner was dismissed. The ironically named Frederick Bent, appointed in 1879, was fired for corruption in 1880, the complaint being that 'Mr Bent has been guilty himself of grave offences against the very laws which he was appointed to support,' an indirect way of stating that the commissioner had gone into the liquor trade.[79]

Some appointees had legal training but were in all probability selected as much for their political connections as their legal qualifications.[80] Others were railway employees, and a few were North-West Mounted Police (NWMP), the latter appointed in British Columbia where Mounties were actively policing sections of the railway by the mid-1880s.[81] All appointees shared demanding working conditions characterized by isolation, difficult law-enforcement duties, responsibility for vast geographical areas, limited assistance, and requirements for reporting to Ottawa. Commissioners were directed to make references to Ottawa over minor matters, financial details in particular. The policy led to difficult situations. Government processes for administering the statutes were cumbersome and slow and commissioners were frequently out of contact with their superiors for extended periods of time. Decisions on detailed aspects of commissioners' activities might ultimately be referred to the ministers responsible and this could leave conscientious appointees waiting many weeks for answers to questions. The overall effectiveness of the policy of imposing prohibition relied largely on the initiative shown by appointees in the field. While their postings varied in terms of difficulty, their work ethos and aptitude for the task helped to settle how vigorously the government's prohibition policy would be enforced in any location.

Granting Processes

Decisions to issue orders-in-council appear to have been largely a result of political requests during the decades of the 1870s and 1880s. Applications from contractors and the timing of proclamations clarify that most occurred after demands were made by contractors building the railway.[82] Departmental mechanisms were in place within the federal government for processing applications for proclamations of prohibition, but political processes appear to have trumped administrative systems in terms of the issuance of orders-in-council. The records of applications suggest that the cabinet relied on requests before proclaiming the statute and that requests were normally granted – at least under Conservative governments – if they related directly to the main line of the Pacific Railway and involved relatively remote areas of construction. Refusals tended to occur when part of the line was constructed through inhabited areas of the country or when lines were feeder or secondary ones and not part of the main route.[83]

The process of petitioning in relation to the Peace Act was fairly standard. The applicant addressed a formal letter, either through an influential intermediary or directly to a minister,[84] with a complaint about labourers and liquor. The letter included claims about the impact of liquor-related problems on the progress of the public work and the absence of established society in the area of construction. The first proclamation demonstrated the elements required and, as the request was brought to cabinet by Macdonald as minister of justice in 1869, may have been drafted under his direction. In relation to the Red River Road, Macdonald reported – based on a complaint from Simon J. Dawson,[85] the engineer officially supervising construction of the road – that 'some 200 men are now employed under Superintendent Dawson in the construction thereof. That this work is within the District of Algoma, where but little provision has yet been made for the preservation of the peace, and the protection of life and property. That the steamers and other vessels trading in Thunder Bay carry thence and sell to the Indians and laborers [sic] intoxicating liquors. That scenes of violence and outrage, and other serious consequences have been the result and that obstruction to the progress of the work is apprehended from these causes.' This proclamation under the Peace Act, as well as two more relating to the road and one to the government-funded Intercolonial Railway, were issued under the Conservative government before it fell in 1873.[86]

An example of a failed request under the Liberal government came from contractor John W. Sifton working on an early stage of the government-built Pacific line.[87] Written from Selkirk, Manitoba, in September 1878, his letter, forwarded through David Mills, appeared to make a good case for proclamation: 'At present we are doing a large amount of work on the Selkirk Station ground and at this place on the Town Flat. There are several squatters and three of them are selling liquor and we find nearly [sic] impossible to carry on the work so long as liquor is being sold so close by. There have been rows and troubles for the past month and except we can get some redress we may well be obliged to stop the work.' Secretary of State Richard Scott directed his deputy to prepare an order-in-council, a move contrary to apparent Liberal policy, but the application failed when Mackenzie's government was defeated in a general election the same month.[88]

Under the Conservatives, two proclamations were made for about four hundred miles of government line in northern Ontario and Keewatin[89] in 1878 and 1879, before the formation of the CPR in 1880. Requests made after 1880 by contractors or officials writing directly on behalf of the privately owned CPR were normally granted. Three written requests from the general manager of the Canadian Pacific Company, Cornelius Van Horne, were all successful: one described problems in relation to the line running north of Lake Superior; two others were supported by letters from CPR employees or contractors at the scene. Concerning a situation in British Columbia in 1884, Van Horne (an American) wrote to Macdonald, as minister of the interior: 'The fair reputation which Canada enjoys for the observance of the laws and maintenance of order is seriously jeopardised by the operation of the whiskey traders who are really composed of bad characters from South of the Boundary.'[90]

Many railway entrepreneurs, including owners or contractors, as well as engineers, moved from one project to another across North America; most knew their way around the practicalities of construction including hiring labour and keeping order among large groups of working men.[91] Whether or not they had previous experience in Canada, contractors working along the Pacific line requested proclamations under the Peace Act. An entrepreneur in the situation of Josiah Whitehead, carrying out his first contract for the federal government on an early stage of Pacific Railway construction, was sufficiently informed to demand proclamation.[92] But this did not mean that contractors working for the government were always confident of having requests granted. Though he had earlier sat as a Liberal MP, Josiah Whitehead's application was one of those refused by the Mackenzie government. This decision was in line with apparent Liberal policy and may also have been a result of the section of the track concerned – a branch line down to Pembina from St Boniface. There were occasional refusals as well under the Conservatives. In 1881, when contractor James Worthington applied for a proclamation to cover work on the extension of the Canada Central Railway from Mattawa to Callander to meet the Pacific Railway, he took the precaution of swearing a two-page statutory declaration detailing his problems. Possibly the rejection of his application the previous year had driven him to seek legal advice. Explaining that 1,500 men were at work on the extension, he stated:

Fifth – that the works of construction have been and are still seriously retarded by the illicit sale of intoxicating liquors along the line by parties who follow the construction of the Line and continue their illegal traffic causing grave breaches of the peace quarrelling and fighting – among the men and leading to the commission of crimes of a more serious nature.

...

Seventh – That it is impossible to carry on the construction of the Railway Works satisfactorily and restrain intemperance and prevent breaches of the peace among so large a body of men in so remote and unsettled a Locality unless the sale of intoxicating Liquor can be prevented.[93]

Worthington's application was again refused, perhaps because the work was on a line within a partly settled area of Ontario. The province could justifiably have claimed that local criminal justice could be provided by Ontario officials and a federally imposed prohibition would have overridden Ontario's right to issue liquor licences.

The conclusion must be that granting prohibition along the main line of the Pacific Railway had become a routine process for a Conservative government after 1878. Once a suitable application or a complaint was received from a credible source, the cabinet would issue an order for the length of line complained of *and* for remaining stretches of the same section or sections, although these might be distant and inactive. And officials would be appointed. Proclamations were then left in place, sometimes indefinitely, until or unless requests for withdrawal were received. Besides the impact on railway labourers, the effects included, on the one hand, frequent confusion among contractors and federal civil servants over which sections of the Pacific line were under prohibition at any time and, on the other, irritation among local citizens resident along the line of the railway where prohibition continued in force when local works were no longer being undertaken nearby.

Another striking feature is the apparently uncritical acceptance of the operation of the Peace Act, at least in the decades of the 1860s and 1870s. There was no consideration in parliamentary debates of the fairness of imposing selective regimes of prohibition on working men, either at the stage of enactment or during debate on later amendments to the legislation. It appears that the passage of the act in 1869 under the umbrella of Canadian criminal law (and as an apparent re-enactment of colonial law) had given the act considerable legitimacy. In effect, under the guise of criminal law, the state had quietly ensured an effective consensus on the benefits of attempts to control the drinking habits of railway construction workers – at least among those familiar with the legislation. Federal state agents' attempts to *prevent* drunkenness and to control the leisure-time activities of thousands of labouring men, relying on the imposition of a form of local prohibition, would have been unacceptable in urban or less isolated settings.

The level of acceptance must be linked to a general lack of familiarity with the act. Other forms of state coercion were relatively well known to the public: the arrest, trial, and imprisonment of individuals for serious crimes; the suppression of collective disorders through military force; and the public policing of the routine activities of the urban working class, including enforcing by-laws and anti-vagrancy and drunkenness statutes.[94] In contrast, the Peace Act was imposed through regimes of local enforcement largely invisible to the wider Canadian population. The act was unfamiliar because application was mostly to labouring men working in remote areas of railway construction. Even for lawyers, the act formed a very small part of the state's routine arsenal of criminal law, as evidenced by brief references in magistrates' manuals;[95] and it seems probable that only a few (perhaps working for railway contractors or practising in remote areas near the railway line) would have been familiar with the statute. In addition, accounts of disorder on the railways actively misled the reading public. Reporters and contractors commonly referred to the Peace Act as 'The Public Works Act,' implying that liquor controls were a part of general public-works legislation, an approach that effectively masked the fact of discretionary federal government involvement.[96]

If the federal government relied on the two statutes for keeping peace, why was this approach preferred to the traditional method of riot control in which a local authority could call out the volunteer militia?[97] The most direct answer is that, given the remote and inaccessible locations in which railway works were carried out along the Pacific line, there were no local militias and it could have proved difficult to bring in troops – unless disorder occurred along a completed section of the line where troops or militia might be moved in by train.[98] Nor was there always unanimity in regarding local authorities as responsible for organizing a response to labour unrest. One editorial in the *Globe* in 1874 adopted an extreme attitude. The writer, under the heading 'Duty of Keeping the Peace on Public Works,' took the view that contractors should be responsible for their own labourers, saying, 'We are not to be told that a contractor is to gather all the ruffianism [sic] of a continent around him in order to do his work and have at the same time no responsibility as to their behaviour,' to which he added: 'Where should we end if the General Government had to provide extra police whenever some public work was going on?'[99] Even this writer recognized that a volunteer militia called out by local authorities was the final resort in situations of riot.[100] A fuller answer has to be that both the federal state and railway contractors preferred an approach along the Pacific Railway that relied on prohibition. Such interventions by the federal state supported contractors or CPR employees responsible for organizing large bodies of labourers and helped in their view to prevent riot and unrest before they began.

CASE STUDIES OF THE OPERATION OF THE PEACE PRESERVATION ACT

Enforcement of prohibition was viewed as 'necessary' by those involved directly in administering the building of the Pacific line, whether as civil servants, politicians, or contractors, and the act was enforced vigorously by some appointees. Surviving returns of convictions show an apparently active magistracy, fining many labourers or whisky traders and jailing others. Fines ranged from a few dollars to as high as forty. Jail terms, often in lieu of fines, were usually short but this was a result of problems associated with imprisonment of convicted men and the need for their labour. A lack of jail facilities –most public-works locations relied on a log cabin or part of the commissioner's quarters to serve as a jail – a lack of jailers, and the costs of feeding and maintaining jailed prisoners all helped to militate against jail sentences. Arguably, as discussed earlier, enactment of the statute as purely criminal law amounted to something of a deception practised on legislators. But the act was even more deceptive in its use against labourers and their drinking practices and against the whisky sellers providing alcohol. Those accused had no opportunity to question the validity of the laws under which they were prosecuted, usually being unrepresented at trial.

The fact that proclamations were made for remote areas of the country along the Pacific line may have helped to render the statutes uncontroversial but it also made them difficult to administer. The fundamental issue was that support for the policy was inadequate. The federal directives in orders-in-council were clearly stated but implementation tended to be underfunded and dependent on the entrepreneurial skills of particular appointees. The commissioners were expected to make their way to remote posts, acquire housing and jail facilities, find means of enforcing a difficult law (as well as the general criminal law), and handle trials, fines, and imprisonment. They were commonly given jurisdiction over large areas, provided with few direct instructions, restricted in the number of constables they might appoint, and required to satisfy their superiors in

Ottawa with their industry and efficiency as demonstrated in written reports. Application of the two statutes was a classic example of the state's willingness to implement a policy coupled with reluctance to fund it adequately.

Attempts at imposing prohibition in societies where the use of liquor is the norm do not usually operate in straightforward ways and prohibition under the Peace Act in conjunction with the Police Act was no exception. The remainder of the chapter explores three applications under the Peace Act to the Pacific line, two during construction in Ontario, in 1883 and 1884, and one along the line in British Columbia in 1885.[101] In the first case considered, proclamations of prohibition along the railway north of Lake Superior, at Michipicoten, Ontario, in 1884, resulted in liquor-related disturbances. The situation demonstrated inept and ineffectual applications of prohibition by Ottawa and probably weak and reluctant enforcement by Ontario officials. The second and third examples, which involved incidents at Rat Portage, Ontario, in 1883 and Farwell (later Revelstoke) in British Columbia in 1885, show prohibition being applied within provinces by federal enforcement officials but with considerable difficulty.

The latter two cases illustrate the emergence in the 1880s of serious differences between federal and provincial authorities as the provinces began to oppose the presence of federal police officials. Complaints tended to arise within local communities and usually concerned the right to obtain provincial liquor licences; jurisdictional questions were not usually raised in the period. Nonetheless, the federal government remained willing to proclaim the statute without regard to provincial views and withdrew it only reluctantly. Continued imposition of the Peace Act directly worsened relations between local federal and provincial officials in Ontario and British Columbia. Conflicts between federal and provincial officials along the railway line in both provinces demonstrate the absence of a common approach to labour on the Pacific Railway although both levels of government supported the project in principle.

In all three cases, local law and order broke down despite federal proclamations. The evidence suggests that the breakdowns were in part a result of federal involvement in the local administration of justice. Federal interventions and provincial responses no doubt reflected the broader battles between federal and provincial administrations in the 1880s over their power to control everyday life. The tensions between the two levels of government and their conflicting claims of jurisdictional sovereignty extended to construction of the national railway and the availability of liquor along the line. Despite the conflicts and unresolved issues, the federal cabinet remained determined to impose prohibition along the main line of construction wherever possible.

Michipicoten, Ontario, 1884

Michipicoten (southwest of present-day Wawa) was a small settlement on the north shore of Lake Superior. The village was used by the Canadian Pacific Company in 1884 as a depot for construction and for bringing in materials for the line by water. The railway lay almost fifty miles inland, running parallel to the north shore of the lake. The construction of this section of the Pacific Railway was a vast and urgent project by the summer of 1884: vast because the route north of Superior running east to near North Bay (known as the Lake Superior Section and the Eastern Section[102]) stretched for over four hundred miles from the Pic River near Marathon to the start of new construction at Callander, Ontario.[103] It was urgent because construction and improvement of existing track had been repeatedly postponed by the CPR.[104] Both Van Horne, the general manager, and George Stephen, the chairman of the board, recognized the difficulty and expense associated with the railway line where it ran north of Superior.

The challenges on the Lake Superior and Eastern sections in 1884 were enormous.[105] One local commentator estimated late that year that seven thousand men were working on the railway west of Sudbury.[106] The Peace Act had already been proclaimed in force for the entire line of construction along the north shore and one peace commissioner and commissioner of police, Charles McCabe, appointed.[107] Three more specific orders-in-council were authorized by the federal cabinet in 1883, the most crucial being that of December 1883 which re-proclaimed prohibition along a lengthy section of railway construction and appointed a second commissioner, J.C. Gough.[108] In practice, two commissioners were not sufficient. The shoreline locations on Lake Superior perceived as problem areas for the illegal liquor trade shifted over time, following the progress of the line. A moving army of enforcement officials would have been required for prohibition to be effective. What was a major centre of the liquor trade one season might become a semi-abandoned settlement by the next. During their brief heyday, harbours on the north shore – with names like Whiskey Bay, Bechawana Bay, Gargantua Bay, and Gros Cap (testifying to the early Native and French presence on the north shore and the recent ubiquitous presence of liquor) – served as entrepôts. As well as receiving construction materials and supplies for the railway line, the harbours became unofficial settlements selling prohibited goods and services to the labourers. In the 1883 construction season, the most notorious settlement had been Peninsula Harbour but by 1884 Michipicoten had become a major object of news reports and commentary.

Disorder and drunkenness along stretches of railway construction were significant issues for local law officers and CPR officials. Ontario Stipendiary Magistrate Andrew McNaughton, based at Sudbury, informed the *Globe* in October 1884 that large supplies of liquor were being smuggled into construction areas. Peddlars brought in liquor to the route of the Pacific line either on foot or by boat and canoe.[109] Or alcohol could be carried on the trains that brought supplies to the head of the line; kegs, for example, were hidden in barrels of legitimate foodstuffs. McNaughton claimed that, in Sudbury, over two hundred gallons had been seized in the three previous weeks and, in the previous thirteen months, he had imposed fines amounting to over $2,000 for ninety convictions. He added: 'There have been three shooting cases and one man, an Italian, was killed with a stone during a riot. His slayer, Coughlin, is in gaol at Sault Ste Marie.' McNaughton claimed that liquor dealers were in cahoots with railway employees and with local constables. He noted: 'The risks are great, the profits equally so.'[110]

The action of the government in re-proclaiming prohibition under the statute and subsequent moves towards apparent enforcement, together with belated attempts by the province of Ontario to impose prohibition at Michipicoten, appear to have provoked a 'riot' by liquor traders and their allies in the village in October 1884. The new proclamation under the Peace Act in December 1883 applied along the railway line and for ten miles on either side, effectively prohibiting liquor in the railway-construction camps.[111] But the area specified failed to include the village of Michipicoten, the nearby landing used by the CPR, or the rough road connecting Michipicoten to the railway line. This oversight, coupled with the earlier willingness of the Ontario authorities to license the sale of liquor at Michipicoten, had allowed a thriving liquor trade to be established legally in the village. A second, parallel, and more profitable trade was the illicit one, based on carrying liquor from Michipicoten to railway workers along the line.

In the spring of 1884, Van Horne complained formally to the federal government and asked for the Peace Act to be extended to the supply road connecting the line of the railway to the village of Michipicoten. The federal cabinet proclaimed a new order-in-council for the road within three weeks, presumably in response to Van Horne's request, with a previously appointed peace commissioner for the railway line, J.C. Gough, reappointed under the new order.[112] The commissioner's jurisdiction now ran from Michipicoten along the road to the line of the railway and from there west to the River Pic, a total distance of roughly one hundred and sixty miles. The geographical area was promptly extended east as far as Sudbury.[113] These actions gave the commissioner almost three hundred and fifty miles of railway construction line and adjacent areas to supervise as well as the Michipicoten road.[114] Perhaps also in response to Van Horne's demands or, possibly, to an offer from the company, a further peace commissioner, Harry Abbott, an engineer and CPR employee, was appointed for the same sections of line between the River Pic and Sudbury in July 1884.[115]

Liquor peddlers in Michipicoten ignored the prohibition on alcohol and continued to supply liquor to construction workers. According to the Ontario magistrate, Captain George Burden, posted to the village, 'had the proclamation been issued when it was decided to make Michipicoten a supply depot, much, if not all, of the trouble would have been avoided.'[116] But the proclamation and the federal appointments came too late. As a *Globe* reporter characterized affairs, Michipicoten was already 'a perfect sink of iniquity': 'Every other log shanty in it is a whisky hole, where the day is enlivened by free fights, and gambling and robbery and [sic] zest to the evening performances ... Although the place consists of less than a hundred houses it yet has within its borders a score of lewd women, the very offscourings of the world.'[117] The appointments of the two additional commissioners in May and July, coupled with the new proclamation for the road and the village, meant that enforcement of the Peace Act was imminent in Michipicoten. The law-abiding residents of the village most likely anticipated enforcement with a sense of relief while those engaged in trading now-illegal liquor would have feared for their livelihoods. The attempt to shut down the liquor trade precipitated a riot; the appointment of new Ontario constables late in the summer to enforce prohibition at Michipicoten was the triggering factor.

A brief summary of the riot will serve to clarify the federal government's ambiguous role.[118] The 'troubles' began in early October when three new constables, under Magistrate Burden, began to enforce prohibition. A pro-liquor group posted written demands, including ultimatums that the constables leave the settlement; these were disregarded by local officials including Burden. A crowd of about thirty men gathered on the night of 9 October and fired several hundred shots from revolvers and rifles at the CPR office and at Captain Burden's cabin. Both buildings were occupied at the time but, despite repeated shots through the walls of the buildings, no one was injured. After intimidating the officials, the same group broke open the jail and released prisoners, and, during the breaking of the jail, two of the new constables were shot. According to the *Globe*, reporting over a week later on 17 October, a gang of about 'thirty roughs' involved in the liquor trade had taken over control of the settlement. The province responded to an appeal made in person by its own magistrate, sending a force of about a dozen Toronto police to restore order. The police arrived two weeks later, on 22 October, and completed their task within a week by arresting the 'ringleaders' of the riot. The day after they departed, more of the wanted 'outlaws' reappeared in the settlement heavily armed and defied the local constables. They left Michipicoten by steamer, firing from the upper deck in an attempt to hit the CPR agent. Word that they were aboard was telegraphed to the Sault and the four were arrested on arrival.

What was the federal government's reaction to events in Michipicoten? After news of the 9 October 'riot' reached Ottawa, the cabinet removed J.C. Gough as peace commissioner. Presumably the conclusion had been reached that Gough was ineffectual.[119] His replacement was Frank Moberley, a commissioner whose instructions were to take 'vigorous action on the part of the law along this supply road.'[120] Moberley was known for his ability to clean up difficult situations, having been sent into Peninsula Harbour the previous summer to perform a similar task. However, he arrived the day after the four remaining wanted men had boarded a steamer for the Sault, well after the situation at Michipicoten had been dealt with by the force of Toronto police. The *Globe* reported on 4 November, almost a month after the riot, 'Mr. Moberley and a posse are expected at Michipicoten today.'

The federal government's proclamations under the Peace Act presented a law-enforcement challenge to provincial officials already responsible for enforcing the criminal law in small settlements in northwestern Ontario. In the case of Michipicoten, the federal government presumably hoped that its proclamations enforced by Ontario officials could solve the situation, since no federal police appeared until the arrival of Commissioner Moberley in November, a month after the riot. The crackdown at Michipicoten by provincial officials in October appears to have provoked the 'riot' by altering the rules of the liquor trade for local players. The central government was slow to help solve the situation it had created. Perhaps the fact of an Ontario presence in the figure of Magistrate Burden and his decision to go to Toronto in October 1884 to demand help from provincial authorities allowed a delay in any direct federal response. It may be indicative of a degree of federal recognition of the role of prohibition in the troubles at Michipicoten that, in the aftermath of the violence, the federal government agreed to underwrite part of the expense of sending Toronto police to Michipicoten.[121] If this were a riot within a province dealt with by police from the capital of the province, the federal government's willingness to bear part of the costs appeared an admission of, at least, dereliction in not having federal agents present in Michipicoten. Perhaps it also reflected Ottawa's acceptance of partial responsibility for the riot, on account of the belated imposition of the Peace Act in the village and along the road from Michipicoten.

The 'War of Rat Portage,' 1883

The 'war of Rat Portage' erupted in the village[122] as a result of proclamations of the Peace Act within the setting of a long-standing, complex, and increasingly acrimonious political dispute over the location of the northern and western boundaries of Ontario.[123] The boundary dispute was of interest to Rat Portage residents, for the answer would establish whether the village lay in Manitoba or in Ontario. Multiple legal issues grew out of the dispute and affected Rat Portage, including which province was responsible for the administration of justice in the village and where prisoners accused of serious crimes should be sent for trial. One jurisdictional question of particular interest concerned the right to issue liquor licences in the village since this remained a patronage plum.[124]

The background in relation to the liquor situation was that the federal government had issued proclamations under the Peace Act from Rat Portage westward in 1878. The following year, the federal cabinet proclaimed the act for three more railway sections from Rat Portage eastward.[125] The Peace Act provided for an exemption to prohibition 'within the limits of any City' but this did not assist small villages like Rat Portage.[126] Continued imposition of prohibition for five years had become a major source of discontent for would-be sellers of liquor and for residents.

As stated, the legal and political questions surrounding the Manitoba-Ontario boundary issue were complex. Sufficient to say that, as part of the dispute, Macdonald extended the eastern boundaries of Manitoba to the existing western boundaries of Ontario in 1881. The unilateral move placed Rat Portage squarely in Manitoba.[127] While the loss of territory was calculated to offend Ontario, Rat Portage had been considered within the sphere of Manitoba justice even before 1881.[128]An earlier federal act of

1880 had been designed to solve practical problems around the administration of justice during the decade-long dispute. The difficulties included officials charging the same incidents as committed in Ontario or 'Keewatin' or Manitoba, depending on their institutional affiliation.[129] Although Edward Blake had attacked the bill in the House of Commons as outside the powers of the federal government, the justice minister, James McDonald, was undismayed, stating that it was meant only to overcome difficulties.[130] But, as one prescient senator commented during the debate in the Senate: 'It is quite apparent there will be a conflict of authority. The Ontario Government assume that they have the right to appoint justices of the peace and stipendiary magistrates there. The Government of the Dominion disputes that right, and, of course, a conflict arises at once.'[131]

Oliver Mowat, premier of Ontario, was becoming increasingly enraged at the prospect of a threatened loss of territory previously awarded to his province.[132] When Manitoba (encouraged by Macdonald) incorporated Rat Portage as a Manitoban town in 1881, Ontario denounced the move as illegal, claiming that Rat Portage had been 'nominally under Ontario jurisdiction since 1871.'[133] Problems worsened in August when Manitoba began to appoint local officials and established a county court, a jail, and a small police force in the village under Manitoba's jurisdiction.[134] A former Dominion peace and police commissioner, Captain Brereton, settled at Rat Portage to accept a Manitoba appointment as a provincial magistrate. Brereton and federal commissioners of peace and of police continued to enforce prohibition in the area, with Commissioner Charles McCabe resident at Rat Portage beginning in 1882.[135] But McCabe appeared overwhelmed soon after he arrived, reporting that the situation in Rat Portage was worsening, with 'dens of iniquity' increasing in number and 'giving shelter to whiskey peddlars.'[136] Existing tensions between Manitoba and Ontario were exacerbated by talk in 1882 of a federal government decision to re-proclaim the Peace Act. Reimposition of prohibition along the line through Rat Portage would deny both provinces the right to license liquor sellers in the area. As P.B. Waite has commented: 'The ground was laid for the three-way quarrel that culminated in the celebrated Rat Portage affair in the summer of 1883.'[137]

The breakdown of order grew out of the issue of whether alcohol was prohibited or liquor licences could be issued, and which of the competing provincial jurisdictions had the right to issue them. The railway contractors working in the vicinity, Manning, McDonald, McLaren and Company, applied for a proclamation from Cross Lake to English River in 1882, along railway sections that included Rat Portage. According to the minister of justice's report to the Privy Council, the contractors 'represented' that

the Government of Manitoba are about to grant licenses for the sale of spirituous liquors at Rat Portage, in the neighbourhood of works which they are at present prosecuting for the Dominion Government.

That the granting of such licenses and the sale of spirituous liquor in the local-ity named will have a very injurious effect upon the prosecution of these works and the public peace in that part of the Dominion.[138]

The requested order-in-council was issued promptly on 27 October, signed by Macdonald, but then recognized by federal officials as in error because the prior proclamations of 1878 and 1879 were still in place.[139] A number of residents opposed prohibition under the Peace Act. In April 1883 a petition was presented to the federal cabinet signed by thirty-nine people (almost half of the number of heads of households[140]) asking for withdrawal of the Peace Act from the town (see Supporting Documents).[141] The content made it clear that Manitoba had taken a more active role in the town and that the petitioners favoured Manitoba's pro-posed issuance of liquor licences though this conflicted directly with the federal Peace Act favoured by the contractors.[142] During a resulting peri-od of uncertainty over the status of the Peace Act, the situation in Rat Por-tage deteriorated. In May, the mayor, Walter Oliver, reported to Dawson that 'the matter is becoming serious here, as no less than thirty unlicensed saloons are selling liquor in the town of Rat Portage.'[143] He added that the fines imposed by Captain Brereton, under the 'Public Works Act' [sic], were having little effect in controlling the liquor traffic. Macdonald received a telegram from W.H. Plummer at Fort William, a Tory warhorse and fed-eral MP, on 14 June: 'Just arrived from Rat Portage all goes well please have public work [sic] act withdrawn in so far as it applies to town of Rat Portage Causes much irritation without good grits trying to make capital out of it.'[144] The reference to Ontario liberals as 'grits,' and the date of the proclamation withdrawing the Peace Act from Rat Portage ten days later, suggest that the political hints in Plummer's telegram were effective.[145] This was not the end of the matter. Once the Peace Act ceased to apply, the conflict between Ontario and Manitoba over the administration of justice and the right to issue liquor licences came into the open.[146] Even before the order was gazetted in July, Ontario officials had made plans to reassume the administration of justice, appointed a jailer and constables, and planned an Ontario jail.[147] Meanwhile, Manitoba reappointed Captain Brereton and his chief constable, Patrick O'Keefe, as provincial appointees.[148]

According to the *Manitoba Free Press*, the 'war' erupted on 25 July when Captain Brereton tried an accused charged with selling liquor without a Manitoba licence and with introducing liquor without a North-West Territories permit. The accused, Montgomery, 'had applied for and was about to obtain an Ontario licence' to sell liquor, but Brereton, a Manitoban appointee, refused to recognize the application. A Winnipeg lawyer, Hugh McMahon, representing Montgomery, challenged Manitoba's jurisdiction in the disputed territory. When convicted by Brereton, Montgomery elected to go to jail while his lawyer returned to Winnipeg to apply for a writ of habeas corpus.

Tensions between the two set of provincial officials increased on 26 July as a Manitoba special constable was reported arrested by two Ontario constables. On the 27th, rumours were circulating that 'the Manitoba jail was to be broken open to-night to release two men confined therein,' one of whom was Montgomery.[149] The jail was surrounded by a crowd and four prisoners were released with one shot fired; the following morning, an unsuccessful attempt was made to burn the jail down. Meanwhile, a party of Rat Portage 'delegates' took the train to Winnipeg to consult with Manitoba Premier John Norquay and returned on 28 July bringing police reinforcements and the premier with them. Those accused of leading the jailbreak were arrested at night and spirited away to Winnipeg for trial. The premier addressed a large gathering and attempted to calm the residents.

What was the federal government's role in these events? Macdonald, vacationing at Rivière-du-Loup on the lower Saint Lawrence, was kept informed by, among others, his former Dominion police commissioner, Brereton. The latter telegraphed to Macdonald on 27 July: 'My chief [constable] and one constable arrested by Ontario constable. Great excitement among town people.' When Chief Constable O'Keefe telegraphed A.P. Sherwood, the chief of Dominion Police, the message was relayed to Sir John: 'Twenty-five Ontario constables here and fifteen Manitoban they are now arresting one another citizen[s] taking part on both sides a general riot expected you had better come here at once answer only two Dominion constables.'[150] George Burbidge, deputy minister of justice, responded from Ottawa: 'Sir John says to do nothing. It is between Manitoba and Ontario.'[151] But, behind the scenes, Sir John was directing actions at Rat Portage through telegrams to the lieutenant governor and others. On 28 July, he received a reply from Frederick White,[152] the comptroller of the North-West Mounted Police, in Winnipeg, assuring him: 'Chief Provincial Police and twelve sound constables leave here on Saturday for disputed territory. Premier also goes there to arrange [? indecipherable] for local improvements at Rat Portage. Suggest that Public Works Magistrate be ordered to Ottawa. He should not remain in territory.' The demand for removal of Commissioner McCabe was echoed by another correspondent, John Shields, who telegraphed Macdonald from Rat Portage the same day: 'Dominion Stipendiary Magistrate McCabe should be dismissed immediately as he is in sympathy with Ontario officials and does not maintain Dom[inion] authority and backs up Manitoba authority ... Something must be done forthwith. Send Chief Sherwood to act in McCabe's place for six weeks if possible.'[153]

Once the proclamation of prohibition had been withdrawn from the town in June, there was little role left for McCabe to play. Apparently, McCabe's activities had failed to satisfy Conservative supporters in Manitoba and Rat Portage who felt that he had been insufficiently partisan. He was now persona non grata, perhaps something of a scapegoat for events at Rat Portage. The result was a federal order-in-council ordering McCabe transferred from the region of Rat Portage to the Sudbury area.[154] Matters settled down, at least temporarily, in Rat Portage, with the supply of liquor assured and the revenue from licences presumably accruing to both provinces during the boundary dispute.[155]

British Columbia, 1885

A second example of conflict between federal and provincial officials in relation to the Peace Act, this time in British Columbia, shows similarities to the Ontario situation but identifies the issues around federal policing even more clearly. The parallels include railway construction lines near inhabited areas, the presence of local police near railway construction, provincial granting of local liquor licences, local opposition to the Peace Act, and failure of the act to assure prohibition. In British Columbia as in Keewatin, the situation was volatile and included sales of 'illicit' liquor along the railway line and conflict between officials acting for different levels of government. The difference between the two situations was that in British Columbia, unlike the Manitoba-Ontario boundary situation, the federal government had no territorial ambitions on behalf of a second province. Macdonald and his cabinet were ready to settle disagreements and withdraw the Peace Act or, at least, cease enforcing it in some towns and villages, especially in view of provincial claims that B.C. officials were able to assure peace and order in those locations.

The federal government had imposed prohibition under the Peace Act in coastal areas of railway development in British Columbia in 1881 and 1882[156] and then along two hundred miles of railway line from Port Moody on the coast to Savona Ferry, also in 1882.[157] Next, prohibition was proclaimed for the Rocky Mountain sections of the line beginning with the easternmost section in 1884, from the boundary with the North-West Territories running west over the Rocky Mountains for one hundred and seventy miles.[158] Two kinds of appointments were made: for the first time, three NWMP officers, William Herschmer, A.G. Irvine, and Sam Steele, were appointed commissioners of police and commissioners of the peace in May 1884.[159] Appointing Mounties to enforce the Peace Act was a new departure but their usual work in the North-West Territories left them well qualified and practised at confiscating liquor. A year later, in April 1885, a civilian commissioner, Justice of the Peace George Hope Johnston, replaced the Mounties over the same '150 miles west of the provincial line.'[160]

The situation along the railway line in British Columbia under the Peace Act was as difficult as in Ontario and Keewatin, according to Sam Steele of the NWMP. At Laggan in 1884, he found that 'large numbers of gamblers, whisky men, in fact almost every description of criminal ... were wending their way ... and establishing their dens on every creek along the line.' The problems of enforcement, in Steele's view, included the need to catch liquor sellers 'in the act of selling' and the insufficiency of the ten-mile belt on either side of the line, which meant that 'the labourers could go out at any time after they received their month's wages to places outside our belt and spend every dollar ... remaining there for a prolonged spree.'[161] Steele's claims of disorder were supported by others; for instance, there had been earlier complaints from the residents of Yale, British Columbia, who described an influx of railway labourers in 1882, 'a great portion of whom are Chinese ... a considerable element of said increase are men of very loose, disorderly, drunken and vicious habits.'[162]

Johnston, a former B.C. magistrate, soon found himself in conflict with a provincial government official, the redoubtable Gilbert Sproat,[163] appointed stipendiary magistrate at Farwell the same year. Local officials were unwilling to accept Johnston, a civilian Dominion appointee, as a replacement for the NWMP officers and Sproat promptly adopted a policy of harassing Johnston and his constables, even sending letters of complaint to B.C. newspapers. According to Steele, Sproat was doing 'his utmost to bring discredit upon Mr. Johnston and his men, who had at best a hard uphill fight against the lawless element.' Steele's account of the dispute at Farwell between Johnston and Sproat identifies the underlying issue as the province's willingness to issue liquor licences in a location where prohibition had been proclaimed under the Peace Act. Steele's version (and he was a well-informed if not unbiased onlooker) claimed that the province continued to sell liquor licences and 'issued all comers licences to sell "spiritous and fermented liquors" within the [railway] belt already proclaimed under the act. This action gave courage to the liquor men, and many sold who, had they not been granted licences, would not have attempted it.'[164]

When matters came to a head – Sproat had arrested Johnston and his constables – John A. Macdonald appointed Lieutenant-Colonel J.F.M. Macleod, formerly commissioner of the NWMP, to investigate and report on the matter.[165] Macleod's report cited Alexander Campbell's account of the sequence of interactions culminating in Johnston's arrest: it was 'the arrest by the Commissioner of two Provincial Constables which culminated in the arrest by the Provincial Authorities of the Commissioner himself and his officers.' Macleod's report, not surprisingly, tended to side with Johnston, confirming that, based on information from 'Railway officials,' the Mounted Police was a very necessary force while the railway was under construction.[166] Sproat, on the other hand, argued privately with Macleod that B.C. officials were capable of maintaining peace along the line of railway construction.[167] At the same time, local business people were complaining about lost revenue from provincially licensed hotels and taverns within Farwell and pointing out that grading was now complete on the nearby line of the railway. Macleod was forced to report to Ottawa that prohibition under the statute was unwelcome within the town, stating that 'there is a very general dissatisfaction among the inhabitants of the Town of Farwell that the *Peace Preservation Act* is in force there concurrently with the Provincial License Act.' Macleod's solution was to propose withdrawal of the Peace Act from Farwell while maintaining it along the line beyond the town. His recommendation stated that the authorities in Farwell 'have sufficient power to control the liquor traffic.' It was apparently accepted by the federal government.[168]

The decision at Farwell set a pattern for other small towns in British Columbia which followed suit in demanding withdrawal of the Peace Act. Queries were forwarded from B.C. magistrates in Golden City and Donald to the provincial government the following year and resulted in a letter of inquiry from the lieutenant governor to Ottawa. The federal government equivocated, however, stating that the CPR had requested that 'in view of the work of ballasting etc. remaining to be done, the protection of the police might be afforded' in a limited area for the 1886 season. The number of Dominion appointees in British Columbia was nonetheless reduced, from six in 1885 to two in 1886, and in all likelihood the statute was no longer enforced within small towns or villages with provincially licensed taverns.[169]

CONCLUSION

Consideration of the operation of the Peace Act and the Police Act opens a window on a complex sphere of political and administrative activity involving federal government ministers and departmental officials, railway companies and their officials, contractors and their employees, and enforcement officers posted along the line of the Pacific Railway. All of these parties shared a vested interest in suppressing supplies of liquor to labourers and they worked in concert to punish unlicensed sellers, and those in possession of liquor, for the purpose of furthering railway construction. While the administrative scheme demonstrates the growing federal state's capabilities in organizing and overseeing a far-flung branch of the central bureaucracy, it also shows a confused and at times ineffectual enforcement process. In addition, the analysis demonstrates how a statute created for the purposes of responding to labour disturbances could be creatively altered and expanded to serve larger or different goals.

The right of the executive to issue proclamations under the Peace Act was exercised routinely between 1878 and 1885, and in advance of any serious crises. The act, which was transformed into an increasingly draconian piece of criminal law, was viewed as a useful device at the disposal of the federal government. And the proclamations – in conjunction with those under the Police Act – essentially provided a program of government support to contractors building the Pacific Railway. Whether or not applications were as useful in suppressing the liquor supply as the federal government intended, they helped to shape the relations of labour and capital along the railway throughout the period.

While the Peace Act had been introduced in 1869 to reduce the incidence of violence and unrest on government public works – reflecting the crown's responsibility for maintaining the public peace – over the decades after confederation use of the statute became more closely linked to state-security concerns. Transportation infrastructure and the Pacific Railway in particular had assumed the status of *necessary* national endeavours under Macdonald's government. The fate of the Conservative administration had become tied to completion of the railway. And, in the minds of members of Macdonald's cabinet and perhaps of a majority of MPs, maintaining order on the state's major economic project had become identified with the government's general responsibility for the maintenance of order. By the 1880s, any threat to the building of the first transnational railway was considered a threat to the state's economic order *and* its political goals. In effect, the state now began to identify economic order with political order. The approach directly served the interests of railway companies and, in the case of construction of the Pacific Railway, the interests of the government itself.

At first appearance, the Peace Act appears to differ in kind from established state-security measures in Canada; liquor offences committed by railway labourers cannot be compared with direct threats to the fabric of the state. But the statute's routine application to maintain order on the Pacific line became an essential component of government control, part of the effort to achieve a critical state goal. The frequent and continuing applications of the statute provide evidence in support of the claim that parliamentarians' views of the meaning of 'state security' had begun to shift during the period of the late nineteenth century. The change was away from notions of security that were limited to political issues and a preoccupation with insurrection or invasion. The adoption and use of the Peace Act as well as the two other statutes considered, the Act respecting Police of Canada, 1868 and the Blake Act of 1878, underline new state concerns around issues of disorder and internal economic security within the Dominion. The shift is evidenced by a willingness on the part of the federal state to intervene directly in situations threatening disorder. With labour organizations beginning to establish themselves more formally in Canada in the period, disorder among working men increasingly became seen as a threat, not only to individual employers, but also to the economic order, the order upheld by the state. The shift was slow; it became more explicit later and gathered strength after the turn of the century when, for instance, labour unrest and strikes were met by strong shows of government force.[170]

The Peace Act itself raises fundamental issues. For instance, in enacting the legislation in 1869, did Parliament put the interests of executive power before the rule of law by adopting a measure of criminal law that applied only to selected citizens at certain times in certain places? And was the federal government's reluctance to desist in applying the legislation in the face of increasing provincial dissatisfaction in Ontario and British Columbia a part of the 'provincial rights' battle? Certainly, the background of broader issues between federal and provincial administrations places the two statutes within a context of deliberate attempts to expand constitutional jurisdiction. Against this setting of federal-provincial disagreements, the effect of later applications and enforcement was to increase levels of conflict between federal and local police within provinces. But the government remained resolute in its intention of imposing the Peace Act as it saw fit. Despite conflicts and problems of imposition in Ontario and British Columbia, the perceived advantages of the act for the security of railway construction were too great for the government to abandon the policy of prohibition.

NOTES

Jim Phillips, Chris English, and Barry Wright provided very helpful comments on earlier versions of this chapter and the comments of two peer reviewers were greatly appreciated.

1 The act, commonly referred to as the Peace Preservation Act, 1869, was in fact entitled An Act for the Better Preservation of the Peace in the Vicinity of Public Works (SC 1869 c.24).

2 The full title was 'An Act respecting Police of Canada' (SC 1868 c.73).

3 Politicians and contractors alike feared that 'disorder' would occur if supplies of alcohol reached men building the line. The terms 'disorder' and 'unrest' are used to refer to disturbances that contractors believed might grow out of, or be exacerbated by, the use of alcohol.

4 When threats were deemed to be beyond the capacity of regular civil authority. See several essays in the first two volumes of *Canadian State Trials*. Murray Greenwood and Barry Wright have described executive emergency measures as a means to 'effectively bypass legislative and judicial scrutiny': 'Introduction: Rebellion, Invasion, and the Crisis of the Colonial State in the Canadas, 1837–9,' *CST* 2, 32n.5. See in particular, in the same volume, Jean-Marie Fecteau, '"This Ultimate Resource": Martial Law and State Repression in Lower Canada, 1837–8,' 207–47.

5 The War Measures Act, 1914: An Act to Confer Certain Powers upon the Governor in Council in the Event of War, Invasion, or Insurrection (SC 1914 c.2).

See Murray Greenwood, 'The Drafting and Passage of the War Measures Act in 1914 and 1927: Object Lessons in the Need for Vigilance,' in W. Pue and B. Wright, eds., *Canadian Perspectives on Law and Society: Issues in Legal History* (Ottawa: Carleton University Press 1988), 291–307.

6 Derived from 'navigator,' meaning a labourer employed in the work of excavating and constructing earthworks such as canals, railways, drains, etc. (*Shorter Oxford Dictionary*, 1936).

7 No references to public-works appointments under section 1 of the Police Act have been found in standard sources on the history of policing in Canada.

8 Donald Creighton, *John A. Macdonald, The Old Chieftain* (Toronto: Macmillan 1955), chapters 2–4.

9 See chapters in this volume by R. Blake Brown and David Wilson.

10 Macdonald wrote to the general manager of the Grand Trunk Railway, C.J. Brydges, in 1870 referring to U.S. territorial ambitions in the 'West': 'One of the first things to be done is to show unmistakably our resolve to build the Pacific Railway … It must be taken up by a body of capitalists, and not constructed by the Government directly.' See John Macnaughton, 'Life of Lord Strathcona,' in W.L. Grant, ed., *The Makers of Canada Series: Anniversary Edition 10* (Toronto: Oxford University Press 1926), 209. Also, LAC, Macdonald Papers, MG 26A, LTB 13, 980, 28 Jan. 1870, mfm C-28. In contrast, the Liberals, under Alexander Mackenzie, believed that the railway project was irresponsible, an impossibility for the government in terms of cost. See Dale C. Thomson, *Alexander Mackenzie Clear Grit* (Toronto: Macmillan 1960), 124–6.

11 A condition of British Columbia's agreeing to join confederation. See Peter B. Waite, *Canada 1874–1896: Arduous Destiny*, 2nd ed. (Toronto: McClelland and Stewart 1988), 25.

12 See Desmond Morton's argument that the Pacific Railway was needed to serve the Tory government's National Policy: *A Short History of Canada* (Toronto: McClelland and Stewart 2001), 114–15, 200. The National Policy was formally named in 1878.

13 Macdonald was mistaken in claiming that the Pacific Railway would eliminate Canadian dependence on American railroads, since, in fact, the railways tied the Canadian economy more closely to the American.

14 See Louis Knafla's chapter in this volume.

15 The CPR was formed in 1880 and took over construction from the government on most sections of the railway in 1881. For the sequence of construction of the railway, see n.101. Accounts of railway building under the CPR are numerous, but see, for example, J. Lorne McDougall, *Canadian Pacific: A Brief History* (Montreal and Kingston: McGill-Queen's University Press 1968); Valerie Knowles, *From Telegrapher to Titan: The Life of William C. Van Horne* (To-

ronto: Dundern Group 2004); Walter Vaughan, *The Life and Work of Sir William Van Horne* (New York: Century Company 1920); Heather Gilbert, *Awakening Continent: The Life of Lord Mount Stephen, Vol. 1, 1829–91* (Aberdeen: Aberdeen University Press 1965, 1976); W. Kaye Lamb, *History of the Canadian Pacific Railway* (New York: Macmillan 1977).

16 When financing arrangements were at their most vulnerable in 1884, Pope told Macdonald, 'You will have to loan them the money, because the day the CPR busts, the Conservative Party busts the day after.' Quoted by Peter B. Waite in biography of J.H. Pope, *DCB Online*, www.biographi.ca.

17 Macdonald's Papers contain a wealth of telegrams and letters from officials, CPR managers, private contractors, MPs, and others located in areas along the Pacific Railway line. See archival appendix by Judi Cummings for details of the Macdonald fonds.

18 Construction of the line was mostly in remote and inaccessible areas, with the result that there would be difficulties in bringing in militia to respond to serious disturbances. During a strike at Cross Lake, Ontario, in 1879, militia could be brought in by train from Winnipeg. See Binnie, 'Explorations in the Use of Criminal Law in Canada, 1867–92,' PhD thesis, Carleton University,1991, chapter 4; and David J. Hall, 'The Construction Workers' Strike on the Canadian Pacific Railway, 1879,' *Labour / Le Travail* 36 (1995): 11–35. See also Eric Tucker's chapter in this volume for use of militia against strikers and Mackenzie's reluctance to take this action.

19 The exceptional nature of such a position was reflected in a hostile comment by Senator Alexander Vidal in the 1885 Senate debate on an amendment to the Peace Act. Vidal referred to 'the senior member from Halifax, who has such a very great regard for the rights, and privileges and interests of working men' and said: 'I really expected ... that [he] would have risen in his place and protested against this terrible encroachment on their rights as freemen.' Senate, *Debates*, 16 April 1885, 597.

20 Alcohol under ss.11–16 and firearms under ss.2–10. See Supporting Documents of this volume.

21 SC 1870 c.28; SC 1875 c.38. See Supporting Documents.

22 SC 1885 c.80 ss.1, 2.1(4), and 14.

23 The Criminal Code (SC 1892 c.151). Repeal at SC 1950 c.11 s.4.

24 SPC 1845 c.6; renewed SPC 1851 c.76. The first of two pre-confederation statutes relating to public works, 'for the better preservation of the Peace, and the prevention of Riots and violent Outrages at and near Public Works while in progress of construction,' spoke to the shock and concern of legislators and the public after serious disturbances broke out among labourers building the Lachine and the Beauharnois canals in Lower Canada in 1843.

25 Canal projects had at times employed very large groups of men, perhaps the first large-scale labour forces in a society where, as Pentland has suggested, labour 'stood between pre-capitalist and capitalist labour': H.C. Pentland, 'The Lachine Strike of 1843,' *CHR* 29 (1948): 256–7. See, also, discussion in Eric Tucker's chapter in this volume.

26 A force that William and Nora Kelly have referred to as 'the first federal police force' in Canada. See their *Policing in Canada* (Toronto: Macmillan 1976), 18–19.

27 An Act to Prohibit the Sale of Intoxicating Liquors on or Near the Line of Public Works in This Province, SPC 1851 c.126. Both statutes appeared in the CSPC (1859) as c.29 and c.30 following the Public Works Act, c.27, suggesting a close link between the three.

28 The creation of a mounted police force was included in the 1868 bill for first reading but removed and replaced by the appointment of preventive resident 'Peace Commissioners.' See House of Commons, *Debates*, 1868, Bill 77; Senate, *Debates*, 1869, Bill D.

29 The Intercolonial Railway was enshrined in the BNA Act (1867–8 [U.K.] c.3 s.145). Construction relied on a guaranteed loan from the British government and the line ran from Rivière-du-Loup in Quebec to Halifax. See Ken Cruickshank, 'The People's Railway: The Intercolonial Railway and the Canadian Public Enterprise Experience,' *Acadiensis* 16 (1986): 78–100. For proclamation under the Peace Act legislation for the railway, see LAC, RG 2, PC 515, 25 May 1872.

30 As liquor was already prohibited under the North-West Territories Act (see, for instance, SC 1875 c.49 s.74 and 1880 c.25 s.90), the ban on alcohol effectively extended along most of the length of the Pacific Railway main line, from Ontario to the Pacific Ocean.

31 The Department of Public Works was responsible for railways and canals until 1879 when it was divided into the departments of railways and canals and public works (LAC, RG 43).

32 The terms Liberal and Reform are used interchangeably in referring to the federal alliance of George Brown's Clear Grits, the Quebec Rouges, and the Reformers of Canada West.

33 Named for Edward Blake, the former Liberal minister of justice, who introduced the bill in 1878, the act was titled An Act for the Better Prevention of Crimes of Violence in Certain Parts of Canada, 1878 (SC 1878 c.17). See Binnie 'Explorations,' appendix A, 'Statute Listing,' for criminal legislation. Also, Susan Binnie, 'The Blake Act of 1878: A Legislative Solution to Urban Violence in post-Confederation Canada,' in Louis Knafla and Susan Binnie, eds., *Law, Society and the State: Essays in Modern Legal History* (Toronto: University of Toronto Press 1995).

34 For Montreal in 1878 by a Liberal federal government and twice more by Tory governments, for Quebec in 1879, and for Winnipeg in 1882, before being allowed to lapse in 1884.

35 While the federal Riot Act also relied on proclamations – making provision for a local official to order a rioting crowd to disperse – that authority was exercised at the local level, not by the federal government.

36 Martial law as a general rule could be imposed by proclamation but usually only where war was raging and regular courts could not function. See Greenwood and Wright, 'Introduction,' *CST* 2, 25–8, 29; and, in the same volume, F. Murray Greenwood, 'The General Court Martial at Montreal, 1838–9: Operation and the Irish Comparison,' 282–7.

37 Although Irish statutes appear likely to have provided statutory templates, a search of English and Irish statutes found no legislation with content similar to the Peace Act. As legislators and drafters preferred to use existing statutes, more work is needed on the question. Several Irish bills in the decades of the 1840s and 1850s carried similar titles, for instance, 'for the Better Prevention of Crime and Outrage in Parts of Ireland,' but the contents showed no similarity to the Canadian Peace Act. The exact origins of the 1845 and 1851 Province of Canada statutes may lie in different common law sources, and, possibly, titles and contents were drawn from a number of acts.

38 In the case of the Blake Act, regular justice could be augmented by prohibition of weapons and appointments of federal commissioners to issue licences for weapons.

39 For the law on riot, see the chapter by Donald Fyson in this volume.

40 See House of Commons, *Debates*, 4 May 1878, for comments by Devlin, then a moderate Montreal Reform MP and Catholic but, as Wilson points out in this volume, supported by Fenians voters in the late 1860s.

41 The Peace Act affected labouring men in remote areas of the country. The Blake Act in contrast affected the rights of respectable citizens in Montreal and came under immediate criticism in 1878. Not surprisingly, there was a readiness on the part of the Tory government to proclaim the Peace Act routinely while the Blake Act was applied with caution in urban areas by Tories and Liberals alike.

42 The provinces of Ontario and Quebec included both pre-confederation statutes in post-confederation statutory revisions – either ignoring the federal legislation or, more likely, claiming parallel jurisdiction for works constructed *within* a province (*CSPC* 1859). As the Ontario and Quebec administrations were on relatively good terms with the federal government, these moves may not have constituted a problem for Ottawa. (My thanks to a peer reviewer for this point.) However, the 1875 Dominion amendment included a provision for

proclaiming the federal Peace Act when work was being carried out by 'any Province of Canada,' possibly in response to these provincial moves (SC 1875 c.38 s.1).

43 Dale Gibson, 'Development of Federal Legal-Judicial Institutions,' in D.J. Guth and W. Pue, eds., *Canada's Legal Inheritances* (Winnipeg: Canadian Legal History Project 2001), 459–60.

44 House of Commons, *Debates*, 1867–8, 19 May 1868, 745.

45 Blake's opposition was ironic because he later proposed federal intervention in the administration of justice under the Blake Act, 1878 when he argued that his 1878 bill was a 'strengthening' of existing criminal law. This was misleading since earlier legislation dealt only with the unlawful use of certain weapons. Those general controls had been included in an omnibus criminal law bill in 1869 and made stronger, under Blake as minister of justice, in 1877. Offences against the Person Act, 1869, SC 1869 c.20 ss. 72–6. The Firearms Act, 1877, SC 1877 c.30.

46 Under the supervision of the local justices of the peace.

47 Kelly and Kelly, *Policing*, 18–19.

48 For the origins of the secret police in Canada, see the chapter by Andrew Parnaby and Gregory Kealy with Kirk Niergarth in this volume.

49 The second part of the paragraph relies on chapters in this volume by David Wilson and by Andrew Parnaby and Gregory Kealey with Kirk Niergarth, as well as S.W. Horrall's article 'Dominion Policing,' *Canadian Encyclopaedia*, www.thecanadianencyclopaedia.com.

50 Clive Emsley, *Crime and Society in England, 1750–1900* (London: Longman 1987), chapter 8.

51 See N. Rogers, 'Serving Toronto the Good: The Development of the City Police Force, 1834–1880,' in V. Russell, ed., *Forging a Consensus: Historical Essays on Toronto* (Toronto: University of Toronto Press 1984); H. Boritch, 'Conflict, Compromise and Administrative Convenience: The Police Organization in Nineteenth Century Toronto,' *Canadian Journal of Law & Society* 3 (1988): 141–7; G. Marquis, 'A Machine of Oppression under the Guise of the Law: The Saint John Police Establishment, 1860–1890,' *Acadiensis* 16 (1986): 58–77.

52 However, an earlier proposal for a provincial police force, made by a Province of Canada commission in 1854, had been viewed with great disfavour by local municipalities and was rejected. See Paul Romney, *Mr Attorney: The Attorney General for Ontario in Court, Cabinet, and Legislature, 1791–1899* (Toronto: The Osgoode Society 1986), 234–7, and Eric Tucker's chapter in this volume.

53 House of Commons, *Debates*, 24 June 1885, 2020. The positions taken in the bill were justified, according to Caron, by the levels of violence on similar projects in the United States where 'the murders committed on them averaged one a day.'

54 Critics of the bill pointed out that alcohol might have been sold without the knowledge of the principal (ss.12–13.) David Mills was a Reform lawyer, formerly minister of the interior under Mackenzie, later minister of justice in Laurier's cabinet, a law teacher, senator, and briefly a judge of the Supreme Court of Canada (SCC).

55 See two of the three case studies presented later in this chapter, concerning Rat Portage, Ontario, and Farwell, British Columbia.

56 The rebellion occurred between March and May 1885. The debates took place in April and June the same year.

57 The railway's obvious political and economic relevance had been driven home when the partly completed line had been used to convey troops to the North-West to fight the rebellion.

58 Begbie to the minister of justice, LAC, RG 13, vol. 63, p.6, 1885 (1131–1200).

59 Begbie noted that the 'Canada Police Acts 1868 and 1879 contain full and minute directions as to the appointments' while the Peace Act and the Extradition Act were silent in this regard.

60 Overturned earlier, without reasons, by the SCC.

61 No response was recorded in Department of Justice files.

62 These proclamations, in 1869, 1870, and 1873, were for the 'Red River Road' under construction from Thunder Bay to the west (LAC, RG 2, PC 666, 13 Sept. 1869; PC 922, 5 May 1870; PC 807, 8 July 1873). The project was also known as the 'Dawson Route,' for S.J. Dawson, the civil engineer who surveyed the route and supervised the project. Dawson, later a provincial Conservative MPP (1875–8) and a federal Conservative MP (1878–91), was responsible for moving troops along the route during the first Red River rebellion. See *Macmillan Dictionary of Canadian Biography* (*MDCB*) (Toronto: Macmillan 1963), 177. See also Louis Knafla's chapter in this volume. No commissioners were appointed by order-in-council for any of these proclaimed areas.

63 Under construction across New Brunswick, shortly after confederation. See n.29 (LAC, RG 2, PC 515, 25 May 1872). No commissioners were appointed for this line.

64 There were variations within the 'major' category. Certain orders applied along lengthy sections of railway construction, possibly for distances of several hundred miles, and appointed several commissioners of the peace while others applied to a single section of construction and appointed one official.

65 A few 'minor' content items were either erroneous (e.g., a proclamation had already been made for the same section of railway) or in draft form (because they were filed as 'dormant' when not accepted at the late stage of consideration in council). Five proclamations fell into each of these categories, a total of ten.

66 For example, one order-in-council including four appointments and one provision for salary appears as five items in Table 1.

67 Corrections ranged from the exact geographical limits of a proclamation to the authority of a commissioner to appoint constables.

68 Totals are not given because data derive from a content analysis, i.e., orders containing multiple commands are included multiple times. But the number of directives (120) rather than the eighty orders was used to calculate percentages.

69 Orders were most often signed by John A. Macdonald. Other signatories included Archibald Campbell, J.H. Pope, Charles Tupper, and, occasionally, one of four or five other ministers.

70 Table 2 shows proclaimed and draft orders-in-council of which eighty are analysed. The total differs from that in Table 1, where orders are broken down into multiple commands or directives.

71 As stated, some proclamations repeated previous orders for the same sections of railway line. The Conservative cabinet proclaimed new areas under prohibition effectively only eleven times; two proclamations in the total of thirteen for the years 1878–85 were repetitions of previous orders. Departmental officials and contractors had difficulty keeping track of which sections were proclaimed – their communications show considerable confusion.

72 See Table 3. This distance excludes the length of the line across the North-West Territories since prohibition applied there routinely under the North-West Territories Act. See n.30.

73 Two proclamations by the Conservative cabinet, in 1878 and 1879, pre-dated the creation of the CPR. Both related to sections of the line in northern Ontario being built by government contractors.

74 Mackenzie introduced the 1875 bill to broaden its provisions. The resulting amendment allowed Macdonald's government to apply the act fifteen years later in support of the privately owned CPR.

75 Mackenzie's renowned parsimony may have been offended by the federal government's responsibility for paying appointees and the administrative costs.

76 See Waite, *Canada*, 55.

77 Thomas Dowell, contractor on the Hamilton and UW Railway, Josiah Whitehead, building the Pembina Line south from St Boniface to the U.S. border, and John Sifton, building the Pacific Railway in Manitoba. LAC, RG 13, 705/1875, 774/1875, 746/1878.

78 Prohibition was first proclaimed in part of Manitoba in 1878, then eastward into Ontario, and along the Ottawa valley in 1881. The Lake Superior sections were proclaimed in 1883 and 1884 and the interior of British Columbia

in 1881. Proclamations were made for the line to the ocean in 1882 and east across the Rockies in 1884 and 1885.

79 LAC, RG 2, PC 1261, 7 July 1880.

80 For example, the appointments of three Nova Scotia lawyers by James Mc-Donald, Tory minister of justice from 1878 to 1881. McDonald came from Pictou County, Nova Scotia.

81 The NWMP already policed railway construction in the North-West Territories and enforced the permanent general prohibition on liquor provided for under legislation for the territories.

82 Not surprising since it was not until the 1890s that contractors holding government contracts were prohibited from contributing to federal election campaigns.

83 Three requests after 1878 for proclamations on other works resulted in no action. Two were for intra-provincial railway projects and the third was from the lieutenant governor of the North-West Territories requesting that bringing liquor into the territories by train be prohibited. As noted, liquor was already prohibited in the territories. LAC, RG 2, PC 1282, 26 Oct. 1880; RG 2, PC 30, 24 Jan. 1884; and RG 2, PC 848, 21 July 1885.

84 Usually to the minister of public works before 1879 (or to the minister of railways and canals after this date) or to the minister of justice.

85 See Louis Knafla's chapter in this volume for background on the construction of the Red River Road.

86 For the Red River Road, see LAC, RG 2, PC 666, 12 Sept. 1896; PC 922, 5 May 1870; PC 1061, 18 June 1870; PC 807, 8 July 1873. (The third proclamation amended and corrected the first.)

87 John Wright Sifton, born in Upper Canada, went west in 1875 and became a Manitoba MLA in 1878. He was the father of Sir Clifford and Arthur Lewis Clifton (*MDCB*).

88 The request was subsequently granted by the new Conservative cabinet in response to a request from the Department of Public Works – probably based on Sifton's earlier complaint. LAC, RG 13, 746/1878, 14 Sept. 1878; RG 2, PC 1066, 20 Dec. 1878.

89 Keewatin was the federal government's term for a large tract of land between Ontario and Manitoba claimed by both provinces.

90 LAC, RG 28, Van Horne Letter Book no. 6, 18 Nov. 1884.

91 See Richard White, 'Losing Ventures: The Railway Construction Contracts of Frank Shanly, 1860–75,' *CHR* 79 (1999): 237–60; R.B. Fleming, *The Railway King of Canada: Sir William Mackenzie, 1849–1923* (Vancouver: UBC Press 1991).

92 Whitehead obtained the contract for the Pembina Line in 1873 but work was delayed until 1878–9. LAC, RG 13, 774/1875. An experienced British

contractor, he went bankrupt attempting to build the Pacific line across northern Ontario where he encountered muskeg and 'bottomless' lakes. He was a federal Liberal MP from 1867 to 1872. *Canadian Directory of Parliament,* LAC, 1968.

93 LAC, RG 13, 327/1881, 1019/1881.

94 For collective disorders, see J.J.B. Pariseau, *Disorders, Strikes and Disasters: Military Aid to the Civil Power in Canada, 1867–1933* (Ottawa: Nat.Def HQ, Dir of History, 1973); Desmond Morton, 'Aid to the Civil Power: The Canadian Militia in Support of Social Order, 1867–1914,' *CHR* 51 (1970): 407–25; Don Macgillivray, 'Military Aid to the Civil Power: The Cape Breton Experience in the 1920s,' *Acadiensis* 3 (1979): 45–64. Also see Eric Tucker's chapter in this volume. For the background to urban policing in the period, see Marianna Valverde, *The Age of Soap, Light and Water: The Age of Moral Reform in English Canada, 1885–1925* (Toronto: McClelland and Stewart 1991). For sources on urban policing, see Greg Marquis, 'Towards a Historiography of Canadian Policing,' in Knafla and Binnie, eds., *Law, Society and the State.*

95 S.R. Clarke's *The Magistrates' Manual* (Toronto: Carswell 1875), 504, was out of date when it stated, contrary to the amendment of 1870, that weapons and alcohol sections of the statute both came into force when proclamations were issued under the act. James Crankshaw's *A Practical Guide to Police Magistrates and Justices of the Peace* (Montreal: Whiteford and Theoret 1895) was more accurate but devoted only three lines to the statute.

96 The same error was common in railway contractors' usage, for instance, in applications for proclamation.

97 See chapters by Eric Tucker, Ian Robertson, and Don Fyson in this volume for issues associated with calling out the militia. For public-order offences more generally, see concluding chapter in this volume by Desmond Brown and Barry Wright.

98 This was the situation during strikes at Cross Lake, Ontario, in 1879 and at Beaver, British Columbia, in 1884. For Cross Lake, see Binnie, 'Explorations'; Hall, 'Construction Workers.' For Beaver, see Sam Steele, *Forty Years in Canada* (Toronto: McClelland, Goodchild and Stewart 1915), 196–201.

99 *Globe,* 25 May 1874.

100 The work referred to was on the Welland Canal. Reliance on local militia forces was more feasible on canal construction since it tended to take place in areas that were relatively developed.

101 It is helpful at this point to set out the rough sequence of construction of the Pacific line in summary form. The government's Red River route, or Dawson Road, to the west was begun in 1867 to run from Lake Superior to Red River. The railway line from Selkirk, Manitoba, south to the American

border, the Pembina Line, was contracted by the government in 1873 (to Josiah Whitehead) but not begun until 1878–9. The Red River route was replaced by a government-built railway beginning in 1875. (Whitehead won a government contract for part of this project but went bankrupt on account of cost overruns in 1880.) In 1879 the government contracted with Andrew Onderdonk to build across British Columbia; the work began in 1880 and was completed to government standards in 1884. Onderdonk was then hired by the CPR to upgrade the line. In 1880 the newly incorporated company contracted with the government to complete part of the line and took control in 1881 of three major government-built sections, the Pembina Branch, the line constructed from Selkirk east to Cross Lake, Keewatin, and the Canada Central Railway line from Brockville via Renfrew to Mattawa. The latter became part of the 'Eastern Section' of the railway running to Sudbury. The CPR built along the line where gaps existed, from Selkirk to British Columbia, Port Arthur/Fort William to Sudbury, and Mattawa to Callendar. Part of the government line from Cross Lake to Port Arthur was too poorly built to be handed over and work was continued there by the government until 1883, although a section from Cross Lake to Rat Portage was handed over in 1882.

102 The term 'Eastern Section' was established in the first clause of the Canadian Pacific Company's contract with the government of Canada. The section from Selkirk east, to north of Lake Superior, was termed the 'Lake Superior Section.' House of Commons, *Journals*, 1880–1; RG 14, E-1 (R1025–2–7–E), 1880–1.

103 This was, more correctly, the junction of the Pacific Railway with the terminus of the Canada Central Railway, which ran to Ottawa and Brockville and which had been extended to meet the Pacific Railway.

104 After 1880, the CPR opted to build easier sections of track across the prairies (costs overran even there) to provide evidence of rapid progress and to obtain revenue from transportation along completed track. It was commonly rumoured that the company would default on building the western mountain stretches and on completing the partially built northern Ontario sections of the line. By 1884, under great financial difficulties and pressure from the federal government, work began north of Lake Superior.

105 Van Horne reported in December 1883 that contractors on the Eastern Section were employing 9,500 men between Port Arthur and Lake Nipissing. LAC, RG 28, III 20, vol. 1.

106 Magistrate McNaughton of Sudbury, *Globe*, 29 Oct. 1884.

107 The entire line had been proclaimed from Sudbury to River Pic (one hundred miles west of Michipicoten) the previous summer (LAC, RG 2, PC 1711, 28 July 1883). Peace Commissioner Charles McCabe had been appointed in

1882 (PC 1282, 7 July 1882). McCabe was based at Rat Portage in Keewatin, i.e., several hundred miles west of Michipicoten, and appears to have had no responsibility for the north shore line.

108 LAC, RG 2, PC 2234, 5 Nov. 1883; Peace Act in force from River Pic to Michipicoten.

109 The international border ran about seventy miles from the uneven shoreline, so enterprising citizens from Michigan and Minnesota or even Wisconsin could join Canadians in the illegal liquor trade.

110 *Globe*, 29 Oct. 1884.

111 LAC, RG 2, PC 2480, 10 Dec. 1883.

112 For Van Horne's letter, see Supporting Documents. For order: LAC, RG 2, PC 1174, 27 May 1884.

113 LAC, RG 2, PC 1226, 2 June 1884.

114 A second commissioner, Raymond Bruyère, had been appointed in May but his commission was withdrawn. LAC, RG 2, PC 771 and PC 1126, dated 12 April 1884 and 2 June 1884, respectively.

115 No correspondence has been found in relation to Abbott's appointment. There is an obvious conflict of interest for a CPR employee to be appointed as peace and police commissioner. The arrangement between the government and the CPR can only be surmised in the absence of access to CPR archives but, in a departure from the normal pattern (where a salary figure was stated in the order), a note attached to the proclamation said: '"and Mr. Abbott's salary to be paid by the Canadian Pacific Company."' LAC, RG 2, PC 1257, 8 July 1884.

116 *Globe*, 13 Nov. 1884.

117 *Globe*, 20 Oct. 1884.

118 For a detailed account, see Binnie, 'Explorations,' chapter 4.

119 LAC, RG 2, PC 1980, 14 Oct. 1884. No record of allegations against him has been found but Gough received no further appointments as a commissioner.

120 Ibid.

121 A federal government record shows payment of forty-two dollars for transportation by steamer of six policemen to Michipicoten, presumably part of the cost for moving the police along the north shore from the Sault. LAC, RG 13, vol. 61, 1278/1884.

122 Rat Portage was a settlement on the north shore of Lake of the Woods, based on lumbering with some mining. Permanent white settlement began there in 1876 because of railway construction and the need for lumber; a gold strike in 1882 encouraged more settlers. See W.L. Morton, *Manitoba: A History* (Toronto: University of Toronto Press 1957), 218; official Kenora website: www.kenora.ca/portal/tourism.

123 The boundary dispute is one of the 'provincial rights' cases between the federal government (which furthered the case for Manitoba) and Ontario. See Robert C. Vipond, *Liberty and Community: Canadian Federalism and the Failure of the Constitution* (Albany: SNUY 1991), 170. The dispute, begun before confederation, came to the fore in the 1870s after the creation of the North-West Territories in 1869 and Manitoba in 1870 and intensified with the development of the North-West. The disputed area of Keewatin had been awarded to Ontario in 1878 by a commission of inquiry agreed to by Ontario and the Dominion. The decision located Ontario's western boundary at Lake of the Woods, placing Rat Portage within Ontario. The dispute continued, nonetheless, for a further eleven years. The federal government under Macdonald worked in opposition to Ontario's claims, disallowing an Ontario statute providing for the administration of justice in the area that included Rat Portage, enacting federal legislation for the same purpose, and encouraging Manitoba to assert control in the territory. The issue of the boundary between Ontario and Manitoba was heard before the Judicial Committee of the Privy Council in 1884 and finally settled in 1889. See *Proceedings before the Imperial Privy Council re Boundary of Ontario* (Toronto: Warwick and Sons 1889).

124 I am grateful to one of the peer reviewers for emphasizing this point.

125 Sections 42, 41, and 25 were now proclaimed. As the railway line ran through Rat Portage, the village was in the middle of five sections of proclaimed line that ran from Selkirk, Manitoba, to near Prince Arthur's Landing and Fort William, a distance of about four hundred and fifty miles.

126 SC 1869 c.24 s.1.3.

127 See LAC, RG 13, A4, Correspondence Miscellaneous Departments, 1867–81.

128 The accused in more serious cases at Rat Portage were being sent to Winnipeg for prosecution since the village was closer to a high court judge in that city (about one hundred and thirty miles by train) than to a police magistrate in Prince Arthur (Thunder Bay), Ontario (about three hundred and twenty miles). The practice of sending serious cases to Winnipeg continued in the early 1880s without practical opposition from Ontario; on two occasions, in June 1882 and January 1883, residents of Rat Portage charged with murder were tried in Winnipeg. See History of Policing, Winnipeg Police Service, www.winnipeg.ca/police/history/.

129 SC 1880 c.36, An Act respecting the Administration of Criminal Justice in the Territory in Dispute between the Governments of the Province of Ontario and of the Dominion of Canada. The Dominion had disallowed an Ontario statute governing the administration of justice in the area. SO 1879 c.19, An Act respecting the Administration of Justice in the Northerly and Westerly

Parts of Ontario. *Dominion and Provincial Legislation, 1867–1895* (Ottawa: Government Printing Bureau 1896).

130 House of Commons, *Debates*, 3 May 1880, 1939.

131 Senator Scott of Ottawa. Senate, *Debates*, 5 May 1880.

132 Mowat, infuriated by Manitoba's moves in the disputed area, stated: 'It is absolutely necessary that we should go and take possession, that we should assume the duty of enforcing the laws there unless some satisfactory provisional arrangement can be made.' Ontario, *Debates of Legislature*, 27 Jan. 1882.

133 The details of Ontario's position, its actions and appointments of local officials, are set out in a lengthy report, 'Report of the Attorney General of Ontario (Oliver Mowat) to the Lieutenant-Governor of Ontario, 29th September, 1883,' AO, RG 75, vol. 16, *Ontario Orders in Council, 1883.*

134 Winnipeg Police Service, 'History of Policing.' The officials included a local coroner and constables.

135 Based on Department of Justice records for the period. LAC, RG 2, PC 1282, 7 July 1880.

136 LAC, RG 13, A4, Correspondence Miscellaneous Departments, 1867–81.

137 Waite, *Canada*, 118.

138 The contractor was building sections 15, 42, and 41 of the line. See LAC, RG 2, PC 2116, 27 Oct. 1882.

139 The order was not gazetted and was filed marked 'error.'

140 Rat Portage was recorded in the 1881 census as consisting of 89 'households' and 92 'families.' Thirty-nine signatures was a considerable number as some residents were probably illiterate. See LAC, 1881 Census, mfm. C-13283, Province of Keewatin, District no. 192, The Territories, B No. 2, Rat Portage, 1–14.

141 The petition was forwarded with the assistance of Simon J. Dawson, now a federal MP. For the full text, see Supporting Documents in this volume.

142 LAC, RG 2, PC 850, 11 April 1883; RG 13, A2, vol. 1886, 976/1883.

143 LAC, RG 13, vol. 1866, 976/1883.

144 Both S.J. Dawson and W.H. Plummer were faithful Tory MPs based in the District of Algoma. Both were intimately involved with planning election strategies for that part of the country (LAC, Morgan, MG 29, D61: vol. 7, 2273–8; vol.17, 6611–16).

145 LAC, RG 2, PC 1462, 26 June 1883. Two weeks passed before withdrawal of the proclamation under the Peace Act was gazetted, and only after further urgings from Manitoban Tories to the prime minister. LAC, Macdonald Papers, mfm C-1762 189062–3; 120369–71; LAC, RG 13, A-2, vol. 18866, 976/1883.

146 LAC, Macdonald Papers, vol. 34, letter to J.H. Pope, 4 July 1884.

147 AO, MS 203(1) RG 3, vol. 16/347, 366, 377, 383, 440.

148 Oliver letter to Dawson, 5 May 1883, LAC, RG 13, A-2, vol. 18866, 976/1883.

149 This account draws from the Winnipeg *Free Press*, including 28 July 1883.

150 LAC. Macdonald Papers, vol. 34, 28 July 1883.

151 LAC, RG 13, vol. 468, 1252/1883.

152 For White, see R.C. McLeod, *The NWMP and Law Enforcement 1873–1905* (Toronto: University of Toronto Press 1976), 41–2.

153 AO, Macdonald Papers, reel 12, 13062–164, for the problems at Rat Portage; White's telegram is at 13100.

154 See LAC, RG 13, 1344/1883, August 1883. McCabe's name disappears from departmental records, suggesting that he may have declined the appointment to Sudbury.

155 According to Sam Steele, the NWMP were ordered to Rat Portage in July 1883 (Steele, *Forty Years*, 1734). White's telegram does not suggest that the police at Rat Portage were Mounties. Another source reports friction at Rat Portage in September 1883, with militia summoned from Winnipeg (J.J.B. Pariseau, *Disorders, Strikes*, 7–8, 81).

156 Labourers hired by contractor Andrew Onderdonk had been working there since 1880. At Farwell, they included survivors from among 2,000 Chinese labourers brought to British Columbia to work on the railway. See Margaret A. Ormsby, *British Columbia: A History* (Vancouver: Macmillan 1958, 1971), 281. Brereton was sent west in 1881 as a peace commissioner appointed to enforce the act in the Yale and Whitemouth areas. LAC, RG 2: PC 78, 3 Jan. 1881; PC 215, 5 Feb. 1881; PC 302, 28 Feb. 1881.

157 In effect, up the Fraser and Thompson rivers, along the line of the railway.

158 At the request of the CPR. Exceptionally, in an 1884 order, the proclamation was extended to twenty miles, instead of the usual ten on each side of the line (and then revised to ten miles in 1885), the explanation being that 'the width being named being insufficient to afford immunity from the presence of liquor sellers.' LAC, RG 2, PC 1233, 2 June 1884; RG 2, PC 1759, 8 Sept. 1884; RG 2, PC 777, 11 April 1885; RG 2, PC 1236, 2 July 1885.

159 See Bill Waiser's chapter in this volume for references to Irvine and Steele's actions during the North-West rebellion of 1885.

160 See: LAC, RG 2, PC 985, 6 May 1884; PC 1110, 16 May 1884; Johnston's appointment, PC 1236, 2 July 1885. In response to the Riel rebellion, NWMP officers were transferred to the territories but returned to British Columbia in the fall and were appointed for additional areas. RG 2, PC 1815, 24 Sept. 1885.

161 Steele, *Forty Years*, 186.

162 This petition, addressed to the governor general (with signatures including

those of three JPs), demanded fewer quashings of convictions by the B.C. Supreme Court and appeared to result in the extension of prohibition under the Peace Act to the village of Yale. A proclamation was issued two months later. LAC, RG 13, vol. 52, 1882/476, March 1882; LAC, RG 2, PC 906, 3 May 1882.

163 Sproat, a liberal and well-educated Scot, had previous experience as an administrator and land-claims commissioner in British Columbia and dedicated himself to the Kootenay after 1883 (*DCB Online*). For Sproat's earlier career, see Douglas Harris, *Landing Native Fisheries: Indian Reserves and Fishing Rights in British Columbia, 1849–1925* (Vancouver: UBC Press 2008), 24–59.

164 Steele, *Forty Years*, 187, 234.

165 Macleod, a Conservative appointee of Macdonald's as commissioner of the NWMP, resigned in 1880 but remained a stipendiary magistrate for the territories until 1886 when he became one of the first members of the territorial Supreme Court. Steele acted as Macleod's assistant during resolution of the dispute between Johnston and Sproat. Roderick G. Martin, 'Macleod at Law,' in J. Swainger and C. Backhouse, eds., *People and Place* (Vancouver: UBC Press 2003). For Macleod's appointment, see LAC, RG 2, PC 1647, 3 Sept. 1885.

166 The report is found in multiple sources, e.g., LAC, RG 2, PC 2215, 27 Oct. 1885; RG 13, vol. 62, 1885 (391–500), 6.

167 See Patricia Roy, 'Law and Order in British Columbia in the 1880s: Images and Realities,' in R.C. McLeod, ed., *Swords and Ploughshares* (Edmonton: University of Alberta Press 1993), 55–90.

168 No proclamation to this effect is recorded.

169 LAC, RG 6, series A-1, vol. 64, p.17, file 14296; RG 2, 1886–0205G. Again, no proclamations to this effect are recorded but the statute appears not to have been applied along the line in British Columbia after May 1887.

170 See Eric Tucker's discussion in this volume. See also Desmond Morton, *Aid to the Civil Power*; J.J.B. Pariseau, *Disarders, Strikes*; Don Macgillivray, *Military Aid*.

6

Street Railway Strikes, Collective Violence, and the Canadian State, 1886–1914

ERIC TUCKER

Imagine the following scenario, which repeated itself with remarkable frequency in North American cities in the decades that bookmarked the turn of the twentieth century.[1] Late one night a group of street railway drivers and conductors met to discuss their work grievances.[2] Wages were low, hours were long, working conditions were poor, and discipline was rigid and often arbitrary. They decided to form a local branch of the Amalgamated Association of Street Railway Employees (AASRE) and began organizing their fellow workers.[3] Within a matter of days, the employer caught wind of their activities and fired some of the instigators, allegedly for misconduct. Nevertheless, the vast majority of the drivers and conductors joined the union and shortly thereafter a list of demands was presented, including a wage increase, reinstatement of the discharged men, establishment of a grievance procedure, and recognition of the union. The street railway company refused the demands and was especially adamant about not recognizing the union. Newspapers carried the exchange and local officials and prominent citizens attempted to bring the parties together. There was considerable public sympathy for the men. Not only were they familiar figures to the citizens who regularly rode the streetcars, but they were employed by a reviled monopoly that failed to provide service at promised or expected levels, was constantly in conflict with the city over street repairs and fares, and was widely viewed as corrupt and avaricious. While negotiations were proceeding, the company prepared for a strike by contracting with a private firm that specialized in operating street railways with strikebreakers imported from other cities.

When the strike started, members of the union donned their uniforms and paraded along the street railway lines, bearing banners and pins emblazoned with the slogan 'We will walk.' Large crowds composed of a cross-section of the city's working population greeted them and took up the slogan. Many newspaper editorialists, local officials, clergymen, and even local business owners expressed their support for the strikers, the latter sometimes refusing to sell provisions to the strikebreakers while providing goods on credit to the striking workers and their families.

Soon, however, the street railway company attempted to restore operations. Cars operated by strikebreakers carrying armed security guards attempted to leave the car barns but were impeded by crowds gathered outside. Teamsters slowly drove across the tracks, further impeding the cars' progress and making them and the strikebreaking operators and security guards easier targets for the objects and opprobrium cast in their direction. The local police were undermanned to deal with the situation and could do little to clear the crowds. A few of the more enthusiastic rock throwers, young boys often, were arrested, but it quickly became apparent that the cars could not operate and service was stopped. Notably, striking workers played a small role in these confrontations.

At this point, the street railway company pressured local officials to take stronger measures to restore law and order. Newspaper editors also emphatically declared that hooliganism and mob behaviour could not be condoned. These low-level street confrontations, however, continued for several more days, until the street railway company decided to force the issue by operating its cars on a Friday night, notwithstanding pleas from local officials that it was not safe to do so. As the streetcars emerged from the barns, crowds again blocked their way, but this time the violence escalated into full-scale rioting. Streetcars were destroyed and the street railway's offices were invaded and ransacked. Police were overwhelmed and the police commissioners met in emergency session. The mayor was dispatched to read the Riot Act and the militia was requisitioned. By the next morning, the militia arrived and the rioting ended. In the meantime, efforts to end the strike were stepped up and shortly thereafter a compromise agreement was reached, which provided for a small wage increase and the establishment of a grievance procedure but no formal recognition of the union as the men's bargaining agent.

In Canada between 1886 and 1914, thirteen of the seventeen street railway strikes or lockouts that occurred in nine different cities were accompanied by significant public disorder (see Table 1). Of course, in this period, as in others, some disorder was not uncommon during strikes and lockouts. Striking workers often sought to deter workers from taking their places, using a variety of tactics ranging from peaceful persuasion to bribes to threats and intimidation to assault. Employers also hired thugs to attack strikers. The level of disorder, however, was usually low and it was largely confined to the parties directly involved in the conflict. Coal mining strikes were an exception insofar as the whole community, populated largely by miners and their families, often became involved. The unique feature of street railway strikes was that the participants in the street confrontations represented a cross-section of the city's working-class population, making them community displays of solidarity for striking workers.

Street railway strikes were often the occasion for the most serious incidents of public disorder in a city's history. The challenge to public authorities, however, was not just in the scale of the disorder but also in the disjuncture between the behaviour that a significant portion of the working-class community felt was legitimate in the circumstances and what the law formally tolerated. Public officials confronted with this disorder had to negotiate between the disparate zones of community and legal toleration. How much disorder would they tolerate before mobilizing the coercive power of the state to protect the right of the street railways to operate with strikebreakers and how much coercive power were they prepared to deploy to impose the law's order? These are the central questions this chapter addresses, but, before turning to the street railway strikes, it will be helpful to examine briefly the development of the state's power to maintain civic order in the second half of the nineteenth century.

STATE RESPONSES TO WORKERS' COLLECTIVE DISORDER BEFORE 1914

Broadly speaking, the repertoire of state responses to workers' collective action consisted of a mixture of conciliation and coercion. State conciliation involved attempts to assist workers and employers to find a mutually acceptable resolution to their dispute. Sometimes conciliation was legally required prior to strikes or lockouts, as in industries covered by the 1907 Industrial Dispute Investigation Act (IDIA),[4] but more commonly conciliation occurred on a voluntary basis, whether pursuant to trade-dispute

Table 1: Street railway strikes, Canada, 1886–1914

Place	Date	Issue	Union	# of Employees	Mediation	Disorder	State Response	Strike Outcome
Toronto, Ont.	March 1886 (3 days)	Firing of union members	Knights of Labor	300	City councilors	Crowds blocked tracks; cars damaged; confrontations with police; police and citizens injured	Police attempted to keep tracks clear and protect co. property; arrests resulting in fines and imprisonment	Union members reinstated
Toronto, Ont.	May–June 1886	Firing of union members	Knights of Labor	300	None	Crowds blocked tracks; cars damaged; confrontations with police; police and citizens injured	Police and mounted police attempted to keep tracks clear and protect co. property; arrests resulting in fines	Strike lost, union disbanded
Hamilton, Ont.	Sept. 1892 (3 days)	Firing of union members	Local association	807	None	None	None	Compromise: improved conditions, discharged men paid off; strikers subsequently laid off
London, Ont.	Oct. 1898 (15 days)	Firing of union members; working conditions; union recognition	Amalgamated Association of Street Railway Employees (AASRE)	110	None	Cars pelted, operators taunted	None	Compromise: reinstatement, improved conditions, right to join union but no recognition

Table 1: (*Continued*)

Place	Date	Issue	Union	# of Employees	Mediation	Disorder	State Response	Strike Outcome
London, Ont.	May–Nov. 1899	Firing of union members; working conditions; union recognition	AASRE	110	None	Escalating crowd violence leading to riot (8 July)	Riot Act read; Militia called up; arrests resulting in fines and imprisonment	Strike lost
Toronto, Ont.	June 1902 (3 days)	Firing of union members; working conditions; union recognition	AASRE	1,000	Board of Trade	Large crowds blocked cars; stones thrown; cars damaged	Militia called up but strike settled before they arrived; arrests	Union win: right to organize recognized; grievance procedure; wage increase
Montreal, Que.	Feb. 1903 (2 days)	Firing of union members; wage increase; union recognition	Montreal Street Railway Employees Association of North America	1,200	Committee of city council	Minor crowd violence	Local police; few arrests	Union victory
Montreal, Que.	May 1903 (4 days)	Wages and working conditions; grievance procedure; union recognition; closed shop	AASRE	1,500	Mediation by mayor refused by employer	Minor crowd violence	Local police; few arrests	Company victory; Feb. agreement restored; local association replaces AASRE

Table 1: (*Continued*)

Place	Date	Issue	Union	# of Employees	Mediation	Disorder	State Response	Strike Outcome
Cornwall, Ont.	June 1905 (7 days)	Wage increase	?	22	Federal Department of Labour under the Conciliation Act	None	None	No change in wages
Winnipeg, Man.	March 1906 (9 days)	Union recognition; wages	AASRE	254	Winnipeg Ministerial Association	Crowd violence; rioting; strikebreakers assaulted pickets	Riot Act read; Militia called up; arrests resulting in fines and imprisonment	Compromise
London, Ont.	July 1906 (21 days)	Discharge of union members; work conditions	AASRE	100	Ontario Railway and Municipal Board (ORMB)	None	Local police; strike sympathizer arrested and fined for calling motorman a scab	Union loss
Lévis, Que.	Sept. 1906 (2 days)	Discharge of union activists	National Union of Motormen and Conductors	40	None	None	None	Union loss
Hamilton, Ont.	Nov. 1906 (26 days)	Discharge of union president; failure to comply with prior arbitration award	AASRE	180	ORMB Arbitration	Escalating crowd violence leading to riot	Riot Act read; militia called up and deployed; arrests resulting in fines and imprisonment	Arbitration of disagreement by ORMB produces compromise

Table 1: (*Concluded*)

Place	Date	Issue	Union	# of Employees	Mediation	Disorder	State Response	Strike Outcome
Winnipeg, Man.	Dec. 1910 (15 days)	Discharge of union officers	AASRE	550	IDIA before strike; prominent citizens after	Escalating crowd violence	Local police; arrests resulting in fines and imprisonment	Terms not disclosed; strikers rehired
Port Arthur / Fort William, Ont.	May–June 1913 (1 month)	Discharge of employees; wage increase	Amalgamated Union of Electrical Car Workers of America	85	IDIA (before strike commenced)	Crowd violence; one sympathizer shot and killed by police another woulded	Local police; arrests	Union loss
Halifax, N.S.	May 1913 (4 days)	Wage increase	AASRE	140	City Board of Control	Crowd violence; car wrecking	Local police; arrests	Compromise
Saint John, N.B.	July 1914 (5 days)	Discharge of union officer and men	AASRE	136	Municipal official	Crowd violence; sympathizer shot in leg by police officer	Riot Act read; soldiers charged crowd; troops requested; arrests	9 of 11 discharged workers reinstated

legislation, such as the Railway Labour Disputes Act,[5] or on an ad hoc basis. While conciliation played a role in the prevention and settlement of street railway strikes, the focus of this chapter is on the control of strike-related activity, an area that was addressed through the state's repertoire of coercive responses.

State coercion could be invoked in response to violations of the workplace, marketplace, or civic order of liberal capitalism. Workplace order refers to the system of property and contract that provided the legal ground rules governing relations between workers and employers; marketplace order refers to the law governing exchange relationships outside the workplace; and civic order refers to the law governing behaviour on the street.[6] State coercion was directly implicated in the workplace order through the law of master and servant, which treated servants' breaches of the contract of employment as a crime punishable by imprisonment. In the period of street railway strikes covered by this chapter, however, employee breaches of contract had been largely decriminalized, and, even though some provincial master and servant statutes treated employee breaches as punishable offences, there is no evidence that striking street railway workers were ever prosecuted for their violation. Hence the development of this branch of coercive labour law will not be explored here.[7] Also, because they were not used in street railway strikes, this chapter will not examine the developing economic torts or labour injunctions, even though they were available during the period under discussion to protect the workplace or the marketplace order and were clearly a form of direct state coercion that could lead to the deployment of police and the arrest and prosecution of workers for being in contempt of the court's order.[8]

The focus here is on the historical development of the repertoire of coercive state powers exercised in response to the challenges to civic order posed by workers' collective action, whether it be the actions of striking workers or their sympathizers in working-class communities. In pre-confederation Canada, coercive state force was most frequently directed at the actions of unskilled or 'rough' workers.[9] Lacking monopolies of skill or stable organizations, common labourers such as canallers, railway labourers, shipyard workers, and raftsmen found it difficult to counter their exploitation by unscrupulous contractors or to resist the effects of intense labour market competition simply by withdrawing their labour and more or less peacefully discouraging other workers from taking their places. Typically, these workers were hired onto large crews in rural areas, and their plebian traditions countenanced violence which not only threatened their employers' physical security and property but also challenged the thin ranks of the legal authorities. In addition, many of these workers came from the racialized groups of the time – especially the Irish – who were viewed as violence-prone by Canadian elites.[10] For example, during a strike by Irish workers on the Beauharnois Canal in 1843, troops were called out and fired on the canallers when they attempted to march on the homes of contractors after failing to disperse following a reading of the Riot Act.[11] At least five canallers were killed and many others were wounded. Twenty-seven were taken into custody.[12] Subsequently, the Legislative Assembly enacted a statute aimed at containing disorder in the vicinity of public works 'on which large bodies of labourers are congregated and employed.'[13] The act provided for the disarming of labourers and the establishment of a mounted police force. Magistrates thereafter made frequent use of military and special police forces at the first sign of unrest on public works.[14]

The legal arrangements for policing strikes in other settings during the pre-confederation period, however, remained problematic, at least from the point of view of local authorities. Policing in general was a local responsibility initially under the control of the magistrates in Quarter Sessions. Beginning in the 1830s, municipal councils of incorporated cities appointed police officers, but this system fostered partisanship that proved to be particularly problematic when the source of the disorder was rooted in sectarian conflict. Moreover, parsimonious councils were often reluctant to appoint a sufficient number of officers for routine law enforcement, let alone to deal with episodes of public disorder.[15] As well, before 1855, local authorities lacked the power to requisition the militia in some British North American jurisdictions, including the Province of Canada, and central authorities were often reluctant to do so.[16]

These difficulties manifested themselves during an 1851 strike of railway labourers building the Great Western Railway (GWR) near Dundas, Ontario. To enforce their demand for an increase of wages, labourers marched through the streets of Dundas, armed with bludgeons and threatening workers who would not join their work stoppage. The local police could not control the crowd. In response, the local elite called a public meeting, which was addressed by Allan MacNab, a leading promoter of the GWR and prominent Tory politician, and sponsored a petition that called upon the government to dispatch troops to 'overawe the turbulent, afford protection to the peaceable and industrious, and in case of necessity, aid the Civil power in enforcing the laws.'[17] No troops were deployed, however, and it is unknown just how the conflict was resolved.

In 1854 MacNab became the Canada West leader of the coalition government of the Province of Canada, which shortly thereafter established a commission to investigate 'the best means of re-organizing the militia of Canada, and providing an efficient and economical system of Public Defence and to report upon an improved system of Police for the better preservation of the public peace.' MacNab was one of the commissioners. The commissioners recommended that one or more local magistrates should be authorized to requisition the militia and that militia members should be sworn in as special constables under the command of the magistrate while on duty. The commissioners also recommended that the municipality be responsible for the lodging and expenses of the men. Finally, the commission investigated the system of policing generally and found that affairs were 'in anything but a satisfactory state.' The causes of the problem included 'the practice of permitting the men to live among, instead of isolating them from, those against whom they may be required to act.' The commission recommended the establishment of a provincial police force that municipalities could rely upon by taking up a share of its expense.[18] The legislature subsequently enacted a new militia act implementing the commission's recommendations in that regard, but the proposal to establish a provincial police force was defeated because of alarm over the force's centralizing tendencies, which were seen to pose a threat to the liberties of the people. Instead, in 1858, an amendment to the Municipal Corporations Act removed control over the police from municipal councils and vested it in local police boards composed of the mayor, the police magistrate, and the recorder.[19]

In post-confederation Canada, the federal government was vested with authority over the militia and the criminal law.[20] One early priority was to re-establish the legislative foundation for the maintenance of public order. The 1868 Militia Act included the provisions from the 1855 Province of Canada statute giving local authorities the power to requisition the militia and making the local municipality responsible for the militia's costs.[21] That same year the government also re-enacted the Riot Act,[22] and the following year it passed the Peace Preservation Act, a composite of earlier Province of Canada statutes regulating the sale of liquor and the carrying of weapons around public-works projects.[23]

The depressed economic conditions that prevailed through most of the 1870s fuelled a sharp rise in collective violence, involving both labour and interethnic conflict. Local officials called out the militia during strikes on numerous occasions, including strikes by coal miners in Nova Scotia (1876) and British Columbia (1877), locomotive engineers (1876–7), and

Lachine canal workers (1877). In order to avoid having to bear the cost, local officials sometimes sought to convince the federal government to initiate the call-up, but Liberal Prime Minister Alexander Mackenzie was unenthusiastic about becoming involved. For example, he resisted demands that his government requisition troops to intervene in the Grand Trunk Railway strike of 1876–7 or the Lachine canal strike of 1877. The return of the Conservatives under John A. Macdonald ushered in a new era and troops were called out in response to a minor disturbance during a strike of railway construction labourers at Cross Lake in the Keewatin district in 1878 as well as during rioting between French and Irish longshoremen in Quebec City that same year. In part, the difference in approach was rooted in an urban-rural distinction: whereas municipalities normally could be expected to be responsible for policing and its costs, in rural areas, especially in strikes on work projects having national significance, the federal government not only saw itself as having a greater role to play but also had less tolerance for disorderly conduct that interfered with such works' completion.[24] In fact, the rural-urban distinction was partially embedded in law, since the Peace Preservation Act could not be invoked in municipal areas. However, in the face of an escalating incidence of armed violence in urban areas, especially sectarian riots, the federal government enacted legislation against the improper use of firearms in 1877, and the following year it passed the Blake Act, which drew on the Peace Preservation Act and imperial legislation aimed at restricting the possession of arms in Ireland. Essentially, that act restricted the carrying of weapons and firearms in designated localities and empowered authorities to conduct searches to find concealed weapons. It was subsequently proclaimed in force in Quebec City following rioting between rival French and Irish longshoremen in 1879, apparently its only use in response to labour violence.[25]

The militia was not widely viewed as an effective force and on at least one occasion a question was raised about the appropriateness of having members of labour organizations in the ranks. Pressure began to develop in some quarters to professionalize the army, including the creation of a permanent force, but progress was slow and by 1913 the size of that force had reached 3,100 while the militia numbered 74,000. Moreover, concerns were raised about the problems of holding municipalities responsible for the cost of paying for military aid. An 1883 amendment authorized the government to advance these expenses, and in 1904 the crown became responsible for recovering the expenses from the municipality, rather than the commanding officer. The 1904 amendment also required the mayor or county warden to be among the three officials signing the requisition. Finally, it stipulated that the permanent force, if available, was to be called in before recourse was had to the militia.[26]

This was the federal repertoire for enforcing public order that was in place during the street railway strikes from 1886 to 1914,[27] but, as John Weaver has noted, 'the North American pattern of law and order was at root a municipally based one.'[28] Yet, while local police forces bore the major responsibility for handling collective disorder, their size and capability varied considerably. The police force of each municipality was governed by a police commission composed of the mayor, the police magistrate, and a county court judge. Although this provided the police with some insulation from local politicians, decisions about how to deploy police, where to set the limits of toleration for disorder, and when to call for military assistance were strongly influenced by local politics. As well, criminal justice was primarily administered on a local level. Minor criminal charges were prosecuted before police magistrates, although for some offences the accused could elect trial by judge and jury, which took them out of the magistrate's court and into a higher one. Magistrates exercised a pretty free hand in their bailiwicks, which allowed them considerable discretion to determine the boundaries of legal strike-related conduct as well as the severity of the penalties for those who were convicted.[29]

In part, the power of the magistrates to interpret the law derived from its ambiguities. For example, at the same time that the Conservative federal government enacted the Trade Union Act, granting workers immunity from prosecution for conspiracy for combining to increase their wages, it also passed the Criminal Law Amendment Act, which made it a criminal offence for workers to threaten, intimidate, molest, or obstruct masters or workmen from engaging in lawful activities. Molestation and obstruction was defined to include persistent following and watching and besetting.[30] Organized labour objected that the law would be used by 'unprofessional magistrates' to restrict legitimate trade-union activity and began a campaign for its repeal.[31] Amendments were enacted in 1875 and 1876 that narrowed the scope of criminal liability by exempting peaceful picketing from the definition of 'watching and besetting,' by specifying that criminal intimidation had to be accompanied by the threat of violence, and by providing that prosecutions for criminal conspiracy could not be maintained unless the acts were punishable by statute.[32] Notwithstanding these amendments, magistrates still were left with leeway in determining what constituted criminal intimidation or other public-order offences such as disorderly conduct. The omission of the peaceful-picketing exemption in the watching and besetting provision re-enacted in the 1892 Criminal Code gave the magistrates even greater scope for deciding the boundaries of lawful conduct.[33] Moreover, because magistrates' decisions were rarely appealed, they operated with minimal supervision by the superior courts.

PUTTING THE LAW TO WORK: STREET RAILWAY STRIKES, 1886–1914

With this background, we can now turn to the operation of local justice in street railway strikes between 1886 and 1914. The focus of the analysis shifts from the development of instruments of coercion available to local authorities to contain worker and other popular manifestations of collective disorder to the question of when and how they were used. What were the social and political limits of toleration? How much coercive force was to be used to limit collective action when it came to be viewed by local authorities as exceeding the zone of legal and social or political toleration? Finally, how were differences over the zone of toleration negotiated in the polarized context of labour conflict?

It will be helpful to begin by clarifying why disputes over the zone of toleration were both so sharp and so common in strikes and lockouts. The basic objective of the parties to a labour dispute is to generate economic pressure that will force the other side to accept terms and conditions that it otherwise would reject. Street railway companies sought to defeat their unionized workers by hiring non-union workers and continuing to provide service, activities that were legally protected. Freedom of contract dictated that employers were at liberty to hire replacement workers. For the most part, the problem facing street railway companies was a practical one. Hiring replacement workers from the local labour market was a dicey business since new recruits were vulnerable to being legally persuaded or unlawfully intimidated to quit by striking workers and their sympathizers. American detective agencies identified a business opportunity for the provision of professional strikebreakers, and one company, Jim Farley's, specialized in breaking street railway strikes.[34] These services came to be widely used in Canada and were perfectly legal as long as strikebreakers were not imported under contract from the United States in violation of the Alien Labour Act.[35] Although striking workers often alleged that this law was being violated, the railway companies always insisted that strikebreakers were obtained from other Canadian cities, and no prosecutions under this act were ever initiated in a street railway strike.[36]

Once the strikebreakers were in place, the focus of the conflict shifted to the streets. For the street railway companies, maintenance of civic order was essential to allow them to provide service and thereby render the strike ineffective. For striking workers, the dilemma at this point was how to make their strike effective when the law governing civic order severely limited their ability to disrupt their employers' operations. It was clearly illegal for striking workers or their sympathizers to physically damage the property of the street railways, to prevent streetcars from travelling along the tracks, to assault or intimidate strikebreakers, or to interfere with members of the public who wished to use the service. As a matter of law, striking workers' options were limited to withdrawing their own labour and peacefully persuading other workers not to take their places and members of the public not to use the streetcars.[37] Moreover, it was also strategically important for street railway workers to maintain as much public support for their cause as they possibly could.

The pattern of events that followed was described at the outset, and will not be repeated here, except to note that the striking workers themselves largely stayed well within the bounds of legality and enjoyed much public sympathy but that crowds of supporters increasingly became more aggressive and the bounds of legality began to be crossed. The question for local officials, including mayors, council members, police chiefs, magistrates, and police commissioners, was what to do about it. But, before exploring in more depth the state's response to the collective violence accompanying street railway strikes, we first need to understand better who was involved and the causes of the violence. It is important to reiterate that the striking workers were not the main participants; indeed, as noted earlier, the union distanced itself from the crowd and denounced the violence. By all accounts, the crowds themselves were comprised of a cross-section of the working-class population of the community in which the strike occurred. The ethnicity of the crowd received little comment, except in the Lakehead where the press emphasized the role of Finnish and Hungarian immigrants 'inflamed by socialist agitation' in the violence, leading the Ottawa *Journal* to comment: 'The "bad actors" in the industrial world in America almost invariably are foreigners, men who do not seem to understand to the full what law means in this country.'[38] The presence of women and girls was frequently noted as well as that of respectable classes. For example, commenting on the riots in Hamilton, Police Chief Alexander Smith expressed his disappointment 'that so many respectable citizens and their wives were seen on the streets.'[39] There is, however, also general agreement that while women and girls played a supporting role, men and particularly young men took the lead in the more aggressive crowd actions.[40]

Why were street railway strikes so violent? There is the obvious point that the opportunities for workers and the public to confront the employer directly were markedly greater in street railway strikes simply because much of the work was performed on public streets rather than on private property. The challenge of providing security in these circumstances was far greater than in other industrial settings, since it was not enough simply to prevent trespassing on, or ensure access to or egress from, a particular piece of private property. Rather, security had to be provided to a fleet of cars that travelled on rights of way granted over public streets, an undertaking that most police forces lacked the resources to accomplish even if they were committed to do so.

Of course, opportunity alone hardly explains the incidence and extent of collective violence during street railway strikes; we must also consider people's motivations. A variety of views has been offered to explain crowd violence, some of which focus on the breakdown of normal constraints while others emphasize the sources of discontent and the cultural and ideological factors that legitimize the use of violence in particular contexts.[41] In street railway strikes, doubtless the gathering of excited crowds, often on Friday night or Saturday afternoon, provided a more permissive environment for displays of youthful rebelliousness and bravado,[42] but a narrow focus on crowd psychology would miss the more important influences that explain the usually high incidence of collective violence.

One factor that has been noted in many studies is the unpopularity of street railway companies. Although most street railways were private businesses, their operations were by their very nature public. They obtained monopoly franchises with the cities that contained provisions regarding service, road maintenance, and fares, all issues that regularly became contentious. As Robert Babcock notes, 'the location of lines, the efficiency of service, and the fares charged were a constant concern of the citizenry' and street railway companies were commonly portrayed in the press as rich monopolists exploiting the public.[43] For example, just days before the Halifax street railway strike in 1913, the Halifax *Herald* campaigned against provincial legislation that, it claimed, benefited the tramway company at the expense of the citizens of Halifax, running a cartoon on its front page showing the 'Grafter' stepping on the 'People' as the provincial government stood by laughing (see Figure 1).[44] The fact that Montreal interests owned the company likely exacerbated people's sense that they were being exploited.

Figure 1: Halifax *Herald*, 14 May 1913

The Halifax Tramway's $2,000,000 Water Bill Has Passed

This view of the street railway companies fed into an older producerist ideology, which saw the world divided between producers and monopolists, so that the workers' interests were viewed as more consonant with those of the broader community.[45] The personal relationships that often developed between passengers and motormen and conductors who ran the same route for years strengthened community support for street railway workers, even as those communities were becoming increasingly class-divided.[46] As well, the willingness of community members to participate in collective disorder reflected widespread support for the basic demands being made by the striking workers: a right to collective representation, a grievance procedure, a living wage, reasonable hours of work, and basic amenities like seats. The reasonableness of the union's demands was strengthened by its willingness to submit all outstanding differences to arbitration. Indeed, the AASRE, the union that represented street railway workers, recognized that this stance legitimized their bargaining in the eyes of the public and required local unions to demand binding arbitration as a condition of receiving financial support for a strike.[47] Finally, the street railway companies' choice of tactics, in particular the use of 'scab' labour and the hiring of professional strikebreakers, violated the moral economy (or what the Montreal *Gazette* referred to as 'a false moral code'[48]) of the crowd and, at least for a moment, created conditions in which a substantial number of individuals were prepared to vent their outrage by drawing on older traditions of rough justice that violated official norms of civic order which, when enforced, clearly favoured the company.[49] Phillips Thompson, a lawyer turned labour journalist, captured this sentiment in commenting on the disturbances surrounding the 1886 Toronto street railway strike: 'Whenever there is long continued and deep-seated injustice – wherever human rights are defied and trampled upon, there will be aroused a spirit of resistance which sometimes may overpass its legitimate bounds ... But we do say that however misled or inconsiderate or even criminal some actions done in the heat of the conflict between Labor and capitalism may be, the responsibility for those actions rests on the individuals, and the system which provoked them.'[50]

It also must be remembered that strike sympathizers were not the only ones to violate the law or engage in acts of intimidation and violence. Professional strikebreakers had a well-established and well-deserved reputation for taking matters into their own hands without much regard for law. For example, during the 1906 Winnipeg strike, Thiel detectives were accused of attacking not only peaceful picketers and sympathizers but also the mayor and city solicitor. As well, strikebreakers frequently brandished guns and in Halifax and Saint John they fired on a crowd as it approached car barns, in the latter case injuring at least one person.[51] The perpetrators of these actions could have been arrested and charged with a variety of criminal offences, but there is no indication that the police ever intervened. Union supporters sometimes pointed to these provocations as the cause of crowd rioting, although they did not make a point of their probable illegality.[52]

While collective violence against the street railways had some legitimacy on the street, it was denounced from every 'respectable' quarter, including the striking union officials who understood that tolerance for disorder was limited and so carefully tried to keep their parades and picketing within the bounds of the law. So when unlawful conduct occurred they were quick to condemn it. For example, on the day following the first riot in the 1906 Winnipeg strike, Fred Fay, a representative of the international office of the AASRE in town to assist with the strike, issued a statement promising that 'everything possible will be done to prevent the destruction of property and the injury of the cars' and that the union would 'explain to the men of the city the absolute necessity of doing nothing to injure our cause in the minds of the public, who must be the final court of appeal in the matter.'[53] Also, newspapers that previously expressed sympathy towards the union and were critical of the street railway's conduct roundly condemned the violence. The Halifax *Herald*, which as we saw was quite hostile towards the railway, nevertheless splashed a headline across its front page the morning after rioting occurred that freely mixed news with editorial comment: 'Rioters for Time in Partial Control at Halifax but Law and Order Must Be Maintained.'[54]

Faced with escalating violence, the mayor and municipal officials came under increasing pressure to regain control of the streets. The street railway companies demanded better police protection and often received support from local business groups and newspapers. For example, after rioting in Montreal significantly reduced the ability of the company to provide service, the Board of Trade held an emergency meeting at which it passed a resolution calling the mayor's attention to the fact that the law was being 'systematically and openly violated' and demanding that the police be instructed to enforce it vigorously. On the same day, an editorial in the *Gazette* decried the laxity that some police officers had shown. 'For the police force the question of the day is not one of struggle between a railway corporation and its men. It is a matter of preserving order in the city, and of maintaining the authority of the law over disturbing elements.'[55]

Similarly, the *Globe*, which earlier had expressed a somewhat sympathetic view of the union's position, strongly denounced the violence on Toronto streets in its post-riot editorial, titled 'The Strike and Public Order': 'In British communities we do not plead for the preservation of the peace and the recognition of the law. We compel respect for the law and due submission to public authority ...The supreme duty of the moment is to maintain that authority inviolate and unimpaired.'[56]

Thus, even though it was clear that strict maintenance of civic order favoured the street railway company,[57] respect for the rule of official law was presented as a neutral and paramount value. Indeed, one legal commentator reflecting on recent street railway strikes reified the law to make the point: 'The law is bound to protect itself. It cannot be violated on any pretext without injury to society at large, and to the weakening of its legitimate and necessary authority. It must not allow such scenes of lawlessness as have been witnessed in the streets of large cities, not only because they are a violation of the law, but because they let loose passions which give rise to further excesses, and bring about disregard for all lawful authority.'[58]

Yet the law did not protect itself; public authorities did and they had to determine where to draw the line and how to enforce it, and on these questions there was often some disagreement. On the one hand, the street railway was often unpopular and local officials were sometimes wary of being seen to be taking their side; on the other, civic order was clearly being disturbed and the rights of the streetcar owners were being violated. As the level of disorder escalated, so too typically did the enforcement effort as the imperative of maintaining civic order increasingly trumped other considerations. As the London *Free Press* put it, 'the rights of property and the public peace must be preserved at all hazards and at any cost.'[59] Still, the question of how far to go remained.

Often the first response would be to make better use of local police. More officers would be deployed on the cars and at key intersections and more arrests would be made. For example, the Montreal *Gazette*, which had been critical of earlier police efforts, noted a 'commendable increase in the efficiency of the police force in meeting the serious situation it is called upon to face.'[60] No further action was required to restore civic order. Intensification of the enforcement effort by police did not usually involve greater use of force. In particular, even though police routinely carried guns, they rarely used them, and then mostly for personal defence when individual officers were being overwhelmed by a crowd.[61] For example, during the Saint John strike, an officer fired his gun and wounded a member of the crowd who had attacked him when he attempted to arrest a rioter. Police also fired their weapons during the 1906 Hamilton strike in similar circumstances, but no one was hurt.[62] The only fatality occurred during the 1913 strike in Fort William/Port Arthur. A crowd of strike sympathizers had attacked a streetcar and assaulted the driver. The police arrested a man for throwing a brick and took him to a local station house. Shortly afterwards, a large crowd, estimated at two thousand, gathered outside the station and began throwing rocks through the windows and battering the door. The sergeant and five police who were present fired warning shots; when that failed to stop the crowd, a second volley was fired, killing Joseph Stefarico (earlier reported as Mike Smorak) and wounding John Tulk.[63] There was no local criticism of the shootings. The local and national press blamed the 'foreigners' and 'agitators' for the violence, while local labour spokesmen cautioned fellow workers to keep the peace. Only *Cotton's Weekly*, the official organ of the Socialist Party of Canada, in an article entitled 'Masters Shooting Their Slaves in Port Arthur,' asked: 'How long will this beastly law stand which allowed a uniformed savage to haul out guns and blaze away into a crowd of toilers? How long do the masters think that their pet law will be able to be enforced?'[64]

Even the most committed police force often lacked the resources to cope with the demands being placed upon it to maintain order and keep the street railways operating. The strongest and most controversial response was for local officials to call out the militia in aid of the civil power.[65] This was first done in the context of a street railway strike in London in 1899. Several weeks into the strike, after escalating sabotage aimed at interfering with the company's efforts to operate the street railway with imported and armed professional strikebreakers, full-scale rioting broke out on a Saturday. Crowds estimated at 2,500 stopped streetcars, chased away their terrified operators, and destroyed several cars. Arrests by local police and pleas from the mayor convinced many to disperse, but, when large crowds reassembled in the evening and attacked more cars, Mayor John Wilson gave in to pressure from the company and read the Riot Act. Police were still unable to disperse the crowd and later that night the mayor called up the militia in aid of the civil power. A small squad of thirty-two soldiers of the 1st Hussars, a militia unit headquartered in London, was dispatched under the command of Colonel J.E. Holmes. The crowd greeted their arrival with jeers and Holmes ordered his men to fix bayonets. With twenty police officers in front of them, the formation moved forward and the crowd dispersed. It reassembled a short distance away and a second charge was needed to clear the streets. Militia companies from surrounding municipalities subsequently sent a total of one hundred militia troops the next day and regular troops in Toronto were put on alert. Three thousand rounds of ammunition were issued to the soldiers, but there was no further need for the troops to take to the streets since efforts to physically prevent the streetcars from running came to an end. The soldiers remained on duty for twelve days before returning to their barracks.[66]

The actions of local officials were sharply criticized from a number of quarters, some surprising. For striking workers and their sympathizers, the use of military force was seen to be an intervention on behalf of the railway and its efforts to break the strike and impose its workplace order.

London workers staged a procession mocking the company's lawyer and local director for their role in having the militia called out, while the international union's newspaper proclaimed, 'If President Everett thought that by getting the militia out he could scare Johnny Canuck into submission, he was very badly mistaken.' Less expectedly, a number of local newspapers also published editorials criticizing the decision of the mayor to call in and keep the troops available at a cost to the city of about $4,000, while the police magistrate, Edward Parke, who was absent from the city at the time of these events, accused the mayor of being frightened into this action, which tarnished the reputation of the city.[67]

Controversy also followed the 1902 decision of the Toronto police commissioners (Mayor O.A. Howland, Judge J.E. McDougall, and Magistrate Rupert Kingford) to call in 1,400 militia, following a Sunday afternoon and evening during which tens of thousands of citizens gathered on the streets and physically prevented the railway from running cars with strikebreakers. The troops included seven hundred cavalry brought in by special trains from Niagara and seven hundred troops drawn from city infantry regiments. Colonel Buchan, who helped lead the troops called up in London, was placed in command.[68] The troops were deployed around the city and were greeted by a mixture of cheers and hisses. Their presence put an end to any attempts to interfere with the operation of the cars and later that day the short strike was settled quickly. The troops brought in from Niagara returned to their bases Monday night.[69] The bill for the troops came to nearly $2,000.[70]

The Toronto Trades and Labor Council unanimously passed a resolution strongly disapproving of the police commission for 'unwarrantedly and prematurely' calling out the militia. One exasperated delegate, after recounting the recent use of the militia in other strikes, suggested that it might be time 'labour organizations took steps to meet these men on their own grounds, armed and equipped their own members to fight the armed forces so frequently and unjustly called upon by capital.' Even the *Globe* acknowledged that there 'appears to be a general opinion that the calling out of the troops to keep order in the city during the street railway strike was an error.' In its view, the 'use of force ought to be kept out of sight as much as possible' and it would be preferable to strengthen the capacity of the regular police to maintain order.[71] Clearly, in this case, the authorities' limits of toleration were much narrower than those of the community.[72]

The decisions to call up the military in aid of the civil power in Winnipeg (1906), Hamilton (1906), and Saint John (1914)[73] were not as controversial, but this may be because officials had become somewhat more cautious and acted only when it became abundantly clear that local police could not control the situation. For example, in Hamilton low levels of disorderly conduct were tolerated for weeks, despite demands from the street railway company for protection. Not even an exchange of gunfire, or admissions by Chief of Police Smith that the police could not protect the company's operations, convinced Mayor Sanford Biggar to call in the militia, a position endorsed by the Hamilton *Spectator*.[74] It was not until full-fledged rioting erupted when the company decided to run cars on a Friday night, including physical confrontations with police officers and the laying of a dynamite charge across the tracks, that Mayor Biggar relented.[75] Similarly, Halifax municipal officials resisted the demand of the Halifax Tramway Company to call out the troops, even after rioting occurred during the 1913 strike.[76]

The response to the presence of the military very much depended on the role they played.[77] In Toronto, 'the moral effect' of the troops' presence, as Toronto's Chief Constable H.J. Grasett put it, was sufficient to end the disturbances and so there was nothing in their conduct to criticize.[78] Similarly, in Winnipeg, the nearly three hundred regular troops remained mostly in the background, except on the Friday afternoon after the mayor read the Riot Act. When the crowd did not disperse, the command 'Ready' was given and the troops loaded their rifles. At that point, the crowd scattered and no further action was taken. Although the troops remained on duty for two more days, the police were able to handle further disturbances without their assistance.[79]

In Saint John, however, eight members of the Royal Canadian Dragoons were in town to conduct cavalry training and were called out during the disturbances. They charged through the crowd and the Saint John *Globe* reported that their action inflamed the crowd. 'Savage cries of "Kill the Cowards" broke forth on all sides and in a short time the bolder spirits of the mob were flinging stones and other missiles at the troops.' Some soldiers were injured and the unit retreated. The strike was settled before reinforcements from Halifax arrived.[80]

The soldiers used in the Hamilton strike of 1906 had been called up from Toronto and London on Saturday morning after an evening of riotous behaviour that was beyond the ability of the local police to contain. They were under the command of Colonel Septimus Denison, the younger brother of George Taylor Denison, the Toronto police magistrate who had dealt harshly with rioters during the 1886 street railway strike.[81] When rioting resumed Saturday evening, the sheriff read the Riot Act and the police charged into the crowds, freely swinging their batons. The cavalry followed them, with their swords drawn, under orders to strike with the broadside only those who resisted. Eventually, the crowd was dispersed and numerous arrests were made. Colonel Denison issued a warning that was prominently displayed on the front page of the *Spectator*. 'If we are called out to-morrow we will clear the streets at any cost, and people, for their own safety, had better be in their homes.' In an interview he also expressed surprise at the antagonism he and his troops encountered from 'seemingly good citizens' in response to the demand that they vacate the streets. 'I fail to see where there is justification for such conduct.'[82] Those 'good citizens,' including several aldermen, were just as quick to criticize the actions of the police in particular, accusing them of being overzealous in their use of force. Indeed, an editorial in the Hamilton *Spectator* characterized the police use of force as 'injudicious,' noting that 'it was not in the interest of citizens generally that the police should act as if every man, woman and child in the city were a personal enemy.' In contrast, the actions of the troops did not attract similar criticism, although some merchants refused to sell provisions to the troops or found their teamsters unwilling to deliver to them if they did.[83]

An alternative to calling up the military was to increase the capacity of the local police by swearing in special constables. For example, during the May 1903 street railway strike in Montreal, firemen were sworn in as special police without any controversy.[84] The issue became far more contentious during the 1906 strike in Winnipeg when a provincial magistrate, Alexander McMicken, was alleged to have sworn in 100 strikebreakers at the railway company's request. At this point, the boundaries between public and private action became obviously and uncomfortably blurred. The *Free Press*, which was sympathetic to the strikers, expressed alarm at this action, especially after receiving reports that special police assaulted peaceful citizens: 'It is a very serious fact that there are walking about the streets of Winnipeg over one hundred strangers, armed with guns, who are possessed of the extensive powers of special police ... That they should be clothed with the powers of the law to maltreat and insult peaceable citizens is intolerable.'[85]

The matter was brought to the attention of the provincial attorney general who suspended McMicken a few days later pending an investigation of his actions.[86] As well, several strikebreakers, including their leader, Louis Christiansen, were arrested for assault.[87] The maintenance of law and order was widely viewed as a matter for the properly constituted authorities and the practice of swearing in strikebreakers as special constables was not repeated in subsequent street railway strikes during this period.[88]

The authority of professional strikebreakers and private security forces, even when they were not sworn in as special constables, however, was often ambiguously defined, perhaps, deliberately so. Armed private detectives provided by Thiel's or other agencies were often prominently deployed by the street railways on their cars or around railway property precisely to deter interference with street railway operations. Thus, during the street railway strike at the Lakehead, the following front-page notice appeared in the press:

Don't mix in a crowd that shows hostility to the men operating the street cars.

The officers on every car are armed with automatic guns and are authorized to shoot into any crowd that attempts to destroy street railway property.[89]

Fortunately, the actual legal limit of the powers of private police to use lethal force was never tested.

Courts were the other institution involved in the maintenance of street order through their power to punish those who were arrested and charged with offences arising out of their participation in collective disorder. Police magistrates were most frequently involved in street railway strikes, both as members of police commissions and as judges where the charges were relatively minor. County court judges were also sometimes members of police commissions and triers of more serious cases or of cases where the accused elected trial by jury.[90] Superior court justices rarely heard cases arising out of the disorder, although this did not prevent some Ontario justices from expressing their hostility towards unions in grand jury addresses delivered after the 1886 street railway strikes. The propriety of judges using this forum to express political views, however, was questioned and the practice seems to have stopped.[91]

The severity of the sentences imposed varied quite considerably depending on the predilections of the individual magistrate or judge, as well as on his assessment of the seriousness of the individual act, the level of disorder, and the need to send a clear message that unlawful behaviour was unacceptable. For example, Magistrate Denison dealt quite harshly with those who were brought before him for their actions arising out of the two 1886 Toronto street railway strikes and from the bench warned: 'The peace of the city must be preserved at any cost. No organization would be allowed to establish mob law as long as there was an officer of the peace in the Dominion.'[92] By way of contrast, Magistrate Daly in Winnipeg dealt far more leniently with those charged with strike-related offences in 1906 and 1910, the majority being given small fines, although he increased the penalties as the strike progressed. 'It was well enough to let those off easy who, in the preliminary stages of the strike, might have been carried away with excitement, but the excitement has somewhat subsided, and more severe lessons are to be taught.' Jail sentences were for the most part meted out only to those convicted of assaulting police officers.[93] This pattern was also evident in the aftermath of the Montreal strike in May 1903. Those who were charged with relatively minor offences, including intimidation, loitering, insulting the police, and disturbing the peace, were tried in Recorder Robert Stanley Weir's court and those convicted were given fines ranging from $2 to $10. On the other hand, Joseph Limoges, an ex-member of the city police who was charged with assaulting a streetcar conductor and enticing a crowd to interfere with a police officer, was brought before Judge Edouard Lafontaine in Police Court where he was convicted and sentenced to six months at hard labour.[94] Similarly, in the aftermath of the Hamilton riots, Judge Colin Snider handed down his harshest sentence to Judson Ryerson (eighteen months) for assaulting a police officer.[95]

In London, a significant number of accused elected trial by jury and their cases were put over to the next general sessions of the peace, presided over by Judge Edward Elliott, which were not held until December 1899, five months after the riots.[96] The first case was that of John Sherlock, a cigar maker, accused of throwing stones at streetcars. A number of fellow cigar makers testified on his behalf, claiming they were in his company and did not see him throwing stones. Nevertheless, Sherlock was convicted on the basis of evidence given by several police officers. Following his conviction, Judge Elliott took the opportunity to express his view that while unions were legal they had no right to prevent a man who does not belong to a union from working: 'No man had the right to obstruct or intimidate another or to obstruct the public conveyances or interfere with the property of the employer. The men who chose to strike had a perfect right to do so, but they had no right to prevent other men taking their places or ask the employer not to engage new men.'[97] Judge Elliott imposed a fine of $500 or eighteen months' imprisonment. Sherlock raised the funds from friends and supporters to pay the fine, but the harsh sentence had its intended impact, since nine other accused pleaded guilty and received fines ranging from $15 to $50. Sherlock subsequently petitioned for a reduction in his sentence, which the province's attorney general viewed favourably on the ground that the penalty was excessive compared to those imposed on others found guilty of similar offences.[98]

It is unclear whether the ethnicity of the accused played a role in the courts. The names of the accused were overwhelmingly of British origin, except in Montreal where a substantial number were French. There was, however, no noticeable difference in the treatment of French and English by the Montreal courts and no press comment on the ethnicity of the rioters.[99] In Winnipeg none of those arrested in 1906 had non-British names, but some did in 1910. Wasyl Baran, identified in the newspaper as 'a foreign-born resident,' received the heaviest sentence by far, nine months' imprisonment, for throwing a whisky flask at a streetcar. Magistrate Daly, however, did not refer to Baran's ethnicity, and later that day he discharged Matweg Hykawy on the basis of the evidence of his friends that he had left the streetcar before a window was broken.[100]

Strikebreakers arrested for their alleged law breaking usually slipped out of town before their cases came to trial or before the trial was completed. The case against Louis Christianson, the Thiel detective agency supervisor involved in the 1906 Winnipeg street railway strike who was charged with assault, did go to trial and Christianson testified in his own defence. The trial was adjourned, however, when two police officers left the courtroom 'through a misunderstanding' before they could testify. The strike was settled the next day and no further reports of the trial have been found.[101]

CONCLUSION

Maintaining civic order during street railway strikes presented a serious challenge to public authorities. While for the most part striking workers remained within the limits of legal toleration for collective action, sympathetic members of the communities they served often did not. Large crowds gathered in the streets and interfered with the running of the streetcars, in some cases by simply obstructing their path, in others by throwing projectiles, breaking windows, attacking strikebreakers, or engaging in other acts of sabotage. For their part, street railway companies insisted that authorities protect their rights, but they were quick to take the law into their own hands by hiring replacement workers (on at least some occasions in violation of the Alien Labour Act) and contracting private security forces that threatened to use and sometimes used force against striking workers and their supporters.

Over the course of the nineteenth century, the state at all levels strengthened its coercive capacity to deal with strikes and collective disorder. Municipal police forces grew (albeit unevenly) and started bearing arms routinely, more federal criminal laws dealing with public disorder were passed, and the military was enlarged and professionalized. However, unlike on public-works projects of national significance described in Susan Binnie's chapter in this volume, the federal government was unwilling to become directly involved and also did not provide local officials with power to obtain proclamations giving them extraordinary powers to prevent or even suppress public disorder. Instead, municipal officials, including mayors, aldermen, police chiefs, and low-level judges, faced the question of when and how to use the powers available to them when a significant and respectable portion of the population collectively violated the legal zone of toleration. As this chapter demonstrates, their response was not consistent. In Toronto, official tolerance for strike-related collective disorder was thin and got thinner with each successive strike. Officials in some other cities, including Hamilton and Winnipeg, were slower to put the law's coercive apparatuses in motion and judges treated those arrested more leniently. As a result, rowdy street demonstrations and interference with street railway operations persisted for weeks at a time.

Finally, we might ask about the larger implications of these events for our understanding of the role of state coercion in response to strike-related collective violence. On the one hand, in all cases coercive force was eventually used to suppress collective violence and vindicate the civic order central to Canadian capitalism.[102] We can conclude, therefore, that despite the different capacities of local law enforcement and the lack of zeal that officials often exhibited in maintaining civic order at the level demanded by street railway companies, once local officials made the decision that collective disorder would no longer be tolerated, the coercive force of the state, including if necessary military aid to the civil power, could be and was mobilized to end it. Yet, on the other hand, this study also demonstrates that between the formal zone of legal toleration and the point at which coercion was mobilized, there was some scope for unruly community displays of solidarity with striking workers. The availability of this space helped street railway workers secure a foothold for their union at a time when craft unions were under attack and new industrial unions were struggling to become established.[103]

NOTES

A SSHRC research grant provided funding for this paper and two Osgoode Hall Law School students, Christopher Donovan and Mark Dunn, provided research assistance. I am also grateful to Craig Heron for allowing me to read and reference a chapter of his forthcoming study, 'The Workers' City: The Remaking of Working-Class Hamilton, 1880–1940.' Helpful comments on earlier versions of this chapter were provided by the editors of this volume, as well as by the members of the Toronto Labour Studies Group.

1 For an overview of Canadian street railway strikes, see Christopher Armstrong and H.V. Nelles, *Monopoly's Moment* (Toronto: University of Toronto Press 1986), 214–17; and Peter D. Lambly, 'Working Conditions and Industrial Relations on Canada's Street Railways: 1900–1920,' MA thesis, Dalhousie University 1983, chapter 2. For the United States, see Scott Molloy, *Trolley Wars* (Washington D.C.: Smithsonian Press 1996); Robert H. Babcock, '"Will You Walk? Yes We'll Walk!": Popular Support for a Street Railway Strike in Portland, Maine,' *Labor History* 35 (1994): 372; Sarah H. Henry, 'The Strikers and Their Sympathizers: Brooklyn in the Trolley Strike of 1895,' *Labor History* 32 (1991): 329; Robert E. Ziegler, 'The Limits of Power: The Amalgamated Association of Street Railway Employees in Houston, Texas, 1897–1905,' *Labor History* 18 (1977): 71.

2 The account that follows is based on an amalgam of all the street railway strikes discussed in this chapter.

3 Street railway drivers and conductors were all men during this period. As well, they were largely of British descent outside Quebec and of British and French descent in that province.

4 SC 1907 c.20.

5 SC 1903 c.55.

6 For a discussion of the dimensions of liberal order and the challenges posed by workers' collective action that draws on street railway workers as a case study, see Eric Tucker, 'Who's Running the Road: Street Railway Strikes and the Problem of Order in Liberal Capitalism,' unpublished manuscript, 2009.

7 Douglas Hay and Paul Craven, 'Introduction,' in P. Craven and D. Hay, eds., *Masters, Servants, and Magistrates in Britain and the Empire, 1562–1955* (Chapel Hill: University of North Carolina Press 2004), 1; Paul Craven, 'Canada, 1670–1935: Symbolic and Instrumental Enforcement in Loyalist North America,' in ibid,, 175; and '"The Modern Spirit of the Law": Blake, Mowat, and the Breaches of Contract Act, 1877,' in G. Blaine Baker and Jim Phillips, eds., *Essays in the History of Canadian Law, Volume VIII: In Honour of R.C.B. Risk* (Toronto: Osgoode Society for Canadian Legal History / University of Toronto Press 1999), 142.

8 For a discussion of the development of labour injunctions in Canada during the period of street railway strikes under discussion in this chapter, see Eric

Tucker, 'The Faces of Coercion: The Legal Regulation of Labour Conflict in Ontario in the 1880's,' *Law and History Review* 12 (1994): 277; Eric Tucker and Judy Fudge, 'Forging Responsible Unions: Metal Workers and the Rise of the Labour Injunction in Canada,' *Labour/Le Travail* 37 (1996): 81. Railway companies occasionally threatened legal action against municipalities for breaching franchise agreements during strikes. On the history of the labour conspiracy law, see Eric Tucker, '"That Indefinite Zone of Toleration": Criminal Conspiracy and Trade Unions in Ontario, 1837–1877,' *Labour/Le Travail* 27 (1991): 15.

9 On the distinction between the respectable and the rough, see Bryan D. Palmer, *Working-Class Experience*, 2nd ed. (Toronto: McClelland and Stewart 1992), 56–63.

10 Bryan D. Palmer, 'Labour Protest and Organization in Nineteenth-Century Canada, 1820–1890,' *Labour/Le Travail* 20 (1987): 61, 62–7; Peter Way, *Common Labour* (Cambridge: Cambridge University Press, 1993), esp. chapter 8; H.C. Pentland, 'The Lachine Canal Strike of 1843,' *CHR* 29 (1948): 255; Ruth Bleasdale, 'Class Conflict on the Canals of Upper Canada in the 1840's,' in Michael S. Cross and Gregory S. Kealey, eds., *Pre-Industrial Canada 1760–1849* (Toronto: McClelland and Stewart 1982), 100; William N.T. Wylie, 'Poverty, Distress, and Disease: Labour and the Construction of the Rideau Canal, 1826–32,' *Labour/Le Travail* 11 (1983): 7.

11 The Riot Act (1 Geo. 1 c.5) was originally passed in Great Britain in 1714 and allowed local authorities to declare a gathering of twelve or more people to be unlawfully assembled. It also authorized the use of deadly force against those who failed to disperse forthwith after the act was read. The act was part of the received law in Canadian colonies. For a discussion of the reception of English criminal laws, see F. Murray Greenwood and Barry Wright, 'Introduction: State Trials, the Rule of Law, and Executive Powers in Early Canada,' in F. Murray Greenwood Barry Wright, eds., *CST* 2, 11–22.

12 Elinor Kyte, Sr, *British Regulars in Montreal* (Montreal and Kingston: McGill-Queen's University Press 1981), 58–9; Way, *Common Labour*, 248–52; Jean Hamelin, Paul Larocque, and Jacques Rouillard, *Repertoire des Grèves dans la Province de Québec au XIXe Siècle* (Montreal: Presses de l'École des Haute Etudes Commerciale 1970), 9–10; Confédération des syndicats nationaux and Centrale de l'enseignement du Québec, *History of the Labour Movement in Quebec* (Montreal: Black Rose Books 1987), 41.

13 SPC 1845 c.6, preamble. Although the measure passed with only two opposed, the bill aroused considerable controversy in debate. *Debates of the Legislative Assembly of United Canada*, 11 and 13 Feb. 1845. More generally, see Bleasdale, 'Class Conflict'; Palmer, *Working Class Experience*, 60–3; W. Thomas Matthews, 'The Myth of the Peaceable Kingdom: Upper Canadian Society

during the Early Victorian Period,' *Queen's Quarterly* 94 (1988): 383-401; *History of the Labour Movement in Quebec*, 41; William N.T. Wylie, 'Poverty,' 25–9.

14 Way, *Common Labour*, 257–63; Bleasdale, 'Class Conflict,' 127. Other accounts of state responses to protest and strike activity by groups of 'rough' workers in the first half of the nineteenth century include: Linda Little, 'Collective Action in Outport Newfoundland: A Case Study from the 1830s,' *Labour/Le Travail* 26 (1990): 7 (sealers); Charles Bruce Fergusson, *The Labour Movement in Nova Scotia before Confederation* (Halifax: Public Archives of Nova Scotia 1964), 18–21 (colliers); Edith Burley, *Servants of the Honourable Company: Work, Discipline, and Conflict in the Hudson's Bay Company, 1770–1878* (Toronto: Oxford University Press 1997), chapter 6; Hamar Foster, 'Mutiny on the Beaver: Law and Authority in the British Fur Trade "Navy,"' *Manitoba Law Journal* 20 (1991): 15.

15 Paul Romney, *Mr Attorney: The Attorney General for Ontario in Court, Cabinet, and Legislature 1791–1899* (Toronto: The Osgoode Society 1986), 231–9; Allan Greer, 'The Birth of the Police in Canada,' in Allan Greer and Ian Radforth, eds., *Colonial Leviathan: State Formation in Nineteenth-Century Canada* (Toronto: University of Toronto Press 1992), 17.

16 By SPC 1846 c.28 s.14, the governor of the province was given the power to call out the militia but was not required to do so in any particular circumstance. Government officials in pre-confederation Nova Scotia were less reticent about calling out the militia in the context of coal strikes, in part because of the colony's fiscal dependence on coal royalties, but also because of its commitment to the maintenance of law and order. For a brief discussion of the government's coercive response to an 1864 coal miners' strike that included calling out troops, see Fergusson, *Labour Movement*, 25–6.

17 Michael B. Katz, 'Profile of an Elite: The Response to the Railway Strike of 1851,' in 'Canadian Social History Project,' Interim Report no. 5, Working Paper no. 33 (Toronto: Department of History and Philosophy of Education, Ontario Institute for Studies in Education 1974), 243. On MacNab, see *DCB Online*, http://www.biographi.ca/.

18 'Report of the Commissioners Appointed to Investigate and Report upon the Best Means of Re-Organizing the Militia of Canada, and Providing an Efficient and Economical System of Public Defence and to Report upon an Improved System of Police for the Better Preservation of the Public Peace,' *Journals of the Legislative Assembly of the Province of Canada* (1855), appendix X.X. Also, see John Victor Barkans, 'Labour, Capital and the State: Canadian Railroads and Emergent Social Relations of Production, 1850–1879,' MA thesis, McMaster University 1976, 164–7. He also notes that, in the absence of readily available public police forces, the railways maintained their own at

considerable expense. For example, the Great Western set aside £2,569 for its police force by 31 May 1854.

19 SPC 1855 c.77 ss.38, 39; Romney, *Mr. Attorney*, 234–9; Nicholas Rogers, 'Serving Toronto the Good: The Development of the City Police Force, 1834–84,' in Victor L. Russell, ed., *Forging a Consensus* (Toronto: University of Toronto Press 1984), 116. The recorder was a local judge, such as a county court judge.

20 The Constitution Act, 1867 (U.K.), 30&31 Vic. c.3 s.91.

21 Militia Act, SC 1868 c.40.

22 SC 1868 c.70. The act authorized justices, justices of the peace, sheriffs, and mayors to read the Riot Act when twelve or more persons 'unlawfully, riotously and tumultuously assembled together, to the disturbance of the public peace' (s.1).

23 SC 1869 c.24. For further discussion, see Susan Binnie's chapter in this volume.

24 Again, see Susan Binnie's chapter.

25 Act to Make Provision against the Improper Use of Firearms, SC 1877 c.30; The Better Prevention of Crimes Act, SC 1878 c.17; Susan W.S. Binnie, 'The Blake Act of 1878: A Legislative Solution to Urban Violence in Post-Confederation Canada,' in Louis A. Knafla and Susan W.S. Binnie, eds., *Law, Society and the State: Essays in Modern Legal History* (Toronto: University of Toronto Press 1995), 215. On the use of the militia, see Desmond Morton, 'Aid to the Civil Power: The Canadian Militia in Support of Social Order, 1867–1914,' *CHR* 51 (1970): 407; J.J.B. Pariseau, *Disorders, Strikes and Disasters: Military Aid to the Civil Power in Canada, 1867–1973* (Ottawa: National Defence Headquarters 1973); and Lt.-Col. J.H. Allan, 'Military Aid of the Civil Power in Canadian Industrial Disputes 1876–1925' (Occasional Papers on Canadian Defence Policy and Civil-Military Affairs, Royal Military College of Canada 1972). On the various strikes, see Ian McKay, 'The Crisis of Dependent Development: Class Conflict in the Nova Scotia Coalfields, 1872–1876,' *Canadian Journal of Sociology* 13 (1988): 36–41; Lynne Bowen, *Three Dollar Dreams* (Lantzville, B.C.: Oolichan Books 1987), 149–75; J.I. Cooper, 'The Quebec Ship Labourers' Benevolent Society,' *CHR* 30 (1949): 336; Susan W.S. Binnie, 'Explorations in the Use of Criminal Law in Canada, 1867–1892,' PhD thesis, Carleton University 1991, 184–201; David J. Hall, 'The Construction Workers' Strike on the Canadian Pacific Railway, 1879,' *Labour/Le Travail* 36 (1995): 11; Desmond Morton, 'Taking on the Grand Trunk Railway: The Locomotive Engineers Strike of 1876–7,' *Labour/Le Travail* 2 (1977): 5.

26 SC 1883 c. 1; SC 1904 c.23. See Morton, 'Aid,' and his *Ministers and Generals* (Toronto: University of Toronto Press 1970); J.L. Granatstein, *Canada's Army* (Toronto: University of Toronto Press 2002), 24–52.

27 The public-order statutes discussed above, as well as others, were included

in the 1892 Criminal Code, SC 1892 c.29, parts V and VI. For more discussion, see Barry Wright's and R. Blake Brown's chapters in this volume.

28 John C. Weaver, *Crimes, Constables, and Courts: Order and Transgression in a Canadian City, 1816–1970* (Montreal and Kingston: McGill-Queen's University Press 1995), 14.

29 Ibid., 19; Greg Marquis, *Policing Canada's Century: A History of the Canadian Association of Chiefs of Police* (Toronto: The Osgoode Society 1993), 27–40; Gene Homel, 'Denison's Law: Criminal Justice and the Police Court in Toronto,' *Ontario History* 73 (1981): 183; Philip Girard, 'The Rise and Fall of Urban Justice in Halifax, 1815–1886,' *Nova Scotia Historical Review* 8, no. 2 (1988): 57.

30 An Act to Amend the Criminal Law relating to Violence, Threats and Molestation, SC 1872 c.31. These statutes, which were passed partly to embarrass prominent Liberal George Brown who had launched a prosecution against striking printers at his newspaper, the *Globe*, were copies of British statutes passed the year before. On the background to the strike and the legislation, see Tucker, 'Indefinite Zone,' 31–41.

31 *Ontario Workman*, 27 March 1873. See Tucker, 'Indefinite Zone,' 42–7.

32 SC 1875 c.36; SC 1876 c. 37.

33 Judy Fudge and Eric Tucker, *Labour before the Law* (Toronto: Oxford University Press 2001), 25–8.

34 Stephen H. Norwood, *Strikebreaking and Intimidation* (Chapel Hill, N.C.: University of North Carolina Press 2002), 45–63. Also, see Edward Levinson, *I Break Strikes!* (New York: Robert M. McBride 1935), and Robert Michael Smith, *From Blackjacks to Briefcases* (Athens, Ohio: Ohio University Press 2003), 39–54.

35 SC 1897 c.11. For background and discussion, see James J. Atherton, 'The Department of Labour and Industrial Relations 1900–1911,' MA thesis, Carleton University, 1972, chapter 9; William Renwick Riddell, 'Labor Legislation in Canada,' *Minnesota Law Review* 5 (1921): 243.

36 For example, in Hamilton, the union retained George Lynch-Staunton KC as counsel to see about obtaining an injunction to prevent the strikebreakers from operating the streetcars in violation of the Alien Labour Act. The company denied the allegation. There is no indication that any legal proceeding was initiated. Hamilton *Spectator*, 6 Nov. 1906, 1. In Winnipeg, striking workers also complained that strikebreakers were being illegally imported from Chicago, and W.N. Reeves, president of the local trades council, wrote the federal minister of labour who advised there was no officer responsible for the enforcement of the act but that any person, with the consent of the provincial attorney general, could lay charges. The matter ended there (Winnipeg *Free Press*, 3 April 1906, 1). Also see *Free Press*, editorial, 'Our Disorderly Special Constables,' 31 March 1906, 4, where the allegation is repeated.

37 The legality of boycotts was unclear at the time, but no legal actions were brought against street railway unions for organizing them. For a discussion of this issue, see Tucker, 'Faces,' 308–29; Tucker and Fudge, 'Forging,' 107–10.

38 Untitled memorandum, Strike and Lockout Files, LAC, RG 27, reel T-2690, vol. 302, file 73; Ottawa *Journal*, 13 May 1913. For similar comments, see *Morning Herald* (Fort William), 13 May 1913, 2. On the hostility of local elites in the Lakehead to foreigners, see Jean F. Morrison, 'Community and Conflict: A Study of the Working Class and Its Relationships at the Canadian Lakehead, 1903–1913,' MA thesis, Lakehead University, 1974, 242–50, and 'Ethnicity and Violence: The Lakehead Freight Handlers before World War I,' in Gregory S. Kealey and Peter Warrian, eds., *Essays in Canadian Working Class History* (Toronto: McClelland and Stewart 1976), 143.

39 Hamilton *Spectator*, 24 Nov. 1906, 1. For similar observations, see Babcock, 'Saint John,' 18, and Palmer, 'Give Us,' 121. The chief's language captures the dominant understanding that women, who were still denied the franchise, were not full citizens. See Veronica Strong-Boag, 'The Citizenship Debates: The 1885 Franchise Act,' in Robert Adamoski, Dorothy E. Chunn, and Robert·Menzies, eds., *Contesting Canadian Citizenship* (Toronto: Broadview Press 2002), 69.

40 For example, Babcock, 'Saint John,' 18.

41 For a useful discussion, see Judy Torrance, *Public Violence in Canada* (Montreal and Kingston: McGill-Queen's University Press, 1986).

42 For example, an editorial in the *Globe*, commenting on the sentencing of rioters in the Hamilton street railway disturbances, suggested, 'The conscious personality of the individual was absorbed and lost in the unconscious personality of the crowd.' The editorial was republished in the Hamilton *Spectator*, 22 Dec. 1906, 6. Also, see Craig Heron, 'Boys Will Be Boys: Working-Class Masculinities in the Age of Mass Production,' *International Labor and Working-Class History* 69 (2006): 14–15.

43 Babcock, 'Saint John,' 6. Hamilton *Spectator*, 5 Nov. 1906, 5, noted at the beginning of the strike that since the company had 'exhibited no particular desire to give the people the best street car service,' the public would be slow to accept its position in the dispute. More generally, see Michael J. Doucet, 'Mass Transit and the Failure of Private Ownership: The Case of Toronto in the Early Twentieth Century,' *Urban History Review* 6, no. 3 (1978): 3; Christopher Armstrong and H.V. Nelles, *The Revenge of the Methodist Bicycle Company* (Toronto: Peter Martin 1977); R.W. Kostal, 'Conservative Insurrection: Great Strikes and Deep Law in Cleveland, Ohio, and London, Ontario, 1898–1899,' in Baker and Phillips, eds., *Essays in the History of Canadian Law, Volume VIII*, 289.

44 The legislation allowed the company to increase its capitalization. The Halifax

Herald claimed that the amount allowed was well beyond what was required for planned expansion and thus 'watered' the value of existing stock.

45 See, for example, Shelton Stromquist, *A Generation of Boomers* (Urbana: University of Illinois Press 1993), 174–87 (explaining support for striking railway workers in the 1870s).

46 Molloy, *Trolley*, 35–8. The insight about the strong link between the working class and the wider community originated in Herbert G. Gutman, *Work, Culture, and Society in Industrializing America* (New York: Knopf 1976), which is cited as a factor in street railway strikes by Palmer, 'Culture,' 216; Babcock, 'Will You Walk?'; Ziegler, 'Limits of Power'; Henry, 'Strikers and their Sympathizers,' 352.

47 Sidney Harring, 'Car Wars: Strikes, Arbitration, and Class Struggle in the Making of Labor Law,' *New York Review of Law and Social Change* 14 (1986): 849.

48 'Lessons of the Strike,' Montreal *Gazette*, 29 May 1903, 6.

49 E.P. Thompson, 'The Moral Economy of the English Crowd in the Eighteenth Century,' *Past and Present* 50 (1971): 76; Palmer, *Working-Class Experience*, 66–9; Scott W. See, 'Nineteenth-Century Collective Violence: Toward a North American Context,' *Labour/Le Travail* 39 (1997): 13. For a discussion of the changing nature of and response to popular disorder in the transition from less to more divided societies, see Paul A. Gilje, *The Road to Mobocracy* (Chapel Hill: University of North Carolina Press 1987).

50 *Palladium of Labor*, 3 April 1886, 1.

51 Kostal, 'Conservative Insurrection,' 297; Winnipeg *Free Press*, 31 March 1906, 1; Lambly, *Working Conditions*, 121; Saint John *Globe*, 24 July 1914, 8.

52 For example, see Hamilton *Spectator*, 24 Nov. 1906, 1.

53 *Free Press*, 30 March 1906, 11.

54 Halifax *Herald*, 17 May 1913, 1.

55 *Gazette*, 25 May 1903, 6 (quote), 11 (Board of Trade).

56 *Globe*, 23 June 1902, 6.

57 The *Gazette*, 'Lessons of the Strike,' 29 May 1903, 6, did not shy away from this point: 'The lesson is that the strike is a comparatively hopeless method of settling grievances when law and order is strictly maintained.'

58 W.E. O'Brien, 'Labour Legislation,' *Canada Law Journal* 41 (1905): 732.

59 London *Free Press*, 'Stern Repression in Order,' 10 July 1899, 4.

60 'Law and Order,' *Gazette*, 26 May 1903, 6.

61 It is unclear whether most police forces routinely carried guns at this time and practices may have varied from city to city. For example, in Hamilton police began to carry guns routinely in 1904 but used them only in exceptional circumstances. See Weaver, *Crimes*, 122–3. Saint John police were armed in 1872.

See Greg Marquis, 'A Machine of Oppression under the Guise of the Law: The Saint John Police Establishment, 1860–1890,' *Acadiensis* 16 (1986): 64.

62 Babcock, 'Saint John,' 18; *Globe*, 24 Nov. 1906, 1. There was also a report that a police officer fired a gun at a window breaker during the 1910 Winnipeg strike. See *Free Press*, 21 Dec. 1910, 1.

63 A coroners' jury was subsequently unable to determine whether the man was killed by a police bullet or missile from the crowd. See *Daily Times-Journal* (Fort William), 12 May 1913, 1; ibid., 20 May, 1; and LAC, Strike and Lockout Files, RG 27, reel T-2690, vol. 302, file 73.

64 *Cotton's Weekly*, 22 May 1913, 3. Also, see *Morning Herald*, 13 May 1913, 4; *Daily Times-Journal*, 12 May 1913, 4; LAC, Strike and Lockout Files, RG 27, reel T-2690, vol. 302, file 73.

65 Generally, see Morton, 'Aid.'

66 London *Free Press*, 10 July 1899, 1, 3, 6. The additional soldiers were from the 21st, 22nd, 29th, and 30th battalions of the Royal Canadian Regiment of Infantry.

67 *Motorman and Conductor* (August 1899), 612 (quote). Also, see *Industrial Banner*, 'Terrorism!' (July 1899), 1 ('It is too bad that Mayor Wilson flew off the handle and lost his head'); Kostal, 'Great Strikes,' 302–3; Palmer, 'Give Us,' 120–2.

68 *Globe*, 23 June 1902, 1. The mounted troops were drawn from the 1st Hussars (London) (250), 2nd Dragoons (Niagara District) (250), Governor-General's Body Guard (150), and the Toronto Mounted Rifles (50). The local infantry were from Queen's Own Rifles (300), Royal Grenadiers (200), and the 48th Highlanders (200).

69 *Globe*, 24 June 1902, 2.

70 Toronto City Council Minutes, 1902 (Toronto: Carswell 1903), 670. There was some controversy over the extent of the city's financial liability. See LAC, RG 13, vol. 2313, file 205/902.

71 *Globe*, 24 June 1902, 10 (TLC meeting), 28 June 1902, 6 (editorial, 'Police and Militia').

72 It is also notable that the two previous street railway strikes in Toronto, both in 1886, were handled by the local police, which at the time included a mounted unit. The mayor at the time was William Howland, and in the second strike he acted decisively to prohibit street gatherings. Police Magistrate Denison also handed down harsh penalties to those who were arrested for strike-related offences. William Howland's younger brother, O.A. Howland, was mayor in 1902. See Tucker, 'Faces,' 297–308, and Desmond Morton, *Mayor Howland: The Citizen's Candidate* (Toronto: A.M. Hakkert 1975), 44–56.

73 The socialist journal, *Cotton's Weekly*, 6 Aug. 1914, 1, noted that H.H. McLean,

president of the Saint John street railway, was also a member of Parliament and a lieutenant-colonel in the army, leading it to observe that he 'is in a position to rob the workers of St. [sic] John's because of his private ownership of wealth, he is where the laws are made saying whether the capitalists or the workers shall get the rewards arising from the labor of the workers, and he is where he can command soldiers to shoot down workers if the workers dare protest against the laws made by McLean and his class in favor of McLean and his class.'

74 Hamilton *Spectator*, 13 Nov. 1906, 6; 16 Nov., 6.

75 Palmer, 'Give Us,' 120; Heron, 'The Workers' City'; Hamilton *Spectator*, 6–26 Nov. 1906.

76 The street railway was having a serious dispute with the city prior to the strike. The Halifax *Herald* characterized the company's demand as 'a serious menace which should be resisted to the utmost' (20 May 1913, 6) and later congratulated the mayor in 'firmly refusing to suffer the situation to be dangerously complicated by the calling out of the Military' (21 May 1913, 6). An amendment to the Militia Act in 1904 that increased the financial accountability of municipalities for the cost of troops may have made officials somewhat more reluctant to take this step, although overall the use of troops in strikes between 1904 and 1914 increased. See Morton, 'Aid,' 422–3.

77 After the 1904 Militia Act, the permanent force was to be called first before recourse was had to the militia, and it was indeed used in the three instances troops were requisitioned to aid the civil power in street railway disputes between 1906 and 1913. The press coverage of military aid in street railway strikes, however, did not clearly distinguish between militia and permanent troops and there was no suggestion that permanent troops behaved differently than the militia.

78 Toronto City Council Minutes, 1903 (Toronto: Carswell 1904), appendix C, 'Annual Report of the Chief Constable for the Year 1902,' 51.

79 Colonel Evans, District Officer Commanding M.D. No. 10, to Secretary, Militia Council, 2 April 1906, in LAC, RG 24, vol. 6514, HQ 363–9. The troops were mostly drawn from the RCMR (82), the 13th Field Battery (53), and the 90th Regiment (151).

80 Saint John *Globe*, 24 July 1914, 1.

81 See Tucker, 'Faces,' 299–301.

82 Hamilton *Spectator*, 26 Nov. 1906, 1, 3, 4. Also, see Morton, 'Aid,' 424–5.

83 Hamilton *Spectator*, 26 Nov. 1906, 6; Heron, 'Workers' City'; John C. Weaver, 'Social Control, Martial Conformity, and Community Entanglement: The Varied Beat of the Hamilton Police Force, 1895–1920,' *Urban History Review* 19 (1990): 115. There is some suggestion in the newspaper accounts that the

troops were reluctant to use force and that the ground troops refused to make a bayonet charge after being ordered to do so by Colonel Denison. See Hamilton *Spectator*, 26 Nov. 1906, 4. Note also that the Hamilton TLC's platform issued after these events called for an inquiry into police behaviour. No mention was made of the militia. See Hamilton *Spectator*, 19 Dec. 1906, 6. The platform also called for municipal ownership of all public utilities and opposed granting the Cataract Power Company, owner of the street railway, any further concessions.

84 Montreal *Gazette*, 26 May 1903, 5.
85 'Our Disorderly Special Constables,' *Free Press*, 31 March 1906, 4. The issue of the legality of their use of firearms was never raised.
86 *Free Press*, 2 April 1906, 7.
87 *Free Press*, 2 April 1906, 1.
88 Earlier, private detectives had been sworn in as special constables in London during the 1899 street railway strike, leading the *Industrial Banner* (July 1899, 3) to ask, 'Does the Street Railway Own London?'
89 *Daily News*, 13 May 1913, quoted in Morrison, 'Community,' 244.
90 For a brief description of these courts' criminal jurisdiction, see Romney, *Mr Attorney*, 283–4.
91 Tucker, 'Faces,' 301–4. Also, see Kostal, 'Great Strikes,' 305–6.
92 *Mail*, 15 March 1886, 8. For a more extended discussion, see Tucker, 'Faces,' 298–301.
93 For example, see *Free Press*, 3 April 1906, 7; 7 April 1906, 18 (quote); 19 Dec. 1910, 17; 22 Dec. 1910, 17.
94 Montreal *Gazette*, 27 May 1903, 9; 28 May 1903, 7.
95 Hamilton *Spectator*, 20 Dec. 1906, 1. He also sentenced James Moran and Alexander Thompson to twelve months' imprisonment for being in an unlawful assembly.
96 The phenomenon was not unique to London. In other cities, however, I was unable to locate subsequent newspaper reports of the trials.
97 London *Free Press*, 15 Dec. 1899, 6.
98 Ibid.; AO, RG4-32, file 1900/933.
99 For example, see Montreal *Gazette*, 28 May 1903, 7.
100 *Free Press*, 29 Dec. 1910, 7.
101 *Free Press*, 7 April 1906, 18.
102 Kostal, 'Great Strikes,' 310, makes a similar point.
103 Craig Heron, 'The Second Industrial Revolution in Canada, 1890–1930,' in Deian R. Hopkin and Gregory S. Kealey, eds., *Class, Community and the Labour Movement: Wales and Canada, 1850–1930* (St. John's: LLAFUR/CCLH 1989), 48.

PART THREE

The North-West Rebellions

7

Treasonous Murder:
The Trial of Ambroise Lépine, 1874

LOUIS A. KNAFLA

As this, in all probability, is the last opportunity I shall ever have on earth of addressing you ... The sentence of the law upon you is that you be taken to the place where you now are to the common gaol of this Province, and there be kept in solitary confinement until the twenty-ninth day of January, 1875, and on that day, between the hours of eight and ten o'clock in the forenoon, you be taken thence to the place of execution, and there be hanged by the neck until you are dead, and may the God of pity have mercy upon your soul.
– Edmund Burke Wood, chief justice of the Court of Queen's Bench at
Winnipeg, Manitoba, 4 November 1874, sentencing Ambroise Lépine[1]

The 1874 trial of Ambroise Lépine for the murder of Thomas Scott in the Red River resistance of 1869–70 was long and complex and involved a number of major questions. What law was in force in the Red River colony in March 1870? What was the legal status of the 'provisional government' (PG) of Red River? What were the actual facts in the arrest, trial, and execution of Scott under the alleged auspices of Lépine? What British, imperial, Dominion, and provincial statutes were relevant for Lépine's trial in Winnipeg in 1874? Which witnesses were allowed to testify, and what evidence was admissible in court? What weight was given to contradictory or conflicting evidence to cause reasonable doubt? Was the chief justice prejudicial towards certain witnesses? Could a conviction for murder be obtained without a body? Did Chief Justice Wood adhere to traditional rules of law in his instructions and address to the jury? Finally, as Lépine was acting on the behalf of the PG, why was he, and not Louis Riel, tried, and tried for murder instead of treason?

The trial of Louis Riel for treason in 1885 took place within a complex background of long-standing, unresolved issues as outlined by Jack Bumsted in this volume. The context resembles in many ways that of the trial of Ambroise Lépine twelve years earlier. The severe winter of 1883–4, which helped fuel the bitter agitation in the Saskatchewan valley, was not unlike that of 1868–9 in Red River. The desire of the Métis for a homeland in 1884 was an attempt to make good what was lost in 1870. The seizure of Fort Carlton by the Métis in March 1884 that launched the North-West rebellion was not unlike the capture of Fort Garry in December 1869 that opened the Red River resistance.[2] The petition to Ottawa of the North-West Settlers' Union in December 1884 was in the spirit of the Bill of Rights of January 1870. Some of the ex-Ontarians who were in the Manitoba militias that fought the Métis and Cree at Duck and Frog lakes in 1885 may well have been those who came to demolish the Métis force from Red River in August 1870. While the Dominion got their man (Riel) in 1885, its failure to get him in 1873 led to a stand-in for his trial, Lieutenant Lépine. Perhaps the government learned from that trial as well. While Lépine had outstanding defence counsel, whose tactics and political savvy enabled him to escape execution in 1873, Riel was not so fortunate. As Bumsted explains, Riel's team was weak, and this, along with the other factors explored by Bob Beal and Barry Wright, also in the present volume, facilitated his conviction (just as political calculations facilitated his execution). Had the government learned something from 1873? The Lépine trial can be seen as a microcosm of Riel's: a state trial that was programmed for conviction.[3]

Lépine's 'murder' trial was preparatory for a potential treason trial of Riel for leading the resistance of 1869; it was also the first major trial in the history of the new province of Manitoba and can be considered among the early state trials in the history of the new Dominion. Its significance for both governments, as Bumsted has argued elsewhere, was to identify and flesh out responses to all possible defences of Riel and his legal counsel.[4] Even if the government failed to convict Lépine, the lessons gained would be useful if it had the opportunity to try Riel. Thus, while the charge was murder, the proceedings, from the original contemplation of treason to the final amnesty, had all the features of a state trial that measured the legitimacy of the actions of a new province and nation.

For a number of English Canadians in 1869–70, Riel was the real obstacle to the grand quest of bringing the Red River colony and the North-

West Territories (NWT) into Canada. Ontarians were settling around Portage La Prairie, and their westward movement was seen as a natural extension of their homeland, with mixed-bloods moved to reserves – views that were expressed explicitly in their local press.[5] For John Mac-Dougall, the lieutenant governor-in-waiting who assisted in drafting the terms for the transfer of Rupert's Land, the region was 'Ontario's West' and the Métis were 'ignorant' 'firebrands' who had to be stopped from overrunning it.[6] According to Adam Mercer, a young new settler, the Métis were best 'exorcised' since Manitoba would support an agrarian population of twenty-five million. Riel was 'Little Napoleon,' a man with a black heart who shot Scott as if he were a dog.[7] For Donald A. Smith, special commissioner for the Dominion and imperial governments, the solution was to have the Natives and Métis 'swamped' by settlers, but Riel, their leader, stood in the way.[8] The Reverend George Young, founder of the Methodist church in the colony, led a crusade against the Catholic 'half-breeds.' Stories of these 'savages' struck fear into the hearts of Ontario settlers.[9] Riel was a 'megalomaniac,' according to the Reverend R.G. MacBeth, and he remembered vividly, at age eleven, his brother running in from the churchyard crying out 'The French are Coming!'[10]

While Riel was at the forefront of the Métis movement to form a British province, Lépine, an 'easy-going giant,' was the largely unknown adjutant-general of the PG who, by virtue of his position, presided over Scott's court martial in March 1870. Scott was charged and convicted of threatening and striking Riel and the guards, and shot by a firing squad. Lépine was not present at the execution and Scott's body was never found. Nonetheless, more than three years later, in September 1873, Lépine was arrested, had a preliminary hearing before Police Magistrate Louis Bétournay in the town of Winnipeg in October, was sent to the provincial prison at the Stone Fort, and was indicted by a grand jury *de medietate linguae* in November before Justice J.C. McKeagney. Lépine stood trial before the Manitoba Queen's Bench at Winnipeg in February 1874, but McKeagney deferred the hearing until the appointment of new chief justice in June, and Lépine was finally tried in October.

This chapter explores the trial of Lépine as the first state trial in the new Canadian west. Questions concerning the criminal law in Prince Rupert's Land in 1869, the provisional government under which Scott was tried, the circumstances that brought Scott to his execution in 1870, and the subsequent events that caused Lépine's arrest in 1873 are assessed in the first half of the chapter because they are integral to an understanding of his trial. The second half of the chapter presents a full analysis of that trial and of the proceedings for amnesty, and it closes with conclusions on the case's significance.

A QUESTION OF JURISDICTION:
THE CRIMINAL LAW OF PRINCE RUPERT'S LAND IN 1869

The complexities of and controversies around the status of criminal law in Rupert's Land in the years before the Hudson's Bay Company (HBC) ceded its royal charter of 1670 to Great Britain, which granted it to the Dominion of Canada on 15 July 1870, have been examined by a number of scholars without agreement.[11] The subject is one that deserves an interpretive overview for a full understanding of Scott's execution and the later staged trials of the participants.

Originally, under the charter, the HBC was granted full sovereignty (ownership in fee simple) over all land that drained into Hudson Bay and jurisdiction over all disputes arising therein.[12] The question of HBC jurisdiction arose in the late eighteenth century, when the fur trade expanded westward. Several acts of the imperial Parliament from 1765 to 1775 gave jurisdiction over that area to any adjoining colony. The Canada Jurisdiction Act of 1803 was enacted to resolve such questions in the 'Indian Territories,' where it was intended to apply to the trading region of the North-West Company (NWC). That act permitted the lieutenant governor of Lower Canada to appoint justices of the peace (JPs) for such districts, with trial in Lower Canada where the company was headquartered.[13] Immediately, the NWC challenged HBC posts on James Bay. Thus, the HBC directors sought a legal opinion on whether the act applied to Rupert's Land.

The 1803 legal opinion was given by some of the leading British jurists of the period – Samuel Romilly, Vicary Gibbs, Thomas Lord Erskine, and Francis Hargrave.[14] They concluded that the land claim and jurisdiction of the HBC were valid, but perhaps the exclusive trading rights were not. They suggested, however, that English courts would probably reject the legal fiction of trying a case from Rupert's Land in England or Lower Canada.[15] Thus, when Thomas Douglas, Earl of Selkirk, considered a settlement in the Red River area in 1805–9, he sought a further legal opinion on the extent of the 1803 act. A similarly prominent group of jurists wrote in unanimity that the act did not apply to the charter of 1670 or to any part of Rupert's Land.[16] The governor-in-council could appoint constables and JPs as in England, and hear cases, but was not advised to do so for capital crimes. This view was reiterated by the same group in an opinion given in 1811.[17] Thus, the London Committee of the HBC devolved its legal powers to the governor and council of Rupert's Land. When Governor Miles Macdonell asked Selkirk for instructions in 1813, he was told that in cases of murder he could either send the case to London or hear it locally according to English law, saving a report to the crown for any sentence.[18]

There had been long-standing issues of law and politics and of lawlessness and struggles for domination in the region. After Governor Robert Semple and twenty Red River colonists were killed by NWC employees at Seven Oaks in 1816, confusion over their trial venues (Upper Canada or Assiniboia?) produced a report by a special committee of the House of Commons that led to the Jurisdiction Act of 1821. Meanwhile, trials occurred at several places in the Canadas and in London, and there was only one conviction.[19] The Colonial Office threw out the case slated for England because the crime was not covered by the statute of Henry VIII that provided for the trial in England of capital felonies in British lands beyond the mother country.[20]

The 1821 act was framed just after the NWC amalgamated with the HBC. Its major purpose was to confirm the exclusive trading privileges in the charter of 1670 and extend them west to the Pacific Ocean.[21] It also empowered the crown to appoint JPs for HBC and Native lands with jurisdiction over all criminal offences except any felony punishable by death, life, or transportation (which had to be tried in Upper Canada).[22] While section 5 said that the 1803 act encompassed all HBC lands, the final section, 14, stated that it did not infringe upon any of the rights, authority, or jurisdiction of the company under its charter. The London Committee again sought a legal opinion for clarification. Jurisdiction was confirmed, but the company was advised, yet again, not to try capital cases in Rupert's Land.[23] Since the Colonial Office had declined to appoint JPs, the London Committee authorized the governor and any two councillors to act as a court with local juries, but to send any capital cases to Upper Canada.[24] Edward Ellice, a major draftsman of the 1821 act,[25] gave evidence to the select committee on the HBC in 1857. He stated specifically that, while the major intention of the 1821 act was to extend the new amalgamated company's control of the fur trade to the Pacific, it was also designed to protect its rights and jurisdiction under the charter and not to extend any Canadian jurisdiction over its lands.[26] Accordingly, Colonial Secretary Lord Bathurst instructed the governor of Assiniboia to 'administer justice according to the law of England under the provisions of the Charter.'[27]

Many less serious disputes after 1821 were settled by informal master-servant law and arbitration. Local by-laws were first drafted in 1832 and consolidated in 1836, and standing rules and regulations for Rupert's Land and all Indian Territories were published at Norway House in June 1837.[28] Additional substantive law for local regulations was put into place by the HBC civil and criminal law regulations of 1839, which were amended afterwards.[29] The Assiniboia Council revised the date of English law reception from 1670 to 1851,[30] the intent being to preserve and extend English law. Meanwhile, the British act of 1859, which expanded the powers of JPs in Indian Territories to hear all matters except capital felonies (reserved for Upper Canada or British Columbia), specifically excluded Rupert's Land.[31] JPs in both jurisdictions held courts of summary procedure and a General Quarterly Court (GQC) similar to quarter sessions in England.[32] All appointments were made by the company's London office, and a civil police force of volunteer, militia-style officers was created.[33] Law-enforcement issues became paramount in the region.[34] As a result, Governor Sir George Simpson and the HBC Council wrote the Colonial Office in 1849 that the crown could appoint JPs to hold trials in Rupert's Land and the Indian Territories, but not for capital cases.[35] For example, the famous Mackenzie River murder case of 1837 was tried in Lower Canada in spite of the difficulties of transport and communication, and resulted in questionable legal process and debilitating human results.[36] When Simpson testified before a parliamentary select committee in 1857 for a renewal of the company's grant of trading privileges, he reported only nineteen instances of homicide since 1821. The one case that required a trial was in the Indian Territories.[37] By 1867, the opinion of the HBC's legal counsel still was that capital cases must be tried in the Canadas.[38]

Therefore, outside the Assiniboia colony, the law of Rupert's Land was the law of England as of 1670, while in the Indian Territories it was that of British Columbia or the Canadas. The imperial Parliament's repeal of the Canada Jurisdiction Act in 1872 confirmed the statute law of England as of 1670 for Rupert's Land, as did its specific repeal of clause 5 of the 1859 act in 1874.[39] Rupert's Land entered the NWT under the Dominion in July 1873 and stipendiary magistrates (SMs) were sent out in the great trek of 1874.[40] The strength of English law in the NWT was confirmed by the act of 1886 that promulgated the law of England of 1870.[41] David Mills, future minister of justice, held that the lands west of Canada were subject to three jurisdictions – Rupert's Land, the Indian Territories, and the district of Assiniboia.[42] But Justice Killam of the Manitoba Queen's Bench, and later of the Supreme Court of Canada, held that the criminal law of the whole region was always the criminal law of England.[43] Killam's opinion was confirmed by J.E. Cote, the prominent Alberta lawyer and legal historian who later researched the statutes of England and Canada and came to the same conclusion.[44] The exception, of course, was always capital cases.

A QUESTION OF LEGITIMACY:
THE PROVISIONAL GOVERNMENT 1869–70

The conflict arising between the end of the Council of Assiniboia in December 1869 and the installation of a provincial government after the transfer of the lands of the HBC to the Dominion in July 1870 informed the status of the provisional government. The legitimacy of the actions of both the opponents and proponents of rapid union with the Dominion of Canada, and of whether the PG presented a security threat to the Dominion, is difficult to determine definitively. Soon after confederation, Sir John A. Macdonald's government sought a parliamentary resolution to expand Canada west to the Pacific. Introduced with the bombastic oratory of William McDougall, minister of public works, on 4 December 1867, the resolution passed after a week's debate. The proponents were the 'Canadians' in Red River and their Ontarian brethren,[45] notably the notorious John Christian Schultz.

After the relatively peaceful 1850s, the 'Canadian Party' under Schultz assailed the HBC and threatened the life and culture of mixed-bloods. 'Dr' Schultz listed himself as 'physician and surgeon.' He became a land speculator and allegedly tried to overthrow the PG, which was attempting to protect the property rights of all residents. According to HBC Governor William Mactavish, every Canadian official who arrived in the colony 'was too intimate of Doctor Schultz.'[46] In 1866 he held a meeting of five to demand a new government, and used his newspaper the *Nor'Wester* to preach sedition.[47] After Scott's execution, Schultz went to Toronto and, besides receiving cash gifts that he never accounted for, gave rousing speeches before crowds of thousands, showed what he claimed was the rope that tied Scott's hands and called upon his listeners to incite riot in the colony. He also made large land claims for property allegedly lost in 1869–70.[48] A devout mason and anti-Catholic, he was elected MP in 1870 and advocated the extermination of Métis. He paid mobs to burn effigies of Riel and Lieutenant Governor Archibald in the streets of Winnipeg and to attack poll booths in Métis areas. The high standing of English Canadians was shown later that year when a recent immigrant, Alex McLean,

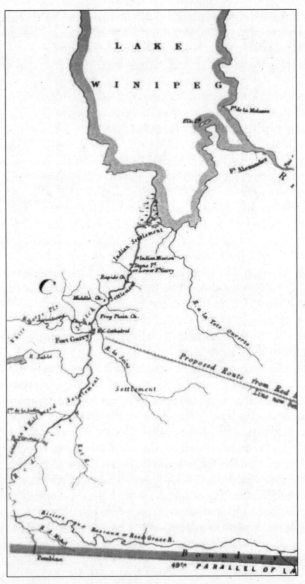

The Red River settlement, 1858. From 'Plan Shewing the Proposed Route from Lake Superior to Red River Settlement Compiled from the Maps of Messrs Dawson and Napier.' Crown Lands Department, Toronto, 23 May 1858. Copy at the University of Calgary, McKimmie Library, Map Room, G3401.S1 SVAR-A 18/1.

was tried for the manslaughter of a Métis trader and found not guilty. Prepared for a guilty verdict, his supporters had planned an escape at the courtroom door.[49]

The famine and storms of the summer of 1868 devastated the colony and brought relief funds from Canada, Britain, and the United States. In June 1869 the Dominion stepped in to build a road from Thunder Bay to Red River to provide employment, without apprising the HBC, and contactor John Snow gave workers chits payable at Schultz's store at inflated prices.[50] When Parliament met to ratify terms for the transfer of HBC lands to the Dominion,[51] the mixed-bloods met in July to consider the matter. Discussions of land ownership proved contentious since some francophone settlements had not been formally granted by the HBC, and Snow staked land already occupied for his own and Schultz's use.[52] Almost four hundred settlers of Portage la Prairie, just outside the colony, took matters into their own hands and created a government of 'Manitoba' with Thomas Spence as president. The colonial secretary wrote from Downing Street to condemn their 'illegal' activity.[53] Meanwhile, Mactavish, who was also governor of Rupert's Land and the District of Assiniboia, had not been informed of how or when the transfer would take place.

The appointment of McDougall as lieutenant governor-in-waiting, and of a council to assist him, along with the arrival of a team of surveyors led by Colonel John Dennis to survey all lands including those of residents, alienated mixed-bloods and many settlers. Mactavish wrote London headquarters in late August that this would lead to opposition. But Joseph Howe, secretary of state for the provinces, wrote McDougall on 20 September instructing him to report on the laws, tax system, and land status of the colony and to be ready to assume power 'in anticipation' of a formal transfer.[54] McDougall aggravated the situation by sending a shipment of arms for his police force. Meanwhile, Howe, a Maritimer who opposed confederation because colonists had not been consulted, visited Red River in early October. Meeting McDougall, who was approaching the border as he left, Howe portrayed him as 'a great satrap' leading his force with a display of 'pomp' that was 'a great blunder.'[55] The U.S. State Department noted unrest over McDougall's assumption of office, predicting a possible revolt and raising the possibility of U.S. annexation.[56] As we shall see, there were representations urging such actions from 1866. Thus, the North-West crisis was connected to Fenian conspiracies, a long-standing security concern in eastern Canada examined elsewhere in this volume.[57] When Mactavish visited Ottawa, he waited days for an interview and said that that no one would listen to him about the problems he faced.[58]

McDougall's premature journey caused a group of Mètis to meet at the house of their spiritual leader, Abbé Janvier Noel Ritchot, on 16 October 1869 to plan strategy. Calling themselves the 'National Committee of the Métis of the Red River,'[59] and bolstered by the return of the boat brigades from the west, they sought to enact the 'laws of the prairies' with a militia. The Council of Assiniboia, lacking a formal transfer of power, met on 25 October and discussed the impasse for eight hours, with Riel and John Bruce presenting the case against McDougall's entry without negotiations with Ottawa.[60] A memo from Colonel Dennis to McDougall on 27 October summed up the situation: anglophones accepted Canadian rule, but, since they had not been consulted, they would not fight against either Métis or Natives.[61] But McDougall also heard from a group of Winnipeg townsmen organized by his protégé Charles Mair and Schultz, who told him that they would provide safe conduct. When McDougall reached Pembina on 30 October, he heard from Mactavish that the only prudent course was to stay there. The Métis, blocking the border, prevented Captain Donald Cameron, who was to head the new police force, from entering. A few days later, Ambroise Lépine appears in the record, leading a party of mixed-bloods to warn McDougall not to cross the border, while another Métis force seized Fort Garry.

Lépine's rise in the Métis movement was occasioned by his close personal, family, and religious ties to Riel. Lépine's father was an engagé of the HBC, and his mother, Marie-Ann Pellerin, was the daughter of an English fur trader and a local Native woman. Educated at the Collège de Saint-Boniface, Lépine married Cécile Marion, of French Canadian and Métis descent, and they began farming in St Boniface. A tall man – 6'3" – with prodigious strength, he was 'of superb appearance' and extraordinarily muscular. He was also level-headed: mild with lesser men, he was unsparing of the strong who wronged him.[62] He supplemented his income with freighting and hunting. On his return to the Red River settlement on 30 October from an expedition to Fort Pitt, he learned that the Métis, led by Riel, had delayed the transfer of Rupert's Land to negotiate terms of union with the Canadian government. He rode with others, apparently in the lead, to turn back the lieutenant governor designate, McDougall, at the border.

On 6 November, Riel, secretary of francophone mixed-bloods, sent a letter to the anglophone mixed-bloods asking them to elect representatives to meet and discuss the present state of the country. The 'Convention of 24' met on 16 November at the courthouse, guarded by 150 armed men. [63] HBC Secretary Joseph James Hargrave read a proclamation declaring their actions unlawful and ordering them to disperse or be considered guilty of rebellion.[64] After a circuitous discussion, the convention was adjourned for the autumn court session. It resumed, deadlocked on McDougall's entry, and adjourned on 24 November until the transfer date of 1 December. In the meantime, Riel had seized HBC documents and had Roger Goulet, collector of customs, hand over his papers. The francophones had decided on a PG, and the anglophones, meeting separately on 26 November, concluded that McDougall should not enter and that they would work through the HBC Council to elect an executive to negotiate terms with the Dominion. On that day the Dominion postponed the transfer until 30 June 1870 to allow time for a peaceful possession.

McDougall wrote to Mactavish and Howe throughout November that, if the transfer did not go through, he would be in an embarrassing position indeed, in that, as he later admitted, his various proclamations would be illegal. Macdonald wrote him on 27 November, after hearing of Métis opposition and his expulsion, that the transfer would not go through and the administration of Assiniboia was now Britain's responsibility. But McDougall's proclamation of 1 December, issued at the Stone Fort and nailed to fence posts at the border,[65] declared the transfer official and his authority lawful and commissioned Colonel J.S. Dennis to take Fort Garry by force. The new situation of possible resistance and bloodshed suggested that postponement was the only viable alternative. While these proclamations were being issued, Howe and Macdonald were writing McDougall that his actions alone cancelled the transfer and that he was invading Great Britain, a 'foreign country.' As Howe wrote to McDougall on 4 December, he had used the queen's name without her authority, making his proclamations and commissions blatantly illegal. When Colonial Secretary Lord Granville heard of the deferral, he observed that sending McDougall was a 'grievous error' and would be 'injurious.'[66]

Hotter heads prevailed. When Captain Charles Boulton and Schultz refused Colonel Dennis's plea to avoid force, the Métis were prompted to take Fort Garry on 6 December – paradoxically on the day Governor General Sir John Young proclaimed a general amnesty.[67] The PG then acted to fill the vacuum left by McDougall's abolition of the HBC administration. The 'Declaration of the People of Rupert's Land and the North-West' of 8 December announced a new government under the 'God of Nations.'[68] Given their status as British subjects, there would be no entry into confederation without negotiation of rights and liberties. The two linguistic sides met that night, and, after considerable discussion, Riel presented his 'Bill of Rights.' The next morning, McDougall's commission was read to Colonel Dennis, who was authorized to arrest or attack anyone who opposed the government. Meanwhile, Schultz was organizing Canadians at his home. Riel responded by having Lépine lead a large group of armed Métis to Schultz's house on 7 December; the Canadians were arrested and sent to the fort.

The PG was proclaimed on 10 December in a formal ceremony with a flag-raising, boys' brass band, and parties. When Mactavish was asked his opinion, he replied: 'Form a government for God's sake, and restore peace and order in the Settlement.'[69] Most of the community agreed that there should be no handover without negotiating terms of the transfer into confederation, and on Christmas Day, Bruce, who was ill, resigned the presidency in favour of Riel. Curiously, Lépine was noted as wavering in his support.[70] Meanwhile, on McDougall's instructions, Colonel Dennis, before returning to Pembina, gave a commission to Joseph Monkman, a Native, on 16 December to incite tribes to rise against the Métis and kill them. When Macdonald heard of this, he told Bishop Alexandre-Antonin Taché to intercept Monkman at Dominion expense, and Granville expressed disbelief that McDougall would issue such orders. It was also alleged that Schultz aimed to raise Sioux warriors.[71] Howe wrote further that McDougall's attempt to seize Rupert's Land was 'by conquest' and that Dennis was a 'reckless' man who 'precipitates' war against Natives, Métis, and the United States.[72]

On the 27th, the day of Commissioner Smith's arrival, the PG was reorganized with Lépine as adjutant-general and a force of 500–600 armed men was raised.[73] Lépine was given orders by the militia council on 8 January to lead the brigade captains in maintaining peace and order in the settlement. While several emissaries came from Ottawa, none apart from Donald Smith had official papers; On 19 January, in -20 degree Fahrenheit weather, a meeting of over 1,000 people was held in the Fort Garry courtyard to hear the commissioner. Thomas Bunn was elected chairman, Riel interpreter, and Judge John Black (recorder of the GQC) secretary. Smith, who had been given no negotiating powers, simply stated that there would be an amnesty if they gave up their arms. He agreed to carry their wishes to Ottawa. Reporting later to Howe, Smith said that, as a house prisoner, he met many residents who had been threatened by Riel, and characterized the Boulton and Schultz parties as rash, unorganized, and useless. He also spent £500 to bribe mixed-bloods to oppose the PG.[74] After sixty men had been set free on oaths, Schultz escaped and took refuge in the Reverend MacBeth's house at Kildonan.[75] He set out to break up the PG, urging people to reverse their support. Other prisoners escaped by early February and took refuge at Portage la Prairie.

The PG Council asked that twenty representatives from each of the two linguistic groups be elected from their districts on 21 January and meet at the courthouse on the 26th. This 'Convention of Forty,' with English- and French-language secretaries and translators, voted unanimously a resolution of loyalty to the crown provided that 'rights, properties, usages and customs be respected.'[76] The convention also proposed a draft Bill of Rights, a bilingual legislature, and courts. A group of three men, led by Judge Black, was sent to Ottawa in early February by a renewed PG to negotiate terms of entry into confederation. Winnipeg townsmen celebrated on the 10th, and on the 11th the Dominion cabinet agreed to negotiate.

Scott, who had escaped through the efforts of Mrs Schultz,[77] joined others who had been released earlier at Portage la Prairie. On the 12th an armed force of about three hundred Canadian 'Liberators' at Kildonan led by Schultz, and about one hundred at Portage la Prairie led by Boulton, marched to release the other prisoners and bring down the PG.[78] A consensus saw the force as futile.[79] Smith said that the 'great majority' of English and Scottish denounced the resistance and 'bitterly complained of those who had set it on foot.'[80] Macdonald wrote that it was 'foolish' and 'criminal.'[81] Schultz's associates, however, sent 'runners' to begin war at different points throughout the province and several were arrested. Upon discovering the dispatches, the Métis demanded that an instigator, William Gaddy, be shot. After leading him to the fort, moderates prevailed. Lépine and Elzéar Goulet had him feign death and arranged an escape.[82]

While the remaining prisoners were released on the 15th on oaths not to act against the PG, towards the morning of the 16th Schultz's force passed through Winnipeg with arms and ladders to attack the fort. A group of Portage men led by Scott and Mair stopped at the house of Riel's cousin Henri Coutu, where Riel often slept overnight, to capture him but he was not there. Meanwhile, Métis agent Norbert Parisien, who had accidentally shot and killed an Ontarian, was caught fleeing near Kildonan church by Scott, who beat him mercilessly with a large staff. Parisien died six days later.[83] On the 17th, Schultz's associates gathered forty-eight armed men (including Scott) two miles from Fort Garry. Marching by Winnipeg through large snow drifts, they were intercepted by PG soldiers and arrested. Three days later, Lépine overwhelmed Boulton's force and arrested them as prisoners of war. Boulton was tried for armed resistance to the PG by court martial. He was found guilty and sentenced to be shot. Riel, receiving numerous requests for mercy, sent Smith to the rebel settlements to have them recognize the authority of the PG and its military court. They did and Boulton was pardoned.[84] While HBC officials, especially Mactavish, were protecting the Canadians, Schultz and Scott did not see it that way.[85] Scott regarded the HBC's conduct as weak, and continued to berate and threaten his Métis guards.[86] The history of the 'Scott affair' over the next two weeks marked the defining moment in the life of Ambroise Lépine.

A QUESTION OF MURDER:

THE TRIAL, EXECUTION, AND DEATH OF THOMAS SCOTT, 1870

The execution of Thomas Scott was a grisly event whose story is much recounted in academic and popular history as well as children's stories.[87] While Scott's trial was never fully addressed in the proceedings against Lépine, the execution was made the principal highlight by both the prosecution and the chief justice. It is therefore important to present the record on Scott's trial, which is still controversial, and its inflammatory impact on the public mind.[88]

Aged thirty-eight, Scott was an unlikely Protestant hero. A transient labourer, he was a large northern Irishman who immigrated in his early thirties to Ontario where he served in the militia. His parents were tenant farmers on the estate of Frederick Blackwood, Lord Dufferin, who later observed that Scott was 'a violent and boisterous man such as are often found in the North of Ireland.'[89] He came to Red River for work in 1869 and led a road gang's revolt for higher wages by threatening to drown their boss John Snow, who was rescued by Métis. Members of the gang were tried before Judge Black on 18–19 November for assault and convicted.[90] Later barricaded in the Winnipeg house of Dr Schultz, who 'enrolled' him in the cause,[91] he was captured by Riel and incarcerated several times; during these periods of imprisonment, he taunted his captors to kill him, threatened and fought with guards, and made a few daring escapes. Afterwards he told the Portage people lurid tales of his treatment.

Riel took Scott prisoner again, along with Major Boulton and forty-six others, on 18 February 1870 after they had tried to seize him while on their way to the Stone Fort, which was ransacked by the Métis a week later. In prison, Scott was so violent on the 28th that the guards dragged him out and were about to 'sacrifice' him when a councillor intervened.[92] Riel investigated the incident the next day, but Scott's outbursts were

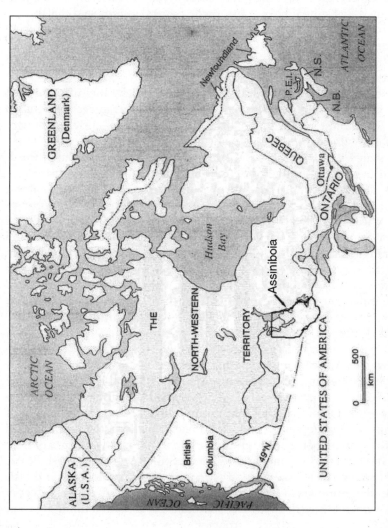

Canada in 1869–70. Modified by Louis Knafla from Roderick Stewart and Neil McLean, *Forming a Nation: The Story of Canada and Canadians*, Book 2 (Toronto: Gage Educational Publishing 1978), 31.

such that the guards put him in irons and demanded an immediate court martial. When Riel tried to obtain a promise of peaceful conduct in return for his release, Scott jeered and insulted him, inciting fellow prisoners to do the same.[93] Alexander Begg, corroborated by others, reports that Scott threatened Riel's life if he ever escaped.[94] Several guards said that, on the day of the trial, Scott tried to strike Riel, and told the judges they were cowards and would not dare condemn him to death. While Riel did not want him killed, the guards said they would shoot him if the court did not order it.[95]

The court-martial panel of six judges appointed by Riel was presided over by Lépine as adjutant-general, and Scott was arraigned on 3 March 1870. The earliest detailed account was by Joseph Nolin, Riel's secretary and chief witness. With most of the two-hour proceedings in French, Nolin stated that Riel acted as the interpreter, summarized the proceedings in English, and allowed Scott to respond but not to summon witnesses. The Reverend Young, who was not there, claimed that Scott did not understand the language and was not allowed to speak.[96] Young's account was reiterated by Donald Smith, Adam Mercer, and others.[97] Riel had nothing to do with the decision except to plead for mercy before and after judgment. Abbé Ritchot moved a guilty verdict with punishment by death, seconded by André Nault; Elzéar Goulet and Joseph Delorme agreed; Elzéar Lagemodière and Jean-Baptiste Lépine voted for exile; and Ambroise Lépine declined to vote.[98] Condemned to be shot the next day at 10:00 a.m., Young's intercession delayed the execution until sometime after 12:00 noon.[99]

The execution was carried out by six men with muskets (hunting rifles) from 60–70 feet, some of whom were intoxicated, and attended by 150–200 people who turned up outside the fort's walls. Some said that Scott did not die until evening, when Lépine allegedly shot him to finish the work. Others said he lived one to two hours after the first shot.[100] What probably happened comes from Nault, the man who commanded the firing squad. Some men withdrew the caps from the nipples of their guns and did not fire. Three bullets struck Scott, two in the breast. Before Nault could go over to see if Scott was dead, François Guillemette, a little intoxicated, ran over to the body, turned it over, and fired a revolver at the head. Some say the shot went into an ear; others, into an eye. The body was placed in a rough carpenter's box 5'8" long, nailed shut, and carried into the fort. Nault remained with it for two and a half hours and heard no sounds.[101] American Major H.N. Robinson reported that Scott was alive five hours later. Doubting that death had occurred, Riel, accompanied by Robinson and a sentry, went to the shed where the body was being kept; there, they found the box containing Scott, from which blood was dripping onto the snow. The boards of the box were not well joined, and Robinson said he heard with horror this voice from within: 'Oh, let me out of this! My God! How I suffer!'[102] He retreated, Riel called the sentry, they walked out, and a moment later there was a shot.[103]

The next morning, Young came to the fort with Bishop Robert Machray and asked to have the body for burial, but Riel refused because Lépine was in charge and would not interfere. Instead, the body was taken out of the fort by Goulet and Lagimodière and buried secretly so that no Orangemen could make it a pilgrimage shrine.[104] When Young organized a party to disinter the grave in October, the box was filled with earth and shavings but no body. According to Goulet and Pierre Gladu (a guard at the fort gate), Scott's body was dropped into the Assiniboine River about a quarter of a mile from the mouth of La Seine by three hooded men a week after the execution. Nault, Lagimodière, and Damase Harrison carried the body out of the fort on Dr Schultz's sleigh, cut a hole in the ice, and dropped it in heavy chains, taking oaths never to reveal what they had done. According to A.G. Morice, Nault, who helped Riel remove Scott's body from the fort, buried it in an unmarked grave in St John's Protestant cemetery.[105] Riel said in one of his last confessions with Father Alexis André that the place of burial was not his secret and he was now going to die for what he had done then and not in the 1885 rebellion.[106]

The Reverend Young's account, circulated throughout Ontario, was full of hyperbole: several bullets went through Scott's chest, the snow was 'stained and saturated with his heart's blood,' and his spirit passed quickly to God; the body, quivering in death, then encountered a half-drunken officer who fired a revolver at the head.[107] Young had had a spiritual conversion in 1840 after serving in the Upper Canada Dragoons during the 1837–8 rebellions. Of United Empire Loyalist stock, he said that his life was governed by divine 'interposition.'[108] Inspired by a talk of the Reverend George McDougall in the autumn of 1867 on the need for missionaries, he resigned his post in Toronto and went west to establish the first Methodist church and school in Red River for English settlers.[109] Young saw Scott as a potential convert and his account noted that he had conducted 'spiritual exercises' with him.[110] He wrote immediately to Scott's family after his death as well as to his contacts in Toronto, and contributed to the famous 'Resolution of Toronto Orangemen' published in the *Globe* on 13 April 1870 to avenge the execution, rescue the colony from popery, and bring the murderers to justice.[111]

Was Scott simply an unruly man who aggravated his captors? Bumsted argues that he threatened his guards physically but was not one of the Canadian leaders or of the inner circle; and there was no evidence that he drank, was actually in the Orange Order, or was anti-Catholic or anti-French.[112] Scott was, as Riel put it, a transient Canadian newcomer among 'strangers.'[113] Riel and Lépine said that throughout 1869–70 they tried to disarm rather than fight the people who made war against them.[114] Riel, pressured by Métis guards, had threatened to shoot a prisoner before but had relented, putting his credibility in question. His decision not to intervene in Scott's case kept Natives and mixed-bloods in his coalition; the execution established quiet and made 'Canada respect us.'[115] Sir Wilfrid Laurier, in a speech to the House of Commons on 15 April 1874, said that Scott's execution was a political act flowing from the sentence of a court that had a de facto existence.[116] Justice A.G.B. Bannatyne, widely respected, said the region was never more peaceful until Colonel Garnet Joseph Wolseley's arrival, and business never better.[117] For some, the spilling of Scott's blood demonstrated the authority of the PG and 'the sovereign authority of a state.'[118]

The Scott affair did not affect relations between Lépine and Riel. After the events of 1870, Riel spoke of 'double joy' in seeing Lépine in December 1870. He wrote of their joint attendance at meetings called to plan resistance to the Fenian raids expected by September-November 1871. He also wrote of their activities at St Paul in May 1872. Though Lèpine had not been present at Scott's execution and Scott's body was never found, more than three years later he was arrested for Scott's murder. When Riel heard of Lépine's arrest, he wrote to Joseph Dubuc of 'a grand injustice,' an assessment with which Dubuc agreed, and outlined how important it was for the country to have impartial trials for Lépine, Nault, and Lagimodière.[119]

A QUESTION OF TIME:
THE 1870–3 INTERLUDE AND FENIAN RAID

The government that Riel and the people of Assiniboia had created was not undone by the Scott affair. The court martial that Lépine had presided over was an interlude in the operation of the colony's legal system during which the PG, under attack, embraced military justice.

The recorder of the GQC during the 'troubles' of late 1869 through the spring of 1870 was John Black, a Scottish solicitor who came to Red River from New South Wales, becoming deputy to Adam Thom and president of the court in 1862. He presided over the council meetings of October-December 1869, the convention that established the PG, and the drafting of the Bill of Rights in January-February 1870, and was one of three delegates sent to Ottawa to negotiate with the Dominion.[120] The petty courts were busy, and Black delivered humane substantial justice, presiding over two murder trials in 1866 and 1868.[121] Black's court sat through mid-December 1869, and, since the convention met in the courthouse, it was adjourned in November for the GQC sittings. The February session was not held owing to uncertainty over HBC jurisdiction. Thus, Lépine's authority as adjutant-general under a perceived state of martial law held sway in the chaotic months of March and April until the GQC resumed its functions in June under a new recorder, Francis Johnson, who previously had been a recorder (1854–8) and was persuaded to return after serving as a Quebec Superior Court judge.[122]

Meanwhile, in February 1870, the PG established a new court structure comprising additional magistrates and JPs, five petty courts, a new district court, and a supreme court.[123] Alexander Ross was appointed chief justice on 26 March and a revised law code was passed on 4 April. The GQC was scheduled to return to its sittings in June, but, because of a lack of business or because of the prevailing uncertainty, it did not. The new district court did sit in late June, however, under Justice Bannatyne (who was sympathetic to Riel's cause and later warned him of the warrant for his arrest and helped raise bail for Lépine) and two associate magistrates.[124]

The settlement was calm after Scott's execution. The first PG council sat on 9 March, a resolution was passed pledging loyalty to the queen, and on the 15th a List of Rights was presented to the Dominion.[125] Bishop Taché, returning from a Vatican Council in Rome, read a telegram from Secretary of State Howe stating that the list of rights was acceptable in general and that the council should send delegates to Ottawa to finalize the details.[126] Taché also brought a verbal general amnesty from the prime minister.[127] When the delegates set off for Ottawa on 24 March, however, all was not well in the east. The Toronto *Telegraph* and *Globe* were passionate over Scott's death. Schultz and others arrived on 7 April, and a crowd of 6,000 passed resolutions for 'Loyalists' to quell the 'Revolt.'[128] Thomas Scott's brother, Hugh, assisted by a new group of Ontario nationalists who called themselves 'Canada First,' swore out a warrant to arrest the delegates for aiding and abetting the murder and sent it to Ottawa. When the delegates arrived on 14 April, they were arrested, but the grand jury found no true bill.[129] Recognized only as representing Red River, the delegates stated that they could not negotiate without an amnesty for all illegal acts. In April, negotiations for the Manitoba Act proceeded, with Dominion representatives suggesting that amnesty would be given. When Abbé Ritchot returned from Ottawa in June with a copy of the bill for the Manitoba Act, he confirmed George-Étienne Cartier's statement that the PG should continue to govern until the arrival of Archibald, the lieutenant governor designate. The PG used this opportunity to pass laws on courts, police, customs, and roads.[130] The Manitoba Act was passed by Parliament on 12 May, with Black and his associates assisting in drafting the final terms. It received royal assent on 22 June, and an imperial order-in-council transferred the colony to Canada on 15 July.[131]

The formation of Colonel Wolseley's militia in May alarmed Riel: its arrival in Manitoba on 24 August 1870 was perceived as an armed conquest. Riel and others fled in advance. Wolseley had appointed Commissioner Smith as acting lieutenant governor until Archibald's arrival, and Smith issued warrants for Riel's arrest on 2 August. His posted 'Orders for the Day' referred to the resistance leaders as 'bandits' and 'brigands.' Orangemen broke into Riel's house, Baptiste Lépine and Nault were beaten and left for dead, and Goulet and Guillemette were killed. Francis Cornish, later prosecuting counsel for the crown, hired men throughout 1870–1 to watch for Riel and others who returned across the border to visit relatives, and to search hotels, while the Ontario government offered a $5,000 reward for Riel's capture.[132]

Lieutenant Governor Archibald, a Nova Scotian viewed as a conciliator by Cartier, arrived on 2 September 1870 and proclaimed the new government on the 6th amidst growing disorder. The following year, William O'Donoghue split with Riel over U.S. intervention, although the falling out dated back to the final months of the PG. In January 1871 O'Donoghue carried a secret petition to President Ulysses Grant and turned to the Fenian Brotherhood, enlisting the help of John O'Neill and J.J. Donnelly.[133] When O'Donoghue invaded the province on 5 October, with O'Neill and thirty-five men from Minnesota, several Métis companies helped defend the province, one under Riel and another under Lépine. Archibald resisted repeated demands to issue warrants for the arrest of Riel and others, assuming that an amnesty was coming. He paid them and thanked them unofficially for their services and then urged them to leave the province.

Meanwhile, the GQC continued to sit for the new province and faced the challenge of responding to a new phase of the crisis in the form of external security threats from the United States. The Fenian 'invasion' was to mark the final raid in that crisis examined in the chapters by Blake

Brown and David Wilson in this volume. Joseph Royal and Joseph Dubuc, the first two practitioners admitted to the Law Society of Manitoba, acted as defence counsel for the November 1871 trials of three Métis who were arrested for assisting in the Fenian raids on Pembina. Two were acquitted, and another was found guilty of lawless aggression under the Fenian legislation and sentenced to death – but given a conditional pardon and banished.[134] O'Donoghue and his American raiders were arrested by a Métis group and escorted back across the border.

The last session of the GQC sat in May 1872, after which the Supreme Court of Manitoba took over under Chief Justice Alexander Morris, who opened its first session on 8 October. The first trial was the prosecution of Cornish by Dubuc for leading English rioters (paid by Schultz) in the federal election of September 1872. Dubuc was beaten by the English outside the courthouse. None of the rioters was indicted because witnesses were afraid to come forward and testify.[135]

With a growing movement in Ontario to recall Archibald for favouring Riel and Lépine, and the political vacuum caused by Cartier's death on 20 May 1873, Macdonald's government advised Attorney General Henry Joseph Clarke to issue a warrant for the arrest of Riel for Scott's murder on 15 November. Riel, forewarned, escaped to New York, was re-elected as MP, and escaped again. Nault, Elzéar Lépine, Joseph Delorme, and Ritchot were arrested for treason-felony in Ottawa on 27 May 1874 after Ambroise Lépine's indictment, and released shortly afterwards for lack of evidence at the preliminary hearing.[136]

THE TRIAL OF AMBROISE LÉPINE

Preliminary Proceedings

The original strategy to indict Riel for high treason before the Manitoba Queen's Bench was thwarted by his escape. This made the likelihood of a Red River jury convicting Riel's associates of high treason doubtful, leaving a charge of murder as the preferred action.[137] The ensuing trial of Lépine was long, taking eleven days and several nights. The Canada First version of events leading to the trial saw the PG installing a Roman Catholic, French-speaking mixed-blood province on Ontario's doorstep in opposition to its 'manifest destiny' to incorporate the colony into either Ontario or the Dominion for the expansion of a Protestant, English-speaking state. That version would be severely tested.

The legal process began with an information laid against Riel, Lépine,

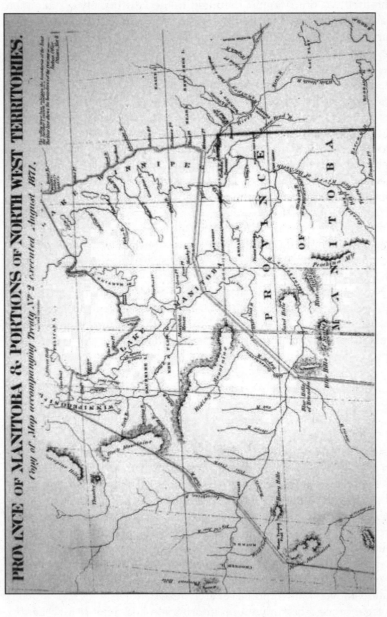

Manitoba and parts of the North-West Territory, 1871. From 'Province of Manitoba and Portions of North West Territories. Copy of Map accompanying Treaty No. 2 executed August 1871' (Ottawa: Queen's Printer 1871).

and others for Scott's murder before JP John H. O'Donnell at Winnipeg on 15 September 1873.[138] O'Donnell had been imprisoned at the Stone Fort with Scott during the disturbances of 1869–70. He had also been at the house of Dr Schultz with Scott and those who had surrendered to the Métis in December 1869, and was released when William N. Farmer was imprisoned. Farmer had been part of the armed band of Canadians who marched from Portage la Prairie to the settlement in February 1870 to release prisoners like O'Donnell and were seized on their return.

Lépine's rapid rise was due to the trust of the men he served with and his close personal ties to Riel. After the Scott affair and the Fenian invasion, during which he had led volunteers in defence of the colony, he spent the next few years on his farm.[139] Arrested on 17 September 1873 while playing with his children, Lépine offered no resistance. With O'Donnell stripped of his office because of his alleged 'private' initiative in arresting Lépine, and with Riel – running successfully for federal seats and notorious for crossing the border – fast becoming a source of friction in Manitoba and Ontario, the provincial and Dominion governments saw this prosecution as a means of bringing closure to the Scott affair.[140]

The preliminary hearing was before SM Bétournay and JP Gilbert McMicken at the Fort Garry courtroom on Friday, 26 September, 1873. Bétournay, the presiding judge, had no judicial experience and no knowledge of the common law or of the courtroom.[141] The much-experienced McMicken, on the other hand, had long service operating Macdonald's security networks against the Fenians, having created a 'Western Frontier Constabulary' for undercover agents who worked the borderlands from 1865 to 1871. Sent to Manitoba to keep tabs on Governor Archibald, McMicken befriended Cornish and became a land speculator until grievances over his work forced him out as JP after the hearing.[142]

The prosecution counsel was Francis Evans Cornish, assisted by his law partner W.B. Thibeaudeau. Cornish, a Conservative Orangeman, was aligned with Schultz and opposed to Riel and the Métis, and arranged for Lépine's arrest in 1873.[143] The defence team was comprised of Joseph Royal, his law partner Joseph Dubuc, and Marc-Amable Girard, all Catholics and sympathetic to Riel and the Métis cause.[144]

The defence focused on two issues: jurisdiction and a politicized charge of murder because a treason charge could not be maintained. They began with a motion to adjourn on the question of jurisdiction, arguing that Rupert's Land was imperial territory between the resignation of the HBC government of Assiniboia in December 1869 and the order-in-council of July 1870, that capital criminal cases were reserved for the courts of Upper and Lower Canada, and that the Manitoba Act was not retroactive. Bétournay responded that, since the question of jurisdiction was up to a higher court, he would consider evidence only on the preliminary charge of murder, and proceeded to examine witnesses for five days.[145] Arguments that the PG replaced the HBC as the de facto authority in Red River, and that the Dominion had negotiated with its delegates, were raised later before a parliamentary inquiry in 1874. That material, however, was already in public hands by the time of Lépine's trial in autumn 1874.[146]

The initial arguments for the defence were that there was only proof of Scott's wounding, no proof that those wounds caused his death, and no body. The hearing ended with Lépine's prepared speech in French on 9 October. He held that the charge, after more than three years, was political, not legal, aimed at 'the political man' 'and not the pretended murderer.' The proceedings trampled upon arrangements made by the Dominion, and he alone could not be held responsible for acts of his government.[147] In contemporary terms and formalities aside, this was, for Lépine and the Métis, a 'state trial'[148] involving the legitimacy of their government. When Bétournay closed the hearing on the 14th before a packed courtroom, he held that Scott's execution was proved – there was no political element and no 'pretended government.' This was a 'man-made case.' Lépine was placed in gaol for the next criminal assize of Oyer and Terminer and Gaol Delivery to be held at Winnipeg.

That summer saw several outbreaks of violence on the Red River frontier. A Sioux massacre at St Joe's, just west of Pembina, and other border outrages on the heels of the Fenian invasion, had placed all local authorities on a state of alert.[149] An extra term of the Queen's Bench was held to allow a grand jury to determine whether Lépine should be indicted. It was opened on 12 November by Justice John Charles McKeagney, an Irishman from Nova Scotia. His French-language skills were virtually nil, despite his claim to be bilingual. Macdonald admitted that he was 'not fit for a judge' after his appointment and contemporaries deemed him barely competent as lawyer or judge.[150] One can only guess how he handled the testimony, most of which was in French. Three days later, the grand jury of twelve, of whom one-half were half-breeds (three were francophones), indicted Lépine.[151] Allowed by Attorney General Clarke to plead not guilty subject to the question of jurisdiction, Lépine did so.

The court sat on 17 November for a demurrer on jurisdiction by the defence,[152] with Attorney General Clarke acting for the crown. Considered a man without principle, he agitated Archibald by trying to control appointments to the new bar and directing the courts. Clarke was also accused of conspiring with Cornish to instigate Lépine's arrest. Reckless, intemperate, and opportunistic, he was seen as 'an irascible lawyer' with a bitter, scolding tongue.[153] Anti-French, in one trial when Dubuc switched to the French language, he rose up and exclaimed: 'Stop; not another word like that or I will hurl you out of the window.'[154]

Royal maintained that the province had no authority to hear the case since the British North America Act of 1867 dispensed with the jurisdiction of the HBC and Rupert's Land was not transferred to the Dominion before 15 July 1870. Thus, jurisdiction lay with Ontario or Quebec. Clarke argued that the HBC transferred all its authority to the Dominion in the Imperial Act of 1868; that the imperial statutes of 1803, 1821, and 1859 merely provided Lower and Upper Canada with concurrent jurisdiction;[155] and that the 1859 act applied only to the Indian Territories. He also said that the BNA Act, c.105, implied the continuance of the powers of HBC courts until further Dominion legislation, and that this provision was repeated in the acts of 1869–71.[156] He argued that the Manitoba Act of 1871 referenced the GQC and extended its power to any subsequent court established by the new province.[157] He also said that the GQC had exercised jurisdiction over felonies without opposition in the past.[158]

The defence counsel maintained that the Manitoba Queen's Bench lacked jurisdiction on matters that had occurred in Rupert's Land prior to July 1870.[159] Moving chronologically from the 1670 charter to 15 July 1870, they posited that all trials in the monarch's dominions were under the Great Seal of England. From the origins of Rupert's Land through the 1850s, legal officers of the HBC had jurisdiction over all criminal matters including capital offences. However, in an impressive interpretation, the defence argued that the colony was not part of HBC lands under the charter and that the courts of Rupert's Land therefore had no jurisdiction over capital cases in that region.[160] The 1859 act enabled the crown to authorize justices to try all but capital cases in Rupert's Land and the territories, the latter being reserved to the superior courts of the colonies.[161] McKeagney, with his judicial experience on the ecclesiastical side of the law, withheld the question of jurisdiction until the appointment of the new chief justice. The result was that Lépine's trial did not get under way until June 1874 after Edmund Burke Wood's appointment.

Trial Arguments and Witnesses

Chief Justice Wood, on opening the June 1874 session, was decisive. He heard a summary of the arguments for and against jurisdiction, and then read a lengthy opinion that he had prepared in the interim.[162] He recited the prosecution's brief and ruled in its favour that the jurisdiction of the GQC, inclusive of capital felonies, continued until the transfer to Canada of 15 July 1870 and then until the creation of the Manitoba Queen's Bench. He did not reply to the objections of the defence on the issue of jurisdiction over capital felonies, possibly because he wished to see his new position as part of an uninterrupted succession to the GQC as the high court of Rupert's Land.[163]

Wood was the son of an Irish American farmer-teacher. Losing an arm, he became a teacher, articled in Hamilton, clerked, and was called to the bar in 1854. A well-known criminal and equity lawyer in Brantford, he was ambitious, abrasive, and self-confident with an eye for business. Elected MPP in 1863, he made his money with the Buffalo and Lake Huron Railways, and the *Globe* called him 'an active paid agent of the Grand Trunk.' A Liberal, he became provincial treasurer in 1867 and a leading reformer. Resigning in 1872, he went federal the next year. His booming voice, the 'Big Thunder,' helped bring down the Macdonald government over the Pacific Scandal. According to contemporaries, he was near bankruptcy, a heavy drinker with a luxurious and dissolute lifestyle who neglected his law practice. The chief justiceship enabled him to rescue his career and resolve his financial crisis.[164]

Lépine was bound over for trial to October 1874. With Cornish heading the prosecution, Dubuc assisted the defence team led by Sir Joseph Chapleau, French Canada's most celebrated trial lawyer, who was appointed to defend Lépine and his Métis compatriots at the behest of Bishop Taché and Royal.[165] Chapleau travelled to Winnipeg at his own expense and argued without fee. Engaged to a bilingual English Protestant, he postponed the wedding to defend French culture and the Catholic faith in the west.[166] Besides Dubuc, Chapleau was assisted by Amédée-Emmanuel Forget, who was later to assist Riel in his 1885 treason trial.[167]

The jury would be crucial, and the documentation for its selection is incomplete. The crown challenged four possible jurors, the defence sixteen, but the records fail to indicate the length of the panel list or how many challenges the defence was allowed. In the end there were six Métis, four English mixed-blood, and two English jurors. According to an observer, Wood promised them extra pay if they did 'good work.'[168] Cartier wrote that he doubted any half anglo-francophone jury would convict Lépine. But the Métis summoned as witnesses were all loyal to the Manitoba government, few were close associates of either Riel or Lépine, and most could not remember who did what and when. While a record of the Scott court martial was made, it did not survive, and the only witness who testified to it was recorder Nolin.

The trial testimony confirms that Scott's execution was the occasion of a large public ceremony. But there was uncertainty over who was in the firing squad and who gave the order to fire. Many agreed that the squad members had taken drink. Most agreed Scott was alive after the first volley; he was probably killed by a pistol shot to the head, and his body was put into a rough wood box. As noted earlier, what happened that night was unclear, as well as what eventually happened to the body. Otherwise there was much conflicting testimony which was left for legal counsel on both sides of the bar to put together for the long-suffering jurors.

Counsel had four months to decide upon and prepare their witnesses for examination, and the witnesses chosen revealed their litigation strategies. Cornish's opening speech stated as fact that Scott and his associates were peaceful Canadian citizens, the colony was in the hands of the Dominion at the time of Scott's killing, and those who arrested, gaoled, and killed him were 'murderers and assassins.'[169] The prosecution called sixteen witnesses, of whom eight were prisoners and five were of little consequence, in examinations that took six and a half days and an evening (38–68).[170] Eight testified on Scott's execution, with one having served on the court martial and two on the PG. Of the eleven who discussed Scott, five did not know him. Of the eleven who discussed Lépine, six did not know him. Seven testified that Riel was in charge, five did not see Lépine at the execution, and only William Chambers and the Charette brothers said they saw him there. On cross-examination, Chambers said he could not swear that he saw Lépine. The defence brought in witnesses who were there and testified that neither Charette was seen near the execution.[171]

It appears that the prosecution strategy was to deny the existence of the PG and use witnesses to highlight the horror of Scott's killing. The fact that its witnesses did not know Scott or Lépine well, were of two minds on Lépine's role, gave no credible testimony of his involvement in Scott's death, and contradicted each other would not have given strong support for conviction. Moreover, there was no concerted attempt to prove malice aforethought on Lépine's part to meet the contemporary standard of mens rea for culpable homicide.

Unable to make headway on the question of jurisdiction, defence counsel developed a strategy that focused on the legitimacy of the PG and the court martial over which Lépine presided. This reflected their view that the murder trial was a disguised political trial. The defence brought thirteen witnesses over three days.[172] Eight testified to the authenticity of the PG as a de facto government of the day – that it was necessary to keep the peace in the period succeeding the Council of Assiniboia and preceding the province of Manitoba. Six of these witnesses were well-known men who served in high office in church and state. They confirmed the history of the troubled months of December 1869 to March 1870, Governor Mactavish's surrender of authority, the elections that brought representatives of English- and French-speaking delegates to a convention, the election of officers, the passing of laws, the election and sending of delegates to Ottawa to negotiate terms of entry, promises of amnesty from Ottawa and London, and a peaceful administration of the region until the arrival of Wolseley's expedition in August 1870. Four of those witnesses were members of the Council of Assiniboia. The impact of their testimony, however, was lessened by the chief justice, who refused to allow the presentation of written evidence of the PG, correspondence with Ottawa, and notes of negotiations for entry and the rights that were incorporated into the Manitoba Act.[173]

The key, and last, witness for the defence was Bishop Taché, who was carried in dramatically on a stretcher. A Lower Canadian whose ancestors Louis Jolliet and Pierre Gaultier had explored the west, he joined the Oblates in 1844 to convert the Natives and was sent to Hudson Bay and James Bay. Settling in St Boniface in 1845, he studied Cree and Athapaskan and was made bishop in 1850. He established new missions and fifteen new parishes, promoted Métis education, and sat on the Council of Assiniboia from 1858. Lobbying for the Métis in Ottawa en route to the Vatican Council in December 1869, and revered by all parties, he was called back in February 1870 to persuade the Métis to accept a transfer to the Dominion.[174] Taché had met with Mactavish in December 1869, and he confirmed the governor's mental health, his request for the inhabitants to form a government, and his personal promises of amnesty (82–4). This evidence also confirmed the prior testimony of Thomas Bunn, Alex McLean, A.G.B. Bannatyne, Xavier Pagé, and the Reverend Ritchot (70–89). Wood ruled this evidence inadmissible as 'hearsay,' over the objections of defence counsel.[175]

As the defence focus on the legitimacy of the PG and its proceedings was frustrated, its other major argument concerned Lépine's culpability for murder. Here, the task was to demonstrate the character of the accused. Five witnesses who knew Lépine testified to his good and gentle character, five testified that he was known as simply one guard among many, and Taché noted his refusal to leave the country after the warrant for his arrest even at the prime minister's 'urgent request' (84). The defence also called witnesses whose testimony contradicted important details around Scott's execution and the disposal of his body, coupled with lengthy cross-examinations of prosecution witnesses that cast doubts on their credibility. Four who were close to the execution place testified that Lépine was not there, and three confirmed details of how Scott was shot and either killed or not killed. They also had one witness each for whether Scott's voice was heard within his box. While Cornish cross-examined eleven defence witnesses, and Wood five, six of those interventions seemed to confirm the defence case.[176] In contrast, the defence cross-examined eleven of the major prosecution witnesses and integrated that testimony into its summation.

How did legal counsel sum up for the jury? The defence began on Friday, 23 October, at 3:00 p.m., as Royal addressed the jury in English for four hours with a two- hour recess for dinner (84–95). His opening line was that this was a 'state trial' (84) and his role was to evaluate the evidence. Surveying the testimony of thirteen prosecution witnesses, he said it was amazing that so many intelligent people could not agree on Lépine's role or what happened to Scott. Tracing the geography of the fort, he explained why there were discrepancies: some witnesses looked through dirty windows, some from behind the crowd, and others from buildings several hundred yards away. The Reverend Young said he did not know the French language but stated in English what Riel and others said in French! Young saw holes in Scott's coat when he was shot, but the gunsmith Chambers saw no bullet holes. Alexander Murray gave a precise description of events, but through a keyhole! Duncan Nolin, who was excited, says he saw Lépine there, but not Young, whom everyone saw. Joseph Nolin, secretary for the court martial, admitted that Lépine, while presiding, said nothing at the trial. And John Bruce, who did not see Lépine anywhere, wrote letters to the press reporting from edited hearsay (87–92).

Rehearsing the testimony of defence witnesses, Royal demonstrated how agreed they were on the formation of the PG and its role in the history of the colony, and on Lépine's quite limited role in the whole affair. Some notable witnesses brought documents to prove their testimony but the chief justice would not allow the jury to see them. Royal closed with the comment that four brave men died in this affair, but Scott might still be alive!

Chapleau gave his summation on legal points in French at 9:30 p.m. (95–102). Wood tried to prevent him from addressing the jury in French, but he persevered.[177] Chapleau spoke until midnight before a packed courtroom. He rehearsed in great detail the contradictions and discrepancies in the prosecution's case and witnesses' testimony, and emphasized the crown's inability to prove that Lépine was actually at the execution. If Lépine was guilty of Scott's death, but said nothing at the court martial and did not participate in the shooting, then hundreds of residents were just as guilty. The jurors must ask themselves, he said, why three years elapsed before Lépine was arrested for this alleged killing. Also, why did the chief justice refuse to allow any documents to be produced for the defence, but gave the crown every latitude to prove its case? And why was this case not being tried before a bench of three to five independent judges of Ontario or Quebec? He closed with the legal concept of 'reasonable doubt' and argued that Lépine's acquittal would preserve continuity with the successful early years of the province (102).

According to witnesses, Chapleau's oratory brought 'murmuring' around the audience, even from those who did not understand French (98). While some historians have considered it boring and ineffectual,[178] it was printed in its entirety in Le Métis on 5 December 1874. Wood, however, was not going to leave the night to the defence. Regardless of the hour, he allowed Cornish to make his opening remarks before adjourning that long day's session, thus dampening Chapleau's effect as the participants walked away into the night.

The court resumed Saturday morning with the prosecution's addresses to the jurors. Cornish began in English, his arguments centring on his belief that Scott was dead and that Lépine had caused this death, and on Riel's repeated statements that the PG required a life to convince the Dominion of its legitimacy. He carefully picked out the testimony of those who agreed with his version of the events. The records of the court martial run by Lépine were, Cornish said, 'destroyed'; Lépine and others plied guards with drink to perform their duties; Scott was shot and the discrepancies irrelevant; Riel promised the body for Christian burial but Lépine refused to give it up. As Scott's mother and brother believed he was killed, so should the jurors (103–7)!

The prosecution case was closed in French by junior counsel Stewart Macdonald. He depicted the Scott trial as one where Riel was the accuser, chief witness, prosecutor, and judge, where the court comprised Riel's henchmen, and where Scott was not allowed to hear the evidence in his language or to testify himself. The jurors must act as one body, he said, not as individuals. If Lépine was a 'participator,' then he was guilty (107). Their decision would 'be echoed all over the civilised world' (108). Since

Lépine has a 'perverted and tyrannical mind,' they must vote for the law that says 'thou shalt not kill.' 'The day of retribution has come at last' (110).

The Trial Decision: Chief Justice Wood and a Question of Justice

The defence strategy aimed at casting sufficient doubt in jurors' minds about the crown's evidence and, if not successful at trial, at raising matters that could serve well on appeal. The chief justice saw this de facto state trial as one to make his career and reputation, with a lieutenant governor post possibly in the offing. His charge to the jury must have been prepared in advance, or over Sunday, since he delivered it on the following Monday morning, speaking for five hours in English (10:00 a.m. to 4:00 p.m.) with a one-hour break for lunch (110–23). Stating that he would address the law, leaving the facts to the jury, he devoted most of his speech to providing the jurors with the events they should consider noteworthy and to noting what facts were correct and incorrect. His long charge was a summation of the major points of the prosecution interspersed with language strongly implying that the activities of Riel and 'his' PG were treasonous.

With regard to the HBC, Wood stated that Mactavish had no right to surrender his legal authority, which the PG had captured and usurped. There were no real elections. He ruled out of hand the whole case of the PG, calling it only 'a thing,' and advised erroneously that the government had to be de jure and not de facto to justify trial by court martial.[179] Boulton was not actually tried by a court but sentenced and released only at Riel's order, and Scott was trapped into becoming a prisoner. Further, the chief justice saw no 'British law and organization' in the PG. It exhibited 'guns,' 'men under command,' and 'the terror of the community' (116).

With regard to Scott, the chief justice argued that this was a killing with malice aforethought, and thus murder regardless of what the jurors might think. Wood had taken prolific notes on the case, but he stated in his charge that he had no need to read them. Scott's scuffles with the guards were set up to warrant his trial. According to Nolin, no proof of rebellion was given to the court martial. If Lépine agreed with the sentence, he was culpable. Riel had told Scott privately that he must die but Riel went to Lépine that night to 'correct' the minutes,[180] the two were in communication, and this was all that was necessary in law for a guilty verdict. With regard to whether Scott was dead, those inconsistencies in the testimony were irrelevant as everyone acted afterwards as if he were dead. The prisoner and his confederates had the body in their hands, and what they did with it only they could say. Thus, the evil here was like 'an event that took place 2,000 years ago' (120). Like Christ, Scott was set up to be executed. Lépine and others got the guards drunk so that they would have the courage to shoot Scott, which made Lépine as guilty as those who shot him, whether he was there or not. Finally, he told the jurors, only if they believed that Scott was alive today could they find the prisoner not guilty. Wood's address was described as brilliant by many. But his approach resembles that of Chief Justice William Osgoode, a judge who was well rewarded for his effort in the 1797 David McLane treason trial.[181]

Critical to Wood's perspective on the trial is an interesting document in his notebooks. The first eight pages comprise a memo from the Reverend George Young, signed 'Yours most blessedly.' It provides a virtual character assassination of Riel, Lépine, and the Métis. The provisional government was managed by an 'intimidated convention,' 'the elements protested by a fearful storm of wind'; some prisoners were forced to haul excrement out of the prison under armed guard 'to invoke disobedience, and then blood would be shed'; and Scott's death on that 'Black Friday' was matched by Elzéar Goulet's drowning – drunk and boastful, he 'took the cramps' – at the spot where 'he sank Scott's body' six months before.[182]

The jury went out at 4:30 p.m., and the defence counsel left for dinner expecting a long deliberation. When the jury returned two and a half hours later, Wood had the decision read before a packed courtroom without defence counsel. Tears streamed down the faces of those assembled.[183] According to one observer, the jurors reached their verdict of guilty 'only a few minutes after their retirement' and notified Wood that they 'demanded their supper,' which would account for their being out for two hours.[184] A surprised defence counsel returned to the courtroom. Chapleau responded promptly with objections to set aside the verdict: the jury was instructed that there was no evidence that Lépine acted as an officer of an accepted government; the jury was not allowed to hear evidence of Canada and Britain's acceptance of that government; the jury was told erroneously that the PG was not accepted by the people of the settlement; and documents proving acceptance of the PG by the HBC and Dominion were not allowed.[185]

Wood summarily overruled them. A motion to set aside the verdict on the question of jurisdiction and a faultily empanelled jury was presented for a possible appeal. Other objections, such as Farmer sitting on the grand jury and its linguistic imbalance, were also left for appeal. Finally,

Wood deferred to the jury's recommendation for mercy and the execution was reprieved, leaving the matter to Ottawa and the governor general. While the chief justice was clear in his mind on a sentence to match the crime, the case was going to receive a political resolution.

The defence was more successful in the trials of André Nault and Elzéar Lagimodière, who were prosecuted after Lépine. Neither of their trials, however, was reported by the court,[186] and our only record is that of Wood's scribbled court notes.[187] Nault and Lagimodière were high on the prosecution's list after Lépine.[188] Their trials took place following Lépine's, on 27–31 October, with the summing-up on Saturday the 31st.[189] The evidence and arguments were similar to those in Lépine's trial, but the lists of witnesses were shorter.[190] Wood's three-hour charge to the jury on Monday, 2 November, was also similar to his former one. However, after Chapleau's defence of Nault and Lagimodière, the jury could reach no verdict. Disgruntled, the chief justice sent them back, stating they must agree! With the proceedings adjourned again until 9:30 p.m., they returned with foreman Robert Massey, saying they had only a 7–5 vote for conviction.[191] The chief justice then allowed them to eat, with instructions to resume the next morning at 10 a.m. to reach an agreement. The foreman, however, intervened and told Wood that not only were they not in agreement but they would never be. Thus they were dismissed. Chapleau requested bail for the prisoners, and the court was adjourned to the next morning, forcing Wood to declare a mistrial and discharge the jury. He ruled the application for bail 'untenable,' and only several months later would he allow Attorney General Dubuc to enter a *nolle prosequi* on the case.[192] Wood delivered Lépine's sentence the next day, and Chapleau returned to Montreal for his wedding and to lead the movement for Lépine's pardon.[193]

The role of the chief justice in these cases should be seen within the larger canvas of his activities in Winnipeg after his arrival in the new province. Wood took his seat on 10 June 1870, the day after he was admitted to the bar, and postponed the court for a week. Shortly after arrival, he met Dr Schultz and borrowed money from him to buy and complete a 'palace' that Schultz had begun. One of his first judicial acts was to help Schultz escape a conviction of perjury.[194] And just after the Lépine trial, in an information on a writ of mandamus charging that Schultz had sworn falsely in a case involving Native residents, McKeagney ruled for the writ and Wood held him in error.[195] The chief justice saw his role as restoring the authority of the bench and the primacy of common law. To prove it he demanded a price on the head of Riel.[196]

Wood's stature in the province diminished quite rapidly. Within his first year he was accused of cowing witnesses on the stand and considered short-tempered and arbitrary, 'a judicial dictator.'[197] Rumours of his financial difficulties had reached the new Liberal prime minister, Alexander Mackenzie, as early as December 1874, when he wrote a letter to Lieutenant Governor Alexander Morris inquiring of details of Wood's debts to Schultz. Complex litigation ended up in the Supreme Court, where Chief Justice William Ritchie held that Wood had no grounds for relief, and Justice John Gwynne added that he 'must abide by the consequences of his own impudence.'[198] Within three years of the Lépine trial, Morris wrote a letter about Wood's conduct to the secretary of state, reporting acts of public drunkenness and charging him with allowing his moral opinions to trump the rule of law, disenfranchising hundreds of voters on 'petty quibbles,' admitting unsworn statements given him on the street and according them greater weight than statements sworn in court, using abusive language in court, changing dates on documents, withholding punishments on convicts he preferred, and refusing to follow precedents even when they came from the Supreme Court. Wood's appeal to his federal supporter Edward Blake was met with a short, terse note.[199]

Later, in 1876, Wood sent to Ottawa a damning report on the actions of the new province's executive in the years 1870–3.[200] He alleged that during those years the executive had 'contemptuously opposed any proceedings being taken against the murderers of Scott,' even warning officials not to take any applications for their arrest, and he asserted that the courts there had no jurisdiction (which was solely in the hands of the imperial authority). The governor's reply was that 'Wood has not confined himself to his duty' and has published a report that is 'utterly ill-founded.'[201]

When a case of assault came up against Lépine's brother Maxime in 1880, Wood discharged the mixed-blood jury that returned a not-guilty verdict and berated its members. He wanted to become lieutenant governor, but Mackenzie refused. One of the charges mentioned by Attorney General Royal in a document presented to the legislature on 4 March 1881 was that Wood had prepared a list of half-breeds for Lépine's trial who were his enemies. Wood responded by drafting a response – an attack on the petitioners – which he printed and sent across the country. In the end, Schultz, now an MP, introduced a motion in the House of Commons to print the petition against Wood but Edward Blake delayed it. After he was paralysed by what appears to have been a stroke, calls for Wood's removal were put aside for a committee's investigation into his conduct. He died on 7 October 1882 before the committee was convened.[202]

AN AMNESTY FOR RESISTANCE:
THE REDEMPTION FOR TREASONOUS MURDER

The Lépine trial verdict was not appealed because defence counsel had prepared for the possibility of a political resolution. On 10 December 1874, a month after three political trials, the new governor general, Lord Dufferin, transmitted a large file to Colonial Secretary Henry Herbert, Lord Carnarvon, to settle the questions of 1869–70.[203] Whether Lépine was fairly tried was never noted for discussion. Immediately after Chapleau's honeymoon, he presented a motion in the Quebec Legislative Assembly asking the governor general to pardon Lépine; it passed unanimously on 18 December.[204] Meanwhile, Riel wrote to Alphonse Desjardins, a New York State senator, of his hope that the Quebec and Manitoba legislatures would save Lépine's life.[205]

Back in February 1870, Governor General Young had written to Bishop Taché that the imperial government wanted the territories settled peacefully and the current matter resolved. That summer, after the Dominion witnessed the acceptance of the PG and the outrage of Ontarians, Secretary of State Howe asked Taché for his advice. The bishop replied that he had promised the insurgents, and Riel and Lépine in particular, a full amnesty for all breaches of law including the murder of Scott. Lord Dufferin, Young's successor, reported that the original amnesty proposal was thought to be just for political offences and conditional upon dispersal of the insurgents before Scott's execution. Taché replied that local people were convinced that Riel was a patriot, that his group brought Manitoba into confederation, and that the bishop's promises should be kept. But, since the people of Ontario now thought differently, Dufferin proposed a lesser sentence.[206]

The problem of amnesty was for the imperial government. Young's proclamation of 6 December 1869 stated that no legal proceedings would be taken against any of the parties 'implicated in these unfortunate breaches of the law.' He wrote as much in letters to Taché as he left Ottawa, and Cartier's letter to Taché of 5 July 1870 said that the queen's intention was still clear. The U.S. consul believed an amnesty was coming, as did Manitoba's later lieutenant governor Royal and Premier Marc Girard. But Schultz would not allow that politically, and the Liberals used the issue in the next election, which had been spearheaded by Blake, a supporter of Canada First who detested Riel.[207]

In 1872 both houses of the Manitoba legislature passed a resolution requesting amnesty. When Riel went to Ottawa to take his seat in the spring of 1874, Blake, the premier of Ontario, offered a $5,000 reward for his arrest. In Parliament, Schultz seconded a motion stating that, since Riel had been charged with murder and presented for trial by a grand jury, he be expelled,[208] which was carried. Then 252 petitions with 58,568 names flooded the cabinet. A dossier of the Committee of the Privy Council was sent to the crown on 4 December 1874. 'On the North-West Question' concluded, after a study of juristic writings, that the disputed acts called for a general amnesty according to the law of nations because both races in the Manitoba legislature believed an amnesty was promised. Carnarvon told Dufferin that he concurred with the jury verdict and recommendation, and would offer Lépine a pardon after a suitable time in prison with loss of civil liberties. Mackenzie was saved from a dilemma when Dufferin issued a proclamation of amnesty and commuted the death sentence without direction from the cabinet, which opposed it. Dufferin sent his recommendation to the Colonial Office on 10 December 1874: two years in prison and permanent forfeiture of political rights. He recommended the same to the minister on 15 January 1875, and in due course he received an imperial order-in-council instructing him to prepare an amnesty to resolve 'vehemently international antagonisms' and 'tranquilize the public mind.'[209] The sentence was commuted on 15 January 1875, four days before the execution date.

The movement for amnesty was led by influential Quebeckers in addition to Chapleau. Luc Letellier de Saint-Just, a powerful French Canadian Liberal politician who had served as minister of agriculture in the Province of Canada and fought for confederation, was appointed to the Senate in 1867. Instrumental in gaining Lépine's commutation, he became lieutenant governor of Quebec in 1876.[210] Joseph-Alfred Mousseau was a prominent Montreal lawyer, writer, and journalist who defended confederation with Conservative zeal, seeing French Canadians as its authors. Elected to Parliament in 1874, he moved the February 1875 amendment to Mackenzie's resolution on a general pardon for the resistance leaders, speaking for five hours.[211] Much was at stake here: for Quebec political figures and Macdonald's political allies, for Cartier's conception of Quebec's role in confederation, and for the protection of French culture and the Catholic faith in the west.

Dufferin's action also provoked a serious constitutional issue concerning self-governing dominions. Colonial ministers were responsible for advising the governor general and this had not been done in the Lépine case. The question was raised in the House of Lords in April 1875, with the result that the process was deemed politically expedient and not a precedent.[212] Edward Blake, the new minister of justice, went to London to discuss recasting the governor general's instructions. He obtained a reaffirmation of the principle and new instructions. Then, in February 1875, Mackenzie introduced a motion in the Commons that Riel and Lépine receive a full amnesty with five years' banishment, which carried after acrimonious debate.[213] Chief Justice Wood followed a year later with requests for rewards for those who apprehended Scott's 'murderers.'[214]

When Lépine was offered a release from prison in June 1875 if he would leave Canada for five years, he refused. He thus served out his sentence until 26 October 1876. Writing with relief that Lépine was granted amnesty 'as promised,' Riel noted the 'perfidy' of Macdonald and the lobbyists of Ontario.[215] In the spring of 1876 he wrote to Lépine's wife to pay his respects and express his hopes for Lépine's speedy release from prison, and later that autumn he deemed him a man whose spirit would never abandon him. He considered all of the accused to be his family.[216] Writing to Lépine's mother, Julie, in February 1877, he gave his respects to all the Lépines and said that he would love to spend just a half-hour with his 'great friend.' A year later, his wish was fulfilled as he spent several days with Lépine, his brother Maxime, and other Métis 'in pure pleasure' at the St Joseph Hotel in Pembina. Riel had brought them presents from Dubuc. Later, Riel and Lépine attended the annual fêtes of Métis held by the Société Saint-Jean-Baptiste.[217]

After his release from prison on 26 October 1876, Lépine maintained close contact with Riel and Taché, remaining active in the French-speaking community. Having participated in the creation of the Union Saint-Alexandre to protect Métis interests, he was elected vice-president of the Société Saint-Jean Baptiste in 1878. When Riel tried to involve him in uniting the Métis and Natives of the NWT into a confederacy, he refused and remained with his family in St Boniface. Several tragedies struck Lépine in later years. A fire destroyed the farm in 1891, poor harvests left his family nearly penniless, and by 1902 he was homesteading with his sons near Forget, Saskatchewan. In 1908 his wife Cécile died and he moved in with his children. The next year he was in Winnipeg, destitute, and sometime after 1909 he sold his homestead and bought a summer resort near

Lake of the Woods. He lived there with a granddaughter. Having his civil rights restored without restrictions, he moved back to St Boniface and died aged eighty-eight at the local hospital in 1923. Buried in the St Boniface cemetery next to Riel, the funeral was attended by many brethren and dignitaries.[218] The 'sleeping giant' had outlived all his antagonists.

CONCLUSIONS

The complexities of Red River, the contemplation of treason charges, and the array of interests at play around Manitoba's entry into confederation suggest that Lépine's was a political state trial 'dressed down' as a murder trial. The events are a minor echo of the Fenian crisis examined in a previous section of this volume and, more significantly, prefigure the chapters that follow, flagging a number of unresolved issues that would play out in the 1885 crisis. The long delays in the trial process suggest that both government and prosecution were unprepared, and undecided, on how to proceed. There were more than three years between the alleged crime and the information and preliminary inquiry in September-October 1873, a long hiatus until Wood's hearing on jurisdiction in June 1874, and yet more delay until the trial in October. Since the trial calendar was set by the prosecution and the court, the deficiencies are readily apparent. The defence counsel, meanwhile, prepared extensively, establishing a systematic strategy that would be effective for the jurors as well as for an eventual appeal or plea for amnesty.

There were a number of real problems for the prosecution. The PG was the only governing authority in the colony from December 1869 to July 1870. The Dominion was culpable in sending McDougall to the colony prematurely, and was caught in a time warp as communications to and from England, Ottawa, and Fort Garry took months at a time when days and weeks were critical. While a few capital cases had been heard in the colony before, legal opinion was clear that such trials were not in accord with statute law. It was well known that Scott was a violent man who had threatened to kill Riel and others, and that he was nurtured by Schultz. It was also clear that the man sought in this affair was Riel and not his friend Lépine.

Most modern writers who have written on the trial have been quite critical of Lépine's defence. Ideally, the defence would have hoped to defend him against the charge of treason, in which event they could have based their case on the continuity of the PG in the legal history of the colony from a government de jure to de facto and back to de jure with all its documentation entered as evidence. Some historians would have had the defence team focus on this even if it was not in the cards they were dealt.[219] The defence has also been criticized for not distinguishing between murder and high treason, and for arguing that the charge was wrongly made. Again, that would not have met the defence of murder. So what was their strategy? To establish the necessity of a PG, and thus the legitimacy of the court martial that Lépine presided over, while the HBC, Britain, and Canada chewed over the transfer of Rupert's Land; and to stress the character of the accused – a strong, quiet, and soft-spoken man who wished no one ill will, fought for his country, and did not have the mind of a killer. Lastly, there was the lack of credibility of the prosecution's witnesses as revealed in cross-examination. The seeds of doubtful evidence were planted not only for the jurors but also for those who would examine the record closely after them.

A number of conclusions can be drawn from this complex case. First, it is clear that the leaders of Canada First, representing many of the Ontario Orangemen, wanted Riel tried for treason in forming and leading the PG and having Scott arrested and executed. But, once Riel escaped their warrants, which was predictable given his high esteem in sections of Manitoba and in Quebec, they fell back upon arresting the still relatively unknown Lépine. Second, the trial can be considered a state trial, and one that rehearsed the history of the formation of Manitoba as a province. The promoters of the prosecution sought, through testimony, to imprint their version of the new province upon the Dominion. Third, the players in the trial did not live up to their billing. While the defence team had notable and talented legal counsel, the prosecution was limited by what it had to work with. By January 1875, Clarke and Cornish had 'stained' reputations, Schultz too was well known for his bully tactics to foment an Orange takeover, and Chief Justice Wood was deep in controversy and troubles both on and off the bench. With the trial transcript at hand, and knowledge of the facts behind it, one can see that no arrest of Riel for treason would have had any prima facie credibility by January 1875. The sordid Scott affair had reached its nadir.

Most of the information that has been provided above was well known to a closely knit community of some 1,600 Europeans and the Dominion cabinet.[220] There is little doubt that legal officers who examined the Lépine file after the trial found serious discrepancies in the arrest and trial of the prisoner, in the evidence given, in the testimony of prosecution witnesses, and in the roles of Schultz and Wood. Regardless of Orange propaganda, an amnesty for all of the alleged 'traitors' was the only viable outcome. Manitoba was still a province dominated by mixed-bloods and Natives, the French language, and the Catholic Church. The sinews of confederation were woven on the incorporation of nothing less.

The legal process against the leaders of the PG began in the autumn of 1873, just as the Macdonald government was in the midst of the Pacific Scandal and a massive international commercial and financial crisis. Perhaps the government of the new Dominion hoped, by rewriting the origins of Manitoba through a state trial, for a successful demonstration of state authority in its march to the west. Winning the prosecution and conviction of Lépine, however, was a shallow victory. Mackenzie's new government had no obligation to Orange interests, the local victors became tainted goods, and the Dominion acceded to British notions of justice. State authority might be reified through a state trial, but the task was fraught with difficulty.

NOTES

1. *Preliminary Investigation and Trial of Ambroise D. Lépine for the Murder of Thomas Scott, Being a Full Report of the Proceedings in This Case before the Magistrates' Court and the Several Courts of Queen's Bench in the Province of Manitoba*, Elliott and Brokovski comp. (Montreal: Burland-Desbarats Lithographic for the Parliament of Canada, 1875; Preface dated Winnipeg, 4 Jan.1875), 126–7. (See volume's Supporting Documents.)

2. The name Fort Garry refers to two places. The original, built by the HBC in 1821 near the later town of Winnipeg, was destroyed by flood in 1826 and rebuilt farther down the Red River below the rapids in 1831. Called the Stone Fort, later it was referred to as Lower Fort Garry. The original, rebuilt in 1835 and called Upper Fort Garry, is referred to here simply as Fort Garry.

3. 'The Scott Murder. The Trial for Which Louis Riel Is Denounced' was the large bold headline in the Ottawa *Free Press*, reprinted in the New York *Times*, on 11 April 1874.

4. J.M. Bumsted, manuscript, 'Trying Riel in Absentia: The Queen v. Ambroise Lépine,' 169–85. I wish to thank Jack Bumsted for sending me a copy of this essay prior to its publication.

5. *Daily Free Press*, 7 Sept. 1874, 4, and 7 Aug. 1874, 2.

6. John McDougall, *In the Days of the Red River Rebellion: Life and Adventures in the Far West of Canada (1868–1872)* (Toronto: William Briggs 1903 [1983 repr.], 115–18.

7. Adam Mercer, *The Canadian North-West: Its History and Troubles* (Whitby: Rose Publishing 1885), 195, quotes at v, 205–8.

8 Donald Smith's report to Howe, 12 April 1870, in E.H. Oliver, ed., *The Canadian North-West: Its Early Development and Legislative Records* (Ottawa: Government Printing Bureau 1914), 1: 920–7.

9 Rev. George Young, *Manitoba Memories: Leaves from My Life in the Prairie Province, 1868–1884* (Toronto: William Briggs 1897), 144–7.

10 Rev. R.G. MacBeth, *The Making of the Canadian West: Being the Reminiscences of an Eye-Witness* (Toronto: William Briggs 1898, 2nd ed., 1905), 64 and 32 respectively.

11 H. Robert Baker, 'Creating Order in the Wilderness: Transplanting the English Law to Rupert's Land, 1835–51,' *Law & History Review* 17, no. 2 (1999): 209–46; Russell Smandych and Karina Sacca, 'The Development of Criminal Law Courts in Pre-1870 Manitoba,' *Manitoba Law Journal* 24 (1996): 201–57; Hamar Foster, 'Long-Distance Justice: The Criminal Jurisdiction of Canadian Courts West of the Canadas, 1763–1859,' *American Journal of Legal History* 34 (1990): 1–48; Louis A. Knafla, 'From Oral to Written Memory: The Common Law Tradition in Western Canada,' in Knafla, ed., *Law & Justice in a New Land: Essays in Western Canadian Legal History* (Toronto: Carswell 1986), 35–42; Desmond Brown, 'Unpredictable and Uncertain: Criminal Law in the Canadian North West before 1886,' *Alberta Law Review* 17 (1979): 497–512. The ideas and interpretations of the authors above have been incorporated into the following discussion, with citations of my reading of the original sources where relevant.

12 Oliver, ed., *Canadian North-West*, 1: 135–53. It should be noted that, while the charter did not confer HBC jurisdiction over Natives, the company did try to involve them at the local level.

13 Canada Jurisdiction Act (G.B.), 43 Geo. III (1803) c.138.

14 Romilly was the top criminal lawyer, and criminal law reformer, of his time; R.A. Melikan, 'Samuel Romilly,' *Oxford Dictionary of National Biography* (Oxford: Oxford University Press 2005), online ed. (hereafter *ODNB*]. Gibbs was a brilliant lawyer who had defended successfully those accused of treason in the famous state trials of the 1790s, and would become solicitor general in 1804 and attorney general in 1805: R.A. Melikan, 'Vicary Gibbs,' *ODNB* (2004). Erskine, champion of parliamentary and law reform who was famous by 1800, would become lord chancellor by 1806: David Lemmings, 'Thomas Erskine, First Baron,' *ODNB* (2004). Hargrave, legal writer and legislative draftsman, was the foremost legal scholar and legal historian of the era: J.H. Baker, 'Francis Hargrave,' *ODNB* (2004).

15 Cited from the original report discussed in Foster, 'Long-Distance Justice,' 13–14.

16 Cited in Smandych and Sacca, 'Development of Criminal Law Courts,' 212n.38. In addition to Romilly and HBC lawyers William Cruise and George

Holyrod, George Bell was the leading Scottish jurist and an expert on British mercantile law: W.M. Gordon, 'George Joseph Bell,' *ODNB* (2004). James Scarlett, brother of the chief justice of Jamaica, was a prominent young barrister who would become chief baron of the Exchequer: G.F.R. Barker, 'James Scarlett,' rev'd Elizabeth A. Cawthon, *ODNB* (2004).

17 See 'Case of Opinion' in Smandych and Sacca, 'Development of Criminal Law Courts,' 212–13.

18 Oliver, ed., *Canadian North-West*, 1: 178–83; and ibid., 'Instructions Relative to Judicial Proceedings' (1814), 186–8.

19 Patrick Brode, *Sir John Beverly Robinson: Bone and Sinew of the Compact* (Toronto: University of Toronto Press 1983), 43–52.

20 (G.B.) 33 Hen. VIII (1540) c.23, which was cited frequently in British colonies in the later nineteenth century. The Colonial Office opinion is in Foster, 'Long-Distance Justice,' 26.

21 Many royal charters sought parliamentary confirmation after the abdication of King James II in 1688. A statute did confirm the HBC charter for twenty years but it was not renewed. However, numerous statutes from 1708 to 1798 acknowledged those privileges.

22 An Act for Regulating the Fur Trade, and Establishing a Criminal and Civil Jurisdiction within Certain Parts of North America (G.B.), 1–2 Geo. IV (1821) c.66, ss.10, 12. The company had to post a bond of £5,000 for performance.

23 R. Harvey Fleming ed., *Minutes of Council, Northern Department of Rupert's Land, 1821–31*, Hudson's Bay Company Record Society, 3 (Toronto: Champlain Society 1940), app. A, 333–4.

24 Oliver, ed., *Canadian North-West*, 1: 219–23.

25 Senior law partner in Ellice, Inglis and Compny – London agents for the NWC – and a negotiator for the amalgamation of the HBC and the NWC in 1821, Ellice was an MP who was the parliamentary legal expert on Canada. He was a future secretary-treasurer and secretary for war in the Whig cabinets of the 1830s, and an MP for forty years: Gordon F. Millar, 'Edward Ellice,' *ODNB* (2004).

26 Great Britain, Parliament, *Report of the Select Committee of the Hudson's Bay Company* (London: Queen's Printer 1857), 324–38.

27 Quoted in Oliver, ed., *Canadian North-West*, 1: 221.

28 Ibid., 1: 266–78 and 755–72 respectively.

29 Amended in 1841, 1852, 1862: 'The Local Laws of the District of Assiniboia,' in Oliver, ed., *Canadian North-West*, 1: 295–306, 369–79.

30 Consolidated Statutes of Manitoba, 44 Vic. (1880–1) c.79.

31 (G.B.) 22–3 Vic. (1859) c.26 s.4. The colony was divided into judicial districts with JPs, sheriffs, constables, and a General Quarterly Court in 1835. HBC lands were given a more formal legal structure in 1839. Rupert's Land ob-

tained a governor-in-chief, council, recorder, and four sheriffs, while the colony had a governor, council, and two sheriffs.

32 Smandych and Sacca, 'Development of Criminal Law Courts,' 210n.32. Their records have not been examined for this matter.

33 The best account of the developing 1830s legal system, from original central records, is Baker, 'Creating Order.'

34 A major law-enforcement issue throughout 1839–67 concerned Natives. The GQC heard 161 criminal cases, of which 37 per cent involved Natives directly and 59 per cent involved the sale or gift of alcohol to them. Adam Thom, appointed recorder of the GQC in 1839 and continuing in this role until he was retired by the London directors in 1851, also generated controversy. Most historians who have read his record agree that he was unsuccessful. A Scot with no knowledge of the French language and little background in English law, he acted summarily on his own, abused judicial process, and defied his council. He was retired by the London directors in 1851 because the people would no longer accept him. The directors rejected his comprehensive civil and criminal code as well as his 'Observations on the Law and Judicature of Rupert's Land' (1840), a poorly researched document with more laws inapplicable to Rupert's Land than relevant. In his defence, English law of 1670 was beyond his learning. Since Thom tied his court to Fort Garry, Governor George Simpson was disappointed with his failure to exercise jurisdiction throughout the land. See Smandych and Sacca, 'Development of Criminal Law Courts,' 242–8 and tables 1–3 at 250–7; and Baker, 'Creating Order,' nn.64–84 at 228–34.

35 *British Parliamentary Papers, Hudson's Bay Company*, vol. 19 (Dublin: Irish University Press 1969), 41.

36 Hamar Foster, 'Sins against the Great Spirit: The Law, the Hudson's Bay Company and the Mackenzie's River Murders, 1835–1839,' *Criminal Justice History* 10 (Westport, Conn.: Meckler 1989), 23–76.

37 Foster, 'Long-Distance Justice,' 36–8, for a discussion of Simpson's testimony.

38 Montague Bere in *The Wolverine Case*, 3 May 1867, in Foster, 'Long-Distance Justice,' 45–6.

39 (G.B.) 35–6 Vic. (1872) c.63, and (GB.) 37–8 Vic. (1874) c.35, respectively.

40 (Can.) 36 Vic. (1873) c.34. For the stipendiary magistrates, see Roderick G. Martin, 'The North-West Mounted Police and Frontier Justice, 1874–1898,' PhD thesis, University of Calgary 2005, 87–99, 139fl.

41 (Can.) Vic. (1886) c.25 s.3.

42 House of Commons, *Debates*, 24 March 1879, 679.

43 *Sinclair v. Mulligan, Manitoba Law Reports* 3 (1886): 485.

44 J.E. Cote, 'The Introduction of English Law into Alberta,' *Alberta Law Review* 3 (1964): 263fl.

45 For the general information on the pre-1869 government here and below, see

J.M. Bumsted, *Trials & Tribulations: The Red River Settlement and the Emergence of Manitoba* (Winnipeg: Great Plains Publications 2003), 172–88; George G.F. Stanley, *The Birth of Western Canada: A History of the Riel Rebellions* (Toronto: University of Toronto Press, 1960, 2nd ed., 1992), 44–174.

46 Stanley, *Birth of Western Canada*, quote at 54.

47 According to J.J. Hargrave, secretary to the governor of Assiniboia. See Stanley, *Birth of Western Canada*, 528.

48 See the depositions of Bannatyne and Dennis in the 'Report of the Select Committee on the Causes of the Difficulties in the North-West Territory in 1869–70,' *Journals of the House of Commons*, 8 (Ottawa: Government Printer 1874), app. 6.

49 Henri de Trémaudan, *Hold High Your Heads*, Elizabeth Maguet, trans. (Winnipeg: Pemmican 1982), 55. Born in Upper Canada, he attended Victoria College 1860–1 but left without a degree. A large, strong man, he went to Red River in 1861 as a fur trader, a line of work that ended in 1864 with several lawsuits. He appeared often before the GQC of Assiniboia as plaintiff and defendant as well as accused. Sued by a creditor for non-payment in 1863, he beat up the bailiff sent to arrest him. Gaoled for the next GQC, he was broken out and dared the court to re-arrest him. He sued his brother-in-law in 1865 and refused arbitration. Proprietor of the *Nor'Wester* from 1864 to 1868, he opposed the HBC, defied its courts, and became a leader of the Canada First party that wanted the colony annexed to Ontario. Gaoled for failing to abide by a judgment for debt in January 1868, he was freed by an armed party led by his wife. He again dared the authorities to re-arrest him, which was not done, although a petition signed by residents disapproved of letting him go free. According to the Reverend Young, Schultz had 'a wonderful history' with 'a life of suffering.' See, in general, Lovell Clark, 'Sir John Christian Schultz,' *DCB*, 12: 949–54; the deposition of Bannatyne in 1868: 'Report of the Select Committee' (1874), app. 6; and Young, *Manitoba Memories*, 121. He later fought for Native land and welfare and mellowed towards the Métis.

50 Stanley, *Birth of Western Canada*, 54.

51 An Act for the Temporary Government of Rupert's Land and the North-Western Territories when United with Canada, 22 June 1869, in Oliver ed., *Canadian Northwest*, 2: 672–4.

52 W.L. Morton, *Alexander Begg's Red River Journal and Other Papers relative to the Red River Resistance of 1869–1870* (Toronto: Champlain Society, 1956), 240 (25 Dec. 1869), 156.

53 Oliver ed., *Canadian North-West* 2: 873–8.

54 Ibid., 878–80.

55 Quoted in Bumsted, *Trials & Tribulations*, 193.

56 Stanley, *Birth of Western Canada*, 59–60.

57 For the Fenian conspiracies and raids into New Brunswick, Quebec, and Ontario in 1867–8, and the threats posed by Irish nationalists, Catholics, and U.S. Civil War veterans, see the chapters by David A. Wilson and R. Blake Brown in this volume.

58 Account of Alexander McArthur, *Causes of the Rising in the Red River Settlement*, 1:1 (Winnipeg: Manitoba Historical Society Publications, 1882), who accompanied Mactavish. McDougall did not know the mixed-bloods.

59 Trémaudan, *Hold High Your Heads*, 63–4. Ritchot had volunteered to be the priest of the Métis parish of St Boniface in 1862. He recorded the parish's deliberations in 1869–70 and was the chaplain of its military forces; Riel was the parish's councillor. Appointed a delegate of the PG to Ottawa in 1870, he was arrested for Scott' execution but released for lack of evidence. A forceful negotiator, he assisted in the drafting of the Manitoba Act of 1870 and devoted his life to the church, education, and the rights of Métis and Natives. See Philippe R. Maillot, 'Noël-Joseph Ritchot,' *DCB*, 13: 876–8. He called the committee the 'Métis Society,' and it had representatives from each parish.

60 Oliver, ed., *Canadian North-West*, 1: 615–18, quote at 617. They demanded 'English liberties' – no government without representation.

61 Dennis was a surveyor and militiaman from the region of lakes Huron and Superior who had his troops retreat in the Fenian Niagara raid of 1866, with the result that he lost thirty-four men and was labelled a coward. Sent by McDougall to Red River in 1868, he lived with Schultz and threatened the Métis. When he could not control his men on being faced with Riel, he escaped to Ottawa without paying them. Later he became the Dominion's first surveyor general, surveyed lands to the Rocky Mountains, was appointed deputy minister of the interior, befriended mixed-bloods and Natives, and introduced the homestead laws to immigrants. See Colin Frederick Read, ' John Stoughton Dennis,' *DCB*, 11: 244–6.

62 The quote is from *Begg's Red River Journal*, 465. See, in general, Gerhard J. Ens, 'Ambroise-Dydime Lépine,' *DCB*, 15: 587–9.

63 Riel's convention account: C.A. Harwood, ed., *Canadian Antiquarian and Numismatic Journal*, 3rd ser. (1909), vol. 6, nos. 1–2.

64 Oliver, ed., *Canadian North-West*, 2: 890–2.

65 Trémaudan, *Hold High Your Heads*, 75.

66 Stanley, *Birth of Western Canada*, quote at 78.

67 Calendar of State Papers, 33 Vic. (G.B. 1870), no. 5, report no. 12, pp. 43–4.

68 Oliver ed., *Canadian North-West*, 2: 893–900, 900–1, 904–6, respectively.

69 Alexander Begg, *The Creation of Manitoba, or, A History of the Red River Troubles* (Toronto: Hunter, Rose 1871), 269.

70 Morton, ed., *Alexander Begg's Red River Journal*, 240 (25 Dec. 1869).

71 In the report of Sir George-Étienne Cartier to the imperial government, 8 June 1870, in 'Report of the Select Committee' (1874), app. 6: 176, 19, 135, 146, respectively.

72 Oliver, ed., *Canadian North-West*, 2: 910–13.

73 *Begg's Red River Journal*, 80 (27 Dec. 1869).

74 Oliver, ed., *Canadian North-West*, 2: 919–36 (12 April 1870).

75 MacBeth, *Making the Canadian West*, 59–60.

76 Quoted in Bumsted, *Trials & Tribulations*, 208.

77 F.H. Schofeld, *The Story of Manitoba* (Toronto: S.J. Clarke 1913), 3: 5.

78 Ibid., 1: 270. For a larger estimate, including 200–300 Natives: *Begg's Red River Journal*, 536–7. See Henry Woodington, *Diary of a Prisoner in the Red River Rebellion* (Niagara: Historical Society Publications, no. 25, 1913), 37.

79 Macbeth, *Making the Canadian West*, 75.

80 D.A. Smith's Report in Oliver, ed., *Canadian North-West*, 2: 927.

81 Joseph Pope, *Memoirs of the Right Honourable Sir John Alexander Macdonald G.C.B.* (New York: AMS Press 1971), 2: 62.

82 *Begg's Red River Journal*, 537–8. Goulet later drowned in the Red River attempting to escape a stoning by volunteers of Colonel Garnet Wolseley's expedition.

83 Trémaudan, ed., Riel, 'Affaire Scott,' 228–9n.1.

84 *Begg's Red River Journal*, 318 (20 Feb. 1870), and 538–9.

85 John H. O'Donnell, *Manitoba: As I Saw It from 1869 to Date* (Winnipeg: Clark Brothers 1909), 29–34.

86 Lewis H. Thomas, 'Louis Davis Riel,' *DCB*, 11: 740.

87 R.W.W. Robertson, *The Execution of Thomas Scott* (Don Mills, Ont.: Burns and MacEachern 1968). Scott was later honoured in 1902 with 'The Scott Memorial Orange Hall' at 216 Princess Street, Winnipeg, which stands today.

88 For the historiography, see Bumsted, *Trials & Tribulations*, 9–16; and the earlier account of A.H. de Trémaudan, ed. and trans., 'The Execution of Thomas Scott,' *CHR* 6, no. 3 (1925): 224–5.

89 J.M. Bumsted, 'Why Shoot Thomas Scott? A Study in Historical Evidence,' in his *Thomas Scott's Body and Other Essays on Early Manitoba History* (Winnipeg: University of Manitoba Press 2000), 197–209.

90 J.A. Snow, *Canadian Government Road Supervisor vs. Some of His Working Men*, in 'Report of the Select Committee' (1870), app. 6: 48. Scott, on leaving the courtroom, said it was a pity they had not thrown him in the river.

91 O'Donnell, *Manitoba As I Saw It*, 29–30.

92 *Begg's Red River Journal*, 113–16.

93 *Le Métis*, III, 38 (28 Feb. 1874).

94 Begg, *Creation of Manitoba*, 302; *Begg's Red River Journal*, 326; and L'Abbé
Dugas, *Histoire véridiques des faits qui ont preparé le mouvement des Métis à la
Rivière Rouge en 1869* (Montreal: Librairie Beauchemin 1905; repr. Ottawa:
National Library of Canada, 1978), 156; respectively.

95 Trémaudan, ed., Riel, 'Affaire Scott,' 231n.1–2.

96 O'Donnell, *Manitoba As I Saw It*, 29–30, 40–1; and Young, *Manitoba Memories*.
According to A.-H. de Trémaudan (who interviewed numerous partici-
pants), Young recited alleged facts which 'only existed in the fertile imagi-
nation of the reverend gentleman,' and those were popularized by Adam
Mercer. See Trémaudan, ed., Riel, 'Affaire Scott,' 232; Oliver, ed., *Canadian
North-West*, 1: 205fl.; and Mercer, *Canadian North-West*.

97 Trémaudan, ed., Riel, 'Affaire Scott,' 232.

98 Stanley, *Birth of Western Canada*, from Nolin's original French text at 104–5.
Elzéar and Jean-Baptiste Lépine were Ambroise's brothers, as was Maxime.
They escaped with Riel, but Maxime, who remained close to Riel, joined
the rebellion in 1885 and was arrested, tried and convicted of treason, and
pardoned after one year in prison. Elzéar Goulet and François Guillemette
were drowned/killed by Wolseley's troops. As Joseph Delorme was an HBC
official and Ritchot a prominent priest under Taché's protection, they were
arrested after Ambroise Lépine in May 1874 but then quickly released and
never tried. This left Nault and Lagimodière as the only ones left to prosecute after Lépine.

99 Smith's report in Oliver, ed., *Canadian North-West*, 2: 933.

100 *Begg's Red River Journal*, 331–2 (8 March 1870).

101 Trémaudan, ed., Riel, 'Affaire Scott,' 233n.1.

102 Young, *Manitoba Memories*, 138–9.

103 Bumsted, *Thomas Scott's Body*, 6.

104 Trémaudan, ed., Riel, 'Affaire Scott,' 233n.1.

105 A.G. Morice, *A Critical History of the Red River Insurrection* (Winnipeg: Canadian Publishers, 1935), 293–5.

106 'A Conversation with Father André and Father McWilliams, 16 November
1885,' in George F.G. Stanley, ed., *The Collected Writings of Louis Riel/Les Écrits
Complets de Louis Riel*, vol. 3, *1884–1885* (Edmonton: University of Alberta
Press 1985), 583.

107 Young, *Manitoba Memories*, 144–7. According to the introduction by his
friend the Reverend Alexander Sutherland, the autobiography is based simply on Young's eye-witness account: 3–6, the quote at 137.

108 Ibid., 14. Born in 1821, Young was ordained in the Wesleyan Methodist

Church in 1846 and held various appointments in Upper and Lower Canada for twenty-one years.

109 Michael R. Angel, 'George Young,' *DCB*, 13: 1122–3.

110 Young, *Manitoba Memories*, 132–5. The chapter title: 'The Climax of Crime and Cruelty.' Young was concerned with compatriots suffering from close confinement, some in frozen conditions, in the winter of 1869–70. He left bibles for those in peril and visited them frequently. He considered the guards drunkards and heathens.

111 Ibid., 141–2. Young wrote to Scott's brother, Hugh, in Toronto and his aged mother in Ireland. Hugh went insane and was sent to the Toronto asylum, where he died. See J.E. Rea, 'Thomas Scott,' *DCB*, 9: 707–9.

112 Bumsted, *Thomas Scott's Body*, 197–209. My view is that this is rather complimentary given all of the contemporary evidence.

113 Ibid., 209.

114 'Report of the Select Committee' (1874), app. 6: 202.

115 Bumsted, *Thomas Scott's Body*, 204.

116 Ulric Barthe, ed., *Wilfrid Laurier on the Platform* (Montreal: Turcotte and Menard 1890), 39.

117 Alexander Begg and W.R. Nursey, *Ten Years in Winnipeg: A Narration of the Principal Events in the History of the City of Winnipeg from the Year A.D. 1870 to the Year A.D. 1879, Inclusive* (Winnipeg: Times Printing 1879), 1: 481; Trémaudan, ed., Riel, 'Affaire Scott,' 234n.1.

118 Thomas Flanagan, *Louis 'David' Riel: Prophet of the New World* (Toronto: University of Toronto Press 1996), 33.

119 Riel to Dubuc, in Stanley, ed., *Collected Writings of Riel*, 1:110–18 at 116 (12 Dec. 1870), 145–50, 159–60; 1: 211–16 (1 June 1872); 1: 283–4 (17 Sept. 1873); 1: 285–7 (c. 22 Sept. 1873); 1: 386–94 (c. 10–29 Sept. 1874); respectively.

120 Lionel Dorge, 'John Black,' *DCB*, 10: 69–70.

121 *The Nor-wester*, 11 Sept. 1862, letter to the editor. One verdict was guilty with commutation.

122 Dale and Lee Gibson, *Substantial Justice: Law and Lawyers in Manitoba 1670–1970* (Winnipeg: Peguis Publishers 1972), 43–5, 55–60, 69–70.

123 *The New Nation*, 18 Feb. 1870.

124 J.E. Rea, 'Andrew Graham Ballenden Bannatyne,' *DCB*, 12: 44–7.

125 Oliver, ed., *Canadian North-West*, 2: 915–18. A proclamation was also issued that pardoned all political offences and reinstated the HBC's business regimes.

126 *New Nation*, 2 April 1870.

127 'Report of the Select Committee' (1874), app. 6: 18–22.

128 *Globe*, 7 April 1870.

129 Stanley, *Birth of Western Canada*, 117. Colonial Secretary Granville also intervened.

130 Marcel Giraud, *The Métis in the Canadian West*, George Woodcock, trans. (Edmonton: University of Alberta Press 1986), 378–9.

131 An Act for the Temporary Government of Rupert's Land and the North-
West Territories when United with Canada, 33 Vic. (1870) c.3, in Oliver, *Canadian North-West*, 2: 964–72, and 939–63 for all the documents.

132 The United States forbade Wolseley's entry, requiring his force to march
across northern Ontario and leaving his men disgruntled. Riel and others
were warned of threats on their lives from scouts. Trémaudan, *Hold High
Your Heads*, 96–106.

133 O'Donoghue, an Irishman, was raised in New York as a boy and, on meeting an Oblate at Port Huron in 1868, offered to serve the church in the west.
Anti-British, he took part in the Métis protest and was elected to the convention for St Boniface on 16 November, was made treasurer of the PG on
17 December, and was elected to the second convention in January 1870.
He participated with Lépine in the capture of Canadians from Portage la
Prairie who planned to overthrow the PG. Witnessing Scott's execution, he
helped draft the Bill of Rights but became dissatisfied with Riel for being
pro-British. Aided by Fenian leaders in drafting a constitution for Rupert's
Land with himself as president, he recruited an army of labourers from Minnesota. When their raid failed, he remained in the United States as a teacher.
George F.G. Stanley, 'William Bernard O'Donoghue,' *DCB*, 10: 556–7.

134 Roy St George Stubbs, *Four Recorders of Rupert's Land* (Winnipeg: Peguis
Publishers 1967), 77–9.

135 Gibsons, *Substantial Justice*, 94–8.

136 *Begg's Red River Journal*, 742–3 (11 May 1870).

137 Memorandum of Sir George Étienne Cartier, 8 June 1870, 'Report of the Select Committee' (1874), app. 6: 171–8. See Bumsted, 'Trying Riel,' 169–70.

138 *Lépine Trial*, 5–6. It should be noted that many criminal charges were being
laid throughout the period from the autumn of 1873 to the summer 1874.
The *Free Press* reported that the attorney general was bringing in invoices of
$1,000–$1,500 every term for prosecutions that were left on the table: 9 July
1874, 4.

139 See MacBeth, *Making the Canadian West*.

140 Bumsted, 'Trying Riel,' 170.

141 Dale Brown, *The Court of Queen's Bench of Manitoba 1870–1950: A Biographical
History* (Toronto: University of Toronto Press 2006), 68–70; and Willie, *'These
Legal Gentlemen': Lawyers in Manitoba, 1839–1900* (Winnipeg: Legal Research
Institute 1994), 63–4. Although he was to have seven volatile years on the

bench before his violent end – run over by a horse and attacked by his own pit bull mastiff – he still could not maintain order in court.

142 Carl Betke, 'Gilbert McMicken,' *DCB*, 12: 675–80. McMicken was 'kicked upstairs' with appointments to the posts of assistant receiver general and inspector of federal prisons in Manitoba, and served in these capacities until his retirement from government office in 1878.

143 From Upper Canada and a former mayor, Cornish had at various times faced charges of bigamy, assault, and public drunkenness. Defeated in provincial politics, he moved in 1872 to Winnipeg, where he kidnapped an opponent on the eve of the election and stole a polling book on election day – see *The Manitoban*, 21 Sept. 1872; Willie, *These Legal Gentlemen*, 67, 86–7; Hartwell Bowsfield, 'Francis Evans Cornish,' *DCB*, 10: 197–8.

144 After attending the Montreal seminary and a Jesuit college, Royal studied law with Cartier and wrote for his newspaper. He was called to the bar in 1864, helped found *Le Nouveau Monde* in 1867, and began to publish correspondence from Riel's associates in 1869. He went to Winnipeg with Bishop Taché in 1870 on a fact-finding tour for *Le Nouveau Monde*. Convinced of the justice of Riel's movement, he launched *Le Métis* at St Boniface in 1871 and was a mediator between Archibald and the resistance. Royal was MLA and speaker in 1871, provincial secretary in 1872, and councillor of the NWT in 1873. Afterwards he was minister of public works and attorney general. He prepared legislation on a wide range of subjects and represented the province in federal negotiations. Supporting mixed English and French governance, he became lieutenant governor in 1888. See A.I. Silver, 'Joseph Royal,' *DCB*, 13: 910–13.

Dubuc studied at the Petit Séminaire de Montreal with Riel in 1858–65. Receiving his BCL from McGill in 1869, he was called to the bar and went to Manitoba at Riel's request in January 1870. Partnering there with Royal, he was appointed attorney general in 1874 and later a councillor of the NWT and chief justice of Manitoba. See Diane Paulette Payment, 'Sir Joseph Dubuc,' *DCB*, 14: 313–14; Willie, *These Legal Gentlemen*, 78–9, 82–100; and Brawn, *Queen's Bench of Manitoba*, 92–113.

Girard articled in Boucherville, became a bilingual notary, and practised in Lower Canada for twenty-six years. A follower of Cartier and Taché, he was recruited with Royal when the Manitoba Act was passed in 1870. Elected MLA by acclamation for St Boniface East, he was appointed provincial treasurer by Governor Archibald. The first barrister appointed in 1871, Girard encouraged Riel to run for Parliament in 1873 and 1874, and spoke on his behalf when the Commons expelled him. The first French senator and first councillor of the NWT, he was chosen by Lieutenant Governor Morris as Manitoba's first premier. Attempting to keep the English and French together, Girard made Dubuc attorney general just after he had acted for Lépine. When Lépine was found guilty in November, Girard and Dubuc's positions were untenable as Riel's friend and adviser respectively. Girard, resigning as premier, was elected MP by acclamation in December 1874. See G.O. Rothney, 'Marc-Amable Girard,' *DCB*, 12: 369–72.

145 *Lépine Trial*, 7–8.

146 'Report of the Select Committee' (1874), app. 6. The report, called the 'Blue Books,' was discussed briefly in the *Free Press*, 24 Aug 1874, 2.

147 *Lépine Trial*, 8–9.

148 For definitions, see *CST 1*, 3–54.

149 See, for example, *Free Press*, 6 July 1874, 1.

150 K.G. Pryke, 'John Charles McKeagney,' *DCB*, 10: 475–6; Willie, *These Legal Gentlemen*, 62–3; Brawn, *Queen's Bench of Manitoba*, 51–66. Called to the bar in 1838, he was probate judge of Cape Breton from 1848 to 1867, a surrogate in Vice-Admiralty, and an MP in 1867. He was appointed to the Manitoba Court of Queen's Bench in January 1873, a post he held for eighteen months, as a reward for splitting the Catholic vote in Nova Scotia.

151 It included Farmer because of a shortage of names on the jury panel.

152 *Lépine Trial*, 10–17.

153 Clarke, an Irishman, was a bilingual Catholic who practised law in Montreal until the California gold rush of 1858, which he covered as a journalist before moving on to El Salvador. Returning to Montreal, he established a reputation as a criminal lawyer. Unsuccessful in politics, he captained the Volunteer Rifles in the Fenian raids of 1866. He moved to Manitoba in 1870 as Archibald's assistant, ran for the assembly, and was elected and appointed attorney general on the strength of his debating skills. As the first president of the bar, he earned the dislike of Lieutenant Governor Morris in 1872 when he left his wife for a married woman. Resigning after the trial, he moved to California again and stayed there for three years before returning to Winnipeg, where he later acted as counsel for twenty-five of Riel's followers in the 1885 rebellion. See Lovell C. Clark, 'Henry Joseph Clarke,' *DCB*, 11: 192–4; Willie, *These Legal Gentlemen*, 65.

154 *Free Press*, 9 July 1874, 4.

155 (G.B.) 31–2 Vic. (1868) c.105; (G.B.) 41 Geo. III (1803) c.138; 1–2 Geo. IV (1821) c.66; 22–3 Vic. (1859) c.36.

156 The 1869 act, c.3 s.5, and the Manitoba acts of 1870 (c.3) and 1871 (c.16).

157 (Can.) 34 Vic. (1871) c.16.

158 *Lépine Trial*, 16. Later, confusion led the Manitoba legislature to declare that the English law of 15 July 1870 had been in force in the province – (Man.)

38 Vic. (1875) c.12, which was later endorsed by the Dominion Parliament: (Can.) 51 Vic. (1888) c.33 s.1.

159 *Trial of Ambrose Lépine at Winnipeg for the Wilful Murder of Thomas Scott. Question of Jurisdiction*, Thomas P. Foran, ed. (Montreal: Lovell Printing 1874), 1–15 (1 Dec. 1874). I assume this to be a defence of the first question at law, of jurisdiction, published after Wood's sentence, perhaps for the amnesty plea as well as public opinion.

160 *Trial of Lépine*, Foran ed., 10–13.

161 Ibid., 14–15; 31–2 Vic. c.105, in Oliver, ed., *Canadian North-West*, 2: 937–9.

162 The chief justice kept extensive notes on the trials that he heard in June-October 1874, and the notebooks are found in AM, MG 14, B42. Notes on this trial are in vol. 1 at pp.2–78, then later in the volume at a new numbered page 1, and in vol. 2 at pp.1–85. The notes are barely legible and have been used only where they contain information additional to that in the printed accounts.

163 This interpretation is derived from Wood's judicial reasoning in the charge he gave to the trial jury, cited below.

164 Willie, *These Legal Gentlemen*, 66, 88; and Brawn, *Queen's Bench of Manitoba*, 71–91, where he is attributed to have suffered from 'ataxie locomotrice progressive' before leaving Brantford (88).

165 Of working-class origins, Chapleau was born in Lower Canada in 1840. Distinguished in appearance and talents, he was educated in philosophy before being trained in law in Montreal and called to the bar in 1861. Specializing in criminal law, in fifteen years he won twenty-one of twenty-two murder cases. A talented dramatist with a melodious voice, he was passionate in the courtroom and had a great effect on juries. He was elected in 1867 with the Liberal-Conservative Cartier party.

166 Later Quebec provincial secretary and Conservative premier, he became Macdonald's secretary of state in 1883 and was lieutenant governor of Quebec at the end of his career. Andrée Désilets, 'Sir Joseph Adolphe Chapleau,' *DCB*, 12: 172–82; Kenneth J. Munro, *The Political Career of Sir Adolphe Chapleau, Premier of Quebec 1879–1882* (Queenston: Edwin Mellen Press 1992), 33–4.

167 A Quebecker then aged twenty-seven, he had articled at Chapleau's law office, was called to the bar in 1871, and accompanied Chapleau to Winnipeg. Forget was charming, considerate, and witty, with an inquiring mind and diplomatic skills. Legal colleagues thought he had a brilliant career in the courtroom. After the trials, as an ardent Liberal dedicated to the west, he was appointed secretary of a commission to enumerate mixed-blood land grants in May 1875 and was appointed secretary and clerk of the new coun-

cil of the NWT in October 1876. He became assistant Indian commissioner in 1888, deputy superintendent general of Indian affairs in 1893, lieutenant governor of Saskatchewan in 1905, and senator for Alberta in 1911. E. Brian Titley, 'Amédée-Emmanuel Forget,' *DCB*, 15: 368–71.

168   *Globe*, 28 Oct. 1874, 3; the observation is at 26 Oct. 1874, 4. According to the *Free Press*, there was 'a great deal of standing aside and challenging': 14 Oct. 1874, 2.

169   *Lépine Trial*, 37-8. Future references in the text are to the page numbers of this trial record. The other sources that have been used for the trial include Wood's notebooks in AM, MG 14, B42; the Winnipeg *Free Press*, which published daily accounts from 14 October to 4 November; and the Toronto *Globe*, which printed daily summaries of the trial that it received by telegram from 23 October to 11 November, interrupted for six days by prairie fires and a sleet storm.

170   From Tuesday, 13 October, through Saturday, 17 October, Monday, 19 October, and Tuesday, 20 October a.m.

171   Michel Dumas and Paul Proulx, in *Lépine Trial*, 77, 80.

172   Ibid., 68–84, from Tuesday afternoon, 20 October, through Friday a.m., 23 October.

173   *Lépine Trial*, 74, 78–9, 83–4, for the evidence of Nolin, Ritchot, and Taché.

174   While Taché prevented civil war, the amnesty promise failed. Distrustful of Liberal politicians, he shared the Natives' sense of injustice while seeking their conversion and westernization. A promoter of education and language rights, he aimed to create a string of French parishes stretching to the Rockies. Jean Hamelin, 'Alex-André-Antonin Taché,' *DCB*, 12: 1002–12.

175   Much of that evidence was corroborated in correspondence and government documents that Wood would not allow in court. According to the *Free Press*, these assurances were well known in the spring of 1870: 25 Aug. 1874, 2.

176   Namely, Bunn (70), Bannatyne (72–3), Charles Nolin (74), Xavier Pagé (75), Narcisse Marion (75–6), and Michel Dumas (76–7).

177   Munro, *Chapleau*, 34.

178   Such as Bumsted, 'Trying Riel,' 181–2, and George F.G. Stanley, *Louis Riel* (Toronto: Ryerson 1963), 210–11, on why their arguments were weak because of the language problem.

179   Throughout, as reported in the *Free Press*, 27 Oct. 1874, 2.

180   It appears that the 'minutes' that were the 'record' of the court were lost, probably in the dispersal of the PG on the heels of Col. Wolseley's Ontario expedition. There is no evidence that they were deliberately discarded.

181   S.R. Mealing, 'William Osgoode,' *DCB*, 6: 557. For Osgoode in the McLane trial, see Louis A. Knafla, 'The Influence of the French Revolution on Legal

Attitudes and Ideology in Lower Canada, 1789–1798,' in Pierre Boulle and Richard A. Lebrun, eds., *Le Canada et la Revolution Francaise* (Montreal: Centre interuniversitaire d'études europeenes 1989), 83–102.

182 AM, MG 14, B42, vol. 1, memo of four folios.

183 *Free Press,* 2 Nov. 1874, 2.

184 *Free Press,* 27 Oct. 1874, 3, and *Globe,* 6 Nov. 1874, 4, respectively.

185 According to Maggie Siggins, *Riel: A Life of Revolution* (Toronto: Harper Collins 1994), 173.

186 *Manitoba Law Reports,* vol. 1, or *Carey's Manitoba Reports 1875–1883* (Toronto: Carswell 1884).

187 AM, MG 14, B42, vol. 2, 1–36, beginning 9 Oct. 1874.

188 André Nault in Trémaudan, ed., Riel, 'Affaire Scott,' 224–5. According to Tom Flanagan, who has examined the Riel papers, Trémaudan was not always accurate.

189 *Free Press,* Tuesday, 3 Nov., 1874, 3; and Wednesday, 4 Nov., 1874, 3.

190 Wood notes the examinations of witnesses for the queen in the following order: Joseph Nolin, James Anderson, Reverend Young, Baptiste 'Charrell,' Duncan Nolin, 'Alix' Murray, Pierre Gladu, and Michael 'Duncas' (the first of whom is cross-examined by Chapleau, the rest by Royal). The notes then come to an abrupt end: AM, MG 14, B42, p. 36.

191 Reported in the *Globe,* 5 Nov. 1874, 1.

192 Munro, *Chapleau,* 33–4. The 'untenable' quote is from the *Free Press,* 4 Nov. 1874, 3.

193 Ibid., 35. After the amnesty, the riding of Provencher asked him to be their MP, but he declined: 37.

194 *R. v. Schultz, Carey's Manitoba Reports* (1874), 32.

195 *The Queen v. Schultz* (1875), *Judgments in the Queen's Bench Manitoba,* Wood, CJ, comp. Daniel Carey (Calgary: Burroughs and Company, repr. 1918), at 70–1 (13 Nov. 1874 and 5 Jan. 1875).

196 Munro, *Chapleau,* 34.

197 Willie, *These Legal Gentlemen,* 48.

198 John C. Schultz and Edmund Burke Wood, on appeal from the Court of Queen's Bench, Manitoba, 6 *SCC Reports* (1882): 585–634. Ritchie held that the evidence was clear that the parties agreed, 'being on terms of friendship and intimacy.' Wood was either 'deluded' if he thought this was an arms-length relationship of which he knew no details, or 'entirely ignorant' (Ritchie at 610, 614–15, Gwynne at 631–2). Wood began negotiations with Schultz for property in late June 1874. He made a deposit on 7 July and they came to a final agreement for a deed and mortgage of $5,926 on 12 August. When the house was completed, the mortgage was assigned to other parties. By May

1875, Woods was sending Mackenzie telegrams for financial help. Eventually he agreed to have monthly payments of $100 taken from his salary. He alleged that Schultz took advantage of his confidence to insert larger sums and items not included in the agreement, sued Schultz, and won. Schultz appealed on a writ of error to the Supreme Court of Canada.

199 NAC, MG 14, B42/1/101, 25 July 1875.

200 AM, MG 12/B1, no. 40 (a copy of the report at Government House, Winnipeg).

201 AM, MG 12/B1, no. 36 (29 June 1876).

202 Yet he was a bencher of Ontario and became president of the Manitoba Historical and Scientific Society. Roy St George Stubbs, 'Hon. Edmund Burke Wood,' in Douglas Kemp, ed., *Historical and Scientific Society of Manitoba*, ser. 3:13 (Winnipeg, 1958), 27–47; J. Daniel Livermore, 'Edmund Burke Wood,' *DCB*, 11: 934–5; Brawn, *Queen's Bench of Manitoba*, 71–91.

203 Sessional Papers, *The Case of Ambroise Lépine: Correspondence between the Earl of Dufferin, the Earl of Carnarvon, Joseph Howe and Others 'relating to the Commutation of the Sentence of Death Passed on Ambroise Lépine, for the Murder of Thomas Scott, at Fort Garry'* (Ottawa, 1875). The *Globe* wrote immediately that it expected the sentence to be commuted: 4 Nov. 1874, 2. In a longer article, it advised that the pardon should not be absolute, since peaceful, land-holding Métis members of the jury had found Lépine guilty: 10 Nov. 1874, 2. It added that vindicating the law was not incompatible with mercy.

204 *La Minerve*, 19 Dec. 1874, for the speeches; and 20 Dec. 1874, for the motion and vote.

205 Stanley, ed., *Collected Writings of Riel*, 1: 423–6 (9 and 20 Jan. 1875).

206 See the papers and correspondence submitted to Dufferin: Sessional Papers, vol. 7, 2nd Session of the 3rd Parliament of the Dominion of Canada, Session 1875 (Ottawa), no. 11, 1–44.

207 Stanley, *Birth of Western Canada*, 145–56, the quote at 146; and Ben Forster and Jonathan Swainger, 'Edward Blake,' *DCB*, 14: 76–7.

208 *Journals of the House of Commons*, 1874, vol. 8, p. 64.

209 Stanley, *Birth of Western Canada*, 168–71 and 27–34 (8 Feb. 1875), respectively, in that order.

210 Robert Rumilly, 'Luc Letellier de Saint-Just,' *DCB*, 11: 520.

211 Andrée Désilets, 'Joseph-Alfred Mousseau,' *DCB*, 11: 624.

212 Great Britain, Hansard, 1975, ser. 3, vol. 223, 1071–6.

213 *La Minerve*, 8 March 1875; House of Commons, *Debates*, 1875, 1: 50, 135–6.

214 AM, MG 12/B11, no. 1281, Wood to Secretary of State R.W. Scott for Lieutenant Governor Morris (15 July 1876).

215 Stanley, ed., *Collected Writings of Riel*, 1: 428–330 (1 Feb. 1875).

216 Ibid., 1: 456–7 (May 1875); 1: 472 (21 Oct. 1875); 1: 474–6 (6 Dec. 1875).

217 Ibid., 3: 186–8 (21 April 1878); 3: 204–5, Riel to Julie (2 May 1879); 3: 289, Riel
     to Prudhomme (25 June 1783).

218 His work to establish the historical committee of the Union Nationale Mé-
     tisse Saint-Joseph du Manitoba in 1909 contributed to the publication of Au-
     guste-Henri de Trémaudan's *Histoire de la nation métisse dans l'Ouest canadien*
     in 1935. Ens, 'Lépine,' 587–9.

219 For example, the works of Stanley and especially Bumsted cited above.

220 There were approximately 5,720 French Métis, 4,080 English Métis, and 560
     Natives in the colony: Red River Census, 1870.

8

Summary and Incompetent Justice: Legal Responses to the 1885 Crisis

BOB BEAL and BARRY WRIGHT

The justice system in all the 1885 rebellion cases demonstrated elements of harshness and carelessness unusual for the day. Prosecutors used their discretion to select the most repressive available laws, and they fully exploited existing procedural expedients. This is surprising given that Prime Minister John A. Macdonald, Justice Minister Alexander Campbell, and Deputy Minister of Justice George Burbidge were all knowledgeable about and sincerely interested in the integrity of the criminal justice system, and Macdonald himself had experience with high-profile political trials. While the need to assert firm Canadian control over the North-West may explain the harsh justice, it does not explain the carelessness. The capable prosecution team generally outmanoeuvred defence counsel in many of the 1885 cases, but carelessness is illustrated best by the incompetence of the judge who heard most of these cases.

More than two hundred were held in custody initially, and of the 130 Métis, Indian, and white settler suspects who continued to be held on charges, the government proceeded in 84 cases.[1] The War Measures Act in the First and Second World Wars affected larger numbers overall, but 1885 was arguably a deeper, more serious national-security crisis, and second only to the 1837–8 Canadian rebellions in terms of the number of political offences charged and the complexity of prosecutions. The trial and execution of Louis Riel for high treason was the most prominent response to the 1885 rebellion, and a number of studies have assessed the legal issues raised in that case. The other 1885 cases, including less well-known ones examined here, raise additional legal and procedural questions, many of which cannot be answered definitively.

Treason-felony convictions resulted in penitentiary terms for many of Riel's associates and for Indian leaders One Arrow, Big Bear, and Poundmaker, as well as for some Indians who were not leaders. Eleven Indians were sentenced to death for murder in relation to the events, of whom eight were hanged at Battleford while three had their sentences commuted to penitentiary terms. Those three joined forty-one Indians and thirty-six Métis in Manitoba's Stony Mountain Penitentiary. (See tables in the volume's Supporting Documents.)

The Riel case, which J.M. Bumsted examines in the next chapter, has attracted by far the most scholarly attention. The Indian trials, which Bill Waiser examines in a subsequent chapter, have emerged from relative neglect in recent years.[2] The same cannot be said of the remaining cases involving the leading Métis rebels (many of whom were members of Riel's council) and white settler supporters. Yet they were a major focus of the government's overall legal strategy in response to the crisis and remained important to it, even as Riel and the Indian leaders came to serve as the primary public examples. In the end, many of the convictions for serious political offences resulted from coerced confessions, Riel's conviction for high treason serving as a powerful motivation for the remaining Métis prisoners to plead guilty to the lesser offence of treason-felony. While firm exemplary justice was balanced by attempts to minimize further aggravation of settler, Catholic, and francophone disaffection, the Indian cases entailed fewer political complications, driven as they were by the perceived need to reassure anxious settlers. No 'white rebels' associated with the crisis were convicted.

This chapter sets the scene for the following chapters about the 1885 crisis. We examine the government's overall prosecution strategy, deal with some of the lesser-known prosecutions of 1885, and assess the actions of the judge, prosecutors, and defence lawyers in these cases. We analyse the specific processes used against the Métis councillors (members of the provisional government council at Batoche), the revealing prosecution of Magnus Burston, and the cases of the 'white settler rebels' William Henry Jackson and Thomas Scott. The latter case, relatively neglected in the existing literature, is presented in particular detail, with Scott's capable defence resulting in the government's biggest prosecutorial failure. Each of these processes was unique in some ways among the 1885 cases, but they also illustrate factors that affected all the cases.

PROSECUTION POLICIES, LEGAL OPTIONS, AND PERSONNEL

Justice Minister Alexander Campbell assured Prime Minister John A. Macdonald that the government response to the rebellion would be handled with appropriate political and legal diligence. 'We shall take great care, I think, to satisfy the Country that the prosecution is well done ... any want of thoroughness in this respect would be unpardonable.'[3] There was concern about whether the non-capital treason-felony offence, which Ottawa adopted twenty years after it had been enacted in the United Kingdom, would be politically palatable in Riel's case, but Macdonald was also worried about the applicability of high treason charges and procedural complications in the North-West Territories. He told Campbell to 'look carefully at the Treason-felony act. I think there may be some difficulty applying the Statute to Riel's case. I hope we shall not be obliged to have recourse to the Statute of Edward. The proceedings are complicated & perhaps can not be applied in the NW.'[4] In expressing concerns about the applicable substantive law and procedures, Macdonald wished to avoid complications that would derail the proceedings. He wanted the quickest and simplest way to put the events of 1885 behind the country.

Towards the end of June 1885, the Department of Justice had worked out a detailed initial strategy, as set out in Campbell's instructions (see Supporting Documents) to Deputy Minister George Burbidge, and carefully selected a prosecution team. Riel and other leading men among the prisoners, including, as Campbell put it, white and 'half-breed' leaders and Indian chiefs, were to be prosecuted for treason. Indians who caused death during the insurrection were to be prosecuted for murder. Campbell anticipated guilty pleas after a certain number of convictions, noting that the team should report for further instructions at that stage. He also noted that the government's objectives would be met by thirty to forty convictions and that special attention should be paid to the possible role of white insurrectionists.[5] The instructions made no distinction between high treason and treason-felony charges, but charges under a third possibility, the Fenian Act, had been abandoned by this point. The prosecution team refined and modified Campbell's directions in the field during the proceedings.

Law and Procedure in 1885

There were three political offences relating to levying war against the state in Canadian law that had potential application to the 1885 crisis.

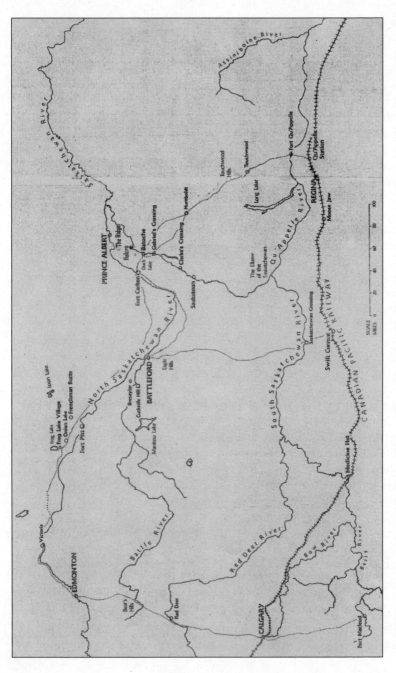

The North-West in 1885. Modified version of map in Rudy Wiebe and Bob Beal, eds., *War in the West: Voices of the 1885 Rebellion* (Toronto: McClelland and Stewart 1985).

High treason was based on the 1352 Statute of Treasons, adopted during the reign of Edward III, and was considered the most serious offence in English law.[6] It set out three main categories of treason and the one applicable to the events of 1885 was that of levying war against the sovereign. The rebellion was not an attack directly on the sovereign, but judges had construed such events to infer an attack on the sovereign, although this construction on levying of war also placed a greater burden on prosecutors to prove intent. In all cases, the prosecution had to show overt acts on the part of the accused related to levying of war.[7] Treason-felony was a non-capital version of the offence, developed in the nineteenth century to supplement high treason.[8] A third possible offence applicable to the situation was the unique Canadian quasi-treason offence of lawless aggression, known widely, after its use in the mid-1860s, as the Fenian Act.[9] All three were considered for use in 1885.

Macdonald's early reservations about high treason initially led Justice Minister Campbell and prosecution team leader Burbidge to consider charging Louis Riel under the Fenian Act.[10] That act, examined in more detail in the chapters by Blake Brown and by Desmond Brown and Barry Wright in this volume, originated in Upper Canadian legislation passed in 1838, designed to deal with a perceived gap in the law concerning foreign invaders from countries at peace with Britain who levied war but who did not seem to owe allegiance and therefore were not liable for treason.[11] While this law was useful against armed invaders and supporters who crossed the border, Riel's entry into Canada in 1884 was peaceful so offences under the Fenian Act would be difficult to prosecute. There were concerns, too, about Riel's U.S. citizenship and repercussions from the United States and Britain if Riel were tried under it.[12]

The offence for which Riel was ultimately tried has received a great deal of historical comment. Some of this displays little insight into applications of high treason on other occasions and deficient understanding of the reception of English law. The suggestion, expressed most recently in George Goulet's eccentric interpretation,[13] that the government dragged out an obscure medieval law that had questionable status in Canada to avoid trying Riel under more humane legislation and ensure he was hanged, neglects the fact that this law was applied widely in British North America as well as in Britain itself in the late eighteenth and early nineteenth centuries, and that treason-felony supplemented rather than replaced high treason. There is little doubt that the medieval Statute of Treasons applied to the North-West, as Desmond Brown has noted,[14] just as it did to the rest of the Dominion and British empire where English criminal law was received. Edward III's statute is referred to in the 1868 Dominion Treason-Felony Act, and Burbidge's *Digest of the Criminal Law* later makes explicit note that it was the law of Canada. High treason was also included, the main offences from the Edward III statute restated in modernized language, in the 1892 Canadian Criminal Code.[15] Macdonald's initial concerns about the high treason offence may have related to the failure of the Canadian government to explicitly transfer the statute of Edward III to the North-West Territories, but it applied nonetheless as the result of reception there in 1670.[16]

Little attention has been paid to the constructions around treason law and how these migrated to the modern treason-felony offence, matters examined in greater detail in the Brown and Wright chapter. While proof of overt acts and intent was necessary for high treason, the reach of the offence was extended by constructions such as Britain's temporary Treason Act, 1795,[17] renewed to deal with activities and advocacy associated with Napoleonic as well as French revolutionary intrigues. The British Treason-Felony Act, passed in response to the 1848 upheavals in Ireland and fears of Chartist agitation, also served as a permanent replacement for that temporary legislation and aimed to overcome the reluctance of juries to convict for the capital offence of high treason. It did not replace the 1352 statute. Rather, it converted the modern legislated constructions (such as conspiracies and even advocacy that attempted to alter the nature of the crown's authority or to commit rebellion) into a lesser, non-capital form of treason. As we discuss in the case of the Métis councillors below, the treason-felony offence also facilitated summary justice by providing a lesser form of treason to which to plead guilty. Neither the Treason Act, 1795 nor the Treason-Felony Act, 1848 applied in the British North American colonies, but Canada adopted a version of the latter in 1868 and explicitly extended it to the North-West.[18]

The procedural issues were complex, as Macdonald knew. After 1869, the new territorial courts were to send capital cases to Manitoba or British Columbia for trial. The 1880 North-West Territories Act changed this to allow for the territorial trial of capital cases and felonies by information, without a grand jury indictment, before a stipendiary magistrate and six trial jurors.[19] The procedural reforms attempted to resolve the legal ambiguities caused by the 1869 transfer to Canada of the Hudson's Bay Company territories that subsequently plagued the Ambroise Lépine case examined in the previous chapter. The territories remained essentially a colonial jurisdiction, as reflected in departures from the usual British and non-territorial Canadian practices.

Defence counsel opened Riel's case by objecting to the trial of capital offences before a stipendiary magistrate and a six-man jury, and this was the basis for the eventual appeal, an issue that figures prominently in some of the existing scholarship reviewed in Bumsted's chapter.[20] But the issue of jurisdiction had been resolved by the Connor murder case shortly before, although Riel's lawyers remained determined to pursue it while that conviction was under appeal.[21] This simplified version of the regular administration of justice was not unusual in a comparative colonial context. As Justice Minister Campbell's brief to the Judicial Committee of the Privy Council put it: 'It should be sufficient to say that the legality of the tribunal by which he [Riel] was tried had been affirmed by the Privy Council, the highest court in the Empire [in *Connor*] ... It has been said that a jury composed of six only, and the absence of a grand jury, are features so inconsistent with the rights of British subjects that the prisoner still had grounds for complaint; but, as was pointed out in the Privy Council, the same crime may be tried elsewhere in the British Empire, notably in India, without any jury, either grand or petty, and this mode of trial has been sanctioned by the Imperial parliament.'[22]

The territorial procedures could not be challenged on legal grounds, but this did not mean that justice was fair. The resort to vague informations and the abbreviated pre-trial review of the crown's cases had profound implications that reverberated throughout the proceedings. It placed defence counsel at an enormous disadvantage and facilitated a form of summary justice. The egregious implications for the accused may not have been so obvious with the administration of routine cases, where expedient procedure under frontier conditions was an important aim of the North-West Territories Act. But they became vividly apparent in political trials, particularly on charges of treason.

British constitutional standards were compromised in jurisdictions such as the North-West Territories and the unfairness of the procedures may be assessed on these broader grounds. In the wake of the Glorious Revolution of 1688–9, and the continuation of Restoration era anxieties about the possible return to Tudor and Stuart excesses prompted by the infamous treason trials conducted by Judge George Jeffreys in the late 1680s, those accused of treason acquired significant procedural rights, celebrated as part of the constitutional advances of the period.[23] The 1696 Treason Trials Act included the right to defence counsel (not extended to felony cases until the nineteenth century), access to a copy of the indictment five days before arraignment, and a list of the jury panel two days before trial. At least two witnesses were required for each treason alleged in the indictment.[24]

Unfortunately, this important liberalizing legislation was not part of the criminal law of the territories since it was enacted after the 1670 reception date. This deficiency underscored the compromised nature of colonial justice, which fell well short of the standards that would have been experienced in Ottawa or London. Macdonald himself made similar arguments about special procedures violating the liberalizing spirit of the 1696 act as a young defence counsel in Kingston in 1838 in a roughly parallel situation that involved the expedient of trying civilians by courts martial on levying-war charges.[25] And, while not legally bound to do so, the crown could have exercised the discretion to try the cases outside Regina or even the territories if it chose, on the technical grounds of pre-confederation imperial legislation that had not been repealed, or by a special commission of oyer and terminer, as was done in Upper Canada in 1814 and 1838.

The Prosecution Team and Defence Counsel

George W. Burbidge, appointed deputy minister of justice in 1882 and architect of the 1892 Criminal Code, assembled a formidable prosecution team that was responsible for organizing the crown's strategy for the 1885 trials. Individual responsibilities varied among the cases. Christopher Robinson led for the crown at the Riel trial, supported by Britton Bath Osler of Toronto, Thomas Chase-Casgrain of Montreal, and David Lynch Scott of Regina. Burbidge's legal expertise and detailed knowledge of government policy gave Justice Minister Campbell the confidence to delegate much of the decision making to the prosecutors in the field.[26]

Robinson, son of Family Compact leader John Beverley Robinson (the father had prosecuted the 1814 treason trials as attorney general, drafted the 1838 emergency legislation and presided as chief justice over a number of the leading treason trials that followed), was one of the country's leading barristers. The younger Robinson had repeatedly refused judicial office and represented the Canadian government in international cases.[27] He was not a criminal law specialist. But the presence of Osler, widely regarded as one of the leading criminal lawyers of the period, more than compensated for Robinson's lack of experience in the area. Osler had the added advantage of being a Liberal, which helped to offset the appearance of partisan political bias.[28] Chase-Casgrain was promoted by Adolphe Caron, minister of militia and defence. A young partner at Caron's firm, he represented French Canadian interests. Scott, mayor of Regina, represented local interests.[29] Alexander David Stewart of Hamilton, Ontario, generally considered to be Canada's most progressive and efficient police chief, was the chief investigator for the prosecution team, and it was in his name that many of the informations were sworn.[30]

There is little doubt about the prosecution team's effectiveness as advocates of the government case. But questions remain about the exercise of their additional responsibilities as officers of the court, notably their lack of intervention concerning Judge Hugh Richardson's persistent misdirection to juries, noted below, about levying war under the treason-felony offence. The defence lawyers, whom we discuss in the context of specific cases below, and who are further examined in Bumsted's chapter, were outclassed by this formidable prosecution team (with the exception of Henry J. Clarke who acted for Tom Scott). Beyond the general pattern of weak defences, the capabilities of the judge who heard most of the cases in 1885 stands out as a concern.

The Judge

As Bob Beal and Rod Macleod point out, it cannot be said that Hugh Richardson was biased against Métis or Indians.[31] However, Richardson was careless, lazy, and irresponsible. He faced situations in 1885 that were well beyond his abilities.

Richardson began his legal career in southwestern Ontario and was a crown prosecutor for some years. In 1872 he became chief clerk in the Department of Justice.[32] His contemporaries did not regard him highly. Surveyor William Pearce recalled that Justice Minister Edward Blake made Richardson a stipendiary magistrate in the North-West Territories simply to get him far away from Ottawa, where he would, presumably, do little damage.[33]

Richardson, at Regina, was not the only judge available for the 1885 trials. Charles Rouleau of Battleford, who heard some of the cases discussed in Waiser's chapter, could have been pressed into wider service. He had suffered losses in 1885 and expressed his biases at the time, certainly more openly than Richardson, but he also possessed a large law library and prided himself on his knowledge of the law.[34] He was capable of handling the complex legal issues raised in political trials, and would have been a better choice than Richardson on these grounds, something that should have been obvious to the prime minister and justice minister. An additional advantage of using Rouleau would have been that he was a Conservative Catholic francophone from Quebec. As we noted earlier, too, a special commission could have been established to hear the cases. Trials in Ontario or Quebec might even have been possible, but politically unpalatable, under provisions of the Imperial Jurisdiction Act, 1821.[35] There is no evidence that these alternatives were considered.

It was routine in treason cases for judges to cite leading authorities to define the laws of treason to juries. The usual authorities cited were Michael Foster and Matthew Hale, but others such as the standard *Archbold's Pleading* were used. They all defined treason law clearly for most situations, particularly regarding the necessity of showing aiding and abetting, not mere presence, key in some of the 1885 cases. Richardson cited no authorities during his 1885 trials, not even *Archbold's*, a basic reference work every criminal lawyer kept close to hand.

Richardson's peculiar incompetence is obvious in several different aspects of the cases over which he presided. We present here some examples from the cases examined in this chapter.

Richardson took little active part in the trial of William Henry Jackson, Riel's non-Métis secretary, but at the beginning prosecutor B.B. Osler had to remind him that the jury must be called before the trial began.[36] At the end of the trial, Osler himself gave the directions to the jury, quoting the relevant portion of the Criminal Procedure Act regarding insanity. Then, Richardson, given his turn, quoted exactly the same words and said little else to the jury.[37] There were numerous objections during the treason-felony trial of alleged white rebel Tom Scott but Richardson was reluctant to rule on them. He was concerned about the possibility of appeal, and much of what he said in court was more comment than ruling. During the testimony of Hillyard Mitchell, for example, defence lawyer H.J. Clarke said: 'I ask my question be taken down, and I ask for your Lordship's ruling, and I know exactly what will be the result.'[38] Richardson did not make a note at that point.[39] A shorthand reporter made transcripts of the 1885 trials. But in the North-West Territories in 1885, the trial record legally consisted of the information, the exhibits, and the judge's notes. The judge was required to take notes of the evidence and of the legal rulings he made during trial. That was the record that would be available to an appeal court. Richardson, however, noted only four instances where he made rulings during the Scott trial, and ignored some rulings he did make.[40] The judge's duty to the record, and to the appeal court, was clear. This was not mere carelessness on Richardson's part; it was likely deliberate.

Richardson's silence at points during the trials is also illustrative. When in the Scott case defence witness Charles Nolin, inexpert in the English language and confused by exchanges between crown and defence, demanded to be examined in the French language, prosecutor B.B. Osler

Hugh Richardson. From John Hawkes, *The Story of Saskatchewan and Its People Vol. 1* (Regina, 1924), 569. (Library and Archives of Canada, C-031192)

declared: 'The witness has answered intelligently questions put to him in English. The jury are satisfied he has had a fair examination.'[41] The judge said nothing, although it was his responsibility to rule. When Cree-speaker William Paquin was cross-examined during the same trial, defence lawyer H.J. Clarke requested that the witness be examined through an interpreter in his own language. Osler retorted that 'the witness is answering in English very well,' though defence lawyer W.V. Maclise pointed out that Paquin did not understand the English word 'neutral.'[42] Given the conceptual differences between the English and Cree languages, Maclise probably had a good point, and the question of alleged neutrality was an important one for the crown. But Judge Richardson said nothing.

Richardson's charge to the jury at the end of the Scott trial was inept, bordering on bizarre.[43] He appears not to have prepared for the most important speech at a treason trial. He rambled. He dealt with matters that were not the jury's concern. He dealt with other matters that seemed to have appeared from thin air. Where he dealt, extremely briefly, with the evidence in the case, he got it wrong. He did not give the jury instructions about particular evidence as he had promised earlier in the trial. He espoused his incorrect understanding of the laws of treason. He digressed (his own description) into peculiar territory, explaining to the jury that he was not a 'creature.'[44] No one in the court had accused Richardson of being a 'creature' (this might have happened during jury selection and if the term had been used it would have been in the older sense of a dependant of powerful persons). Richardson stated: 'At some of the earlier stages of this trial – I regret to say – charges were made, or assertions were made, indicating, first, that I was simply a creature, and, secondly, that you, gentlemen, were all creatures. Well, now, true it is I may be a creature, that is, I may hold a commission which may be put back at a moment's notice, but while I do hold it, while I do hold such a commission, I think I feel that until I have shown myself a creature, I am not liable to that charge.'[45]

Richardson explained the prosecution of a treason-felony charge to the jury by saying that 'it is a cardinal principle laid down in the law books that the Queen is the people.'[46] The books certainly did not say that. Richardson stressed to the jury that the treason-felony offence was modern law, unlike high treason. But he only briefly quoted the relevant clause of the treason-felony statute. He did not explain it, expressing impatience at revisiting 'this verbiage which covers two or three sheets of foolscap paper.'[47]

Richardson cannot be faulted for his explanation of the crown's burden of proof and the doctrine of reasonable doubt during his jury charge in the Scott trial. But his review of the evidence was, in his own words, 'general and cursory.'[48] Richardson failed to explain how a letter, which as we shall see was the cornerstone of the crown's case and a major point of contention between counsel, related to the law of treason (and he was probably incapable of doing so).[49] Richardson simply told the jury that, if they were convinced that Scott was a party to the resolutions passed at certain meetings and to the contentious letter, 'from a legal standpoint, I must tell you that there is evidence sufficient to sustain a conviction upon the law which I have read to you.'[50] That was going farther than even the crown was willing to go.

The Scott trial highlighted Richardson's inept jury charges, but his incompetence had become evident in previous cases. Richardson's jury charges in the cases of Cree chiefs One Arrow and Poundmaker involved minimal direction about the law of treason and the evidence required for conviction, avoiding the regular defence contention that the crown had to show participation beyond mere presence during rebellion. The pattern of incompetent jury directions became obvious with the Scott case, and it featured also in the next treason-felony trial, that of Chief Big Bear. There, Richardson explicitly instructed that mere presence among armed rebels was evidence of constructive levying of war, going well beyond what was contemplated for the treason-felony offence and contradicting all accepted precedent.[51] As Big Bear's counsel, Beverly Robertson, repeatedly tried to point out, mere presence during rebellion did not constitute evidence of treason. The accused had to be shown to have been actually aiding and abetting rebellion, and mere presence did not put the onus on him to demonstrate innocence.[52] Richardson dismissed Robertson's arguments out of hand. A fairly quick glance at a standard legal source, or even out-of-court discussions with the prosecution team at the 1885 trials, would have shown Richardson that Robertson was correct. But Richardson obstinately persisted in his misunderstanding of the law.

SUMMARY JUSTICE

The crown did not extend to the accused the protections of the Treason Trials Act, 1696[53] and was not required to do so because it was not part of the law of the North-West Territories, a technically sound position in law but a questionable one on broader constitutional grounds. The form of 'summary' or abbreviated justice the Métis councillors experienced underscores this point.[54] One of the egregious practices that the 1696 legislation sought to discourage was behaviour such as Judge George Jeffreys's encouragement of guilty pleas in the aftermath of Monmouth's rebellion.[55] Temporary pardoning legislation passed in Upper Canada in 1838, examined in the previous volume, bypassed the spirit of the 1696 act with the same objective as Jeffreys had.[56] No such special emergency legislation was required in the North-West Territories, but had the 1696 act applied, it might well have prevented the coercion of guilty pleas in the cases of the Métis councillors.

The vague informations under North-West Territories procedure facilitated summary justice. The availability of the treason-felony offence also helped. The new law enhanced not only the prospects of jury convictions but also the pursuit of plea bargains by providing a lesser treason offence to which the accused could plead guilty.

The Métis Councillors and Guilty Pleas: The Church Puts the Fix In

As it became clear that a powerful example would be made of Riel, government prosecutors moved to remove the other Métis accused from the limelight, seeking to minimize publicity around those participants in the rebellion.

The Métis who had been members of the provisional government council at Batoche were highly motivated to plead guilty to treason-felony as soon as there was a sense of the outcome of Riel's trial for high treason. For their advisers and defence counsel, the odds of throwing the accused on the mercy of the crown were better than courageous defiance. A consequence was further vilification of Riel as the councillors were portrayed as more distanced from him than they had in fact been or as unwitting victims of his delusional ambitions. Guilty pleas meant an easy job for defence counsel, who merely had to present mitigating circumstances for sentencing. They also meant a very easy job for the crown, avoiding the delays, costs, risks, and negative publicity that would ensue from full trials. They were cheap convictions, but convictions for treason nonetheless. Such summary justice was also part of the balance between exemplary justice and lenient mercy sought by governments aiming to appear confident in their exercise of authority. The strategy was certainly not unprecedented, but it was constitutionally questionable.

The guilty pleas were extracted under the impression that charges of high treason were likely. This strategy is not obvious in Justice Minister Alexander Campbell's instructions to the crown prosecutors, which refer in general terms to treason without distinguishing between high treason and treason-felony.[57] As Bumsted notes in his chapter, Riel's defence team remained in the dark about the precise offence, not realizing that he was being tried for high treason until the matter was clarified towards the end of the first day of his trial. Informations were associated with controversial crown prerogative powers that bypassed usual regular pre-trial indictment procedures, powers that were to be exercised circumspectly after the late seventeenth century. Informations were nonetheless relied upon widely in colonial contexts. The informations the prosecution team issued against the councillors charged them with intending to levy war to compel the queen to change her measures and counsels as evidenced by an overt act of levying war 'at and near' Batoche on 26 March and other days, a charge applicable to either high treason or treason-felony.[58] There was no reference to the relevant legislation. A full indictment procedure involving a grand jury would have clarified details of the charges before trial, and under the 1696 act the defence would have received ample notice.

It is unclear if the government ever intended to proceed against the councillors with high treason charges. Again, Campbell's instructions anticipated guilty pleas once sufficient examples had been made (after some convictions, he expected that many accused would plead guilty, and that after thirty or forty convictions the government would consider revising or dropping charges).[59] But the pursuit of 'summary' justice for as many accused as possible developed before Riel's trial, as the prosecutors refined their strategy 'on the ground.' Prosecutors realized early on that they would have trouble making strong cases against the accused other than Riel. On 18 July, Burbidge informed Campbell by telegram that the prosecution had decided to proceed under the treason-felony statute partly because of anticipated difficulties in persuading juries to convict on capital charges.[60] B.B. Osler told his brother, an Ontario appeal judge from whom Osler was asking advice during the proceedings,[61] that the crown wanted to take the easier route of treason-felony prosecutions to avoid the complexities of high treason proceedings.[62]

Burbidge was probably correct in anticipating that high treason charges against the Métis councillors would have resulted in at least some acquittals. Some of the councillors were prominent members of the Saskatchewan business community. Riel was an outsider compared to people such as Emmanuel Champagne and Alex Fisher, whom some jurors might have associated with or done business with. As noted earlier, British experience with jury acquittals in cases involving constructions of high treason was a major reason for creating the treason-felony offence.

The councillors and their lawyers were not told of this change. They believed that they faced high treason charges unless they pleaded guilty to treason-felony. No one was prepared to press matters by calling the government's bluff, especially as Riel's trial unfolded and it appeared that the government was resolute in taking a harsh approach. Councillor Philippe Garnot recalled his lawyer telling him: 'The Crown has offered that if you plead guilty, you will be charged with treason-felony. But, if you refuse, you will be charged with high treason and several of you will be executed.'[63] Unlike the prosecutors, the defence team led by W.V. Maclise concluded that the crown had ample evidence for high treason convictions before Regina juries. One of the lawyers, Daniel Carey, wrote Archbishop A.-A. Taché: 'The Crown has decided to indict them all for High Treason, and the proof in every case being complete, and the Regina juries being very hostile, we have no doubt that sentences of death would be recorded against them all.'[64]

The church took a leading role in the cases of the councillors, and the priests had considerable influence among the North-West Métis. Archbishop Taché hired Winnipeg lawyer Daniel Carey to assist the councillors; the excitable Father Alexis André was giving them advice. For the church and its priests, Louis Riel had not merely committed treason against the queen. Much more important, he had committed treason against the pope. Riel had declared that the Church of Rome had fallen and the mantle of St Peter resided with Montreal bishop Ignace Bourget (who died just before the Riel trial began).[65] Riel encouraged the Métis to adopt new liturgies, and he had physically taken control of the church at Batoche on 19 March.[66] The priests had strong motives to persuade the councillors to plead guilty. By pleading guilty, they would be confessing their sins, renouncing Riel and his new religion, and returning to the bosom of the true church. It was necessary for the priests to portray the Métis councillors as ignorant dupes of the deluded Riel rather than as true converts to a heretical religion.

One of the temporary holdouts to the plea-bargain deal was Philippe Garnot, who was secretary of the 1885 provisional government, a French Canadian who had been not long in the North-West.[67] He was probably not so much under the sway of the local priests as were his comrades. When Garnot announced he intended to fight the charges, 'Father André then had the goodness to tell me that I would be hanged.'[68]

The main group of Métis councillors was brought before the court on 4 August, just after Riel's trial finished. That group all pleaded guilty. It was only then that there was clear reference to a felony offence, as the court clerk recorded the plea and declared: 'You say you are guilty of the felony with which you stand charged.'[69] Prosecutor Christopher Robinson then requested delay for submissions on sentencing.

The remaining charges against a relatively small number of prisoners used the same formulation of intending to levy war as evidenced by overt acts of actually levying war or, in a few cases such as Scott's, treasonous letters. Three councillors held out against the plea bargain, Moïse Ouellette for one day (5 August)[70] and Garnot and Alexis Lombarde until 12 August, before pleading guilty.[71] Despite the clarification of 4 August, it appears that the apprehension of capital charges of treason continued. As Garnot recounted: 'I told them that I could not consider myself guilty and could not conscientiously plead guilty and that, if I was hanged, it would be more as a victim of the hatred for my nationality.'[72]

More courageous counsel might well have challenged the crown in many of these cases, especially the cases of the holdouts. But they bowed to what seemed a merciful offer, and the defence team Maclise led focused on the relatively simple task of preparing affidavits to present mitigating circumstances for the sentencing.[73] Most of those who had been prisoners of the Métis defendants, such as Métis Charles Nolin and surveyor John Astley, made out positive affidavits about their treatment at the hands of the accused. Fathers Vital Fourmond, Louis Cochin, and Alexis André demonized Riel as an instigator who seduced the hapless Métis from their allegiance to the crown and the true church.[74] Archbishop Taché wrote a confidential letter to Judge Richardson pleading for compassion for the Métis.[75]

The parallel between Riel's heresy and treason reinforced the ideology or symbolic public rhetoric of justice tempered by mercy. Spiritual confession complemented the secular objectives of justice and, with guilt acknowledged, the men threw themselves upon the mercy of both God and Ottawa.

By 13 August, the affidavits were complete. On the following day, eleven prominent Métis (Garnot, Pierre Parenteau, Pierre Henri, Maxime Lépine, Albert Monkman, Philippe Gariepie, Alexandre Cayen or Cadieux, Jim Short, Baptiste Vandal, Pierre Vandal, and Maxime Dubois) were sentenced to seven years' imprisonment. Moïse Ouellette, Pierre Gariepie, and Alexander Fisher received three years and four others were sentenced to a year (Joseph Arcand, Ignace Poitras the elder and the younger, and Moïse Parenteau). Eight, including Alexis Lombarde, were conditionally discharged. The crown decided not to proceed against six others, including André Nolin whose father, Charles, was the crown's star witness in the Riel trial.[76]

A few other Métis remained in jail, but none faced trial apart from Magnus Burston. On 8 September, Louis Goulet appeared in court on charges of treason-felony in relation to the Frog Lake killings,[77] along with five others from Breysalor, near Battleford, implicated with Poundmaker's Indians (Charles and James Bemner, Henry and Baptiste Sayer, and William Frank). All were released because of insufficient evidence.[78] Proceedings against Abraham Montour and André Nault, implicated along with Goulet in events at Frog Lake, were repeatedly delayed until 5 October because of problems with witnesses. Then, Burbidge informed Maclise of a telegram that indicated the minister's decision to stay proceedings by issuing a nolle prosequi.[79] Of these comparatively minor cases, Burston, the last treason-felony trial heard by Judge Hugh Richardson, stands out because of the questions it raised.[80]

Magnus Burston: Hardly Even a Participant

Métis Magnus Burston was an employee of Duck Lake storekeeper Hillyard Mitchell who had gone to Batoche on 21 March as an emissary from North-West Mounted Police (NWMP) Inspector Lief Crozier. Mitchell continued to work for Crozier during the early part of the rebellion, and he left Burston in charge of the store while he was away.[81]

Burston was an extremely minor character during the rebellion. He had clearly not been involved in any fighting, and he was certainly not a leader, nor even a person of influence. It is difficult to know now why the crown bothered to proceed against him. Historians have almost entirely ignored the prosecution of Magnus Burston, but the proceedings illustrate a number of issues that flowed through all trials in 1885.

The crown charged Burston with intending to levy war as evidenced by two rather vague, unspecific overt acts. The crown alleged that Burston had, on 26 March and other days, conspired to levy war at Duck Lake. This was to be supported by evidence that Burston assisted the Métis looting Mitchell's store and that he had a hand in setting Mitchell's house on fire. The crown also alleged that Burston had, on 3 April and other days, further conspired to levy war at Duck Lake. That was a reference to evidence it hoped to produce linking Burston with the rebels at Batoche.[82] On the first overt act, defence evidence would strongly challenge the crown evidence. On the second, the crown produced almost no evidence at all.

D.L. Scott appeared for the crown in the Burston case. He was the weakest among the prosecution team in the courtroom, but he was also responsible for organizing the evidence before Burbidge and the others arrived from the east.[83] Ill-prepared for the Burston case, he did not, for example, know the locations of some things that were familiar to anyone with knowledge of the area.[84] T.C. Johnstone of Winnipeg appeared for Burston. He had been the junior member of Riel's defence team, but he had previously handled the sensational Connor murder case that raised the question of jurisdiction in capital cases.

Johnstone elected trial by judge alone for Burston. No evidence exists to show why he did that. The crown's case was weak and the defence case was reasonably strong, but Burston faced a judge whose misunderstanding of the treason law could result in conviction on weak evidence. Johnstone might have been wary of the attitude of Regina juries towards Métis and Indians. But in mid-September, a Regina jury acquitted Chief White Cap after hearing evidence that was significantly stronger than that the crown had against Burston, on charges that were much more connected with actual fighting.

As they had in the case of Tom Scott, another non-combatant charged with treason-felony, the crown presented evidence that a rebellion had occurred. Two prisoners of the Métis, John Astley and William Tompkins,[85] testified that the Métis 'were in open rebellion,'[86] the purpose of which was 'to start a new government.'[87] Astley also testified that, while he was prisoner at Duck Lake on 26 March, he saw Burston 'going backwards and forwards in the [Mitchell's] store with the half-breeds whenever they wanted any stuff out.'[88] But then he testified, on direct examination, that he could not see the store from where he was being held; he merely saw Burston going towards the store.[89] Astley said that he saw Burston subsequently at Batoche, but 'he was just walking around' unarmed.[90] He further testified that Hillyard Mitchell told him that he had left Burston in charge of the store.[91]

The crown's main witness was Métis Patrice Fagnant, who had extensive contact with Burston at Duck Lake on 26 March. He testified in French at length, but his testimony was highly confusing and unreliable. No one in the court appears to have known how to deal properly and effectively with translated evidence. D.L. Scott directed his questions to the translator rather than through the translator to the witness, with the result that most of the crown's evidence amounted to hearsay given by the translator.[92] Surprisingly, Johnstone did not object to this, and Judge Richardson said nothing. Johnstone's cross-examination was inconsistent in this regard.[93]

Several buildings were set ablaze at Duck Lake on 26 March, beginning with the telegraph office and including Mitchell's store and house. Fagnant testified that Burston contributed to burning down the house.[94] He said that an initial fire in Mitchell's house was burning out when Burston went into the house and relighted it with pieces of paper.[95] Defence witnesses very strongly challenged that evidence, testifying that Burston was not even inside Mitchell's house. On cross-examination, Fagnant testified that Burston directed him to take windows off the house to save them for Mitchell and that he removed a hand rake from the property.[96]

The defence called seven witnesses. Six of them were examined in either French or Cree, but the translation problems were not acute because the testimony was brief, establishing that Burston did not participate in the Battle of Duck Lake nor was he subsequently associated with the rebels.[97] Indian Department farm instructor John Tompkins also testified for the defence. He said that Burston removed from Tompkins's farm some of Tompkins's property and some government property to protect it during the rebellion.[98] Using archival sources other than the prosecution's files, Beal and Macleod conclude that Burston had removed many of the goods from Mitchell's store and taken them to his own home for safekeeping before the Métis seized the town of Duck Lake.[99] The defence did not produce witnesses to this, and, under the rules of the day, Burston could not testify in his own defence. One would think, though, that Hillyard Mitchell, who had testified in other cases, was available to the defence, and it is surprising he was not called as a witness.

As the crown closed its case, Johnstone asked the judge to discharge Burston for lack of evidence, on the basis that, though he may have been present, he in no way aided and abetted treason. There was no need for defence evidence, Johnstone said: 'The only evidence against him is the evidence of the last witness [Fagnant] and I submit that unless his evidence is corroborated your honor could not convict; and the evidence of Mr. Tomkins [sic] merely shows that although he had a gun on the day of the rebellion [26 March] he was not at the fight at all. He was taking charge of these buildings; and afterwards, the evidence of this man Fagnant shows that he took the windows off the building to save them for Mr. Mitchell, so that the only evidence given goes to show that the prisoner was there in the performance of the duty of looking after Mr. Mitchell's property.'[100] The evidence against Burston was his presence. He appeared to be merely doing his job and not in any way aiding and abetting treason. As we noted earlier, during the trials of the Indians accused of treason-felony in 1885, defence lawyer Beverly Robertson attempted to challenge Judge Richardson's understanding of the treason law, most pointedly at the end of the trial of Chief White Cap, where he noted that a person's mere presence during rebellion did not constitute evidence of treason and that evidence was required of actually aiding and abetting rebellion.[101]

Richardson dismissed Johnstone's request for a discharge by saying: 'I think I shall call upon you, Mr. Johnstone, for your defence. Of course it is not necessary, even that the man should have arms. You will recollect those Fenian cases, where a man was with the party, a newspaper reporter and a doctor. I think the prisoner will have to exculpate himself.'[102]

The Fenian cases of 1866 did not say what Richardson thought they said. Evidence in those cases showed that the reporter and doctor might not have been at the events merely in their professional capacities but rather may have been leading Fenians themselves. The judges in those 1866 cases ruled that there was enough evidence of that to go to a jury, not that mere presence was sufficient in itself.[103] There was a significant difference between how Richardson applied his fundamental misunderstanding of the treason law in the previous cases and in Burston's case. In previous cases, he had expressed his view generally during directions to the juries, in a manner that was not technically a matter of record and therefore difficult to appeal. In the Burston case, he made an explicit ruling on Johnstone's submission. That could have been a clear matter of appeal, if the judge had done his legal duty and noted it as part of the trial record. But Judge Richardson did not note it.[104] It appears, as happened previously, that the judge crafted the record to protect himself against appeal.

Richardson made another ruling during the Burston trial, when Johnstone objected to part of Scott's re-direct examination of John Astley about a conversation Astley had with Hillyard Mitchell.[105] Richardson began to note evidence of the contentious conversation but quickly had second thoughts and crossed out what he had written, without getting to the objection or his ruling on it.[106] It appears, as happened during the trial of Thomas Scott, that the judge deliberately edited the record.

Neither the crown nor the defence summed up at the end of the Burston trial, but Johnstone made a technical objection to the wording of the information, noting that the matter could still be raised at that late stage: 'I submit the information is insufficient, as it does not give the words of the statute, it does not use the word "feloniously," and the want of the word "feloniously" in an information for larceny is held to be fatal. The same rule should govern in informations for treason.'[107] Johnstone did not press the matter, suggesting that it might be a clerical error, but uncharacteristically Judge Richardson noted the objection.[108] On appeal the matter would have been the fault of the prosecution, not the judge. There was to be no appeal, since Richardson reserved his judgment and acquitted Burston two days later. But the matter indirectly raises a question that goes to the heart of the cases of summary justice. If full indictments had been the norm in the North-West Territories, and defence counsel had been less intimidated by Riel's trial and looked more carefully at the precise charges the crown intended to pursue, would as many men have pleaded guilty?

THE WHITE REBELS

The prosecution team from Ottawa faced a major political hurdle when they arrived in Regina near the beginning of July 1885. More than eighty Indians and forty Métis were in jail waiting for trial, but only two white men had been charged, Will Jackson and Tom Scott. The newspapers, especially the Conservative-leaning Toronto *Mail*, were running stories about 'white rebels' whom the government had not bothered to capture. Instead, it was victimizing downtrodden Indians and persecuting French-speaking Catholics who stood up for their rights, so said sections of the popular press, especially in Quebec. Justice Minister Alexander Campbell's instructions were emphatic: 'It may be, and from the information which the Government has, it seems probable, that the rebellion has been encouraged actively by whites, particularly of Prince Albert. Nothing in the whole duty entrusted to you is, I apprehend, more important than that we should, if possible, find out some of the men who have, with far better knowledge than the half-breeds and Indians, stirred them up to rebellion and your special attention is asked to this point.'[109] This matter, aside from preparation of the Riel case, was the major priority for the prosecution team. But the prospects of finding white rebels who could convincingly be charged with treason-felony did not look good.

Categories such as white, half-breed, and Indian were widely used, but communities in the North-West in 1885 were complex, something easterners did not appreciate. Racial background was often less significant than community identification.[110] Tom Scott was a white man, but he was associated with the English half-breed community. Will Jackson was in the process of joining the Métis community. Philippe Garnot, who was tried with Riel's other councillors, was a French Canadian who joined the Métis community at Batoche. Despite their association with other communities, Jackson and Scott were important to the government's prosecution team because they were Protestant English-speakers who could be portrayed as white settlers.[111]

The government's preoccupation with this element of the rebellion reflected more than a concern for the appearance of equal justice for all rebels regardless of background.[112] The government was anxious not only to deal with criticism in Quebec but also to discount the view that rebellion was an expression of more general dissatisfaction with the government's administration of the territories. Western discontent involved complex and sometimes contradictory tensions. Balanced against sensitivities about the perception of racial and linguistic bias, the need for salutary examples from active disaffected white settlers, and the impression of equal justice for all rebels was the danger of admitting that western alienation ran deep and well beyond the marginalized.

North-West grievances went beyond Métis concerns about land and economic and cultural rights. They extended beyond the boiling discontent in Indian communities brought on by the disappearance of the buffalo and the lack of assistance they knew had been promised in the treaties but not delivered. White settlers were demanding political and economic reform. In 1883 and 1884, for example, segments of the Manitoba and North-West Farmers' Union proposed either seceding from confederation and forming a new colony or inviting the United States to annex western Canada, views that later fuelled the newspaper stories of settler involvement in the rebellion.[113] The Métis were drawn into supporting the emerging settler resistance in circumstances that were very different from their resistance to the Canadian takeover in 1869–70. Riel's appeal for Indian support badly frightened many farmers and immigrants, as Riel knew it might, destroying prospects of a broad front.[114]

Investigations focused initially on documents that government troops captured at Batoche. These yielded sufficient evidence to charge Scott and Jackson, but Burbidge sought out more evidence and other suspects. Two investigators were sent to Prince Albert to conduct interviews, and newspapers were pressured to reveal sources about other white rebels. The crown decided to proceed quickly against Jackson when consensus emerged about his insanity.

The information prepared against Jackson, the first to be preferred for treason-felony in 1885, was carelessly written. It had been prepared, when the prosecution team began organizing the trials, as a model for all the treason-felony charges.[115] But the drafter simply took the only full formulation of a treason-felony charge contained in *Archbold's Pleading*[116] and worded it so that Jackson was charged with intending to depose the queen, as evidenced by an overt act of intending to levy war.[117] Such a complex formulation might lead to trouble if a rigorous defence were mounted. What the drafter had apparently not noticed was that *Archbold's* added in italics: 'Add counts charging a compassing to levy war, in order to compel the Queen to change her measures and counsels, or otherwise according to the facts.'[118] The prosecution team quickly simplified the informations. By the time the first of the Métis councillors came to court, the informations charged the defendants with intending to levy war, as evidenced by overts acts of actually levying war, but, as noted earlier, they did not explicitly state that the prosecution was under the treason-felony statute.[119]

It is a requirement in treason trials (except for purely conspiracy allegations, which were not at issue for the events of 1885) that the crown prove actual levying of war, not merely contemplated levying of war. During most of the treason-felony trials of 1885, the crown paid only cursory attention to the requirement that there be evidence of actual rebellion. But, in the prosecution of Thomas Scott, it was clear that Scott had not even been at the scene of actual fighting. The crown, therefore, had to show that his activities contributed to actual war.[120] The first two witnesses the crown called at the Scott trial had been prisoners of the Métis at Batoche and testified about the fighting.[121] But they did not testify about the intent of the fighting, which was also a requirement, and neither the crown nor defence called witnesses who could capably testify about the Métis object in taking up arms, whether it was, in law, riot for redress of local grievances or levying war for a broader purpose.[122]

William Henry Jackson: Dealing with an Unhinged Agitator

At first glance, William Henry Jackson seemed to be an important part of solving the government's political problems and confronting accusations of selective prosecution. He was from Prince Albert, allegedly a hotbed of white rebellism.[123] A political radical, a young, energetic agitator for all worthy causes, he was secretary of the Settlers' Union, one of several such groups in the west that had been badgering Ottawa for reforms. He was also the personal secretary to Louis Riel.[124]

Jackson had been active during the months leading up to the 1885 rebellion, trying to gain white settler support for Riel and the Métis movement. He wrote and signed one of the most obviously treasonous of Riel's communications, a plea for help from the Indians written as rebellion broke out, which began: 'Justice commands us to take up arms.'[125]

The problems of prosecuting Jackson as a white rebel became apparent the moment he was arrested, when the Battle of Batoche ended on 12 May. Jackson was not found with the fighters or among the Métis families. He was found imprisoned with the men the Métis had captured. General Frederick Middleton soon learned that Jackson had been confined because Riel believed his young disciple had become insane as the rebellion began.[126] After his capture, Jackson's behaviour seemed to confirm Riel's diagnosis.[127]

William Henry Jackson grew up in a strict Methodist environment in Wingham, Ontario. While he was taking classics at the University of Toronto, the Jackson family encountered financial difficulties and moved west to Prince Albert. Will's father, Gething, became a homesteading farmer. His brother, Eastwood, became the town's pharmacist. Will dropped out of university in 1883 to join them, and immediately became involved in the volatile world of western Canadian politics.[128]

Jackson visited Louis Riel as soon as Riel returned to Canada in the summer of 1884, and the two became close friends. Riel and the South Branch Métis, on the South Saskatchewan River near Prince Albert, were delighted to have the well-educated, well-spoken, and enthusiastic young man on their side. Jackson moved to the South Branch and lived at the home of Moïse Ouellette, one of the community's leaders, where he fell in love with sixteen-year-old Rose Ouellette.[129]

The early months of 1885 were intense for Will Jackson, and the events probably brought latent mental instability to the fore. He believed in the philosophy of American activist Henry George, the single-tax, all-property-should-be-held-in-common Prophet of San Francisco who was popular at the time, especially among radical labour groups. George attributed all man's problems to the evil of rent. But Louis Riel, who called himself the Prophet of the New World and was Jackson's new hero, promoted a finely tuned philosophy of Aboriginal title, something that directly contradicted George's philosophy.[130] By his own account, Jackson's arguments with Louis Riel on this point drove him to the verge of insanity.[131]

Jackson faced a bigger intellectual conundrum in early 1885. In order to marry Rose Ouellette and to become closer to Riel and the Métis, he converted to Catholicism. For his family, that was the moment Will became entirely insane.[132] For strict Methodists such as the Jacksons, the pope and everything papist were evil, and so, from their point of view, Will had forsaken any hope of salvation. One could not possibly do that voluntarily – one had to be insane. Jackson struggled with all this, trying to reconcile the Sermon on the Mount[133] (which Methodists saw as a call to social action and not as encouraging obedience to secular authority) with his newfound belief in papal infallibility.[134]

Then, another blow added to Jackson's intellectual dilemmas. Riel announced that Rome had fallen and the new pope was Montreal bishop Ignace Bourget.[135] Jackson was trying to balance Jesus Christ's Sermon, Pope Leo XIII, and Riel's new pope. He had also come to believe that Riel had supernatural powers.[136] By the time he got to Regina after the rebellion, it was obvious to everyone that Jackson was not just eccentric; he was not in his right mind. From jail, Jackson wrote a letter to Lieutenant Governor Edgar Dewdney, who dutifully forwarded it to Prime Minister Macdonald with the helpful comment: 'I think he *is* crazy.'[137] Even the editors of the Toronto *Mail*, who had been pushing stories of white rebels, thought Jackson was non compos mentis, that he 'is now said to have become quite imbecile.'[138]

When B.B. Osler arrived in Regina in July, he received a letter from Liberal opposition leader Edward Blake whom Jackson's parents had contacted, pleading with him to intervene to get help for their son.[139] The crown had a strong case against Jackson. Review of the Batoche papers yielded ten documents implicating him directly in the rebellion and interviews yielded three witnesses to his activities at the rebel camp, though he had not taken part in any fighting.[140] But on 18 July, prosecution team leader George Burbidge asked NWMP physician Augustus Jukes to assess Jackson's mental state, along with a local doctor of Jukes's chosing, Robert Cotton. By 21 July, Burbidge had decided that Jackson was legally insane and the crown should accept a plea of not guilty by reason of insanity. He asked the doctors to advise whether it would be in Jackson's interest to send him to an asylum in hope of a cure or simply to return him to the care of his family. He also asked if 'the excitement and strain which may be produced by his trial is likely to be attended by serious results.'[141] Burbidge might have been worried too that, if the prosecution waged a full trial against Jackson, forcing his lawyer to try to make the insanity defence successful, the government might be viewed as persecuting an insane white man for the sake of having a white man in the dock, something that would add to the political problems.

The doctors recommended Jackson's committal to the Selkirk asylum in Manitoba,[142] a step that would necessitate a formal, if perfunctory, trial. Burbidge worried about how Jackson might be treated. On 21 July he telegraphed prominent Winnipeg lawyer J.B. McArthur: 'Have had reports from surgeon respecting Jackson. If you will come at once think his case can be disposed of. You had better make enquiries as to what conveniences are afforded for insane prisoners in the temporary asylum at Selkirk.'[143] Jackson's father, Gething, had retained McArthur, writing: 'Willie received such cruel treatment at the hands of Riel that his mind is quite unhinged and he is sinking into idiocy.'[144]

Jackson was the first of the 1885 accused other than Riel to be tried. His case, which came to trial on 24 July during a break in the Riel proceedings, seemed simple. According to everyone involved, except the man himself, Jackson was crazy. When he came to court, he refused to answer to his name and declined to answer any other questions. But after the charge was read, he said: 'As far as responsibility of mine about what you call rebellion, I have always declared myself perfectly responsible, that is to say, as Riel's secretary, and I wish to share his fate whatever that may be.'[145] Jackson probably was not volunteering to be hanged; he knew very well that was not a possibility.[146]

Despite the crown's strong case against Jackson, evidence of his participation in the rebellion was merely alluded to during his trial. Prosecutor B.B. Osler called Eastwood Jackson, Will's brother, whom the Métis had incarcerated along with Will and other prisoners. Eastwood's testimony was brief; he was obviously trying to be very cautious where his brother was concerned, and the lawyers did not press him. He testified that 'from the time he was christened in the Roman Catholic Church he has been insane.' Asked to elaborate on cross-examination, Eastwood referred to his encounter with his brother at Batoche shortly after the Battle of Duck Lake on 26 March. 'He hardly knew me when I first saw him, he was always praying,' and, from 'his general actions and appearance,' Eastwood knew he was insane. He said that Will 'became worse after his capture by Middleton.'[147] Eastwood Jackson had previously given the prosecution team a lengthy deposition. The deposition was much more candid than was the testimony he gave from the witness box. In taking the deposition, the prosecutors were more interested in Eastwood's knowledge of the activities of Chief Big Bear (who had a meeting with Riel in 1884 at the Jacksons' Prince Albert home, above Eastwood's drug store[148]), Louis Riel, and various Métis. But in the deposition, Eastwood made one telling comment about his brother's state-of-mind. Eastwood had been among a group of Prince Albert residents whom the Métis allowed to retrieve the bodies of the dead from the battlefield at Duck Lake. He took that opportunity to go to Batoche to see his brother. Will was so disconnected from reality, Eastwood said, that he did not even know that rebellion had broken out and people had lost their lives in a battle:

My brother did not seem at that time to know anything of the battle and I doubt whether he even knows of there having been any blood spilt.

My reason for thinking my brother did not know of any battle having occurred was the fact that he offered to carry a parcel to William Napier in Prince Albert whom I knew at the time to have been slain in the battle and whose body was amongst those bodies in the sleigh waiting for us at the door.[149]

For Jackson's defence, J.B. McArthur called the two doctors, Jukes and Cotton, who had reported to Burbidge. Cotton mentioned that he had spoken to Albert Monkman, one of the Métis leaders, and to Louis Riel about Jackson's condition at the time of the rebellion. But the doctors' testimony mainly concerned his mental state at the time they examined him. Jukes's testimony was the more detailed of the two:

Q. What do you say as to his mind? A. When he was first brought down he showed occasional symptoms. I was under the impression that he was insane, not only from my own observation but from what I heard and from what I was told by the officer who came down with him from Batoche. During the time he has been in the guard room, on account of the quiet and repose since he came down, he improved very much, and I formed the impression that he would be restored with proper treatment. Since the commencement of the arrangements for this trial, news of which reached him, I have noticed that he is very much worse. To-day I consider him better than at any time for four weeks, but I am still under the same opinion that he is laboring under a mild form of insanity, which is curable under proper treatment ...

Q. [by Osler on cross-examination] Is he so insane that it would be fair to say he was not responsible for his actions? A. There are times when I consider he would be quite responsible. To-day he spoke and reasoned with me in a manner that was very clear, but only three days ago he was dazed; his mind seems to be dazed. I don't think that to bring him at a moment's notice that he would be capable of conducting his trial or doing justice to himself in any manner.

Q. To a considerable extent your opinion is that he could not control his actions? A. I have never seen anything about him to give me the impression that his actions were uncontrollable, it is rather his mental hallucinations, his ideas. He holds peculiar views on religious matters in connection with this trouble, and in connection with the new religion of which he thinks Riel is the founder, and which he thinks it is his duty to sustain.[150]

The jury found Jackson not guilty by reason of insanity. He was committed to the Selkirk Lunatic Asylum. There, the medical superintendent, David Young, did not consider him a very serious or dangerous lunatic and allowed him a fairly free rein. On 1 November 1885 Jackson simply walked away from the asylum and went to the United States to continue his colourful career as an 'Agitator, Disturber, producer of Plans to Make Men Think, and Chronic Objector,' under the name Honoré Joseph Jaxon, a person born in a buffalo-hunting camp among the Métis.[151]

Sandra Bingaman has emphasized the contrasts between how issues of mental state were handled at Riel's trial and Jackson's trial, and indeed the French press later seized upon Jackson's fate compared to Riel's as an example of discrimination against French-speakers.[152] The key difference was that there was consensus about Jackson. Was Will Jackson 'really crazy'? In 1885 the science of psychiatry was in its infancy, but the doctors who examined him, the prosecutors, his family, his friends, Louis Riel, and his lawyer probably had the correct instincts.[153]

Thomas Scott: No White Rebel

With a failure to find other white rebels who could convincingly be charged with treason-felony, and Jackson in the lunatic asylum, the prosecution team was left with trying to make the strongest possible case against Tom Scott.[154]

Scott was a leading figure in the English-speaking communities between the Métis settlements at the South Branch and Prince Albert.[155] Those communities included Red Deer Hill and Halcro, near the South Saskatchewan River about two-thirds of the way from Batoche to Prince Albert. They were collectively known as The Ridge, the name used in the charges preferred against Scott, and included the Lindsay school and the St Catharine's church/school where the community held meetings in 1885. Scott was from the Orkney Islands. He came to western Canada in the 1870s in the employ of the Hudson's Bay Company (HBC).[156] He left the HBC to become a manager with Stobart and Company, a major merchant firm in the North-West.[157] He was also a farmer, and his 300-acre farm was considered one of the most prosperous in the area, on very valuable and strategic land.[158] Shortly after the rebellion, he married Mary Jane Isbister, the daughter of English Métis leader James Isbister, one of the four-man delegation that went to Montana in 1884 to bring Louis Riel back to Canada. In 1885 Scott was living on his farm at The

Ridge with his mother-in-law and was postmaster at Kirkpatrick, west of Prince Albert on the North Saskatchewan River, some distance northwest of The Ridge.[159]

Scott was a very active link between The Ridge communities and the Métis, and in gaining English support for the Métis agitation.[160] But when rebellion broke out, Scott did not participate and may have tried to help the government forces. The NWMP arrested Scott and held him in the Prince Albert jail, although General Middleton released him on his own recognizance when he arrived at Prince Albert.[161]

The strongest evidence the crown had against Scott was a letter he had probably written on 23 March, three days before the Battle of Duck Lake but well after the Métis had begun organizing the rebellion and taking prisoners,[162] to the Métis at the South Branch. It read: 'At a meeting held at the Lindsay school to-night, which was largely attended, the voice of every man was with you, and we have taken steps which, I think, will have a tendency to stop bloodshed and hasten a treaty. We will communicate with you inside of forty-eight hours after you get this. Notify us of any steps, if any is liable to take place.'[163]

A few days before this meeting, The Ridge communities had sent a delegation led by Scott to the South Branch to see what the Métis were planning. The delegation returned with a letter from Riel and the Métis to which the one quoted above was a reply:

The Ottawa Government has been maliciously ignoring the rights of the Original Half-Breeds [meaning both English half-breeds and Métis] during fifteen years. The petitions which have been sent to that Government on that matter and conserning [sic] the grievances which all classes have against its policy are not listened to, moreover the Dominion has taken the high-handed way of answering peaceful complaints by reinforcing their Mounted Police. The avowed purpose being to confirm in the Saskatchewan their Government & usurpation of the rights and liberties of all classes of men except these assistant oppressers [sic] the Hudson's Bay Company and Land Speculators.[164]

The letter from the Métis was mild in tone but it ended with the statement: 'Justice commands [us] to take up arms.' The Ridge communities held a number of meetings during this period. The strong consensus appears to have been to continue voicing support for Métis rights but to stay out of any fighting.[165]

The prosecution team knew their case was weak. They sent their Scott file to Stephen Brewster, an English solicitor living at Prince Albert, for a second opinion. Brewster reviewed the evidence and suggested the charges be dropped:

The case against Scott seems to be founded as far as I can judge on suspicion with perhaps a little ill feeling combined, he no doubt is a man who has taken considerable interest in the movement so lately taken by many in this district with regard to obtaining what they considered their legal rights and which up to a certain point they advanced by constitutional means, and he no doubt is a man somewhat biggotted [sic] and rum sighted: and has spoken in a tone somewhat louder than his fellows[;] that he has not criminated himself I am unable to say, but from the evidence adduced I cannot advise that his case be proceeded with at present.[166]

Not only could the crown investigators find no stronger evidence against Scott, but, despite their best efforts, they could find no other white rebels. The fact is that there were no white rebels. There were a number of whites who sympathized strongly with the plight of the Métis and Indians, and quite a large number who agreed with Louis Riel about such things as provincial rights. There were a large number who voiced grievances about timber dues and land regulations. The prosecutors charged Tom Scott, against the advice of their outside assessor, because he was the only person they could find (aside from the insane Will Jackson) who might, just possibly, be made to look like a white rebel.

The Conservative-leaning Toronto *Mail*[167] propagated the myth of the white rebels in the North-West. The newspaper published a series of six long articles in June and July, penned by correspondents 'W.G.' and 'F.B.M.,' both of whom claimed to be from Prince Albert.[168] The series concluded that the rebellion was 'the outcome of cold-blooded calculation on the part of Riel and his white associates.'[169] It decried 'the operations of those white rebels, against whom the Minister of Justice has not yet thought fit to proceed.'[170] For most of the series, the authors did not put many names to specific actions, with the exception of allegations against Gething Jackson, Eastwood Jackson, Will Jackson, and Tom Scott, the easy targets.[171]

If any of the specific, serious allegations presented in the *Mail*'s series had been true, the crown's investigators would have found evidence during their work leading up to the trials.[172] Prince Albert residents organized the 1884 meeting at which Riel spoke. Some Prince Albert residents probably donated money to help bring Riel back to Canada in 1884. Will Jackson canvassed Prince Albert for signatures for the Métis Bill of

Rights.[173] But beyond that, the prosecution team found not an iota of evidence for any of the claims. No evidence is extant in the prosecution files or in any other archival records to support the allegations. The disconnect between the results of their investigations and the stories in the *Mail* exasperated the prosecution team at Regina. B.B. Osler demanded to know who wrote the stories, threatening to charge the newspaper as an accomplice to treason if it did not provide names.[174] The white rebels series ended abruptly on 6 July.[175]

Scott's trial began on 8 September and ended on 10 September. He was not charged with taking up arms himself. In fact, the evidence from both crown and defence showed that he had opposed taking up arms. Proof was required of overt acts and the crown had to prove that his activities led to war, in addition to his having the intent to levy war.[176] He was charged with activities that allegedly had the effect of aiding and abetting those in arms at Batoche.[177] Except for the Riel trial, Scott's was the longest and most thorough; the crown and defence each called nine witnesses.[178] The trial was also remarkable for what Beal and Macleod describe as 'one of the most bombastic speeches ever heard in a Canadian courtroom.'[179]

At the beginning of the Scott trial, defence lawyer H.J. Clarke presented an argument that the North-West Territories courts did not have jurisdiction, as had Riel's lawyers.[180] But he did it in a much different way. He emphasized such things as eighteenth-century treaties between Britain and France (Utrecht in 1713 and Paris in 1763), the Royal Proclamation of 1763, the Quebec Act of 1774, the Constitutional Act of 1791, and the Jurisdiction Act of 1821. It was a clever historical discourse that left the easily perplexed Judge Richardson wondering if Clarke was arguing that the North-West was under French jurisdiction, rather than Canadian or British.[181] In reply, B.B. Osler dismissed Clarke's analysis as an 'interesting historical lecture.'[182]

Crown witness John McNiven, who lived in the neighbourhood of The Ridge, testified that he had attended the 20 March meeting at the Lindsay school and that Scott chaired it. He further said that the meeting secretary, William Miller (who would be a defence witness), had declared that the Métis of the South Branch were in arms. According to McNiven, the meeting was called 'to see what steps might be taken for the settlers as a rule to protect themselves against the outbreak.' He said that the meeting resolved to send a delegation to the South Branch and that the meeting ended with three cheers for the delegation and three cheers for Louis Riel.[183] The crown called no other witness to that meeting.

The crown called also William Craig, who had been secretary of a meeting at the St Catharine's school on 22 March. He testified extensively, but cautiously, about that meeting.[184] He said that he warned the English half-breeds about the dangers of siding with the Métis, that the fight was not between the Métis and the police but between rebels and Canada. However, he also testified that he knew most of the English half-breeds would not fight against their Métis cousins and that the best hope was to persuade them to remain neutral. On cross-examination, he agreed with defence lawyer W.V. Maclise's suggestion: 'You stated that you knew the position of neutrality was blameable, but yet was the best that could be done.'[185] Craig said that NWMP Commissioner Acheson Irvine later told him that 'he thought I had done the best that could be done under the circumstances.'[186] Craig also testified that Scott had described the letter sent by the South Branch Métis meeting. H.J. Clarke objected because the crown had not produced the letter but Richardson allowed the testimony because Craig described what Scott had said the letter said rather than the letter itself.[187] Craig's most contentious testimony concerned a course of action that Scott allegedly suggested at the meeting. Volunteers had organized at Prince Albert and gone to reinforce the police at Fort Carlton. Scott, said Craig, suggested that the volunteers should lay down their arms. 'The expression used was to leave the French half-breeds and mounted police to settle the matter among themselves.'[188] When it came their turn, the defence would put a different colour on what Scott had suggested and meant.

Of all the meetings the English Métis held among themselves at The Ridge and with the Métis at Batoche, the most important was that of 23 March at the Lindsay school and concerned the letter that was the cornerstone of the crown's case. But the crown led no evidence about the meeting itself or the context of the letter, presumably content to leave inferences as to its meaning and context up to the jury, assisted, of course, by B.B. Osler's interpretation during his closing address.

Witness Tom McKay was at Batoche when Scott arrived there on 21 March leading the three-man delegation from The Ridge. He had accompanied storekeeper Hillyard Mitchell from Fort Carlton with a message from NWMP Superintendent Lief Crozier to Riel.[189] Except for establishing Scott's presence (he recognized Scott's voice but said he did not actually see him at Batoche that day), McKay's evidence did not do much.[190] The crown also called a young clerk from the Winnipeg post office to identify Scott's signature on documents allegedly produced in his capacity as Kirkpatrick postmaster.[191] H.J. Clarke objected strongly to the evidence of Charles Tuck, whom he derided as a 'cabin boy'[192] and a 'sweep,'[193] who could not even testify that Scott even was a postmaster, let alone identify handwriting. As its last witness, the crown called as a handwriting expert former banker A.L. Lunen.[194] On direct examination, Lunen identified Scott's signature on documents presented to him, including the contentious 23 March letter. But Clarke easily confused him on cross-examination, including presenting him with one or two forgeries of Scott's signature.[195] The crown also led evidence of one alleged event that happened before any of the overt acts contained in the information against Scott. John Astley testified that he had seen Scott in Prince Albert on 17 or 18 March in the company of H.S. Moore, who organized the volunteers to reinforce the police at Fort Carlton.[196] Astley said that Scott was encouraging Moore not to raise volunteers 'but let the police and halfbreeds have it settled between themselves.' The defence strongly challenged that testimony in its own evidence, and Astley was not a reliable witness. He had appeared as a crown witness in other rebellion cases, where he was prone to exaggeration and was developing a reputation as the crown's 'hired gun,' as H.J. Clarke was to point out.[197]

When the crown closed its case, Clarke told the judge that since the crown had failed to show that Scott was in even the most remote degree identified with an act of rebellion, there was no case of levying war to go to the jury.[198] Judge Richardson refused to stop the trial.[199] Clarke then asked advice. He wanted to open with an address to the jury, but he needed to be careful, especially in case of an appeal. Prosecutor B.B. Osler advised that it was proper to open with an address before calling defence evidence, but if he did so, he would be confined in his closing address to simply summing up defence evidence: 'The inconvenience that I have found in defence is that you cripple your reply by your being confined to summing up your evidence, but in the Riel case they opened and closed that way.'[200]

Clarke wanted to put the defence evidence in a political context, and he wanted the jury to have the context before they heard the evidence. He wanted to take a page from the playbook of the famous English state trials defence lawyers by not only advocating for his client but advocating for his client's cause. He had probably read the legendary Thomas Erskine's defence of Lord George Gordon after the 'Gordon Riots' of 1780.[201] The mobs Gordon incited attempted to burn down London, but, as with Thomas Scott, Gordon's intent was peaceable political protest, and he tried to calm his followers when they got out of hand. Erskine's defence was said to have 'not only instantly dispelled all feeling of exhaustion and lassitude from the minds of the Jury, the Judges, and the bystanders, but, while he spoke, they all seemed to be inspired with a new etherial existence, and they listened as if addressed by some pure intelligence of heaven, who had appeared to instruct them.'[202] Clarke sought to emulate that performance, and, in the view of the *Manitoba Free Press*, nothing in the history of Canadian state trials could compare to his opening speech:

The Scott trial will probably be the most memorable of the state trials; at all events it is proving the most interesting to spectators. There were several scenes in the court to-day between Messrs. Clarke, Q.C., and Osler, Q.C., and altogether it was the most stormy session witnessed since the commencement of the trials. Objections were taken time and again by the defense and all the rulings were against the Crown. As the case stands at present Scott is virtually acquitted, and to-morrow will probably see the end of the case. Clarke spoke for three hours, and his is considered the greatest speech of the whole trials. It was a strong indictment against the Dominion Government.[203]

Clarke began by putting his client squarely in the history of struggles against tyranny, not someone passively waiting for justice but one who actively sought justice, peaceably, of course. He traced the history of the western grievances against Ottawa, grievances that Clarke said the government had ignored for fifteen years. He told the jury that the crown was alleging that the people of the west had no grievances at all and that it was the defence's duty to show the opposite:[204]

Now, gentlemen, when we are told that these people had no grievances, I admit that it is but my simple duty to prove to you that they had grievances, that they had very strong grievances, that men who were in the prime of life fifteen years ago, the father [sic] of young children, that their sons have grown up to be young men with their families in turn around them, and that the man who was in the prime of life fifteen years ago is now old and grey, and his life nearly worn out, and still the claim that he had to the piece of waste land in the North-West Territory he is still waiting for the adjustment of; and we are told by the representatives of the Crown that these people had no grievances![205]

The grievances were, of course, not at issue in Scott's trial for treason-felony. The crown was not alleging that the people of the west had no grievances against Ottawa, and it was not the duty of the defence to show that they did. The only legal issues concerned Scott's actions, and whether those actions contributed to a levying of war with intent to levy war.

But, as Beal and Macleod write: 'Clarke knew that a good political speech might move a jury ... He might have suspected even that one or two on the six-man jury harboured a secret wish that they had had the courage to do what Scott had done.'[206] Clarke told the jury that, when the Métis of the South Branch took up arms, the people at The Ridge quite naturally tried to find out what was happening 'and by that means to be in a position to preserve the peace and to avoid the shedding of blood.'[207] Clarke continued to heap scorn on the crown evidence, especially the handwriting evidence. He also took the crown to task for arguing the subthesis that it was illegal to advocate neutrality during a treasonous levying of war, that it was everyone's duty to inform the authorities of treasonous plots and otherwise to do everything possible to aid the government. If that were true, Clarke said, then NWMP Superintendent Lief Crozier and Commissioner Acheson Irvine should be charged. Scott was no more guilty of treason-felony than they were.

Not only had the crown presented weak evidence, Clarke told the jury, but it had failed in a fundamental duty. The crown prosecutors had deliberately chosen not to expose the jury to the best possible evidence, evidence that was easily available to them. If Scott was connected with the Métis outbreak, Clarke asked, why did the crown not put Louis Riel in the witness box, or Philippe Garnot, the secretary of the Métis provisional government at the South Branch?

Clarke tackled one strong piece of evidence the crown had presented, John Astley's testimony that Scott suggested to H.S. Moore that the Prince Albert volunteers lay down their arms. Clarke said that Astley was lying, and that Scott's view of the activities of the volunteers was entirely different than Astley suggested, a point he was preparing to lead evidence about.

Two men who had been delegates with Scott from the Lindsay school meeting of 20 March to Batoche appeared as defence witness. Farmer Hugh Ross and Cree William Paquin testified that little actually happened at the Lindsay meeting.[208] The meeting resolved to send the delegation to the Métis 'to see what the state of affairs was, to see if it was true' that the Métis were in arms, Paquin testified.[209] William Miller, who had been secretary of that meeting, testified that the delegation was sent simply to find out what was happening so that settlers at The Ridge could prepare to defend themselves if necessary.[210]

Crown witness John McNiven had testified that the 20 March meeting had ended with three cheers for the delegation and three cheers for Louis Riel,[211] but all three defence witnesses to that meeting did not support him. Paquin and Miller said they heard no cheers at all.[212] Ross testified that he heard cheering outside the school after the meeting, but he did not know the reason for it.[213] Tom McKay had been the crown's only witness to the activities of the delegation from The Ridge at Batoche on 21 March but his testimony was very weak, as we have seen.[214] The basis of all the crown's allegations against Tom Scott was that he had aided and abetted the Métis in rebellion. The only instance the crown presented of Scott actually being in the company of Métis was 21 March, and it is significant that the crown did not present evidence stronger than that of McKay. Ridge delegate Hugh Ross testified that Scott told Riel: 'He would have nothing to do with him after he took up arms.'[215] Even stronger evidence in Scott's favour came from storekeeper Hillyard Mitchell, who had been at Batoche on 21 March as an emissary from NWMP Superintendent Crozier. He testified: 'The prisoner [Scott] said he had been sent there by the English half breeds to find out the cause of the disturbance and get them to stop and disperse, and that if they did not stop they would get themselves into trouble, and they were endangering the lives of the settlers. That is all the prisoner said to me.'[216] While crown witness William Craig had testified that, at the St Catherine's meeting on 22 March, Scott suggested that the volunteers from Prince Albert who had gone assist the police at Fort Carlton put down their arms and remain neutral,[217] defence witness Andrew Whitford testified that was not at all what Scott had suggested. Scott, Whitford said, was worried that, with most of the able-bodied men and most of the arms from Prince Albert moved to Fort Carlton, the town was left defenceless and open to attack from the Métis or Indians.[218]

The defence team thought that their best witness would be the man who organized the meetings on 22 March. Anglican minister Edward Matheson was the first witness they called, but his testimony was not as strong as Clarke and Maclise hoped it would be. Matheson had gone to Fort Carlton on 21 March to hold Sunday services there the next day. When he arrived, Thomas McKay, on behalf of NWMP Superintendent Crozier, asked Matheson to organize meetings at The Ridge.[219] It is obvious that Matheson was a reluctant witness in court. His testimony was exceedingly cautious and unforthcoming, to the extent that Osler thought he was deliberately suppressing evidence. Matheson felt differently about the events than he revealed in the witness box.[220] His problem was that he was terrified of being accused of treason himself. Shortly before the trial began, he wrote to Tom McKay begging him to back up his story, to make sure that everyone knew that Matheson had been acting directly on

Crozier's orders, 'to contradict any charge of disloyalty or rebellion made against my people or myself.'[221] Matheson's surest evidence was about what Scott suggested regarding the Prince Albert volunteers.[222] On cross-examination, B.B. Osler pressed Matheson on that point, but the minister stood his ground. Scott wanted the volunteers to return to Prince Albert, but 'No, not laying down arms.'[223]

In its evidence, the defence ignored entirely the controversial letter of 23 March. They did lead some evidence of the meeting at which the letter was composed, but only to establish that efforts were made to transmit resolutions from that meeting to Crozier at Fort Carlton.[224] On cross-examination, the crown also avoided the letter. Perhaps the prosecutors were afraid of what they might hear if they asked about it.

The theory the defence put forward was that Scott, in his discussions about what the Prince Albert volunteers were doing, had the defence of The Ridge and Prince Albert in mind, and that his suggestions were perfectly sensible in the circumstances. They had excellent evidence in that regard. Defence witnesses testified that the English half-breeds and the people of Prince Albert were afraid of an attack from the Indians. With men and arms removed from Prince Albert to Fort Carlton, that attack was more likely, and more likely to succeed.[225] The defence underlined the strategic location of The Ridge as the point where all three trails converged from the south on the way to Prince Albert.[226] The defence also led evidence that Scott attempted to fight on the government's side in the rebellion. On 26 and 27 March, Albert Porter was at William Miller's house at The Ridge, next door to Tom Scott's farm, attempting to tap into the telegraph line to secure transmissions between Fort Carlton and Prince Albert. Porter testified that Scott arrived there and asked him to telegraph the NWMP commander at Prince Albert with his offer to raise 150 to 200 men 'for the purpose of fighting against the Indians and rebels in defence of Queen and country.'[227]

Clarke's final address to the jury on 10 September was short, and relatively dispassionate by his standards. As B.B. Osler had told him before his opening address, he was restricted to summarizing his own evidence in closing. But Clarke just could not stick to the rules. He spent most of his address heaping scorn on the crown's evidence, especially that concerning the 23 March letter.[228] He lectured briefly on the absurdity of treason law.[229]

Osler's closing address was an anticlimax that Clarke enjoyed interrupting. Osler seems to have been resigned to losing. That did not result from Clarke's bombast, which would have little effect on B.B. Osler. It was the result of the essential weakness of the crown's case. Osler spent most of his address going over the evidence of the 23 March letter. He chided Clarke for suggesting that the crown did not bring its best evidence to court. Louis Riel was a condemned man and would not be a competent witness. He also reiterated the crown's contention that neutrality on the part of the English half-breeds amounted to aiding the Métis rebellion. If Scott had threatened Riel that the English half-breeds would fight for the government, there would have been no rebellion, according to Osler.[230]

On paper, some evidence of Scott's treason-felony looked good, but in practice in the courtroom, even on direct examination, it was borderline at best. The defence witnesses were strong, and H.J. Clarke was stronger. The defence was careful to rebut every crown allegation, covering the four overt acts alleged against Scott more thoroughly than the crown did. The two highly experienced counsel, Osler and Clarke, sparred and insulted one another frequently.[231] It is clear that defence counsel Maclise disliked Osler and, as a westerner, sympathized with lawful agitation for redress of grievances.[232] Maclise often tried to get evidence in through the back door by asking open-ended questions of defence witnesses. He asked about events of 1884, well before the chronology of the overt acts alleged against Scott. He regularly lapsed into leading questions on direct examination. 'You are leading him all the time, it is awful,' Osler sputtered at one point.[233] Maclise and Clarke consistently pushed the boundaries through their questioning. The defence was trying to deflect the jury's attention away from specific actions towards the general frustrations with Ottawa that had been building for years, frustrations the jurors themselves might have felt.

As noted earlier, Judge Richardson was reluctant to rule on the numerous objections. His rambling charge to the jury in the Scott case was bizarre in places (asserting he was not a 'creature'), demonstrated a negligent attitude towards the law (expressing his impatience with the 'verbiage' of the Treason-Felony Act), and, in his 'general and cursory' review of the evidence, failed to explain the relevance of the letter that was key to the crown's evidence of treason and a major point of contention between counsel.[234] After deliberating for thirty minutes, the jury acquitted Tom Scott, to no one's surprise, except perhaps Judge Richardson's. The spectators cheered.[235]

CONCLUSION

Although the two white anglophones who were most directly connected to the rebellion were not found not guilty, there is no evidence that the outcomes of the Jackson and Scott trials were the direct result of a discriminatory agenda. Nevertheless, this failure to bring the settler element of the rebellion to account compromised the image of even-handed justice in symbolic terms, a setback to key objectives of the government's prosecution strategy. There are also doubts about the success of the government's other objectives in its orchestration of the 1885 proceedings. Resistance was squashed but did the proceedings reflect a fully legitimate exercise of the rule of law? They certainly did little to calm grievances or solidify prairie allegiance to Ottawa.

Jackson and Scott benefited from influential advocates and effective counsel, something that could not be said for most of the other accused. There would be other instances of questionable judicial conduct. But, unlike the Scott case, this would clearly work against the accused, who faced jurors who came from different communities, who were less likely to identify with the accused, and who were more likely to regard the accused with suspicion. In this manner, privilege and identity gave real meaning to the presumption of innocence and the benefit of reasonable doubt.

The Riel trial has always been the focus of popular and scholarly commentary. But the other cases are rich with legal and constitutional issues and reflect the complexity of the grievances that precipitated the 1885 crisis. The crown consistently pursued the harshest options that were practically available. The prosecution team was highly capable, and, with the exception of Clarke in the Scott case, they outperformed defence counsel, a pattern that is amply illustrated in the two following chapters in this volume. Judge Richardson's incompetent conduct of the Scott trial proved true to form, his uncertain grasp of the law to be manifested in the other treason felony trials he presided over. Though defence counsel Beverly Robertson was confident of Chief Big Bear's prospects the day following Scott's acquittal, he underestimated the damaging impact of Richardson's approach to treason law. In the larger scheme, most of the treason convictions in 1885 were obtained by a summary form of justice, as the Métis councillors were coerced into confession by the threat of high treason and the prospect of the terrible fate that Riel faced.

NOTES

1 See RG 13, F2 (Records Relating to Louis Riel and the North West Rebellion, 1873–1886), LAC, for complete lists.
2 See Bob Beal and Rod Macleod, *Prairie Fire: The 1885 North-West Rebellion* (Edmonton: Hurtig 1984), chapter 17.

3 Campbell to J.A. Macdonald, 18 May 1885, MG 26A (Macdonald Papers), vol. 197, 82814, LAC.

4 Macdonald to Campbell, 19 May 1885, MG 27, I, C2 (Campbell Papers), LAC.

5 Campbell to Burbidge, Robinson, Osler, Casgrain, and Scott, 20 June 1885, *CSP*, 1886, no. 43, 12; Campbell to Burbidge, 20 June 1885, MG 26A, vol. 197, 82880, LAC. The instructions, reproduced in this volume's Supporting Documents, were made public in response to an address of the House of Commons requesting all instructions and communications sent by the government to Judge Richardson, staff of the court, and prosecution counsel. The Department of Justice responded that no such communication was given by the minister of justice or officer of the Department of Justice to Judge Richardson or to court staff. *CSP*, 1886, no. 43, 11.

6 25 Edw. III st.5 c.2 (England).

7 For a through discussion of the historical development of the treason of levying war, see Bob Beal, 'Attacking the State: The Levying War Charge in Canadian Treason Law,' MA thesis, University of Alberta 1994.

8 11–12 Vic. c.12 (U.K.).

9 31 Vic. c.14.

10 A draft information against Riel specified four counts under the Fenian Act and one for murder ('Draft Charge under 31 Vic c.14 & for Murder,' RG 13, F2, 2644–50, LAC). For more details, see Beal, 'Attacking the State,' 93–4. As Beal notes (93, citing examples that included Winnipeg *Daily Times*, 18 May and 19 June 1885; *Canada Law Journal*, 21 June 1885), public opinion seemed equally divided between the appropriateness of the Fenian Act and the treason-felony statute, while few commentators expected trials for high treason under the Edward III statute.

11 As explained in the chapter by Desmond Brown and Barry Wright in this volume, allegiance could be extended by way of a finding of British birth held to prevail over subsequent naturalization (natural allegiance) or residency under the temporary protection of the crown (local allegiance). The legislation created levying-war offences that could be tried in the regular courts as an alternative to military justice.

12 Beal, 'Attacking the State,' 93–6. See also Jeremy Ravi Mumford, 'Why Was Louis Riel, a United States Citizen, Hanged as a Canadian Traitor in 1885?' *CHR* 88, no. 2 (2007): 237.

13 George R.D. Goulet, *The Trial of Louis Riel: Justice and Mercy Denied* (Calgary: Telwell 1999).

14 D.H. Brown, 'The Meaning of Treason in 1885,' *Saskatchewan History* 28, no. 2 (1975): 65.

15 See Supporting Documents (1868 treason-felony legislation); George W. Burbidge, *A Digest of the Criminal Law of Canada* (Toronto: Carswell 1890), 55–6;

Criminal Code, 1892, 55–6 Vic. c.29 s.65. Burbidge had obtained the 1877 edition of Fitzjames Stephen's Digest in 1883. It assisted him in the preparation of the Revised Statutes and in devising responses to the 1885 crisis, and it was the basis of his published Digest started in 1887. See the Brown and Wright chapter in this volume.

16 English laws were received in the territories with the Hudson's Bay Company's 1670 charter. Under the North-West Territories Act (43 Vic. c.25), neither English laws passed after reception in 1670 nor Canadian law applied automatically apart from those set out in the statute itself. The statute of Edward III therefore applied through reception in 1670 rather than by virtue of Canada's jurisdiction. The complex processes of colonial reception of English law are examined in more detail in F. Murray Greenwood and Barry Wright, 'Introduction: State Trials, the Rule of Law, and Executive Powers in Early Canada,' of *CST 1*, 3–51; and, in the context of the North-West, in the chapter by Knafla in this volume.

17 36 Geo. III c.7 (U.K.). See the Brown and Wright chapter in this volume for details.

18 31 Vic. c.69.

19 43 Vic. c.25 s.76.

20 See J.M. Bumsted's chapter in this volume, and Beal and Macleod, *Prairie Fire* 292–4, 297. To guard against attempts to free Louis Riel, Minister of Militia and Defence Adolphe Caron ordered him sent for trial at Winnipeg. Campbell and Burbidge quickly pointed out that Riel could not be tried in Manitoba (after 1880 the Manitoba courts served only as a route of appeal). Caron changed his instructions accordingly to avoid a technical error in the government's case, not as a design to deny Riel a full, half-French-speaking jury, as some have argued.

21 Territorial jurisdiction in capital cases under the 1880 act had been challenged in the murder case of James Connor but his conviction was upheld on appeal, and Connor was executed days before Riel's trial. (Connor is named 'John' in Beal and Macleod, *Prairie Fire*, and Beal, 'Attacking the State.') See 'The Queen v. James Connor,' RG 13, F2, LAC ('Magistrate's report re James Connor murder of Henry Mulaski at Moose Jaw, North West Territories on 6 April 1885'); *Manitoba Law Reports* 2 (1885): 235. See also *The Queen v. Louis Riel, Manitoba Law Reports* 2 (1885): 321, and *Riel v. the Queen, Appeal Cases* (1885), 675.

22 Alexander Campbell, 'Memorandum respecting the case of the Queen v. Riel, prepared at the request of the Committee of the Privy Council, 25 November 1885,' *CSP*, 1886, no. 43, 2–11. This position was accepted by the Privy Council in *Riel v. the Queen, Appeal Cases* (1885), 675.

23 While the special treason trial provisions were not adopted in the 1689 Bill of Rights (1 Wm. & Mary sess.2 c.2), they were introduced with the 1696 Treason Trials Act (7–8 Wm. III c.3).

24 Beal, 'Attacking the State,' 39–42; James Ray Phifer, 'The Reform of the Use of Political Crime in England, 1689–1696,' PhD thesis, University of Colorado 1975; Alexander H. Shapiro, 'Political Theory and the Growth of Defensive Safeguards in Criminal Procedure: The Origins of the Treason Trials Act of 1696,' *Law and History Review* 11 (1993): 215.

25 The charges were under the under the analogous offence of lawless aggression. See Barry Wright, 'The Kingston and London Courts Martial,' in *CST 2*, 130–59.

26 Desmond Brown describes Burbidge as the 'guiding hand' of the 1885 prosecution. 'He was largely, if not wholly, responsible for arranging that Riel alone among the accused was charged under the medieval English statute of treasons … rather than under the Canadian treason-felony statute.' *DCB*, 13:135–6.

27 Patrick Brode, 'Christopher Robinson,' *DCB*, 13: 882–4. For J.B. Robinson: Patrick Brode, *Sir John Beverly Robinson: Bone and Sinew of the Compact* (Toronto: University of Toronto Press 1984).

28 Patrick Brode, 'Britton Bath Osler,' *DCB*, 13: 795–6; Beal and Macleod, *Prairie Fire*, 292.

29 Desmond Morton, ed., *The Queen v Louis Riel* (Toronto: University of Toronto Press 1974), xii; Beal and Macleod, *Prairie Fire*, 292.

30 Beal and Macleod, *Prairie Fire*, 296–7.

31 Ibid., 331; Beal, 'Attacking the State,' 104. Some commentators on the Riel trial, such as Desmond Morton and J.M. Bumsted, are also critical. Shelley Gavigan takes a favourable view of Richardson, based on her recent assessment of his activities in more routine cases and administration of 'low law.' See Shelley Gavigan, 'Criminal Law on the Aboriginal Plains: The First Nations and the First Criminal Court in the North-West Territories, 1870–1903,' SJD thesis, University of Toronto 2008, 86–94. Thomas Flanagan asserts that Richardson's 'competence and conscientious dedication remain unquestioned,' a statement with which we, obviously, disagree strongly. See Thomas Flanagan, 'Hugh Richardson,' *DCB*, 14: 870–2.

32 'Hugh Richardson,' Henry J. Morgan, *Canadian Men and Women of the Time: A Handbook of Canadian Biography* (Toronto: William Briggs 1898), 856.

33 Early in his career as a North-West Territories judge, Richardson demonstrated his carelessness and irresponsibility towards the law during a peculiar soap opera that entertained the citizens of Battleford. Richardson's daughter, a minor, fell in love with North-West Mounted Police Constable Henry R.

Elliott and the parents objected to the romance. Elliott and three other constables took the young woman from Richardson's home, and Elliott married her.
Richardson charged Elliott with the offence of abducting an heiress against
her will (24–5 Vic. c.100 s.53) and offences under the Mounted Police Act
(32–3 Vic. c.20 s.54). See Wilbur F. Bowker, 'Stipendiary Magistrates and the
Supreme Court of the Northwest Territories, 1876–1907,' in Marjorie Bowker,
ed., *A Consolidation of Fifty Years of Legal Writings, 1938–1988* (Edmonton: University of Alberta, Faculty of Law 1989), 708.

   Elliott and two other constables then deserted, taking with them a prisoner,
government horses (including one belonging to NWMP Inspector James
Walker, Elliott's commanding officer), and other government property. The
group headed to the United States, but some months later Elliott surrendered
at Fort Walsh in the Cypress Hills and was tried on theft charges at Battleford
in December 1878. Inspector Walker appeared as prosecutor, victim, and main
crown witness and Hugh Richardson tried the case. Newspaper proprietor
Patrick Gammie Laurie wrote: 'The Stipendiary Magistrate [Richardson]
charged the jury at some length, and very strongly against the prisoner, after
which the jury retired. After about five minutes' deliberation they returned a
verdict of Not Guilty.' *Saskatchewan Herald*, 30 Dec. 1878, 1, 7.

34 Louis A. Knafla, 'Charles-Borromée Rouleau,' *DCB*, 13: 907–9. 'Legal scholarship was the hallmark of his judicial career. His library contained an outstanding collection of legal sources and texts. He had all of the major British,
Canadian, and American treatises covering the full range of legal actions, a
complete set of Canadian and territorial law reports, and all the Canadian
statutes in both French and English editions. On the bench he revelled in the
trial process.'

35 2 Geo. IV c.66 (U.K.).

36 *CSP*, 1886, no. 52, 'Queen v. Jackson,' 340.

37 Ibid., 344.

38 *CSP*, 1886, no. 52, 'Queen v. Scott,' Hillyard Mitchell evidence, 132.

39 'Trial of Louis David Riel[,] High Treason[,] Rebellion 1885. At Regina before
Judge Richardson[.] July 20th 1885,' 'Queen v. Scott,' MG 3, D1–2 (Louis Riel
Collection), 65–66, AM. The title here is that on the first page of this document. The first few pages of the document consist of very carefully worded
and neatly handwritten (not in Richardson's hand) instructions to the judge
and the court clerk covering nineteen points from beginning to end of the
Riel trial. For example: '5. S.M. [Stipendiary Magistrate] – Ask Prisoner if he
has been furnished with a copy of Charge, Panel of Jurors, and list of witnesses for the Prosecution. 6. Clerk – (Arraign Prisoner) Louis Riel, you stand
charged as follows. – (Read Charge).' Following the script for the Riel trial are

Richardson's own notes for all the 1885 trials over which he presided. When this document reached the Archives of Manitoba, it was not identified as containing the judge's notes, but it is clear that this is what it contains. In citations following, we refer to this document as 'Richardson trial notes.'

40 Richardson trial notes, 'Queen v. Scott,' MG 3, D1–2, 54–74, AM.

41 *CSP*, 1886, no. 52, 'Queen v. Scott,' Charles Nolin evidence, 152.

42 Ibid., William Paquin evidence, 145.

43 As Bob Beal points out in 'Attacking the State,' British and Canadian judges sometimes did give out-of-the-ordinary or biased jury directions in treason cases. But Richardson's behaviour seems to have been without direct precedent.

44 *CSP*, 1886, no. 52, 'Queen v. Scott,' Hugh Richardson directions, 169.

45 Ibid. This was likely a reference to the provision in the North-West Territories Act mandating the judge to himself pick the jury panel. 43 Vic. c.25 s.75 ss.9.

46 Ibid.

47 Ibid.,169–70.

48 Ibid.,170.

49 Ibid.,171.

50 Ibid.,172.

51 *CSP*, 1886, no. 52, 'Queen v. Big Bear,' Hugh Richardson directions, 230–3; Beal, 'Attacking the State,' 104. This construction extended liability in a fashion similar to less serious cases of riot involving assemblies for the redress of local grievances.

52 Bob Beal covers this in 'Attacking the State,' 104–9. He also covers more generally in that work the development of the aiding-and-abetting rule.

53 7–8 Will. III c.3 (U.K.).

54 In common law jurisdictions, the term 'summary justice' usually refers to non-jury trials before magistrates. Here, the term is used more generally to denote the exploitation of abbreviated regular procedure (six-man juries presided over by a judge who lacked independence and expertise) and the deliberate management of proceedings to promote plea bargains or coerced confessions.

55 See Robin Clifton, *The Last Popular Rebellion: The Western Rising of 1685* (London: M.T. Smith 1985), chapter 8.

56 1 Vic. c.10 (Upper Canada) aimed to avoid having the courts bogged down with time-consuming trials and to reduce the risk of acquittals by encouraging confessions in return for assurances of lenient treatment. In both England and Upper Canada, such assurances proved false in many cases. For Samuel Lount and Peter Matthews in 1838, it led to the noose: see Paul Romney and Barry Wright, 'The Toronto Treason Trials, March-May 1838,' in *CST 2*, 62–7 and 88.

57 See Supporting Documents (Campbell to Burbidge, Robinson, Osler, Casgrain, and Scott, 20 June 1885, *CSP*, 1886, no. 43, 12).

58 *CSP*, 1886, no. 52, 'Queen v. Parenteau and Twenty-Five Others,' 368–9.

59 See Supporting Documents (Campbell to Burbidge et al.).

60 Beal, 'Attacking the State,' 101; Beal and Macleod, *Prairie Fire*, 308; Burbidge
to Campbell, 18 July 1885, RG 13 F2, letterbook, LAC.

61 'Featherson Osler,' Morgan, *Canadian Men and Women of the Time*, 788.

62 Osler to 'Fern,' 2 Aug. 1885, F 1032, Mu2303, AO. The two-witness rule for
cases of high treason did not apply in cases of treason-felony.

63 'Mémoire de Ph. Garnot (1886, Février),' 71.220, PAA.

64 Carey to Taché, 3 Aug. 1885, RE 3641, SAB.

65 'Petite Chronique de St. Laurent. Extraite du registre pour la Mission de
St. Laurent établie en 1871 sur la branche Sud de la Saskatchewan proche
Carlton,' R 500, 125/1a, SAB. This is a copy of the original in 71.220,
PAA.

66 Beal and Macleod, *Prairie Fire*, 142–3.

67 Donatien Frémont, *Les Secrétaires de Riel: Louis Schmidt, Henry Jackson, Philippe
Garnot* (Montreal: Éditions Chantecler 1953), 123–4.

68 'Mémoire de Ph. Garnot (1886, Février).'

69 *CSP*, 1886, no. 52, 'Queen v. Parenteau and Twenty-Five Others,' 369.

70 *CSP*, 1886, no. 52, 'Queen v. Quellette,' 344–5.

71 *CSP*, 1886, no. 52, 'Queen v. Lombarde and Garnot,' 337–8.

72 'Mémoire de Ph. Garnot (1886, Février).'

73 See *CSP*, 1886, no.45c, 'Return to an address of the House of Commons for
copies of all the depositions or other evidence submitted in favour of Half-
breeds or Metis … 13 May 1886.'

74 *CSP*, 1886, no. 52, 381–408. Henry J. Clarke later claimed he had actually
written the affidavits of André, Fourmond, and Nolin. George F.G. Stanley,
Louis Riel (Toronto: Ryerson Press 1963), 342. That is unlikely; the affidavits
read differently. In any case, the claim must be put in the context of Clarke's
penchant for exaggeration and self-aggrandizement, as well as the fact that he
made the claim while trying to persuade John A. Macdonald to appoint him
to the bench.

75 Taché to Richardson, 11 Aug. 1885, RE 3641, SAB. Taché labelled the letter
'Strictly Confidential' and wrote: 'I know it is a delicate matter to interfere
with the exercise of your important functions, and it is for this reason that I do
so in a strictly confidential way. No one knows that I am writing to you.' Taché blamed the federal government for the rebellion rather than, as his priests
were doing, Riel. That undoubtedly resulted from Taché's lingering bitterness
resulting from the Manitoba Act negotiations of 1870 and the subsequent Riel

amnesty controversy. Raymond J. A. Huel, *Archbishop A.-A. Taché of St. Boniface: The 'Good Fight' and the Illusive Vision* (Edmonton: University of Alberta Press 2003), 103–41.

76 Affidavits and Sentences, *CSP*, 1886, no. 52, 381–408; see table compiled from this source in the volume's Supporting Documents.

77 *CSP*, 1886, no. 52, 'Queen v. Louis Goulet,' 346–7.

78 *CSP*, 1886, no. 52, 'Queen v. Charles Bremner et al.,' 347–8. If the crown had known what would happen, it might have tried harder to convict Charles Bremner. While Bremner was in jail at Battleford, General Middleton and some of his officers pilfered Bremner's furs as spoils of war. An outraged Bremner complained all the way to a select committee of the House of Commons, and Middleton was forced to leave Canada in disgrace. Desmond Morton, 'Frederick Dobson Middleton,' *DCB*, 12: 798–802; Frederick Middleton, *Parting Address to the People of Canada* (Toronto: Hunter, Rose 1890).

79 *CSP*, 1886, no. 52, 'Queen v. Abraham Montour and Andre Nault,' 338-40.

80 Two treason-felony trials were held at Battleford subsequently before Judge Charles Rouleau. Beal, 'Attacking the State,' 108–9.

81 Beal and Macleod, *Prairie Fire*, 143–4, 153.

82 *CSP*, 1886, no .52, 'Queen v. Burston,' 348–9.

83 Louis Knafla, 'David Lynch Scott,' *DCB Online*, http://www.biographia.ca.

84 For example, D.L. Scott did not know the location of Henry Walters's store (on the west side of the South Saskatchewan River across from Batoche). *CSP*, 1886, no. 52, 'Queen v. Burston,' William Tompkins evidence, 352. He appeared confused about the relationship between Scott's home (northeast of Duck Lake) and the village of Batoche. *CSP*, 1886, no. 52, 'Queen v. Burston,' Peter Lavallée evidence, 365.

85 This name is consistently misspelled 'Tomkins' in the transcript.

86 *CSP*, 1886, no. 52, 'Queen v. Burston,' John Astley evidence, 349.

87 Ibid., William Tompkins evidence, 352.

88 Ibid., John Astley evidence, 350.

89 Ibid.

90 Ibid., 351.

91 Ibid., 350.

92 Ibid., Patrice Fagnant evidence, 354–6.

93 Ibid., 356–8.

94 Ibid., 355–8.

95 Ibid., 356–8.

96 The serious difficulties with Fagnant's testimony are illustrated in this exchange on cross-examination (*CSP*, 1886, no. 52, 'Queen v. Burston,' Patrice Fagnant evidence, 358):

Q. Ask him if that was the time that they carried off the hand-rake – the witness and the prisoner?

Mr. Scott – He says he did not carry off a hand-rake.

By Mr. Johnstone:

Q. Ask him if he saw a hand-rake that day? A. No.

Q. He did not see one at all? A. He seen it outside of the house.

Q. Ask him if he took it away when he took the windows? A. No, he went and left it at the mill.

Q. He took the rake away? A. Yes, he took the rake away, and went and left it at the mill – the witness did.

Q. Did he take it away that day, when the buildings were on fire? A. He says that is the time.

Q. Ask him if the prisoner was coming in the gate at the time he was taking the rake away? A. He did not see him coming.

Q. Well, where was he [Burston] personally when he, the witness, took the rake away? A. He says he thought it was the windows you asked him about. He says he never took the little hand-rake; he left it there. He says he meant the windows he took to the mill.

97 Ibid., Peter Levallée evidence, 364–5; Joseph Arcand evidence, 367–8; Moïse Parenteau evidence, 368; Jerome Ledeau evidence, 363; Peter Tourond evidence, 361–2. Jerome Ledeau testified that he saw Burston on the road fixing a sleigh about one hundred feet from Mitchell's house when the telegraph office was burning. Ledeau did not see Burston when Mitchell's house was on fire. But Peter Tourond did. He testified that Burston continued to work on the sleigh on the road the entire time the house was ablaze. Both Ledeau and Tourond testified there were many people milling around the buildings at the time, and they could not tell who was responsible for the fires.

98 Ibid., John Tompkins evidence, 365–7.

99 Beal and Macleod, *Prairie Fire*, 153.

100 *CSP*, 1886, no. 52, 'Queen v. Burston,' T.C. Johnstone submission, 360.

101 *CSP*, 1886, no. 52, 'Queen v. White Cap,' Beverly Robertson address, 55–6.

102 *CSP*, 1886, no. 52, 'Queen v. Burston,' Hugh Richardson response to T.C. Johnstone submission, 360.

103 Beal, 'Attacking the State,' 88–90.

104 Richardson trial notes, 'Queen v. Burston,' MG 3, D1–2, 121, AM.

105 *CSP*, 1886, no. 52, 'Queen v. Burston,' John Astley evidence, 352.

106 Richardson trial notes, 'Queen v. Burston,' MG 3, D1–2, 118, AM.

107 *CSP*, 1886, no.52, Queen v. Burston, Johnstone submission, 368.

108 Richardson trial notes, 'Queen v. Burston,' MG 3, D1–2, 118, AM.

109 See Supporting Documents (Campbell to Burbidge et al.).

110 'Country-born' was also used in the Red River area but 'English Métis' became the preferred term by English-speakers for this community and is what
Riel usually called them. 'Half-breed' is considered derogatory in modern
usage but it was widely used to describe North Americans of mixed ancestry. 'Métis' in French simply means half-breed, a word that can be applied
to people of racially mixed ancestry and even hybrid plants. The English
'half-breed' (mainly of Scottish descent) and French Métis communities recognized each other as cousins, and they sometimes worked closely together.
But there were significant differences between the two communities, most
notably in language and religion but also in economics. In 1885 in the North-
West Territories, there were 20,556 people of British Isles origin; 1,520 people
of French origin; 1,404 English half-breeds; 3,387 Métis; 20,170 Indians; and
1,325 others (mainly European). Canada, Department of Agriculture, *Census
of the Three Provisional Districts of the North-West Territories* (Ottawa: Maclean,
Roger 1886), 10–11.

111 Sandra Estlin Bingaman, 'The Trials of the "White Rebels,"' *Saskatchewan
History* 25, no. 2 (1972): 41–54, surveys these two particular cases. While both
Jackson and Scott reflected the same prosecutorial priority, Bingaman (41)
emphasizes the contrasts. 'Scott's was preceded by vitriolic press war …
whereas Jackson's caused almost no comment until after the Riel proceeding, July 30 to August 1, with which it was then contrasted by the French
papers in Quebec. Scott's trial dragged on for two days … while Jackson's
lasted only a few minutes.'

112 B.B. Osler made a point of this in his opening address at the Scott trial. *CSP*,
1886, no. 52, 'Queen v. Scott,' Osler opening address, 78.

113 Beal and Macleod, *Prairie Fire*, 34–5. In the newspaper coverage following
the rebellion, all the alleged white rebels were said to be Liberals, not a Conservative among them. 'The Rebellion: About the White Rebels Who Co-op-
erated with Riel. Many Double-Dyed Renegades. How They Betrayed First
the Half-Breeds and Then the Government,' Toronto *Mail*, 18 June 1885, 4;
'Riel's White Supporters,' Toronto *Evening News*, 8 July 1885, 1. In response
to the Conservative-leaning Toronto *Mail*'s speculations about 'white rebels,'
the Liberal *Manitoba Free Press* sarcastically called Tom Scott 'a white Grit.'
'Dangerous Proceedings,' *Manitoba Free Press*, 27 July 1885, 2.

114 From the time of his return to Canada in the summer of 1884 to just before
rebellion actually broke out, Riel was very cautious in his dealings with the
Indians. For example, Cree Chief Beardy invited Riel to attend a council at

Duck Lake in July 1884. But Riel would agree only to meet the chiefs a few days before the general council began, seeking to maintain a low profile in his Indian relations. Beal and Macleod, *Prairie Fire*, 114–15. Some white settlers were sympathetic to the Indians' plight, but most had contrary interests and many were also terrified of them.

115 'Draft Charge – Treason Felony,' n.d., RG 13, F2, 3146–61, LAC.

116 *Archbold's Pleading and Evidence in Criminal Cases* (London: H. Sweet 1886), 841.

117 *CSP*, 1886, no. 52, 'Queen v. Jackson,' 340.

118 *Archbold's Pleading*, 1886, 841.

119 *CSP*, 1886, no. 52, 'Queen v. Parenteau and Twenty-Five Others,' 368–89.

120 *CSP*, 1886, no. 52, 'Queen v. Scott,' B.B. Osler opening address, 79.

121 Ibid., evidence of William Tompkins and John Astley, 81–4.

122 This topic is covered thoroughly in Beal, 'Attacking the State.' The crown also called George Young, one of General Middleton's staff officers, for evidence of rebellion and the documents seized at Batoche used during the Scott trial. *CSP*, 1886, no. 52, 'Queen v. Scott,' George Young evidence, 84–5. Charles Nolin was called as a defence witness, and could have testified about this, but he was not asked about it.

123 Riel had been warmly received at a well-publicized meeting in Prince Albert in the summer of 1884. Beal and Macleod, *Prairie Fire*, 112–14.

124 Jackson is the subject of a recent biography by historian Donald B. Smith, *Honoré Jaxon: Prairie Visionary* (Regina: Couteau Books 2007). While we disagree here with some of Smith's characterization of Jackson (Jaxon), and with his analysis of the 1885 proceedings against him, Bob Beal wishes to thank Don Smith for his assistance over many years, particularly in researching the life and adventures of this fascinating historical figure.

125 *CSP*, 1886, no. 52, 'Queen v. Jackson,' 341–2. Riel derived this injunction from Matthew 10:34: 'Think not that I am come to send peace on earth: I came not to send peace, but a sword.' As Beal and Macleod point out, the next verse in Matthew was worrisome for Will Jackson: 'For I am come to set a man at variance against his father, and the daughter against her mother, and the daughter in law against her mother in law.' *Prairie Fire*, 142.

126 Ibid., 165–6.

127 Ibid., 306–7.

128 Smith, *Honoré Jaxon*, 27–31.

129 Beal and Macleod, *Prairie Fire*, 129–30; Smith, *Honoré Jaxon*, 34–43.

130 Beal and Macleod, *Prairie Fire*, 132–3; William H. Jackson to 'My dear family,' 19 Sept. 1885, MG 3, C20–1, no. 4, AM. This long letter contains Jackson's description of this particular intellectual crisis and the others he endured.

131 Will Jackson to Albert Monkman, 2 Feb. 1885. Extracts of this letter are quoted in a letter from his brother, T.E. Jackson, to the Toronto *Globe*, 2 July 1885, 6.

132 *CSP*, 1886, no. 52, 'Queen v. Jackson,' Eastwood Jackson evidence, 342.

133 Matthew 5–7.

134 Jackson to 'dear family,' 19 Sept. 1885, MG 3, C20–1, no. 4, AM.

135 Beal and Macleod, *Prairie Fire*, 142.

136 Jackson to 'dear family,' 19 Sept. 1885, MG 3, C20–1, no. 4, AM.

137 Jackson to Dewdney, 17 June 1885, MG 26A, vol. 107, 43219, LAC.

138 'Riel's Backers,' Toronto *Mail*, 1 June 1885, 4. On the other hand, as Jackson was being escorted to Regina, a *Mail* correspondent reported: 'He endeavours to keep up the crazy dodge, but many think him quite rational.' 'Rebel Prisoners,' Toronto *Mail*, 18 June 1885, 1.

139 Osler to Blake, 1 July 1885, RG 13, F2, letterbook, LAC.

140 RG 13, F2, LAC.

141 Burbidge to Deane, 18 July 1885; 20 July 1885, RG 13, F2, letterbook, LAC. Inspector Richard Burton Deane had charge of the NWMP jail in Regina. Burbidge communicated with the doctors through Deane.

142 The Selkirk asylum was just then being built, and inmates were being housed in a temporary asylum at Lower Fort Garry.

143 Burbidge to McArthur, RG 13, F2, letterbook, LAC.

144 'The Northwest Troubles,' Montreal *Gazette*, 26 June 1885, 1.

145 *CSP*, 1886, no. 52, 'Queen v. Jackson,' 340.

146 Shortly after his escape from the asylum, Jackson sent a letter to his sister, Cicely, enclosing a message for John A. Macdonald in which he offered to hang in Riel's place. But by then he was safely in the United States. Jackson's hometown newspaper, the Wingham *Times*, published the message to the prime minister. It is printed in Louis Blake Duff, 'Amazing Story of the Winghamite Secretary of Louis Riel,' *Western Ontario History Nuggets* 22 (1955): 6–7. A copy of this is in MG 3, C20–2, AM.

147 *CSP*, 1886, no. 52, 'Queen v. Jackson,' Eastwood Jackson evidence, 342.

148 Beal and Macleod, *Prairie Fire*, 116; Smith, *Honoré Jaxon*, 36–8.

149 Thomas Eastwood Jackson deposition, RG 13, F2, 3361–9 at 3666, LAC. The Jacksons probably knew William Napier as a neighbour and through their Liberal connections. Also killed at the Battle of Duck Lake was Skeffingham Elliot, a Prince Albert lawyer and nephew of Liberal opposition Leader Edward Blake. Napier was Elliot's law clerk, a nephew of British General Charles Napier. See Beal and Macleod, *Prairie Fire*, 159.

150 *CSP*, 1886, no. 52, 'Queen v. Jackson,' Augustus Jukes evidence, 343.

151 'The Investigation into the Cause of the Escape of W.H. Jackson, an Insane

Patient, Confined in the Lower Fort Garry Asylum,' *CSP*, 1886, no. 2, schedule 21, 51–5. Curiously, Young argued that he had the authority to keep or release Jackson at his own discretion because Jackson's warrant of committal was the same as those for 'ordinary cases of lunacy.' But the warrant for Jackson's committal seems quite clear, directing the Selkirk Asylum to keep Jackson 'as a dangerous lunatic, until the pleasure of the Lieutenant-Governor ... is known or until the said William Henry Jackson is discharged by law.' MG 3, c.20–1, no. 2, AM. Reading not very finely between the lines of Jackson's letter to 'my dear family' of 19 Sept. 1885, it is obvious he was planning to escape. The self-description used here is from the 29 Oct. 1908 issue of Jackson's newsletter, *Fair Play and Free Play*. Jackson/Jaxon's subsequent career is covered in Smith, *Honoré Jaxon*.

152 Bingaman, 'The Trials of the White Rebels,' 46–7.

153 Jackson's family was most anxious to keep him in treatment, hoping for a cure. After his flight to the United States, the family wanted him recovered and returned to the care of the asylum. While their letters to Dr Young were polite and pleading, their lawyer, J.A. McArthur, was blunt. 'Your conduct in this case will create a great scandal,' he told Young. Cicely Jackson (Will's sister) to Young, 4 Nov. 1885, MG 3, C 20–1, no. 8, AM; A.L. Morrison (Cicely's friend) to Young, 7 Nov. 1885, MG 3, C 20–1, no. 9, AM; McArthur to Young, 10 Nov. 1885, MG 3, C 20–1, no. 10, AM. Will Jackson probably suffered from a condition modern psychiatry terms 'borderline personality disorder' as reflected in his reaction to intellectual and personal stress. From the asylum, he wrote his family: 'I wish to learn two things without further delay, Guitar playing in case of my becoming blind, & wood-carving in order to keep myself in literature should I be confined here for a lengthy period.' Jackson to 'dear family,' 19 Sept. 1885, MG 3, C20–1, no. 4, AM. There was nothing wrong with Jackson's eyesight (he did not even wear glasses). Borderlines such as Jackson can easily convince themselves that extreme improbabilities are real possibilities and typically need to rationalize their actions; simply wanting to learn to play guitar is not enough. Perhaps even more improbable was the fact that voracious reader Will Jackson needed an excuse, learning woodcarving, to keep reading.

154 He was no relation to the Thomas Scott of Red River resistance fame. H.J. Clarke made the point that the government seemed to need an 1885 victim named Thomas Scott. *CSP*, 1886, no. 52, 'Queen v. Scott,' H.J. Clarke opening statement, 122–3.

155 Beal and Macleod, *Prairie Fire*, 146; *CSP*, 1886, no. 52, 'Queen v. Scott,' Hugh Ross evidence, 136; Alexis André evidence, 147.

156 *CSP*, 1886, no. 52, 'Queen v. Scott,' Hugh Ross evidence, 135; H.J. Clarke

opening statement, 112; Agreement between Thomas Scott and the Hudson's Bay Company, 28 Feb. 1870, A.32, vol. 52, HBCA.

157 'The Rebellion' (interview with Thomas Scott), Toronto *Mail*, 13 July 1885, 4.

158 *CSP*, 1886, no. 52, 'Queen v. Scott,' Thomas McKay evidence, 99; H.J. Clarke opening statement, 112. In the winter of 1884–5, Scott sold 150 pigs, 1,500 bushels of oats, 1,600 bushels of wheat, and a quantity of potatoes. 'Riel's Secretary' (interview with Thomas Scott), Winnipeg *Sun*, 23 March 1885, 4. Scott, of course, was not Riel's secretary. The reporter mixed him up with Will Jackson. The account of the interview was written on 17 March, well before the Battle of Duck Lake, from Fort Qu'Appelle.

159 *CSP*, 1886, no. 52, 'Queen v. Scott,' Thomas McKay evidence, 99; John Mc-Niven evidence, 87; 'The Rebellion' (interview with Thomas Scott), Toronto *Mail*, 13 June 1885, 4; Bob Beal's interview with Lyle Jones of Saskatoon, great-grandson of Thomas Scott and Mary Jane Isbister, 9 Dec. 2007. Scott also told the newspaper he was a Conservative, not a Liberal. Scott's first wife's name was Sarah Thompson. She was from Ontario and died in 1882 or 1883. *CSP*, 1886, no. 52, 'Queen v. Scott,' John McNiven evidence, 87. Philosophically, the Métis, especially the more politically knowledgeable among them, were closer to the Conservatives than the Liberals. (Louis Riel was a Conservative member of Parliament.) Conservative philosophy admitted such things as community rights, and Old Tories such as John A. Macdonald believed strongly in the protections of minority rights in the English constitution. In contrast, Liberal philosophy of the day was very much laissez-faire economics with a strong sense of individual responsibility. The 1885 rebellion caused more Métis to vote Liberal than might have otherwise been the case. Diane Payment, *Batoche (1870–1910)* (St Boniface, Man.: Les Éditions du Blé 1983), 104–7.

160 Beal and Macleod, *Prairie Fire*, 146–8.

161 See S.E. Bingaman, 'The North West Rebellion Trials, 1885,' MA thesis, University of Saskatchewan 1971.

162 Beal and Macleod, *Prairie Fire*, 147–8.

163 *CSP*, 1886, no. 52, 'Queen v. Scott,' 61.

164 'To the English Half-Breeds of Red Deer Hill, St. Catharine & St. Paul,' 21 March 1885, in Thomas Flanagan, ed., *The Collected Writings of Louis Riel* (Edmonton: University of Alberta Press 1985), vol. 3, 53–5.

165 Beal and Macleod, *Prairie Fire*, 145–8.

166 RG 13, F2, 2535–7, LAC.

167 John A. Macdonald and John Sandfield Macdonald founded the *Mail* as a Conservative alternative to the Liberal *Globe*. But before 1885, the *Mail* began

professing independence, though it still favoured the Conservatives editori-
ally. Douglas Fetherling, *The Rise of the Canadian Newspaper* (Toronto: Oxford
University Press 1990), 80–1; Paul Rutherford, *A Victorian Authority: The
Daily Press in Late Nineteenth-Century Canada* (Toronto: University of Toronto
Press 1982), 59–61.

168 W.G. stories: Toronto *Mail*, 18 June 1885, 4; Toronto *Mail*, 20 June 1885, 4; Toronto *Mail*, 23 June 1885, 4; Toronto *Mail*, 30 June 1885, 4. F.B.M. stories: Toronto *Mail*, 2 July 1885, 4; Toronto *Mail*, 6 July 1885, 5. Though F.B.M. started
up as soon as W.G. left off, it is unlikely they were the same person. The
writing styles are similar but also significantly different. And F.B.M. seems
to have had not as good a grasp of local affairs as W.G. had, though F.B.M.
wrote that he discussed the matters with W.G. before he began writing. The
Conservative Winnipeg *Times* picked up at least two of the W.G. stories from
the *Mail*: Winnipeg *Times*, 23 June 1885, 3; Winnipeg *Times*, 25 June 1885, 3.
The *Times* also ran two letters-to-the-editor from 'Veritas' of Prince Albert
that were of much the same tenor as the white rebels stories. These letters
were mainly a vicious attack on Prince Albert shoemaker J.C. MacKenzie,
named in the white rebels stories, whose son had been one of the Prince
Albert volunteers killed at the Battle of Duck Lake. Veritas, 'The Grit Agitators,' Winnipeg *Times*, 29 June 1885, 3; Veritas, 'A Nest of Traitors,' Winnipeg *Times*, 10 July 1885, 3. MacKenzie refused to reply to the anonymous
attacks, but he named two employees of the crown timber office in Prince
Albert whom he thought responsible. 'The Prince Albert Rebels,' Winnipeg
Times, 29 July 1885, 1. The series opened with: 'It is well known, at least by
loyal people here, that all the rebels in this insurrection were not in the rifle
pits at Batoche's. White settlers, some of them men in a good position in life,
had quite as much to do with instigating the rising as Riel himself, and perhaps more.' 'The Rebellion,' Toronto *Mail*, 18 June 1885, 4.

169 F.B.M., 'A Nest of Traitors,' Toronto *Mail*, 6 July 1885, 5.

170 F.B.M., 'A Nest of Traitors,' Toronto *Mail*, 2 July 1885, 4.

171 There is a very short, general list in W.G., 'The Rebellion,' Toronto *Mail*, 18
June 1885, 4. The *Mail*'s W.G. wrote that everything had begun with railway
routes. He alleged that Liberals had inside information that the Alexander
Mackenzie government (1873–8) would build the transcontinental through
Prince Albert, and those insiders then bought land along the route. When
the Conservative Macdonald government changed to the southerly route in
1881, the investments of those settlers were destroyed. Those people then
became extremely embittered against the Macdonald government and conspired to raise rebellion against it. W.G., 'The Rebellion,' Toronto *Mail*, 18
June 1885, 4.

172 The crown hired Samuel Bedson, warden of Stony Mountain Penitentiary and transport officer for General Middleton's column during the rebellion, and William P. Sharp to investigate the white rebels' situation at Prince Albert. Burbidge to Bedson and Sharp, 23 July 1885, RG 13, F2, letterbook, 179–80, LAC.

173 All copies of the Bill of Rights were probably destroyed before the rebellion began. None is known to exist. But Beal and Macleod identify a list of demands supplied by a correspondent to the Toronto *Mail* as probably the Bill of Rights. Beal and Macleod, *Prairie Fire*, 135–6. The newspaper called it a 'Revolutionary Bill of Rights,' but there was nothing at all revolutionary about it. Toronto *Mail*, 13 April 1885.

174 Osler to [*Mail* general manager] Christopher Bunting, 3 Aug. 1885, RG 13, F2, letterbook, 229–31, LAC. The newspaper did not divulge the names.

175 F.B.M., 'A Nest of Traitors,' Toronto *Mail*, 6 July 1885, 5. It is obvious that more articles in the series were contemplated, but they never appeared.

176 Beal, 'Attacking the State,' deals with overt acts in the context of treason law.

177 The counts (see Beal and Macleod, *Prairie Fire*, 146–8 for more details) were:

- Compassing and intending to levy war against the queen, at Batoche on 20 March and other days, in order to force the queen to change her measures and counsels;
- Compassing and intending to levy war against the queen, at Batoche on 20 March and other days, in order to put force and constraint on Parliament.

Each of these counts was supported with allegations of the same four overt acts:

- Conspiring and consulting on 20 March and other days to levy rebellion (meeting of the English Métis at the Lindsay school, chaired by Tom Scott, resolving to send a delegation, including Scott, to the South Branch. The wording was designed to cover events shortly before 20 March and the journey of the delegation the next day).
- Conspiring and consulting on 22 March to levy rebellion (the English Métis held two meetings, organized by Anglican minister Edward Matheson, at the Lindsay school and the St Catharine's church, where the delegation reported and the community decided on further action).
- Expressing and declaring an intention to levy war on 23 March at The Ridge by publishing a letter addressed to those then in open rebellion (the English Métis met again at the Lindsay school and passed resolutions and

there Scott may have written the highly contentious letter to the South Branch Métis).

- Aiding and abetting those in open rebellion on 23 March at The Ridge (this overt-act allegation was designed to cover further the events of the 23 March meeting, the reception of a Métis delegation the next day at The Ridge, and subsequent events. The crown did not lead any evidence specifically supporting the fourth of these alleged overt acts).

178 *CSP*, 1886, no. 52, 'Queen v. Scott,' 60–172.

179 Beal and Macleod, *Prairie Fire*, 318.

180 *CSP*, 1886, no. 52, 'Queen v. Scott,' H.J. Clarke opening address, 64–76. Clarke clearly knew the history very well (though he did get the date of the Treaty of Utrecht wrong) and was able to mould it to suit his purpose.

181 Ibid., H.J. Clarke submission, 73.

182 Ibid., B.B. Osler submission, 73.

183 Ibid., John McNiven evidence, 87–90.

184 Ibid., William Craig evidence, 91–8.

185 Ibid., 97. The English half-breeds unanimously passed a resolution at that meeting declaring their neutrality when it came to fighting but reiterating their support for 'all lawful means' for redressing grievances. 'Resolutions,' 22 March 1885, IV-9 (Buck Papers), SAB.

186 *CSP*, 1886, no. 52, 'Queen v. Scott,' William Craig evidence, 97.

187 Ibid., 92–3.

188 Ibid.

189 Beal and Macleod, *Prairie Fire*, 144–5.

190 *CSP*, 1886, no. 52, 'Queen v. Scott,' Thomas McKay evidence, 98–101.

191 Ibid., 85–7.

192 Ibid., H.J. Clarke opening statement, 114.

193 Ibid., H.J. Clarke closing address, 163.

194 Ibid., A.L. Lunen evidence, 101–2. The crown also asked witness John McNiven to identify Scott's signature. Ibid., John McNiven evidence, 87–8.

195 Ibid., H.J. Clarke closing address, 158.

196 Ibid., John Astley evidence, 84.

197 Clarke told the jury: 'You must remember this[:] that when a man becomes so extremely useful about a court of justice as Mr. Astley has become lately, even the most credulous juryman would begin to doubt all about it.' Clarke compared Astley, very unfairly, to notorious English false witness Titus Oates of seventeenth-century Popish Plot fame. Ibid., H.J. Clarke opening address, 122.

198 Ibid., H.J. Clarke argument, 102.

199 Ibid., Hugh Richardson ruling, 102.

200 Ibid., B.B. Osler's argument, 103.

201 T.B. Howell, ed., *A Complete Collection of State Trials and Proceedings for High Treason and Other Crimes and Misdemeanors* (London: Longmans 1816), vol. 21, 485 at 562–7 and 587–621.

202 Henry Flanders, 'Lord Erskine,' *University of Pennsylvannia Law Review and American Register* 48, no. 6 (1909): 353–71.

203 *Manitoba Free Press*, 10 Sept. 1885, 1. It is interesting that Clarke had the newspaper reporter so enthralled that he reported Richardson's rulings as mainly favouring the defence. The opposite was true.

204 *CSP*, 1886, no. 52, 'Queen v. Scott,' H.J. Clarke opening statement, 103–23.

205 Ibid., 107.

206 Beal and Macleod, *Prairie Fire*, 318–19.

207 *CSP*, 1886, no. 52, 'Queen v. Scott,' H.J. Clarke opening statement, 113.

208 Ibid., Hugh Ross evidence, 137; William Paquin evidence, 143.

209 Ibid., William Paquin evidence, 143.

210 Ibid., William Miller evidence, 154.

211 Ibid., John McNiven evidence, 90.

212 Ibid., William Paquin evidence, 140; William Miller evidence, 154.

213 Ibid., Hugh Ross evidence, 137.

214 Ibid., Thomas McKay evidence, 98–9.

215 Ibid., Hugh Ross evidence, 140.

216 Ibid., Hillyard Mitchell evidence, 132.

217 Ibid., William Craig evidence, 92–3.

218 Ibid., Andrew Whitford evidence, 152.

219 Ibid., Edward Matheson evidence, 124–5.

220 This is obvious in the letter-to-the-editor he prepared in response to the *Mail's* white rebels series, but which he apparently did not send. Undated, unsigned draft, A. M421, SAB.

221 Matheson to McKay, 27 Aug. 1885, A. M421, SAB. McKay replied the same day, reassuring Matheson. McKay to Matheson, 27 Aug. 1885, A. M421, SAB. His experience as a witness, and especially B.B. Osler's sniping at him, did not do Matheson's peace of mind any good. After the trial, he wrote a similar letter to Lief Crozier. Matheson to Crozier, 29 Sept. 1885, A. M421, SAB.

222 *CSP*, 1886, no. 52, 'Queen v. Scott,' Edward Matheson evidence, 126.

223 Ibid., 129.

224 Ibid., Hugh Ross evidence, 141; William Miller evidence, 153.

225 Ibid., Hugh Ross evidence, 139; William Paquin evidence, 144–6; Alexis André evidence, 147; Charles Nolin evidence, 150.

226 Ibid., Albert Porter evidence, 136; Charles Nolin evidence, 148; William Miller evidence, 154.

227 Ibid., Albert Porter evidence, 134.

228 Ibid., H.J. Clarke closing address, 157–63.

229 Ibid., 61–2.

230 Ibid., B.B. Osler closing address, 164–8.

231 During the evidence of Edward Matheson, B.B. Osler objected to leading questions, and H.J. Clarke retorted: 'When the learned gentleman sits there in all the dignity of his own importance and thinks he is going to shut us up he makes a mistake.' Ibid., Edward Matheson evidence, 126. When Clarke objected that Osler was putting words in Alexis André's mouth, Osler responded: 'I may say that I have been practising at the bar for a great many years, and I never knew of such professional conduct before, as I have had from the learned senior on the other side. I have never known a man so careless of what is right in professional conduct as the learned counsel.' Ibid., Alexis André evidence, 150–1. When Clarke again complained that Osler was trying to put words in the French-speaking Charles Nolin's mouth, Osler shot back: 'A barrister of a year's standing ought to know better than to interfere' with cross-examination. Clarke responded: 'It is not a cross-examination. You are making out an examination-in-chief, and you are giving evidence.' Ibid., Charles Nolin evidence, 150.

232 See, for example, ibid., Edward Matheson evidence, 124.

233 Ibid., Hugh Ross evidence, 140.

234 Ibid., judge's directions, 168–71.

235 *CSP*, 1886, no. 52, 'Queen v. Scott,' 172; Beal and Macleod, *Prairie Fire*, 321.

9

Another Look at the Riel Trial for Treason

J.M. BUMSTED

The high treason trial in 1885 of Louis Riel has been the subject of considerable debate and controversy since the day it began. The substance of the debate has not much changed since 1885. Government critics then and since have insisted that Riel did not receive a fair trial. Malcolm Cameron, Liberal MP for Huron, maintained in a lengthy speech in the House of Commons in 1886 that 'Louis Riel was executed contrary to law, contrary to the plainest principles of British law and British justice, and in obedience to a power that is not responsible to Parliament.'[1] Government defenders have been equally vehement that he was appropriately treated. According to Sir Hector Langevin in the same Commons debate in 1886:

In this case, we did not create a new tribunal to try Louis Riel; he was not tried by a court martial, but he was tried by a court established by the law of the land as any other man would have been tried, whether he was called Riel or called by another name, whether he had French blood in his veins or English or Scotch or Irish blood. It was not a question of nationality – it was a question of an accused prisoner put upon his trial for the crime of high treason. He was tried before that tribunal; every opportunity was given him to defend himself; his own counsel admit that these opportunities were as great as could be expected.[2]

The debate has taken on added import in recent years, as various groups lobby for a posthumous reconsideration of the guilty verdict of the jury and the subsequent execution of Riel, usually on the grounds of inequity.[3] A substantial contemporary literature has been augmented by much modern literature,[4] so that we now know considerably more about both the trial and the history of Canadian law.[5] Nevertheless, there is still no definitive assessment of the case and such an assessment is elusive. The subject remains controversial, with a number of major points based on irreconcilable assumptions about the nature of fairness, and others still shrouded in mystery or uncertainty. Riel's defence is raised as a particular concern in this chapter, which revisits some of the key legal issues and evaluates existing interpretations of them.

BACKGROUND

Riel's reputation has changed substantially over the years. Although he has always been revered in Manitoba by the Métis, most historians in English Canada were hostile to him until George Stanley's *The Birth of Western Canada* was published in 1936. In recent years, his reputation has altered from historical to mythological.[6]

Louis Riel emerged from obscurity in Red River in 1869 to lead a Métis resistance against the annexation of the settlement by Canada, which had earlier purchased the entire North-West from the Hudson's Bay Company (HBC). He became president of a provisional government replacing the HBC in December of that year, and was well on the way to negotiating peacefully Red River's admission into Canada with the Canadian government when he permitted an informal court martial to sentence one Thomas Scott, a Canadian from Ulster, to death. Why he allowed Scott to be executed is still not entirely clear.[7] The public in Ontario reacted to Scott's death with extreme anger, and Riel found himself on the run, officially not because he had been a rebel against the crown but because he had committed murder. Riel was formally indicted for Scott's murder in 1873 and, as we have seen in Louis Knafla's chapter in this volume, an information was laid in Winnipeg against his lieutenant of 1870 – Ambroise Lépine – who was subsequently tried and convicted of the crime. The Canadian government offered Riel an amnesty, provided he stayed out of the country for five years. Riel went into exile in 1875, but he did not remain outside Canada, suffering a nervous breakdown late that year and spending eighteen months in several facilities for the insane in Quebec between 1876 and 1878. His illness was complicated by his insistence that he was a prophet of God seeking the reform of the Roman Catholic Church, thus adding a religious dimension to his dementia. Riel eventually became sufficiently better to return to exile in the United States in

1880, moving to Montana in 1880, marrying, and becoming an American citizen in 1882.

In the decade after 1875, the North-West had become a seething mass of discontent, with most residents singularly unhappy with the Canadian government. The interests of Canada in the North-West, particularly under Sir John A. Macdonald, were focused on agricultural settlement, both as an outlet for excess eastern population and as a stimulus to the development of a truly transcontinental nation. A major problem faced the Dominion in the North-West, however. The government did not have the money to develop the territories as quickly as it, and the incoming settlers, would have preferred. The attempt to finance the building of a transcontinental railway helped to push the Macdonald government out of office. Finding the large number of surveyors necessary to survey the land in advance of settlement, and the money to pay them, proved extremely difficult. Paying the compensation required to extinguish Aboriginal title to the land was almost impossible.

On the surface, Dominion policy concerning the Native inhabitants of the North-West Territories was simple and sensible. Canada acknowledged Aboriginal rights to land of the 'Indians' – though not the Métis – and was prepared to negotiate treaties extinguishing those rights in exchange for reserves, often located on the most marginal and least fertile land. These treaties not only freed the more desirable land for settlement but enabled the Canadian government to continue to pursue its pre-confederation policy of settling First Nations people on the land as farmers in the hopes of eventually assimilating them into mainstream Canadian society. The Aboriginal peoples of the west were caught in an inexorable process of change. The buffalo were rapidly disappearing, the victims of overhunting, the arrival of settlement and new technology, and probably some sort of bovine disease epidemic. Whatever the reasons, most Aboriginal leaders knew that their traditional way of life was disappearing forever. But the Department of Indian Affairs expected them to become self-sufficient virtually overnight. It did not supply the reserves with enough food to prevent starvation and disease, and it complained when the desperate people slaughtered their livestock for something to eat. The reserve lands tended to be marginal, the assistance supplied was inadequate, and the attitude of many of the 'Indian agents' (the government's representatives on the reserves) was basically unsympathetic. By the early 1880s, the west was a virtual powder keg of Aboriginal discontent. Cree leaders in what is now Alberta sent a letter to Sir John A. Macdonald (who was minister of the interior and head of Indian affairs as well as prime minister) telling him that they were destitute and that their motto was, 'If we must die by violence let us do it quickly.' The winter of 1883–4 was particularly severe, and many were starving. Some Indian agents wrote to Ottawa, but nothing was done. In June 1884 Big Bear and his followers, with many others, travelled to Poundmaker's reserve for discussions, after which some 2,000 people took part in the religious ritual known as the 'thirst dance.'

Like the First Nations, the Métis had been systematically pushed to the margins. The Macdonald government had created Manitoba as a province only under duress, and the prime minister regarded the mixed-bloods as needing merely to be 'kept down by a strong hand until they are swamped by the influx of settlers.'[8] And swamped they were. As thousands of new settlers, mainly from Ontario, arrived in the province, the land rights that had been guaranteed to the Métis were gradually whittled down, and much of the land promised the Métis in 1870 – about two million of the two-and-a-half-million acres (809,370 out of 1,011,715 hectares) – ended up in the hands of speculators. By 1885, Ontario-born settlers outnumbered Métis five to one in Manitoba, and only 7 per cent of the province's population was of mixed-blood origin. The extent to which deliberate government policy was responsible for the plight of the Métis has been one of the most bitter historical controversies ever seen in Canadian historiography. Many Métis headed farther west, often to the Saskatchewan valley, where they formed several mission settlements, including Qu'Appelle, Batoche, and Duck Lake.[9] But the buffalo were becoming scarce. French, English, and Scottish mixed-bloods in the region demanded grants similar to those given to the mixed-bloods under the Manitoba Act. As in Red River a decade before, the arrival of government surveyors sparked fear and uncertainty as to whether the river-lot holdings of the Métis would be allowed to survive in a square-survey system. Part of the problem was that the surveying was not happening fast enough, not just for the Métis (who sought exemptions from it), but for the European settlers as well.

By the early 1880s, the Europeans in the region were becoming as restive as the First Nations and the Métis, although for different reasons. Their concerns were more political. In March 1883 the Qu'Appelle settlers' rights association passed resolutions calling for parliamentary representation, land-law reform, proper legislation for settlers, and government assistance for immigrants. In December of that year, a Manitoba and North-West farmers' union was organized in Winnipeg. A motion for repeal of the BNA Act and the formation of a 'new confederacy of the

North-West Provinces and British Columbia' was only barely defeated. A Bill of Rights was drawn up, which was summarily rejected in Ottawa.

In the late spring of 1884, the despairing Métis turned to their old leader, Louis Riel. He had apparently put his life back together when a delegation from the Saskatchewan country visited him in Montana on 4 June. They told him of all the grievances that were burdening the peoples of the region, explained that agitation was developing against the Canadian government, and pleaded with him to return and lead them. Within a month, Riel and his family were in Batoche and he was initiating a peaceful movement of protest against Canadian policies. By December 1884, Riel and W.H. Jackson (secretary of the North-West Settlers' Union) had drafted a long petition, with twenty-five sections, which they sent to Ottawa. The document concluded by requesting that the petitioners 'be allowed as in [1870] to send Delegates to Ottawa with their Bill of rights; whereby an understanding may be arrived at as to their entry into confederation, with the constitution of a free province.'[10] Ottawa acknowledged receipt of the petition but made no other response. Riel was mistaken in thinking that the tactics that had worked – under special conditions – in 1869–70 could be repeated fifteen years later. He was equally mistaken in believing that he had the support of all the people in the region. As soon as signs of armed confrontation appeared, the European settlers quickly disassociated themselves from Riel's movement, and the First Nations moved in their own direction.

On 21 March 1885 Riel sent a letter to Superintendent L.N.F. Crozier of the North-West Mounted Police at Fort Carlton, which was manned by a force of Mounted Police and volunteers. The missive demanded that the fort surrender, on pain of attack by Riel and his men. Crozier refused. On 26 March, Gabriel Dumont, Riel's military 'general,' intercepted a small detachment from Fort Carlton near Duck Lake. When Crozier heard of this action, he left the fort with as many men as he could muster. This force met Riel and 300 Métis on horseback before it reached Duck Lake. Startled, Crozier gave an order to fire. Thirty minutes of gunfire exchanges followed, during which lives were lost on both sides. Riel wrote a letter to Crozier blaming him for the battle. 'A calamity has fallen upon the country yesterday,' he insisted. 'You are responsible for it before God and man.'[11] He then appealed to the Cree to assist him. He got more than he had anticipated. Poundmaker's men broke into buildings in Battleford, terrifying settlers, and the Cree warrior Wandering Spirit (Kapapamahchakwew) led a band that attacked Frog Lake, where nine were killed.

Prime Minister Macdonald was determined to crush this uprising quickly, and sent a military force under Major-General Frederick Middleton – by way of the new Canadian Pacific Railway – to put it down. Many of the troops came from Winnipeg militia units composed of ex-Ontarians. Lieutenant-Colonel William Otter relieved Battleford, but he was fired on by Aboriginal warriors at Cut Knife Hill and had to withdraw. A battle with the Métis at Fish Creek delayed the march on Batoche, where Middleton intended to confront Riel. But on 9 May the Canadian force of eight hundred men arrived at Batoche, where they quickly defeated Riel, Dumont, and about two hundred armed Métis. The uprising was over by 12 May.[12] Riel, thinking that any proceedings would serve as a platform for his cause, surrendered and was taken into custody by the Canadian army. Initially, he was ordered to Winnipeg by Militia and Defence Minister Adolphe Caron, but new instructions, telegraphed 21 May, sent Riel to Regina instead to stand trial along with other leading members of the resistance. The government's prosecution strategy, options on charges, and prosecuting lawyers are examined in detail in the previous chapter by Bob Beal and Barry Wright and the question of venue is examined below.

Riel was the first to face trial on 20 July, on high treason charges that surprised Riel, his defence team, and indeed much of the public. There are numerous contemporary and modern accounts of his trial so a bare outline is presented here.[13] Riel's lawyers (Quebec lawyers François-Xavier Lemieux, Charles Fitzpatrick, and James Greenshields, and local lawyer T.C. Johnstone) opened by objecting to the venue and the special territorial procedures for the trial of a capital case. After a brief adjournment, and further arguments from Johnstone about the wording of the information and Riel's nationality, the prosecution notified him that the six preferred counts of levying war (three as a British subject, and three as a foreigner owing local allegiance under the temporary protection of the crown) did not relate to the Fenian or Treason-Felony acts but were for high treason under the statute of Edward III. Faced with this and Judge Hugh Richardson's rejection of their jurisdictional arguments, Riel's defence team decided that their best option was the defence of insanity. They requested an extended adjournment to call witnesses and medical specialists.

Richardson granted a week only, refusing Riel's request for the appearance of indicted fugitives in the United States such as Dumont (which would have entailed pardons) and of government officials and supporting documents concerning Métis claims. Riel began to part ways with his counsel, writing Prime Minister Macdonald directly to describe his team as well intentioned but unable to understand his cause. Jackson's case, examined in the previous chapter, came up during the adjournment and his not-guilty verdict on grounds of insanity only reinforced the defence team's commitment to the insanity defence. The court reconvened on 28 July with a jury of six (two merchants, four farmers, all anglophone) selected from a panel of thirty-six. As crown witnesses testified about Riel's leadership of the uprising, Fitzpatrick focused on extracting admissions of Riel's erratic behaviour. Charles Nolin, Riel's relative and a close associate until 1885, proved the crown's most effective witness, and prompted Riel's active participation in the proceedings and rupture with his counsel. Defence witnesses such as the priests Alexis André and Vital Fourmond and provisional government secretary Phillipe Garnot testified to Riel's madness and the defence's medical evidence was more authoritative than that of the crown. However, B.B. Osler's effective questioning of the defence's expert witnesses, evoking the possibility that Riel's eccentric conduct might be attributed to deception, was probably decisive for the jury. The defence and crown addresses to the jury were eloquent and Judge Richardson's charge was cautious. Fitzpatrick's impassioned speech was followed by Riel's (which, while lengthy, also seemed the product of a sane mind) and then Christopher Robinson's lucid and logical summation for the crown. The jury withdrew for an hour and returned a verdict of guilty with a recommendation for mercy. After a further speech from Riel, Richardson sentenced him to death, the execution to be carried out on 18 September.

Lemieux and Fitzpatrick led the appeal in the Manitoba Court of Queen's Bench, on jurisdictional and procedural grounds. The arguments were unanimously rejected and Riel was reprieved until November as the case was taken directly to the Judicial Committee of the Privy Council, which indicated on 22 October that it would not hear the appeal. The government had decided to let the law run its course and did not intervene with a pardon, despite the jury's recommendation of mercy. With the legal issues apparently decided, the matter became one of politics, and the calculation was that outrage in Quebec would dissipate and no serious international repercussions would ensue given the lack of British and American intervention. On 31 October a commission of doctors was appointed to determine whether Riel's mind had given way since the trial, whether his reason had deteriorated to such an extent that, despite his sanity being confirmed by three courts, he was no longer able to know right from wrong and therefore not accountable for his offences, but the preponderance of opinion was negative. Despite his refusal to recant his

Louis Reil addressing the jury during his trial for treason, Regina, 1885, by O.B. Buell (Library and Archives Canada, C-001879)

heresies, the attending priests gave Riel the sacraments, on the basis that his aberrations were a symptom of his insanity. The warrant for his execution arrived on 15 November and he was hanged the next morning.

LEGAL ASSESSMENTS

Interpretations that focus on the legal issues arising out of Riel's case include studies by Desmond Brown, Louis Thomas, Bob Beal and Rod Macleod, and, most recently, Jeremy Mumford. There are other, more controversial, legal examinations. Thomas Flanagan and Neil Watson, in 'The Riel Trial Revisited: Criminal Procedure and the Law in 1885,' note that a primary government concern in 1885 was that the Riel trial should be perceived to be fair.[14] They add that two crown prosecutors would have preferred special legislation to create a special commission, and, as a fallback, recommended trying him under the North-West Territories Act of 1880 (43 Vic. c.25), 'following its provision as closely as possible and giving the accused every protection or privilege provided by any law not clearly inconsistent with it.' Here and in subsequent publications, Flanagan has tried to define the debate on the trial by setting two standards.[15] First, he insists that any trial study and evaluation must place the trial within context of law and judicial practice of 1885, rather than modern presumptions. Secondly, any trial study must evaluate rules of conduct followed by participants in the trial, but not the outcome of the trial, which is an open process. 'Strictly speaking, there is no such thing as a fair or unfair outcome; there is only a fair (impartial) or unfair (biased) process,' he has written.[16] The hypothetical question to be answered, Flanagan argues, is whether 'Riel was tried in the same way as would any other man who had committed similar actions in the same jurisdiction.'[17]

Such standards, while sounding reasonable, necessary, and legitimate, really raise more questions than they answer. They are, in the end, little more than Flanagan's formulation of the rules for interpretation of the evidence, and, it is suggested here, designed to present the government in a favourable light. While historians can agree that present-day standards should not be introduced into any evaluation of the Riel trial, particularly given that the rights of the accused in criminal proceedings have been enhanced over the more than one hundred years since 1885, placing the trial within the context of law and judicial practice of 1885 is no easy matter. In the first place, what law and what judicial practice provide the context? Are we talking only about the law and practice in the North-West Territories, or does the context include Canada, or even extend to the wider British empire and beyond? In the second place, are we talking about usual practice or best practice? These are important questions, since one of the problems with the Riel trial is that it was conducted in a jurisdiction in which criminal procedures were unusual by Canadian standards and to which some important modern English and Canadian criminal laws had not been formally extended or introduced. One might have supposed that some of these legal extensions were at least partly what the prosecutors were talking about in their recommendation noted earlier. Beal and Macleod have commented on the 'highly complex legal issues' that resulted from the absence of full integration of the North-West Territories into the Canadian legal system, many of them 'not fully grasped by any of the lawyers on either side although they included some of the best legal minds of the era.'[18]

Moreover, are we talking about ordinary criminal trials or unusual trials for high treason? Trials for high treason had long included special procedural protections for the accused designed to curb the Tudor and Stuart abuses by way of the 1696 Treason Act. Unfortunately, that act was passed over twenty five years after the territorial reception date for English law (the Hudson's Bay Company's charter for Rupert's Land) and was not explicitly extended with the declared applicable Dominion legislation under the 1875 and 1880 North-West Territories acts. While the Treason Act applied elsewhere in British North America, earlier Canadian state trials examined in previous volumes of this series cannot be characterized by best practice; there was much fudging of evidence and arbitrary decisions by the courts.[19] There are really no standards of comparison for high treason trials conducted in Canada in 1885, since Riel was the only insurrectionist of that year tried under the 1352 Statute of Treasons. The other 1885 convictions were for the lesser offence of treason-felony, as were the 1848 Irish treason trials and the 1883 English cases involving the Fenian 'dynamiters.' The one vaguely comparable American case – the trial of the presidential assassin Charles Guiteau – provides little evidence of contemporary best practice since the law was different (the definition of treason was explicitly restricted by the U.S. constitution).[20] To see Riel's trial even in the context of regular indictable offence or felony procedure, as Flanagan and Watson do in 'The Riel Trial Revisited,' is clearly to stack the cards in favour of heavy-handed government practice and tactics. While Flanagan and Watson refer to 246 British and pre-confederation Canadian trials for high treason, most were conducted under emergency legislation which explicitly and temporarily extended definitions of treason or adopted special procedural expedients.

As we shall see, the government may have had the right to try Riel under the 1352 statute, but it was not obliged to do so. British practice by this time tended to lenience towards insurrectionists charged with offences analogous to classic heads of treason (for example, the lesser offence of treason-felony), and harshness with those charged with non-political criminal offences like murder committed in a political context. In cases involving the attempted assassination of nineteenth-century monarchs by demented young men – there were a number of such cases – the British simply put them into institutions and threw away the key. Riel and his colleagues were not pardoned after 1870, so went the argument, because they had committed murder. But in 1885 Riel was not a murderer because he had been granted an amnesty.

The question that should be posed becomes: What decisions did the government make about the trial in areas where it had options and is there a pattern to those decisions? We need to know not whether Riel was tried legally, but whether he was fairly dealt with by the government, which had a series of options both within and without the context of the trial. The government chose to try Louis Riel under a statute that provided only one outcome for a guilty verdict – condemnation to death – although it was not obliged to do so. No amount of apologetics can turn this into anything other than a loaded strategy.

At the same time, it has to be emphasized that – apart from the recommendation of the prosecutors and the requirements of politics – the crown was under no special obligation to bend over backwards to be fair to Riel, whatever various contemporaries said and thought. The crown was obliged to follow the applicable eighteenth- and nineteenth-century statutes and the appropriate forms of the law. These were not the same thing as the due-process standards of the modern criminal trial. Nor could formal legal requirements be superseded by an obligation to seek equitable justice. The charge of high treason was essentially a political decision, not a legal one (although it also had to be a legally sound one). It set in motion a series of legal consequences. After Riel's conviction, the outcome entailed yet another political decision, one that was not necessarily just.

The hypothetical question whether Riel was tried in the same way as would any other man who had committed similar actions in the same jurisdiction is thus both a bit disingenuous and more than a bit unsatisfactory. In the first place, Riel could not possibly be disentangled from his reputation and his history, and to raise the question in this way is to stack it against Riel. The question is not whether Riel was treated as any other accused in his position would have been, but whether he should or could have been treated as any other accused party, given his acknowledged leadership role as well as the government's previous experiences with him and attitudes towards him. One of the key historic points about high treason and rebellion was that governments often treated leaders more leniently than the rank and file, for political reasons, especially when they had not been personally involved in atrocities. Since the age of Machiavelli if not before, governments have recognized the dangers of creating martyrs.

The argument that the Canadian government acted in most instances in the only way possible given the law of the time is untenable given the fact that it had choices. What the Canadian government did in the Riel trial may have been legal given the law of the day, but there were sufficient instances in which it might have acted differently to suggest that the government was indeed out to get Riel and probably eager to satisfy the hostility to Riel of eastern voters. In a paragraph discussing various denunciations of the legitimacy of the trial, Flanagan and Watson quote L.H. Thomas – who had earlier argued that the trial was political – as writing that 'the government, exploiting the venerable sanctions of an outmoded legality, arranged a trial which satisfied most of the technical requirements of the legal process, but which in reality was designed to assuage the paranoic fears and passions of Ontario voters.' Flanagan and Watson insist that if 'these views are even approximately correct' – apparently including the Thomas statement with the denunciations – then 'Canada would have much to be ashamed of; and presumably the government should grant Riel a posthumous pardon.'[21] It would appear that the underlying agenda for Flanagan (and his collaborator) is therefore to argue that the trial was not unfair and that Canada has nothing to be ashamed of. Whether these are the appropriate issues is a different matter entirely. While we ought not to introduce modern conceptions into our considerations, we are certainly entitled to introduce contemporary standards of fairness and to argue that the government, while acting in a strictly legal fashion, was still unfair because it chose to be unfair. Neither of Flanagan's 'standards' deals with the question of the political nature of both the crime and the punishment. Louis Riel may have been tried and condemned legally, but not even Flanagan really tries to argue that he had, by some inexorable objective standard, to be executed.

What does need to be discussed in any re-evaluation of the Riel trial is the standing of counterfactual arguments which have been raised in other legal assessments by Thomas, Brown, Beal and Macleod, and Mumford, as well as George Goulet and Ronald Olesky. As any lawyer knows, a brilliant chain of legal logic can be instantly undone if the court does not accept its basic premise. However compelling the argument – and that about the necessity of a jury of twelve seems to me to be abstractly quite compelling in the Riel case – it is not compelling at all if it has been consistently rejected by the court and the appellate courts in the case at issue. The matter is a bit different when the arguments were not actually advanced in the case. To insist, for example, that Riel's lawyers ought to have adopted a different defence strategy – and there is little doubt that they should have done so – is a counterfactual. It would not have been accepted as grounds for overturning a verdict by almost any appellate court in the British empire. At the same time, to claim that certain arguments or procedures were not tried because they were 'legally dubious' does not mean that they ought not to have been tried. Moreover, the real question is the venue of the re-evaluation. Are we limited to a perspective from a venue of some abstract appellate court sitting in 1885 – say the Supreme Court of Canada, which never heard the case – or are we in an even more abstract court of international 'justice' imaginatively conceived as the Nuremberg court actually was embodied in 1945?

SPECIFIC LEGAL ISSUES

Riel was tried by the law of the North-West Territories, which in several ways was different from the norm elsewhere in Canada. It called for trial of any infraction by a stipendiary magistrate of the territories and a justice of the peace before a jury of six men. The specific procedural implications are discussed below but it should be noted that expedients in the administration of justice in the North-West originated in an attempt to confront practical challenges of geographical distance and shortage of legal personnel in a frontier setting. While similar expedients were common in British colonial settings, they represented a departure from the standards of due process in English criminal law that more developed jurisdictions emulated. And, while the procedure followed in Riel's trial may not have been unusual for the trial of 'routine' offences in a frontier setting, high treason was not a routine offence. It was a special offence, the most serious in English law, heavy with constitutional associations as reflected in the procedural protections set out in the 1696 legislation. However, the territories' procedure can be said to violate only the 'constitutional spirit' of the 1696 Treason Act since it had not been adopted as law in the North-West at the time of Riel's trial.

The Question of Venue

There are several interesting questions around venue and jurisdiction. Did the government have to try the case in the North-West Territories? The 1873 North-West Territories Act specified Manitoba as the venue for capital trials, and, although this provision was dropped in the 1880 amended act which created a local court system, it was not expressly repealed. Flanagan offers the negative argument that there is 'no evidence that anyone in 1885 regarded the provision as alive.' But silence is not the same as positive statement. As we have seen, the government quickly changed initial orders to hold Riel in custody in Winnipeg. Beal and Macleod argue that the government was obliged to do so because Riel could not be legally tried in Manitoba (where he would face a full jury, half French-speaking). While the Manitoba courts remained a route of appeal after 1880, the execution of James Connor in Regina on 17 July 1885, days before Riel's trial, appears to have confirmed the jurisdiction of the territorial courts in capital cases.[22] Incidentally, a Manitoba trial before twelve jurors, six anglophones and six francophones, would not necessarily have found in favour of Riel, as the murder trial of Ambroise Lépine in 1874 had demonstrated.[23]

Perhaps a better question would be, could the government have moved the venue, possibly by way of a special commission outside the regular court sessions (as was often done in treason trials), on the grounds that the accused might not receive a fair trial in the North-West Territories? The refusal to change the venue does not necessarily depend on the government's total inability to do so. There may have been political reasons for not changing the venue, but these are different from legal ones. The Riel lawyers argued for a venue in Ontario or British Columbia on two grounds, both of which were technical: first, the composition of a jury in the North-West Territories was different than elsewhere in the Dominion, to the defendant's disadvantage, and secondly, prior imperial legislation (the Canada Jurisdiction Act, 1803 and the Fur Trade Act, 1821), never explicitly repealed, precluded the trial of capital offences in the North-West Territories. Argument two was probably always a non-starter, since for any court to concede this jurisdictional point would have been to create chaos in the system of justice as practised in the west since 1870. The Manitoba court in 1874 had decided against similar arguments on behalf of Ambroise Lépine.[24] On the other hand, while the jury system of the North-West Territories may have been legally defensible, as Flanagan observes, the government need not have rested content with it. The crown rebutted the arguments, and the magistrate accepted the rebuttal. Flanagan is wrong to imply that the imperial legislation had not previously been challenged – it had in the Lépine case, although here too the decision had gone against the defendant. The government's position on jurisdiction may have been legally sound but it remains the case that it had options and could have decided to move the venue to demonstrate fairness.

Whether there was some reason that the defence did not argue these issues explicitly in terms of fairness and justice – rather than solely in technical terms – is another question. Whether the court properly understood that what Riel's lawyers were really claiming was that he could not get a fair trial in Regina – or whether the lawyers were trying to claim through technicalities that Riel could not get a fair trial in Regina – must be left open, but it appears likely that Justice Richardson was able to be obtuse about the matter because of the way the objections were phrased. The defence lawyers may have tried to be too clever by half on the venue question.

Pre-Trial Hearing

The Canadian psychiatrist R.E. Turner first raised the question of a pre-trial hearing for Riel at a symposium held in Vancouver in 1964. Turner argued that 'it is a matter of law and procedure at the outset of a trial to consider whether the accused is fit to stand trial.' He pointed to a section from the 1869 Dominion criminal law consolidations, later adopted in the 1892 Canadian Criminal Code.[25] The point was reiterated by L.H. Thomas in his 1977 article on the Riel trial. Flanagan notes that the reason there was no such hearing in Riel's case was because Canadian rules of criminal procedure had to be specifically extended by statute to the North-West Territories, and the provisions governing fitness to stand trial had not been so extended. Apart from the obvious observation that this failure suggests a neglect of the region by the Canadian government, there is also the question of whether the absence of statutory enactment necessarily meant that a pre-trial hearing was as 'legally dubious, if not impossible' as Flanagan contends. The legislation elaborated the common law that was within the jurisdiction of court, and, given the modern law elsewhere, who knows what the court might have accepted? Flanagan argues that the way the crown dealt with the lack of pre-trial process for Riel's secretary William Henry Jackson was to try him and to allow the jury to find him not guilty by reason of insanity. But, as the chapter by

Beal and Wright indicates, Jackson's circumstances were distinct, and it remains unclear why the crown dealt with him as it did.[26] Once again we have to conclude that the crown may have had choices, which it opted not to pursue. Another pre-trial issue, resulting from the special procedures set out in the North-West Territories acts, was reliance on the expedient of informations rather than full indictment procedure, a matter, as we shall see, that put the defence at a disadvantage in preparing to meet the charges against Riel.

Jury Composition

Flanagan argues that the jury was chosen fairly from the neighbourhood of the trial, which was composed almost entirely of people of British stock. This begs the question, however, because one of the reasons the government might have preferred Regina as the venue was the composition of the surrounding population, which might be less sympathetic to Riel. As Beal points out, using this universe as the pool for the jury also meant that the jurymen knew Judge Richardson, and might pay more attention to his charge to them than otherwise.[27] Whether local attitudes could have been made the basis of a request for change of venue is another matter entirely. Further, the difference between six and twelve jurors is, of course, a matter of no small importance in a capital case since a larger panel increases the likelihood that one or more jurors will refuse to convict. Again, the North-West Territories Act of 1875, as amended in 1880 – which specified the size of the jury and provided other exceptional powers of advantage to the crown – pre-dated the Riel trial, but it was legislation that the crown was prepared to use to full advantage.

The Choice of Judge

Hugh Richardson was the presiding judge.[28] He was a stipendiary magistrate appointed at the pleasure of the government, without one of the significant formal protections of judicial independence (tenure according to good behaviour determined by Parliament) confirmed under the British North America Act, 1867. The defence pointed this out as part of its request for a change of venue. One MP observed in the House of Commons debate in 1886 that 'it was an unhappy choice to select, of the three or four judges, the person who filled the position of the political adviser, the political law officer, to the Government in the Territories to be the judge in this particular trial.' This was particularly true since one of the complaints leading to the rebellion was about the administration of justice, or the lack of it. Richardson did not speak French. He was receiving a salary as legal adviser to the lieutenant governor and was not inclined to have any independent views, as his decisions and actions demonstrate. His references to the McNaghten rules in directions to the jury and on the treason-felony offence in other cases examined in the Beal and Wright and Bill Waiser chapters suggest his limitations as a jurist. Most important, Richardson was not a judge experienced at conducting controversial trials. The government was within its rights to select Richardson to try the Riel case, but it did have a choice. Flanagan argues that Richardson was well intentioned, but surely a man being tried for his life on charges of high treason ought to be able to expect something more than merely good intentions from the bench. Richardson was the perfect judge for a government looking to execute Louis Riel, although it might have been different had Riel's defence chosen to defend Riel's actions rather than to blame them on insanity.[29]

Liability and the Charges

Two quite different issues arise over the charges. First, there is the statute under which the charges were laid, and secondly, there are the charges themselves. The Canadian government had a choice of three statutes under which it might lay charges against Riel. It chose the most serious of the applicable offences, proceeding under the 1352 Statute of Treasons (25 Edward III stat. 5 c.2). Death was the only possible outcome of a guilty verdict, unless there was a reprieve on the execution of sentence which made the condemned eligible for a pardon, conditional on a secondary punishment (such as imprisonment – a number of those convicted of high treason in the Canadas in 1838 were transported). Written hundreds of years before the establishment of a British empire, the 1352 statute's language might have been regarded as anachronistic, but it remained the basis of the substantive law of treason, until supplemented by the lesser offence of treason-felony in the mid-nineteenth century. As Desmond Brown pointed out in 1975, it was still the major treason statute in force in the North-West Territories in 1885, and indeed the basic elements of the legislation were preserved with modernized language in the 'high treason' provisions of the 1892 Criminal Code, with the treason-felony offence becoming the lesser offence of 'treason.'[30]

Liability for treason was limited to subjects of the realm. Riel had become a U.S. citizen and renounced his allegiance to Britain. The complex issues of foreign citizenship and continuing allegiance raised by the Riel case have been recently examined in detail by Jeremy Mumford. One of the later elaborations of treason law was the development of the doctrine of local allegiance. According to Matthew Hale, writing in the seventeenth century (although his work was not published until 1736), 'if an alien the subject of a foreign prince in amity with the king, live here and enjoy the benefit of the king's protection and commit a treason, he shall be judged and executed, as a traitor, for he owes a local allegiance.'[31] Another basis for extending liability was the doctrine of natural or perpetual allegiance, applied to British-born subjects who became naturalized citizens of another country. As Blackstone put it, 'natural Allegiance is therefore a debt of gratitude, which cannot be forfeited, cancelled or altered by any time, place, or circumstance.'[32] This categorical position was increasingly questioned after the American Revolution and the uncertainty around the doctrine was resolved in Britain by section 6 of the Naturalization Act of 1870 (33 Vic. c.14 s.6), which declared that if any British subject became naturalized in some other state, he would be 'deemed to have ceased to be a British subject and be regarded as an alien.' This legislation was virtually cloned by the Canadian Parliament in its Naturalization Act of 1881 (44 Vic. c.13), although the Canadian legislation allowed British subjects naturalized in a foreign state to continue to be British subjects, providing they had declared the same and taken an oath of allegiance within two years after the passage of the act. While the Naturalization Act was not explicitly extended to the North-West Territories, the doctrine nonetheless had some modern status. The Department of Justice crafted the charges so that Riel could be found liable under either extension of allegiance, although Riel would have to be found resident long enough to be considered under the protection of the crown. Unfortunately, defence counsel chose not to pursue the issue of nationality, despite Riel's own view that he was not liable as a U.S. citizen, and instead made the strategic decision to focus on the defence of insanity. Washington could have pressured London on the matter, as it had done in the case of the Fenians in 1866, but, as Mumford shows, chose not to do so.[33]

Charges other than high treason were considered by the Dominion government and Department of Justice. The crown might have proceeded against Riel under the Lawless Aggressions Act, also known as the Fenian Act, of 1867 (31 Vic. c.14), which, as noted elsewhere in this volume, created a capital political offence for aliens from a nation at peace with Canada who levy war. This was an offence equivalent to the 'levying war' head of treason, while liability for criminal acts by enemy combatants was governed by martial and international law. Proceeding under this statute required the government to prove that Riel was a naturalized citizen of another country, 'a responsibility the Crown did not choose to assume,'[34] probably out of desire not to provoke international difficulties with the United States.

The crown could also have proceeded under the Canadian treason-felony statute of 1868 (31 Vic. c.69), as it did in most of the other cases in 1885. Flanagan argues that the 'actual wording of the statutes' displays 'very little practical difference in the charges' between the 1352 Statute of Treasons and the 1868 treason-felony statute – but also notes that few British trials under the latter involved overt acts of war or insurrection, but only actions related to insurrection. Thus, to proceed under treason-felony would have been 'unusually lenient.' The offences were in fact quite different. As noted elsewhere in the volume, the treason-felony offence derived from 1848 British legislation (11&12 Vic. c.12) passed to formalize temporary elaborations of treason law to widen its reach (to include conspiracies as well as overt acts) and to increase the prospects of conviction (juries found it easier to convict an accused not facing capital charges). All of Riel's compatriots ended up facing this lesser offence. While Brown and Flanagan can both agree that employing the 1352 statute was quite legitimate, neither demonstrates its absolute necessity. The decision on the charge was a political one. Beal and Macleod argue that 'in the circumstances of 1885, when dozens had died because of Riel's actions, it would have been inconceivable to charge Riel with any offence that did not carry the death penalty.'[35] This left either the 1352 Statute of Treasons or the Lawless Aggressions Act. But surely this is to surrender to public opinion.

Prime Minister Macdonald, Justice Minister Alexander Campbell, and George Burbidge, deputy minister of justice and leader of the prosecution team, initially favoured Lawless Aggressions Act charges against Riel and informed public opinion of the time was divided between that charge and treason-felony.[36] However, the Lawless Aggressions Act option was later rejected, as noted above. Goulet insists that the charges based on Riel as a British subject should have been dismissed, since it was never proven that he was a British subject. Whether or not this assertion is correct, Riel's citizenship was never tested at any point in the proceedings, an instance of dereliction of duty by the defence. Riel was thus judged by the jury without any evidence on this point. The omnibus charges against Riel were never unpacked by the judge, and may well have perplexed the jury, as they have perplexed others commenting on the case.

The Defence

Riel's defence team was unprepared for high treason charges, and, placing their hopes on the insanity defence, they failed to make arguments that might have come out of more diligent research in treason law. While the closing speech by Charles Fitzpatrick, a later minister of justice and chief justice, was widely celebrated as one of the most eloquent ever in a Canadian courtroom and achieved a jury recommendation for mercy, Lewis Thomas gives Riel's counsel a mixed review, suggesting that the defence failed to explore possible avenues as they faced the more experienced prosecutors. This criticism could be made even more emphatically. After the setback of the first day's opening arguments about the court's jurisdiction in capital cases (a matter that had been previously decided in the crown's favour) and the irrelevant matter of Riel's status under the Lawless Aggressions Act, the defence team unanimously concluded that the only chance of saving Riel was the insanity defence. A number of key issues were not pursued, including the discredited doctrine of perpetual allegiance and the question of whether Riel was resident in Canada sufficiently long enough to come under temporary protection of the crown as discussed above.

The defence's initial confusion over the charges was in some respects unsurprising since the lack of the usual indictment process in the North-West Territories contributed to it. The brief information relied upon referred to levying war but failed to indicate whether it was under the Lawless Aggressions Act, treason-felony, or high treason under Edward III. Nor was the crown obliged to inform Riel and his lawyers precisely what statute the allegations of levying war would come under. The pleadings, based on standard forms from *Archbold's*, did not distinguish between levying war for high treason and treason-felony (derived from an English text, they were unlikely to apply to the Lawless Aggressions Act, which might have signalled that the case was not going to be tried under it). Late in the first day, as Johnstone was presenting defence arguments about Riel's status in the context of the Lawless Aggressions Act and responding to questions from Judge Richardson, prosecutor B.B. Osler intervened and noted that they were proceeding on high treason under 25 Edward III.[37] While the territorial procedural expedients contributed to this remarkable confusion, it was nonetheless the responsibility of the defence to insist that the charges be clarified before the trial began. The defence was perfunctorily handled and this was one of the main reasons for any failure of justice in 1885.

The defence team was not chosen by Riel, nor did he fully accept them, particularly as they quickly put all their efforts into an insanity defence. The Riel Defence Committee in Ottawa had originally approached Charles Fitzpatrick, François Lemieux, and J.N. Greenshields. The crown paid their rail expenses to Regina and, under pressure, offered to pay the expenses of witnesses within the territories coming to Regina. Of the three, only Lemieux was an experienced criminal lawyer with substantial trial experience, and he did not head the defence. That task went to Charles Fitzpatrick, whose experience in capital cases was certainly limited. In Regina the defence team recruited Thomas Cooke Johnstone, a local lawyer whose employment was designed to add experience with the North-West Territories legal system.

Riel expressed some reservations over the team from the outset. He wanted a defence based upon 'the merit of my actions,' in effect justifying his rebellion in terms of the misconduct of the Canadian government in the west. Flanagan insists that Riel's preferred strategy was 'legally hopeless because a government's mistakes can never be a sufficient defence against the charge of treason, at least as long as the same government continues to rule, and every lawyer would doubtless agree in principle.'[38] At the same time, this is surely a good example of the weaknesses of Flanagan's approach. While such a defence might defy the government's own legal assertions and assumptions, the real point is that there was a wild card in the equation: the jury. The jury needed to be given some reason to defy the government and the charges that would be given it by the judge to find the defendant guilty. The government had chosen to go for death by charging high treason, which had always been a difficult charge to sustain because of the understandable reluctance of juries to condemn men to death by finding them guilty, especially when government maladministration was involved in producing the acts for which they were being tried. Despite the defence's failure to present any decent reasons for sympathizing with Riel, the Regina jury found him guilty but asked for mercy. As Flanagan and others such as Desmond Morton point out, if the jury thought Riel might be insane, they should have returned a verdict of not guilty by reason of insanity. So, in recommending mercy, they were apparently suggesting that the rebellion 'while perhaps not justifiable, was understandable in view of the government's dilatory handling of settlers grievances.'[39] One juror wrote to Edward Blake commenting on the 'dilatoriness of Sir John Macdonald, Sir David McPherson, and Lieutenant Governor Dewdney,' and another said many years later that the jury often commented on the need to have the minister of the interior (Sir

John A. himself) in the prisoner's box.[40] Had the jury been given more reasons for finding the rebellion justifiable, it might well have decided otherwise. A defence based on the inadequacies of the government, were it made strongly and persistently enough, might well have swayed a jury that was already predisposed to blame the government and give a verdict according to conscience. Such a defence in a different context had been rejected at the murder trial of Ambroise Lépine, but in that trial the presiding judge had refused to admit any evidence of government cheating and lying that could not be substantiated with documentary evidence, and the defence had no documents, only oral testimony by various witnesses that the government had lied to them. The same ruling might have been given in 1885, but if Flanagan and Watson are right that the government was really prepared to give the defence some latitude, a defence based on the merits of Riel's actions might have made some sense and some headway. A spirited defence of the rebellion might well have forced the crown into showing its hand totally, instead of being allowed to present itself persistently as the generous protector of the rights of the accused.

As we have seen, after the bungled first day of trial, Riel's lawyers applied to the court for a postponement to produce witnesses and documents and requested funds to bring them to Regina. The affidavit for adjournment filed on 21 July 1885 in Riel's name listed the material witnesses required and the papers needed to 'prove that the agitation in the North-West Territories was constitutional and for the rights of the people of the said North-West.'[41] There were also two separate affidavits from Fitzpatrick and Lemieux about the need for witnesses to testify as to Riel's sanity. Some of the witnesses had been actively involved in the rebellion and had escaped out of the country. The crown insisted that it had no authority to give such individuals a safe conduct to testify in this trial. More to the point, the crown was totally dismissive of the question of documentation. Robinson insisted that the large number of petitions and documents held in Ottawa were, he believed, 'utterly inadmissible under any circumstances, as a defence in this case.' After all, continued Robinson, 'we hear, for the first time, that an application for redress on constitutional grounds is evidence to form a justification for armed rebellion.' 'If those documents were here they would be opposed as wholly inadmissible,' he said, but they had not actually been applied for. As for the correspondence seized at Batoche, these papers were state documents and could not be released. Riel's certificate of naturalization was not relevant to the crown's case, Robinson maintained.

Robinson moved from a variety of arguments against delay and mag-

The jury of six at Louis Reil's trial, Regina, 1885, by O.B. Buell (Library and Archives Canada, PA-118759)

nanimously offered for the crown to pay the expenses of any witnesses living in the territories.[42] The crown also offered a week's delay, presumably for the production of witnesses and documents. An interesting sequence of statements then ensued, in which Greenshields (who had argued the case for the delay) apologized for the 'vehemence and warmth with which I had urged the application for the adjournment,' all the while still insisting that 'the result of this trial largely depends upon whether this application is granted or refused.' Greenshields had actually earlier commented that endeavours to obtain information had been frustrated by the government, a statement that one of the crown attorneys had instantly challenged. Almost immediately after this 'apology' from Greenshields, Fitzpatrick accepted, on his own responsibility, the crown offer of a delay. This may well have been one of the key turning points in the trial. The crown had certainly exposed its hand to some extent here, announcing that it would oppose any attempt to introduce evidence of the previous efforts of the people of the territories to get grievances answered as a justification for the rebellion. It is worth noting, however, that the defence had backed off this line of attack at the first sign of crown assertiveness, which meant that Justice Richardson did not have to rule on the admissibility of the documents. Fitzpatrick had jumped instead with alacrity on an offer of a week's delay, not enough to permit the documentation from Ottawa to be produced. The reader of the trial transcript can hardly help but suspect that Robinson and Fitzpatrick had silently worked out a deal on the floor of the courtroom. It was hardly one in Riel's best interests, as the junior member of the defence team must have recognized full well. More and continued pressure on all the points in this defence initiative was what was required, not least to force Justice Richardson into rulings that could be challenged on appeal. Instead, the defence focused on the insanity defence.

Riel's Madness and the Insanity Plea

Before the Riel trial in 1885, there had been no serious attempt in Canada to produce legislation defining the meaning of insanity in the context of the criminal act.[43] The treason trial of James Hadfield for his attempt to shoot George III resulted in the passage of English legislation concerning fitness to stand trial and the modern common law insanity defence emerged with the 1843 McNaghten case.[44] The general problem of Riel's madness is an important one in understanding the trial. Probably the most important general difficulty with Riel and madness is the failure of most commentators to appreciate that the question of Riel's mental state is not a single monolithic one, but rather a series of quite separate and distinct questions to be governed by quite separate sets of criteria. On the one hand, there is the question of whether or not Riel was truly mad. The general assumption is that this is the question which needs to be posed in terms of his 1885 trial for treason. Unfortunately, it is not, for several reasons. The plea of insanity that Riel's lawyers attempted to employ in his defence in 1885 was a very specific legal one, based upon the McNaghten rules, which presumed sanity unless the accused was unable to distinguish right from wrong at the moment of the commission of the crime for which he was being tried. Riel could have been insane and still able to distinguish right from wrong, which appears to have been the conclusion of the court in 1885. The Regina court did not in 1885 have to make any judgment on the overall state of Riel's mental health, but only on his ability to distinguish right from wrong at the moment of his criminal act. There were thus other possible conclusions that might have been reached. He could also have been insane at some point in the past, but was now able to distinguish right from wrong, or was sane but for some reason or another unable to distinguish right from wrong while committing his crime (thus suffering from what in popular parlance is called 'temporary insanity').

A second whole group of problems with Riel's mental state revolves around his spiritual state, and its relationship to his insanity. Louis Riel experienced visions and heard voices, some of which told him to found a new church of which he would become the leader. History is full of people who had visions and heard voices and were impelled by these experiences to found new churches, and not all of them are universally regarded as mad. That Riel is treated differently from Joseph Smith, say, or Emanuel Swedenborg, or Paul, or Jesus Christ himself, is a product of a number of factors. One is that Riel never successfully created a new church and therefore never had its historians to serve as apologists for his spiritual and emotional state while in the act of creation. A second related factor is that Riel was a public rebel who was manifestly unsuccessful in his rebellion in 1885, and that failure – and his execution for treason – has tended to cloud the whole question of his visions. Riel was not a visionary who confined his activities to the spiritual or even the religious realm. Perhaps the most important reason, however, why Riel's visions are not taken as completely legitimate revolve around both his Catholicism and the very nature of Catholicism. Many quite orthodox Catholics have had visions, which in form if not in content have been similar to those of Louis

Riel. It was not the 'roaring like a bull' that made Riel's experiences unacceptable but his mission to become his own pope. Riel himself was an ambivalent Catholic. He wanted the solace of orthodoxy through religious practice and the excitement of pursuing his visions. He wanted to be a 'good Catholic' who rejected the pope and the hierarchy of the church. These were quite incompatible, and have tended to damage his historical reputation. Riel was clearly acting on the basis of what he thought was divine revelation, whatever the other manifestations of his mental condition. Even the Catholic Church would allow that conventional definitions of insanity and sanctity are not necessarily incompatible. Although at this stage in his life Louis Riel may have been 'certifiably insane,' this does not automatically mean that his spiritual experiences were less than divinely inspired. The doctors who examined and observed him at the time may have described his behaviour in non-religious terms, but Louis Riel was still a prophet and seer. Any excessive behaviour does not by itself invalidate his claim to sanctity.

From the time of his institutionalization to his execution, but especially while in Longue Pointe and Beauport, Riel attempted to work out the details of what he hoped would be a new religion. The outlines of this religion are to be found in his papers, both as notes on his visions/experiences and as a series of drafts of a total religious and theological system, the 'Massinihican.' As was usually the case with religious reformers, Riel's religion was based on his various spiritual experiences – 'I am in direct communication with my creator,' he wrote Bishop Ignace Bourget in 1876 – which provided him with a sense of mission and convinced him that he was an heir to the biblical prophets of the Old Testament, most notably David.[45] At his most extreme, Riel saw himself as a combination of prophet, priest, king, and pontiff. The chosen people were the Métis, the descendants of the Ten Lost Tribes of Israel and the heirs of the French Canadians; the papacy itself would ultimately be transferred to St Vital, Manitoba. He developed a version of the Mosaic law that included a number of major reforms, including the reintroduction of circumcision and the Saturday Sabbath, as well as new rules for marriage, including an acceptance of marriage between brother and sister, polygamy (but only for males), and a married clergy. Much of his early thinking was based on numerology, and Thomas Flanagan suggests that his later drafts of the 'Massinihican' were influenced by contemporary concepts of theosophy.[46] One of Riel's principal teachings at the end of his life was that all mankind would be saved, a spirit of universalism quite common among Protestant sectarian reformers in the late eighteenth and nineteenth centuries.

Society has always had great difficulties in coming to terms with religious visionaries. To deny prophetic utterance and even the possibility of new revelation would be to deny both the Old Testament and the New Testament of the Bible. That a prophet like Moses might come down from a mountaintop with fresh instructions from God has to be allowed by believers, and was the basis of much of the creation of new religious sects in the eighteenth and nineteenth centuries. As soon as Riel's religious system is described, its parallels to other new metaphysical and cultic religions in North America are obvious.[47] For example, Henry Alline, the Nova Scotian who founded the Free-Will Baptists, had a whole series of visions which instructed his movement.[48] Alline was also a universalist. Then there is the case of Joseph Smith. In 1823 an angel named Moroni appeared to Smith and directed him to a stone box, in which were found a set of thin plates covered with engraved characters. The angel also provided the Urim and the Thummim, the spiritual 'glasses' through which Smith was able to read what was written on the plates.[49] The result was the Book of Mormon, which offered an entirely new religion and provided a justification for polygamy for males. Consider, too, Mary Baker Eddy, the founder of Christian Science, who had spiritual experiences and regarded herself as the mouthpiece of God.[50] There were plenty of precedents for Riel's specific teachings, such as polygamy, the Saturday Sabbath, and clerical marriage. Such reforms are echoed in various of the nineteenth-century fringe religions, and Riel's insistence that all humankind would be saved even found expression in more mainstream Protestantism of the century.

Turning to the plea of insanity, introduced by Riel's lawyers as the essential ingredient of their defence, meant that in the absence of legislation, any plea for insanity would be governed by the English common law, which in effect meant an application of the McNaghten rules formulated by the House of Lords. Daniel McNaghten, who had shot to death Sir Robert Peel's secretary under the mistaken impression that he was Peel himself, was acquitted by a jury after a brilliant defence by Alexander Cockburn. The defence counsel persuaded the judges that they should allow medical evidence that a person of otherwise sound mind could harbour a delusion that carried him beyond self-control, even though he knew the difference between right and wrong. The acquittal, which included a lifetime sentence to mental institutions, was heavily criticized. As a result, a rule (or rather a series of rules) was formulated. The rules were actually a series of answers by a panel of judges to a series of hypothetical questions relating generally to the insanity defence. They were deliberately drafted to deal with the McNaghten defence of 'partial insanity,' and the key element of their response was that 'at the time of the committing of the act, the party accused was labouring under such a defect of reason, from disease of the mind, as not to know the nature and quality of the act he was doing, or if he did know it, that he did not know he was doing what was wrong.'[51] But, in answer to another question about the testimony of medical experts who had never seen the prisoner before the trial but who were present for the whole trial and the examination of witnesses, the answer was basically that such testimony was at the discretion of the judge. This opened the door for expert witnesses to be asked hypothetical questions. Many expert lawyers and judges recognized almost from the outset that there were problems with the McNaghten rules. As one American jurist argued in 1871, it was impossible for a court to 'lay down an abstract general proposition, which may be given to the jury in all cases, by which they are to determine whether the prisoner had capacity to entertain criminal intent' because 'it is an attempt to find what does not exist, namely, a rule of law wherewith to solve a question of fact ... No formal rule can be applied in settling questions which have relation to liberty and life, merely because it will lessen the labor of the court or jury.'[52] The common law was nonetheless adopted in Canadian courts and the rules influenced the 1892 Canadian Criminal Code provisions. Any uncertainly about the rules was not shared by Judge Richardson in the Riel trial. He charged the jury in the exact words of McNaghten and informed them that this was indeed the law. Richardson was clearly acting within bounds in so informing the jury, but he might have done otherwise and his assertion was certainly open to challenge. One of the defence witnesses had certainly opened the door to another conclusion.

Dr Daniel Clark of the Toronto Asylum, testifying as an expert medical witness for the defence, had simultaneously admitted that Riel could distinguish right from wrong and added, 'I would convince any lawyers if they will come to Toronto Asylum, in half an hour, that dozens in that institution know right and wrong both in the abstract and in the concrete, and yet are undoubtedly insane; the distinction of right and wrong covers part of the truth; it covers the larger part of the truth, but the large minority of the insane do know right from wrong. It is one of those metaphysical subtleties that practical men in asylums know to be false.'[53] Under cross-examination, Clark maintained that Riel knew right from wrong 'subject to his delusions,' an important distinction that certainly might have been pursued further. Instead, Clark, on cross-examination by the defence, insisted that Brigham Young (another religious leader with a mania) was perfectly sane, which might have led to a discussion of whether deciding on the question of sanity when dealing with religious prophets was really a useful enterprise. Clark also got led by the crown into a discussion of whether Riel was malingering, and this was a question no expert witness who had not observed the accused for months could possibly answer. In an 1887 article on Riel, Clark insisted that the legal profession 'can not discern any valid evidence that does not tally with a metaphysical and obsolete definition.'[54] As Goulet points out, Clark was a bad defence witness simply because he did not believe in the McNaghten rules and so could not phrase his testimony in the appropriate language. Like other Canadian 'experts' on mental illness of the time, however, Clark treated the subject entirely in rationalist terms. Religious visions were delusions, not manifestations subject to different laws.

A major consideration in the Riel trial is that Riel and his lawyers, as suggested earlier, had a continuing major disagreement over the principal strategy of the defence, the insanity plea, to which Riel was unalterably opposed. In the course of the trial, Riel made clear that he did not agree with his lawyers, and they did their best to shut him up. George Goulet emphasizes the shortcomings of Riel's lawyers in relying on the insanity plea (which was bound to be shaped by the court's unquestioning acceptance of the McNaghten rules and the judge's instructions to the jury in this regard).[55] As Goulet suggests, the reliance on the insanity plea (to which Riel was himself opposed) meant two things: first, that the defence spent much of its time in examination and cross-examination trying to establish that Riel was mentally unbalanced (in effect a deluded fool) instead of focusing on the misdeeds of the government, and therefore, second, that they did not struggle as hard as they might have to establish an alternate line of defence, chiefly one rooted in Riel's own desire for a trial based 'on the merit of my actions.' One of Riel's counsel even asserted to the court, 'I do not want to justify the Rebellion.'[56] The lawyers also insisted that they took instructions not from Riel but from unnamed 'others.' These 'others' were probably the Riel Defence Committee in Ottawa. Their defence team's strategy was, of course, a disaster for Riel that he had in no way authorized and that he argued against in both his addresses to the jury. He even thanked those who had helped undermine the insanity plea. When the insanity plea collapsed, however, the defence had little else to fall back upon.

From Riel's perspective, there were several objections to a plea of insanity. One was that it would undermine his religious credibility with his Métis followers, many of whom believed that he was indeed the prophet of the New World. Another objection was that Riel did not believe he was insane. As the seventeenth-century playwright Nathaniel Lee had earlier written, 'they called me mad, and I called them mad, and damn them, they outvoted me.' In his two speeches to the jury, Riel suggested the outlines of a defence based on his actions. Three observations can be made about Riel's arguments. First, as far as was humanly possible, his own lawyers attempted to discredit Riel's perfectly rational discussion of the politics of the rebellion and his reasons for the rebellion by presenting him as insane. Secondly, Riel was forced to spend far too much time and energy defending his sanity. Thirdly, the defence did not call many witnesses or introduce documentation attempting to demonstrate the truth of Riel's criticisms of government policy in the west. Indeed, it allowed the crown to evade the production of evidence that Riel regarded as essential to his case. On one level, Riel behaved quite rationally in his leadership of the military resistance to Canada in 1885. On another level, of course, he believed that his ultimate mission was divinely inspired and in these terms might well have been regarded as unable to distinguish right from wrong in the context of that mission.

The Appeal

Riel's conviction in the court of the North-West Territories under the North-West Territories Act of 1880 was appealed to the Court of Queen's Bench of Manitoba, as specified in the 1880 statute. The appellate court could not acquit. It could either confirm the conviction or call for a fresh trial. The three judges who heard the appeal – Lewis Wallbridge, Wardlaw Taylor, and A.C. Killam – were all Tory appointees. Another judge of the court who might have been sympathetic to Riel – Joseph Dubuc – was deliberately absent. The lawyers who brought the appeal included Fitzpatrick and Lemieux, as well as a Manitoba lawyer named John S. Ewart. The court ruled that it could hear the appeal but could not have Riel brought to Winnipeg during its deliberations.

The three Manitoba justices all praised the zeal and adequacy of the defence, obviously overlooking the blatant evidence in the proceedings that Riel had disagreed profoundly with his lawyers over strategy. The defence raised four grounds to the appellate court, two technical and two substantive. George Goulet admits the weakness of the technical objections, one of which claimed that the information had been taken before the wrong magistrate and the other that notes of the trial had been taken in shorthand instead of in full and had been fleshed out later by the court stenographer. A better ground might have been the problems of French translation during the proceedings in a court that was supposed to be bilingual. This certainly hampered the testimony of one of the expert witnesses, Dr François Roy of the Beauport Asylum. When Roy hesitated to give categorical answers about the nature of the disease from which Riel suffered, the defence pointed out that if the witness was having trouble understanding the questions he should answer them in French. The sneering response of Osler, who had been examining for the prosecution, leaps out from the printed page. 'If the man wants to hide himself under the French he may do so.' The defence was soon complaining about the translations that were being given to the jury of Roy's testimony. Osler answered that it was for the defence to produce a translator for a witness whose testimony required one. The defence further objected that, although the answers were being taken down in French, they were going to the jury in English. Osler replied, 'The witness can explain himself in English but was told not to do so; it is not my difficulty.' According to one MP in the 1886 debate over Riel, defence counsel F.-X. Lemieux offered a number of other examples of translation problems.[57] Why he did not use these as part of the appeal is a question we cannot answer.

The first substantive ground of appeal questioned the jurisdiction of the court. This point had been argued at great length before Judge Richardson and dismissed. The Manitoba court agreed with Judge Richardson. To find otherwise would have been to question a decision rendered by two of these three judges in another appeal on similar grounds, and might have turned the whole administration of justice in the west into chaos. Finally, the appellate judges turned down the defence plea of insanity. They made a special point of noting that Riel's lawyers were not complaining about unfairness, or about the charge of the magistrate to the jury, almost as though these would have been important matters had they been raised. Goulet observes that the defence had not complained about the failure to produce documents which Riel insisted that he needed to make his case, or indeed about its failure to call witnesses deemed essential by Riel. This absence of complaint was related, of course, to the line of defence taken by his lawyers, to which those same lawyers could hardly point.

Nowhere in the appeal was mentioned the involvement of one of the Manitoba justices – Lewis Wallbridge – in planning the crown strategy to prosecute Riel. Nor could this point possibly have been made, since the involvement was behind the scenes and was discovered by a researcher more than a century after the event.[58] Wallbridge had not only given important advice to the government about the venue of the trial, however, but had also helped orchestrate appeal proceedings in another case involving the Regina court which provided a precedent for the appellate court's decision in the Riel appeal. Although he admits that judges gave private advice to the government in this era, Ronald Olesky asserts that 'Wallbridge's behind-the-scenes conduct certainly went beyond the law, even by standards of his own time.' Wallbridge should have disqualified himself, but he doubtless did not expect his private involvement to become public knowledge. Whether this conflict of interest is sufficient reason for posthumously overturning the Riel conviction is another matter entirely. The question of a pardon on this basis turns not on one piece of evidence but rather on whether one either believes that the crown – as Olesky charged in his article on the Riel case – 'exercised its prosecutorial discretion unfairly' or that for some other reason Riel did not get a fair trial.

The Riel conviction was subsequently taken, by a petition for leave to appeal, from the Manitoba Court of Queen's Bench to the lords of the Judicial Committee of the Privy Council, sitting in London. In that petition, the whole question of Riel's insanity was omitted, and the grounds of appeal were reduced to jurisdiction and the shorthand recording process, with still no complaint about the facilities for translation in what was supposed to be a bilingual court. The Privy Council committee noted that neither the facts of the trial nor Riel's commission of high treason were being contested. It observed that the only fact argued before the jury was whether Riel was not guilty by reason of mental infirmity, that the jury had 'negatived that defence,' and that it was not now being argued that such a decision was incorrect. The committee insisted that to doubt the jurisdiction of the court (which meant doubting the right of the Canadian legislature to enact the North-West Territories Act of 1880) would have been quite mischievous. As to the recording process, there was 'no complaint' of inaccuracy or mistake from Riel's lawyers. Given the feebleness of the petition, its rejection was inevitable.[59]

Post-Appeal Actions

In the 1886 debate over Riel in the House of Commons, one of the critics of the government (Guillaume Amyot) pointed out that the legislation under which Riel had been tried specified that, in the case of a sentence to death, the magistrate 'shall forward to the Minister of Justice full notes of the evidence with his report upon the case, and the execution should be stayed until such report is received and the pleasure of the Governor thereon is communicated to the Lieutenant-Governor.' As Amyot noted, 'the execution is not left by the Government to take its course, as in ordinary cases, but must be ordered by them.'[60] The phrase 'the pleasure of the Governor' in practice meant 'the decision of the cabinet.' Lord Dufferin had acted on the death sentence of Ambroise Lépine in 1875 on his own initiative, but that action was presumably with the consent of a government which did not wish to be involved in a decision on the matter. In 1885 the Macdonald government could not really avoid sanctioning any sentence of death which it had worked so hard to get.

The cabinet would hardly have taken seriously any argument that Riel had been justified in his resistance to the law, but there remained the question of Riel's mental state at the time of the resistance. As noted earlier, the government appointed a medical commission to examine Riel's sanity before he was executed. The jury, of course, had recommended mercy. Perhaps the best discussion of the government's treatment of the medical commission is in Flanagan's *Riel and Rebellion*. Here Flanagan points out in considerable detail how the government had manipulated the commission. The prime minister gave private instructions in advance to one member of the commission, Dr Michael Lavell. More to the point, two of the members of the commission, Dr Lavell and Dr François-Xavier Valade, came to opposite conclusions on the critical matter of whether Riel was indeed an 'accountable being.' The cabinet ignored Valade's testimony, and ordered execution. In the debates in the Commons, the government manipulated Valade's report for public consumption. Curiously enough, despite this episode which he himself condemns, Flanagan insists that 'the government made a legally defensible decision in the end' because all the doctors agreed that Riel was legally accountable under the McNaghten rules.[61] Beyond the question of the government's bad faith – which in this instance even Flanagan admits – is the larger point that the government had a choice, which it exercised on strictly political grounds. It need not have executed Riel. It need not have pardoned him outright either. It could have commuted his sentence to a lengthy term of imprisonment, issued a conditional pardon on the basis of the jury's recommmendation of mercy, or ordered a retrial because of legal arguments that could have been made, the latter requiring some further action by the defence that it did not undertake. A pardon was a political decision, one that has been examined by numerous historians. However, the failure of the defence to make legal arguments could have prevented this outcome.

CONCLUSIONS

The existing procedures in the North-West Territories tilted the playing field in the crown's favour, and the departures from the prevailing British norms of due process were particularly egregious in the context of high treason charges, but such an assessment in the circumstances is a constitutional rather than a legal one. The crown effectively pursued its responsibilities to secure conviction. The same cannot said of Riel's defence counsel. The defence team failed to pursue a number of legal issues and it is perhaps here that we see the main reason for the failure of justice in 1885.

Two connected observations need to be made about the defence team. First, the two senior counsel did very well in their post-Riel legal lives. Fitzpatrick rose to be chief justice of Canada, Lemieux to become chief justice of Quebec. This is not to suggest that they were being directly rewarded for their services in the Riel case, but it is to suggest that these men were ambitious establishment lawyers who were not likely to want to play too dirty with the system, particularly by attempting to expose its western policy as so poor as to lead directly to rebellion. Politicians in the House of Commons might make this case, but lawyers seeking to avoid blotting their copybooks could hardly do so. The possibility of unspoken and implicit collusion between crown and defence, particularly in very political trials, is one of the open secrets of the legal profession. Fitzpatrick and Lemieux, when they first met with Riel in June 1885, must have been relieved to discover that he seemed quite irrational, for it meant that they could employ a defence that essentially blamed Riel for the rebellion rather than a defence that blamed the government. Malcolm Cameron, in his speech in the House of Commons on the Riel case in 1886, does a far better job of defending Riel than his lawyers did in 1885, but that was because Cameron went after government policy. What Riel did not have on his defence team was a maverick professional defence lawyer, a Clarence Darrow or Horace Rumpole-type character whose sole goal in life was not the Canadian equivalent of 'taking silk' but defending his client by whatever means proved necessary. Such a lawyer would either have been given considerable leeway by the crown or broken down the crown's professions of fairness. As it was, the possibility of a real defence of Riel was never really raised, except by the accused and, perhaps, by James Greenshields.

As George Goulet put it, Riel was 'deprived of his right to make full answer and defence,' but not so much by the crown as by his own lawyers.[62]

This raises an interesting question about any posthumous action on the conviction and sentence of Riel for treason. Flanagan seems to operate on the assumption that, if he can demonstrate that the crown committed no heinous examples of unfairness, there would be no reason for posthumous redress. But surely the defence can be equally responsible for a miscarriage of justice. I do not think the case has really been made that the crown was fair (legally sound decisions are not necessarily fair). Every time it had a choice it opted for the course of action least favourable or most hostile to Riel. But, in the end, Riel's own lawyers were the people who were most responsible for his failure to receive justice in 1885.

NOTES

1 House of Commons, *Debates*, 1886, 105.
2 Ibid., 72.
3 In June 1998 Bill C-417 (An Act respecting Louis Riel) was introduced in the Canadian Parliament as a private members' bill, sponsored by one member of each political party. It sought to reverse the conviction of Riel and recognize him as 'a Father of Confederation and the Founder of the Province of Manitoba.' It was not adopted.
4 Much of the literature on the trial concentrates on the madness question. For a sampling, see H. Gilson and Dr. Bourque, 'La Folie de Riel et la justice anglaise,' *L'Union médicale du Canada* 14 (1885): 561–4; H. Gilson, 'Étude sur l'état mental de Louis Riel,' *L'Encéphale* 6 (1886): 51–60; Daniel Clark, 'A Psycho-Medical History of Louis Riel,' *American Journal of Insanity* 44 (1887–8): 33–51; Clark, 'A Few Canadian Cases in Criminal Courts in which the Plea of Insanity was Presented,' *Transactions of the American Medico-Psychological Association* 2 (1995): 183–90; W.W. Ireland, *Through the Ivory Gate* (Edinburgh: Bell and Bradfute 1889); C.K. Clarke, 'A Critical Study of the Case of Louis Riel,' *Queen's Quarterly* 12 (1905): 379–88, 13 (1905): 14–26; Frank W. Anderson, 'Louis Riel's Insanity Reconsidered,' *Saskatchewan History* 3 (1950): 104–10; Harold Knox, 'The Question of Louis Riel's Insanity,' *Collections Historical and Scientific Society of Manitoba*, ser 3: 6 (1951); E.R. Markson, 'The Life and Death of Louis Riel: A Psychoanalytic Commentary,' *Canadian Psychiatric Association Journal* 10 (1965); 246–52; E. Desjardins and C. Dumas, 'Le Complexe medical de Louis Riel,' *L'Union médicale du Canada* 99 (1970): 1656–61; Simon N. Verdun-Jones, '"Not Guilty by Reason of Insanity": The Historical Roots of the Canadian Insanity Defence, 1843–1920,' in L.A. Knafla, ed., *Crime and Criminal Justice in Europe and Canada* (Waterloo, Ont.: Wilfrid Laurier Press

1981), 179–218. Riel's trial is also considered at some length in every biography of the man as well. The reaction to the trial and execution in Quebec – not really considered in this chapter – may be followed in A.I. Silver, *The French-Canadian Idea of Confederation 1864–1900* (Toronto: University of Toronto Press 1982).

5 The modern literature that focuses on a broad range of legal issues includes Desmond Morton, 'An Introduction,' in *The Queen v. Louis Riel* (Toronto: University of Toronto Press 1974), vii–xxxv; D.F. Brown, 'The Meaning of Treason in 1885,' *Saskatchewan History* 28 (1975): 65–73; Lewis H. Thomas, 'A Judicial Murder – The Trial of Louis Riel,' in Howard Palmer, ed., *The Settlement of the West* (Calgary: University of Calgary Press 1977), 37–59, 239–41; Bob Beal and Rod Macleod, *Prairie Fire: The 1885 North-West Rebellion* (Edmonton: Hurtig 1984; 2nd ed., 1994), 293–305; Thomas Flanagan, *Riel and the Rebellion: 1885 Reconsidered* (Saskatoon: Western Producer Prairie Books 1985); Ronald L. Olesky, 'Louis Riel and the Crown Letters,' *Canadian Lawyer*, February 1998; George R.D. Goulet, *The Trial of Louis Riel: Justice and Mercy Denied* (Calgary: Tellwell 1999); Jeremy Ravi Mumford, 'Why Was Louis Riel, a United States Citizen, Hanged as a Canadian Traitor in 1885'? *CHR* 88, no. 2 (2007): 237–62.

6 Among the chief authorities are: Alexander Begg, *The Creation of Manitoba* (1871); [Joseph Edmund Collins,] *The Story of Louis Riel the Rebel Chief* (Toronto: J.S. Robertson and Brothers 1885); Charles Arkoll Boulton, *Reminiscences of the North-West Rebellions, with a Record of the Raising of Her Majesty's 100th Regiment in Canada* (Toronto: Grit Printing and Publishing 1886); W.F. Bryant, *The Blood of Abel* (Hastings, Neb.: The *Gazette Journal* 1887); George Young, *Manitoba Memories: Leaves from My Life in the Prairie Province, 1868–1884* (Toronto: William Briggs 1897); A.G. Morice, 'Á propos de la mort de Scott,' *Les Cloches de Saint Boniface* 13 (1914); Georges Dugas, 'Encore la mort de Scott,' *Les Cloches de Saint-Boniface* 13 (1914); Edwin E. Kreutzweiser, *The Red River Insurrection: Its Causes and Events* (Gardenvale, Que.: Garden City Press, n.d.); A.G. Morice, *A Critical History of the Red River Insurrection* (1935), passim; George F.G. Stanley, *The Birth of Western Canada: A History of the Riel Rebellions* (Toronto: University of Toronto Press 1936); William McCartney Davidson, *Louis Riel 1844–1885* (Calgary: Albertan Publishing Company 1955); Joseph Howard, *Strange Empire: Louis Riel and the Métis People* (New York: William Morrow and Company 1952); Robert E. Lamb, *Thunder in the North* (New York: Pageant Press 1957); E.B. Osler, *The Man Who Had to Hang: Louis Riel* (Toronto: Longmans Green and Company 1961); G.F.G. Stanley, *Louis Riel* (Toronto: Ryerson Press 1963); Robert Walter Weir Robertson, *The Execution of Thomas Scott* (Toronto: Burns and MacEachern 1968); Hartwell Bowsfield, ed., *Louis*

Riel: The Rebel and the Hero (Toronto: University of Toronto Press 1971); Peter Charlebois, *The Life of Louis Riel in Pictures* (Toronto: NC Press 1978); J.E. Rea, 'Thomas Scott,' *DCB*, 9: 707–9; Thomas Flanagan, *Louis 'David' Riel: 'Prophet of the New World'* (Toronto: University of Toronto Press 1979, rev. ed. 1994); Lewis H. Thomas, 'Louis Riel,' *DCB*,11: 736-52; Bernard Saint-Aubin, *Louis David Riel: Un destin tragique* (Montreal: Les Éditions la Presse 1985); Maggie Siggins, *Riel: A Life of Revolution* (Toronto: McClelland and Stewart 1994); J.M. Bumsted, *Louis Riel v. Canada: The Making of a Rebel* (Winnipeg: Great Plains Publications 2001); Jennifer Reid, *Louis Riel and the Creation of Modern Canada* (Albuquerque: University of New Mexico Press 2008).

7 See my 'Thomas Scott and the Daughter of Time,' *Prairie Forum* 23, no. 2 (1998): 145–70, and 'Why Shoot Thomas Scott? A Study in Historical Evidence,' in *Thomas Scott's Body and Other Essays on Early Manitoba History* (Winnipeg: University of Manitoba Press 2000).

8 Quoted in D.N. Sprague, 'The Manitoba Land Question, 1870–1882,' in J.M. Bumsted, ed., *Interpreting Canada's Past*, vol. 2 (Toronto: Oxford University Press 1986), 4.

9 David Lee, 'The Métis: Militant Rebels of 1885,' *Canadian Ethnic Studies* 21, no. 3 (1989): 1–19.

10 Quoted in Thomas, 'Louis Riel,' 746.

11 Bowsfield, ed., *Louis Riel: The Rebel and the Hero*, 116.

12 The best survey of the rebellion is Beal and Macleod, *Prairie Fire*. But see also Walter Hildebrant, *The Battle of Batoche: British Small Warfare and the Entrenched Métis* (rev. ed., Regina: Canadian Plains Research Centre 1999).

13 There are numerous newspapers reports of the proceedings. The case is reproduced in the Canada Sessional Papers and in Morton, *The Queen v. Louis Riel*, who also provides a comprehensive summary of the proceedings (xiii–xxv). A number of other modern studies, such as Beal and Macleod, *Prairie Fire*, also offer useful summaries that emphasize different aspects of the trial.

14 Thomas Flanagan and Neil Watson, 'The Riel Trial Revisited,' *Saskatchewan History* 34 (1981): 57–73.

15 Flanagan, *Riel and the Rebellion*; Flanagan, *Louis 'David' Riel*.

16 Flanagan, *Riel and the Rebellion*, 118.

17 Ibid.

18 Beal and Macleod, *Prairie Fire*, 292.

19 For evidence on this point, see *CST 1* and *CST 2*.

20 Charles Rosenberg, *The Trial of the Assassin Guiteau: Psychiatry and the Law in the Gilded Age* (Chicago: University of Chicago Press 1995).

21 Flanagan and Watson, 'The Riel Trial Revisited,' 58.

22 Beal and Macleod, *Prairie Fire*, 293–4. Connor, also named John, was convicted

of murder in Regina in a case presided over by Richardson and defended by
Johnstone. Johnstone made the similar arguments in Riel's case, although
Connor had been appealed to the Manitoba Court of Appeal and the Judicial
Committee of the Privy Council, both of which upheld the conviction.

23 See Louis Knafla's chapter in this volume.
24 Ibid.
25 32–3 Vic. c.29 s.102, An Act respecting Procedure in Criminal Cases and Other
Matters relating to Criminal Law, which provides: 'If any person indicted for
any offence be found insane, and upon arraignment be so found by a jury empanelled for that purpose, so that such person cannot be tried upon such indictment, or if, upon the trial of any person so indicted, such person appears
to the jury charged with the indictment to be insane, the Court, before whom
such person is brought to be arraigned, or is tried as aforesaid, may direct
such finding to be recorded, and thereupon may order such person to be kept
in strict custody until the pleasure of the Lieutenant-Governor be known.'
26 See also Donald B. Smith, 'William Henry Jackson: Riel's Secretary,' *The
Beaver*, spring 1981, and Cyril Greenland and John Griffin, 'Riel's Secretary:
Another Case of Involuntary Confinement,' *Canadian Psychiatric Association
Journal* 23 (1978): 469–77.
27 Bob Beal, 'Attacking the State: The Levying War Charge in Canadian Treason
Law,' MA thesis, University of Alberta 1994.
28 See Thomas Flanagan, 'Hugh Richardson,' *DCB*, 14: 7770–1; also Roderick
Martin, 'Lords of the Western Bench,' in Louis Knafla and Rick Klumpen-
hower, eds., *Laws and Societies in the Canadian Prairie West, 1670–1940* (Calgary:
Reynolds 1997), 158–9.
29 Enos Stutsman's treatment of Recorder John Black in Red River in an 1868
murder trial reminds us of what can happen when inexperienced judges encounter highly skilled lawyers.
30 See Brown, 'The Meaning of Treason in 1885'; and the chapter by Desmond
Brown and Barry Wright in this volume. Goulet, *The Trial of Louis Riel*, 189–
202, attempts to cast doubts on the applicability of the 1352 statute.
31 Matthew Hale, *The History of the Pleas of the Crown* (London, 1736), 1: 133.
32 Blackstone, *Commentaries on the Laws of England* (12th ed., rev., 1795), 4: 81.
33 Mumford, 'Why Was Louis Riel.' As Mumford explains, the American press
did not identify him as an American citizen and the Riel case marked the
beginning of a long retreat from protecting U.S. citizens facing prosecutions
abroad.
34 See *The Queen v. Louis Riel*, 67, and the chapter by Blake Brown in this volume
for applications of the legislation in 1866 and uncertainties about its applicability to British subjects, issues tested in *Regina v. McMahon*, 26 Upper Canada

Queen's Bench 195 (1866). See also F. Murray Greenwood,. 'The Prince Affair: "Gallant Colonel" or "The Windsor Butcher"?' *CST* 2, 160–87.

35 Beal and Macleod, *Prairie Fire*, 296.

36 See Beal and Wright's chapter in this volume. The initial draft charges were duplicated to cover Riel as both an alien and as a British subject joined with others and being in arms to levy war in battles at Duck Lake, Fish Creek, and Batoche. The information eventually preferred six counts of levying war under Edward III treating Riel as a British subject, three counts under the doctrine of perpetual allegiance, and three under the doctrine of temporary protection/local allegiance.

37 The edition used by Burbidge was *Archbold's Pleading and Evidence in Criminal Cases*, J. Jervis ed. (London, 1874). See Beal, 'Attacking the State,' 97–8.

38 Ibid., 130.

39 Flanagan, *Riel and the Rebellion*, 136.

40 House of Commons, *Debates*, 1886, 255; W.M. Davidson, *The Life and Times of Louis Riel* (Calgary: Albertan Printers 1951), 104.

41 *The Queen v. Louis Riel*, 59–62.

42 Ibid., 53–6.

43 Verdun-Jones, '"Not Guilty by Reason of Insanity."'

44 (1843) 8 E.R. 718. See Daniel N. Robinson, *Wild Beasts & Idle Humours: The Insanity Defense from Antiquity to the Present* (Cambridge, Mass.: Harvard University Press 1996), esp. 163–91; Joel Peter Eigen, *Witnessing Insanity: Madness and Mad-Doctors in the English Court* (New Haven, Conn., and London: Yale University Press 1995).

45 Riel to Bourget, 15 May 1876, George F.G. Stanley, General Editor, *The Collected Writings of Louis Riel/Les ecrits Complets de Louis Riel* (Edmonton: University of Alberta Press 1985), 2: 17.

46 Thomas Flanagan, 'On the Trail of the *Massinihican*: Louis Riel's Encounter with Theosophy,' *Canadian Journal of Church History* 37 (1995): 89–98.

47 In general, consult Richard Kyle, *The Religious Fringe: A History of Alternative Religions in America* (Downer's Grove, Ill.: Intervarsity Press 1993).

48 J.M. Bumsted, *Henry Alline 1748–1784* (Toronto: University of Toronto Press 1970).

49 Fawn Brodie, *No Man Knows My History: The Life of Joseph Smith the Mormon Prophet* (2nd ed., rev., N.Y.: Alfred A. Knopf 1982), 39–40.

50 Julius Silberger, Jr, *Mary Baker Eddy: An Interpretive Biography of the Founder of Christian Science* (Boston: Little, Brown 1980).

51 Justice Tindall's answer, quoted in Robinson, *Wild Beasts*, 172–3.

52 Quoted in ibid., 179.

53 Quoted in Verdun-Jones, '"Not Guilty by Reason of Insanity,"' 189.

54 Goulet, *The Trial of Louis Riel*, 139.
55 Ibid., 242–63.
56 *The Queen v. Louis Riel*, 229.
57 House of Commons, *Debates*, 11 March 1886, 79.
58 Olesky, 'Louis Riel and the Crown Letters.'
59 For the text of this decision, see House of Commons, *Debates*, 1886, 75–6.
60 Ibid., 79.
61 Flanagan, *Riel and the Rebellion*, 145.
62 Goulet, *The Trial of Louis Riel*, 267.

10

The White Man Governs: The 1885 Indian Trials

BILL WAISER

When Louis Riel dropped to his death – some might argue, martyrdom – on 16 November 1885, many Canadians considered his execution the final act in the North-West rebellion. After all, the Métis leader had precipitated the armed showdown with the Canadian government by declaring a provisional government at Batoche in the late spring of 1885, and it symbolically ended with his hanging in Regina almost exactly eight months later. Popular fascination with Riel and his fate, however, has tended to deflect attention away from how Ottawa dealt with prairie Indians in the aftermath of the rebellion. Indian Affairs officials had been searching for a way to crush any remaining vestiges of First Nations autonomy, especially among the Plains Cree, and deliberately used the Indians' apparent involvement in the rebellion to justify a number of repressive measures. Twenty-eight reserves were identified as disloyal, even though in several instances the bands had taken no part in the fighting and simply fled their homes in fear of what might befall them. Measures for the future 'management' of Indians were also secretly adopted, including the requirement that Indians not leave their reserves without first securing a pass. Above all, those First Nations individuals brought to trial were to feel the sting of the full force of the law. This government retribution – and the great suffering that accompanied it – was wholly unjustified. Most Indians had staunchly stood by the queen during the rebellion, and yet in the aftermath the Canadian government treated them as outlaws in their own country. It was as if the First Nations, and not Riel and his followers, were the culprits.

THE REBELLION[1]

The First Nations of the western interior had never been more vulnerable in their relations with Ottawa as they were following the 1885 North-West rebellion. It should not have been that way. In the summer of 1884, exiled Métis leader Louis Riel had returned to Canada at the invitation of the mixed-blood and white settlers of the Saskatchewan country to secure redress of a number of grievances. At first, Riel sent petitions and letters to Ottawa, but by the late winter he increasingly began to advocate more provocative measures in the naive belief that he could repeat the success of the Red River resistance fifteen years earlier – only this time with the collective might of a grand Indian-Métis alliance. Riel made his move on 19 March 1885 when he declared the formation of a provisional government at his Batoche headquarters and demanded the surrender of forts Carlton and Battleford. One week later, a small Métis party under Riel's 'general' Gabriel Dumont clashed with a combined force of North-West Mounted Police (NWMP) and civilian volunteers near Duck Lake.

The battle of Duck Lake is often cited as the opening salvo in Canada's first and only civil war. The clash was significant for a number of reasons. First, it made a negotiated settlement impossible and effectively forced Riel and his Métis followers to fight a rebellion they could not win. And the reason they could not win is that the Conservative government, upon learning of the Mounted Police's routing, quickly mobilized a large militia force to put down the insurrection; Prime Minister John A. Macdonald may have ignored western grievances, but war was another matter. The swiftness of the government response was also motivated in part by its misguided belief that the Métis could count on Indian support. The Duck Lake battle had taken place on that part of the Carlton trail which ran through Beardy's reserve; Indians were also spotted in Métis ranks. It was easy for Canadian officials to conclude, then, that the Cree had joined forces with Riel and that they were actually dealing with a combined Indian-Métis insurgency that could sweep across the western interior. Little did they realize that the majority of the region's First Nations wanted nothing to do with the rebellion – they were not prepared to break their treaty pledge to live in peace – and that most Indians at Batoche had been taken there against their will. Michel Dumas, the farm instructor at the nearby One Arrow reserve and future secretary of Riel's governing council, for example, ordered the Willow Cree to slaughter their cattle and join the Métis.

This fear that the North-West rebellion, like a prairie fire, might not be contained was fuelled by events elsewhere. Upon hearing of the Duck Lake battle, chiefs Little Pine and Poundmaker decided to lead a delegation to Fort Battleford, at the junction of the Battle and North Saskatchewan rivers, to confirm their allegiance to the crown and secure rations for their hungry bands. But by the time the Indians reached Battleford on 30 March 1885, all of the town's 500 residents had taken refuge in the small police stockade in the belief that the incoming Cree had warlike intentions. Little Pine and Poundmaker patiently waited all day for the local Indian agent to meet with them. Only when it became apparent that their mission to Battleford had been in vain did some of the Indians help themselves to provisions and other items in the abandoned stores and homes before heading back home late that night. From the vantage point of the stockade, it appeared to the frightened residents that they were under siege – how else would one explain the looting if Cree intentions were peaceful? The Indians had done nothing, however, to harass the townspeople; the telegraph line, for example, was not cut. Yet this same telegraph line would be used by the beleaguered residents of the stockade to plead with Canadian authorities to send someone to rescue them before it was too late.

Three days later, the horrifying news of a massacre at the tiny hamlet of Frog Lake, along the North Saskatchewan River near the present-day Alberta-Saskatchewan border, made things seem even worse. Chafing at the hands of a mean-spirited Indian agent, several of the more aggressive members of Big Bear's band decided to take advantage of the police defeat at Duck Lake by taking the residents of Frog Lake prisoner and helping themselves to much-needed rations. But the plan turned into a murderous rampage on the morning of 2 April 1885, when Wandering Spirit and his warriors found alcohol during their looting spree and turned their guns on their hostages. By the time Big Bear, who had been away at the start of the trouble and pushed aside by the warrior society, could stop the carnage, nine men lay dead, including the Indian agent, the farm instructor, and two Catholic priests. Although the killings at Frog Lake had not been orchestrated by Riel, the link between the two seemed obvious; it was as if the rebellion virus had infected the North Saskatchewan country. The other victim that tragic morning was Big Bear, who had been spearheading a diplomatic offensive to force the government to honour its treaty promises. Even though he exercised only limited authority over his followers, as chief, the government held him personally responsible for the murders.

Such was the situation that faced Major-General Frederick Middleton, the sixty-year-old commander of the Canadian militia who was handed the task of organizing and leading the 8,000-strong punitive force against Riel. 'Old Fred,' as he was mockingly called by his men, decided from the outset to concentrate his army's energies on the Métis stronghold at Batoche, believing that a quick knockout blow there would effectively end the rebellion. He consequently started north from Fort Qu'Appelle on 6 April with the first of the troops in the field, confident that any resistance would melt away like the spring snow once his force arrived in rebel territory. The events in the Battleford and Pitt areas, however, forced Middleton to amend his plan. On 11 April, he instructed Lieutenant-Colonel W.D. Otter and his 500 men to proceed directly from Swift Current to North Battleford, instead of descending the South Saskatchewan River to Batoche as originally arranged. Another assault force would march north from Calgary to Edmonton and then eastward along the North Saskatchewan River. Middleton largely regarded these secondary columns as a security measure; his sights remained firmly fixed on Batoche.

The Métis, in the meantime, made no attempt to draw on their familiarity with the countryside and conduct a guerilla campaign, but calmly prepared to meet the Canadian response by building an elaborate system of trenches at Batoche. This decision to lie in wait on Métis home ground was made at the urging of Riel; as a prophet with a divine mission, he believed that God was on his side and that there was nothing to fear from the approaching army. Indeed, the only action that Riel approved in the first few weeks of the campaign was the dispatch of messengers to outlying Indian reserves with an invitation to join him. This search for First Nations recruits – by force in the case of the Whitecap Sioux at Moose Woods – was made necessary because too many of the local Métis refused to take part in the troubles; only an estimated 250 of a total regional Métis population of some 1,500 were prepared to defend Batoche. How much military support the Indians actually offered Riel, however, is debatable; not only were many aged and even more poorly armed than the Métis, but most were there reluctantly.

Middleton captured Métis headquarters on 12 May 1885 after a four-day battle that amounted at times to little more than skirmishing. In fact, the final assault on the village was over in minutes, largely because the remaining defenders had all but exhausted their ammunition and were unable to offer any resistance. Many paid with their lives. Whereas Middleton lost only eight men during the battle, the Batoche dead may have numbered as many as two dozen. Riel was much luckier. He had prayed for a miracle throughout the siege and had initially escaped with Gabriel Dumont, but he decided to surrender three days later in a bid to take his cause to the courts (the consequences of which are examined in J.M. Bumsted's chapter in this volume).

The fall of Batoche was the first Canadian victory of the North-West campaign. The troubles were far from over, though – there was still the matter of Poundmaker and Big Bear. Following their unsuccessful pilgrimage to Battleford, the Cree had anxiously gathered on the Poundmaker reserve in early April along a creek not far from the base of Cut Knife Hill. Far from joining the rebel cause, as events in late March had implied, the local bands were just as frightened and confused by events as the townspeople cowering in the fort. Like their white counterparts, they had essentially come together for defensive reasons. This uneasy calm was shattered following the arrival of Colonel Otter's relief column at Battleford on 24 April. Disappointed that he had not seen any action on his march north from Swift Current and determined to punish the Indians for their apparent siege of Battleford, Otter assembled an attack force of about 325 men, complete with two cannons and a Gatling gun, and planned to storm the sleeping Cut Knife camp in the early hours of 2 May. But the Indians were alerted to the coming of the troops and mounted a counter-attack which proved so effective that Otter's retreating force might have been wiped out if not for Poundmaker's restraint of the warriors.

Two days after the surprise Otter attack, the Cut Knife camp was visited again –this time by a group of Métis emissaries who had been sent by Riel to bring the Indians to Batoche in preparation for the showdown with Middleton. Poundmaker had steadfastly avoided such a commitment since the Métis leader's return to Canada the previous summer, but he was effectively taken prisoner and forced to go along. The Cut Knife party, however, soon abandoned its plan to return to Batoche when, on reaching the east end of the Eagle Hills, just south of Battleford, the Métis agents learned of Batoche's fall and Riel's surrender. It now fell to Poundmaker, the diplomat, to reach a settlement with Canadian authorities, and on the morning of 26 May, exactly two months after the Duck Lake skirmish, he proudly led his people into Battleford to submit to a waiting General Middleton.

That left Big Bear, who had been busy adding to his list of supposed rebellion crimes. On 15 April, less than two weeks after the brutal Frog Lake slayings, Wandering Spirit and his warriors moved against Fort Pitt in order to secure the area and gain access to much-needed food and provisions. Yet, instead of attacking the defenceless post, the Indians, at Big Bear's urging, allowed the Mounted Police detachment to escape aboard a scow down the ice-choked North Saskatchewan River to Battleford. The remaining occupants of the post, including several families, were taken hostage and joined a growing camp, eventually numbering around 1,000 people, back at Frog Lake. Nothing more was done. The Cree made no attempt either to move eastward to Batoche or to prepare for an eventual Canadian response. As in the case of the Cut Knife camp, they waited peacefully in the region to see how the rebellion would unfold.

The answer was soon forthcoming in the form of the Alberta Field Force headed by Major-General T.B. Strange. On 20 April 1885 the 1,000-man column had left Calgary for the North Saskatchewan country, and, despite encountering not a hint of Indian resistance along the trail, they marched into Fort Edmonton like liberating heroes. Not until 26 May, however, did the force finally arrive in the Fort Pitt district – just in time to interrupt a 'thirst dance' which the Cree were holding for spiritual guidance at the base of Frenchman Butte. The arrival of the troops threw the camp into turmoil, and, under Wandering Spirit's guidance, the Cree moved a few miles north to a more defensible position along the valley of Red Deer Creek. The battle of Frenchman Butte, as it was incorrectly named at the time, started on the morning of 28 May, when Strange shelled the Indian pits on the north side of the creek valley and then ordered his men forward into the ravine. But Wandering Spirit had chosen his position well and Strange had to abandon the frontal assault in favour of using his cannon to inflict whatever damage he could; both sides eventually withdrew after a few hours of skirmishing.

The Indians were thoroughly shaken by the intensity of the assault and decided to flee north through the muskeg-riddled forest rather than face the troops again. They eventually reached the southwest corner of Loon or Makwa Lake on 2 June. But any hope of safe haven was dashed the next morning when an advance party of about sixty men under NWMP Inspector Sam Steele swooped down on the unsuspecting Indians and their prisoners who were camped at the lake narrows. The fight at Steele's Narrows, the final battle of the rebellion, lasted little more than half an hour, but it seemed to break any remaining Indian resistance. The camp divided in smaller groups which went their separate ways, while the last of the prisoners were released.

The flight of the Indians kept the Canadian troops busy for most of June. With the capture of Riel and the surrender of Poundmaker, General Middleton was determined to apprehend Big Bear and bring the campaign to a successful conclusion, even if it meant tying up his troops for several weeks in a seemingly futile chase. He consequently moved to Fort Pitt with a large force and ordered three other columns north: Commissioner A.G. Irvine of the NWMP would march from Prince Albert to Green Lake; Colonel Otter from Battleford to Turtle Lake; and General Strange from Frog Lake to Cold Lake. But the largest manhunt in Canadian history came up empty-handed. In fact, it was only because the fugitive Indians decided that they could not wander in the northern wilderness for much longer that they either gave themselves up at the nearest community or sought asylum in the United States. These defections meant that Big Bear was effectively abandoned by the time he surrendered to authorities near Fort Carlton on 4 July; by that point, the old chief had been reduced to a shell of his former self, while his strategy for dealing with the Canadian government lay in total ruin.

PUNISHING THE FIRST NATIONS

Edgar Dewdney, Indian commissioner and lieutenant governor for the North-West Territories, was well aware that the majority of Indians had remained aloof from the Métis during the rebellion, while only a few bands were driven to the rebel side by a mixture of force and lies. In a long, reflective letter to Prime Minister Macdonald in early June 1885, Canada's most senior official in the west laid the blame for much of the death and destruction over the past few weeks on the pernicious activities of Riel and his emissaries. He also severely criticized the behaviour of those settlers who had abandoned their homes in panic and confusion and, in doing so, created the false impression that the insurgents were carrying the day. 'That they [the Cree] ever thought, intended or wished that the uprising should have reached the proportion it has,' he emphatically told Sir John, 'I do not believe.'[2]

But Dewdney's understanding of the Indian situation had its limits. In the same letter, he advised the prime minister that the 'break[ing] loose' of a few bands had turned 'a Half-breed revolt of small magnitude into an uprising of large dimensions.' According to the commissioner, the country had come perilously close to 'an Indian war from one end of the Territories to the other.'[3] Dewdney realized that this assessment of the situation was totally unrealistic and dangerously misleading. Nor was he sympathetic to the bands that had been tampered with by Métis agents and were innocent of any misconduct. Why should he be? Watching the conflict unfold from the territorial capital, Dewdney saw in the rebellion an unprecedented opportunity to rid himself and the Canadian government of troublesome Indian leaders and their nagging call for revision of the treaties. Though privately he knew better, it was to his advantage to portray the Indians as reckless allies of Riel who would cause trouble in the future unless reined in.[4]

Dewdney's campaign against the Indians began to take shape in mid-June 1885, well before hostilities in the North Saskatchewan country had officially come to an end. He sent three letters to the prime minister in the space of seven days. In them, he reported that Indian Agent Ansdell Macrae had found several incriminating notes that Riel had sent the Cree in the Battleford district, including the one calling on them to destroy the fort.[5] He also urged Lawrence Vankoughnet, the deputy superintendent general of Indian affairs, to withhold annuity payments from the Indians until he could determine who had 'participated in anyway whatever in the late rebellion.'[6] He even went so far as to suggest the breaking up of several reserves. 'Some bands have violated the terms of the treaty made with them,' Dewdney concluded, 'and ... it will be for the govt to say what will be done with them and their reserves.'

This tough talk found a receptive audience in Ottawa, and on 3 July, the day before the surrender of Cree chief Big Bear, Dewdney was instructed to 'quietly collect evidence' against all Indians suspected of any wrongdoing, no matter how trivial.[7] Local agents and farm instructors had already been doing this, for they looked upon the troubles as a chance to strengthen their own hand over their charges, as well as extract a measure of revenge against recalcitrant chiefs and individuals. In the Battleford district, for example, Macrae had been visiting the outlying reserves since late May, collecting evidence and lining up witnesses for the expected trials of those who had been involved in the fighting at Cut Knife.[8] To the south, meanwhile, in the Qu'Appelle district, Treaty 4 agent Allan McDonald was demanding that the File Hills chiefs and headmen be deposed for allowing the slaughter of twenty head of cattle on the four reserves. His earlier concern for the bands' welfare, especially when the Canadian troops had first arrived in the region in April, had given way to intense anger and suspicion. There was no room in his heart for leniency; the guilty parties had to be harshly punished. 'Action of this kind will settle all difficulties in the future,' McDonald implored, 'an example ... must be made.'[9] Dewdney agreed, and at a Regina hearing in early July, two of the File Hills chiefs, Peepeekisis and Starblanket, were reprimanded for being off their reserve.[10]

Hayter Reed, Dewdney's ambitious assistant, was given the job of determining the loyalty of the bands. Reed had been in the field since late March 1885, spending almost two months hunkered down in Prince Albert with NWMP Commissioner William Irvine before proceeding westward to join Frederick Middleton, the commander of the Canadian Field Force, at Battleford and later Fort Pitt. In fact, the assistant Indian commissioner was in the Loon Lake area when the last of the Frog Lake prisoners were released. Reed would play a crucial role in deciding the Indians' fate in the months ahead. Writing to Dewdney from Fort Pitt on 23 June, he described the Plains Cree as the 'leading demons' during the rebellion and recommended that the government 'not ... feed them an ounce until next spring.'[11] Even harsher measures would follow. 'One of the great faults of our [military] leaders,' Reed counselled Dewdney in the same letter, 'is that they do not understand the Indian character, and do not know when he is defeated, and when to follow up an advantage.' Reed thought he did. And he had the power do something about it.

Reed returned to Regina convinced that only a program of repression against the First Nations would set things right.[12] He was personally offended by the Indians' conduct. How dare they cast off the government hand that fed them? He also believed that they enjoyed far too much freedom and that drastic measures were necessary in order to squeeze every last savage ounce out of them. As a result, Reed tackled the task of determining who had been unfaithful with a vicious enthusiasm; all agents were called upon to submit a summary report for each band, emphasizing any transgressions.[13] He also started work on a list of recommendations for future management of the Indians that would ultimately shape and inform his career as Dewdney's successor. The Canadian military had had their crack at subduing the Cree. Now it was Reed's turn.

PREPARING FOR THE TRIALS

While this covert campaign against the Indians took shape, preparations were also under way for a series of trials in Regina. The most famous trial – both then and now – was that of Louis Riel, who appeared in a Regina courtroom on 20 July charged with committing high treason. Guided by the hand of God, Riel had surrendered to General Middleton three days after the fall of Batoche in the naive hope that he could use his trial as a platform for his cause. Although his lawyers claimed that their client was insane, the Métis leader's eloquent closing address to the jury was not that of a madman. He was found guilty and sentenced to death.[14]

The mass exodus of lawyers, journalists, and other interested parties from Regina following Riel's prosecution did not mean that the court docket was empty. What has been widely overlooked or simply ignored is that another 129 people were being held on rebellion-related charges: eighty-one Indians, forty-six Métis, and two whites. These arrests and detentions (also examined in the Bob Beal and Barry Wright chapter in this volume) were part of the Macdonald administration's strategy to divert attention from its mishandling of western affairs; primitive Native peoples, not government mismanagement, had spawned the recent unrest.[15] This interpretation dovetailed nicely with the needs of the Indian Affairs Department. If a large number of Indians were convicted as rebels, Dewdney and Reed would enjoy a relatively free hand in the future. That the majority of those charged were innocent was immaterial.

Much has been written about the fairness of Riel's trial and whether justice was served (see the previous chapter by Bumsted).[16] The Indian trials, in comparison, have been little studied.[17] This does not mean, though, that the Canadian government was not vitally interested in what happened to the First Nations defendants. As early as 18 May 1885, a week before Cree chief Poundmaker surrendered to General Middleton at Fort Battleford, Alexander Campbell, the federal minister of justice, assured the prime minister that his department 'shall take great care ... that the prosecution is well done.'[18] Prime Minister Macdonald was not so confident, and in his response the following day he raised concerns about whether the English statute of treason (25 Edward III stat.5 c.2) was applicable in the circumstances, let alone operative in the North-West Territories. The answer was forthcoming one month later in the justice minister's instructions to his deputy, George Burbidge, and the prosecution team of Christopher Robinson, Thomas C. Casgrain, Britton B. Osler, and David L. Scott. Any Indians who had killed people would face murder charges, while chief and head men implicated in the troubles were to be prosecuted for treason – as would 'leading half-breeds or white men.' Campbell also claimed that 'the object of the Government' would be realized by 'a certain number of convictions.'[19]

These instructions suggested that the Macdonald government was determined to make an example of the Indians and thereby guarantee the safety of western settlement, one of the prime minister's cherished national policies. Indeed, the Indians were the only ones in Campbell's instructions to be singled out for murder charges, which, like treason, carried the death penalty. Even then, it was not clear whether the prosecution was expected to make a distinction between those who had actually committed the alleged murders or participated in the killings by their mere presence. The other troubling aspect of the instructions is that treason-felony, a non-capital offence punishable by life imprisonment or a lesser term, seems not to have been considered, at least at first, as a possible charge.

The British government had introduced treason-felony in 1848 in response to the revolutions in continental Europe and especially the failed uprising in Ireland inspired by a group of nationalists known as 'Young Ireland.' This lesser, non-capital form of treason was designed to provide a more palatable alternative to jurors who had been found in the past to be uncomfortable with high treason's death sentence. At the same time, the new offence was more flexible, and in that sense, more useful, in that it expanded the scope of acts against the state that were considered treasonous. Canada incorporated treason-felony into the criminal law with the Dominion consolidations in 1868 and made it applicable in the North-West Territories five years later. In other words, the offence was part of the prosecution arsenal and should have been considered, particularly given the parallels between the 1848 Irish uprising and the 1885 North-West rebellion. The Canadian government considered this and other options, as noted in the chapter by Beal and Wright, but proceeded first with high treason in handling the rebellion trials.

This desire for retribution remained strong even after Deputy Minister of Justice Burbidge arrived in Regina in early July to work up the case against Riel. Within days of his arrival, he wired Ottawa that Manitoba's Stony Mountain penitentiary should be enlarged to accommodate all the new prisoners.[20] Upon further reflection, though, it was decided to proceed with treason-felony charges against the Métis councillors and First Nations chiefs. Burbidge justified this change in strategy in a telegram to the minister of justice on 18 July. He indicated that the prosecution team, after reviewing the evidence, believed that treason charges would be difficult to substantiate in all instances and that some of the cases could result in acquittals.[21] Treason-felony, on the other hand, carried a greater chance of conviction, especially since the accused were more likely to simply plead guilty to the lesser charge and thereby avoid joining Riel on the scaffold.

The adoption of treason-felony in place of treason certainly made legal sense. But there were also political considerations for modifying the charge. In the case of the Métis, the Macdonald government preferred to place primary blame on Riel for the rebellion and, in doing so, deflect attention away from Métis grievances. That is why Riel was the only one to be charged with high treason and why the Métis councillors were given the option of pleading to treason-felony in the interest of getting their trials over as quickly as possible and without controversy. As for the First Nations leaders, the government clearly wanted to punish the chiefs so that their followers would never be led astray again. But convicting them of treason and sending them to their death was going too far and would likely serve to poison government-Indian relations for years, if not decades. The desired effect could be achieved just as effectively through a treason-felony conviction and a prison sentence. It would send a clear message that chiefs would be personally held responsible for the actions of their followers and would be taken away from their bands and caged like animals if necessary.

Indians who had committed murder and other alleged crimes, however, were not to be treated so leniently. In fact, whereas the Macdonald government was prepared to see the Métis defendants as poor, simple men who had been manipulated by Riel, it reserved its most severe punishment for the Indians. The earliest indication of how the Indian defendants were to be treated differently occurred at Battleford in mid-May, well before the fighting was over in the Frog Lake-Fort Pitt theatre. Inspector Francis Dickens, as senior NWMP officer, presided over a series of preliminary hearings to decide whether those Métis being held in detention at the fort should proceed to trial. No such hearings were held for the Indian prisoners.[22] The prime minister also interfered in the judicial process when he directly instructed Burbidge to indict those who had been involved in the Frog Lake killings with murder and not treason-felony.[23] The image of a wild, lawless west was one of the last things that the Canada government needed as it struggled to attract settlers to the region in the 1880s, and Macdonald sought to undo the damage by demonstrating that those who had committed murder would be punished accordingly.

In assessing the trials, it is important to understand that the First Nations defendants were unfamiliar with the court system and its procedures and, as a consequence, failed to challenge testimony, free themselves from self-incrimination, or appeal verdicts. The Canadian system of determining guilt and assigning punishment was completely foreign to the Indians. They also understood little, if any, English, and often did not know what was being said or argued, especially since the court translator was used sparingly.[24] It began with the difficulty of translating the charge of treason-felony: 'feloniously and wickedly did conspire, consult, confederate, assemble, and meet together with divers other evil-disposed persons ... to raise, make and levy insurrection and rebellion against our said Lady the Queen within this realm.'[25]

Most Indians stood before the court alone. Only a handful of the accused had legal counsel – and only then after Sandford Fleming, the former Canadian Pacific Railway engineer-in-chief, raised the matter of legal representation for the Indians with Lawrence Vankoughnet of Indian affairs. Prime Minister Macdonald, in turn, sought the advice of his attorney general, who believed that it would be 'eminently fair' to provide Poundmaker and the other wards of the crown with a lawyer from western Canada.[26] This defence counsel was not expected to make any difference to the outcome of the trials. The Indian defendants also did not have the benefit of political pressure as exerted by francophone members of Parliament and the Roman Catholic clergy on the Métis' behalf. It did not help that the juries were composed of white, Protestant settlers, the same people who had lived in fear of an Indian attack during the rebellion.

THE REGINA TRIALS

The first major Indian trial – for treason-felony – was that of One Arrow, the Willow Cree chief who had been forced to go to Batoche, along with several of his men, after the declaration of Riel's provisional government at Batoche on 19 March 1885. Beverly Robertson, an experienced Winnipeg lawyer who had been hired by the federal government in mid-July, handled his defence. Robertson had to juggle his new duties with a busy private practice and did not arrive in Regina until a few days before One Arrow's 13 August trial. Things started badly. The elderly chief found the proceedings thoroughly confusing, even more so when the treason-felony indictment was translated as 'knocking off the Queen's bonnet and stabbing her in the behind with the sword.' There was no Cree equivalent for words such as conspiracy, traitor, or rebellion. 'Are you drunk?' a perplexed One Arrow reportedly asked the court interpreter.[27]

The case against One Arrow rested on the contention that he had openly associated with the Métis at Batoche and thereby breached his treaty 'allegiance to the Government, the country, and the Queen.'[28] Not one prosecution witnesses was able to say, however, that the Willow Cree leader had actually fired a shot or was even directing his band at Duck Lake and Batoche. And when the government's star witness, surveyor John Astley, testified that he had seen One Arrow and Riel talking together, the defence pointed out that Astley did not understand a word of Cree. It did not matter, though, whether the aged chief had actively participated or not. Because of Judge Richardson's expansive interpretation of treason-felony, One Arrow's mere presence in the rebel camp sufficed. Besides, as Astley casually remarked, the chief had the reputation for being a 'worthless hound' who was 'more fond of loafing around than working.'[29]

At the conclusion of the crown's evidence, Robertson tried to have the charge withdrawn, maintaining that 'not a tittle of evidence'[30] had been produced to link One Arrow directly to the uprising. Failing that, he tried to counter the suggestion that the chief had been disloyal by appealing to the jury's prejudices. 'An Indian has no notion of the nature of civilized society ... no notion of the importance of maintaining law and order,' he admonished the jury. 'Let us show that we really are superior to the unhappy race to which he belongs.'[31] But it was hopeless. 'I cannot acquire his confidence,' Robertson remarked candidly to the jury. 'I don't know the Indians well enough, and I have not been able to get anyone to assist me.' He continued, 'The most that I can do is to sit here and watch the case made by the Crown, appeal to you to consider it leniently, and to bear in mind the difficulties of this poor man's position.'[32]

Armed with Richardson's suspect description of the offence, the six-man jury required only a few minutes to return with a verdict of guilty. One Arrow was remanded for sentencing late the next afternoon. At this point, the real story behind the band's presence at Batoche began to emerge. When asked by Judge Hugh Richardson whether he had anything to say, an overwrought One Arrow tried to explain through the court interpreter that he could not have taken up arms or painted his face because he had just lost a grandchild. He also claimed that his fighting days were long past and that he would never break his treaty pledge. 'All that was said against me was thrown upon me falsely,' he asserted. 'I was taken to the place, Batoche's, to join Riel by Gabriel [Dumont]. I did not take myself to the place. They took me there ... I know that I have done nothing wrong, I can't see where I have done anything wrong against anybody so I beg of you to let me go, to let me go free.'[33] Since there was no one to corroborate his account, One Arrow's plea sounded like a last-minute fabrication to save himself. Certainly, the judge was unmoved, and, in keeping with the jury's recommendation that no mercy be shown, he sentenced One Arrow to three years in the Manitoba penitentiary.

It was a harsh outcome, given the circumstances, but even more so when compared with the treatment of several of the Métis defendants. An hour before One Arrow learned his fate, Judge Richardson had passed sentence on twenty-six Métis rebels who had been rounded up in the weeks after the conflict. These men, mostly rank-and-file followers of

Riel, had first come before the court as a group on 4 August (see Beal and Wright). Although most had pleaded guilty to treason-felony at the time, the prosecution requested that sentencing be delayed until the judge had had an opportunity to consider the particular circumstances of each individual case; the crown argued that the prisoners had been 'led away by evil counsels.'[34]

When the court convened for sentencing on 14 August, no less than thirty affidavits had been secured by the defence – many sworn out by leading local citizens –attesting that the Métis defendants were a poor, ignorant lot who were not responsible for their actions. Father Alexis André, who had verbally wrangled with Riel, for example, declared that, except for a few hard-nosed disciples who had fled the country, 'not one of the other half-breeds had the least idea or suspicion that there was any probability or danger of rebellion.'[35] Hudson's Bay Company clerk Lawrence Clarke also made a lengthy, emotional appeal on behalf of the group immediately prior to their sentencing, in which he argued that the prisoners did not even understand the nature of the charge against them. 'We are not dealing with cultivated intellect,' Clarke told the judge. 'We are dealing with wild men of the territories ... who were in the habit from early days ... to follow a leader in the territories, to follow a leader in the buffalo hunt, to follow a leader wherever they went ... and they looked up to that leader as their hope.'[36] Judge Richardson then read his decision, sentencing eleven men to seven years, three to four years, and four to one year. He discharged the remaining eight on the understanding that the court might recall them at a later date. They joined another four men, who had been released in early August. Adolphus Nolin, who had been at Frog Lake and Cut Knife, was one of these men. Apparently, the Métis could be excused for being in Clarke's words, 'the creatures of circumstances,'[37] whereas One Arrow could not.

Chief Poundmaker's trial followed three days later. Ottawa was determined to proceed with the prosecution, even though Dewdney had known since mid-May, some two weeks before the chief's surrender, that Poundmaker had no control over the Assiniboine warriors who had killed two white men in the Battleford area and that the Cut Knife camp had been divided into war and peace factions.[38] The Indian commissioner was also aware that Crowfoot, the influential Blackfoot chief, felt great distress at his adopted son's arrest and was anxious about his fate. Nothing, not even the truth, however, would deter Ottawa from proceeding with its plan to decapitate the Cree political movement. Almost a year and a half earlier, in February 1884, Dewdney had complained to the prime minister that Poundmaker was 'a leader in mischief' and that he sought 'freedom from the wiles of this cunning individual.' He had added, 'If any trouble arises, on his head will rest much of the guilt.'[39] The Macdonald government now believed that it had more than enough evidence to remove Poundmaker from the scene and thereby rob the Battleford bands of their leadership.

The crown's case against Poundmaker was seductively simple – he was Riel's ally. In his opening statement to the jury, prosecutor David Scott, a Regina barrister, maintained not only that Poundmaker had conspired with the Métis leader but that 'war was actually levied by him' on three distinct occasions: the month-long siege of Fort Battleford, the engagement with Colonel Otter's force at Cut Knife, and the capture of the government supply train southeast of the Eagle Hills. The most damning piece of evidence, though, was Poundmaker's name on a letter, found at Batoche, asking Riel to send reinforcements to help take Fort Battleford.[40] So confident was the prosecution of its case that Scott claimed that the more serious charge of high treason could have easily been proven.[41]

The prosecution's first witness was Robert Jefferson, the reserve farm instructor who was married to Poundmaker's sister. His appearance on behalf of the crown was controversial since he himself had initially come under prosecution scrutiny because of his presence in the Indian camp. But, in the end, it was decided that he could be more useful as a witness against the chief – and for good reason. Jefferson was the one who had prepared the letter of support to Riel, and in his testimony he maintained that Poundmaker had willingly agreed to have his name on it. But, under intense questioning by Beverly Robertson about the matter, Jefferson first expressed confusion, then reported that he could not remember, and finally confessed that he could be mistaken. It was also pathetically clear during his testimony that he feared for his life in the Cut Knife camp and did what the Métis leaders told him to do without asking questions.[42]

Other evidence over the course of the two-day trial revealed that there was a reasonable, alternative explanation for the behaviour of Poundmaker and his followers. When Scott tried to prove that the band had deserted its reserve in the wake of the Duck Lake battle and planned to sack Battleford, one of the prosecution's own witnesses had to admit under cross-examination that the Indians regularly performed begging dances for the townspeople and that none of these visits had resulted in vandalism, let alone violence.[43] And when Scott tried to evoke sympathy for the hundreds of frightened people who had taken refuge within the police stockade walls in late March, Peter Ballendine and William McKay, both residents of the community who had remained outside the fort, were forced to divulge under oath that they had heard from a messenger that the Indians were coming to Battleford to see Indian Agent John Rae.[44] Robertson similarly dissected the crown's version of the other two instances of Poundmaker's war activities, while at the same time eliciting names and descriptions of the otherwise shadowy Métis agents who had been specifically dispatched to the region to bring the local bands to Riel's side.

In his address to the jury, Robertson continued to hammer away at the idea of an alternative version of events in the Battleford area, claiming that 'Poundmaker's influence, such as it was, was always exercised in the interests of peace and humanity –always, but there was a stronger influence here, an influence that he could not countervail, the influence of those half-breeds with the Stonys [sic] at their back.'[45] As in the One Arrow case, Robertson also publicly questioned the fairness of trying an Indian in a white man's court. 'I ask you to remember,' Robertson pleaded with the jury, 'that this poor man is an Indian, that although he is defended here, he is very imperfectly defended ... if I had a white man to defend ... it would be a very different thing.'[46]

The prosecution, in response, took direct aim at the suggestion that Poundmaker was 'perfectly helpless'[47] and raised the question again and again that, if Poundmaker was so loyal, if he was truly a man of peace, then why did he not surrender at either Battleford or Cut Knife? Osler also reminded the jury that the evidence clearly supported the charge of treason-felony given 'the company he kept ... the aid he gave.' And, as for the suggestion that Poundmaker had been pushed aside by the warrior society and had little influence in the Cut Knife camp, Osler insisted that he was still personally accountable for his actions.

Before sending away the jury, Judge Richardson reviewed the damaging evidence against Poundmaker. He then suggested that the chief should be found guilty if he was caught up in the troubles in any way. It was a glaring misinterpretation – not simply a misunderstanding – of the law. And the judge certainly should have known better. As a stipendiary magistrate for nine years, with over 250 cases to his credit, Richardson should have referred to the authorities on treason-felony if he was in any way unclear about the law. Clearly, there were precedents that should have given him direction. But, as Beal and Wright argue in their chapter, Judge Richardson failed to properly discharge his duties in the rebellion trials he presided over – to the point of being lazy, if not incompetent. In fact, he seemed at times just as confused about the law and procedure as the Indian defendants.

With Richardson's prompting, the jury quickly delivered a guilty verdict. Before being sentenced, Poundmaker was given the opportunity to address the court. 'Everything that is bad that has been laid against me this summer,' he replied through the interpreter, 'there is nothing of it true ... I did everything to stop bloodshed. If I had not done so there would have been plenty of blood spilled this summer ... and now that I have done so ... I will have to suffer for their sakes, that I have saved the lives of so many. So I shake hands, gentlemen, with the whole of you.'[48] Sadly, these efforts earned him a three-year prison term at Stony Mountain. It could have been much worse. Judge Richardson, himself a former resident of Battleford, suggested in his pre-sentence remarks that Poundmaker was fortunate because he could have been charged with high treason and sentenced to death. The Cree chief did not see it that way. As he was hustled out of the courtroom, with the judge's sentence barely off his lips, Poundmaker shouted, 'I would prefer to be hung than to be in that place.'[49]

Poundmaker's conviction did little to appease Battleford. P.G. Laurie, editor of the *Saskatchewan Herald*, angrily denounced the trial as a 'farce' and the sentence as 'ridiculously short.'[50] This same bitterness coloured an editorial some three weeks later, in which Laurie suggested that Poundmaker had received 'what is the Indians' highest ambition to attain – plenty to eat and nothing to do ... He said he preferred death to imprisonment, and it is a pity he was not accommodated.'[51] The Toronto-based *Week* saw the trial in an entirely different light. After reviewing a summary of the key testimony, 'Lex' concluded that the crown's case was 'very weak and inconclusive.'[52] In particular, the columnist noted that Poundmaker was actually on his reserve while camped at Cut Knife and that it was the Canadian military that attacked the Indians. 'Considering the whole case,' Lex observed, 'it is very doubtful whether there has not been a great injustice done to a man who was our friend throughout ... and yet this man is condemned as a felon to imprisonment for three years, and because he is an Indian not a voice is raised to say one word for him.'[53]

Defence lawyer Beverly Robertson could not have agreed more. But the sentiments expressed in the article were no substitute for reality, a reality that seemed to have no place for justice for and understanding of the Indian situation. And it did not take much reflection for Robertson to realize, especially after the demoralizing outcome of the One Arrow and Poundmaker trials, that his efforts were futile in the face of Judge Richardson's open-ended interpretation of treason-felony and that it was just a matter of going through the motions as quickly as possible.

He consequently wrote the crown counsel upon his return to Winnipeg and instructed them to 'be ready to try a considerable number of Indians in rapid succession the next time I come up to Regina and let me know at least a few days beforehand what overt acts are charged against them respectively.'[54]

The next series of Regina trials got under way in mid-September. Big Bear, looking lost and confused after more than two months in custody, first appeared before Judge Richardson on 3 September, but, because Robertson had still not returned from Winnipeg, the judge postponed the trial for eight days. In the interim, settler Thomas Scott was acquitted of treason-felony, a verdict that suggested that white defendants were to be treated differently by the court. According to surviving prosecution documents, the crown considered the case against Big Bear to be weak.[55] In fact, in his opening remarks, David Scott suggested that he might not be able to show that Big Bear was in charge of his band or that he had played a part in the Frog Lake killings. As in the trial of One Arrow, however, the prosecution was content to base its case on guilt through association. 'You must understand,' Scott lectured the jury, 'that if he were acting with these parties at that time in open rebellion against the Government of the country ... then ... he was in open rebellion against the Government of the country and ought to be punished.'[56] Ironically, the case against Big Bear might have been dismissed on a technicality if Robertson had properly prepared for his defence. The formal indictment gave the wrong date for the siege of Fort Pitt – an error that was repeated several times by the crown.[57]

The trial itself confirmed that Big Bear, like Poundmaker, had done everything within his power to promote peace. Several former captives testified for the defence that Big Bear had tried to use his limited influence to restrain the young warriors in his band. These white witnesses included W.B. Cameron, who had been spared during the Frog Lake murder rampage. In fact, the image that emerged from the testimony was that the Cree chief was anything but a rebel: he tried to stop the slaughter at Frog Lake, he arranged for the emergency evacuation of Fort Pitt, he was several miles behind the lines at Frenchman's Butte, and he kept a protective eye on Wandering Spirit's prisoners. Unfortunately, such evidence, no matter how favourable, could not counteract his reputation as a troublesome leader whose band had committed one of the vilest acts in Canadian history. This was glaringly apparent during the hearing, when defence witness and former hostage Henry Halpin reported that Stanley Simpson, another prisoner, had confronted him in private for agreeing to appear on Big Bear's behalf. 'He thought it was strange, very strange, any white man should get on the defence of an Indian,' Halpin told the court. 'His idea was that Indians should have been hung.'[58] Simpson was the only prosecution witness to testify that Big Bear spoke in favour of the rebellion on several occasions. But his reliability was thrown into serious doubt when Robertson was able to demonstrate on cross-examination that Simpson did not understand Cree.

In his address to the jury, Robertson tried a different tack from the two earlier trials and argued that Big Bear was obliged to remain with his band even though he disagreed with the warriors' actions. He could not simply leave, especially during a time of crisis, when the war chief had assumed leadership. This explanation of Indian behaviour was barely understood, much less believed, by the jury. It was also flatly contradicted by Richardson's loose definition of treason-felony, in which overt acts of insurrection or even active involvement in a rebellious conspiracy were not necessary to prove guilt. Instead, the jury preferred the prosecution's interpretation, as voiced by Scott in his closing address, that it was Big Bear's duty 'not to be found in the rebel camp, but to be found where law and order prevailed.'[59] And, in keeping with past decisions, they found the elderly chief guilty after only a few minutes' deliberation – but this time recommended mercy.

This verdict set the stage for Big Bear's last and perhaps finest speech as leader of the Plains Cree. Returning to court two weeks later to be formally sentenced, he used the occasion to protest his innocence and at the same time make a special plea on behalf of his people. 'I think I should have something to say about the occurrences which brought me here in chains,' he began.

I knew little of the killing at Frog Lake beyond hearing the shots fired. When any wrong was brewing I did my best to stop it in the beginning. The turbulent ones of the band got beyond my control and shed the blood of those I would have protected ...When the white men were few in the country I gave them the hand of brotherhood. I am sorry so few are here who can witness for my friendly acts. Can anyone stand out and say that I ordered the death of a priest or an agent? You think I encouraged my people to take part in the trouble. I did not. I advised against it ... I look around this room and see it crowded with faces far handsomer than my own. (Laughter) I have ruled my country for a long time. Now I am in chains and will be sent to prison ... At present I am dead to my people. Many of my band are hiding in the woods, paralysed with terror. Cannot this court send them a pardon? My own children! – perhaps they are starving and outcast, too, afraid to appear in the light of day. If the government does not come to help them before the winter sets in, my band will surely perish. But I have too much confidence in the Great Grandmother to fear that starvation will be allowed to overtake my people ... I am old and ugly, but I have tried to do good. Pity the children of my tribe! Pity the old and helpless of my people! I speak with a single tongue; and because Big Bear has always been the friend of the white man, send out and pardon and give them help! How! Aquisanee – I have spoken![60]

A profound silence followed his last word, only to be shattered by Judge Richardson's sentence – three years at Stony Mountain penitentiary.

The next pair of trials were something of a farce. On 16 September, nine members of Big Bear's band, who had been arrested near Fort Carlton, were tried for treason-felony. This was not the first time that the court had dealt with more than one defendant, but, because of the difficulty in pronouncing the Cree names, the men were each assigned a number. In the resulting chaos, the lawyers and witnesses were never sure if they were talking about the same person.[61] Robertson, meanwhile, did not bother to mount a defence; he called no witnesses and declined to make a closing statement. In the end, all nine were found guilty and sentenced to two years.

An almost identical scene took place the next day – this time for five Indians, one from One Arrow's band and four from Whitecap's. Once again, the defendants were given numbers, and even though there were fewer of them, the trial was equally confusing, since the two bands had arrived at Batoche at different times. Judge Richardson had no problem keeping things straight and sentenced four of the men to three years for being in the rebel camp; the fifth, the Hole, a member of Whitecap's band, received only six months. These sentences were consistent with the punishment of the three chiefs. But what was curious, if not revealing, is how André Nault and Abraham Montour, two of Riel's agents, had been treated in the same courtroom only days earlier. Charged with treason-felony for their part in events at Frog Lake and Frenchman's Butte, the pair had their hearing postponed because of the absence of witnesses; the case would later be silently dropped.[62]

The last Regina trial was that of Whitecap, the Dakota chief who had been conscripted by the Métis in early April. General Middleton had detained and interrogated Whitecap after the fall of Batoche but released him upon hearing his story. Once the government's lawyers discovered that the chief had been a member of Riel's governing council, however, the Mounted Police took him into custody until his trial for treason-felony on 18 September.[63] Whitecap's situation was identical to that of One Arrow; he had been present at Métis headquarters and was, according to the crown, little better than the rebels themselves – especially since he was the only Indian member of Riel's governing council. But, unlike at One Arrow's hearing, Robertson had a white witness, the Dakota-speaking Gerald Willoughby of Saskatoon, who verified that Whitecap and his band had been kidnapped by a large Métis force and that the citizens of Saskatoon were helpless to stop it. And, whereas One Arrow had been characterized as a worthless hound, Willoughby described Whitecap as a loyal Indian who was always a welcome guest in homes throughout the district.[64]

This kind of testimony was hard to refute. In fact, in Department of Justice notes about the trial, prosecutor Scott scribbled, 'coercion of half breeds,' on one of the pages.[65] Robertson, by this time, had become thoroughly cynical about the process and began his address to the jury with a stinging attack on the objectivity of the court. 'Since the conviction of Big Bear,' he observed sarcastically, 'I have felt that it is almost a hopeless task to obtain from a jury in Regina a fair consideration of the case of an Indian. It has seemed to me it is only necessary to say in this town to a jury, there is an Indian, and we will put him in the dock to convict him.'[66] A frustrated Robertson also finally took issue with Judge Richardson's questionable interpretation of the law and twice interrupted his biased instructions to the jury. He did not need to worry, though. The jury returned within fifteen minutes with a verdict of not guilty. Richardson, who normally lectured the accused before passing sentence, seemed surprised by the acquittal and pronounced simply, 'You are now a free man again.'[67]

THE BATTLEFORD TRIALS

The Macdonald government had planned to hold all the rebellion trials in Regina. But once it weighed the costs of transporting all the prisoners and witnesses to the territorial capital, it decided that it would be more expedient to schedule the last set of hearings in Battleford, where some sixty Indians were in custody by early August.[68] This change of venue made a mockery of the remaining trials. Still smarting from the so-called siege, Battleford residents expected – even demanded – the severest possible punishment.[69] But this vengeance came at the cost of fair trials. The accused were not only bewildered by the court proceedings but had no access to defence counsel. The presiding judge, on the other hand, was

Dakota Chief Whitecap in captivity, 1885, by O.B. Buell (Library and Archives Canada, PA 182241)

prepared to set aside due process and, with it, any suggestion of presumed innocence in the interests of quick, at times harsh, sentences.

Judge Charles Rouleau was called upon to dispense this crude justice. It was an unfortunate twist of fate. A year earlier, Hayter Reed had privately criticized Rouleau for giving a one-week sentence to an Indian who had assaulted a farm instructor on one of the local reserves. 'Rouleau has been but a short time in the country,' a disappointed Reed had written Dewdney, 'and not ... yet grasped the Indian question.'[70] But events in Battleford that spring had remedied this 'shortcoming.' Not only had Rouleau fled to Swift Current fearing for his life, but his home, including his valued collection of legal books, had been destroyed by fire just before the arrival of Otter's column. And when he resumed his duties at Battleford it was with a kind of blinkered vengeance. Protesting that General Middleton had been far too kind, he bluntly told Dewdney, 'It is high time ... Indians should be taught a severe lesson.'[71] He would be the one to do so, especially since he doubled as judge and jury at most of the trials and the defendants were without legal counsel.

The first prisoner, led in irons into criminal court on the morning of 22 September, was Wandering Spirit, described by the *Herald* as 'one of the greatest murderers that ever walked on two legs in America.'[72] He was lucky to be alive. Shortly after his surrender at Fort Pitt, Big Bear's war chief had tried to commit suicide by plunging a knife into his chest, puncturing his left lung.[73] Over the next two months, while he recuperated slowly in the Battleford jail, Wandering Spirit seems to have resigned himself to his fate – even allowing himself to be baptized and given a Christian name.[74] His much-anticipated appearance for murdering Frog Lake Indian agent Tom Quinn proved anti-climatic. As soon as the indictment had been entered and translated, the man whose very stare had struck terror in hearts quietly pleaded guilty. It was over in a matter of minutes. So too were the hearings for Itka and Man Without Blood, the Assiniboine warriors accused of killing farm instructor James Payne and farmer Barney Tremont respectively. Brought before Rouleau on 5 October, they both pleaded guilty and were sentenced to join Wandering Spirit on the scaffold on 27 November.

The other murder trials were just as speedy – even when the defendants pleaded not guilty. There was no attempt to understand why or how the slayings had occurred; it was simply a matter of assigning guilt and doling out the punishment. On 1 October, for example, Round the Sky elected to be tried by Rouleau for killing Father Léon-Adélard Fafard at Frog Lake. Three other Cree, who were there that fateful morning, testified that the defendant had delivered the coup de grâce. After Round the Sky had heard the evidence against him, he declined to cross-examine the witnesses, claiming instead that they had told the truth.[75] Rouleau then promptly sentenced him to hang. Bad Arrow and Miserable Man were treated the same way two days later, when they too refused to challenge the crown's witnesses. Nor did a lack of evidence act as a deterrent to the judge's decisions. On 9 October, Little Bear was convicted of the murder of George Dill, even though he claimed that he had intentionally missed his target. He had been seen riding after the trader on his horse and firing in his direction.[76] In all, eleven Indians were condemned to death in a two-and-a-half-week period.[77] One week before the mass hanging at Battleford, the largest in post-confederation history, Prime Minister Macdonald mused in a confidential letter to the Indian commissioner, 'The executions ... ought to convince the Red Man that the White Man governs.'[78]

Rouleau's treatment of the other Indian prisoners, especially those from Big Bear's band, was equally ruthless. He seemed to believe that no punishment was too severe for the Cree – even if the length of sentence contradicted standard practice. The Idol, one of Lucky Man's councillors, received six years for stealing an Indian Department horse, while God's Otter, who had a mare from Fort Pitt in his possession, was given four. Three of the men who had placed their names on the Cut Knife letter to Riel, meanwhile, were sentenced to two years. It did not matter that several witnesses reported that the letter was composed at the insistence of Riel's emissaries.[79] Rouleau's harshest punishment, however, was reserved for those who had committed arson, reflecting the personal outrage that he and others had felt about the burning of Battleford. On 24 September, Four Sky Thunder, who had decided not to flee to the United States with Imasees, was sentenced to a staggering fourteen years for torching the Roman Catholic church at Frog Lake. Toussaint Calling Bull and Little Wolf were somewhat more fortunate, receiving only ten years for setting fire to a government building and stable respectively. One can only wonder how Poundmaker, Big Bear, One Arrow, and the other Indian defendants might have fared if all of the trials had been held at Battleford.

THE WHITE MAN GOVERNS

By the fall of 1885, then, the Macdonald government had made great advances in its campaign to subdue the Plains Cree. Choosing to ignore repeated Indian protestations of loyalty – not to mention numerous acts of allegiance – Ottawa deliberately portrayed the rebellion as the work of the Métis traitor Riel and his brutal Indian henchmen. They were common allies in an evil cause, rebels who had to be punished – not only for bringing the Saskatchewan country to the brink of a full-scale war but also for breaking their treaty promises and turning against the very government that sustained them. Ottawa's response was swift and methodical. While Indian Affairs officials secretly gathered information on the conduct of western bands in preparation for the imposition of new repressive policies, the courts were used to intimidate the Indian population in one of the most shameful episodes of Canadian legal history. Not only were influential leaders, such as Poundmaker and Big Bear, imprisoned for crimes they did not commit, but scores of other Indians received unusually severe sentences (summarized in the volume's Supporting Documents) with little justification except for their race. It was as if Ottawa had declared war on the First Nations – a war it was determined to win, at whatever the cost. And in the long run, it has. The imprisonments and executions have left a lasting legacy with First Nations people. Twenty-eight bands, identified as disloyal in 1885, still carry the stigma of having broken their sacred agreements with the crown to live in peace. The official record and many history books, meanwhile, leave the unmistakable impression that the Indians participated fully in the fighting and, in some instances, took the lead. How else can one explain the large number of Indian convictions for rebellion crimes? As he was about to be led away in chains, Big Bear eloquently summed up the sorry situation of his people: 'I always thought it paid to do all the good I could. Now my heart is on the ground.'[80]

NOTES

1 This section on the North-West rebellion is largely taken from the author's contribution to *Canada: Confederation to Present*, CD-Rom (Edmonton: Chinook Multimedia 2001).
2 LAC, John A. Macdonald Papers, vol. 107, 43110–18, E. Dewdney to J.A. Macdonald, 3 June 1885.
3 Ibid.
4 J.L. Tobias, 'Canada's Subjugation of the Plains Cree, 1879–1885,' in J.R. Miller, ed., *Sweet Promises: A Reader on Indian-White Relations in Canada* (Toronto: University of Toronto Press 1991), 231–2. Prime Minister Macdonald looked upon the rebellion in much the same way. He later told Governor General Lansdowne, 'We have certainly made it assume large proportions in the pub-

lic eye. This has been done however for our own purposes, and I think wisely done.' LAC, Macdonald Papers, vol. 23, 271–2, J.A. Macdonald to Lansdowne, 3 Sept. 1885.

5 GA, E. Dewdney Papers, box 2, f.38, 566–7, E. Dewdney to J.A. Macdonald, 16 June 1885; LAC, Macdonald Papers, vol. 107, 43166, Dewdney to Macdonald, 22 June 1885; 43171, 23 June 1885.

6 LAC, Government Archives Division, Department of Indian Affairs, RG 10, vol. 3584, f.1130, E. Dewdney to L. Vankoughnet, 19 June 1885.

7 Ibid., L. Vankoughnet to E. Dewdney, 3 July 1885.

8 Ibid., vol. 3584, f.1130, pt. 1A, J.A. Macrae to E. Dewdney, 10 June 1885.

9 Ibid., vol. 3710, f.19550–3, A. McDonald to E. Dewdney, 29 May 1885.

10 D. Light, *Footprints in the Dust* (Battleford: Turner Warwick 1987), 506.

11 LAC, Macdonald Papers, vol. 107, 43180–3, H. Reed to E. Dewdney, 23 June 1885.

12 S. Carter, *Lost Harvests: Prairie Indian Reserve Farmers and Government Policy* (Montreal: McGill-Queen's University Press 1990), 145.

13 See, for example, the list that Agent McDonald provided for his agency. LAC, RG 10, vol. 3710, f.19, 350–1.

14 See J.M. Bumsted's chapter in this volume and D. Morton, *The Queen v. Louis Riel* (Toronto: University of Toronto Press 1974).

15 S.E. Bingaman, 'The North-West Rebellion Trials,' MA thesis, University of Regina 1971, 3.

16 See, for example, D.H. Brown, 'The Meaning of Treason in 1885,' *Saskatchewan History* 28, no. 2 (1975): 65–73; and T. Flanagan and N. Watson, 'The Riel Trial Revisited: Criminal Procedure and the Law in 1885,' *Saskatchewan History* 34, no. 2 (1981): 57–73.

17 See Bingaman, 'The North-West Rebellion Trials,' and B. Beal and R.C. Macleod, *Prairie Fire: The 1885 North-West Rebellions* (Edmonton: Hurtig 1984), 309–17. The most complete source is B. Stonechild and B. Waiser, *Loyal till Death: Indians and the North-West Rebellion* (Calgary: Fifth House 1997), the basis for this study. A broader perspective is provided by S.A.M. Gavigan, 'Criminal Law on the Aboriginal Plains: The First Nations and the First Criminal Court in the North-West Territories, 1870–1903,' SJD thesis, University of Toronto 2008.

18 LAC, Macdonald Papers, vol. 197, 82818, A. Campbell to J.A. Macdonald, 18 May 1885.

19 Ibid., vol. 197, 82880, A. Campbell to J. Burbidge, 20 June 1885. See Supporting Documents.

20 Bingaman, 'The North-West Rebellion Trials,' 30.

21 LAC, Government Archives Division, Department of Justice, RG 13, B2 , vol. 1–22, G. Burbidge to A. Campbell, 18 July 1885.

22 Bingaman, 'The North-West Rebellion Trials,' 7–8.
23 Ibid., 110.
24 Only selected questions and answers were translated for the Indian defendants. See, for example, *Sessional Papers*, 1886, no. 52, 'Rebellion Trials,' 7.
25 Ibid., 13.
26 LAC, Macdonald Papers, vol. 290, 133119–20, L. Vankoughnet to J.A. Macdonald, 15 June 1885; 133121, A. Campbell to J.A. Macdonald, n.d.
27 Beal and Macleod, *Prairie Fire*, 309.
28 'Rebellion Trials,' 15.
29 Ibid., 19. On Richardson and his expansive definition of treason felony, see Bob Beal and Barry Wright's chapter in this volume and Bob Beal, 'Attacking the State: The Levying War Charge in Canadian Treason Law,' MA thesis, University of Alberta 1994.
30 Ibid., 25.
31 Ibid., 26–7.
32 Ibid., 28.
33 Ibid., 32–3. In complete contradiction to the testimony at the trial, Richard John, the great-great grandson of One Arrow, is claiming today that the chief willingly supported Riel and actively participated in the rebellion. J. Lagimodiere, 'Historians Chided for Misinformation,' *Eagle Feather News* 10, no. 9 (2007): 1, 6.
34 Ibid., 370.
35 Ibid., 382.
36 Ibid., 375.
37 Ibid., 374.
38 LAC, RG 10, vol. 3710, ff.19350–3, J.A. Macrae to E. Dewdney, 14 May 1885.
39 Ibid., Macdonald Papers, vol. 212, 90043, E. Dewdney to J.A. Macdonald, 16 Feb. 1884.
40 Instead of fleeing to the United States with Gabriel Dumont, Michel Dumas, and Norbert Delorme, Joseph Jobin, the Métis agent who helped prepare the letter, quietly returned to the Bellevue district (near Batoche) and died there in 1891. He was never brought to trial for his role in the rebellion.
41 'Rebellion Trials,' 263–5.
42 Ibid., 280. Jefferson knew what had happened in the Battleford area during the rebellion but apparently decided not to speak up on Poundmaker's behalf to avoid getting himself in trouble with the Indian Affairs Department.
43 Ibid., 273.
44 Ibid., 279–302.
45 Ibid., 380.
46 Ibid., 328.

47 Ibid.

48 Ibid., 336.

49 Ibid., 337.

50 *Saskatchewan Herald*, 24 Aug. 1885.

51 Ibid., 14 Sept. 1885.

52 'Lex,' 'Poundmaker's Trial,' *The Week*, 10 Sept. 1885, 645.

53 Ibid., 646.

54 Quoted in Bingaman, 'The North-West Rebellion Trials,' 43.

55 Ibid., 36.

56 'Rebellion Trials,' 175.

57 Light, *Footprints*, 521.

58 'Rebellion Trials,' 218.

59 Ibid., 231.

60 Quoted in W.B. Cameron, *The War Trail of Big Bear* (London: Ryerson 1927), 222–4.

61 See, for example, 'Rebellion Trials,' 249–51.

62 Ibid., 338–41. The condemned Miserable Man apparently implicated Nault, but nothing was done. Bingaman, 'The North-West Rebellion Trials,' 185.

63 D. Morton and R. Roy, eds., *Telegrams of the North-West Campaign* (Toronto: Champlain Society 1972), 375 [A.P. Caron to F. Middleton, 7 July 1885].

64 'Rebellion Trials,' 45–50.

65 LAC, Government Archives Division, Justice, RG 13, ser. F-2, vol. 820, 3388.

66 'Rebellion Trials,' 51–2.

67 Ibid., 60. Richardson was known to be lenient towards Aboriginal offenders in routine cases.

68 Bingaman, 'The North-West Rebellion Trials,' 14.

69 See, for example, *Saskatchewan Herald*, 25 May 1885: 'Good and loyal Indians are among the things of the past ... there are none at present'; and 22 June 1885: 'the last remnant of this fiendish band [Poundmaker's] should be wiped out of existence ... put a price on their heads.'

70 GA, Dewdney Papers, box 4, f.66, 1398–1401, H. Reed to E. Dewdney, 4 Sept. 1884. For background on Rouleau, see Louis A. Knafla, 'Charles-Borromee Rouleau,' *DCB*, 13: 907–8.

71 GA, Dewdney Papers, box 4, f.66, 2508, C.B. Rouleau to E. Dewdney, 12 June 1885.

72 *Saskatchewan Herald*, 26 Oct. 1885.

73 Ibid., 20 July 1885.

74 Light, *Footprints*, 514.

75 *Sessional Papers*, no. 52a, 1886, 'Battleford Trials,' 6.

76 Ibid., 8.

77 Eight of the eleven condemned Indians were eventually executed; the other three had their sentences commuted. The mass hanging, with a high scaffold that made the executions visible outside, was a contravention of the 1868 federal statute (in effect after the execution of Patrick James Whelan) that ended public executions.

78 GA, Dewdney Papers, box 2, f.38, 587–8, J.A. Macdonald to E. Dewdney, 20 Nov. 1885.

79 Ibid., 22–3.

80 Quoted in Cameron, *War Trail*, 223.

PART FOUR

Securing the Dominion

11

'High-handed, Impolite, and Empire-breaking Actions': Radicalism, Anti-Imperialism, and Political Policing in Canada, 1860–1914

ANDREW PARNABY and GREGORY S. KEALEY
with KIRK NIERGARTH

Surveillance and intelligence-gathering operations that targeted political dissidents were a part of the Canadian state from its inception. This is not surprising. Not only had such practices – furtive, repressive, and legal in equal measure – long served military and diplomatic objectives in British North America, but the development of a Canadian system of political policing was tied to Canada's status as an outpost of the British empire. Indeed, early political police structures in Canada were modelled after those created in other colonial contexts and, by the 1860s, agents of the Canadian state had become integrated within an imperial network of intelligence gathering and sharing.[1] Furthermore, it was the mobilization of anti-colonial activists, whose primary target was Britain itself, that spurred the Canadian government to develop and expand a political police force that could serve the interests of both the Dominion and the empire.

In the late 1860s, in the aftermath of the American Civil War, North American Irish radicals became the principal focus of Canadian secret police operations. If the Fenian threat helped boost the idea of confederation, it also provided the impetus to normalize the use of spies and spymasters as part of the federal civil service.[2] British imperial personnel, however, remained significant players in Canadian intelligence gathering, just as the imperial tie shaped the way the Canadian state perceived its enemies. This pattern persisted into the early 1900s when South Asian radicals in Canada agitated for an end to British rule in India. While the

Dominion had become geographically larger and economically more complex by this time, the Canadian state remained willing to engage in political policing to maintain the security of the British empire.

This chapter focuses on the careers of spymaster Gilbert McMicken and spy William Charles Hopkinson. It examines the influence of imperial politics on Canada's early forays into political policing, as well as the overt and covert methods deployed by the Canadian state to curb the growth of anti-colonial activism at home and abroad.

GILBERT McMICKEN AND THE FENIANS

With an ideological pedigree that stretched back to the United Irish rebellion in the 1790s, the Irish Republican Brotherhood (IRB) was founded in Dublin in 1858. It was an avowedly revolutionary organization that was committed to overthrowing British rule in Ireland and establishing an Irish republic.[3] Yet, as its leaders understood well, success at home required the support of Irish immigrants abroad, most notably in the United States where tens of thousands of Irish men and women, many of whom had fled Ireland during the depths of the Famine, swelled the ranks of working-class populations in New York, Boston, Chicago, Detroit, and Cincinnati.[4] Thus, seven months after the IRB's founding, an American support group, the Fenian Brotherhood, was established. As David Wilson notes elsewhere in this volume, Fenianism found a receptive audience in Canada as well. In Toronto, members of the Hibernian Benevolent Society, an Irish self-help organization founded by cooper and tavern keeper Michael Murphy, created a clandestine Fenian circle in 1859. Its members were mostly working class, and, like their counterparts south of the border, they were drawn to a heady mix of camaraderie, nationalism, and collective action at a time when politics often turned on the power, privileges, and prejudices that differentiated the Orange from the Green. 'It is time to cast off the habiliments of wretchedness and come forth clothed in the manly garb of equality,' the Hibernian's newspaper, *Irish Canadian*, exclaimed. 'We Irish will yet stand erect in Canada.'[5]

The British empire took action against Irish nationalism on both sides of the Atlantic in 1865. In Ireland, alarmed by the steady growth of the IRB and the arrival of Irish American veterans of the U.S. Civil War, British officials raided the organization's offices, closed its newspapers, and arrested many of its high-profile members. In Canada, John A. Macdonald, attorney general and minister of militia affairs in Upper Canada, aware that American Fenians were debating the politics of 'freeing Ireland on the plains of Canada,' empowered Gilbert McMicken, the head of the Western Frontier Constabulary, to covertly investigate the Fenian organization on both sides of the Canadian-American border. 'The Fenian action in Ireland is serious and the Imperial government seems fully alive to it,' Macdonald observed. 'We must not be caught napping.'[6]

McMicken's Canadian résumé, at first glance, seems unsuited to a career in political policing compared to the military credentials of Colonel Frederick William Ermatinger, who was McMicken's equivalent in Lower Canada. With border security of paramount concern, however, McMicken's personal experience and political ties help explain his selection by Macdonald. After his arrival in Canada in 1832 and marriage into a prominent family in 1835, McMicken's career in business was directly connected to cross-border transportation, communication, and trade.[7] McMicken eventually became both a civil servant and a politician. He had received his first government appointment as a customs inspector in 1838 and was elected to the Upper Canadian Legislative Assembly in 1857. He was a loyal ally of Macdonald, who had arranged for him to be appointed an excise officer in Windsor only two months before choosing him to head Canada's first undercover security force, the Western Frontier Constabulary, in 1864.[8] McMicken's varied cross-border activities and connections prepared him to lead a force created initially to reassure U.S. officials of Canadian neutrality during the American Civil War, after a group of Confederate soldiers had launched a raid on St Albans, Vermont, from Canadian soil.[9] By the end of the Civil War, McMicken had about fifteen undercover operatives patrolling the border under his command.[10]

The Fenian threat prompted McMicken to increase significantly the number of Canadian secret police. By 1870, approximately fifty agents, working both in the United States and in Canada, were attending Fenian meetings, frequenting 'Irish Saloons,' and shadowing suspected 'Irish Rebbles.' Fragmentary evidence suggests that McMicken's recruits were usually men in their late twenties and early thirties who possessed military and/or police backgrounds; of the eighteen agents who can be positively identified, seven were Irish (six Roman Catholics), six were Scottish (one Roman Catholic), and five were English (all Protestants). Paid relatively well, many informants nonetheless took up employment in the areas under their supervision in order to allay any suspicions of how they were supporting themselves and what were their real motives. 'I was impressed with the idea that he was capable and had proven his being a very intelligent Irish Roman Catholic,' McMicken wrote to Macdonald, assessing the credentials of one of his latest recruits. 'This, in connection with his integrity and loyalty, led me to engage his services for a time. He was to put himself in communication with the British Consul there [Buffalo] and be instructed by him and through him by me.'[11]

When it came to monitoring the machinations of Fenian rebels in the United States, the Canadian government worked cheek by jowl with British consular officials in several large American cities, most notably in Buffalo, a key border crossing, and New York, a hive of Green activity. The British consuls in these cities, H.W. Hemans and Sir Edward Mortimer Archibald respectively, recruited a network of informants and were often in direct contact with McMicken's men. Consular officials channelled information to various British officials, including the colonial secretary (who, in turn, informed police forces in London and Dublin), the commander of British forces in North America, the lieutenant governor of New Brunswick, and the governor general of Canada, Lord Monck. Combined, the Canadian government and British diplomats marshalled a far-flung and eclectic battery of informants. Drawn from inside and outside the Fenians' ranks and scattered along the Canada-U.S. border, it pumped information through the capillaries of communication that linked governments and law-enforcement agencies on both sides of the Atlantic.[12]

By April 1866, when the Fenians attacked Campobello Island, New Brunswick, the Canadian government was well informed about both American and domestic Fenian activity.[13] Patrick Nolan, one of McMicken's most reliable informants in Chicago, had been recalled to Toronto where he submerged himself in the local Green scene. Nolan learned that there were approximately seventeen Fenian lodges in Upper Canada, nine of them in Toronto; that, while the Hibernian Benevolent Society and the Fenians were not the same thing, there was substantial overlap between the two organizations; and that the ubiquitous Michael Murphy was indeed a Fenian and was in touch with like-minded individuals in the United States.[14] In March 1866 Nolan reported that Murphy and a coterie of supporters were preparing to leave the city to assist their American comrades in a cross-border raid of some kind.[15] At Campobello, the Fenian raiders were met by the combined force of six British warships and scores of U.S. troops and easily turned back. North of the border, Michael Murphy and a group of supporters, who had been under surveillance since they left Toronto, were apprehended in Cornwall, Upper Canada, on their way to assist their American counterparts.[16] McMicken had no fewer than four agents keeping tabs on the prominent Irish leader at the time of his arrest.

The Fenian's defeat at Campobello did not, however, dampen the organization's enthusiasm for the 'Canada option.'[17] They launched more successful attacks in June 1866, one in Upper Canada (Ridgeway and Fort Erie) and another in Lower Canada.[18] This time Canadian authorities were forewarned, but they were not, surprisingly, forearmed. Poor communication between government, secret service, and military officials, coupled with conflicting reports from some secret agents, generated a mix of confusion and complacency in official circles. The failure of the secret powers of state to prevent these attacks prompted the Canadian Parliament to make use of the more conventional repressive tactics examined in Blake Brown's chapter in this volume. On 8 June it amended the 'quasi-treason' offence of lawless aggression, originally enacted in Upper Canada after the rebellions of 1837 and 1838. Detailed in the throne speech and given royal assent on the same day, the changes permitted the government to try by military court martial any foreigner or British subject who took up arms in the province. It also suspended habeas corpus for a year, enabling police in Upper and Lower Canada to arrest dozens of men suspected of Fenian sympathies without the burden of due process (see Supporting Documents). Parliament later passed legislation 'to authorize the seizure of Fire Arms collected for purposes dangerous to the public peace' and made a huge military appropriation – $1,897,085 on a total budget of $7,003,236 – which included $100,000 for 'detective and secret service work.' It added an additional $50,000 and $75,000 in 1867 and 1868 respectively.[19]

In the wake of the Fenian attacks of 1866, Macdonald pushed ahead with significant changes in the operation and structure of the secret service. Of particular importance was the establishment of more independent and reliable sources of intelligence. The career of informant Henri LeCaron highlights this new priority well. Born in England to a modest family, LeCaron, whose real name was Thomas Beach, worked in France as a banker in the late 1850s, eventually leaving Europe for North America in 1861 to fight for the Union Army in the Civil War. Once in the United States, Beach, who was in his early twenties, enlisted in the 8th Pennsylvania Reserve as a private and adopted the name Henri LeCaron. After the war, he settled in Illinois and later took a position as a medical officer at the Illinois State Penitentiary. On the basis of his military credentials and knowledge of Fenianism – he had served with Irish soldiers in the Union Army – LeCaron was recruited by British officials in the autumn of 1867 to be a paid informant. Early on, he reported directly to the British Home Office, but, as he wormed his way into the Fenians' inner sanctum, he looked for a closer, more secure contact, and wrote to the Canadian government. Macdonald, apparently impressed with LeCaron's connections, authorized McMicken to hire him for $150 a month, but warned: 'A man who will engage to do what he offers to do, that is, betray those with whom he acts, is not to be trusted.' Macdonald's scepticism was misplaced. From the date of his recruitment, LeCaron, dubbed by one biographer 'The Prince of Spies,' provided the Canadian government with copious and prescient intelligence, often on a daily basis.[20]

Additional changes to the secret service were spurred on by the assassination of journalist, member of Parliament from Montreal, and 'Father of Confederation' Thomas D'Arcy McGee on 7 April 1868. McGee's death, as David Wilson explains elsewhere in this volume, led to the arrests of some seventy Hibernian leaders on suspicion of Fenian sympathies. In addition to the intimidation of suspected Fenians, the assassination prompted the ruling Conservatives to create the Dominion Police in May 1868 with a mandate to protect government buildings, investigate federal crimes such as mail theft, and undertake political policing. The foundation of a permanent Canadian secret service had thus been laid: it had an institutional home in the form of the newly minted Dominion Police force, possessed a stable source of funding, and, significantly, depended more and more on the expertise of its own well-paid and highly placed agents – not the British diplomatic service.

When rumblings of another Fenian invasion emerged in 1869 and 1870, government officials enjoyed almost complete knowledge of Fenian planning. LeCaron was in the thick of things, stashing guns and ammunition at key border points while simultaneously communicating the Fenians' whereabouts to McMicken. (On one occasion, two government informants reported on LeCaron's actions, unaware that the highly respected Fenian commander was himself an undercover agent.) Not surprisingly, then, when about two hundred Fenian soldiers finally crossed the border from Vermont on 25 May, they were met by a sizable Canadian force – one that had been called up and prepared well in advance – and were easily defeated. In the fall of 1871, McMicken was personally involved in thwarting another perceived Fenian threat, this time in Manitoba, where a raiding party of between forty and eighty men with Fenian connections was captured by American authorities before it reached the Canadian border. In McMicken's own account of this apprehended insurrection, he describes, in a style fit for Boy's Own Annual, his surreptitious journey from St Paul, Minnesota, to Fort Garry, Manitoba, during which he slipped by the Fenian raiders en route; his assistance to the lieutenant governor of Manitoba, Adams George Archibald, in raising a militia of 'loyal Canadians'; and his unflagging devotion to queen and country.[21]

What McMicken called the 'abortive raid' on Manitoba was not, officially, a Fenian operation. Organized by William Bernard O'Donoghue, who had served as treasurer of Louis Riel's provisional government during the Red River rebellion of 1869–70, the attack was not sanctioned by the leadership of the Fenian Brotherhood in Canada or the United States, though O'Donoghue did gain the support of Fenian generals John O'Neill and J.J. Donnelly. O'Donoghue later explained that he viewed the action as an attempt to revive Riel's rebellion of 1869. The raiders clearly anticipated that they would gain the support of Manitoba's Métis community, with whom they shared both a religion and an anti-colonial perspective. A Fenian-Métis alliance was precisely what Archibald and McMicken feared, but it failed to materialize. Riel and other Métis leaders, in this instance, remained loyal to the government. A grateful Archibald became infamous in the eyes of Ontario Orangemen for shaking hands with Riel after inspecting Métis troops who volunteered to help defend the province against O'Donoghue's Fenian-assisted incursion.[22]

As it happened, the so-called Fenian threat to Manitoba only hastened McMicken on a journey already in progress. Even before the fateful handshake with Riel, Prime Minister Macdonald and other federal politicians were concerned that Lieutenant Governor Archibald was too sympathetic to Métis demands that they be granted the lands guaranteed them in the Manitoba Act. McMicken was dispatched to, as he put it to Macdonald, ensure that 'actual settlers' received land without enraging 'French half breeds' over violations of their 'fancied rights.'[23] In addition to his duties as Dominion Police commissioner, then, McMicken was appointed to a number of civil-service offices in Manitoba: he was simultaneously an agent of the Dominion lands branch, the province's assistant receiver general, the secretary of the Intercolonial Railway commission, and an immigration officer. While in Manitoba, as Macdonald's intelligence agent, McMicken surreptitiously monitored both Archibald's activities and the security threat posed by the Métis. As lands agent, McMicken proposed a scheme for a random distribution of lands to the Métis that undermined the arrangements already made by Archibald.[24] When Canada's sovereign interests shifted from border security to westward expansion, McMicken's combined bureaucratic and security career travelled on a parallel track – a blending of roles that foreshadowed the tactics deployed by the federal government in the early decades of the next century.

That the use of undercover agents had become so routine by the late 1860s and early 1870s underscores just how uncontroversial the emergence of the secret service was among Canada's political classes. The only dissent came in 1877 when Alexander Mackenzie's Liberal government investigated Macdonald's (ab)use of the secret service fund. Yet at issue was not the legitimacy, purpose, or secrecy of the fund, but simply its misappropriation. During his tenure as a political leader, Macdonald expressed no reservations about creating a secret police; indeed, he exerted a firm grip on his subordinates, personally controlled the secret service fund, and developed the mechanisms necessary to gather intelligence in recognition of personal, national, and imperial interests. Significantly, the constellation of forces arrayed against the Fenians – domestic and imperial – were still at the disposal of the Canadian state in the early 1900s when it confronted another anti-colonial movement that hoped, like the Fenians, to strike a blow for independence at home by generating support in North America. Even specific strategies, like the overt and covert actions undertaken by McMicken, were reactivated, as the Canadian government sought to resolve its 'Hindoo crisis' on the west coast and, in so doing, help preserve the stability of British rule – the Raj – in India.

WILLIAM CHARLES HOPKINSON AND THE 'HINDOO CRISIS'

Between 1857 and 1914, a period bracketed by the revolt of Indian soldiers serving in the Bengal army – the Great Mutiny – and the outbreak of the First World War, British officials in London and Calcutta undertook a far-reaching inquiry into many areas of imperial policy, including the administration of land, settlement, and the military and Indian access to education, the civil service, and other political institutions. At the same time, Indians – many of whom were educated at newly created schools and universities – remained politically active. By the turn of the century, pockets of collective action, increasingly dedicated to Indian self-determination, had emerged at home and abroad. In England, France, Germany, Switzerland, and the United States, South Asian radicals mixed with left-wing and liberal intellectuals, socialists and trade unionists, and other immigrants and exiles. They rejected the moderate approach charted by the Indian National Congress, which was founded in 1885, and articulated instead a vision of independence achieved through militant tactics. Canada, like other nations where South Asian immigrants pooled, was home to a vibrant radical milieu.[25]

Between 1904 and 1908, about 5,200 South Asians, most of whom were Sikhs from the Punjab, immigrated to British Columbia. Drawn by the promise of work and wages in the industrializing west, they arrived at a time of intense anti-Asian agitation. Spurred on by the inflammatory rhetoric and violent demonstrations of many white British Columbians, actions that only intensified as the local economy faltered in 1907, the federal government sought to curtail Asian immigration by raising the head tax on newcomers from China and negotiating a 'gentleman's agreement' with Japanese authorities. For the ruling Liberals, the outright exclusion of South Asian immigrants posed a problem, for, unlike the Chinese and Japanese, they were British subjects and, at least in theory, possessed all the rights and freedoms associated with that status.[26] The broader connection between the plight of South Asians in Canada and the political (in)stability of the Raj was also a key concern. A Canadian ban on Indian immigration would have revealed the hollowness of the rights the Raj claimed to guarantee and fanned the flames of anti-imperial sentiment among South Asians at home and abroad.[27]

In March 1908 William Lyon Mackenzie King, the young deputy minister of labour, was dispatched to England to confer with British and Indian authorities about Canada's immigration policy. King found that imperial officials agreed that it was 'natural' that the Canadian government should wish to restrict Asian immigration: 'That Canada should desire to remain a white man's country is believed to be not only desirable for economic and social reasons,' he reported, 'but highly necessary on political and national grounds.' On the other hand, King reported that all thought it was best to avoid 'enacting legislation in either India or in Canada which might appear to reflect on fellow British subjects in another part of the empire,' since 'nothing could be more unfortunate ... than that the impression should go forth that Canada ... is not deeply sensible of the obligation which citizenship within the empire entails.' Fortunately, according to King's analysis, the 'dovetailing' of new Canadian immigration restrictions with Indian emigration laws created an 'effective bar' to further South Asian immigration to Canada.[28] Especially effective, King thought, would be the Canadian order-in-council PC 27, passed on 8 January 1908, which prohibited the entry of immigrants who did not travel by 'continuous journey' from the country of their birth to Canada. Since the only company that had been selling a 'through ticket' from India to Canada was the Canadian Pacific Railway, and since the government had used its influence to convince this company to stop selling such tickets, PC 27 achieved its purpose: between 1908 and 1915 only about 100 South Asians were admitted to Canada.[29]

If PC 27 was politically sly, it was legally dubious. Declared invalid by the British Columbia Supreme Court even while King was praising it in England, the government moved quickly to replace it with a reworded order-in-council, PC 662. The measure was put on firmer legal footing on 27 May 1908, when it was underpinned by an amendment to the Immigration Act passed in the House of Commons.[30] If the government's extraordinary efforts to maintain the 'continuous journey' stipulations dampened the spirit of anti-Asian agitation in British Columbia – so toxic in the months and years leading up to Ottawa's intervention – on the other side of the racial divide, members of the South Asian community were incensed. Not only did the 'continuous journey' requirements cut them off from family and friends who wished to join them in Canada, but it cast in bold relief the emptiness of the crown's claim that all British subjects were equal before and under the law. That the Sikhs had remained loyal to the Raj during the Great Mutiny of 1857 and had played a key role in the Indian army in subsequent decades only added insult to injury. In this hothouse of intolerance and confrontation, nationalist, anti-British sentiments started to germinate – drawing many in the South Asian community, including a small yet influential group of Western-educated students and entrepreneurs, into a political debate that was at once local and global in its consequences.

Mindful of the situation in British Columbia and the broader politics of imperial rule in India, especially at a time when unrest was rocking parts of the Punjab and Bengal, the federal government was anxious to keep tabs on this pocket of agitation, both for its own benefit and for the benefit of its counterparts in London and Calcutta. Its principal resource in this regard was William Charles Hopkinson. The son of a British officer in the Indian army and a Brahmin mother, Hopkinson was born in Delhi in 1880. At the age of sixteen, he joined the Indian police, working first in the Punjab, then later in Calcutta from 1901 to 1907, two locales that, during this period, were seedbeds for various political movements. Fluent in English, Punjabi, Hindi, and other Indian languages, Hopkinson left the Calcutta police force sometime in 1907 and surfaced in British Columbia later that year (or early in 1908), taking up a permanent position as an interpreter with the Vancouver immigration service in February 1909.[31] Shortly after his arrival, yet several months before officially taking up his post in the immigration service, the diminutive former detective had convinced local authorities to shut down a night school for South Asian workers in New Westminster and a newspaper called *Free Hindusthan*, which routinely published anti-British material. Both were run by Taraknath Das, a young activist and university graduate who at one time played a role in nationalist protests in Calcutta against the partition of Bengal.[32] Fragmentary evidence suggests that Hopkinson had been on the radical's trail for some time – more than likely at the behest of India's Department of

Criminal Intelligence, which was created in 1904. Whatever the impetus for Hopkinson's journey to North America, the Canadian Department of the Interior, which was responsible for immigration, and the federal cabinet understood just how valuable his skills were in managing potential political unrest, both as an interpreter and later as a spy.[33]

Having all but stemmed the flow of South Asian immigrants to British Columbia, the Canadian government next considered a plan that would relocate those who had already arrived. In the fall of 1908, Ottawa devised a plan to transplant South Asians from British Columbia to British Honduras. The scheme was first formulated by J.B. Harkin, private secretary to the minister of the interior, the summer before. 'It has been pretty well established that physically and mentally the Hindoo is unfitted to compete successfully with whites or with other Orientals in a country like this,' Harkin told W.D. Scott, the superintendent of immigration. '[This proposal] avoids the possibility of a precipitation of trouble in India consequent on the return of Hindoos enraged at their treatment in British territory.'[34] The federal government concurred, and, within weeks of receiving the Colonial Office's blessing, it permitted Harkin to assemble a delegation to investigate the feasibility of the central American colony as a home for British Columbia's South Asians. The special group included Hopkinson, who was brought on board as a secretary and interpreter, and two representatives from the city's South Asian community: Sham Singh, a Hindu, and Hagar Singh, a Sikh. It travelled to Belize in late October. From Harkin's and Hopkinson's point of view, the trip, which lasted several weeks, was a great success. The demand for agricultural labour in British Honduras was higher than expected, and by all accounts the South Asian delegates were impressed by the working conditions there and desirous of seeing the scheme through. Or so the trip's organizers thought. Upon returning to Vancouver, Sham Singh and Hagar Singh rejected the relocation plan and went so far as to accuse Hopkinson of trying to bribe them into delivering a more positive assessment. Harkin, who was not in British Columbia at the time the delegates made their views public, was incensed. 'Evidently agitators [are] at work,' he informed W.W. Cory, the deputy minister of the interior, after receiving an assessment of the situation in Vancouver from Hopkinson. 'It is to be regretted that the efforts of the Government to better their condition and ensure their welfare in another part of the British Empire should be thus thwarted by foreign influence, over which we seem to have little control,' Cory replied.[35]

The 'mischievous agitator' in question was Teja Singh, an articulate, multilingual, and highly educated Sikh who came to Vancouver in October 1908 and quickly emerged as a local leader.[36] Shortly after the delegation's return from British Honduras, the suspected seditionist made several speeches outlining his opposition to the relocation plan, the existence of corruption in the immigration service, and, more ominously from the government's point of view, 'the present unrest in India.' Teja Singh's remarks, whereabouts, and personal relations were carefully tracked by Hopkinson and forwarded to local officials with the Department of the Interior who, in turn, kept senior bureaucrats, cabinet members, and the prime minister well informed.[37] Not surprisingly, all of this was of great concern to the governor general, Lord Grey. Like his predecessors at Rideau Hall, he was an aristocrat, a veteran of the civil service, and an official link between Ottawa and London. As such, he handled the voluminous correspondence that flowed back and forth across the Atlantic and advised the Dominion government on issues of national and imperial concern. Indeed, when it came to this particular realm of political affairs, Lord Grey's opinion still carried considerable weight on Parliament Hill, despite the largely ceremonial and administrative character of his position. 'A vigilant watch must be maintained on all events, statements, and newspaper reports which, if repeated in India, might be likely to inflame the minds of those who are tools and victims of sedition,' he cautioned the prime minister in early December 1908.[38] Sound intelligence was, of course, key to this approach, and the governor general worked hard to ensure that it found its way to the Colonial Office and India Office in London and the Department of Criminal Intelligence and viceroy in Calcutta. (The words 'Copy Sent To India' are stamped on many of these documents.)[39]

But Lord Grey was not the only imperial official to play a decisive role in the expansion of political policing in Canada. When Ottawa first proposed the idea of relocating South Asians, Colonel E.J. Swayne, governor of British Honduras and an 'Old Indian officer,' was in London on other business; evidently, he offered up his colony as a possible solution to Canada's 'Hindoo' problem. On his way back to Belize in early December 1908, the governor travelled via Canada and met with the governor general and prime minister, and later undertook his own investigation of 'matters affecting the East Indian Community in British Columbia.'[40] Less anxious than Lord Grey about the potential risks posed by the likes of Teja Singh, Swayne nevertheless possessed strong opinions on the future of South Asian immigration to Canada. It should be 'controlled,' he wrote forcefully, because 'the terms of close familiarity which competition with white labour has brought about, do not make for British prestige.'

Swayne understood well that, for a small, yet influential group of whites and South Asians, familiarity did not breed contempt; rather, on occasion, it produced solidarity.[41] 'Socialists of a very undesirable type have made it their business to tamper with the East Indians in Vancouver,' he wrote bluntly, referring specifically to the radical Industrial Workers of the World (IWW) and the Socialist Party of Canada (SPC).

The return of the Sikhs to the Punjab amongst their friends, spreading as they will, new, ill-digested socialistic ideas, and the familiar knowledge of such defects amongst their white fellow labourers, such as labour rivalry would have been only too ready to pick out, cannot but tend to re-act amongst the military classes of the Punjab, to the detriment of British prestige. As – when all is said and done, looking at our position in India as a whole, it must be recognized that it is by prestige alone that India is held and not by force, the importance of a circulation of labour between Vancouver and India as affecting that prestige is such, I submit, as cannot be wisely overlooked.[42]

In this regard, he concluded, in addition to 'strictly limiting' immigration from India to Canada, it was crucial that the 'doings of the Brahmin section be closely watched' on an ongoing basis. 'I do not think that a better man than Mr. Hopkinson of the Calcutta police could be found for this work,' Swayne stated, recognizing the importance of having another old India man on the job. 'I suggest Mr. Hopkinson be appointed as Dominion police officer on special duty at Vancouver, for the special purpose of this enquiry, and the Government of India be asked to place him in official communication with the head of the Calcutta police in order to further this work.'[43]

With the support of the Department of the Interior, the governor general, and the governor of British Honduras, Ottawa officially hired Hopkinson early in 1909. He was given a permanent position in the immigration department in Vancouver and was assigned to the Dominion Police, although he did not receive a formal commission in the federal force until 1911. For $100 per month, he was expected to keep tabs on the South Asian community and undertake regular duties as an interpreter. Ottawa was certainly pleased with its new agent. So, too, no doubt, were imperial officials. Just months before Hopkinson was hired, Lord Morley, the secretary of state for India, had written to Lord Minto, the viceroy, and lamented the absence of knowledgeable undercover agents. 'The whole Indian field is absolutely unfamiliar, in language, habits, and everything else,' he said. 'In short, both you and I can easily understand that the ordinary square-toed English constable, even in the detective branch, would be rather clumsy in tracing your wily Asiatics.'[44]

Between 1909 and 1914, Hopkinson was exceptionally busy. His activities, which were initially confined to British Columbia's Lower Mainland and southern Vancouver Island but later expanded to include Washington state, Oregon, and northern California, were many and varied: he attended suspicious meetings and rallies in order to 'find out their latest move and the methods they are adopting for the bringing out of their countrymen from India'; monitored the movements of community leaders and their supporters within the province and across the Canada-U.S. border; and kept tabs on foreign-language newspapers. Taraknath Das's *Free Hindusthan*, which was then based in Seattle but printed locally with the assistance of the Socialist Party of Canada, was of particular interest; so, too, was *Swadesh Sewak* (Servant of the Country), a Gurmukhi-language monthly published out of Vancouver by Guran Ditta Kumar, a former college instructor from Calcutta who arrived in British Columbia in 1907.[45] Kumar, a self-described 'Punjabi Buddhist' and 'Worker in the cause of Temperance and Vegetarianism,' first came to Hopkinson's attention as a possible 'agitator' nearly two years later. At that time, he was living in Victoria and running a grocery store that had been set up with the assistance of his friend Taraknath Das. The link between the two men, which was common knowledge within the South Asian community, prompted Hopkinson to pay a visit to Kumar's modest operation in the provincial capital in August 1909. Disguised as a lumberman looking for labourers, the new Dominion Police investigator discovered not only that Kumar sold *Free Hindusthan* and the radical, London-based *Indian Sociologist*, but that he was in constant contact with the ubiquitous Teja Singh and Taraknath Das, who was then living in Washington State. The following November, Kumar surfaced in Vancouver, opened the 'Swadesh Sewak Home,' and started publishing a newspaper by the same name early in 1910. Hopkinson kept tabs on him at all times. 'The tone of this paper gradually became more and more objectionable,' one government official's report concluded, based in part on Hopkinson's assessments. 'It was addressed principally to the Sikhs in the Indian Army in their own language, and was being sent out to India in considerable numbers.'[46]

Hopkinson's modus operandi – the reading of seditious publications, the tracking of suspected agitators – was the stock-in-trade of political policing; it would have been easily recognized by the likes of Patrick Nolan or Henri LeCaron. But Hopkinson was not simply an undercover agent, he was an immigration inspector as well, and this dual role was fraught with both tension and danger at a time when Ottawa was making use of its wide-ranging discretionary powers to curtail immigration from Asian countries.[47] Hopkinson, like other immigration inspectors, possessed the authority to admit, reject, or initiate deportation proceedings against new immigrants – powers that were invaluable for someone concerned both with the administration of immigration policy and with limiting the development of seditious behaviour. In this important respect, not only was Hopkinson deeply lodged in the day-to-day controversies surrounding the enforcement of the landing restrictions for South Asian immigrants, but, ironically, his very actions in this regard helped to stoke the unnerving anti-British sentiment that had prompted the federal government to hire him in the first place. For Hopkinson, carrying out this dual role would in the end prove deadly.[48]

From the moment that the federal government imposed the 'continuous journey' restrictions in 1908, the South Asian community mounted a sustained campaign to overturn it, a development that enhanced the profile of committed radicals and brought moderates in touch with more militant ideas and tactics. One of the men who was particularly forceful in his denunciation of federal immigration policy, and Hopkinson's role in implementing it, was Chagan Kairaj Varma, a native of the Porbander district in Gujarat state who came to Canada on a tourist visa in January 1910 after spending several years working in Japan and Hawaii. Known in British Columbia by the Muslim name Hussain Rahim, the middle-aged, Westernized Hindu quickly assumed a leadership role in the South Asian community – an ascent that was driven, in part, by his own ongoing conflict with the immigration service.[49] Shortly after turning up in Vancouver, Rahim, who was interviewed by Hopkinson upon his arrival, established the Canada India Supply and Trust Company and applied for permission to stay in the country. Immigration officials responded to this request by arresting Rahim and initiating deportation proceedings against him. 'You drive us Hindus out of Canada and we will drive every white man out of India,' he said after being apprehended. Hopkinson, for one, took this threat seriously. Later that same day, city police located a notebook belonging to Rahim that contained information about explosives and the names of activists from other countries. In the weeks and months that followed this startling revelation, both men found themselves in court as Rahim, like other 'Hindoos' before him, challenged the government's deportation order – successfully arguing that particular elements of the orders-in-council that curbed South Asian immigration exceeded the scope of authority available to the federal government under the Immigration Act.[50] Writing to the prime minister and imperial authorities, including Lord Crewe, secretary of state for India, in 1910, the Hindustani Association, a self-help organization that assisted in Rahim's legal defence, laid bare the wider political significance of this narrow technical argument: 'As British subjects, we demand our inalienable rights to reside more freely in the British Empire and request immediate redress against high-handed, impolite, and Empire-breaking actions of local authorities.'[51]

For Hopkinson, Rahim's legal victory was infuriating for many reasons, not the least of which was that it heightened his prestige in the South Asian community, called into question the legitimacy and effectiveness of the immigration branch, and, by virtue of the issues at stake, provided further grist for the anti-colonial mill. 'The failure ... of the Department to deport Rahim from Canada has so bolstered up his position in the Hindu community here as to make him a leader and a counsellor in respect to all matters concerning their community,' he informed his Ottawa-based handler, W.W. Cory. 'Canada would be well rid of Rahim and the exposure of his true character would have a very beneficial effect on [the] community.'[52]

Significantly, the 'true character' that Hopkinson had in mind was not simply Rahim's obvious commitment to the 'liberty, equality, and fraternity of the Hindustani Nation' but his immersion in Vancouver's vibrant left-wing milieu, which was then dominated by the Socialist Party of Canada and the Industrial Workers of the World. Indeed, as the tone and content of his intelligence reports filed in the wake of the court case suggest, Hopkinson became increasingly preoccupied with this cross-fertilization of socialist and anti-colonial politics that Rahim in particular embodied – eventually discovering that he joined the SPC shortly after arriving in the country, helped to form a South Asian local, and, drawing on the resources of the Canada India Supply and Trust Company, posted bail for several members of the IWW jailed during the free-speech fights in 1912. 'The Hindus have up to the present never identified themselves with any particular Political party and the introduction by Rahim of the socialist propaganda into this community, is, I consider a very serious matter, as the majority of these people are uneducated and ignorant and easily led like sheep by a man like Rahim,' Hopkinson wrote in April 1912. 'The danger to the country is not here but the question is what effect will all these Socialistic and Revolutionary teachings have on the people in India on the return of these men primed with Western methods of agitation and Political and Social equality.'[53]

Hopkinson knew well that Rahim, as important as he was in Vancouver, was but one cog in a much larger political machine: there were South Asian men 'primed' with both 'Western methods of agitation' and ideas of 'political and social equality' operating up and down the west coast. Not surprisingly, then, Hopkinson eventually broadened his area of surveillance to include Seattle, Portland, San Francisco, and Berkeley, where Lala Har Dayal, a Delhi-born, Oxford-educated nationalist and the founder of the Ghadar (Mutiny) Party, was lecturing in Indian philosophy. Hopkinson was certainly familiar with Har Dayal prior to this trip, but it was not until the British consul general in San Francisco informed him that the university instructor was linked to both the assassination attempt on the viceroy, Lord Hardingue, on 23 December 1912 and the IWW that he placed him under constant surveillance. By February 1913, the file on this suspected agitator had ballooned considerably, and Hopkinson, who was increasingly adamant that Har Dayal was one of the most dangerous men around, more dangerous than Taraknath Das, was dispatched to London by the federal government to report on the current state of anti-colonial agitation on the Pacific coast.[54]

Acting largely on the basis of his brief, British and Canadian authorities agreed that Hopkinson should be more secure, both institutionally and monetarily. As a result, in addition to his existing relationship with the Canadian government, Hopkinson was placed on the India Office's payroll – the money coming out of the Department of Criminal Intelligence's budget – and ordered to report directly to the former superintendent of police for Bombay, J.A. Wallinger, who was in England at the time working in the area of intelligence and imperial defence. Canada's new governor general, the Duke of Connaught, was not impressed with this new arrangement. 'It is highly ... undesirable that this work should be dependent on the existence of a single individual,' he informed the Colonial Office. 'In the first place, Mr Hopkinson has to cover the entire country from San Francisco to New York and from the Canadian to the Mexican frontiers. In the second place, the entire system – if system it can be called – is dependent on one man. If any thing happens to Mr Hopkinson, the work would automatically collapse.' For the governor general, the best way to proceed was to transfer Hopkinson to the Indian government. After all, he stated, the uber-agent's work was both costly and increasingly about imperial, not national, concerns. Wallinger disagreed, and argued persuasively that 'the permanent transfer of Mr Hopkinson to the Indian Government would entirely destroy Mr Hopkinson's usefulness. He is now, by very reason of his multifarious offices ... in a position to do some delicate work for us without having suspicion drawn upon himself. Once he is removed from these offices he would be a marked man.'[55]

There was certainly an element of truth in Wallinger's assessment. By virtue of his 'multifarious offices,' Hopkinson was indeed in a position to carry out 'delicate' intelligence work among South Asians up and down the west coast, just as he had been doing for the better part of six years. At the same time, however, the former police superintendent was dead wrong on the question of anonymity: if anything, Hopkinson's dual role as immigration officer and undercover agent kept him in the public eye. At no time was this more obvious than during the spring and summer of 1914 when Gurdit Singh, a Sikh entrepreneur, and 376 passengers – 340 Sikhs, 24 Muslims, and 12 Hindus – challenged the federal government's ban on South Asian immigrants by sailing into the port of Vancouver on board the *Komagata Maru* on 23 May. 'We are British citizens and we consider we have a right to visit any part of the Empire. We are determined to make this a test case and if we are refused entrance into your country, the matter will not end here,' Gurdit Singh told the local press, shortly after dropping anchor. 'What is done with this shipload of my people will determine whether we shall have peace in all parts of the British Empire.'[56]

Immigration officials did with this batch of immigrants what they had done to scores of others since the federal government first introduced selective landing requirements: they refused to allow them on shore. This action, coupled with Gurdit Singh's resolve to overturn the ban, prompted a long and sometimes violent stand-off which ended on 23 July when the passengers of the *Komagata Maru*, after facing down an attempt by Canadian authorities to seize the ship by force, decided to return to India. Throughout this incident, Hopkinson handled the negotiations between those on ship and those on shore – including senior immigration officials and the immigrants' allies, the so-called 'shore committee' which was led by Hussain Rahim.[57] From the perspective of many in the South Asian community, the entire *Komagata Maru* affair simply reinforced their belief that a toxic combination of fear, loathing, and racial hatred was at the core of both Canadian immigration policy and the broader white society that sanctioned it. What was more, it reaffirmed graphically the hypocrisy of the British empire. Sikhs and Hindus simply did not possess the same rights and freedoms as free-born Englishmen – whether in Canada or in India. And Hopkinson, by virtue of his role as an immigration officer and secret agent, was as guilty as anyone in defending this condition of inequality.

In the months that followed the *Komagata Maru*'s departure, several of Hopkinson's informants were murdered. Another of Hopkinson's supporters, Bela Singh, was attacked while praying at the Sikh temple in Vancouver. In response, he shot and killed two people, including the priest, and wounded seven others before surrendering to the authorities. On 21 October 1914 Hopkinson himself was murdered. While waiting outside a Vancouver courtroom to testify in defence of Bela Singh, he was shot and killed by Mewa Singh, a man who had been apprehended during the summer stand-off trying to smuggle arms into Canada but who later became an informant for Hopkinson.[58] '[He] is the last man one would have suspected of committing the deed,' Malcolm Reid, Hopkinson's superior at the immigration branch, wrote to Ottawa. 'No doubt, however, he was influenced by the local Hindu community. The man is now perfectly cheerful in his cell and to all intents and purposes seems glad he has murdered Hopkinson.'[59] Glad, perhaps, because this was not simply an act of revenge, but an act of greater political and religious significance, spurred on, in part, by the Ghadar Party's call to arms that accompanied Britain's declaration of war in August; 'it was the duty of a good man to give his life for a good cause,' Mewa Singh said just weeks before he was hanged for his crime. Hopkinson was given a lavish funeral by the municipal and federal government – approximately 2,000 people marched in the procession – and his widow received a lump-sum payment from the Indian government. The money came from its secret service fund, for Indian, British, and Canadian authorities wanted to keep Hopkinson's activities hidden.[60]

CONCLUSION

Few institutions mirror a nation's political culture, the working logic of its government, and the preoccupations of its leaders more than its secret police – in terms of its status, modus operandi, and declared enemies.[61] Even at its birth, Canada's secret service faced no challenge or debate among the Canadian political class: the prerogative of the federal government to monitor potentially subversive citizens surreptitiously was underwritten by the 'peace, order and good government' provision of the British North America Act of 1867, which allowed for a highly centralized state and made available to the prime minister and his cabinet a wide range of emergency powers – executive and administrative – to confront threats to the political and economic status quo. The suspension of habeas corpus, political arrests without charges, mail seizure, secret agents, perhaps even agents provocateurs – all were present in the formative years of the new nation-state and all went virtually unopposed, the lone dissenting voices being those of the victims. The profound suspicion so prevalent in Victorian England of spies, spying, and secrecy found few reflections in the Canadian outpost of empire. Here, fears of oligarchy were less evident than fears of republicanism: it was republicanism, bound up in broader agendas of French Canadian and Irish nationalism, that was cast as the antithesis of the new nation-state. That new nation-state, largely imposed from above, and extended westward with a remarkable ruthlessness, contained a secret service from its inception.

If decades passed between when the Canadian political police mobilized against Fenians and when it directed its efforts against South Asian radicals, features of these responses bear marked similarities. What is perhaps more striking than the common surveillance and infiltration tactics of agents and informants is the way in which these secret activities were coordinated with more conventional uses of state power. Elsewhere in this volume, David Wilson concludes that, against domestic Fenians, the Canadian government used the suspension of habeas corpus with moderation and restraint. The limited scope of this *overt* breach of civil liberties, however, was made possible through extensive *covert* intelligence gathering by the secret police. In the early 1870s, while Gilbert McMicken was clandestinely policing the western frontier against further Fenian incursions or Métis rebellion, he was also openly forwarding the expansionist interests of the Dominion government as a lands agent. Some forty years later, immigration restrictions and espionage were likewise deployed against South Asians in Canada by a single agent of the state, William Charles Hopkinson.

The links between Canada's colonial legacy and its foray into political policing were extensive. Throughout this period, the federal government was preoccupied with 'suspected seditionists' whose real enemy was the mother country itself. While Irish and South Asian radicals possessed different histories of oppression under British colonialism, and drew on different cultural and religious resources to mount their political challenges, their activities abroad were very similar. Leavened by the freedom available to them outside their respective homelands, they dedicated considerable intellectual and financial resources to raising people's consciousness, articulating a vision of national independence, forging links between those in exile and those at home, and taking action. While the government found its embryonic secret service useful in policing these pockets of anti-colonial agitation, it also relied heavily on Britain's extensive diplomatic corps in the United States and the imperial civil service to gather and disseminate information. Not only were consular officials, many of whom operated their own undercover agents, important in this regard, but so too were the various governors general who served as Canada's head of state – in particular Lord Monck and Lord Grey. A position of little significance today, the governors general possessed extensive knowledge of imperial politics, served as important conduits for the copious intelligence that flowed between Ottawa and London, and were strong advocates of political policing as a means to solve both national and imperial problems. Only in the immediate post-war period, when Canada's internal security problems changed and its own capacity to monitor dissidents expanded, would the role of this imperial infrastructure diminish.

With the onset of the Great War, the question of who posed a threat to Canada's internal security, and the best way to limit that potential threat, would undergo a decisive shift at the highest levels of the federal government. As Hopkinson's increasing preoccupation with the influence of 'socialistic ideas' suggests, signs of this transformation away from imperial concerns were already present before the outbreak of hostilities in Europe. Indeed, in the crucible of the war years, Ottawa would suspend civil liberties outright, create a new battery of repressive measures, and, under the pretext of mobilizing the nation for war, move to crush its new, more formidable opponent: labour and the left. For the better part of the twentieth century, the Canadian state was preoccupied by the 'red menace.'[62] With the end of the Cold War, and the events of 11 September 2001, however, its focus has shifted to new security threats: anti-globalization activists and suspected terrorists who, for extraordinarily different reasons and in extraordinarily different ways, have mounted a challenge to the global reach of a different superpower, the United States. That Ottawa's response to these challenges has enhanced state power, eroded the balance between different branches of government, blurred the line between legitimate and illegitimate political action, and circumscribed individual and collective rights is clear. What is less appreciated is that this political solution possesses a long history in Canada, one that stretches back well over a century.[63]

NOTES

The authors are grateful to Kirk Niergarth, formerly a post-doctoral history fellow at the University of New Brunswick, for his substantial assistance in preparing this chapter, derived from earlier versions of their research and analysis that appear under the title 'The Origins of Political Policing in Canada: Class, Law, and the Burden of Empire' in *Osgoode Hall Law Journal* 41, nos. 2 and 3 (2003): 211–40; *Prairie Forum* 31, no. 2 (2006): 245–71; and Alexander Netherton, Allen Seager, and Karl Froshauer, eds., *In/security: Canada in the Post-9/11 World* (Burnaby, B.C.: Simon Fraser University Press 2005), 127–67.

1 In the aftermath of the rebellions in Upper and Lower Canada in 1837 and 1838, authorities in Quebec, drawing on the example set by colonial authorities in Ireland and Jamaica, appointed stipendiary magistrates to head up a newly created rural police force, a body charged with the responsibility of collecting political intelligence and pacifying the countryside. Decades later, during the American Civil War, politicians on both sides of the Ottawa River adopted a similar, albeit much smaller version of this system to prevent military recruiters from violating Canadian neutrality. Greg Marquis's 'The "Irish Model" and Nineteenth-Century Canadian Policing,' *Journal of Imperial and Commonwealth History* 25, no. 2 (1997): 193–218, provides an excellent discussion of policing in British North America, including the colonies of Vancouver Island and Newfoundland. See also: Allan Greer, 'The Birth of the Police in Canada,' in Greer and Ian Radforth, eds., *Colonial Leviathan: State Formation in Mid-Nineteenth-Century Canada* (Toronto: University of Toronto Press 1992); Brian Young, 'Positive Law, Positive State: Class Realignment and the Transformation of Lower Canada, 1815–1866,' in *Colonial Leviathan*; and Greer, *The Patriots and the People* (Toronto: University of Toronto Press 1993).

2 The connection between the Fenian invasion and confederation is a staple of the Canadian literature. See, for an early example, C.P. Stacey, 'A Fenian Interlude: The Story of Michael Murphy,' *CHR* 15 (1934): 133–54, and 'Fenianism and the Rise of National Feeling in Canada at the Time of Confederation,' *CHR* 3 (September 1931): 238–61. In the latter, Stacey writes: 'Fenianism provided a most beneficial influence upon the immediate fortunes of the project, by creating at once a popular apprehension of danger which worked strongly against the possibility of a repudiation of parliament's decision, and by engendering eminently favourable conditions for the success of an experiment in nation building.'

3 The literature on the Fenians, in particular, and Irish nationalism, more generally, is massive. For the purposes of this discussion, the best place to start is with John Newsinger's slim volume *Fenianism in Mid-Victorian Britain* (London: Pluto Press 1994); it provides a cogent account of the important debates associated with Feniansim and a thorough bibliography. Also useful are Padraic Kennedy, 'Political Policing in a Liberal Age: Britain's Responses to the

Fenian Movement, 1858–1868,' PhD thesis, Washington University 1996; W.S. Neidhardt, *Fenianism in North America* (University Park, Penn.: Pennsylvania State University Press 1975); Keith Amos, *The Fenians in Australia, 1865–1880* (Kensington: New South Wales University Press 1988); and Brian Jenkins, *Fenians and Anglo-American Relations during Reconstruction* (Ithaca, N.Y., and London: Cornell University Press 1969). Interestingly, Fenian leader James Stephens was also a member of the International Working Man's Association, the so-called First International which included Karl Marx. See Hereward Senior, *The Fenians in Canada* (Toronto: Macmillan 1978), 40–1.

4 On this last point, see Jenkins, *Fenians and Anglo-American Relations during Reconstruction*; David Montgomery, *Beyond Equality: Labor and Radical Republicans, 1862–1872* (New York: Knopf 1967); and Eric Foner, 'Class, Ethnicity, and Radicalism in the Gilded Age: The Land League and Irish-America,' *Marxist Perspectives* 1, no. 2 (1978): 30–1. During the U.S. election of 1868, John A. Macdonald remarked: 'Both Republicans and Democrats will fish for the Irish vote, and therefore wink as much as possible at any action of the Fenian body.' See John A. Macdonald to Col. Ermatinger, 8 Feb. 1868, LAC, John A. Macdonald Papers [hereafter JAMP], MG 26, Letterbooks, vol. 11.

5 In the Canadian context, the Fenian question has been framed in many ways: as an important moment in Canadian military history; as a significant dimension of Irish immigrants' experience in the New World; and, as already mentioned, as a key variable in the debates associated with the act of confederation in 1867. In addition to David Wilson's essay in this volume, see George Sheppard, '"God Save the Green": Fenianism and Fellowship in Victorian Ontario,' *Histoire Sociale / Social History* 20, no. 39 (1987): 129–44; Jeff Keshen, 'Cloak and Dagger: Canada West's Secret Police, 1864–67,' *Ontario History* 79 (1987): 353–77; Peter M. Toner, 'The Home Rule League: Fortune, Fenians, and Failure,' *Canadian Journal of Irish Studies* 15, no. 1 (1989): 7–19; Oliver Rafferty, 'Fenianism in North America in the 1860s: The Problems for Church and State,' *History* 84 (April 1999): 257–77; Brian Clarke, *Piety and Nationalism: Lay Voluntary Organizations and the Creation of an Irish-Catholic Community in Toronto, 1850–1895* (Kingston and Montreal: McGill-Queen's University Press 1993). The quotation from the *Irish Canadian* is taken from Clarke, *Piety and Nationalism*, 175.

6 John A. Macdonald to Cockburn, 2 Jan. 1865 and 7 Feb. 1865, LAC, JAMP, MG 26, Letterbooks, vol. 7; Macdonald to Lord Monck, 18 Sept. 1865, and Macdonald to McMicken, 22 Sept. 1865, LAC, JAMP, MG 26, Letterbooks, vol. 8. Technically, Macdonald's title was attorney general 'for that part of the Province of Canada called Upper Canada.' While the terms 'Canada West' and 'Canada East' were used in the popular press between 1841 and 1867,

Margaret Banks has shown that they had no basis in law and that the terms 'Upper Canada' and 'Lower Canada' remained both officially correct and in widespread use. See Margaret Banks, 'Upper and Lower Canada or Canada West and East, 1841–1867?' *CHR* 54, no. 4 (1973): 473–80.

7 McMicken worked for and with prominent merchants on the Niagara peninsula and was involved in the construction of the Queenston suspension bridge and the extension of Canada's first telegraph line from Toronto to Lewiston, New York. In 1835 he married Anne Theresa Duff, granddaughter of Alexander Grant, who, in Carl Betke's words, 'dominated the early fur trade, the shipping industry, and the Provincial Marine in the Detroit region.' See Carl Betke, 'Gilbert McMicken,' *DCB*, 12: 675–80.

8 The specific nature of the alliance between McMicken and Macdonald is not entirely clear. Carl Betke notes that, days after McMicken received his patronage appointment in Windsor, he wrote to remind Macdonald that he had 'borne contumely and reproach aye even imprisonment and Bonds for your sake.' As quoted in Betke, 'Gilbert McMicken.' Cheryl MacDonald suggests that the two may have been connected through Samuel Zimmerman, the financier and influence peddler who employed McMicken for a time. See Cheryl MacDonald, 'Canada's Secret Police,' *The Beaver* (June/July 1991): 44–9. See also J.K. Johnson, 'Samuel Zimmerman,' *DCB*, 8: 963–7.

9 McMicken developed an especially close relationship with Alan Pinkerton, head of Pinkerton's Detective Agency, and personally intervened, as a magistrate, to facilitate extraditions when Pinkerton detectives had pursued fugitives into Canada. See Dale and Lee Gibson, 'Railroading the Train Robbers: Extradition in the Shadow of Annexation,' in Dale Gibson and Wesley Pue, eds., *Glimpses of Canadian Legal History* (Winnipeg: Legal Research Institute of the University of Manitoba 1991), 71–93.

10 Gilbert McMicken, 'Special Order,' 31 Dec. 1864, LAC, JAMP, MG 26, McMicken Correspondence. See also the various letters between British, Canadian, and American officials in *Correspondence relating to the Fenian Invasion and the Rebellion of the Southern States* (Ottawa: Hunter Rose 1869), in particular: Simon Cameron, U.S. Secretary of War, to the Right Honourable Sir Edmund Head, 24 Oct. 1861; Lord Lyon to Lord Monck, 8 Aug. 1864; Lord Monck to E. Cardwell, Member of Parliament, 23 Sept. 1864; British Legation, Washington, to Seward, U.S. Secretary of State, 26 Dec. 1864.

11 This paragraph, including the material on the social origins of the spies, is drawn from various spy reports contained in LAC, JAMP, MG 26, McMicken Correspondence; the final quotation is taken from McMicken to Macdonald, 9 April 1866.

12 The intelligence-gathering activities of British diplomats are discussed in

David Wilson's essay in this volume. See also Edith J. Archibald, *The Life and Letters of Sir Edward Mortimer Archibald* (Toronto: George N. Morang 1924); William D'Arcy, *The Fenian Movement in the United States* (New York: Russell and Russell 1947); Neidhardt, *Fenianism in North America*; Wayne A. Crockett, 'The Uses and Abuses of the Secret Service Fund: The Political Dimension of Police Work in Canada, 1864–1877,' MA thesis, Queen's University 1982, 66; Leon O'Broin, *Fenian Fever: An Anglo-American Dilemma* (New York: New York University Press 1971), 41–51; Harold A. Davis, 'The Fenian Raid on New Brunswick,' *CHR* 36, no. 4 (1955): 316–34; W.L. Morton, 'Lord Monck and Nationality in Ireland and Canada,' *Studia Hibernica* 13 (1973): 77–100.

13 Monck to John A Macdonald, 10 Nov. 1865, LAC, JAMP, MG 26, Governors General Correspondence, vol. 93; D'Arcy McGee to John A. Macdonald, 2 Nov. 1865, LAC, JAMP, MG 26, Governors General Correspondence, vol. 1.

14 Crockett, 'The Uses and Abuses of the Secret Service Fund,' 40; D'Arcy, *The Fenian Movement*, 97–8.

15 Keshen, 'Cloak and Dagger,' 366.

16 The arrests came at the behest of George-Étienne Cartier, attorney general for Lower Canada, and Alexander Galt, minister of finance, who were anxious to contain the Fenian threat before it spread to their own, largely Roman Catholic, bailiwick. Macdonald was not impressed by his colleagues' actions. Not only did Cartier and Galt lack the necessary information to convict Murphy of treason, but the ministers' intervention scuttled ongoing undercover operations.

17 John A. Cooper, 'The Fenian Raid of 1866,' *Canadian Magazine* 10, no. 1 (1897): 41–55.

18 According to Keshen: 'At the most crucial moment of his career as Stipendiary Magistrate for Canada West, McMicken failed miserably. His presence and that of the frontier force changed nothing. The Fenian raid proceeded as planned, and the government was unprepared.' See 'Cloak and Dagger,' 368.

19 Carl Betke and S.W. Horrall, 'Canada's Security Service: An Historical Outline, 1864–1966,' RCMP Historical Section, 1978, unpublished manuscript in possession of authors, 77–9; Philip Stenning, 'Guns & the Law,' *The Beaver* (December 2000-January 2001): 6–7; D'Arcy, *The Fenian Movement in the United States*, 194–211. On the suspension of habeas corpus, see David Wilson's essay in this volume.

20 Charles Curran suggests that Beach adopted this name in jest: 'Le Caron is argot for "slice of fat bacon." Beach was lean and wiry. It has been suggested that he took the name by way of a joke.' See his 'The Spy behind the Speaker's Chair,' *History Today* 18 (1968): 745–54. That Beach chose a French name at all was likely due to the British government's support of the South during the

Civil War. See also J.A. Cole, *Prince of Spies: Henri LeCaron* (London: Faber and Faber 1984), and Henri LeCaron, *Twenty-Five Years in the Secret Service* (London: Heinemann 1892).

21 Gilbert McMicken, 'The Abortive Fenian Raid on Manitoba: Account by One Who Knew Its Secret History,' *Historical and Scientific Society of Manitoba*, Transaction no. 32, 1887–8 (Winnipeg: Manitoba Free Press Print 1888). See also Ruth Swan and Edward Jerome, 'Unequal Justice: The Métis in O'Donoghue's Raid of 1871,' *Manitoba History* 39 (2000): 24–38; D.N. Sprague, *Canada and the Métis, 1869–1885* (Waterloo, Ont.: Wilfrid Laurier University Press 1988), 75–107; A.H. de Trémaudan, 'Louis Riel and the Fenian Raid of 1871,' *CHR* 2 (June 1923): 132–44; J.P. Pritchett, 'The Origin of the So-Called Fenian Raid on Manitoba in 1871,' *CHR* 10 (March 1929): 23–42.

22 In the aftermath of the raid, three Métis were arrested for assisting the raiders. Two, Isadore Villeneuve and Andre Jerome, were not convicted, but the third, Louison Letendre, was found guilty and sentenced to hang (his sentence was later commuted to twenty years' imprisonment, and in January 1873 he was exiled to the United States). Ruth Swan and Edward Jerome explore the context of these arrests and the harsh treatment of those arrested in 'Unequal Justice.'

23 McMicken to Macdonald, 12 Nov. 1871 and 22 Dec. 1871, as cited in Sprague, *Canada and the Métis*, 98.

24 See Sprague, *Canada and the Métis*, 96–8.

25 This paragraph on the British in India from 1857 to 1914 is drawn from Judith M. Brown, *Modern India: The Origins of an Asian Democracy* (Oxford: Oxford University Press 1994), 1–193. Richard J. Popplewell examines the development of political policing in India under Lord Curzon and, as the title of his book implies, its role in the defence of the empire at home and abroad. See his *Intelligence and Imperial Defence: British Intelligence and the Defence of the Indian Empire, 1904–1924* (London: Frank Cass 1995). On the development of the Indian radical tradition abroad, see Arun Coomer Bose, *Indian Revolutionaries Abroad, 1905–1922: In the Background of International Developments* (Patna: Bharati Bhawan 1971). James Campbell Ker's *Political Trouble in India, 1907–1917* (Delhi: Oriental Publishers 1917 [1973]) is an indispensable source. Ker was a senior officer in the Home Department of the Indian government; he also worked as personal assistant to the director of criminal intelligence. This book is a collection of the confidential documents he amassed during his tenure at the Department of Criminal Intelligence. As such, it details the activities of radicals operating outside India.

26 In October 1907 Prime Minister Wilfrid Laurier told Deputy Minister of Labour Mackenzie King that he thought that imperial authorities would act on

Canada's behalf to stop immigration from India. According to King's account, Laurier 'thought the Chinese were met now by the tax, the Japs wd. be limited by understanding, and the Hindoos would be stopped by an ordinance in India preventing their immigration and which wd. be arranged thro British office.' Laurier had clearly been disappointed in this hope by January 1908, as his government's adoption of specific orders-in-council to prohibit South Asian immigration attests. See the entry for 7 Oct. 1908, LAC, Diaries of Prime Minister William Lyon Mackenzie King [hereafter King Diaries], MG 26-J13, available online at http://king.collectionscanada.ca/EN/Default.asp. The prime minister's sense of the political situation in India is illustrated by a letter sent to Governor General Earl Grey, 11 Dec. 1908, quoted in Governor General of Canada to Colonial Office, 11 Dec. 1908, BL, Asia, Pacific, and Africa Collection (APAC), India Office Records (IOR), Judicial and Public Department Proceedings (JPDP), 320/1909.

27 On the emigration of South Asians to British Columbia, see Hugh Johnston, *The Voyage of the Komagata Maru: The Sikh Challenge to Canada's Colour Bar* (Oxford: Oxford University Press 1979); R. Sampat-Mehta, *International Barriers* (Ottawa: Canada Research Bureau 1973), 125–91; Norman Buchignani and Doreen M. Indra with Ram Srivastava, *Continuous Journey: A Social History of South Asians in Canada* (Toronto: McClelland and Stewart 1985), 4–70; Gucharn S. Basran and B. Singh Bolaria, *The Sikhs in Canada: Migration, Race, Class, and Gender* (Oxford: Oxford University Press 2003), 95–103; Hira Singh, 'The Political Economy of Immigrant Farm Labour: A Study of East Indian Farm Workers in British Columbia,' in Milton Israel, ed., *The South Asian Diaspora in Canada: Six Essays* (Toronto: Multicultural History Society of Ontario 1987), 87; Achana B. Verma, 'Status and Migration among the Punjabis of Paldi, BC and Paldi, Punjab,' PhD thesis, Simon Fraser University 1994; Ninette Kelley and Michael Trebilcock, *The Making of the Mosaic: A History of Canadian Immigration Policy* (Toronto: University of Toronto Press 1998), 142–56.

On anti-Asian agitation in British Columbia, see especially Patricia Roy, *A White Man's Province: British Columbia Politicians and Japanese Immigrants, 1858–1914* (Vancouver: University of British Columbia Press 1989); W. Peter Ward, *White Canada Forever: Popular Attitudes and Public Policy towards Orientals in British Columbia,* 2nd ed. (Montreal and Kingston: McGill-Queen's University Press 1990); Mark Leier, *Red Flags and Red Tape: The Making of a Labour Bureaucracy* (Toronto: University of Toronto Press 1995), 125–42. It is important to note that not all white British Columbians endorsed the politics of Asian exclusion; the radical labour movement and the Protestant missionaries were important voices of tolerance. On the former, see Mark Leier, *Where the Fraser River Flows: The Industrial Workers of the World in British Columbia* (Vancouver:

New Star Books 1990); on the latter, see Ruth Compton Brouwer, 'A Disgrace to "Christian Canada": Protestant Foreign Missionary Concerns about the Treatment of South Asian in Canada, 1907–1940,' in Franca Iacovetta, Paula Draper, and Robert Ventresca, eds., *A Nation of Immigrants: Women, Workers, and Communities in Canadian History, 1840s–1960s* (Toronto: University of Toronto Press 1998), 361–83.

28 Aside from the 'continuous journey' requirements, which will be discussed below, King pointed out that a close reading of the Indian Emigration Act (1883) allowed for the emigration of contract labourers only to a country 'certified' by the governor-général-in-council to have had 'made such laws and other provisions as the Governor General in Council thinks sufficient for the protection of emigrants to that country during their residence therein.' Since no such certification would be made for Canada, King suggested that Canada could 'prohibit the landing in Canada of immigrants who come in violation of the laws of their own country' and thereby eliminate any prospect of contract labourers arriving from India. King was also pleased that the government of India had issued public warnings about the 'risks involved in emigration to Canada.' Finally, King noted that the regulation requiring immigrants to possess $25 could also pose a justification for barring some South Asian immigrants, but 'should this amount prove inadequate it could be increased.' On 3 June 1908, a month after King submitted his report, an order-in-council required South Asian immigrants to be in possession of $200 on arrival. King's report was published as 'Immigration to Canada from the Orient,' Sessional Paper no. 36a, *Sessional Papers*, 7–8 Edward VII 1908. See also Johnston, *The Voyage of the Komagata Maru*, 138; and Sampat-Mehta, *International Barriers*, 131–42.

29 On the arrangement made with the CPR, King recorded in his diary that the minister of labour, Rodolphe Lemieux, told him that 'Canada had doubled her subsidy to the CPR. England not paying as much, a tacit understanding was that immigration from India was not to be encouraged by the Co.' See the entry for 27 April 1908, King Diaries. The immigration figures cited here are contained in Kelley and Trebilcock, *The Making of the Mosaic*, 142–56.

30 The British Columbia judgment, in the case of *Re Narain Singh et al.*, principally determined that the provincial British Columbia Immigration Act (1908) was inoperative because ultra vires. Judge J. Morrison, however, noted that while the governor-in-council had power to 'prohibit the landing in Canada of any specified class of immigrants,' those South Asians who had arrived in British Columbia aboard the *Monteagle* had not been so specified and had a right to land in Canada according to sections 35 and 53 of the Immigration Act. See *Reference Re Narain Singh* (1908) 13 British Columbia Reports 477 (Su-

preme Court); Johnston, *The Voyage of the Komagata Maru*, 138; and Sampat-Mehta, *International Barriers*, 138, 140–2.

31 The biographical information on Hopkinson is drawn from the following sources: Hugh Johnston, 'The Surveillance of Indian Nationalists in North America, 1908–1918,' *British Columbia Studies* 78 (summer 1988): 5 and n.4; Johnston, *The Voyage of the Komagata Maru*, 1, 7, 137n.1, 138n.13; Buchignani, Indra, and Srivastiva, *Continuous Journey*, 25, 30n.42; Popplewell, *Intelligence and Imperial Defence*, 150–1, 163n.25.

Details of Hopkinson's father's career in the army vary widely. Popplewell states that he 'had been one of the military escort of Sir Louis Cavagnari massacred at Kabal in 1879,' leaving Hopkinson and his mother 'stranded at Lahore in the Punjab.' Buchignani, Indra, and Srivastiva suggest that 'Hopkinson's father was a non-commissioned officer in the British Indian army, who was reputed to have been killed by Afghan raiders when Hopkinson was young.' As a result, they assert, Hopkinson was 'raised in India by his Brahmin mother' and was 'fiercely anti-"seditionist."' Johnston, whose work is perhaps the most comprehensive, states in *Voyage* that Hopkinson's father was 'a sergeant instructor of volunteers at Allahabad.'

32 The information on Taraknath Das is taken from: '(Confidential) Memorandum on Matters Affecting the East Indian Community in British Columbia, by Colonel E.J.F Swayne,' BL, APAC, IOR, JPDP, 320/1909. See also: N.N. Bhattacharya, 'Indian Revolutionaries Abroad,' *Journal of Indian History* 50 (1972): 415; Arun Coomer Bose, 'Indian Nationalist Agitation in the US and Canada until the Arrival of Har Dayal,' *Journal of Indian History* 43 (1965): 227. According to Das, *Free Hindusthan* 'advocates the liberal principles of man and puts forth undeniable facts and fights about the exploiting principles of the British government in Hindustan.' This quotation appears in Brij Lal, 'East Indians in British Columbia, 1904–1914: An Historical Study in Growth and Integration,' MA thesis, University of British Columbia 1976, 60–1. On Das, see Bose, *Indian Revolutionaries Abroad*, 48–52; Ker, *Political Trouble in India*, 119–20. Ker's book also contains translations of various articles that appeared in *Free Hindusthan*; see 120–2.

33 There is some disagreement among scholars as to whether or not Hopkinson was sent to British Columbia by Indian authorities. Popplewell argues strenuously that 'the initiative in the surveillance of Indian agitators on the Pacific Coast at this time came entirely from the Canadian side and not from India, let alone from the British government in London.' In *Voyage*, Johnston states flatly that 'he had turned up in Vancouver in 1908 ... an Inspector of the Calcutta Metropolitan police ... officially on leave, but pursuing investigations for the Criminal Intelligence Department [sic] in India.' These statements are not

necessarily contradictory: it is possible that he was sent by the Department of Criminal Intelligence (DCI) in India, but the proposal to place the South Asian community under constant surveillance came first from the Canadian government. On the emergence of the DCI in India, see Brown, *Modern India*, 137–9; Popplewell, *Intelligence and Imperial Defence*, 8–164, esp. 147–64.

34 J.B. Harkin to Superintendent of Immigration, 29 July 1908, BL, APAC, IOR, JPDP, 320/1909.

35 The rise and fall of the British Honduras scheme is chronicled in J.B. Harkin's own *The East Indians in British Columbia: A Report regarding the Proposal to Provide Work in British Honduras for the Indigent Unemployed among Them* (Ottawa: Department of the Interior 1908). See also: Harkin to Superintendent of Immigration, Ottawa, 29 July 1908; Harkin to Ministry of Interior, 16 Oct. 1908 and 6 Nov. 1908; Wilfred Collet, Officer Administering the Government, British Honduras, to Secretary of State of Canada, 19 and 26 Nov. 1908; Collet to Colonial Office, 2 and 3 Dec. 1908; and 'Certified Copy of a Report of the Committee of the Privy Council, Approved by His Excellency the Governor General on 10 December 1908,' BL, APAC, IOR, JPDP, 320/1909.

The final quotation in this paragraph is from Governor General of Canada to Colonial Office, 21 Dec. 1908, BL, APAC, IOR, JPDP, 320/1909. Along with his confidential letter, Lord Grey included a detailed memorandum prepared by W.W. Cory, the deputy minister of immigration, about the relocation plan. The memo [hereafter Cory memorandum] includes excerpts from the telegrams and letters exchanged between Hopkinson, Harkin, and ministry officials after the delegation returned from Belize; see Hopkinson to Harkin, 20 and 23 Nov. 1908; Harkin to Cory, 23 Nov. 1908. Johnston takes up the issue of Hopkinson's alleged corruption in 'The Surveillance of Indian Nationalists,' 6n.11. 'Hopkinson was loyal to British India and Anglo Canada and behaved accordingly,' he concludes. 'One does not need evidence of personal corruption to explain the part he played.'

36 This brief biography of Teja Singh is based on: '(Confidential) Memorandum on Matters Affecting the East Indian Community in British Columbia, by Colonel E.J.E. Swayne'; Buchignani, Indra, and Srivastiva, *Continuous Journey*, 26–7; Johnston, *Voyage*, 12; Bose, *Indian Revolutionaries Abroad*, 52–5. Harkin certainly did not think much of Teja Singh either, referring to him as the 'absolute dictator of the community.' See his *East Indians in British Columbia*, 4.

37 Hopkinson to Harkin, 20 Nov. 1908; Cory to Harkin, 4 Dec. 1908; Vancouver *Province*, 23 Nov. 1908; and Cory memorandum, BL, APAC, IOR, JPDP, 320/1909.

38 On the role of the governor general during this period, see Robert Bothwell, Ian Drummond, and John English, *Canada: 1900-1945* (Toronto: University

of Toronto Press 1987), 111–18; Governor General of Canada, Lord Grey, to Prime Minister Wilfrid Laurier, 3 Dec. 1908, BL, APAC, IOR, JPDP, 320/1909.

39 Governor General of Canada to Colonial Office, 9, 10, 11, and 21 Dec. 1908; Secretary of State for the Colonies to Governor General of Canada, 23 Dec. 1908; and Colonial Office to India Office, 30 Dec. 1908, BL, APAC, IOR, JPDP, 320/1909. See also Johnston, 'The Surveillance of Indian Nationalists,' 9.

40 Colonel Swayne to Governor General of Canada (Confidential), 30 Dec. 1908, BL, APAC, IOR, JPDP, 320/1909. The 'old Indian officer' quotation is from: Colonel Swayne to Officer Administering Government, British Honduras, 20 Dec. 1908, BL, APAC, IOR, JPDP, 320/1909. The most important document in this regard is Swayne's report: '(Confidential) Memorandum on Matters Affecting the East Indian Community in British Columbia, by Colonel E.J.E. Swayne.'

41 On the links between the IWW, the SPC, and the East Indian community in British Columbia, see: Hopkinson to J.B. Harkin, 19 Dec. 1908, BL, APAC, IOR, JPDP, 1309/1909. Prime Minister Laurier was particularly enchanted with Colonel Swayne, remarking in a letter to the governor general after meeting the governor: '[He is] the very embodiment of that most valuable class of officers developed by Indian service, trained for war and civil service, honest and true as the sun's light, modest and firm, devoted to the Empire and equally devoted to those over whom they are appointed to rule. Happy the country served by such men, and no country but England ever produced such men.' See: Laurier to Lord Grey, 8 Dec. 1908, BL, APAC, IOR, JPDP, 320/1909. See also Peter Campbell, 'East Meets Left: South Asian Militants and the Socialist Party of Canada in British Columbia, 1904–1914,' *International Journal of Canadian Studies* 20 (fall 1999): 35–65.

42 '(Confidential) Memorandum on Matters Affecting the East Indian Community in British Columbia, by Colonel E.J.E. Swayne.'

43 Ibid. As a servant of the empire, Swayne was aware of wider, global patterns of political violence linked to radicalism and nationalism, including the Fenian bombing campaigns that took place in Britain in 1881 and 1884, the wave of anarchist bombings that rocked Western Europe and North America in the 1890s, and the nationalist agitation that had been destabilizing parts of India on and off for decades.

44 Quoted in Popplewell, *Intelligence and Imperial Defense*, 129. It is important not to overstate the novelty of this manoeuvre; this was not the first time that Ottawa had been caught between the rock of national politics and the hard place of imperial concerns and used secret agents to help solve the conundrum. That Hopkinson was hired into the ranks of the Dominion Police with little difficulty or debate underscores just how commonplace this practice had

become. At the same time, however, the fact that the British and Indian governments were relying on a Dominion Police officer to track 'wily Asiatics,' instead of fielding their own agents in North America, suggests that intelligence gathering at the imperial level was still a somewhat ad hoc affair.

45 This brief section on the general nature of Hopkinson's duties is based on the following: Hopkinson to Cory, 10 Sept. 1908; 19 Dec. 1908; 4 and 18 Jan. 1909; 15 April 1909; 18 May 1909; 14 Jan. 1910, BL, APAC, IOR, JPDP, 1309/1909; Hopkinson to Cory, 10, 23, and 29 March 1911; 7 June 1911; 4 Aug. 1911; 7 and 8 Dec. 1911, BL, APAC, IOR, JPDP, 6/1604.

46 This section on Kumar is based on: Hopkinson to Cory, 12 Aug. 1909, BL, APAC, IOR, JPDP, 1309/1909; Hopkinson to Cory, 8 and 13 May 1911, BL, APAC, IOR, JPDP, 6/1604; Secretary to the Government of India to Sir Richmond Ritchie, His Majesty's Under Secretary of State for India, 25 Nov. 1911, BL, APAC, IOR, JPDP, 4917/1911. The final quotation in this paragraph is taken from a report entitled 'History Sheet of G.D. Kumar' attached to the secretary's letter of 25 Nov. 1911. The reference to Kumar being a 'Punjabi Buddhist' is taken from Johnston, 'The Surveillance of Indian Nationalists,' 9.

47 On the changing nature of Canadian immigration policy at this time, see Kelley and Trebilcock, *The Making of the Mosaic*, 111–63; Barbara Roberts, *Whence They Came: Deportation from Canada, 1900–1935* (Ottawa: University of Ottawa Press 1988), 1–70. The 1910 revisions to the Immigration Act sought to further insulate from judicial scrutiny those boards of inquiry created under the auspices of the immigration branch; section 23 of the revised act stated that 'no court or judge could interfere with a decision of a Board of Inquiry.' See Johnston, *Voyage*, 18.

48 Hopkinson to Cory, 20 Sept. 1909, and Harkin to Cory, 22 Sept. 1909, BL, APAC, IOR, JPDP, 1309/1909; Hopkinson to Cory, 14 Oct. 1910; 17, 19, and 28 Nov. 1910; 16 March 1912; 28 June 1912, BL, APAC, IOR, JPDP, 6/1064.

49 This brief biography of Rahim is culled from: Hopkinson to Cory, 26 March 1912 and 1 April 1912, BL, APAC, IOR, JPDP, 6/1064; Buchignani, Indra, and Srivastiva, *Continuous Journey*, 36–47; Johnston, *Voyage*, 9–12; and Peter Campbell, 'East Meets Left.' Johnston is dismissive of Rahim's left-wing politics, writing that he 'assimilat[ed], in a half-digested way, the language of class warfare.' For a more sympathetic reading, see Campbell's 'East Meets Left' and *Canadian Marxists and the Search for the Third Way* (Montreal and Kingston: McGill-Queen's University Press 1999), 10–11, 18, 74, 247n.2, and 248n.25.

50 J.H. MacGill, Immigration Agent, to Cory, 28 Oct. 1910; Hopkinson to Cory, 3 Nov. 1910 and 17 Feb. 1911, BL, APAC, IOR, JPDP, 6/1604.

51 Quoted in Lal, 'East Indians in British Columbia,' 65–6. G.D. Kumar was the organization's secretary treasurer.

52 Hopkinson to Cory, 26 March 1912, BL, APAC, IOR, JPDP, 6/1604.
53 Hopkinson to Cory, 22 Feb. 1912; 1 April 1912; 9 May 1912, BL, APAC, IOR, JPDP, 6/1604. Rahim's involvement in the SPC is detailed in Campbell, 'East Meet Left,' 46–50. More on the IWW can be found in Mark Leier's 'Solidarity on Occasion: The Vancouver Free Speech Fights of 1909 and 1912,' *Labour/Le Travail* 23 (spring 1989): 39–66; *Where the Fraser River Flows*; and *Rebel Life: The Life and Times of Robert Gosden, Revolutionary, Mystic, and Labour Spy* (Vancouver: New Star Books 1999).
54 Popplewell, *Intelligence and Imperial Defence*, 150–61.
55 Ibid., 158.
56 See Johnston, *Voyage*, and Popplewell, *Intelligence and Imperial Defence*, 159–61. The quotation is from Johnston, 37–8.
57 By all accounts, Hopkinson carried out his duties well and was largely responsible for keeping a tight leash on the more belligerent and pugnacious elements within government ranks.
58 See Johnston, *Voyage*, 125–36.
59 Reid to Scott, 22 Oct. 1914, BL, APAC, IOR, JPDP, 6/1341.
60 Johnston, 'The Surveillance of Indian Nationalists,' 22–7.
61 On this thought, see David Vital, 'Not Single Spies, but in Battalions: Espionage Uncovered in France, Russia, Britain, and the US,' *Times Literary Supplement* (December 2000): 4–6: 'As more than one old intelligence hand has been moved to observe, few institutions reflect national character and the operative norms of government so closely as a state's intelligence arm, the status granted it, the modus operandi to which it is habituated and the confidence with which it proceeds to its targets in a foreign environment.'
62 See the following articles by Gregory S. Kealey: 'State Repression of Labour and the Left in Canada, 1914–1920: The Impact of the First World War,' *CHR* 73, no. 3 (1992): 281–315; 'The Surveillance State: The Origins of Domestic Intelligence and Counter-Subversion in Canada, 1914–21,' *Intelligence and National Security* 7, no. 3 (1992): 179–210; and 'The Early Years of State Surveillance of Labour and the Left in Canada: The Institutional Framework of the Royal Canadian Mounted Police Security and Intelligence Apparatus, 1918–26,' *Intelligence and National Security* 8, no. 3 (July 1993): 129–48. *The RCMP Security Bulletins*, 8 vols. (St John's: Canadian Committee on Labour History 1989–97), edited by Kealey and Reginald Whitaker, document the extensive surveillance undertaken by the Mounties during this period.
63 On the federal government's response, see Ronald J. Daniels, Patrick Macklem, and Kent Roach, eds., *The Security of Freedom: Essays on Canada's Anti-Terrorism Bill* (Toronto: University of Toronto Press 2001).

12

Codification, Public Order, and the Security Provisions of the Canadian Criminal Code, 1892 '

DESMOND H. BROWN and BARRY WRIGHT

The allocation of criminal law jurisdiction to the Dominion of Canada and eventual codification reflect the perceived central place of criminal law in securing the new federation. The comprehensive political and public-order provisions in the 1892 Code[1] not only were rationalized forms of received English, British North American, and Dominion offences but also articulated the new powers of the central government in support of its nation-securing and nation-building policies. They provided the means, beyond national defence, to respond to the wide array of real and apprehended threats to the union and its development.

Colonial legacies and the anticipated challenges to be faced by the Dominion set the foundation and favourable conditions for codification but the 1885 North-West crisis helped to make it a political priority. The association between criminal law reforms and public-order concerns is seen in other nineteenth-century British jurisdictions. Codification may be understood as a modernized expression of state power, an unrealized key objective of the English utilitarian reformers, reflecting their notion of a 'totalizing' science of legislation that would minimize the archaic discretionary authority expressed in forms like the common law. While the Dominion's assertion of criminal law jurisdiction absorbed many of the nineteenth-century reforms to English criminal law (sometimes at the expense of more appropriate local colonial innovations), Canada codified and England did not. Canada was the first self-governing jurisdiction in the British empire to codify its criminal law, followed by New

Zealand in 1893 and Queensland in 1899, although all were predated by imposed imperial codifications for India and Jamaica. The prospects of codification were greater in British colonial and emerging self-governing jurisdictions that faced complexities arising from the reception of English law, a rudimentary legal profession distant from the sources and culture of the common law, and wide experience of executive manipulation of the criminal law in support of colonial elites. Criminal law reforms had public purposes beyond the efficient management of crime, England's domestic preoccupation. Codification aimed to foster greater compliance with the existing order and to make the rule of law more effective in culturally diverse frontier settings. Public-order crises influenced the projects in India, Jamaica, New Zealand, and Queensland, as well as Canada, and lent political urgency and legislative momentum to codification.

Public-order concerns are amply reflected in the development of the 1892 Canadian Criminal Code and in its prominent and comprehensive security provisions, the focus of this chapter. The modernization of Canada's security laws and their codified form are explained here by way of two contexts; the first situates the general codification project within nineteenth-century British criminal law reform and imperial public-order challenges, while the second places the specific Code provisions within a comprehensive survey of the origins and nineteenth-century development of national-security laws. This chapter serves as the volume's primary reference for these laws, although many are introduced in the previous chapters that examine their applications as Canada developed, in the words of the volume's Introduction, from a collection of dependent British North American colonies into a self-governing Dominion that assumed new responsibilities around matters of territorial integrity and internal and external security. We also see that their codified form can be understood as an expression of modern legal authority. The 1892 Code constrained state powers in some respects (clearer definition of offences, reduction of the place of the common law, rationalized criminal procedures, etc.), but it also further empowered the Canadian state to protect and promote perceived national interests as it updated the classic political offences, consolidated nineteenth-century British and local developments, and added new security measures. Codification was a legal rationalization that sought to widen the reach and enhance the effectiveness of the criminal law. It also aimed, in significant part, to strengthen the rule of law and sovereign authority in support of the Dominion's nation-securing and nation-building priorities.

ENGLISH CRIMINAL LAW REFORM AND BRITISH COLONIAL
SETTINGS

The failure to codify English criminal law was ascribed by the nineteenth-century English law commissioner Andrew Amos to 'codiphobia,' a chauvinistic tendency to see codification as alien to English legal tradition, adhered to by conservative elements of the bar and bench determined to preserve common law powers. Lindsay Farmer describes a related conceptual gulf between common law traditionalists, who saw criminal law as primarily about the protection of private interests, an adjunct to private law, and the utilitarian reformers, who saw it as public law governing relations between the state and citizens, a form of sovereignty that demands clarification.[2] From the broader perspective of political and social theory, notably Max Weber's concept of 'formal legal rationality,' the failure of codification illustrates the 'peculiarities of the English,' the common law exception that persisted in the face of the typical legal forms of modernity.[3] As Farmer, Michael Lobban, and K.J.M. Smith suggest, the dismissal of codification as alien to English legal tradition (its proponents seen as foreigners or philosophical radical interlopers) neglects the prominence of codification in nineteenth-century English criminal law reform debates.[4] It is also myopic, failing to account for codes enacted in other British common law jurisdictions that sought to modernize state authority and make it more effective.

Jeremy Bentham coined the term 'codification.' He dismissed William Blackstone's *Commentaries*, an Enlightenment-inspired attempt to lend rational order to the common law, as no more than 'an elegant palliative to inherently chronic confusion of the common law'[5] which was hopelessly arcane and needlessly complex, the product of random cases and self-serving judges. Criminal law reform involved matters of vital public policy, with enormous impact on public and individual happiness, and required a systematic approach that was properly a matter for Parliament, not the courts. Bentham's 'science of legislation,' as set out in *Introduction to the Principles of Morals and Legislation*, sought fundamental legislative reformulation informed by the rational principles of utility and the objective of deterrence. It left no terra incognita by aiming for the complete definition of offences, defences, and liability set out unambiguously so that law would be perfectly clear to the average person as well as to judges. Bentham's ambitious pannomion aimed for nothing less than the comprehensive regulation of social relationships and sovereign power, with the legislator occupying a position analogous to the 'gaze' in his better-known panopticon.[6]

Bentham's direct influence is much debated.[7] The sweeping institutional and administrative reforms that gained momentum in the 1820s and the decades that followed, including the introduction of the new police, the 'professionalization' of the criminal trial, and the emergence of the penitentiary as the primary site of punishment, resembled more elements of the panopticon than the pannomion. Debates about reforming and rationalizing the criminal law ranged from 'consolidations' (reducing existing criminal law legislation from numerous statutes to one) and 'digests' (more ambitious attempts to present the law, including common law, in an organized fashion) to codification proposals which aimed for more systematic reorganization that abrogated common law elements but fell short of Bentham's conception that sought elimination of the common law and fundamental reform according to utilitarian principles.

Whig reformers were joined by prominent Tories as Robert Peel introduced not only the Metropolitan London Police but also the criminal law consolidation acts of 1827–32, which repealed or modernized hundreds of obsolete statutes and scaled back the death penalty from over 200 to a dozen offences. The reform consensus dissolved after Henry Brougham, appointed lord chancellor after the fall of Wellington's government, launched a criminal law commission in 1833 mandated to produce a single digest of criminal statues, one of common law, and to consider combining both. Lord Chief Justice Ellenborough's implacable defence of judicial powers had already set the tone for conservative elements of the English bar and bench for the remainder of the century, and the common law cause was reinforced by emerging legal scholarship and procedural reforms.[8] The commission's time-consuming committee approach brought out differences among the codifiers, and eight reports culminated in a combined digest in 1845 presented to a Tory government. Judicial opposition frustrated attempts to restart the project and little trace remained of the commissioners' work in Charles Greaves's modest 1861 Criminal Law Consolidation.[9] A final nineteenth-century codification attempt was authored by James Fitzjames Stephen, a conservative utilitarian who favoured pragmatism to conceptual abstraction and accepted judicial discretion as useful and inevitable.[10] His Draft English Code set out all offences but left defences to the common law, and the minimal general part did not attempt to define liability. It was converted into a bill, but the government fell just after its introduction in 1880. Stephen's middle course satisfied neither the progressive codifiers nor the defenders of the common law, Lord Chief Justice Cockburn disingenuously declaring the proposal inconsistent with the idea of codification and that no code was better than a half-baked one.[11]

The failure of Stephen's code ended the prospects for codification in England, perhaps forever, but the prospects were better in other British jurisdictions. The utilitarian reformers were influential in the Colonial Office and related departments and encountered fewer obstacles in overseas colonial 'laboratories.' The imposed imperial codes, the first and most notable being Thomas Macaulay's India Penal Code (IPC), reflected attempts to modernize the colonial state and enhance the legitimacy of imperial authority by making laws more effective and reducing reliance on military intervention. The aim of making the rule of law more effective in new settings was shared by the more autonomous jurisdictions, although it was Stephen's effort, not Macaulay's, that became the main reference for the first wave of codes in self-governing jurisdictions, led by Canada.[12]

Macaulay's short but influential time in India highlights the impact of utilitarianism on imperial policy.[13] Although Macaulay had been a libertarian Whig critic of utilitarian 'enlightened despotism,' he assisted James Mill with the passage at Westminster of a new Charter Act for India in 1833 and embraced Bentham's legal theories upon his appointment as the law representative in the governor general of India's Legislative Council, which in 1835 approved the creation of a law commission mandated to draft a code. Macaulay boasted that his commission was cooking up something that would 'make old Bentham jump in his grave.'[14] The IPC draft was completed by 1837, the purest manifestation and fullest realization of the Benthamite conception of criminal law codification in the nineteenth century, but enactment was stalled until 1860 by conflicting India policies, counterproductive interventions from rival reformers such as Andrew Amos and John Austin, and British expatriate resistance to the idea of having the same legal status as the indigenous populations. The Great Mutiny of 1857 proved decisive for the implementation of the IPC.[15] This first British criminal code was dismissed by the English profession as suitable only for backward overseas colonies where 'it was necessary to keep things simple for the native population and magistrates of limited ability,' but the Colonial Office promoted it elsewhere as a means to make English law more effective in foreign settings and a solution to abuses of justice and over-reliance on costly military responses.[16] Rebellion in Jamaica in 1865 prompted the Colonial Office to commission R.S. Wright to revise and update the IPC. The Jamaica Code was introduced in 1877, enacted elsewhere in the West Indies,[17] and displaced by a new Colonial Office model code only in 1925.[18]

Stephen, not Macaulay or Wright, was to be the main influence on the self-governing jurisdictions, but more importantly, local conditions favoured the prospects of codification. In Canada and in other colonies, the reception of English criminal law and local amendments resulted in complex layers of applicable law. These complexities were compounded by the emergence of new colonies out of the territories of older ones, such as Upper Canada from Quebec and New Brunswick from Nova Scotia, and by the opposite process of colonial union, notably of Upper and Lower Canada in 1840 (prefacing the larger challenge faced in 1867 of reconciling the diverse criminal laws of the British North American colonies, each with different reception dates and subsequent local amendments).[19] Consolidations had simplified the accumulated layers of law but the local legal profession also tended to be amenable to yet further rationalization. The colonial bar and bench were relatively distant from the culture of the common law and faced huge practical challenges accessing the sources of law.[20] Receptiveness to codification was also enhanced by experience of uses of the criminal law to fend off challenges and maintain the authority of local elites, supported by wide executive influence over the colonial administration of justice. Judicial independence was compromised by colonial judges holding office according to royal pleasure (rather than good behaviour as determined by Parliament), frequent reliance on extrajudicial opinions, the practice of appointing chief justices to executive and legislative councils, and controversies surrounding executive influences on juries and the prosecutorial powers of crown law officers.[21] Receptiveness to codification was therefore enhanced by the pressing practical need to simplify the law and make it more accessible as well as by the recognition that it might check the powers of the state by reducing discretionary authority and defining the criminal law more clearly, factors that gave the project a constitutional momentum lacking in England itself where, as Farmer notes, debate focused on the effectiveness of the criminal law with a striking failure to consider how a code might limit state power.[22]

The emerging self-governing jurisdictions were not, however, receptive to imperial urgings to codify. The IPC and succeeding Colonial Office efforts were imposed codifications that involved little local or indigenous input. This did not mean that codification conflicted with aspirations for greater responsible self-government. And Stephen's Draft English Code did not have the same colonialist baggage. The Canadian, New Zealand, and Queensland codes of the 1890s were voluntary efforts that reflected relatively democratic legislative processes and local experience, and it is unsurprising that Stephen was embraced as their primary external reference. His modest, pragmatic approach to codification was loose enough in conception to be easily combined with local consolidations. Local developments and reforms could be accommodated rather than rejected in favour of a purer Benthamite conception.[23]

The self-governing projects represent a distinct trajectory of codification from the imposed codes but they were nonetheless informed by the same English criminal law reform debates. And the nineteenth-century codes share a common basic objective, the attempt to enhance the effectiveness and legitimacy of prevailing authority by expanding the rule of law and reducing discretionary forms of power in culturally diverse frontier settings. Public-order crises underscored the importance of this modernizing objective. The Great Mutiny preceded enactment of the IPC and rebellion preceded the drafting of the Jamaica Code. The 1885 North-West rebellion lent urgency to Canada's large and time-consuming legislative project of codification, just as local difficulties did in the case of New Zealand and Queensland.[24]

CANADA'S CRIMINAL CODE

During the debates leading to the British North America Act, 1867, John A. Macdonald urged uniform criminal law under the proposed federal jurisdiction. The prime minister retained the Department of Justice portfolio in the new government and enacted Dominion consolidations in 1868–9. The rapid and effective assertion of federal criminal law powers was a government priority, associated with enhanced responsibilities for internal and external security, the cohesion of the union, and its territorial integrity. Codification proved to be more elusive, a policy priority only after the 1885 crisis.

There was broad support for Macdonald's view of criminal law jurisdiction. No opposition to it appears in the records of the confederation debates. It is one of the few matters that remained unchanged in successive constitutional drafts.[25] A decentralized federation was widely seen as a contributing factor to the then-raging U.S. Civil War and Macdonald urged avoidance of the dysfunctional American model, drawing a direct relation between criminal law and defence powers: 'One of the great advantages of Confederation is, that we shall have a united, a concerted, and uniform system of defence ... We will have one system of defence and be one people, acting together alike in peace and in war. The criminal law too – the determination of what is crime and what is not and how crime shall be punished – is left to the General Government ... I think this is one of the most marked instances in which we take advantage of the experience derived from our observations of the defects in the Constitution of the neighbouring republic.'[26]

The connection between criminal law and the territorial integrity and stability of the proposed union was also informed by experience. As seen in the previous *Canadian State Trials* volumes, the security crises of 1812–15 and 1837–9 involved a combination of American aggression and fears of internal disaffection and insurrection. The American 'Patriot' raids in the aftermath of the Canadian rebellions were a formative experience for Macdonald. We see in this volume how he orchestrated the 1866 Fenian prosecutions. As prime minister and justice minister, he faced new security concerns in the North-West signalled by the Lépine affair. Growing preoccupation with securing the Dominion's sovereignty over and development priorities in the vast northwestern territories (as the influence of the Hudson's Bay Company declined, American incursions increased, and the British government's obligations to indigenous groups were transferred to Ottawa) is reflected in criminal law reforms and related initiatives such as the North-West Mounted Police, the Department of Indian Affairs, and the economic and public-works measures associated with the 'National Policy.'

The idea of federal jurisdiction over criminal law was not unprecedented. Macdonald also compared the chaotic state of American criminal laws to the United Province of Canada where uniformity was brought to the disparate colonial criminal laws of Upper and Lower Canada (Upper Canada's was relatively benign with 11 capital offences, based on English law received in 1792 as amended by the adoption of Peel's consolidations in 1833, compared to over 200 in Lower Canada, based on largely unreformed English criminal law from 1774).[27] An even larger challenge was faced in 1867, that of reconciling the criminal laws of all the former British North American colonies with the Dominion's assumption of jurisdiction over diverse criminal laws, originating in English law received at different times, amended by colonial legislation, and applied by the colonial courts in different ways according to local conditions. Prior British North American innovations pointed the way for more dramatic rationalization,[28] but the rapid and effective assertion of federal jurisdiction was to be more easily achieved through consolidation than a large, legislative time-consuming codification project.

Consolidation alone was a formidable challenge. Macdonald and his deputy minister, his former private secretary Hewitt Bernard, faced at least three options. Adoption of one of the pre-confederation consolidations seemed to be the easiest course but risked acrimonious debate with the provinces. Striking a commission to draft a consolidation that assimilated the best colonial provisions could be nearly as time-consuming as codification. Macdonald's expedient course, one that was cheap, quick, and avoided political complications, was to turn to Greaves's English consolidation of 1861 as the basis for the new Dominion consolidations. Much of the work was delegated to Gustavus Wicksteed, the House of Commons law clerk, later assisted by Bernard and Judge James Gowan, and the project was completed in 1869.[29]

The new provisions were in some cases a retreat on advances in earlier local consolidations, while new laws were imported that had never been in effect in the colonies, including matters that intruded on provincial jurisdiction. Amending bills proliferated, twenty passing within five years. During this time, Gowan travelled to meet with English and Irish barristers and judges, reformers, and Colonial Office officials, including Wright, then at work on the Jamaica Code.[30] Gowan became a strong advocate of codification and his *Canada Law Journal* was influential, but codification was to be shaped more by political priorities than by law reform debates and professional attitudes.[31] Macdonald's government fell as Gowan returned to Canada. Making little headway with the Liberals, he travelled again to the United Kingdom in 1878 and witnessed early debate on Stephen's Draft English Code.[32] There remained little political appetite for such a large, potentially contentious legislative project when the Tories returned to power and the prime minister took on the Department of the Interior instead of Justice.

A new consolidation was nonetheless drafted as part of the Revised Statutes of Canada in 1884. Passage was delayed by the North-West crisis while Justice department officials struggled with the laws to be applied to those involved. The 1885 crisis was a catalyst, mobilizing the political will to make codification a legislative priority. George Burbidge, the deputy minister of justice, who had published a Canadian edition of Stephen's *Digest* and directly supervised the rebellion prosecutions, joined Gowan in lobbying Macdonald and John Thompson, the new justice minister. Burbidge stressed the urgency and ease of codification, noting that the Draft English Code provided an ideal, ready-made model. Burbidge had relied on *Archbold's Pleadings* for the new consolidation and the 1885 prosecutions, but he found the 1879 version of Stephen's draft code a superior means of organizing a conventional consolidation's mass of unconnected statutes. Once the unexpurgated consolidation was finalized for the government, he began work on a draft code modelled on Stephen's.[33] Further prompting came when Thompson visited London and was encouraged by British ministers to consider the 1880 English bill, and when Mr Justice Henri-Elzéar Taschereau, a Liberal appointee to the Supreme Court of Canada, volunteered to draft a code in six months. Thompson declined

Taschereau's offer but directed Burbidge to begin work on a codification bill.[34]

Burbidge and Robert Sedgewick did most of the drafting, while Thompson set out general guidelines and worked out a strategy for the bill's introduction to Parliament after carefully studying the debates on the Draft English Code bill.[35] Judge Gowan also advised, although his most notable contribution may have been the removal of Lord Chief Justice Cockburn's published criticism of the Draft English Code from Ottawa's Parliamentary Library (confiding to Thompson that it was best kept out circulation to facilitate the bill's passage).[36] The bill essentially combined the Dominion consolidations with the Draft English Code.[37] It embraced Stephen's approach to codification in concept and closely resembled the 1880 bill in organization.[38] In content, Stephen's common law renderings were adopted and most of the statute-derived provisions drew from the 1886 Canadian Revised Statutes. It has been estimated that 40 per cent of the substantive provisions (209 sections) derive from the Draft English Code while 60 per cent (321) are from Canadian sources.[39] The bill was introduced in the spring of 1891 and distributed to MPs, the bench, provincial attorneys general, and leading members of the bar.[40] A revised bill was introduced in April 1892, passing after two months of well-managed committee hearings in which debate focused on the public-order offences of sedition, libel, and riot.[41]

THE PUBLIC-ORDER OFFENCES IN THE CANADIAN CRIMINAL CODE, 1892

As we have seen, the allocation of criminal law jurisdiction to Ottawa was motivated by the view that such powers were essential to the effectiveness of the new federal government's authority, and this drove the rapid passage of the Dominion consolidations. While colonial legacies favoured the prospects of codification, public-order crises helped generate political momentum to make this larger project a legislative priority, a pattern also seen in other British jurisdictions that codified in the nineteenth century. The 1885 rebellion did not cause Canada to codify but it did lend urgency to the project. It focused the official mind, marking an accumulation of a critical mass of challenges to public order and to the territorial integrity, security, and stability of the union. These included the Fenian threat and the earlier North-West rebellion of 1870, as well as broader challenges to social, economic, and political integration and development (ethnic, religious, and regional divisions, sectarian, urban, and labour unrest, and conflict arising out of the expropriation of First Nations territory).

Codification was about more than the efficient management of crime. It was also about enhancing public order and encouraging compliance with Ottawa's authority by attempting to make the criminal law and the rule of law more effective in challenging settings. These matters are best illustrated by the prominent and comprehensive political offences and national-security provisions in the 1892 Code, rationalized laws that, because they deal explicitly with real and perceived security threats, are the provisions most directly relevant to the *Canadian State Trials* series. But they also resonate with many of the more routine criminal offences that are beyond the scope of this study, enforcement by institutions such as the North-West Mounted Police, and administrative regulation by institutions such as the Department of Indian Affairs. The 1885 crisis demonstrated the importance of organized, effective, and comprehensive security measures as an 'ultimate resource,' to use Jean-Marie Fecteau's term from Volume II of this series.

Overview of Provisions and Comparison with Stephen

The security provisions in the 1892 Canadian Criminal Code are expressed in forms that are generally more liberal and less arbitrary and discretionary than their predecessors, yet they also represent more pervasive interventions into the polity, characteristics that reflect the modern rationalization of authority associated with codification. The major political offences appear immediately following the general and introductory parts (Title II, 'Offences against the Public Order, Internal and External,' beginning with Part IV, 'Treason and Other Offences against the Queen's Authority and Person'). High treason (section 65) and its related provisions (section 66, conspiracy; section 67, accessories) are similar to the Draft English Code formulations in slightly more elaborate form. The 1886 Revised Statutes had included reference to the statute of Edward III but curiously specified only compassing the death of the sovereign (perhaps because it was more arcane than levying war or adhering to enemies). While this clarified the status of the medieval statute in Canada, the experience of the 1885 trials underscored the importance to Burbidge of setting out explicitly all three main heads of treason, and the wording of 'adhering' and 'levying' in section 65 of the 1892 Code derives from Stephen. Sections 68 (lawless aggression) and 69 (treasonable offences) are restatements of the earlier Dominion Fenian and treason-felony legislation, carried over in 1886, that extended liability for levying war from overt acts by subjects (high treason) to aliens who do so, as well as to indirect manifestations of insurrectionary intent.

These major political offences are followed, as in the Draft English Code, by a number of minor direct offences against the state. The new offence of intimidating legislatures was added in 1886, following Stephen, and became section 70, accompanied by similar offences directed against the sovereign and military forces (section 71, alarming Her Majesty; and sections 72–5, mutiny and encouraging or assisting desertion). Part IV closes with adoption of the 1889 British official-secrets legislation (sections 76–8, unlawfully obtaining and communicating official information).

Public-order or indirect offences against the state are set out in Parts V–VIII. The main remaining national-security-related provisions here, excluding piracy, fall into two groupings, offences related to breaches of the peace and those related to sedition. The first are found in Parts V and VI, sections 79–98, which consolidate offences relating to unlawful assemblies and riot but in elaborate form to include three basic unlawful assembly and riot offences, riotous damage and destruction to buildings or public works, as well as military training and non-security-related breaches of the peace such as affray and prize fights. Sections 99–119 contain a number of provisions originating in earlier Canadian legislation concerning specific prohibitions around the use of offensive weapons and alcohol. Finally, Part VII, sections 120–6, sets out sedition offences (including administering oaths and spreading false news).

This overview suggests five areas that warrant more detailed examination as Canada's main security-related offences at the end of the nineteenth century: treason, lawless aggression, and official secrets as direct offences against the state, and the indirect offences related to breaches of the peace and sedition. First, however, a brief look at the equivalent provisions of the Draft English Code and Stephen's justifications provides a useful general perspective on the security laws in Canada's 1892 Code.

Stephen's organizational structure and titles are almost identical to the Canadian Code. He restates, in modern language, the three main heads of high treason from the medieval statute, and the lesser treason offence is based on the 1848 treason-felony legislation.[42] A definition of conspiracy and accessories follow, and the procedural protections associated with the 1696 legislation and successors are restated along with a rule against retroactivity. The same minor direct offences against the state follow as in Canada, although there are no official-secrets provisions (which post-date the Draft English Code). A single part sets out breach-of-the-peace offences, less comprehensive than the Canadian provisions. Stephen radically simplified the accumulation of law by setting out a summary offence of riot (three or more assembled in public in breach of the peace) and an indictable offence of riot (twelve or more assembled an hour after a Riot Act proclamation). Similar related offences of riotous damage, destruction of public buildings, and unlawful drilling/training in arms follow but there is nothing equivalent to the 1892 Code's Part VI offences. Stephen's modernized version of sedition replaces the complex legislation and common law with the minor offence (two years' imprisonment) of speaking, publicizing, or publishing matters reasonably calculated to bring the state into contempt or excite disaffection with the aim of encouraging change by unlawful means. Since the Draft English Code does not set out general principles of liability, it is unclear whether the common law on seditious intent is displaced. The Canadian version does not incorporate Stephen's 'reasonably calculated' but does include a similar defence for attempts in good faith to respectfully point out errors and matters believed to cause ill will, to express opinion favouring constitutional change, and to promote change in policy or state matters by lawful means.

Stephen's modernized security provisions are a cautious liberalization of the existing law and many of the modest advances are replicated in the 1892 provisions, although they are also more elaborate and retain significant 'Canadian content.' Stephen articulated his justification for modest reform in his *History*, where two basic positions are set out on political offences. Existing laws reflect the traditional assumption that rulers, as natural superiors, are owed unquestioned allegiance, loyalty, and political deference. Stephen acknowledged that such assumptions have been increasingly challenged by modern notions of popular sovereignty (derived from Locke) that view governments as agents of the people exercising delegated authority. This has profound consequences for political offences since allegiance can justifiably be withdrawn from oppressive governments and criticism is a right:

If the ruler is regarded as the superior of the subject, as being by nature of his position ... the rightful ruler and guide of the whole population, it must necessarily follow ... no censure should be cast upon him likely or designed to diminish his authority. If on the other hand the ruler is regarded as the agent and servant, and the subject as the wise and good master who is obliged to delegate his power to the so-called ruler because being a multitude he cannot use it himself, it is obvious that this sentiment must be reversed. Every member of the public who censures the ruler for the time being exercises in his own person the right which belongs to the whole of which he forms a part.[43]

Stephen expressed inconsistent views on constructive treason and did not limit the offence of treason to levying war as is the case under the U.S. constitution.[44] While expressing doubt about the continuing existence of sedition in modern common law,[45] he chose to retain rather than eliminate it.

In sum, the Draft English and Canadian codes simplify and rationalize the classic political offences and related measures, but in a manner that reflects the sensibilities more of Burke than of Locke. The law is tightened and procedure liberalized but there is also a decisive conceptual shift, beyond threats to the person of the sovereign to a wider array of threats against the abstract state under the rubric of 'public order.' Laws are elaborated accordingly, supported by modern policing and security institutions that enhance the state's ability to identify and assess sources of disorder and potential security threats and deploy alternative legal responses to the classic political offences of treason and sedition.[46]

Treason

As noted above, section 65 sets out treason punishable by death (or high treason), long regarded as the most serious crime in English law and derived from the 1351/2 Statute of Treasons, which included three major heads (along with four other acts against the sovereign). The 1892 Code replicates this arrangement: 'compassing' or plotting the death of the sovereign, 'levying war' or insurrection to depose the sovereign, compelling change in government measures or to overawe Parliament, and 'adhering' to the enemies at war, including encouraging invasion. As we have seen in this and previous volumes, all these heads had been applied in Canada, including in the 1797 trial of David McLane (an expansive view of 'compassing' to include overseas conspiracies to rebel) and the 1814 trials arising out of the War of 1812 (mostly 'adhering'). Levying war was applied in many of the 1838 rebellion trials and, as we see in this volume, to Riel.

Levying war could be prosecuted as a lesser offence than high treason, either as treason-felony, as in most of the other 1885 trials, or as lawless aggression, as was the case in the 1866 Fenian trials.[47] There was no attempt in the 1892 Code to confine 'levying war' to the offence of high treason. At the same time, the experience of 1885 and Stephen's influence appears to have precluded any attempt to confine treason to forms of 'levying war' as was the case in the U.S. constitution. As noted above, Stephen is followed in setting out the terms in which a conspiracy could be considered an overt act of treason (section 66) and converting misprision to accessories after the fact (section 67). Procedural expedients to facilitate treason convictions had been curbed to a significant extent by the protections set out in the 1696 Treason Act (advanced look at the crown's evidence, two-witness rule, right to defence counsel, etc.), which unfortunately, as explained in the earlier chapters by Bob Beal and Barry Wright and J.M. Bumsted, did not apply to the North-West Territories in 1885.

Two other contentious aspects of treason law have been highlighted in this and previous volumes of the *Canadian State Trials* series: extending liability by way of constructions and flexible approaches to allegiance. The 1892 Code resolved neither. Significant constructions were absorbed into section 69, the lesser treason offence punishable by life, which originated in the 1848 U.K. Treason-Felony Act and was extended to Canada in 1868.[48] The particular Canadian solution to issues of allegiance was preserved with the section 68 offence of lawless aggression.

Definitions of treason were extended by way of judicial interpretation or temporary legislative extensions (nine under Henry VIII). In the eighteenth century, the perceived limitations of medieval law, premised on threats to the person of the sovereign, were handled by similar extensions. Interpretations of compassing included overseas subjects seeking to overthrow British colonial rule or advocacy of republican forms of government, and levying war included armed resistance to the government and even armed rioting to pursue more generalized political aims. Pitt's temporary 1795 Treason Act (never adopted in British North America) attempted to put these modern constructions into legislative form but led to spectacular prosecutorial failures.[49] The move towards a lesser offence of treason that included such constructions proved more successful in the longer term. The James Hadfield case in 1800 prompted a bill to create a felony offence of treason (without the special rights associated with high treason), but the most immediate result was creation of the minor offence of 'Alarming His Majesty' and the development of indefinite detention powers for those found unfit to stand trial.[50] As noted in the earlier chapters by Beal and Wright and Bill Waiser, the 1848 Treason-Felony Act was prompted by political crisis (rebellion in Ireland, revolutions throughout Europe, and fears of alliances between Irish nationalists and English Chartists), but it also reflected these longer-standing issues in treason law. Designed to improve the prospects of jury convictions by creating a non-capital version of treason, it also made the modern extensions of liability for treason permanent law in the United Kingdom and Canada.[51]

Treason could be committed only by persons under the sovereign's protection who owed a reciprocal duty of allegiance. Enemy invaders or foreigners from a nation at peace with Britain did not therefore commit treason unless there was a finding of allegiance, either by birth as a British subject or by local residency of a sufficient time that the alien came under the temporary protection of the crown. The doctrine of natural or perpetual allegiance (which prevailed over subsequent naturalization) became increasingly discredited after the American Revolutionary War. Doubts were again raised during the War of 1812 and Chief Justice John Beverley Robinson rejected the doctrine in 1838, a position that helped to justify his lawless aggression legislation examined below.[52] Both doctrines of extended allegiance were applied against Riel, a naturalized American citizen, but, as the Bumsted chapter points out, they were not contested by his counsel, nor did the U.S. government intervene on his behalf as it had done in 1866 with the Fenians.[53]

Lawless Aggression

The problem of allegiance loomed particularly large in Canada, with a long frontier, easy migration, and experience of border raids by armed American residents. Section 68, governing 'levying war by subjects of a state at peace with Her Majesty,' originated as Upper Canada's Lawless Aggressions Act, drafted by Robinson and passed in 1838 during the rebellion and Patriot border raids. As described in Blake Brown's chapter, it became known in the 1860s as the Fenian Act. The original legislation survived a recommended disallowance by the British law officers, was amended in 1840, and was extended throughout the Province of Canada in 1866 and the Dominion of Canada the next year.[54]

In the previous volume of *Canadian State Trials*, Murray Greenwood explored the legal issues in 1838 raised by the pressing problem of foreigners who levied war by armed invasion or inciting violence but came from countries at peace with Britain.[55] To be liable for treason, the raiders had to be found to be British-born subjects or resident and under the crown's protection long enough to owe temporary allegiance. Although some raiders were of recent British or Irish origin, Chief Justice Robinson doubted the validity of the doctrine of natural allegiance. The raiders also resided in the United States and could not be considered under the crown's protection. The situation during wartime was governed by international conventions.[56] The law was unclear about captured invaders from a peaceful state, although recent precedents, including actions by Andrew Jackson, suggested that such land-based pirates or brigands could be executed summarily as 'outlaws' under martial law (this expedient was pursued by Colonel John Prince in response to the invasion of Windsor in late 1838).[57] The problem was compounded when British rebels joined the raiders and the liability of the former under martial law was suspect.[58]

These circumstances led to the passage of the lawless-aggression legislation which created a new political felony applicable to foreign brigands, who could be tried in the regular courts (with allied British subjects facing treason charges for levying war), along with an alternate process to try the offences by foreigners and British subjects alike by courts martial (a reversion to military justice justified on the basis of 1798 and 1838 precedents in Ireland and Lower Canada).[59] It was an improvement over the controversial Jacksonian outlawry concept. Foreigners had also been previously made liable for political offences, by legislation that supplemented prerogative powers of indefinite detention and deportation and included allied British subjects.[60] The British law officers recommended disallowance, motivated in significant part by a concern about relations with the United States, but Upper Canada successfully contested the recommendation.[61] As examined in the previous volume, the law was applied by trial at Niagara and by court martial at Kingston and London and it became a permanent feature of Canadian law.[62]

Official Secrets

In contrast to the medieval origins of treason, the roots of the Code's official-secrets provisions were so recent, derived from adopted U.K. law passed in 1889, that there is nothing comparable in Stephen's Draft English Code. The 1889 legislation sought to create more effective measures against disclosure of sensitive official information by public servants or through publication. Existing administrative measures, civil actions, and criminal prosecutions for larceny were inadequate and strained extensions of sedition or even treason were inappropriate. Mounting concerns about new forms and technologies of espionage and security of government information were sparked by a series of successive leaks to the press in 1887 that proved embarrassing to the government and compromised its intelligence operations. The Admiralty began work on new measures and the Treasury took over the project in 1888. The legislative debate focused on the urgent need for such law in cases of suspected espionage and breaches of official trust by public servants and the inappropriateness of prosecutions for treason felony. Espionage in a wide range of forms and the unauthorized disclosure of official information or 'leakage' became the two main classes of offences set out in a single bill that became law.[63]

The 1892 Code provisions closely follow the 1889 legislation first enacted in Canada in 1890. Section 76 defines government locations and forms of communications and expression. Section 77 creates a dual offence, a minor one punishable by a year's imprisonment, of 'unlawful disclosure' that involves obtaining or possession, by all persons, of official information that, in the interests of the state, ought not to be communicated; and a more serious one punishable by life, of communicating or intending to communicate such information to a foreign state or agent of that state. Section 78 sets out a dual offence of 'breach of official trust' applicable to those holding office or contract with Her Majesty or the governments of the United Kingdom or Canada who lawfully or unlawfully obtain or communicate information contrary to their duty. Communication or attempted communication to a foreign state is punishable by life imprisonment, other cases punishable by a year.

The perceived shortcomings of 1889 legislation (espionage offences required proof of intentional damage to the state, which placed a heavy burden of proof on the crown, and, while leakage required only proof that communication was not in the public interest, it applied only to civil servants and government contractors) led to amending bills in 1896 and 1908. However, successful mobilization of opposition by the press delayed revision until 1911, when more elaborate and sweeping measures were passed in the form of the Official Secrets Act (further amended in 1920). Espionage and leakage continued as the main offences, but protection of military secrets was extended and the provisions expanded to cover information 'for the benefit of any foreign power or other manner prejudicial to the safety or interests of the state.' Leakage was applied to all confidential information, whether classified or not, and liability for it extended to the press and all persons not authorized to receive information. New procedural expedients were introduced, including in camera and reverse onus provisions. Sections 77 and 78 were removed from the Canadian Criminal Code and replaced in 1939 by the Official Secrets Act, based on the 1911 and 1920 U.K. acts (the U.K. legislation saw major amendment in 1986 and the Canadian act saw a series of minor amendments after the Second World War and the Gouzenko affair, with more major revisions implemented with the Anti Terrorism Act, 2001, which retitled the legislation the 'Security of Information Act').[64]

As we will see in future volumes of *Canadian State Trials*, official-secrets legislation proved to be a powerful support for intelligence operations throughout the twentieth century, for the policing and compliance of the public service and the maintenance of government secrecy. The espionage provisions (along with other espionage-related offences that were added after 1892 and remained in the Criminal Code) dealt with situations that were previously considered as treason, but this advance in narrow terms was accompanied by the much more elaborate legal regulation of security concerns. The leakage provisions resemble sedition as a security-related curb on expression, and, although their focus is restricting public access to sensitive information rather than criticism of authority, they were to have a chilling effect on freedom of the press and proved a major obstacle in struggles for open government. Sections 76–8 of the 1892 Code therefore represent a watershed in the development of Canada's modern security laws and an important legal mandate for twentieth-century security operations.

Breaches of the Peace

Collective disorder had long been met by criminal laws of unlawful assembly and riot derived from common law or legislation, backed up by military intervention when civil authority failed. More extreme forms of public disorder gave rise to security concerns and armed popular protest could be prosecuted as treason. Urbanization and industrial and public works had the effect of concentrating popular grievances and opportunities for informal political meetings. The growing prevalence of collective unrest in Britain from the late eighteenth century[65] became apparent in British North America from the 1820s.[66] Popular protest was aimed at, among other things, political/constitutional reform and industrial economic justice, while also reflecting more traditional agrarian grievances as well charivaris rooted in local, cultural, indigenous, and sectarian traditions. While the 'age of revolution' saw a growing public sphere, changing perceptions of acceptable political behaviour, and widening legitimacy of popular opinion, expanding protest also fuelled new official anxieties about public disorder and public displays of violence. Examples of the administration of the laws to manage collective disorder, their nineteenth-century elaboration, and more effective means of enforcing these laws through policing are explored in the chapters by Ian Robertson, Donald Fyson, Susan Binnie, and Eric Tucker earlier in this volume. Stephen's Draft English Code mostly rationalized these laws while Dominion laws and the 1892 Criminal Code also made them more comprehensive, particularly around unlawful assembly, drills, and firearms.

William Holdsworth describes the common law of unlawful assembly and riot, elaborated by legislation from the time of Elizabeth I, in the following terms: 'The offence of unlawful assembly is committed, if there is an assembly [of three or more persons] for an illegal purpose against the peace. Though nothing is done in pursuance of that purpose ... that if they proceed to execute their illegal purpose ... [the assembly] becomes a riot.'[67] By the eighteenth century, difficulties in determining illegal purpose or unlawfulness led to consideration of whether the character of the assembly 'would inspire the average citizen with reasonable fear' and violence was held to be necessary to constitute riot.[68] Riot was also brought within the sphere of constructive treason, resulting in further distinctions noted by Holdsworth: 'In the first place, the object of the riot must be merely a private object ... In the second place, if the aspect of the assembly was not warlike, it could only be a riotous assembly, and its acts of violence could only amount to a riot.'[69] Participants in a riotous assembly must be formed into companies under officers or armed to be considered treasonous. The Riot Act, 1715 enabled governments to avoid recourse to this contentious construction by introducing a new procedure for twelve or more assembled unlawfully in disturbance of the peace, where a mayor, justice of the peace, or sheriff could order dispersal within an hour, with the failure to do so punishable as a felony. Lord Mansfield verified that treason remained an option and Lord Gordon was tried for it in connection with the 1781 riots, but Thomas Erskine's defence resulted in a jury acquittal, Dr Johnson observing that 'he was glad ... Gordon had escaped rather than a precedent should be established.'[70]

Along with the Gordon Riots and Peterloo 'massacre,' the year 1819 saw a dramatic increase in public meetings involving advocacy of public objects that were not obviously threatening or that otherwise failed to come under the terms of the Riot Act. Growing government unease with public disorder resulted in significant changes in the law and its administration, including the displacement of routine sedition prosecutions, elaboration of breach-of-the-peace offences, and the emergence of professional policing.[71] In addition to new legislation, the courts expanded the test of lawfulness of assemblies beyond considering whether such meetings struck the average citizen with reasonable fear to include seditious intent to incite disaffection.[72] Perhaps most significant were the powers of the new police established by Robert Peel. The common law had set out the powers of magistrates, parish constables, and other officials and the duties of ordinary subjects in helping to disperse an unlawful assembly or riot when calls for assistance or the posse comitatus were issued. Riot Act proclamations met by refusal to disperse warranted summoning the militia or army as well as felony prosecutions. Nineteenth-century legislation and police regulations extended such powers, notably preventative policing powers and new procedures for military aid to the civil power.[73]

British North American and Canadian governments also contended with increases in such meetings. In Upper Canada, for instance, popular meetings outside established legislative processes to organize petitions to the crown and imperial government were used to great effect by Robert Gourlay in 1818 and during the late 1820s to address a wide range of grievances.[74] The petitioning movement was renewed by William Lyon Mackenzie in the 1830s and again in the aftermath of the rebellions, notably the 1839 meetings supporting Lord Durham's report.[75] Sectarian unrest was prevalent throughout British North America.[76] Some reforms in this area appeared before the Canadian rebellions (the creation of a police force for Toronto accompanied the adoption of Peel's consolidations and the construction of the Kingston Penitentiary in Upper Canada), but they gained momentum in the aftermath, propelled by events such as the Durham meetings, Rebellion Losses agitation, sectarian violence, and early labour unrest. As Michael Cross puts it, 'law in mid-nineteenth century Canada indeed seemed cobweb-like at times in its inability to contain popular protest. But, like cobwebs, the law spun out in ever greater complexity, with a resiliency and strength which allowed it eventually to enmesh and stifle its opposition.'[77] The rebellions opened the way not only for union and responsible government but also for wider institutional transformations and a more effectively policed order.[78] After 1867, these changes continued apace with the federal government's assumption of criminal law powers (the Riot Act was included in the Dominion Consolidations), the formation of the Dominion and the North-West Mounted Police, and military aid (now under Dominion jurisdiction) to civil power (under provincial and municipal authority).[79] New Dominion legislation, originating in post-rebellion period legislation, included the Peace Preservation Act, 1869 (31 Vic. c.12), for disorder at public works, and the Blake Act (41 Vic. c.17), enacted during 'an especially turbulent decade [1870s] marked by strikes, demonstrations, and sectarian violence' that culminated in the 1877 Montreal riots.[80]

As we have seen, Stephen's 1880 code eliminated the offence of unlawful assembly (the right to peaceful assembly was to be regulated according to routine police powers) and set out a simple distinction between summary and indictable riot (punishable by one and seven years' imprisonment respectively). The 1892 Code provisions preserved three basic offences. Sections 79 and 81 preserved unlawful assembly as summary and indictable offences punishable by a year's imprisonment, defined as three or more persons who cause reasonable fear in others of a tumultuous disturbance of the peace. Riot (sections 80 and 81, an indictable offence punishable by two years' hard labour) was defined as unlawful assembly that has actually begun to disturb the peace tumultuously. Sections 83 and 84 set out a more serious riot offence of twelve or more persons who assemble tumultuously and have triggered a Riot Act proclamation (itself codified), where such rioters obstruct the proclamation or fail to disperse within a half-hour (punishable by life imprisonment). Sections 85 and 86 largely replicate the Draft English Code with separate offences of riotous destruction of buildings (punishable by life, twenty years in Stephen) and riotous damage (punishable by seven years). Section 98 in the 1892 Code was a unique indictable offence, punishable by two years, for persons who incite three or more 'Indians, non-treaty Indians or half-breeds' to make any demand or request of a government official or agent in a riotous, threatening, or disorderly manner or to do any act calculated to cause a breach of the peace.

Stephen's code included the offences of illegal drilling and non-security-related breach-of-the-peace offences such as affray, duels, and prize fights. These matters appear in the 1892 Code but, again, the Canadian provisions are more comprehensive. Elaborate military-training provisions (sections 87 and 88) can be traced to 1838 rebellion era legislation that prohibited military training, imposed restrictions on firearms use, and introduced seizure powers, as well as measures adopted during the Fenian raids and imperial legislation in Ireland. Although the Blake Act, directed at armed sectarian and urban rioting, was temporary and renewed annually until 1883, it accompanied permanent firearms-control legislation (40 Vic. c.30). Part IV of the 1892 Canadian Criminal Code reflects the legacy of these measures by way of the Revised Statues of Canada (cc.148, 149, and 151). Sections 99–101 set out offences concerning the unlawful use and possession of explosive substances. Sections 101–17 set out comprehensive prohibitions on the unauthorized possession, concealment, use, importation, and gift or sale of firearms. Section 102 creates an indictable offence (punishable by five years' imprisonment) for armed activity for purposes dangerous to the public peace. Sections 113, 114, and

115 prohibit armed persons from attending or lurking within one mile of public meetings or lying in wait for persons returning from public meetings. Section 116 restricts the sale, barter, or gift of 'improved' arms and ammunition. Sections 117 and 118 concern the possession of weapons and the sale of liquor near public works.[81]

Sedition

Sedition, as it developed in its modern form, is the crime of verbal, written, or published attacks on the sovereign, his or her government, its institutions, or its officials, with the intent of bringing down the government by unlawful means.[82] As explained in the overview of the offence in the first volume of *Canadian State Trials*, sedition was widely prosecuted before the second quarter of the nineteenth century. It also had broader reach, directed at criticism of the state or political authority intended to promote discontent and disaffection. There was no need to prove actual incitement of public disturbance (unlike treason, which required proof of overt acts against the state). Although it was considered a political misdemeanour, it came with severe but imprecise punishments that included fines, imprisonment, and the pillory. Stephen doubted the legitimate modern existence of sedition as a common law offence in the absence of specific statutory provisions, and, as noted earlier, he acknowledged that Lockean political philosophy implied that the offence should be abolished. He opted to preserve it as a modern offence rather than omit it from the Draft English Code. Although the Canadian Criminal Code bill, drawing from Stephen, promised greater statutory definition of sedition, its sections dealing with this subject, unlike most of the others examined so far, were subject to much parliamentary debate, the result of which, as we shall see, were vague and broad provisions that were later exploited by governments and the bench to suppress labour radicalism. It was only in 1951 (*Boucher v. R.*) that the Supreme Court of Canada, obliged to consider the common law because seditious intent was not defined in the Canadian Criminal Code, specified that there must be an intent to incite violence or create public disorder for the purpose of resisting or disturbing constituted authority.[83]

In Tudor times the courts interpreted the Statute of Treasons, 1351 to include constructive treasons that encompassed public protest and public expression of opposition to the crown, extensions that were supplemented by legislation under Henry VIII. Separate prosecutions for sedition followed largely from Sir Edward Coke's formulation, in his report of

Pickering's Case, prosecuted when he was attorney general in the Court of Star Chamber at the height of its power in 1605, which distinguished between libels against private persons and public figures.[84]

The common law offence of seditious libel, distinct from the criminal libel of defamation and the parliamentary privilege offence of contempt (reflecting Parliament's residual function as a court), became the most prominent form of the offence by the eighteenth century. It evoked unsettled constitutional issues, ranging from freedom of the press and political expression to judicial independence and freedom of the jury's verdict. The late-seventeenth-century constitutional compromises included advances such as the Habeas Corpus Act, 1679, the Treason Act, 1696, and the convention of 'no prior restraint,' which coincided with the demise of licensing and the government's print monopoly and censorship powers. Seditious libel was elaborated by the courts to fill the gap, as reformers fought governments over the reach of post-publication sanctions while judges maintained control over the most contentious questions in a manner that favoured governments and restricted the scope of the jury's verdict. The liberal advance of Fox's Libel Act, 1792,[85] which reiterated the powers of the jury to give a general verdict that included matters of intent and seditious inference, was checked as Britain became embroiled in war with revolutionary France. By an ironic twist, the conviction rates rose, facilitated by prosecutions through ex officio informations which enhanced the powers of the crown to pack juries, among other expedients. Another spate of prosecutions followed in 1816–20 as a response to urban rioting.[86] Indictments were still drawn up in a manner that resembled Coke's rules, but with an added proviso: seditious libel was 'blame of public men, laws or institutions, published with an illegal intention on the part of the publisher.' The common law continued to reflect the traditional presumed duty of deference to rulers rather than the modern notion that governments are agents of the people, who have the right to criticize and should be punished only for false or demonstrably harmful expression.

This began to change with an 1819 enactment[87] that, in a roundabout way, gave the crime a statutory definition similar to that in effect today. In part, it provided that a judge could, after convicting a person of sedition, seize all copies of the offending publication(s), and it described such writing as being '[any] seditious Libel, tending to bring into Hatred or Contempt the Person of His Majesty … or the Government … by law established … or to excite His Majesty's Subjects to Attempt the Alteration of any matter of Church or State … otherwise than by lawful means.'[88] While, in general, the judges had hewn to the letter of the law of the Libel

Act during the Napoleonic Wars, and it had been for the most part juries that had become ex post facto censors of the press,[89] the situation changed in the early post-war period. In the new conditions of peace, Britain lost many of its markets to continental entrepreneurs and rising prices put many more Britons out of work, a situation exacerbated by the Luddite mobs destroying new machinery and by thousands of demobilized servicemen.[90] Large rallies that gave voice to discontent alarmed the government, which intensified the repressive measures instituted during the war. Those prosecuted for seditious conspiracy for expressing the views of such assemblages, including peaceful meetings to draw up petitions to Parliament for redress, were given the same treatment as those who had incited mobs to violence and riot.[91] It is at this point that the bench began to diverge in views and behaviour, some members openly favouring the government's repressive position as a necessary defence of the existing order. Henry Hunt's indictment for seditious conspiracy in 1820 after the Peterloo 'massacre' resulted in conviction and two and a half years' imprisonment. This was despite evidence that Hunt urged the assembly to be peaceful and that the military contingent began the bloodletting, evidence that Justice John Bayley refused to admit.[92] Another 1820 case arising from Peterloo, which involved the radical MP Sir Francis Burdett, resulted in a conviction, heavy fines, and three months' imprisonment for seditious libel for a pamphlet that criticized government action and opinions alleged to constitute an incitement to riot.[93] Both convictions were upheld on appeal.

The demise of routine resort to sedition prosecutions outside of crises, apparent by the second quarter of the nineteenth century in England, occurred about a decade later in British North America, after the Robert Gourlay, Francis Collins, and Joseph Howe cases examined in Volume I of *Canadian State Trials*.[94] This shift reflects an increasingly tolerant political climate and legal developments, including judicial differences over the common law. As noted earlier, governments changed prosecutorial focus, from sedition to less contentious breaches-of-the-peace and unlawful-assembly offences, a move made possible by the development of professional policing which supported the elaboration and more effective enforcement of the latter laws.[95] Reform advocacy of permitting the defence of truth in all libel cases increased through the 1820s and was eventually achieved with Lord Campbell's Libel Act, which in turn led to new pressure to redefine sedition.[96] Legislation enacted from the mid 1820s that enabled working men to combine for their own benefit began to remove labour disputes from the reach of sedition. The political ascendancy of Whigs in the 1830s further legitimatized popular political engagement and criticism. Perhaps most important, governments had decreasing confidence in securing compliant juries, as juror attitudes reflected currents of wider tolerance in public opinion. The threat of jury acquittals, the long-term result of the Libel Act, 1792, became perhaps the most effective check on sedition prosecutions.[97]

While Mr Justice Joseph Littledale's charge to the jury in the 1836 case *R. v. Collins* [98] is an illustration of the broader and more tolerant outlook of some judges, Irish cases in the 1840s were a distinct exception to the trend. Little toleration is reflected in the treatment meted out to Daniel O'Connell, an Irish barrister and nationalist, in 1843 by the Court of Queen's Bench in Dublin. He was charged, inter alia, with seditious conspiracy.[99] O'Connell, who opposed the legislative union of Great Britain and Ireland in 1801, had, over the years, made numerous attempts to have the union repealed by constitutional means similar to those that he had used in the struggle leading to the enactment of the Catholic Emancipation Act, 1829, an achievement for which he was largely responsible. His latest and most successful plan was to politicize the Catholic population of Ireland in a succession of monster rallies at which he explained to his audience the strictly constitutional means by which repeal might be effected. The Conservative prime minister, Sir Robert Peel, grew alarmed by O'Connell's successful agitation and, in October 1843, when a mass meeting was called in Clontarf, 'the meeting was forbidden, and O'Connell told his followers to obey orders.' Peel then 'took a second step. O'Connell was arrested and brought to trial on a long count. The jury was packed [in Dublin in 1843, there was not a single Roman Catholic in the jury], and although there were technical faults in the indictment the verdict went in favour of the government.'[100] Sentenced to a year in prison and fines, O'Connell appealed his conviction in 1844, and the verdict of the law lords, of whom the majority were Whigs, was in his favour.[101] In his judgment, the future Liberal lord chancellor, Lord Campbell, openly laid the blame on the Dublin Court of Queen's Bench for packing the jury.[102] While the government had halted the campaign in the short term and the size of the Irish constabulary was rapidly expanded, growing local discontent and revolutionary movements in Europe inspired a new manifestation of Irish nationalism, the Young Ireland movement. The result was charges against several leading nationalists in March 1848, notably John Mitchel, editor of the *United Irishman*, who advocated Irish independence, by force if necessary. This was followed in April by the passage of the Treason-Felony Act, noted earlier, a response to rebellion, European revolutionary upheaval, and government fears of a coalition between Irish nationalists and English Chartists. Mitchel and Kevin Izod O'Doherty, editor of the *Irish Tribune*, were convicted and transported to Australia.[103]

In 1886, during a period of much labour unrest, what is perhaps the leading case in common law on the definition of sedition was heard in London before Mr Justice William Cave when John Burns and three fellow labour leaders were indicted for, inter alia, 'unlawfully and maliciously uttering seditious words ... with intent to riot, and ... for conspiring together to effect the said objects.'[104] That February 'a monster concourse' of 50,000 in Hyde Park had been broken up by the police. For leading one such group of about 20,000 on a march ending in a riot in London's West End, Burns and three colleagues were arrested for addressing the crowd. It was also proved that they had urged the assemblage to keep the peace and later, when violence had broken out, that they had urged the marchers to disperse.[105] In the course of his remarks during the *Burns* trial, Cave defined the misdemeanour of sedition using a definition of Stephen's that had been freely adapted from the statute of 1819 as well as specifying what was not sedition.[106] His charge to the jury echoed that of Justice Littledale in *R. v. Collins* and diverged from that of Justice William Best in *R. v. Burdett* and the Irish Queen's Bench in *R. v. O'Connell*: 'You must not attach too much importance to the isolated phrases, but you must look at the general gist of the matter. You must consider the object which took them there, the way they set about attaining it, and you must also consider to some extent. as throwing some light upon your decision, whether the riots which actually took place were the natural consequences of speeches delivered on that occasion.'[107] Moreover, Cave went to the heart of the matter when he uttered the short, concise phrase that made *Burns* a leading case: 'In order to make out the offence of speaking seditious words there must be a criminal intent on the part of the accused, they must be spoken with seditious intention.'[108] The jury returned a not-guilty verdict.

Hence, what was deemed to be sedition as of 1886 was the text printed at length in the 21st edition of *Archbold's Pleading and Evidence in Criminal Cases* of 1893,[109] in which Cave was quoted with approval. Generally speaking, in J.F. Stephen's short form, a seditious intention was defined as an intent to alter the ruling institutions by unlawful means; seditious words and writings were those that would bring about the seditious intention, and a seditious conspiracy was one in which two or more persons agreed to commit acts in furtherance of a seditious intention.[110] However, because the state was seen as the extension of the individual, and thus the servant of the people, the right of the subject to criticize the government freely and without restraint was recognized, so long as such criticism did not incite people to commit unlawful acts. That many of the English judiciary had come to accept this view is reflected in *Law Times* in April 1886: 'The result of the Socialist's trial [*R. v.* Burns] was not a surprise to us, nor should we imagine to any of our readers. There was a half-heartedness about the prosecution which became painfully apparent, while the judge plainly, at an early period, showed that he did not think much of the case for the crown.'[111] Yet this view was not unanimous and another editorial in the *Law Journal* suggested that some elements of the profession still adhered to the view that such matters remained a matter for the bench rather than the jury:

The questions for the jury in a prosecution for seditious words, as in a case of defamatory words or writings, are – first, were the words charged spoken? and, secondly, had they the tendency alleged? The learned judge's summing-up was, however, concerned almost entirely with the question of malice, an inference which the law presumes against the utterer of words with a seditious tendency. The only reference to the presumption of law upon which the whole case turned seems to have been in the words: 'The Attorney-General had said that inciting to disorder was the natural consequence of the words the defendants used, and, therefore they were responsible for it. He could not agree entirely as to that. There must be, in order to make out the offence of speaking seditious words, a criminal intent. The words must be seditious and spoken with a seditious intent. Although it was a good working rule to say that a man must be taken to intend the natural consequences of his acts, it was very proper to ask the jury if there was anything to show to the contrary. In some reports Mr. Justice Cave is made to say of this fundamental rule of law that it is a legal fiction.'[112]

In Canada as in England, there was also a divergence of opinion in the legal profession on the question of sedition. This was apparent from the fact that the editorial in the *Law Journal* was printed in full with obvious approval in the *Canada Law Journal* less than a month after its publication in London.[113] But this was not an unexpected reaction since one of the main issues that concerned Canadian legalists at that time was the challenge to the sanctity of contract, most notably by labour movements.[114] On the whole, the weight of legal opinion was heavily on the side of sanctity of contract.[115] If Canadian strikes had developed into riots and property damage had been caused by allegedly seditious speeches to large gatherings, and charges of sedition had been laid, the English common law, as reflected in a number of pre-1840 cases, would have been resorted to.[116] Later legislation, apart from emergency acts passed during the rebellions, included 'An Act respecting Seditious and Unlawful Associations and Oaths' in the Consolidated Statutes of Lower Canada in 1861,[117] one of the acts carried over in an appendix volume of the 1886 Revised Statutes of Canada[118] and in force throughout Canada under Dominion jurisdiction.

If events had turned out differently with the Revised Statutes of 1886, Canada would have had even more advanced sedition law than that set out in *Burns*. As noted earlier, George Burbidge, who was in charge of drafting the 1886 legislation, began with the current volume of *Archbold's*,[119] relied upon in the 1885 North-West rebellions, but then turned to the 1879 version of Stephen's Draft English Code. It defined the offence in much the same words as did the English statute of 1819. Moreover, for the first time since the early seventeenth century, a specific punishment was laid down for the person so convicted: two years' imprisonment.[120] Sedition was similarly defined in Burbidge's draft and the punishment reduced to two years from twenty-one or seven years' imprisonment.[121] As the rebellion exploded in March 1885 and consumed much of Parliament's time, the project was dropped and instead the separate criminal acts became part of the Revised Statutes.[122]

As we have seen, six years after the revision, the Department of Justice combined the 1880 Draft English Code with the existing Canadian laws and introduced the Criminal Code bill.[123] On 8 March 1892 the definitive version was introduced to the House as Bill no. 7 by the minister of justice.[124] As it turned out, sedition was one of the offences that drew considerable parliamentary attention and even more debate than the breach-of-the-peace provisions. All the members who took part in the debate on the bill in the Committee of the Whole, with the exception of Justice Minister John Thompson, were Liberals, and most of them were eminent lawyers destined to hold high judicial office. Imbued with the Whig interpretation of history, they argued their case as though the minister was trying to undermine parliamentary supremacy. Thompson defended the specific provisions that came under attack, relying heavily in doing so on the imperial commissioners, but he was not dogmatic and would generally concede the point in the interest of preserving the prospects of the Code as a whole.[125] Article 102 became a major bone of contention, the first part of which defined a seditious intention as an intention:

(a) To bring into hatred or contempt, or to excite disaffection against the person of Her Majesty, or the government and Constitution of the United Kingdom or any part of it, or of Canada or any Province thereof, or either House of Parliament of the United Kingdom, or of Canada or any Legislature, or the administration of justice; or

(b) To excite Her Majesty's subjects to attempt to procure, otherwise than by lawful means, the alteration of any matter in the State; or

(c) To raise discontent or disaffection amongst Her Majesty's subjects, or

(d) To promote feeling of ill-will and hostility between different classes of such subjects.[126]

Thompson, a former judge of the Supreme Court of Nova Scotia, had experience searching out obscure statutes and dealing with the exasperating problem caused by the archaic procedures specified in such enactments. As minister of justice, he now had the opportunity to remedy the situation and he made the most of it. His objective, he said, was to simplify the law, to get rid of the now meaningless felony and misdemeanour distinction and to put all the criminal law between two covers.[127] In particular, in a reasoned argument in the debate on sedition, he made the point that the distinguished jurists who had revised Stephen's Draft English Code of 1878 had declared that 'this [definition of sedition] is as exact an application as we can make of the existing law' and in addition stated: 'On this very delicate subject we do not undertake to suggest any alteration in the law.'[128] Examination of *Archbold's* shows that the words of the definition are repeated almost verbatim, bearing out the truth of the jurists' assertion.

On the other hand, David Mills, a future minister of justice and member of the Supreme Court of Canada, insisted that the contentious section 'would alter the constitutional law as set out in the trial of Sacheverell' and would thus make any criticism of the queen or her government or ministers a seditious offence.[129] Louis Davies, a future chief justice of the Supreme Court, also harked back to the Glorious Revolution and held that liberty of the subject was inextricably bound up with the common law, which was 'elastic and justly elastic. It is made by the prudence of the people and the constitution.' William Mulock, a future chief justice of the Exchequer Division of the Supreme Court, thought that the section would impair freedom of speech and, in the most reasoned argument of Thompson's opponents, gave what he considered to be examples where free speech would be restricted or forbidden. But, more to the point, he said: 'I trust that the section will be so modified as to put that right beyond all question of controversy. If the Minister will not yield the point now, I give him notice that when the Bill is reported I will move to cut down that clause.'[130]

In succeeding days the remainder of the bill's 981 sections were discussed, amended, or otherwise dealt with and no more really contentious issues arose. By 28 June, the last clauses were up for debate. Parliament was to be prorogued on 9 July , which left only eleven days for the bill to pass the Senate and receive royal assent. Probably for this reason, and because there was agreement as to the disposition of all the other sections, Thompson acceded to Mulock's request and deleted the offending passages that defined a seditious intention, rather than risk an acrimonious and probably extended debate in the House.[131] Subsection 1 was simply and expediently deleted in its entirety. The irony, given the tenor of the opposition criticism, was that persons subsequently charged with sedition were subject to the elastic common law definitions. For the larger cause of getting the Code through Parliament, the punishment for sedition was specified but the offence was not. This meant that it remained defined by common law, which was an ominous portent for the future.

CONCLUSIONS

National security figures prominently in both the general objects of the 1892 Canadian Criminal Code and its specific provisions, although, of course, the Code served many other purposes. As noted above, the Code's provenance included the nineteenth-century English criminal law reform debates and colonial conditions and experiences, influences shared with other British jurisdictions that codified. As in these jurisdictions, Canadian codification was also prompted, in part, by political or public-order crises. All these criminal codes aimed to modernize and rationalize authority by reforming archaic forms of discretionary power and enhancing the place of the rule of law in challenging colonial and frontier situations.

The 1892 Code was also the product of a specifically Canadian public agenda. The factors at work here included the strong position articulated during the confederation debates in favour of centralized federal jurisdiction over criminal law, Macdonald's explicit association of this power with national defence, the challenges of consolidating the diverse criminal laws of the British North American colonies, the assumption of new responsibilities for internal and external security, and associated initiatives to support the sovereignty and development of the federation. Threats to this agenda culminated with the 1885 North-West crisis. Codification became a government priority. Stephen's Draft English Code served as the primary external model, one in which pragmatism prevailed over purity of utilitarian and broader liberal principles, a tendency that continued with the drafting, debate, and passage of the 1892 Code. This ensured the success of the government's bill, unlike Stephen's effort, but at the cost of an unfortunate malleability of certain provisions.

Codification made the criminal law more accessible, rational, and comprehensive, but at the same time it should also be understood as a quasi-constitutional initiative, one that aimed to improve public order and to make the criminal law and prevailing authority more effective and pervasive. It was both a liberal advance and a means of enhancing power. Codification reduced archaic discretionary forms of authority and better absorbed tensions between the rule of law and sovereignty, although it by no means resolved these tensions or eliminated discretion. The prominent and comprehensive national-security provisions set out in Canadian Criminal Code, 1892 serve as the best illustrations of these matters. They directly addressed the internal and external security concerns of the Dominion and reflected the more rational, liberal yet comprehensive qualities of modern state power. They were a mixture of modernized English and local laws filtered through Canadian experiences, J.F. Stephen's political sensibilities, and the more general emerging security preoccupations of modern states.

By 1892, there had been extensive experience in Canada with the major political offences of high treason (from McLane to Riel), treason-felony (the other 1885 trials), and lawless aggression (the 1838 Patriot and 1866 Fenian raids), the unique offence that reflected Canadian preoccupation with the immense border and the ambitions of the U.S. republic and its inhabitants. These classic political offences were updated. Other security provisions in the 1892 Code included new interventions such as the official-secrets offences and elaborated breach-of-the-peace laws, laws that were accompanied by new police and security institutions which supported a more pre-emptive approach to real and perceived security threats along with intelligence gathering and assessment. The new developments rendered the classic political offences increasingly moribund although they remain part of Canada's Criminal Code. Here the persistence of the sedition offences as a viable twentieth-century security measure is particularly surprising, given political advances that suggested demise, but, as we have seen, the opportunity to narrow or eliminate the offence was lost. And, as we shall see in the next volume of *Canadian State Trials*, sedition was used widely against the labour movement in the wake of the Winnipeg General Strike, supplemented by related amendments to the Criminal Code that became the basis for the infamous section 98 (which accompanied the operations of the reorganized security branch of the Royal Canadian Mounted Police and wide resort to deportations under related immigration legislation). Although section 98 was repealed in 1936, the uncertain definition of seditious intent persisted until 1951.[132] The War Measures Act, emergency legislation developed outside the Canadian Criminal Code, was to be the most significant, subsequent development in Canada's national-security laws.[133] This sweeping executive-enabling legislation made it possible to suspend civil rights such as habeas corpus temporarily without subjecting civilians to martial law, while also avoiding the controversy, inconvenience, and risks of temporary emergency legislation and public trials. Treason remained part of the Canadian Criminal Code but nothing like the 1885 prosecutions would be ventured again by Canadian governments.

NOTES

1   55&56 Vic. (Can.) c.29.
2   Lindsay Farmer, 'Reconstructing the English Codification Debate: The Criminal Law Commissioners, 1833–45,' *Law and History Review* 18 (2000): 400.
3   See ibid. on codification in relation to Weber's notion of formal legal rationality as an expression of modern authority. See also generally, Harold J. Berman and Charles J. Reid, 'Max Weber as Legal Historian,' in S. Turner ed., *The Cambridge Companion to Weber* (Cambridge: Cambridge University Press 2000), 32; R. Cotterrell, *The Sociology of Law: An Introduction* (London: Butterworths 1984), 158–68. The common law exception is attributed in part to the late-seventeenth-century British constitutional compromises that promised to check repressive powers, removing one of the incentives that lay behind later modern European criminal law codifications.
4   Farmer, 'Reconstructing'; K.J.M. Smith, *Lawyers, Legislators and Theorists: Developments in English Criminal Jurisprudence, 1800–1957* (Oxford: Clarendon 1998); Michael Lobban, *The Common Law and English Jurisprudence, 1760–1850* (Oxford: Clarendon 1991).
5   Smith, *Lawyers, Legislators and Theorists*, 11 (see also 9–12, for Smith's succinct examination of debates around the reform of substantive criminal law doctrine which informs this summary). William Blackstone, *Commentaries on the Laws of England* (1765–9; repr. Chicago: University of Chicago Press 1966); Jeremy Bentham, *A Comment on the Commentaries and a Fragment on Govern-*

ment (1776), ed. J.H. Burns and H.L.A. Hart (London: Athlone 1977); *An Introduction to the Principles of Morals and Legislation* (1789), ed. Burns and Hart (London: Athlone 1970). Also, R. Cross, 'Blackstone v. Bentham,' *Law Quarterly Review* 92 (1976): 516; S. Milsom, 'The Nature of Blackstone's Achievement,' *Oxford Journal of Legal Studies* 1 (1981): 1; D. Kennedy, 'The Structure of Blackstone's Commentaries,' *Buffalo Law Review* 28 (1979): 205; H.L.A. Hart, 'The Demystification of Law,' in Hart ed., *Essays on Bentham: Jurisprudence and Political Theory* (Oxford: Clarendon 1982), 21.

6 Smith, *Lawyers, Legislators and Theorists*, 20, 28–9; Farmer, 'Reconstructing,' 423.

7 On Bentham's influence, see, e.g., S.E. Finer, 'The Transmission of Benthamite Ideas, 1826–1839,' in G. Sutherland, ed., *Studies in the Growth of Nineteenth Century Government* (London: Routledge and Kegan Paul 1972); H. Benyon, 'Mighty Bentham,' *Journal of Legal History* 2 (1981): 62. For an overview of reforms, see R. McGowan, 'The Image of Justice and Reform of the Criminal Law in Early Nineteenth Century England,' *Buffalo Law Review* 32 (1983): 89.

8 See Smith, *Lawyers, Legislators and Theorists*, 361, 364. James Mackintosh's 1819 committee that paved the way for Peel's consolidations avoided the judges but they were routinely consulted on subsequent criminal law reforms (see ibid., 56–63). See also Desmond H. Brown, *The Genesis of the Canadian Criminal Code of 1892* (Toronto: Osgoode Society / University of Toronto Press 1989), 15–18.

9 See Smith, *Lawyers, Legislators and Theorists*, 136–8; Farmer, 'Reconstructing,' 404–5. See also Brown, *Genesis*, 19–22, and Michael Lobban, 'How Benthamatic Was the Criminal Law Commission?' *Law and History Review* 18 (2000): 427.

10 Stephen later provided an extended defence of this approach, after examination of the Indian Penal Code and Lord Chief Justice Cockburn's critique of the Draft English Code. See J.F. Stephen, *A History of the Criminal Law of England, Volume III* (London: Macmillan 1883), 347–52.

11 Smith, *Lawyers, Legislators and Theorists*, 143–50.

12 For further exploration of the themes in this section, see B. Wright, 'Criminal Law Codification and Imperial Projects: The Self-Governing Jurisdiction Codes of the 1890's,' *Legal History* 12 (2008): 19, and 'Macaulay's Indian Penal Code: Historical Context, Originating Principles, and the Reconstitution of Authority' (forthcoming).

13 Andrew Amos and James Fitzjames Stephen also served in India but Macaulay's role was dominant. His reforms, including the elimination of privileged access of British residents to the civil courts and new education policies, established the dominance of utilitarian policy until the renewal of 'orientalist' policies in the late nineteenth century. See generally, Eric Stokes, *The English Utilitarians and India* (Oxford: Oxford University Press 1959).

14 Macaulay to Thomas Flowers Ellis, 3 June 1835, quoted in Thomas Pinney, ed., *The Collected Letters of Thomas Babington Macaulay, Volume 3* (London: Cambridge University Press 1982), 146.

15 J.F. Stephen made explicit the direct connection between the Mutiny and the successful passage of the IPC – see M.C. Setalvad, *The Common Law in India* (London: Stevens and Sons 1960), 124. See also generally, Stokes, *Utilitarians and India*; K.J.M. Smith, 'Macaulay's Indian Penal Code: An Illustration of the Accidental Function of Time, Place and Personalities in Law Making,' in W.W. Gordon and T.D. Fergus, eds., *Legal History in the Making* (London: Hambleton 1991), 145; Elizabeth Kolsky, 'Codification and the Rule of Colonial Difference: Criminal Procedure in India,' *Law and History Review* 23 (2005): 631; Radhika Singha, *A Despotism of Law: Crime and Justice in Early Colonial India* (Delhi: Oxford University Press 1998).

16 See Graham Parker, 'The Origins of the Canadian Criminal Code,' in D.H. Flaherty, ed., *Essays in the History of Canadian Law, Volume I*, (Toronto: Osgoode Society / University of Toronto Press 1981), 251; 'Some Considerations Preliminary to the Preparation of a Penal Code for the Crown Colonies,' 20 May 1870, NAUK, Colonial Office (CO) 885/3/19. The IPC was adopted in Ceylon, Malaysia, Singapore, and a number of other Asian colonies.

17 M.L. Friedland, 'R.S. Wright's Model Criminal Code: A Forgotten Chapter in the History of the Criminal Law,' *Oxford Journal of Legal Studies* 1 (1981) : 307; Smith, *Lawyers, Legislators and Theorists*, 151–2. Wright updated Macaulay and included a more sophisticated definition of liability. J.F. Stephen critically reviewed Wright's effort while working on his own codification project for the lord chancellor's office.

18 After a false start by J.F. Stephen's son Henry on a new model code to replace Wright, Albert Ehrhardt's successful 1925 effort was largely derived from the Queensland Code. See R.S. O'Regan, 'Sir Samuel Griffith's Criminal Code,' *Australian Bar Review* 7 (1991): 141.

19 See generally the discussion of reception in F. Murray Greenwood and Barry Wright, 'Introduction: State Trials, the Rule of Law, and Executive Powers in Early Canada,' *CST 1*, 11–22. The colonial reception of English law in territories acquired through conquest or discovery and occupation is a complex topic bound up with the imposition of an outside political and legal order. *Calvin's Case* (1608) 77 ER 377 sought to clarify, among other things, questions of allegiance and the legal status of subjects and aliens; and, as the first British empire took shape, it was the basis for the view that, with the establishment of British interests in a territory, subjects were governed by those laws deemed reasonably applicable in local circumstances by the local executive authority, although this was qualified by the view held in the American colonies that

English law after 1497 was not applicable unless expressly adopted by charter or local legislative or judicial recognition. Formal reception followed when settlement reached levels where there were demands for representative legislative institutions and colonial courts to administer the law regularly. In effect, when a colonial legislature was established, English law usually became the foundation of that jurisdiction's law, and the local legislatures and courts were empowered to amend these laws as conditions required, subject to imperial supervision (Colonial Office review and possible British government disallowance, imperial legislation, and, after 1833, appeals to the Judicial Committee of the Privy Council).

20 Local judges, unlike those on the English bench, were among the strongest proponents of codification. As Desmond Brown notes elsewhere (*Genesis*, 42, 71), professional attitudes were shaped in significant part by the difficulties of accessibility to relevant statutes and legal texts, which were scarce and expensive. Institutional holdings were limited and difficult for lawyers to access, let alone judges facing greater distances and more extreme conditions on circuit than their English counterparts.

21 See Greenwood and Wright, 'Introduction,' *CST 1*, 22–3; John McLaren, 'Bowing to no Power but the Supremacy of Law: Judges and the Rule of Law in Colonial Australia and Canada, 1788–1840,' *Australian Journal of Legal History* 6 (2003): 177; Barry Wright, 'Libel and the Colonial Administration of Justice in Upper Canada and New South Wales c.1825–35,' in B. Berger, H. Foster, and A.R. Buck, eds., *The Grand Experiment: Law and Legal Culture in British Settler Societies* (Vancouver: Osgoode Society for Canadian Legal History / University of British Columbia Press 2008), 15; Paul Romney, 'From Constitutionalism to Legalism: Trial by Jury, Responsible Government and the Rule of Law in Canadian Political Culture,' *Law and History Review* 7 (1989): 130.

22 Farmer, 'Reconstructing,' 423–4. The conflict between utilitarians, with their notion of 'enlightened despotism,' and traditional Whigs contributed to the contradictions in nineteenth-century British liberalism. Apart from figures such as Macaulay and Brougham, few Whigs shared the utilitarian enthusiasm for codification in part because of their failure to grasp its possibilities as a check on the powers of the state.

23 The Canadian Criminal Code of 1892 and the New Zealand Code of 1893 preserved Stephen's cautious, narrow conception of codification that retained common law, while the Queensland Code crafted by Samuel Griffith used it more as a jumping-off point, his essentially Benthamite conception ending up resembling Macaulay and Wright more than Stephen. See B. Wright, 'Self-Governing Codifications of English Criminal Law and Empire: The Queensland and Canadian Examples,' *University of Queensland Law Journal*

26 (2007): 39; M.L. Friedland, 'Codification in the Commonwealth: Earlier Efforts,' *Criminal Law Forum* 2 (1990): 145.

24 Growing Maori resistance to land confiscations and indefinite detentions coincided with the drafting of the first New Zealand codification bill in 1883. A general strike and the emergence of the Australian Labor Party fuelled political crisis in Queensland and was the context for former premier and chief justice Samuel Griffith's drafting of the Queensland Criminal Code in 1896–7 (which included provisions that displaced parliamentary privilege and extended 'responsible' judicial oversight over legislative processes) – see Wright, 'Criminal Law Codifications and Imperial Projects,' 37–46. The scale of the public-order crises differed. Thousands were killed during the Mutiny and at Morant Bay. The North-West rebellion of 1885 resulted in fewer casualties, but, as we see elsewhere in this volume, it highlighted the fragility of Ottawa's authority over the North-West and the scale of disaffection. *CST 2* examines conflicts between the rule of law and the resort to emergency powers and military justice after the 1837–8 Canadian rebellions. Public debate on these matters as it developed from the mid-nineteenth century and the Jamaica crisis is examined in Rande Kostal, *A Jurisprudence of Power: Victorian Empire and the Rule of Law* (Oxford: Oxford University Press 2005). While criminal codes were developed, in part, as a means to achieve more effective, legitimate, and modern rule-of-law-based authority, they did not resolve the tensions between sovereignty and the rule of law, as identified by Franz Neumann and highlighted by responses to insurgency in modernizing postcolonial states. See also Nasser Hussain, *The Jurisprudence of Emergency: Colonialism and the Rule of Law* (Ann Arbor: University of Michigan Press 2003).

25 Peter B. Waite, ed., *The Confederation Debates in the Province of Canada*, 2nd ed., (Montreal and Kingston: McGill-Queens's University Press 2006). See also *Parliamentary Debates on Confederation* (Quebec: Hunter Rose 1865), 508, 576–7; Parker, 'Origins,' 252; Brown, *Genesis*, 59–60. The views expressed at the closed conferences in Charlottetown, Quebec, and London are not known, but the section dealing with the matter in the proposed British North America Act remained unchanged in each successive draft, and there is no record of opposition to it in any other published material – see, e.g., *Report concerning the Enactment of the British North America Act of 1867* (Ottawa: King's Printer 1939), annex 4, 52, 70, 91. The Dominion Parliament was given jurisdiction over the criminal law and procedure (30&31 Vic. c.3 c.91), but the actual constitution of the courts of criminal jurisdiction was left to the provinces.

26 Waite, *Confederation Debates*, 24–5.

27 While the Act of Union provided that all the laws of the two jurisdictions

were to remain in effect, Lord Sydenham's administration moved quickly to correct this double standard of justice by repealing all previous criminal legislation and consolidating the criminal law in both provinces, resulting in substantial reform in Quebec: (1840) 3&4 Vic. c.35 s.46 (imperial); (1841) 4&5 Vic. cc.24, 25, 26, 27 (Province of Canada). This was followed by coordinated consolidations in 1859 and 1860. See Brown, *Genesis*, 56–7, 86–9.

28 The Province of Canada consolidation exercise had also given rise to a codification proposal based on Macaulay's IPC from William Badgley, a former attorney general, in 1850. Elsewhere in British North America, Nova Scotia was the first British jurisdiction to collect all applicable statutes in 1804 (antedating the first volume of the British Statutes of the Realm), and New Brunswick, which had also adopted Peel's consolidations acts, was the first British jurisdiction to enact a codified format for all offences in 1849 digest. See Brown, *Genesis*, 74–8, 84–5.

29 (1869) 32&33 Vic. c.18–26 (Canada). Bernard and Gowan (who had corresponded with Greaves) became involved when the scale of the task became clear, but the drafters were put under tight timelines and Macdonald opposed significant changes to the English text. The first bills were introduced in April 1868 but were defeated in the Senate, and were introduced again and passed the following session – see Brown, *Genesis*, 1989, 92–7. See also D.H., Brown, ed., *The Birth of a Criminal Code: The Evolution of Canada's Justice System* (Toronto: University of Toronto Press 1995), 28.

30 Ibid., 29.

31 It was the most influential journal on the profession in this period, generally closely attending English reform debates and dismissing American legal innovations. For instance, the journal paid much attention to Stephen's Draft English Code, which was contrasted with Macaulay's effort, while David Dudley Field's codification of New York criminal law was largely ignored. Unlike England, the journal's advocacy of codification evoked little professional criticism or defences of the common law. See Parker, 'Origins,' 253–5; Brown, *Genesis*, 70.

32 Between 1875 and 1880, fifty additional federal criminal laws were passed, seven of which were amending. See Brown, *Birth*, 31; Brown, *Genesis*, 103–6.

33 Great Britain, Parliament, *Parliamentary Papers*, 'Report of the Royal Commission on the Law Relating to Indictable Offences, 1878–79' [2345], ss.102–3. The Draft English Code is an appendix to this report.

34 Brown, *Genesis*, 106–23; Brown, *Birth*, 31–2; Parker, 'Origins,' 257–9. Burbidge, borrowing heavily from Stephen's digest, published *A Digest of the Criminal Law of Canada (Crimes and Punishment) Founded by Permission on Sir James*

Fitzjames Stephen's Digest of the Criminal Law (1889) to accompany the 1886 Revised Statutes. Gowan visited London again in 1889, following up on Thompson's general discussions.

35 Parker, 'Origins,' 260; Brown, *Genesis*, 120–2; Brown, *Birth*, 33.

36 Parker, 'Origins,' 258.

37 The Department of Justice records (reproduced in Brown, *Birth*) show that the 1880 English bill and the 1886 Canadian Revised Statutes were the primary references. The Greaves consolidation, Stephen's Digest, and Burbidge's edition of the latter were also relied on and there is oblique reference to nine English and American periodical articles on the IPC and the New York and Italian codes. The comprehensive definition of all criminal offences, the ending of the felony and misdemeanours distinction, and the adoption in full of the indictment and summary-offence procedures were identified as the key innovations, and particular Canadian offences were noted (inciting Indians to riotous behaviour, larceny of timber, unguarded ice holes, etc.). See also Parker, 'Origins,' 261–4.

38 The first six titles were the same (the English code had one further preliminary title on procedure while the Canadian bill added several more).

39 Brown, *Genesis*, 123–4 (a larger proportion of procedural matters, about 70 per cent, are based on earlier Canadian sources).

40 Brown, *Birth*, 34–5; Parker, 'Origins,' 265–9. The responses were largely technical, reflecting little by way of principled, theoretical, or public-policy concerns such as effective deterrence or civil liberties. Parker notes submissions from moral reformer D.A. Watt (resulting in further provisions to protect young women from sexual predators) and publisher John King (father of the future prime minister, whose suggestions concerning libel, defamation, and freedom of the press were not incorporated).

41 Parker, 'Origins,' 271; Brown, *Birth*, 37–41. Piqued by his exclusion and distracted by Supreme Court business, Taschereau attempted to emulate Cockburn. His letter to the attorney general in January 1893, published after the bill was passed and proclaimed, was not only badly timed but was also largely lifted from the lord chief justice's critique of the Draft English Code. Sedgewick defended the Canadian Code in a long memo in February 1893, adding that lawmakers were apprised of Cockburn's criticisms and that the drafters agreed with Stephen's view of the impossibility of excluding the common law. See Parker, 'Origins,' 273–6.

42 Vol. 2, sess. 1880, 43 Vic., A Bill to Establish a Code of Offences for England and Ireland, and Procedure by Indictment for the Punishment of Offenders; A Bill to Establish a Code of Criminal Law and Procedure (Criminal Code no.2).

43 J.F. Stephen, *A History of the Criminal Law of England, Volume 2* (London: Macmillan 1883), 299.

44 Although he articulated a principled stand against constructive treasons in his *History*, Stephen included the treason-felony extensions in his draft code and later presided as judge over some of the 1883 Fenian treason-felony trials (involving conspiracies to blow up public buildings) where he expressed an expansive view of intent and conspiracy. In *Denis Deasy et al.* (1883), 15 *Cox's Criminal Cases*, 334, Stephen suggested a reverse onus on reasonable inferences, stating at 342 that 'there was a point in all these cases at which the burden of proof shifts, and if the prosecution proved the prisoners to have been in such circumstance without explanation, left them open to the reasonable inference of the existence of such a conspiracy as they wished to establish, then it might be for the defence to say what they were doing.'

45 Stephen, *History*, 2: 298–9, 375.

46 See M. Lobban, 'From Seditious Libel to Unlawful Assembly: Peterloo and the Changing Face of Political Crime c.1770–1820,' *Oxford Journal of Legal Studies* 10 (1990): 307.

47 The treason-felony and Fenian legislation was explicitly extended to the North-West Territories by 36 Vic. c.34, while the Statute of Treasons was part of the received English laws in effect in 1670 (the Hudson's Bay Company's Charter for Rupert's Land). See previous chapters in this volume and D.H. Brown, 'The Meaning of Treason in 1885,' *Saskatchewan History* 28 (1975): 70.

48 11&12 Vic. c.12 (U.K.), 31 Vic. c.69 (Canada), becoming RSC c.146 s.3 in 1886 and s.69 in 1892.

49 36 Geo. III c.7 (G.B.) – see John Barrell, *Imagining the King's Death: Figurative Treason, Fantasies of Regicide, 1793–6* (Oxford: Oxford University Press 2000). Despite these failures, the legislation was temporarily extended beyond the life of George III in 1817 (57 Geo. III c.6).

50 See R. Moran, 'The Origin of Insanity as a Special Verdict: The Trial for Treason of James Hadfield, 1800,' *Law and Society Review* 19 (1985): 487. Hadfield shot at George III in a theatre and was defended by Thomas Erskine who had secured spectacular acquittals in treason cases the previous decade.

51 While the 1795 Treason Act was never adopted in British North America, Canada adopted the 1848 act in 1868 (see Supporting Documents). Some of the compassing extensions remained high treason but most found their way into the new nineteenth-century treason-felony legislation (e.g., attempts to alter the nature of the crown's authority and conspiracies to commit armed rebellion or compel changes in government measures by force, adhering to hostile foreign powers, and advocacy of invasion). The 1848 offences were punishable by life imprisonment, or no less than two years or transportation

for seven years, and were deployed against Irish nationalists, including newspaper editor John Mitchel, resulting in some of the last cases of transportation to Australia and new efforts to reform the jury – see R. Blake Brown '"A
Delusion, a Mockery and a Snare": Array Challenges and Jury Selection in
England and Ireland,' *Canadian Journal of History* 39 (2004): 20–3. In 2003 the
Guardian newspaper launched an unsuccessful constitutional and legal challenge to the Treason-Felony Act in the House of Lords on the basis that republican advocacy in print of the abolition of the monarchy, even by peaceful
means, remains an offence.

52 See Paul Romney and Barry Wright, 'The Toronto Treason Trials, March-May
1838,' *CST* 2, 64–5, and, in the same volume, Chief Justice Robinson's grand
jury charge, appendix D4, 464–9.

53 Despite Robinson's earlier rejection of natural allegiance, the doctrine appears
to have been indirectly resurrected by Chief Justice W.H. Draper' opinion
in *R. v. McMahon* (1866, 26 Upper Canada Queen's Bench, 195), an appeal
(denied) of the Irish-born McMahon's conviction as a U.S. citizen under the
Fenian Act. As we have seen, Riel's charges were initially framed as if he continued to be a British subject, but three counts on the basis of local allegiance
were added, in recognition of the uncertain modern legal status of perpetual
allegiance and in anticipation of potential U.S. objections (see also Jeremy
Ravi Mumford, 'Why Was Louis Riel, a United States Citizen, Hanged as a
Canadian Traitor in 1885?' *Canadian Historical Review* 88, no. 2 [2007]: 237).

54 (1838) 1 Vic. c.3 (Upper Canada), An Act to Protect the Inhabitants of the
Province from Subjects of Foreign Countries at Peace with Her Majesty; (1840)
3 Vic. c.12 (U.C.) An Act to Alter and Amend. For the 1866 amendments (Statutes Province of Canada, 1866, c.2 . c.4), see Supporting Documents. Before
1866, British subjects could be tried for the offence only by court martial; if
facing the regular courts, they could be tried only for treason (levying war).
The amendment was justified by reference to equivalent felony procedure in
the 1848 U.K. Treason-Felony Act, and in late 1867 that measure was enacted
as the law of the Dominion of Canada (31 Vic. c.14) and included in the Dominion Consolidations (R.S.C. c.146 ss. 6 and 7) before emerging as section 68
in the 1892 Code.

55 F. Murray Greenwood, 'The Prince Affair: "Gallant Colonel" or the "Windsor
Butcher"?' *CST* 2, 160.

56 Grotius, de Vattel, and von Martens held that foreign invaders were to be
treated as prisoners of war if captured and released or deported once the
frontier was pacified. They could not to be put to death summarily or by court
martial except on the grounds of military necessity, and secondary punishments such as transportation could be imposed only for offences committed
during detention. These international rules received modern elaboration

under the Geneva Conventions, although in practice the exception of military necessity was widely exercised (e.g., the U.S. government's recent claimed exemption for the 'unlawful combatants' held at Guantánamo Bay).

57 Coke, Hale, Foster, and Blackstone, as well as the international jurists, suggested that such invading foreigners were to be treated as in wartime unless they could be found to owe allegiance in the jurisdiction invaded. On the other hand, arguments were also made that summary executions were warranted (e.g., two British subjects executed as outlaws by General Andrew Jackson for aiding Native resistance in Florida in 1818 and another executed by the Spanish King Ferdinand for aiding rebels in 1831). Piracy could be tried only if the offence occurred on the high seas. Murder, arson, robbery, and other offences could of course be charged where foreigners entered intent on private gain, plunder, or vengeance, but the situation became murkier when their actions stemmed from political motives. See Greenwood, 'Prince Affair,' 163–5, 179–81.

58 Greenwood, 'Prince Affair,' 161–3. Military authority over civilian British subjects replaced the common law only when and where hostilities made it impossible for the regular courts to function. See Barry Wright, 'The Kingston and London Courts Martial,' CST 2, 130; and F. Murray Greenwood, 'The General Court Martial at Montreal, 1838–9: Operation and the Irish Comparison,' ibid., 279.

59 The Irish and Lower Canada precedents suggested that court-martial proceedings against civilians could be justified outside of war when the regular courts are unable to function owing to the magnitude of the security crisis. See Barry Wright, 'Kingston and London Courts Martial'; Greenwood, 'The General Court Martial in Montreal and the Irish Comparison.'

60 See B. Wright, 'Migration, Radicalism and State Security: Legislative Initiatives in the Canadas and the United States, c.1794–1804,' Studies in American Political Development 16 (2002): 48.

61 Greenwood, 'Prince Affair,' 162, 177–9.

62 Thomas Sutherland was also tried for the offence by court martial in early 1838 but was acquitted. The general courts martial of Kingston and London heard 184 cases of lawless aggression, resulting in seventeen executions and seventy-eight convicts transported to Australia – see Wright, 'The Kingston and London Courts Martial.' After the Niagara trials, uncertainty stemming from the British law officers' negative assessment of the felony version of the offence delayed the trials of the Pelee Island raiders until 1839 – see Greenwood, 'Prince Affair,' 166–9. As seen in this volume of Canadian State Trials, the 1840 amendment eliminated the troublesome requirement that invaders be joined by British subjects levying war and the Fenian crisis resulted in 1866 amendments that extended the act to Canada East (Quebec) and further chan-

ges for the entire Province of Canada (to have retroactive effect and to make British subjects also liable for lawless aggression in the regular courts).

63 53 Vic. c.10 ss.1, 2, 5 (U.K.). For a concise history, see chapter 4 and appendix III of the U.K. Franks Committee, *Report of the Departmental Committee on Section 2 of the Official Secrets Act 1911*, no. 5104 (London: HMSO 1972). See also D.G.T. Williams, *Not in the Public Interest* (London: Hutchinson 1965); J. Aitken, *Officially Secret* (London: Weidenfeld and Nicolson 1971); D. Hooper, *Official Secrets: The Use and Abuse of the Act* (London: Secker and Warburg 1987); R.M. Thomas, *Espionage and Secrecy: The Official Secrets Acts 1911–1989 of the United Kingdom* (London: Routledge 1991).

64 See, e.g., 1&2 Geo. V c.28 (1911 U.K.); 49–50 Elizabeth II, Statutes of Canada (2001), c. 41 pt.2 ss.24–32. See also the Franks Committee, *Report: Reform of Section 2 of the Official Secrets Act, 1911*, no. 7285 (London: HMSO 1978); the Mackenzie Committee, *Report of the Royal Commission on Security* (Ottawa: Queen's Printer 1969); and M.L. Friedland, *National Security: The Legal Dimensions*, for 'The Commission of Inquiry concerning Certain Activities of the Royal Canadian Mounted Police' (the McDonald Commission) (Ottawa: Queen's Printer 1979).

65 Of the extensive literature in the British context, see George Rudé's classic, *The Crowd in History: A Study of Popular Disturbances in France and England 1730–1848* (New York: Wiley 1964); and, on the legal and enforcement dimensions in particular, see Stanley H. Palmer, *Police and Protest in England and Ireland, 1750–1850* (Cambridge: Cambridge University Press 1988); Richard Vogler, *Reading the Riot Act* (Philadelphia: Oxford University Press 1991); and Lobban, 'From Seditious Libel.'

66 For earlier forms of protest, see generally S.D. Clark, *Movements of Political Protest in Canada, 1640–1840* (Toronto: University of Toronto Press 1959), and F. Murray Greenwood, *Legacies of Fear: Law and Politics in Quebec in the Era of the French Revolution* (Toronto: Osgoode Society / University of Toronto Press 1993). There is extensive literature on British North America after the 1820s. For studies with a legal focus, see, e.g., Carol Wilton, 'Lawless Law: Conservative Political Violence in Upper Canada, 1818–41,' *Law and History Review* 13 (1995): 125; Wilton, 'A Firebrand amongst the People: The Durham Meetings and Popular Politics in Upper Canada,' *Canadian Historical Review* 75 (1994): 346; Susan W.S. Binnie, 'The Blake Act of 1878: A Legislative Solution to Urban Violence in Post-Confederation Canada,' in Binnie and L. Knafla, eds., *Law, State and Society: Essays in Modern Legal History* (Toronto: University of Toronto Press 1995), 215.

67 William Holdsworth, *A History of English Law, Volume VIII* (London: Methuen 1925), 324.

68 Ibid., 325–6.
69 Ibid., 328.
70 Ibid., 320–1.
71 Lobban, 'From Seditious Libel,' notes the shift in prosecutorial emphasis from sedition, which saw high rates of jury acquittals, to breaches of the peace and unlawful assembly, laws that could be more effectively pursued with the emergence of professional policing.
72 Holdsworth, *History, Volume VIII*, 327. Stephen rejected this extension and, like the Draft English Code, the Canadian Code did not adopt it either.
73 Holdsworth, *History, Volume VIII*, 329, 331; Stephen, *History, Volume 1*, 201.
74 See Barry Wright, 'The Gourlay Affair: Seditious Libel and the Sedition Act in Upper Canada, 1818–19,' 487–504, and Paul Romney, 'Upper Canada in the 1820s: Criminal Prosecution and the Case of Francis Collins,' in *CST 1*, 505–21.
75 See Wilton, 'Lawless Law' and 'A Firebrand.'
76 See, e.g., Scott W. See, *Riots in New Brunswick: Orange Nativism and Social Violence in the 1840s* (Toronto: University of Toronto Press 1993).
77 Michael S. Cross, 'The Laws Are Like Cobwebs': Popular Resistance to Authority in Mid-Nineteenth Century British North America,' in T. Barnes, P. Waite, and S. Oxner, eds., *Law in a Colonial Society: The Nova Scotia Experience* (Toronto: Carswell 1984), 106.
78 See generally P. Corrigan and D. Sayer, *The Great Arch: English State Formation as Cultural Revolution* (Oxford: Blackwell 1985); A. Greer and I. Radforth eds., *Colonial Leviathan: State Formation in Mid-Nineteenth Century Canada* (Toronto: University of Toronto Press 1992). In these works, new state institutions such as the professional police and the penitentiary and public education and health are examined from the point of view of moral regulation, expert knowledge, and identity formation where traditional affiliations are broken down and compliant modern citizenship is promoted.
79 31 Vic. c.70, An Act respecting Riots and Riotous Assemblies. For pre-confederation military interventions, outside wars, and the 1837-8 rebellions, see LAC, RG 8, Militia Records, vols. 316–19, 'Military Aid at Riots 1800–1870.' It is estimated that, from 1867 to 1933, the military came to the aid of the civil power on at least 133 occasions, with the threat of popular disorder being the main pretext. See Don Macgillivray, 'Military Aid to the Civil Power: The Cape Breton Experience in the 1820s,' *Acadiensis* 3 (1974): 45.
80 See Binnie, 'The Blake Act,' 215.
81 Concerns around external aggression and internal political unrest rather than the regulation of routine crime appear to be the origin of Canada's gun-control laws, themes that seem undeveloped in the existing literature. See, e.g., Philip C. Stenning, 'Guns and the Law,' *The Beaver* (December 2000/January

2001): 6, Samuel A. Bottomley, 'Parliament, Politics and Policy: Gun Control in Canada, 1867–2003,' PhD thesis, Carleton University 2004.

82　1819, 60 Geo. III and 1 Geo. IV c. 8 (U.K.) (An Act for the More Effectual Prevention and Punishment of Blasphemous Libels and Seditious Libels).

83　[1951] 2 DLR 369, 379 per Kerwin J; 380 per Rand J; 381 per Kellock J; 394 per Esty J; 408–9 per Locke J. In *R v Chief Metropolitan Stipendiary Magistrate: ex parte Choudhury* [1991] 1 QB 429, 452, *Boucher* was cited in support of this formulation as the modern common law in the United Kingdom. New Zealand, which like Canada drew from Stephen's Draft English Code, abolished sedition offences in 2007.

84　*The Case of de Libellis Famosis, or of Scandalous Libels* 77 *English Reports*, 250; Holdsworth, *History, Volume V,* 208; *VII*, 336.

85　32 Geo. III c.60 (U.K.).

86　C. Emsley, 'An Aspect of Pitt's "Terror": Prosecutions for Sedition During the 1790's,' *Social History* 6 (1981): 155; F.K. Prochaska, 'English State Trials in the 1790s: A Case Study,' *Journal of British Studies* 17 (1973): 63; Barrell, *Imagining*; Kevin Gilmartin, *Print Politics: The Press and Radical Opposition in Early Nineteenth Century England* (Cambridge: Cambridge University Press 1996).

87　1819, 60 Geo. III c. 8, An Act for the More Effectual Prevention and Punishment of Blasphemous Libels and Seditious Libels (U.K.).

88　1819, 60 Geo. III c.8 s.1.

89　Stephen, *History, Volume 2,* 366.

90　J. Stephen Watson, *The Reign of George III 1760–1815* (Oxford: Clarendon Press 1960), 520ff. See the appendix to *R. v. Stockdale* (1798), Howell, *State Trials*, 23: 294–305, which is an extract from the *Journal* of the House of Lords and which records the debate and the vote on the Libel Act.

91　Llewellyn Woodward, *The Age of Reform* (Oxford: Clarendon Press 1962), 63.

92　*R. v. Hunt* (1820), Great Britain, State Trials Committee, *Reports of State Trials*, New Series (hereafter *State Trials*, New Series), 8 vols. (London: Eyre and Spottiswood 1888–98), 1: 171, 176, 201, 230–1, 488, 494.; see also, Woodward, *Age*, 62.

93　*R. v. Burdett* , *State Trials, New Series*, 1: 170.

94　See the following essays in *CST 1*: Barry Wright, 'The Gourlay Affair'; Romney, 'Upper Canada in the 1820s'; and Barry Cahill, '*R. v Howe* (1835) for Seditious Libel: A Tale of Twelve Magistrates,' 547–75.

95　Lobban, 'From Seditious Libel.'

96　6&7 Vic. c.96.

97　See Wright, 'Libel and the Colonial Administration of Justice,' 19, 28.

98　*R. v. Collins*, 173 E.R. 911.

99　*R. v. O'Connell*, *State Trials*, New Series, 2: 14.

100 Woodward, *Age*, 335–6.

101 Ibid., 336.

102 *R. v. O'Connell, State Trials*, New Series, 5: 903.

103 See also *The Queen v. Mitchell, State Trials*, New Series, 6: 599; *The Queen v. O'Doherty, State Trials*, New Series, 6: 831; Palmer, *Police and Protest*, 490–501.

104 *Cox's Report of Criminal Cases* ... (hereafter Cox's CC) (London: n.p., 1843–1940), 14: 356. For context, see C.K. Ensor, *England 1870–1914* (Oxford: Clarendon Press 1968), 77–84, 134.

105 Ensor, *England*, 101; *R. V. Burns*, Cox's CC, 14: 358.

106 *R. V. Burns*, Cox's CC, 14: 360.

107 Ibid., 367.

108 Ibid., 364.

109 John Jervis, ed. (London: William Bruce 1893), 883–5.

110 Stephen, *History, Volume 2*, 298.

111 17 April 1886, 423.

112 17 April 1886, 217.

113 *Canadian Law Journal* 22 (1886): 175–6.

114 J.F. Newman, 'Reaction and Change: A Study of the Ontario Bar, 1820–1930,' *University of Toronto Law Review* 32 (1974): 62–3.

115 W.S. Gordon, 'Strikes and Strikers in Their Legal Aspects,' *Canadian Law Times* 3 (1883): 367; P. Edwards, 'Breach of Contract by Strikes,' *Canadian Law Times* 13 (1893): 10.

116 See Wright, 'Gourlay,' Romney, 'Upper Canada in the 1820s,' and Cahill, 'Howe,' in *CST 1*; and Barry Wright, 'Sedition in Upper Canada: Contested Legality,' *Labour/Le Travail* 29 (1992): 7, particularly 56–7.

117 1860, 23 Vic. c.10.

118 Acts of the Legislatures of the Provinces Now Comprised in the Dominion of Canada which Are of a Public Nature (Ottawa: Queen's Printer 1887), 255–8.

119 John Jervis (London: H. Sweet 1874).

120 For example, 1819, 60 Geo. III c.8 s.IV specified that a person convicted of sedition shall 'suffer such punishment as may now by law be inflicted in cases of high misdemeanours, or to be banished from the United Kingdom ... for such term of years as the court in which such conviction shall have taken place shall order.' A more meaningful definition is given in *Jowitt's Dictionary of English Law*: 'At common law the punishment is imprisonment for life and forfeiture of the offenders goods.' John Burke, 2nd ed. (London: Sweet and Maxwell 1977), 2: 1191. As late as 1898, that year's edition of *Archbold's* said: 'The punishment for seditious libel is fine and imprisonment.' See Stephen's strictures on the classification and punishment of misdemeanours which are,

he said 'vague to the last degree' and 'practically useless.' Stephen, *History*, *Volume 1*: 489; *Volume 2*: 194; *Volume 3*: 578.

121 A copy of Burbidge's draft code has not yet been discovered. The information about its content has been taken from 'A New Penal Code' published in the Toronto *Globe*, 30 Aug. 1884, 6.

122 Brown, *Genesis*, 110–13.

123 Ibid., 128.

124 Ibid., 131.

125 House of Commons, *Debates*, esp.16–19 May 1892, cols. 2637–917.

126 House of Commons, Criminal Law Bill. no. 7, art. 122, s.1.

127 House of Commons, *Debates*, 12 April 1892, cols. 1313–14.

128 United Kingdom, Parliament, *Parliamentary Papers, Report of the Royal Commission on the Law relating to Indictable Offences*, 1878–9 [2345], 20, 103.

129 Canada, House of Commons, *Debates*, 19 May 1892, cols. 2830–1. Henry Sacheverell was a high Anglican and a Tory. In 1709 he preached a sermon at St Paul's Cathedral in London which was bitterly critical of the Glorious Revolution of 1689 and in which he advocated a) passive obedience to the crown; b) non-resistance, or the obligation (to a high Anglican) to eschew resistance to the lawful sovereign; and c) the theory of the divine right of kings. In his speech Sacheverall compared the Glorious Revolution to the execution of Charles II, rather than to the foiling of the Gunpowder Plot of 1605, as other speakers were prone to do. This and other comments incurred the wrath of the government party, which convicted him for contempt: *R. v. Sacheverell* (1710), Howell's *State Trials*, 15: 2; G. Holmes, *The Trial of Doctor Sacheverell* (London: Eyre Methuen 1973), 62–8.

130 Canada, House of Commons, *Debates*, 19 May 1892, col. 2833.

131 Ibid., 28 June 1892, col. 4344.

132 See Brown, *Genesis*, 152–3. See also D.H. Brown, 'The Craftsmanship of Bias: Sedition and the Winnipeg Strike Trial, 1919,' *Manitoba Law Journal* 14 (1984): 1. Sedition prosecutions also followed the Cape Breton strikes of 1922. During the trial for seditious conspiracy of the leaders of the Winnipeg General Strike, Mr Justice Metcalf presented a conservative rendition of the common law that was at odds with the more liberal *Burns* precedent. The rise in labour unrest during the last years of the Great War and the outbreak of the Winnipeg General Strike prompted a government committee to consider and report on the law of sedition in May 1919. It recommended an amendment to the section 97 provisions on unlawful associations, drawing upon a 1918 order-in-council under the War Measures Act (which declared named organizations illegal and imposed penalties for printing, publishing, or offering for sale any material that advocated the use of violence to bring about

a change in government) and taking advantage of the failure of Parliament in 1892 to define sedition. Section 133 of the Code, defining what constituted 'lawful criticism' of government,' was also repealed. Sections 97A and 97B became law in October (An Act to Amend the Criminal Code, 1919, 9&10 Geo. V., c.46), the origins of the infamous section 98 that was repealed in 1936.

133 See F. Murray Greenwood, 'The Drafting and Passage of the War Measures Act, 1914 and 1927: Object Lessons in the Need for Vigilance,' in W. Wesley Pue and Barry Wright, eds., *Canadian Perspectives on Law and Society: Issues in Legal History* (Ottawa: Carleton University Press 1988), 291.

APPENDICES

Archival Research and Supporting Documents

Appendix A

The Sir John A. Macdonald Fonds: Research Strategies and Methodological Issues for Archival Research

JUDI CUMMING

The archival fonds of all of Canada's nineteenth-century prime ministers, found at Library and Archives Canada (LAC), provide users with rich documentation on the development of the Canadian state, but the Macdonald fonds is one of the most extensive of the period and a particularly important source for the study of many political and legal aspects of pre- and post-confederation Canada. The purpose of this essay is to highlight Macdonald's close association with state security and criminal law issues and its documentation in his papers.

As the fonds of Canada's first prime minister, the Macdonald papers have received more archival attention than other private archival fonds of the period with regard to preservation, arrangement, description, diffusion, and publication either through conventional means – in print – or by exhibition, including online exhibition. Moreover, in view of the weakness, generally, in the acquisition of the archival record related to nineteenth-century legal history, the papers of Canada's prime ministers have become a heavily used source of information on legal developments as well as aspects of security, a major preoccupation of a young nation both before and certainly after confederation. Efforts to obtain archival papers of prominent members of the judiciary, for instance, to augment primary-source documentation on nineteenth-century legal history at LAC proved to be disappointing.[1]

Macdonald's active public life extended from before the rebellions and invasions of 1837–8 (he was a young defence counsel in 1838 at the

Kingston court-martial proceedings) to the introduction of the Canadian Criminal Code bill in 1891. As we have seen in this volume of *Canadian State Trials*, Macdonald supervised the prosecution of the Fenian raiders in 1866, the development of security branch operations, the Dominion consolidations of criminal law, and the legal responses to the North-West rebellion of 1885, in addition to his prominent role in the politics of this period. An example of documentation on security is the extensive correspondence from Gilbert McMicken as well as his security reports. The papers also document constitutional issues associated with the federation of British North American colonies, law reforms, and the defence of the new state. In addition, Macdonald's professional life as a lawyer and his family life are documented.

Users seeking further information in the context of the national-security and legal themes raised in this volume need an understanding of how this material is arranged and described, with particular attention to general, hierarchical description and reference tools called finding aids. Moreover, certain archival principles act as a framework for the arrangement and description of archival material. The concept of the fonds and the hierarchical nature of the arrangement and description of a fonds are essential components of these principles. In addition, users must be cognizant of technological advances in disseminating not only descriptive information about archival material but also information about the availability of archival records in a variety of forms.

ARCHIVAL PRINCIPLES: THE FONDS CONCEPT AND *RESPECT DES FONDS*

The Sir John A. Macdonald papers are referred to as a 'fonds' because they consist of 'the whole of the records, regardless of form or medium ... accumulated and used by a particular individual ... in the course of that creator's activities or functions.'[2] In general, the Macdonald fonds comprises documents that he created and/or received, accumulated, or used. The fonds was arranged according to the principle of *respect des fonds* and therefore requires different research methodologies than those employed to consult library material. Unlike the subject classification of material found in a library, archival fonds of a specific individual, family, or corporate body are 'kept together in their original order, if it exists or has been maintained, and (are) not mixed ... with the records of another individual or corporate body.'[3]

THE PHYSICAL ARRANGEMENT OF THE MACDONALD FONDS

After the death of Sir John A. Macdonald in 1891, his former secretary, literary executor, and later biographer, Sir Joseph Pope, arranged the letters by subject, correspondent, subjects within each year, and in chronological order respectively. Pope's physical arrangement of Macdonald's papers including subject files, correspondence files, miscellaneous material, general letters, letterbooks, personal and family papers, and legal and financial material has been retained by LAC with some adjustment.[4]

Notwithstanding the modern archival practice of not mixing the fonds of two or more persons, some original letters from Macdonald to other persons were placed in the Macdonald fonds and a search of the finding aid entitled 'List of Contents, Volumes 1–593' reveals this fact. Generally speaking, however, original letters written by Macdonald and received by the intended recipient would be preserved in the fonds of the recipient.

Users should be aware that there are physical gaps in the Macdonald fonds which may affect topics related to state security and criminal law reform. For instance, the letterbooks consist of letterpress copies of letters written by Macdonald or his secretaries spanning the period 1855 to 1891. Although Macdonald habitually retained a copy of his outgoing letters in the form of letterpress copies, there are no copies of outgoing letters for the period 1 November 1873 to 2 October 1878 when he was out of office. Nor can the researcher rely on the letterbooks, which cover specific chronological periods, as proof of the preservation of copies of all of Macdonald's outgoing correspondence for those periods. For instance, he wrote to Sir Henry Sumner Maine, an English legal theorist, on 9 April 1867, concerning both Quebec civil law and tense relations between Canada and the United States. Macdonald was in England when he wrote this letter, not in his office, and it does not appear that a copy was kept. Indeed, there is a likelihood that he may not have retained copies of personal letters that he wrote.[5] Moreover, most of his archival papers relate to the period 1867–91 and are relatively thin for the period after the Pacific scandal and before his return to office.[6] The pre-confederation period, including his legal career, is also more sparsely documented.

Over the years since the acquisition of the Macdonald fonds, many letters written by Macdonald to a variety of individuals have been collected by LAC. Such letters have been identified, in archival terms, as 'single items' rather than as fonds. The unit titles of each of these single items commences, 'Letter from Sir John A. Macdonald to ...,' followed by the

name of the recipient. They complement but are not part of the Macdonald fonds.

THE INTELLECTUAL ARRANGEMENT AND DESCRIPTION OF THE MACDONALD FONDS

The intellectual arrangement of the Macdonald papers is hierarchical in
nature, from the general to specific – fonds, series, items, etc. The highest
or fonds-level description corresponding to this arrangement provides
general information about the whole fonds, including outside dates of the
archival material, total linear extent, and the general nature of the contents. The researcher will also find a lengthy list of subject headings at the
end of the fonds description that, taken together, provide an overview of
the breadth of the subject matter of the various parts of the fonds. Some of
these headings refer to issues of security and of law, for example:

Law – Canada – Cases [1835–74], or,
Secret service – Canada [1843–91],
Fenians [1851–91]

Series-Level Descriptions

There are sixteen series-level descriptions linked to the fonds-level description. They describe personal, political, and family papers according
to identifiable series, for example: 'Personal papers. Legal,' 'Political papers. Letter books,' 'Political papers. Correspondence,' 'Political papers.
Subject files,' etc. The series description for legal material describes archival documents connected with his legal practice, consisting of correspondence with his partners along with dockets of legal cases. The political
subject files contain letters to Macdonald on prominent post-confederation topics.

Item-Level Descriptions

At the lowest level of description, thousands of item-level descriptions
have been linked hierarchically to specific series descriptions. These item-
level descriptions relate to individual documents and consist of subject or
nominal information. Researchers may be able to locate these item-level
descriptions by entering the desired subject or nominal information online at: http://www.search-recherche.collectionscanada.ca/archives.

SPECIALIZED FINDING AIDS

Reference tools called finding aids provide description in greater detail than that provided by hierarchical description. As mentioned above, one of the Macdonald finding aids provides an overview of the entire fonds according to the box or volume number(s). The following list contains examples of entries for certain volumes of the fonds:

> Vols. 48 & 49: Confederation – B.N.A. Act – Drafts, 1867;
> Vol. 55: Constitutional Questions, 1860–1873;
> Vol. 146: Secret Service – Correspondence – G.W. Brega;
> Vols. 538–41: Legal Correspondence, 1835–1874, etc.

Another finding aid, prepared at the document level of description, consists of nominal, subject, and chronological indexes, each of which contains approximately 150,000 entries. It is available for consultation in several formats: on paper, on microfilm, and also online as an 'ArchiviaNet Research Tool' in the prime ministers' fonds database. Using the paper-based format of the finding aid, the researcher may physically browse the lists to get a sense of the extent of archival material on any given subject or person, including varied forms of terms relating to specific subjects or authors.

Searching the Macdonald Finding Aid in the Prime Ministers'
Fonds Database

The Macdonald 'index' was originally prepared in the 1960s on index cards using conventional or natural language. At a later date, when automation became possible, this simple language was converted to an in-house vocabulary of terms whose character length was often severely restricted because of the requirements of the automated system. The words that comprise these terms were often abbreviated to just a few letters, for example:

- Econ for Economic, e.g., Econ Cond for Economic Conditions,[7]
- Def for Defence,
- Amer for American,
- Can for Canadian,
- Dom for Dominion,
- but Constitutional for Constitutional, etc.

Unless the precise term, in its automated format, is known for specific subjects or personal names, or an exact part of the term is provided, relevant references or 'hits' in the automated index are unlikely. The researcher cannot retrieve all appropriate hits if more information than is available for retrieval is provided by the researcher for any automated term. For instance, to find references to Louis Riel, the researcher may input Riel or L Riel but not Louis Riel because the full name was not used in the indexes.

Searching by Personal Surname

A researcher conducting a search of the index for information regarding nineteenth-century security issues might seek references to Gilbert Mc-Micken,[8] who figures prominently in the chapters by David Wilson and Andrew Parnaby and Gregory Kealey with Kirk Niergarth. Since he was a close and trusted associate of Macdonald, a search of the index for the name 'Gilbert McMicken' should be rewarding. However, it yields no results. This occurs because the automated index provides the surname of persons and only a first initial. The researcher's strategy here is to provide the least possible amount of correct data in order to avoid a negative result. Using a first initial *with no period* and the correct spelling of the surname, e.g., G McMicken, or just the surname results in approximately five thousand hits! The researcher can narrow and focus the results by placing words in all three fields: date, subject/correspondent, and keyword of the database:

Example: *Date*: 1864
Subject/Correspondent: G McMicken
Keyword: Secret Service

Searching by Subject

Searching by subject can also be difficult without knowing how terms have been entered in the database. If the researcher has used words to form a term and received no or suspiciously few hits, a strategy for locating information on a given topic is to try a reasonable abbreviation of the words in a term. For instance, no result is obtained for the term British North America Act. However, entering this same term in an abbreviated form as BNA Act results in seventy-one hits:

Example: *Date*: 1867
Subject/Correspondent: J Howe
Keyword: BNA Act

Unfortunately, searching by subject cannot automatically be assumed to involve an abbreviation of English words. The term 'Criminal Code,' for example, appears as such in the database. The following is a particular search that resulted in one hit.

Date: 1881
Subject/Correspondent: A Campbell
Keyword: Criminal Code

Searching by more than one possible form of the subject is sometimes highly beneficial. For example, using the term 'American Civil War' will reveal nothing, but 'US – Civil War' or just 'Civil War' will produce various references. Similarly, there are numerous references in the index to the Dominion Police, the security force formed by the federal government after the assassination of Thomas D'Arcy McGee for purposes including the protection of politicians and, under McMicken, intelligence operations against Fenians. Using the term 'Dominion Police' or the abbreviation 'Dom Police' will result in references that may be useful to the researcher.

Limitations of the Automated Macdonald Indexes

The inclusion of abbreviations in the indexes that are not considered today as standard forms of abbreviation means that this database could benefit from a built-in thesaurus to permit the researcher to search for a topic as he or she understands it using English words in common parlance, for example, North-West rebellion. A thesaurus would direct the user to the term that was actually used in the index, 'NW Rebellion.' Some heavily used terms, such as 'Can-Amer Rels' (meaning Canadian-American Relations), might be indecipherable by modern researchers. With the passage of time, index terms that were once in common usage may lose favour with new researchers. Moreover, in the twenty-first century, there may be new terms that were unknown in the time period when the index was created, or else used with a different meaning. There is also inconsistency in some terms, for example, 'Laws – Codification' and 'Codification of Laws.'

AVAILABILITY OF THE SIR JOHN A. MACDONALD ARCHIVAL FONDS

Most of the Macdonald papers are available for consultation on microfilm so that researchers may consult them outside the confines of the archival institution through the inter-institutional loan of microfilm reels by local libraries that participate in this program. Moreover, for those who travel to LAC, they may also be able to consult the Macdonald papers as 'copy-flow.' These are photocopies of the original documents and may be more pleasant to read than microfilm.

Large portions of the microfilmed Macdonald papers are being made available for consultation online as digitized documents. The digital images of these documents will complement their online, hierarchical description, be it series or item, and be located next to those descriptions. This means that, when the researcher consults the hierarchical descriptions of the Macdonald fonds, they will be able to view many of the documents described at the same time. For example, for the series entitled, 'Family papers. Baroness Macdonald,' the series description is accompanied by a digitized version of her diary which the researcher can read, page by page. Digitization presents the possibility for researchers to conduct all of their archival research wherever a computer and web browser are available. The online hierarchical descriptions from fonds to series and from series to item play a critical role in this process.

CONCLUSION

The concept of the archival fonds and its hierarchical arrangement and description is now pervasive in Canadian archival repositories. An understanding of this concept is needed to conduct archival research effectively in the digital age. The Macdonald fonds is one of many archival units in the custody of Library and Archives Canada that are being digitized and rendered accessible via its website.

Acquired prior to the development of modern archival standards, the fonds of Sir John A. Macdonald and its accompanying reference tools in the form of general, hierarchical description and detailed finding aids have undergone many changes over time to take account of evolving standards and technological capacity. As more and more fonds and collections are digitized, archival research will be revolutionized.

While Macdonald was a prominent figure in many of the events examined in this volume, researchers may turn to numerous other relevant fonds at LAC, of a public or private nature, related to specific subjects, particularly their political, legal, or military dimensions. On the North-West rebellion of 1885, for instance, researchers should have recourse to such public records as the *Sessional Papers* and the records of the Department of Justice. In addition, there are private fonds of military officers in the latter quarter of the nineteenth century who served during the 1885 rebellion as well as papers of Louis Riel acquired from a variety of sources. And, of course, on a topic such as Riel there are important archival holdings elsewhere, as explored by Gilles Lesage in the essay that follows.

NOTES

1 The Systematic National Acquisition Programme of the Public Archives of Canada was started in 1967 to locate extant archival papers of Canadian leaders including members of the judiciary. It was most successful in locating twentieth-century archival records since many nineteenth-century records had disappeared, particularly those dating to the last quarter of that century. In part, the loss of nineteenth-century records was due to the introduction of acidic paper which deteriorated rapidly.

2 Bureau of Canadian Archivists, *Rules for Archival Description* (Ottawa: 1990), D-3.

3 *Rules*, D-5.

4 *Manuscript Group 26, Prime Ministers' Papers: Preliminary Inventory* (Ottawa: Public Archives of Canada 1958).

5 Richard Gwyn, *John A. The Man Who Made Us: The Life and Times of John A. Macdonald, Volume One: 1815–1867* (Toronto: Random House Canada 2007), 452.

6 *Manuscript Group 26* (Ottawa: Public Archives of Canada 1958).

7 The researcher needs to enter data once as 'Economic' and once as 'Econ' to retrieve all possible references.

8 McMicken 'led a detective force which prevented Confederate agents from using Canada as a military base. The spy network he established served him ... in the 1860s when as chief commissioner of Dominion Police, he kept the radical Fenian movement under close observation, greatly diminishing its threat to Canada.' Biographical sketch by Edward Butts, in James H. Marsh, ed., *The Canadian Encyclopedia* (Toronto: McClelland and Stewart 2000), 1405.

Appendix B

Archival Sources in Canada for Riel's Rebellion

GILLES LESAGE

Albert Braz, in his 2003 study entitled *The False Traitor: Louis Riel in Canadian Culture*, examines the multiple and varying representations of Riel in English and French literary sources. He writes in his introduction: 'Since his hanging for treason on November 16, 1885, [Riel] has been depicted variously as a traitor to Confederation, a French-Canadian and Catholic martyr, a bloodthirsty rebel, a New World liberator, a pawn of shadowy white forces, a Prairie political maverick, an Aboriginal hero, a deluded mystic, an alienated intellectual, a victim of Western industrial progress, and even a Father of Confederation.'[1]

Riel has been researched over the years from many of these perspectives, and archival materials that document him personally as well as his actions, and the people with whom he interacted, have been fundamental to many publications, as well as to representations of Riel in other media. In fact, so large does Riel loom in Canadian culture that Braz suggests that Riel has made 'it into the company of William Tell, Robin Hood and El Cid.'[2]

Riel's controversial trial in 1885 is still of great interest and, as shown in the chapter by J.M. Bumsted in this volume, has generated much academic debate. The chapters by Louis Knafla, Bob Beal and Barry Wright, and Bill Waiser examine the lesser-known prosecutions of Riel's associates and together these cases demonstrate the complexity of the issues involved. Yet Riel was at the centre of events before and after the North-West rebellion and his trial is the most prominent and the most contentious of the rebellion cases. Indeed, it is the most famous treason trial in

Canadian history. In addition, the historical context of the ongoing Métis struggle in the 1870s and 1880s for recognition as a people continues to inform recent Métis negotiations for governmental acceptance of their collective rights. Riel's trial also continues to provoke popular and political debate, as efforts over the last few decades to obtain a posthumous pardon or to exonerate Riel have demonstrated.[3]

In studying the prosecution of Riel for high treason, it is essential to explore the full range of issues raised at his trial, such as his mental health and his theological positions vis à vis the Catholic Church. It is also important to consider the views of contemporary supporters and detractors of Riel, as well as prevailing laws and procedures, in order to better measure the extent to which justice prevailed or failed to prevail. Archival material is crucial to these and related endeavours. A large number of archival sources is listed below that document the trial itself and also provide background information on the 1885 Métis uprising and on events at Batoche. However, sources are so numerous that no attempt has been made to consider the relevance of these or other archival holdings to the trials of many other accused also prosecuted after the rebellion, whether First Nations, Métis, or white.

SOURCES

Three important sources for the trial record should be noted at the outset. First, many of the main government documents relating to the 1885 proceedings were published in the 1886 Government of Canada *Sessional Papers*, now available online through 'Early Canadiana Online.'[4] Secondly, Desmond Morton's 1974 book, *The Queen v Louis Riel*, reproduces the Riel trial transcripts.[5] Finally, collections of contemporary newspaper reports of the trial are readily available either in library holdings or through online sources.

For Riel's writing, the reader is referred to the five volumes edited by George F.G. Stanley, *The Collected Writings of Louis Riel: Les Écrits complets de Louis Riel*,[6] which contain all of Riel's known writings, including letters, notes, drafts, telegrams, contracts, public notices, agreements, declarations, minutes, ordinances, addresses, proclamations, petitions, briefs, memoranda, autographs, revelations, interviews, diaries, prayers, and poetry.

ARCHIVES

The various archival fonds identified below are grouped geographically, with those located at the national archives, Library and Archives Canada, in Ottawa listed first, followed by those in other archival institutions in the provinces of Quebec, Ontario, Manitoba, and Alberta.

Ottawa

Canadian Psychiatric Association Fonds, Library and Archives Canada, Ottawa. 1854–1979. 1.18 m of textual records.

While the records of this professional association contain very few documents on Louis Riel, they could shed light on the perspectives of the time pertaining to mental health.

The Archival Reference Number is: R3387-0-4-E. To consult or to order copies of documents, reseachers should use the former Archival Reference Number: MG28-I165, vols. 1 to 6.[7]

Edgar Dewdney Fonds, Library and Archives Canada, Ottawa. 1861–1926. 35 cm. of textual records.

Edgar Dewdney was Indian commissioner for Manitoba and the North-West Territories from 1879 to 1888. This fonds consists mostly of correspondence relating to the North- West rebellion,[8] including correspondence from Louis Riel and from political and military figures. Part of the Dewdney records includes a series titled 'Northwest Rebellion,' with correspondence organized in alphabetical order. Some items are numbered and this has led archivists to believe that they were organized with regard to Riel's trial. See also holdings at the Glenbow Archives for Dewdney, identified below.

The Archival Reference Number is: R4505-0-2-E. The former Archival Reference Number is MG 27 IC4.

Fonds François-Xavier Lemieux, Library and Archives Canada, Ottawa. [ca 1819]–1933. 25 cm of textual records.

Sir François-Xavier Lemieux was a renowned Quebec criminal lawyer who defended Louis Riel. This fonds contains correspondence, biographical information, and other documents.

The Archival Reference Number is: R6043-0-5-F. To consult or to order copies of documents, researchers should use the former Archival Reference Number and the volume number: MG 27-IF6, vols. 1 to 3.

Fonds François-Xavier Valade, Library and Archives Canada, Ottawa. 1885. 0.9 cm. of textual records (38 pp.).

This fonds consists of a report on the mental condition of Louis Riel based on an examination while he was in prison at Regina and submitted to Sir John A. Macdonald in 1885; and a letter from Sir John A. Macdonald requesting the report's preparation and transmission in cypher, dated 31 October 1885.

François-Xavier Valade, physician, was one of three doctors responsible for re-examining Louis Riel as a result of the insistence of French Canadian cabinet colleagues of Sir John A. Macdonald. Valade, a well-known practitioner in Ottawa, as well as Dr Augustus Jukes of Regina and Dr Michael Lavell, a specialist in obstetrics and warden of the Kingston penitentiary, were instructed to report to the government on whether Riel was reasonable and accountable for his actions and therefore fit for execution. Valade concluded that Riel was not an accountable being and therefore unfit for execution. However, his testimony was falsified by the ministry in the report submitted to Parliament in 1886 in order to make it appear that he had agreed with the other two doctors who believed that Riel was sane.[9]

The Archival Reference Number is: R7047-0-4-E. The former Archival Reference Number is: MG 27-IJ8. To consult this material or to order copies of documents, researchers should use the former Archival Reference Number. There is one volume.

Gilbert Bagnini Collection, Library and Archives Canada, Ottawa. 1865–1890. 47 photographs.
These photographs document the 1885 trials and include photographs of the North-West Mounted Police barracks, the Regina Court House, the Guard House, other related buildings and locations, some of the jurors, some witnesses, and prisoners and other persons related to the North-West rebellion. They were collected by Christopher Robinson, one of the crown prosecutors at the trial of Louis Riel, and passed down by family descent to Gilbert Bagnini.

The Archival Reference Number is: R8237-0-4-E.

Louis Riel Collection, Library and Archives Canada, Ottawa. 1860–1970. 7.6 cm. of textual records.
This collection contains letters both sent to and received from Louis Riel, as well as poems and other writings of Riel's.[10] It also contains copies of proclamations, minutes, and bills pertaining to political events of the Red River colony, 1869–70, and to the North-West Territories in 1885.

The Archival Reference Number is: R5768-0-1-F. The former Archival Reference Number is: MG 27-IF3.

North West Field Force Fonds, Library and Archives Canada, Ottawa. 1885. 2.5 cm. of textual records.
This material documents the battles of Batoche and includes a list of wounded, receipt books for supplies, and brigade orders.

The Archival Reference Number is: R6625-0-8-E. The former Archival Reference Number is: MG 29 E75.

Records relating to Louis Riel and the North West Uprising (series), Department of Justice fonds. Library and Archives Canada, Ottawa. 1873–1886. 1.1 m. of textual records.
This series consists of correspondence, memoranda, notes, various drafts of poems, prayers, and other Riel papers, as well as notes, warrants, charges, statements and briefs of evidence, magistrate's reports, and an account book of witness expenditures (1885). Many of the documents in this series were among Riel's private papers seized at Batoche on 11 May 1885.

The documents in this series have been described to the item level online and linked hierarchically to the series description. The Archival Reference Number for this particular series in the Department of Justice fonds is: R188-61-1-E, or in French, R188-61-1-F. Researchers should use the former Archival Reference Number for this series, RG 13-F-2, plus the volume number, for purposes of on-site consultation or for copying. RG 13-F-2, volumes 804 to 825 and 2132, are available on microfilms C-1228 to C-1231 (the researcher may be required to use microfilm).

Sir John A. Macdonald Fonds, Library and Archives Canada, Ottawa. 1827–1971. 36.82 m. of textual records. (See preceding essay by Judi Cumming.)
In addition to the textual records, there is also cartographic material, photographs, and a technical drawing (see preceding essay by Judi Cumming).

This fonds consists of the political, personal, and family papers of Sir John A. Macdonald. The political papers document the shaping of a new nation and cover such key events as railway construction, the expansion of national boundaries, and a wide range of other topics including government administration and Native affairs.

There are numerous documents relating to Louis Riel. For the year 1885, the finding aid to the Macdonald papers lists more than 500 references to Louis Riel, relating to such matters as his capture at Batoche, his mental state, legal counsel, trial and execution, and so on.

The former Archival Reference Number is: MG 26-A. To consult this material or to order copies of documents, researchers should use this number plus the volume number and the copyflow or the microfilm reel number. Generally speaking, researchers consult the copyflow or the microfilm for research purposes.

Quebec

Fonds Famille Joly de Lotbinière, Bibliothèque et Archives nationales du Québec. Quebec. 1798–1921. 2.43 m. of textual documents.
This material includes the papers of Henri-Gustave Joly de Lotbinière (1829–1906), who was active in Quebec politics from 1861 to 1885 and in federal politics from 1896 to 1900. In 1885 he corresponded with Major-General Thomas Bland Strange, who organized the Alberta Field Force for the defence of that region. The documents present his views on the Métis rebellion and the resulting course of action taken to deal with Riel. He disagreed with Honoré Mercier's position and relinquished his seat for this reason.
The Archival Reference Number is: P 351.

Fonds de la famille McLeod, Archives of Séminaire St-Joseph. 5 cm. of textual records.
Pierre McLeod was a journalist for two Montreal newspapers, *La Minerve* and *Le Monde*. He was sent to Regina in 1885 to cover Louis Riel's trial. This fonds may contain comments on the trial.

Fonds Famille Mercier, Bibliothèque et Archives nationales du Québec, Montreal. 1772–1987. 6.44 m. of textual records, 409 photographs.
This fonds includes papers of Honoré Mercier, Sr (1840–94), lawyer, journalist, and Quebec politician. Son of a Patriote, a provincial Liberal and leader of the party in 1885, Honoré Mercier was a committed nationalist. His papers include discussion of Riel's break with the Catholic Church, his relationship through blood and culture to French Canadians, and the acquittals of William Henry Jackson and Thomas Scott. Mercier was opposed to Riel's hanging and lobbied Governor General Lord Lansdowne for a pardon for Riel. Also found in this fonds are photographs of Louis Riel's family.
The Archival Reference Number is: P 74.

Fonds François-Xavier Lemieux, Bibliothèque et Archives nationales du Québec. Quebec. 1814–1938. 1.68 m. of textual records.
François-Xavier Lemieux was called to the bar in 1872, and his reputation as a defence lawyer led to his agreeing to defend Louis Riel in 1885.

His professional life is documented in his letters, which also contain notes pertaining to various court cases. Among these are records relative to the Louis Riel trial which include letters from Charles Fitzpatrick (another Riel defence lawyer), Wilfrid Laurier (Liberal federal politician who actively campaigned against the execution of Louis Riel), Honoré Mercier (leader of the Quebec provincial Liberal Party in 1885), and Joseph-Israel Tarte (journalist and politician who was ambivalent about the 1885 *Affaire Riel*).

The Archival Reference Number is: P 145.

Fonds Hector Langevin, Bibliothèque et Archives nationales du Québec, Quebec. 1672–1967. 4.5 m. of textual records.
This fonds documents the political career of Hector Langevin, minister of public works (1879–91) in the Macdonald government. Of particular interest are documents relating to the *troubles du Nord-Ouest* and the execution of Louis Riel. Certain files pertain directly to Louis Riel and events in the North-West in 1884–5.

The Archival Reference Number is: P 134.

Fonds Jacques-Ferdinand Verret, Bibliothèque et Archives nationales du Québec. Quebec. 1857–1947. 1.06 m. of textual records.
Verret, a businessman, poet, and prolific writer, also kept a personal diary. His fonds documents his commercial activities as a businessman and, besides his poetry, includes forty-one volumes of his diary as well as documents pertaining to Louis Riel's execution.

The Archival Reference Number is: P 819.

Fonds Joseph-Adolphe Chapleau, Bibliothèque et Archives nationales du Québec. Montreal. 1885–95. 7 textual records.
Chapleau was secretary of state in Macdonald's government (1882–91). These papers contain newspaper clippings on Louis Riel's hanging and two letters from that period.

The Archival Reference Number is: P 1000, D 100.

Fonds Nazaire Le Vasseur et Arthur Évanturel, Bibliothèque et Archives nationales du Québec Quebec. 1885. 05 m. of textual records.
Both Nazaire Le Vasseur and Arthur Évanturel were members of the 9th Battalion of the Québec Voltigeurs in the Canadian militia and each kept a record of the 1885 campaign. Arthur Évanturel's account of the campaign is in log format: it includes daily information about the temperature, the events of the trip, troop movements, places he went to, and

people he met. Very different in approach, the diary of Nazaire Le Vasseur includes, besides the specifics of the campaign, details pertaining to the culture and customs of the people he encountered. Also included in these records is a study of the Riel rebellion by Jean-Yves Gravel. The Archival Reference Number is: P 52.

Ontario

Centre for Addiction and Mental Health, Queen Street Site Fonds, Centre for Addiction and Mental Health Archives, Toronto. 1888–2004. 4.7 m. of textual records.
The Centre's Queen Street site dates to 1839. Dr Daniel Clark was medical superintendent of the centre from 1875 to 1905 and was called as a defence witness at Louis Riel's trial. In 1887 he published *A Psycho-Medical History of Louis Riel.*[11] The material could provide some insight into the thinking of Daniel Clark on mental health and the perspectives of the time on the same subject.

Deschâtelets Archives, Ottawa
This archives holds the fonds of various Oblate jurisdictions in different provinces of Canada and the personal papers of many Oblates, including Alexis André, Vital Fourmond, Julien Moulin, and Valentin Végréville, all of whom were involved, directly or indirectly, in the 1885 North-West rebellion or in Louis Riel's trial. Alexis André was with Riel in Regina and accompanied him on his way to the gallows. Vital Fourmond was a missionary at Saint-Laurent de Grandin. From 1882 to 1914, Julien Moulin was a missionary at Saint-Antoine de Batoche. He was injured in 1885. Between 1880 and 1885, Valentin Végréville was a missionary in Batoche, Prince Albert, Saint-Louis, and Duck Lake. In 1885 he and Vital Fourmond were taken prisoner by the Métis. The Deschâtelets Archives also include the personal papers of Adrien-Gabriel Morice and Jules Le Chevallier,[12] both of whom wrote extensively on the Métis and the 1885 rebellion. Here as well are records of Alexandre Taché, archbishop of Saint-Boniface, and Vital-Justin Grandin, bishop of Saint-Albert.

Featherstone Osler Family Fonds, Archives of Ontario, 1738–1949. 1.5 m. of textual records.
Britton Bath Osler (1839–1901) was a prosecuting lawyer at Louis Riel's trial. This fonds contains personal and business letters of Osler's which may give insights on the man and his views.
The Archival Reference Number is: F 1032.

Manitoba

Fonds Corporation archiépiscopale catholique romaine de Saint-Boni-face, Société historique de Saint-Boniface Archives, Winnipeg. 1818–2000. 12.8 m. of textual records.
This fonds includes a series for Alexandre Taché, archbishop of Saint-Boniface. The series documents the events of 1885 and Taché's role in relation to the rebellion. The documentation includes Taché's positions on Louis Riel's apostasy via-à-vis the Catholic Church, issues related to Métis grievances in 1884 and 1885, and his efforts to have Riel's death sentence commuted and to defend Métis rights after 1885. Of particular interest is the report commissioned by Taché from Gabriel Cloutier, a member of Taché's secular clergy. This report contains the testimony of many Métis whom Cloutier questioned in 1886 as he travelled across the Batoche region documenting the rebellion and the current condition of the people. Also included in the Taché series is correspondence with Louis Riel, François-Xavier Lemieux, Charles Fitzpatrick, James Greenshields, and fathers Alexis André (Louis Riel's confessor in Regina in 1885), Vital Fourmond, Albert Lacombe, Julien Moulin, Valentin Végréville, and Louis Schmidt. In addition the fonds includes a series for Archbishop Adélard Langevin. Langevin had commissioned a biography of Taché and this led Langevin to contact various people involved in events surrounding Taché's life, including Riel's defence lawyers.

Fonds Louis Riel, Société historique de Saint-Boniface Archives, Winnipeg. 1875–1980. 60 cm. of textual records.
This collection includes many of the original writings of Louis Riel. These were published in 1985 with all other known writings of Riel in G.F.G. Stanley's collected edition.[13]

Fonds La Société historique métisse, Société historique de Saint-Boniface Archives, Winnipeg. 1874–1940. 1.13 m. of textual records.
This fonds includes records assembled for the purpose of preparing a history of the Métis people from a Métis perspective. Auguste Henri de Trémaudan was commissioned to write this history, which was first published under the title *Histoire de la nation métisse dans l'ouest canadien.*[14] The papers include some of Louis Riel's writings and correspondence to him from a number of different people. There is an interview with Gabriel Dumont at the end of the century giving his memories of the events of 1885, including descriptions of the Battle of Batoche and the Battle of Fish Creek.

Fonds Union nationale métisse Saint-Joseph du Manitoba, Société historique de Saint-Boniface Archives, Winnipeg. 1887–1992. 1.9 m. of textual records.
This fonds contains additional materials for the project of a history of the Métis nation from the Métis perspective, which culminated in the publication of Auguste Henri de Trémaudan's book.[15]

George A. Flinn Collection, Archives of Manitoba , Winnipeg. 1884–1935. 3.6 cm. of textual records.
George A. Flinn was a journalist and correspondent for the Winnipeg *Sun*. He kept a diary and took extensive notes during the 1885 Batoche campaign and the Riel trial. The records include an interview with Riel and correspondence with some of the protagonists in the events of 1885. Also included are Flinn's typed memoirs for 1882–5.

Kenneth Hayes – Northwest Rebellion Photograph Collection, University of Manitoba Archives and Special Collections, Winnipeg. 1869–90. 18 photographs.
This collection contains photographs from the 1885 rebellion.
The Archival Reference Number is: A.98-15.

Pitblado Family Fonds, University of Manitoba Archives and Special Collections, Winnipeg. 1836–1977. 2.9 m. of textual records.
Includes documents belonging to Charles Bruce Pitblado, Isaac Pitblado's son, which relate to the rebellion. Charles Pitblado was a Presbyterian minister and a chaplain with the Canadian forces at Batoche. He accompanied Louis Riel, then a prisoner, to Regina.
The Archival Reference Number is: MSS 48.

Alberta

Canadian Pacific Railway, Western Division, Riel Rebellion Telegrams Fonds, Glenbow Archives, Calgary. 1885. 9 cm. of textual records.
The Canadian Pacific Railway Company offered its services to move troops, animals, equipment, and provisions to the North-West Territories during the 1885 uprising. The company also provided communications support. The fonds consists of telegrams received by the company in its Winnipeg Office pertaining to the rebellion.
The Archival Reference Number is: M 2286.

Edgar Dewdney Fonds, Glenbow Archives, Calgary. 1861–1926. 88 cm. of textual records.

This collection includes diaries, reports, and news clippings kept by Edgar Dewdney when he was Indian commissioner (1879–88) and lieutenant governor of the North-West Territories (1881–92). Documenting in particular the North-West rebellion and Louis Riel's trial, it complements the records at Library and Archives Canada.

Jukes Family Fonds, Glenbow Archives, Calgary. 1814–1950. 50 cm of textual records.

Augustus Louis Jukes was a medical doctor stationed at Regina in 1885 who saw Riel often in the Regina jail. He was called as a witness at Riel's trial and declared him to be sane.

Louis Riel Collection, Glenbow Archives, Calgary. 1869–1969. 3 cm. of textual records and six photographs.

This collection includes Samuel Plunkett's letters and photographs and a letter by Dr Romuald Fiset, all pertaining to the North-West rebellion. Fiset had been Riel's classmate in Montreal; he helped to secure funds for Riel's trial and negotiated the services of Fitzpatrick, Greenshields, and Lemieux as Riel's lawyers. Samuel Plunkett served with the Queen's Own Regiment in 1885.

Oblates of Mary Immaculate Province of Alberta-Saskatchewan Archives Fonds, Provincial Archives of Alberta, Edmonton. 1842–1984. 51.5 m. of textual records, 30,000 photographs, 140 cartographic materials, 90 sets of drawings and plans.

This fonds includes administrative records and personal papers of Bishop Vital Grandin and fathers Vital Fourmond, Valentin Vegréville (including an 1885 journal), Julien Moulin, and Jules Le Chevallier, all of whom were Oblate priests in the west at the time of the rebellion. It also includes the journal of the Soeurs Fidèles Compagnes de Jésus of Saint-Laurent during the uprising, the 'Petite Chronique' de Saint-Laurent (1874–1891), Saint-Laurent de Grandin, and surrounding areas (1875–93), and many more records documenting the situation in the North-West leading up to the rebellion. In addition, these records contain documents on Riel, the North-West rebellion, and the ensuing trials, as well as the papers of Jules Le Chevallier, who researched and gathered information for a book on the rebellion.[16] Some of the events are also documented in parish and mission records and these include Onion Lake records (also documents events at Frog Lake) and the *Codex Historicus* of Battleford. A detailed guide to these records, *A Guide to the Archives of the Oblates of Mary Immaculate Province of Alberta-Saskatchewan*, was published by Brian M. Owens and Claude M. Roberto.[17]

Richard Burton Deane Fonds, Glenbow Archives, Calgary. 1847–1962. 12.5 cm. of textual records.
Richard Burton Deane was appointed superintendent of the North-West Mounted Police in 1884. His records include reminiscences of the Louis Riel trial.

Robert Kellock Allan Fonds, Glenbow Archives, Calgary. 1881–1942. 5 cm. of textual records.
This fonds includes Robert Kellock Allan's diary, postcards to his family, and correspondence while he served in the 90th Winnipeg Rifles and participated in the Batoche campaign.

Sisters of the Faithful Companions of Jesus Fonds, Glenbow Archives, Calgary. 1883–1983. 43 cm. of textual records.
This order, established at Saint-Laurent de Grandin in 1885, kept annual records of its activities and some of these records relate in part to the North-West rebellion.

William Pearce Fonds, University of Alberta Archives, Edmonton. 1858–1930. 15.66 m. of textual records.
William Pearce was chief adviser to the Department of the Interior on matters pertaining to the development of the North-West until 1884. He prepared a report on the causes of the North-West Rebellion.

NOTES

The author wishes to express his gratitude to Judi Cumming for her assistance with descriptions and references for fonds in the collection of Library and Archives Canada.

1 Albert Braz, *The False Traitor: Louis Riel in Canadian Culture* (Buffalo, N.Y.: University of Toronto Press 2003).
2 Ibid., 17.
3 Bill C-257, 1999 (to reverse the conviction of Louis Riel) and Bill C-417, 1998

(an exoneration bill). In September 1983 William Yurko, MP, proposed a private member's bill to pardon Louis Riel. In 1996 the House of Commons voted 112 to 103 against a Bloc Québécois' bill rehabilitating Riel. On 13 Feb. 1998 Suzanne Tremblay, MP, presented a motion to declare nul and void the 1885 judgment of high treason. On 3 June 1998 two MPs, Denis Coderre and Reg Alcock, presented a bill to rehabilitate Louis Riel, declare him innocent, and make him a father of confederation. On 21 Oct. 1999 MP Marlene Jennings raised the issue of Louis Riel's death sentence in the House of Commons. In December 2001 Senator Thelma Chalifoux introduced a further bill to exonerate Louis Riel. See Radio-Canada's news clip, 'Une depute à la défense de Riel,' broadcast 13 Feb. 1998, and 'Les Métis et leurs droits ancestraux,' broadcast 19 July 1998, at http://www.archives.cbc.ca.

4 CIHM.

5 Desmond Morton, *The Queen v Louis Riel* (Toronto: University of Toronto Press 1973).

6 George F.G. Stanley acted as general editor of *The Collected Writings of Louis Riel / Les écrits complets de Louis Riel* (Edmonton: University of Alberta Press 1985). It consists of: *Volume 1, 29 December / décembre 1861 – 7 December / décembre 1875*, edited by Raymond Huel; *Volume 2, 8 December / décembre 1875 – 4 June / juin 1884*, edited by Gilles Martel; *Volume 3, 5 June / juin 1884 – 16 November / novembre 1885*, edited by Thomas Flanagan; *Volume 4, Poetry / Poésie* edited by Glen Campbell; and *Volume 5, Reference / Référence*, edited by George F.G. Stanley, Thomas Flanagan, and Claude Rocan.

7 Here and below, when a former Archival Reference Number is given, researchers wishing to consult this material or order copies of documents should use that number plus the volume number and copyflow or mircrofilm reel number.

8 The following terms are used in the English-language historical literature to describe the same events in 1885: 'North-West Resistance,' 'Métis Resistance,' 'North-West Rebellion,' 'North-West Uprising,' and 'Riel's Rebellion'; this volume generally uses 'North-West rebellion.' In French, the expressions 'les troubles du Nord-Ouest,' 'l'Affaire Riel,' and 'la résistance des Métis' are also used interchangeably.

9 See Thomas Flanagan, *The Riel 'Lunacy Commission': The Report of Dr. Valade, Revue de l'Université d'Ottawa* 46 (January-March 1976): 108–27. The article contains references to a number of related documents and includes François-Xavier Valade's report.

10 The fonds contains original documents now published in Stanley's volumes.

11 Daniel Clark, *A Psycho-Medical History of Louis Riel* (Baltimore, Md., Utica, N.Y., 1887).

12 Jules Le Chevallier, *Les missionnaires du Nord-Ouest pendant les troubles de 1885* (Montreal: L'œuvre de presse Dominicaine 1941). This publication includes Gabriel Dumont's interview giving his memories of 1885. See Fonds La Société historique métisse.

13 Stanley, ed., *Collected Writings*.

14 Henri de Trémaudan, *Histoire de la nation métisse dans l'Ouest canadien* (Montreal: Éditons A. Levesque 1935).

15 Ibid.

16 Chevallier, *Les missionnaires du Nord Ouest*.

17 Brian M. Owens and Claude M. Roberto, *A Guide to the Archives of the Oblates of Mary Immaculate, Province of Alberta-Saskatchewan/ Guide pour les archives des Oblats de Marie Immaculée, Province d'Alberta-Saskatchewan* (Edmonton: Missionary Oblates, Grandin Province 1989).

Appendix C

Supporting Documents

1. THE FENIANS

a) Suspension of Habeas Corpus (Brown, Wilson)

29–30 Vic. c.1 (1866, Province of Canada)
An Act to authorize the apprehension and detention until the eighth day of June, one thousand eight hundred and sixty-seven, of such persons as shall be suspected of committing acts of hostility or conspiring against Her Majesty's Person and Government.

[*Assented to 8th June, 1866*]

Whereas certain evil disposed persons being subjects or citizens of Foreign Countries at peace with Her Majesty, have lawlessly invaded this Province, with hostile intent, and whereas other similar lawless invasions of and hostile incursions into the Province are threatened: Her Majesty, by and with the advice and consent of the Legislative Council and Assembly of Canada; enacts as follows:

1. All and every person and persons who is, are or shall be within Prison in this Province at, upon, or after the day of the passing of this Act, by warrant of commitment signed by any two Justices of the Peace, or under capture or arrest made with or without Warrant, by any of the officers, non-commissioned officers or men of Her Majesty's Regular, Militia or Volunteer Militia Forces, or by any of the officers or men of Her Majesty's Navy, and charged;

With being or continuing in arms against Her Majesty within this Province;

Or with any act of hostility therein;

Or with having entered this Province with design or intent to levy war against Her Majesty, to commit any felony therein;

Or with levying war against Her Majesty in company with any other subjects or citizens of any Foreign State or Country then at peace with Her Majesty;

Or with entering this Province in company with any such subjects or citizens with the intent to levy war on Her Majesty, or to commit any act of Felony therein;

Or with joining himself to any person or persons whatsoever, with the design or intent to aid and assist him or them whether subjects or aliens, who have entered or may enter this Province with design or intent to levy war on Her Majesty, or to commit any felony within the same;

Or charged with High Treason or treasonable practices, or suspicion of high Treason, or treasonable practices;

May be detained in safe custody without Bail or mainprize until the eighth Day of June, one thousand eight hundred and sixty-seven, and no Judge or Justice of the Peace shall bail or try any such person or persons so committed, captured or arrested without order from Her Majesty's Executive Council, until the eighth day of June, one thousand eight hundred and sixty seven, any Law or Statute to the contrary notwithstanding; provided, that if within fourteen days after the date of any warrant of commitment, the same or copy thereof certified by the party in whose custody such person is detained, be not countersigned, by a clerk of the Executive Council, then any person or persons detained in custody under any such warrant of commitment for any of the causes aforesaid by virtue of this Act, may apply to be and may be admitted to Bail.

2. In cases where any person or persons have been, before the passing of this Act or shall be during the time this Act shall continue in force arrested, committed or detained in custody by force of a warrant of commitment of any two Justices of the Peace for any of the causes in the preceding section mentioned, it shall and may be lawful for any person or persons to whom such warrant or warrants have been or shall be directed to detain such person or persons so arrested or committed, in his or their custody, in any place whatever within this Province, and such person or persons to whom such warrant or warrants have been or shall be directed, shall be deemed and taken to be to all intents and purposes lawfully authorized to detain in safe custody, and to be the lawful Gaolers and Keepers of such persons so arrested; committed or detained, and such place or places; where such person or persons so arrested, committed or detained, are or shall be detained in custody, shall be deemed and taken to all intents and purposes to be lawful prisons and gaols for the detention and safe custody of such person and persons respectively; and it shall and may be lawful to and for Her Majesty's Executive Council by warrant signed by a Clerk of the said Executive Council to change the person or persons by whom and the place, in which person or persons so arrested, committed or detained, shall be detained in safe custody.

3. The Governor may, by Proclamation, as and so often as he may see fit, suspend the operation of this Act, or within the period aforesaid, again declare the same to be in full force and effect, and, upon any such Proclamation, this Act shall be suspended or of full force and effect as the case may be ...

31 Vic. c.16 (1867, Dominion of Canada) [Renewal and extension of suspension]

[*Assented to 21st December, 1867*]

Whereas certain evil-disposed persons; being: subjects or citizens of Foreign Countries at peace with Her Majesty, have lawlessly invaded this Province, with hostile intent, and whereas other similar lawless invasions of and hostile incursions into Canada are threatened: Her Majesty, by and with the advice and consent of the Senate and House of Common of Canada; enacts as follows:

1. All and every person and persons who is, are or shall be within Prison in Canada at, upon, or after the day of the passing of this Act, by warrant of commitment signed by any two Justices of the Peace, or under capture or arrest made with or without Warrant, by any of the officers, non-commissioned officers or men of Her Majesty's Regular, Militia or Volunteer Militia Forces, or by any of the officers or men of Her Majesty's Navy, and charged;

With being or continuing in arms against Her Majesty in Canada;

Or with any act of hostility therein;

Or with having entered Canada with design or intent to levy war against Her Majesty, to commit any felony therein;

Or with levying war against Her Majesty in company with any other subjects or citizens of any Foreign State or Country then at peace with Her Majesty;

Or with entering Canada in company with any such subjects or citizens with the intent to levy war on Her Majesty, or to commit any act of Felony therein;

Or with joining himself to any person or persons whatsoever, with the design or intent to aid and assist him or them whether subjects or aliens, who have entered or may enter Canada with design or intent to levy war on Her Majesty, or to commit any felony within the same;

Or charged with High Treason or treasonable practices, or suspicions of High Treason, or treasonable practices;

May be detained in safe custody without Bail or mainprize until the first day of December, one thousand eight hundred and sixty-eight, and no Judge or Justice of the Peace shall bail or try any such person or persons so committed, captured or arrested without order from the Queen's Privy Council for Canada, until the day after the termination of the first session held after the first day of December, one thousand eight hundred and sixty eight, any Law or Statute to the contrary notwithstanding; provided, that if within one month after the date of any warrant of commitment, the same or copy thereof certified by the party in whose custody any such person or persons detained under it, be not countersigned, by a clerk of the Queen's Privy Council for Canada, then any person or persons detained in custody under warrant of commitment for any of the causes aforesaid by virtue of this Act, may apply to be and may be admitted to Bail.

[Remaining provisions, sections 2–4, identical except for references to the relevant new institutional bodies]

b) The Fenian Acts (Brown)

The original legislation, Upper Canada's Lawless Aggressions Act, 1 Vic. c.3 (1838), is reproduced in the Supporting Documents of *CST 2*.

The British law officers recommended disallowance of this act (28, 31 May and 21 August 1838) but the legislation was upheld by the British government. The act was amended in 1840 (SUC c.12) and became c.98 of the Consolidated Statutes of Upper Canada. This legislation continued in effect in Canada West in 1866 and was extended to Canada East on 8 June 1866 by way of 'An Act to Protect the Inhabitants of Lower Canada against Lawless Aggressions from Subjects of Foreign Countries at Peace with Her Majesty' (29–30 Vic. c.2).

On 15 August 1866 amending legislation was enacted (29–30 Vic. c.3 for Lower Canada, 29–30 Vic. c.4 for Upper Canada), thus taking effect before the Fenian trials commenced in October. The amendment repealed the third section of the recently passed act for Lower Canada and the same section of c.98 of the Consolidated Statutes of Upper Canada, replacing them with the following provision:

3. Every subject of Her Majesty and every citizen or subject of any foreign state or country who has at any time heretofore offended or may at any time hereafter offend against the provisions of this Act, is and shall be held to be guilty of felony and may, notwithstanding the provisions hereinbefore contained, be prosecuted and tried before the Court of Queen's Bench in the exercise of its criminal jurisdiction in and for any district in Lower Canada [c.4: before any Court of Oyer and Terminer and General Gaol Delivery, in and for any County in Upper Canada] in the same manner as if the offence had been committed in such district [c.4: County] , and upon conviction shall suffer death as a felon.

These amendments were consolidated and replicated in the same language (except necessary revisions of institutional references) when the legislation was enacted for the Dominion of Canada in 1867 (31 Vic. c.14):

An Act to Protect the Inhabitants of Canada against Lawless Aggressions from Subjects of Foreign Countries at Peace with Her Majesty.

[*Assented to 21st December, 1867*]

Whereas in and by the ninety-eighth chapter of the preamble of the Consolidated Statutes for Upper Canada, and further by an Act made and passed in the Session of Parliament of the late Province of Canada, held in the twenty-ninth and thirtieth years of Her Majesty's Reign, and chaptered four, certain provisions are made for the protection of the inhabitants of the part of the said late Province of Canada called Upper Canada, against lawless aggressions from Subjects of Foreign Countries at Peace with Her Majesty ; And whereas in and by two several Acts made and passed in the said Session of Parliament of the late Province of Canada, held in the twenty-ninth and thirtieth years of Her Majesty's Reign, and chaptered two and three respectively, certain provisions are made for the protection of the inhabitants of that part of the late Province of Canada called Lower Canada, against similar lawless aggressions; And whereas it is expedient to continue the operation of the said Acts respectively, and that similar provisions be enacted in respect to the Dominion of Canada – Her Majesty, by and with the advice and consent of the Senate and House of Commons of Canada, enacts as follows: –

1. The ninety-eighth chapter of the Consolidated Statutes for Upper Canada, the said Act made and passed in the Session of Parliament of the late Province of Canada, held in the twenty-ninth and thirtieth years of Her Majesty's Reign, and chaptered four, – and the said two several Acts made and passed in the said Session of Parliament of the late Province of Canada, held in the twenty-ninth and thirtieth years of Her Majesty's Reign, and chaptered two and three respectively, are hereby extended and the provisions thereof declared to be in force throughout Canada as follows, that is to say:

2. In case any person, being a citizen or subject of any Foreign State or Country at peace with Her Majesty, be or continues in arms against Her Majesty, within Canada, or commits any act of hostility therein, or enters Canada with design or intent to levy war against Her Majesty, or to commit any felony therein, for which any person would, by the laws in force in any Province of Canada in which such offence is committed, be liable to suffer death, then the Governor may order the assembling of a Militia General Court Martial for the trial of such person, agreeably to the Militia Laws in force in such Province; and upon being found guilty by such Court Martial of offending against this Act, such person shall be sentenced by such Court Martial to suffer death, or such other punishment as shall be awarded by the Court.

3. If any subject of Her Majesty, within Canada, levies war against Her Majesty, in company with any of the subjects or citizens of any Foreign State or Country then at peace with Her Majesty, or enters Canada in company with any such subjects

or citizens with intent to levy war on Her Majesty, or to commit any such act of felony as aforesaid, or if, with the design or intent to aid and assist, he joins himself to any person or persons whatsoever, whether subjects or aliens, who have entered Canada with design or intent to levy war on Her Majesty, or to commit any such felony within the same, then such subject of Her Majesty may be tried and punished by a Militia Court Martial, in like manner as any citizen or subject of a Foreign State or Country at peace with Her Majesty, is liable under this Act to be tried and punished.

4. Every subject of Her Majesty and every citizen or subject of any foreign state or country, who has at any time heretofore offended, or may at any time hereafter offend against the provisions of this Act, is and shall be held to be guilty of felony, and may, notwithstanding the provisions hereinbefore contained, be prosecuted and tried in any county or district of the Province in which such offence was committed before any Court of competent jurisdiction, in the same manner as if the offence had been committed in such county or district, and upon conviction shall suffer death as a felon.

5. In case any person shall be prosecuted and tried in the Province of Ontario under the provisions of the next preceding section and found guilty, it shall and may be lawful for the Court before which such trial shall have taken place, to pass sentence of death upon such person, to take effect at such time as the Court may direct, notwithstanding the provisions of an Act of the Consolidated Statutes for Upper Canada, intituled: *An Act respecting New Trials and Appeals and Writs of Error in Criminal Cases in Upper Canada.*

2. MANAGING COLLECTIVE DISORDER

a) The Tenant League (Robertson)

The Queen v. Donald McLeod, for attempting to persuade or entice one William Glynn, a soldier in Her Majesty's 16th Regt. of Foot, to desert.

(*source: Royal Gazette* (Charlottetown), 20 Sept. 1865)

The facts of the case lie in a very small compass. On the 15th of the present month the prisoner who was riding on a truck, was met by Miss Ellen Duffy, a young and very intelligent person, near Admiral Bayfield's corner; he enquired of her which was the upper and which the lower road; she having designated both, the prisoner made choice of the lower road, when Miss D for the first time, perceived that there was a soldier on the truck, when she immediately called out to the prisoner 'that was not the right way to the camp, and that they ought to take the Upper Road'; that the prisoner must have heard what she said, for he made some reply, which she did not distinctly hear. Glynn, the soldier, was examined and deposed that he knew the prisoner at the bar, that he met him yesterday evening driving a truck. Prisoner asked him if he was going to the barrack, to which he replied yes. Prisoner told him to jump on the tail of the truck. He did so. Prisoner then spoke of the number of men who had deserted from the Regiment, said it was likely the deserters would not be found. Prisoner said he could partly drop on them – the deserters – said that he would drive him – Glynn – 17 miles into the country if he wished, when he would see somebody whom he, Glynn, knew – mentioned the name of a man 'Goodman,' who had deserted. He also said there were four others who had deserted, and was about to name the place where they were, when the stoppage of the truck prevented him. Witness believed that the prisoner intended to drive him into the country the seventeen miles. He had a couple of glasses, but was not the worse of liquor. Sergeant Allan, of the 16th Regt. & Policeman Brennan were examined as to the capture of the prisoner; and Captain Russel testified that Glynn had no leave of absence.

Policeman Brennan in giving his evidence testified that on returning to town, after the capture of the prisoner, which took place near Mr. Theoph. DesBrisay's gate, that he told the prisoner that he had no right to take away a soldier that way on a truck; to which he answered 'that the Horse and Truck were his own, and that he would take fifty of them if he could.' Prisoner was sober, the soldier the worse of liquor.

The first hearing was on Saturday the 16th. On the prisoner intimating that he wished to call evidence on his defence, he was told that bail for his appearance on Tuesday – this day – himself in £50, and two sureties in £25 each, would be taken, and that subpoenas for his witnesses would be granted him, and that he might employ Counsel if he pleased.

On being put to the bar this day, Tuesday, the evidence was read over to him, as was the clause in the Mutiny Act under which he was tried, and asked what defence he had to make. His reply was 'he was not aware of the law of the case. He never refused any man a ride when asked. He was not aware of any harm in asking a man to ride on his truck. That being confined in Jail, he had no opportunity of sending for witnesses.'

Councillor Theophilus DesBrisay, Esq., who with Richard Heartz, Esq., heard the case, after reminding the prisoner that he had been remanded on Saturday for the purpose of enabling him to procure witnesses, and might have done so – stated that the duty of the court was very plain, and that the evidence was most conclusive against him. That the Court could not believe that he was so ignorant as he pretended to be, after all that had been said and printed respecting deserters. That he must have known that he was doing wrong. That the attempting to persuade or entice men to desert was a serious misdemeanor, and that it was the duty of the Court to mark and punish it when detected. He then sentenced the prisoner to be imprisoned, and kept at hard labor in the Jail of Charlottetown for six calendar months. He reminded him that he had the right of appeal from the decision of the Court, and that it was open to him to apply to the Executive for a mitigation of the sentence.

The Queen v. Henry Green

(*source*: the *Islander* (Charletottetown), 3 Nov. 1865)

The Queen vs. Henry Green for attempting to procure or persuade Peter Macgowan, a Private Soldier in the 2nd Batt. of Her Majesty's 16th Regt. of Foot, to desert. His Worship the Mayor, who, with Mr Councillor DesBrisay, tried the case, observed that the charge was founded upon the 80th section of the Mutiny Act. The words of the Statute are 'Any person who shall, by any means whatsoever, directly or indirectly, procure any soldier to desert, or attempt to procure or persuade any soldier to desert, shall be deemed guilty of a misdemeanor.'

It appeared from the evidence for the prosecution that two separate attempts were made by the defendant to induce soldiers to desert. The first is stated to have taken place on the 8th of August last in a public house kept by one Sweeny, in Charlottetown, where Privates Macgowan, Lamb and Macgrory, and Corporals Macgowan and Mumby were sitting drinking, when the defendant Green came in, and, after treating all the soldiers to drink, threw his purse on the table and said, according to the testimony of Macgrory, 'that any man who wanted to desert he was the man to exchange the clothing. He was the very boy who would do it for him.' According to that of Lamb, Green threw his purse on the table and said, 'that if any man wished to change his clothing there was his purse at his command, and he, Green, would see them safe off the Island. Did not care what creed or profession they were he would stand to them.' Macgrory stated that Green took out his purse and threw it on the table, saying 'there is plenty of money, and as long as the money lasted he would see any of them off the Island.' Corporal Macgowan said Green took a purse out of his pocket and laid it on the table, saying 'that any man who was going to change his clothes he would see him off the Island as long as his purse would stand.' James Keenan, who was called on the part of the defendant, stated that he saw Green take out his purse and throw it on the table, saying 'that he did not care for creed or profession; so far as it would go, a man's principles was all he wanted.' All the witnesses agree in stating that Green was drunk.

The whole of this testimony, observed His Worship, is consistent throughout. The slight discrepancies are its best confirmation, and proves that it is not a tale concocted by the witnesses. Each man gives, as the result of the conversation, the impression made on his mind at the time. Keenan's evidence, so far as it goes, is in complete unison with the others, and he repeats the very words of Lamb about 'creeds and principles,' and those of Macgowan and Macgrory 'as far as it would stand,' alluding to the purse. There can be no doubt as to the truth of this testimony as to the offer of the contents of the purse, and the willingness of the defendant to assist the soldiers (and Macgowan is of the number) off the Island; and there can be as little doubt but that this was – to use the words of the Statute – directly or indirectly, an attempt to procure or persuade Macgowan and the others to desert, and it is in evidence that one of the party to which this offer was made did afterwards actually desert. Now the defence to this charge is, that Green was so utterly drunk as not to be capable of knowing what he was saying or doing, and that no more attention ought to be paid to what he then said than to the ravings of a decided lunatic or insane person. It militates much against this supposition that the language made use of is connected and perfectly rational, and appears to be the result of a previous determination. They are words that, if spoken by a man in his sober senses, would not of themselves excite any suspicion of insanity, and are the words which a man in the class of life of the defendant, wishing to encourage men to desert, would be likely to make use of. The proverb *In vino veritas* is not without an apt signification in the present case.

The second attempt to induce Macgowan to desert is on the 11th October. Macgowan swears that on that day he met Green on the street between the hours of 5 and 6 in the evening; Green asked him if there was any word of Private Moffit – one of the men who had deserted; to which he replied there was no word of him. Green then said there will not be, for it was I put him away, and I buried his clothes by tying a stone to them to sink them. Green then said that if he, Macgowan, was willing to go, he, Green, would put him in the same way. If this statement be correct, then there is no doubt whatever of the guilt of the defendant. To rebut the evidence of Macgowan, the only witness, and upon whose veracity everything in this stage of the case depends, several witnesses are called ...

There was an attempt made to invalidate the testimony of Macgowan, and to make it appear that he was anxious to desert and proposed to Green to assist him, which Green refused to do ... The Court being unanimously of opinion that the charges of attempting to persuade Peter Macgowan, a private soldier in Her Majesty's 16th Regiment of Foot, to desert, has been fully proved, sentence you, Henry Green, to be imprisoned in the Jail of Charlottetown for six calendar months, and during that time to be kept at hard labor.

b) The Riot Act (Robertson, Fyson, Binnie, Tucker)

[Please note that some of the chapters deal with pre-confederation versions of this legislation.]

An Act respecting Riots and Riotous Assemblies 31 Vic. c. 70 (1868, Canada)

[*Assented to 22nd May, 1868*]

Whereas, it is expedient to assimilate, amend and consolidate the Laws in force in the several Provinces of Quebec, Ontario, Nova Scotia, and New Brunswick, in relation to Riots and Riotous Assemblies, and to extend the same as so consolidated to all Canada: Therefore, Her Majesty, by and with the advice and consent of the Senate and House of Commons of Canada, enacts as follows:

1. In case any persons to the number of twelve or more, being unlawfully, riotously and tumultuously assembled together, to the disturbance of the public peace be by Proclamation, in the Queen's name, made in the form in this Act directed, by any one or more Justice or Justices of the Peaces, or by the Sheriff of the District or County, or his Deputy Sheriff, or by the Mayor, or other head officer, or Justice of the Peace of any city or town corporate, where such persons are so assembled, required or commanded to disperse themselves, and peaceably to depart to their habitations, or to their lawful business, and in case such persons to the number of twelve or more (notwithstanding such Proclamation made) unlawfully, riotously and tumultuously remain or continue together by the space of one hour after such command or request, such persons or any of them so continuing together to the number of twelve or more, after such command or request, so made by Proclamation, are severally guilty of felony, and shall be liable to be imprisoned in the Penitentiary for life, or for any term not less than two years, or to be imprisoned in any other goal or place of confinement, for any term less than two years.

2. The order and form of the Proclamation to be made by the authority of this Act shall be as follows, that is to say: The Justice of the Peace, or other person authorized to make the said Proclamation, shall, among the said rioters, or as near to them as he can safely come, with a loud voice command, or cause to be commanded, silence to be, while Proclamation is making; and after that, shall openly and with a loud voice, make, or cause to be made, Proclamation in these words, or like in effect:

'Our Sovereign Lady the Queen chargeth and commandeth all persons being assembled immediately to disperse themselves, and peaceably to depart to their habitations or to their lawful business, upon the pains contained in the Act respecting Riots and Riotous assemblies. – God save the Queen.'

3. Each and every Justice of the Peace, Sheriff, Deputy Sheriff, Mayor and other Head Officer, within the limits of their respective jurisdictions, shall, on notice or knowledge of any such unlawful, riotous and tumultuous assembly of persons to the number of twelve or more, resort to the place where such unlawful, riotous and tumultuous assembly is, and there make, or cause to be made, Proclamation in manner aforesaid.

4. If twelve or more of the persons so unlawfully, riotously and tumultuously assembled, continue together, after Proclamation made in manner aforesaid, and do not disperse themselves within one hour, then every Justice of the Peace, Sheriff, and Deputy Sheriff of the District or County where such assembly may be, and also every High and Petty Constable, and other Peace Officer within such District or County, and also every Mayor, Justice of the Peace, Sheriff and other Head Officer, High or Petty Constable, and other Peace Officer, of any city or town corporate where such assembly may be, and any person or persons commanded to assist such Justice of the Peace, Sheriff or Deputy Sheriff, Mayor, Bailiff, or other Head Officer aforesaid (who may command all Her Majesty's subjects of age and ability to be assisting to them therein), shall seize and apprehend the persons so unlawfully, riotously and tumultuously continuing together, after Proclamation made as aforesaid, and shall forthwith carry the persons so apprehended before one or more of Her Majesty's Justices of the Peace of the District, County or place where such persons are so apprehended, in order to their being proceeded against for such their offences according to law.

5. If in the dispersing, seizing or apprehending or endeavoring to disperse, seize or apprehend any of the persons so unlawfully, riotously and tumultuously assembled, any such person happen to be killed, maimed, or hurt, by reason of their resisting the persons dispersing, seizing or apprehending, or endeavoring to disperse, seize or apprehend them, then every such Justice of the Peace, Sheriff, Deputy Sheriff, Mayor, Head Officer, High or Petty Constable, or other Peace Officer, and all persons who were aiding and assisting them, or any of them, shall be free, discharged and indemnified, as well against the Queen's Majesty, as against all and every other person and persons, of, or concerning, the killing, maiming or hurting, of any such person or persons so unlawfully, riotously and tumultuously assembled as aforesaid.

6. If any person or persons with force and arms, wilfully and knowingly oppose, obstruct, or in any manner let, hinder or hurt, any person or persons who begin to proclaim, or go to proclaim, according to the Proclamation hereby directed to be made, whereby such Proclamation cannot be made, then every such person so opposing, obstructing, letting, hindering or hurting such person or persons so beginning or going to make such Proclamation, as aforesaid, is guilty of felony, and shall be liable to be imprisoned in the Penitentiary for life, or for any term not less than two years, or to be imprisoned in any other gaol or place of confinement for any term less than two years.

7. And every such person or persons so being unlawfully, riotously and tumultuously assembled, to the number of twelve or more, as aforesaid, to whom Proclamation should or ought to have been made, if the same had not been hindered, as aforesaid, who, to the number of twelve or more, continue together, and do not disperse themselves within one hour after such let or hindrance so made, having knowledge thereof, are guilty of felony, and shall be liable to be imprisoned in the

Penitentiary for life, or for any term not less than two years, or to be imprisoned in any other gaol or place of confinement for any term less than two years.

8. No person or persons shall be prosecuted for any offence or offences committed contrary to this Act, unless such prosecution be commenced within twelve months after the offence committed.

9. This Act shall commence and take effect on the first day of January, in the year of Our Lord one thousand eight hundred and sixty-nine.

c) The Peace Act (Binnie)

An Act for the Better Preservation of the Peace in the Vicinity of Public Works, 32–33 Vic. c.24 (1869, Canada)

[*Assented to 22nd June, 1869*]

For the preservation of the peace, and for the protection of the lives, persons and property of Her Majesty's subjects, in the neighbourhood of public works on which large bodies of labourers are congregated and employed: Her Majesty, by and with the advice and consent of the Senate and House of Commons of Canada, enacts as follows:

1. The Governor in Council may, as often as occasion requires, declare by Proclamation that upon and after a day therein named, this Act shall be in force in any place or places in Canada therein designated, within the limits or in the vicinity whereof any Railway, Canal or other public work is in progress of construction, or such places as are in the vicinity of any such Canal or Railway or other work as aforesaid, within which he deems it necessary that this Act should be in force, – and this Act shall, upon and after the day to be named in any such Proclamation, take effect within the places designated in such Proclamation:

2. The Governor in Council may, in like manner, from time to time, declare this Act to be no longer in force in any of such place or places; and may again from time to time declare the same to be in force therein;

3. But no such Proclamation shall have effect within the limits of any City.

2. Upon and after the day to be fixed for such purpose in such Proclamation, no person employed upon or about any such Canal, Railway or other work as aforesaid, within the place or places in which this Act is then in force, shall keep or have in his possession or under his care or control, within any such place, any gun or other fire-arm, or air-gun or any part thereof, or any sword, sword blade, bayonet, pike, pikehead, spear, spearhead, dirk, dagger, or other instrument intended for cutting or stabbing, or any steel or metal knuckles, or other deadly or dangerous weapon, under a penalty of not less than two dollars, nor more than four dollars, for every such weapon found in his possession.

3. On or before the day appointed as aforesaid in such Proclamation, every person employed on or about the Canal, Railway or other work to which the same relates, shall bring and deliver up to some Commissioner or Officer to be appointed for the purposes of this Act, every such weapon in his possession, and shall obtain from such commissioner or Officer a receipt for the same.

4. When this Act ceases to be in force within the place where any weapon has been delivered and detained in pursuance thereof, or when the owner or person lawfully entitled to any such weapon satisfies the commissioner that he is about to remove immediately from the limits within which this Act is at the time in force, the commissioner may deliver up to the owner or person authorized to receive the same, any such weapons, on production of the receipt so given for it.

5. Every such weapon found in the possession of any person employed as aforesaid, after the day named in any Proclamation as that on or before which such weapon ought to be delivered up, and within the limits designated in the Proclamation bringing this Act into force, may be seized by any Justice, Commissioner, Constable or other Peace Officer, and shall be forfeited to the use of Her Majesty.

6. If any person, for the purpose of defeating this Act, receives or conceals, or aids in receiving or concealing, or procures to be received or concealed, within any place where this Act is at the time in force, and such weapon as aforesaid belonging to or in the custody of any person employed on or about any such Railway, Canal or other work, such person shall forfeit a sum of not less than forty dollars nor more than one hundred dollars; one half to belong to the informer, and the other half to Her Majesty.

7. Any Commissioner appointed under this Act, or any Justice of the Peace having authority within the place where this Act is at the time in force, upon the oath of a credible witness that he believes that any such weapon as aforesaid is in the possession of any person or in any house or place contrary to the provisions of this Act, may issue his warrant to any Constable or Peace Officer to search for and seize the same, and he, or any person in his aid, may search for and seize the same in the possession of any person, or in any such house or place:

2. In case admission to any such house or place be refused after demand, such Constable or Peace Officer, and any person in his aid, may enter the same by force by day or by night, and seize any such weapon and deliver it to such Commissioner; and unless the party in whose possession or in whose house or premises the same has been found, do, within four days next after the seizure, prove to the satisfaction of such Commissioner or Justice that the weapons so seized was not in his possession or in his house or place contrary to the meaning of this Act, such weapon shall be forfeited to the use of Her Majesty.

8. Any Commissioner or Justice, Constable or Peace Officer, or any person acting under a warrant, in aid of any Constable or Peace Officer, may arrest and detain any person employed on any such railway, canal, or other work, found carrying

any such weapon as aforesaid, within any place where this Act is at the time in force, at such time and in such manner as in the judgement of such Commissioner, Justice, Constable or Peace Officer, or person acting under a warrant, affords just cause of suspicion that they are carried for purposes dangerous to the public peace; and the act of so carrying any such weapon by any person so employed shall be a misdemeanor, and the Justice or Commissioner arresting such person, or before whom he is brought under such a warrant, may commit him for trial for a misdemeanor, unless he gives sufficient bail for his appearance at the next term or sitting of the Court before which the offence can be tried, to answer to any indictment to be then preferred against him.

9. Every Commissioner under this Act shall make a monthly return to the proper authority of all weapons delivered to him, and by him detained under this Act.

10. All weapons declared forfeited under this Act shall be sold or destroyed under the direction of the Commissioner by whom or by whose authority the same were seized, and the proceeds of such sale, after deducting necessary expenses, shall be received by such commissioner and paid over by him to the Receiver General for the public uses of the Dominion.

11. Upon and after the day to be fixed in such Proclamation, and during such period as the Proclamation may remain in force, no person shall at any place within the limits specified in such Proclamation barter, sell, exchange or dispose of directly or indirectly to any other person, any alcoholic, spirituous, vinous, fermented or other intoxicating liquor, or any mixed liquor, a part of which is spirituous, or vinous, fermented or otherwise intoxicating, – nor shall expose, keep or have in his possession for sale, barter or exchange, any intoxicating liquor:

2. But this section shall not extend to any person selling intoxicating liquors by wholesale, and not retailing the same, if such person be a licensed Distiller or Brewer.

12. Any person who, in contravention of the next preceding section, by himself, his clerk, servant or agent, exposes or keeps for sale or barters, or sells, disposes of, gives or exchanges for any other matter or thing, to any other person, any intoxicating liquor, shall be liable to a fine of twenty dollars on the first conviction, forty dollars on the second, and on the third and every subsequent conviction, to such last mentioned fine and imprisonment for a period of not more than six months.

13. If any clerk or servant or agent, or other person in the employment or on the premises of another, sells, disposes of, or exchanges for any other matter or thing, or assists in selling, disposing of, or exchanging for any other matter or thing, any intoxicating liquor, in contravention of this Act, for the person in whose service or on whose premises he is, he shall be held equally guilty with the principal, and shall suffer the like penalty.

14. If any three credible persons make oath or affirmation before any Commis-

sioner, or Justice of the Peace, that they have reason to believe and do believe that any intoxicating liquor intended for sale or barter in contravention of this Act, is kept or deposited in any steamboat or other vessel, or in any carriage or vehicle, or in any store, shop, warehouse, or other building or premises at any place within which such intoxicating liquor is by Proclamation under this Act prohibited to be sold or bartered or kept for sale or barter, or on any river, lake or water adjoining such place, the Commissioner or Justice shall issue his Warrant of Search to any Sheriff, Police Officer, Bailiff or Constable, who shall forthwith proceed to search the steamboat, vessel, premises or place described in such Warrant, and if any intoxicating liquor be found therein, he shall seize the same, and the barrels, casks or other packages in which it is contained, and convey them to some proper place of security, and there keep them until final action is had thereon; but no dwelling house in which, or in part of which a shop or bar is not kept, shall be searched, unless one at least of the said complainants testifies on oath to some act of sale of intoxicating liquor therein or therefrom, on contravention of this Act, within one month of the time of making the said complaint.

2. The owner or keeper of the liquor seized as aforesaid, if he is known to the Officer seizing the same, shall be summoned forthwith before the Commissioner or Justice by whose warrant the liquor was seized, and if he fails to appear, and it appears to the satisfaction of such Commissioner or Justice, that the said liquor was kept or intended for sale or barter, in contravention of this Act, it shall be declared forfeited with any package in which it is contained, and shall be destroyed by authority of the written order to that effect of the said Commissioner or Justice, and in his presence, or in the presence of some person appointed by him to witness the destruction thereof, and who shall join with the officer by whom the said liquor has been destroyed, in attesting that fact upon the back of the order by authority of which it was done; And the owner or keeper of such liquor shall pay a fine of forty dollars and costs, or be committed to prison for three months in default thereof.

15. If the owner, keeper or possessor of liquor seized under the next preceding section is unknown to the officer seizing the same, it shall not be condemned and destroyed until the fact of such seizure has been advertised, with the number and description of the package as near as may be, for two weeks, by posting up a written or printed notice and description thereof in at least three public places of the place where it was seized;

2. And if it is proved within such two weeks, to the satisfaction of the Commissioner or Justice by whose authority such liquor was seized, that it was not intended for sale or barter in contravention of this Act, it shall not be destroyed, but shall be delivered to the owner, who shall give his receipt therefor [sic] upon the back of the Warrant, which shall be returned to the said Commissioner or Justice who

issued the same; but if after such advertisement as aforesaid, it appears to such Commissioner, or Justice, that such liquor was intended for sale or barter, in contravention of this Act, then such liquor, with any package in which it is contained, shall be condemned, forfeited, and destroyed.

16. Any payment or compensation for liquor sold or bartered in contravention of this Act, whether in money or securities for money, labor or property of any kind, shall be held to have been criminally received without consideration, and against law, equity and good conscience, and the amount or value thereof may be recovered from the receiver by the party making, paying or furnishing the same; and all sales, transfers, conveyances, liens and securities of every kind which either in whole or in part have been given for or on account of intoxicating liquor sold or bartered in contravention of this Act, shall be null against all person, and no right shall be acquired thereby, and no action of any kind shall be maintained either in whole or in part for or on account of intoxicating liquor sold or bartered in contravention of this Act.

17. Any Commissioner or Justice of the Peace may hear and determine in a summary manner any case arising within his jurisdiction under this Act; and every person making complaint against any other person for contravening this Act, or any part or portion thereof, before such Commissioner or Justice, may be admitted as a witness; and if the Commissioner or Justice before whom the examination or trial is had, so orders, as he may if he thinks there was probable cause for the prosecution, the defendant shall not recover costs though the prosecution fail.

18. All the provisions of any Law respecting the duties of Justices of the Peace in relation to summary convictions and orders, and to appeals from such convictions, and for the protection of Justices of the Peace when acting as such, or to facilitate proceedings by or before them, in matters relating to summary convictions and orders, shall in so far as they are not inconsistent with this Act, apply to every Commissioner or Justice mentioned in this Act or empowered to try offenders against this Act, and any such Commissioner shall be deemed a Justice of the Peace within the meaning of any such Law, whether he be or be not a Justice of the Peace for other purposes.

19. Any action brought against any Commissioner or Justice, Constable, Peace Officer, or other person, for anything done in pursuance of this Act, must be commenced within six months next after the fact; and the venue shall be laid or the action instituted in the District or County or place where the fact was committed, and the Defendant may plead the general issue and give this Act and the special matter in evidence; and if such action is brought after the time limited, or the venue is laid or the action brought in any other District, County or place than as above prescribed, the judgment [sic] or verdict shall be given for the Defendant; and in such case, or if the judgement or verdict is given for the Defendant on the merits, or if the Plaintiff becomes nonsuit or discontinues after appearance is entered, or has judgment rendered against him on demurrer, the Defendant shall be entitled to recover double costs.

20. No action or other proceeding, Warrant, Judgement, Order or other instrument or Writing, authorized by this Act, or necessary to carry out its provisions, shall be held void, or be allowed to fail for defect of form.

21. In this Act the word 'Commissioner' means a Commissioner under this Act; the word 'weapon' includes every kind of weapon mentioned or included in the second section of this Act, and all ammunition which can be used with or for any such weapon, and any instrument or thing intended to be used as a weapon; the expression 'intoxicating liquor' means and includes every kind of liquor mentioned or included in the twelfth section of this Act; and the expression 'District, County or Place,' includes any division of any Province, for the purposes of the administration of justice in the matter to which the context relates.

22. This Act shall commence and take effect on the first day of July, in the year of Our Lord one thousand, eight hundred and sixty-nine.

An Act to Amend the Acts for the Better Preservation of the Peace in the Vicinity of Public Works, 38 Vic. c.38 (1875, Canada)

[*Assented to 8th April, 1875*]

Her Majesty, by and with the advice and consent of the Senate and House of Commons of Canada, enacts as follows:–

1. The operation of the Act passed in the Session held in the thirty-second and thirty-third years of Her Majesty's reign and intituled: '*An Act for the Better Preservation of the Peace in the Vicinity of Public Works,*' as the same is amended by the Act passed in the thirty-third year of Her Majesty's reign, intituled: '*An Act to Amend an Act for the Better Preservation of the Peace in the Vicinity of Public Works,*' is hereby extended to any place or places in Canada, within the limits or in the vicinity whereof any railway, canal, road, bridge, or other work of any kind is in progress of construction, and to any place or places at or near which any mining operations are being carried on, and to which the Governor in Council may deem it expedient to apply the provisions of the said Acts – whether such work be constructed or carried on by the Government of Canada or of any Province of Canada, or by any incorporated Company or by an municipal corporation, or by private enterprise: and the expression 'Public Work' in the said Acts or either of them shall hereafter be understood to include any such work as aforesaid, and the Governor in Council shall have the same powers with reference to any such work as with reference to works constructed by the Government of Canada.

d) Peace Act, Illustrative Documents (Binnie)

i) Petition (source: LAC, Secretary of State (PC 850, 1883), file 2132–4)
Letter sent to Simon James Dawson, federal member for Algoma.

> Office of
> The Secretary-Treasurer,
> Rat Portage,
> Manitoba
> 3rd April, 1883

Dear Sir,

   I am requested by Mr. Walter Oliver, Mayor of this Corporation to forward the Petition of the Citizens of Rat Portage re Public Works Act to you; and to ask your influence in adjusting the matter. Mr. Oliver desires me to say that he would be greatly obliged if you would forward the petition to the proper quarter, and recommend its favorable [sic] consideration.

> I am Dr Sir,
>> Yours truly,
>>> Mitchell
>>>> Sec^r Treas^r

…

> House of Commons
> Ottawa, 9th April,
> 1883

Sir,

   I beg leave to enclose a Petition from the Inhabitants of the Town of Rat Portage to His Excellency, the Governor General, praying that the Public Works Act may no longer be made to apply to Rat Portage.

> I have the honor [sic] to be Sir
> Your obdt servant
> S. J. Dawson

…

The Hon The Secretary of State
Unto the Right Honorable the Governor in Council
of the Dominion of Canada _____
The Petition of the property owners and citizens
Of the town of Rat Portage in the County of
Varennes and Dominion of Canada _____
Humbly Sheweth _____

That your Petitioners are true and loyal British subjects and are at all times willing to submit to the laws of the Dominion of Canada but your Petitioners are desirous to submit to Your Honorable Body, the disadvantages under which they are at present placed. _____

That the town of Rat Portage has been recently incorporated by letters Patent of Incorporation from the Province of Manitoba, and Your Petitioners are desirous of possessing such benefits as any other Municipality, and for that purpose wish to see a certain number of Hotels duly licensed for the sale of intoxicating liquor and believe that if such was the case, the illicit traffic in liquor would be stopped to a large extent. _____

That the town of Rat Portage is the centre of a large Milling and Mining District and large numbers of people are daily arriving for the transaction of business.

That it is generally believed that the Public Works Act has been proclaimed in the vicinity of Rat Portage, and as there are at present no Public Works carried on within a long distance of Rat Portage, Your Petitioners feel that Your Right Honorable Body should take such steps to issue a Proclamation that the Public Works Act will be inoperable in the said Town of Rat Portage, as Your Right Honorable Body may deem fit.

May it therefore please Your Right Honourable Body to take these premises into consideration, and to issue a Proclamation that the Public Works Act will have no effect in the Town of Rat Portage and generally to protect the rights of Your Petitioners; and Your Petitioners will ever pray _____

[The following signatures and thirty-six other names:]

Walter Oliver, Mayor

James Wendman, Registrar

Alex^r Mac Talb (Bestable) C.E. for Pac. Ry.

ii) Letter from Cornelius Van Horne to minister of railways and canals, 3 May 1884 (source: LAC, MG 28 III, 2, v.1. Van Horne Letterbook #5, p.907)

Sir,

In prosecuting the work north of Lake Superior, it has been necessary to construct an expensive supply road from the mouth of the Michipicoten River to Dog Lake, a distance of forty-eight miles ... and over this road is carried an enormous quantity of high explosives.

Licenses have been granted by the authorities at Sault Ste Marie to one or more parties for the sale of liquor at the mouth of the Michipicoten River, and our work for a long distance is exposed to an invasion of liquor sellers from this direction. I need not call your attention to the great importance of keeping liquor entirely away from the work; ...

3. THE NORTH-WEST REBELLIONS

a) The Treason-Felony Act (Beal and Wright, Waiser)

An Act for the Better Security of the Crown and of the Government, 31 Vic. c.69 (1868, Canada)

[Assented to 22nd May, 1868]

Whereas it is expedient to assimilate the Statute Laws of the several Provinces of Quebec, Ontario, Nova Scotia, and New Brunswick, respecting offences affecting the security of the Crown and of the Government, and to amend and consolidate the same Therefore, Her Majesty, by and with the advice and consent of the Senate and House of Commons of Canada, enacts as follows:

1. Nothing herein contained shall lessen the force of or in any manner affect anything enacted by the Statute passed in the twenty-fifth year of King Edward the Third [25 Ed. 3 c.2], 'A declaration of which offences shall be adjudged treason.'

2. Whosoever within Canada or without, compasses, imagines, invents, devises or intents death or destruction, or any bodily harm tending to death or destruction, maim or wounding, imprisonment or restraint of our Sovereign Lady the Queen, Her Heirs or Successors, and such compassings, imaginations, inventions, devices or intentions, or any of them, expresses, utters, or declares, by publishing any printing or writing or by any overt act or deed, is guilty of treason, and shall suffer death.

3. If any Officer or Soldier in Her Majesty's army, holds correspondence with any rebel, or enemy of Her Majesty, or gives them advice or intelligence, either by letters, messages, signs or tokens, or in any manner of way whatsoever, or treats with such rebels or enemies, or enters into any condition with them without Her Majesty's license, or the license of the General, Lieutenant-General or Chief Commander, every such person so offending is guilty of treason, and shall suffer death.

4. In all cases of treason, the sentence or judgment to be pronounced against any person convicted and adjudged guilty thereof shall be, that he be hanged by the neck until he be dead.

5. Whosoever, after the passing of this Act, within Canada or without, compasses, imagines, invents, devises or intents to deprive or depose Our Most Gracious Lady the Queen, Her Heirs or Successors, from the style, honour, or royal name of the imperial crown of the United Kingdom, or of any other of Her Majesty's dominions or countries, or to levy war against Her Majesty, Her Heirs or Successors, within any part of the United Kingdom or of Canada, in order by force or constraint to compel her or them to change her or their measures or counsels, or in order to put any force or constraint upon, or in order to intimidate or overawe both Houses or either House of Parliament, of the United Kingdom or of Canada, or to move or stir any foreigner or stranger with force to invade the United Kingdom or Canada, or any other of Her Majesty's dominions or countries under the obeisance of Her Majesty, Her Heirs or Successors, and such compassings, imaginations, inventions, devices or intentions, or any of them, shall express, utter or declare by publishing any printing or writing, or by open and advised speaking, or by any overt act or deed, is guilty of felony, and shall be liable to be imprisoned in the Penitentiary for life or for any term not less than two years, or to be imprisoned in any other gaol or place of confinement for any term less than two years, with or without hard labour.

6. No person shall be prosecuted for any felony by virtue of this Act in respect of such compassings, imaginations, inventions, devices or intentions as aforesaid, in so far as the same are expressed, uttered or declared by open and advised speaking only, unless information of such compassings, imaginations, inventions, devices and intentions and of the words by which the same were expressed, uttered or declared, shall be given upon oath to one or more Justice or Justices of the Peace, within six days after such words shall have been spoken, and unless a warrant for the apprehension of the person by whom such words shall have been spoken shall be issued within ten days next after such information shall have been given as aforesaid; and no person shall be convicted of any such compassings, imaginations, inventions, devices or intentions as aforesaid in so far as the same are expressed, uttered or declared by open or advised speaking as aforesaid, except upon his own confession in open Court, or unless the words so spoken shall be proved by two credible witnesses.

7. It shall be lawful, in any indictment for any felony under this Act to charge against the offender any number of the matters, acts or deeds by which such compassings, imaginations, inventions, devices or intentions as aforesaid, or any of them shall have been expressed, uttered or declared.

8. If the facts or matters alleged in an indictment for any felony under this Act amount in law to treason, such indictment shall not by reason thereof be deemed void, erroneous, or defective, and if the facts or matters proved on the trial of any person indicted for felony under this Act amount in law to treason, such person shall not, by reason thereof, be entitled to be acquitted of such felony; but no person tried for such felony shall be liable to be afterwards prosecuted for treason upon the same facts.

9. In the case of every felony punishable under this Act, every principal in the second degree and every accessory before the fact, shall be punishable in the same manner as the principal in the first degree is by this Act punishable; and every accessory after the fact to any such felony, shall be liable to be imprisoned in any gaol or place of confinement other than the Penitentiary, for any term less than two years, with or without hard labour.

10. This Act shall commence and take effect on the first day of January, in the year of our Lord, one thousand eight hundred and sixty-nine.

b) The Sentencing of Ambroise Lépine (Knafla)

[Chief Justice Wood, Court of Queen's Bench, Winnipeg, Manitoba, 4 November 1874]:

Prisoner, you stand convicted of having, on the 4th of March, 1870, at Fort Garry, in that portion of Rupert's Land which has since become the Province of Manitoba, murdered Thomas Scott. An unlawful, ordinary homicide is a startling and shocking occurrence in a civilized and Christian community at any time, but the killing of Scott is taken out of the category of common homicides. So dreadful and so horrible was it that even those who at first felt disposed to sympathize with the cause of the insurrectionary movement would not believe it possible until the dark deed was perpetrated. The knowledge of it sent a thrill of horror throughout the Dominion of Canada and the civilized world, and struck the hearts of the settlers of Red River with shuddering terror; and although now over four years have passed away, that crime is still regarded by the people of Red River and the Dominion of Canada with unabated abhorrence; and not a solitary individual has ever dared to speak or write a single sentence, I will not say in justification, but even in extenuation, palliation, excuse or apology of its enormity; and the evidence given on your trial, instead of relieving, has added to and increased the dark shadows surrounding that awful tragedy. A jury, the majority of whom are natives of Red River, for two weeks have patiently listened to all that could be said in your defence. Your counsel, most sympathetic, learned, able and eloquent gentlemen, have done all that could be done in your behalf. In your defence they were allowed the widest latitude; but to the credit of human nature and to the honor of the profession be it said, during their entire defence they had not one syllable in justification or apology to offer for the awful crime of which you have been convicted. They did for you all that great ability and great eloquence with the greatest liberty of defence could accomplish. The question of your guilt or innocence was fairly left to that jury by the Court – your counsel having taken no exception to the charge. That jury have pronounced you guilty; and I must say I do not well see how they could have done otherwise. Indeed I do not believe twenty respectable French *Métis* can be found in the whole Red River Settlement who could not have come to the same conclusion – and who do not now approve of the verdict of that jury – whatever native Canadians may say in respect of it. You can claim no consideration on the ground of ignorance or misapprehension. Père Ritchot swears he advised you and others of the risk and the danger you incurred in the movement in which you and your *confrères* were engaged. Long prior to the commission of this offence, you had before you the Proclamation of the Governor General, issued by the order of the Queen, forgiving you and your associates in treason all you and they had done up to that time; *provided you returned to an observance of the laws and obedience to the law-ful authority of this land.* You were assured by the official documents under the hand of the Governor-General and proceeding from the Privy Council of Canada, that all possible grievances, if any existed, should be redressed; that the most generous and liberal policy towards the inhabitants of Red River should be pursued in dealing with the North-West Territories, and in thus carrying out the policy of the Empire – that all their possessory and other rights should be respected; – in short you were informed that the Imperial measure of uniting Rupert's Land and the Indian Territories to Canada had been conceived as much as in the interests of the population of Red River as in that of Canada and the Empire at large. To enforce those views and to render conviction of their truth irresistible, gentlemen of unquestionable integrity and such as must have commanded your confidence and that of the misguided men over whom you assumed to exercise control, or with whom you were associated in your unreasonable and unlawful rebellion to the constituted authority of the country, were sent to you as special commissioners. For what was done by you and your associates from that time onward, whatever may be said as to what was done prior thereto, you and your associates stand before the world without a shadow of excuse or justification. You would not heed the warning – you would not listen to what you knew was the truth. You imprisoned, and I may say from what has been disclosed on this trial, tortured those innocent of even actively opposing your mad proceedings. You robbed Her Majesty's loyal subjects of their property and plundered whatever you could do so with impunity. And, lastly, you crowned the long catalogue of your crimes with the slaughter of Thomas Scott for no other offence than loyalty to his Queen. But it is not my province to say anything by which one additional sting should be added to that remorse which in all charity it is to be hoped that you now experience for the past. I have made all these remarks to prepare you for what I now say to you, that I dare not hold out any hope that mercy will be extended to you for the crime of which you have been convicted. In my heart of hearts I pity your wife and children, your relations and friends. They must keenly feel your situation. Had you taken the advice of your brother Baptiste on that fatal evening of the 3rd of March, you would not now be where you are. It is one of the inevitable consequences of crime to involve all relations and connections in its punishment, and knowing this, it alone should have arrested you in your mad career. *You did not spare poor Scott.* You did not think of, or if you did, you did not regard his poor old mother or his relations. Where his ashes repose you may know, but we do not. Whether his body was made away with so as not to be found, to be set up as a defence as has been done on this trial, or because it was so mangled and mutilated that even you were ashamed it should ever be seen, is unknown. What was done with Scott's body you must know. Taking all the facts in the evidence together, well might the ever-to-be-lamented Sir George E. Cartier, in a private and confidential communication to Lord Lisgar, say, '*The killing of Scott was an excessive abuse of power and cruel brutality.*' The jury have recommended you to mercy. All the exceptions taken by your counsel, together with the entire evidence and proceedings and the recommendation to mercy, will be transmitted to the Secretary of State for Canada and by him laid before His Excellency the Governor-General in Council. In addition to that your counsel will have an opportunity of presenting to the Executive any considerations they may think advisable outside the record. I have but one course left open to me, and that is to pronounce on you the final sentence of the law. I have made the day of your execution more distant than I otherwise might have done in consequence of the distance and the length of time necessary in communication between Manitoba and Ottawa; and to give you ample opportunity for self-examination, for reflecting over your past life, and for preparation for the awful change which awaits you. You, unlike Scott, will not be forced to prepare to leave this and enter the invisible world in a few short hours. When the Rev. Mr. Young came to you like an angel of mercy and with streaming eyes begged you to spare Scott's life only for a few short hours to meet his God, you inhumanely denied and refused his request with a brevity and emphasis in keeping with every act surrounding this human butchery. After Scott's death this same messenger of Heaven, bathed in his tears, went to Riel along with the Bishop of Rupert's Land, and humbly implored Riel to give him the body that he might give it the last sad rites of the Church, intimating that he was about to write to his poor old mother the untimely death of her son, and that it would be consolation to her to know that her son had received Christian burial. Even his heart softened under this appeal. But you, he declared, claimed that you had the disposition of the body and utterly refused to surrender it for burial. To all entreaties to spare life for a brief period before death, and to give up the body for burial after death, you were alike inflexible. Search the annals of barbarous tribes which for centuries have roamed over the vast prairies of the North-West, and in them you will fail to find a parallel in savage atrocity. There is no spirit of vengeance in these proceedings. It is the triumph of law over the unbridled audacity of crime. As this, in all probability, is the last opportunity I shall ever have on earth of addressing you, I thought it is my duty, however painful it might be, to address these plain and candid observations to you that you might realize your true position and prepare to meet your God. The sentence of the law upon you is that you be taken from the place where you now are to the common gaol of this province, and there be kept in solitary confinement until the twenty-ninth day of January, 1875, and on that day, between the hours of eight and ten o'clock in the forenoon, you be taken thence to the place of execution, and there be hanged by the neck until you are dead, and may the God of pity have mercy upon your soul.

(*Source*: *Preliminary Investigation and Trial of Ambroise D. Lepine for the Murder of Thomas Scott, Being a Full Report of the Proceedings in This Case before the Magistrates' Court and the Several Courts of Queen's Bench in the Province of Manitoba*, transcription of the court record reported and compiled by Elliott and Brokovski, Office of the Minister of Agriculture (Montreal: Burland-Desbarats 1874), 124–7).

c) General Instructions to the 1885 Prosecution Team
(Beal and Wright, Bumsted, Waiser)

Department of Justice, Ottawa 20th June, 1885. To Messrs. C. Robinson, Q.C.; B.B. Osler Q.C.; G.W. Burbidge, Deputy Minister of Justice; T. Chase Casgraine and D.L. Scott.

GENTLEMEN, – In the matter of the prosecution of Riel and others, growing out of the recent rebellion in the North West Territories and in which you are engaged as counsel on behalf of the Crown, I have thought it best to send you this note of general instructions:–

(1) Riel and all the leading men among the prisoners – white or half-breed – to be prosecuted for treason.

(2) The Indians who committed the murders to be prosecuted for murder.

(3) Other Indian chiefs and principal men to be prosecuted for treason.

(4) I think that after a certain number of convictions many prisoners will probably plead guilty.

(5) I think it would be well at this stage that you should report to me for further instructions.

(6) The object of the Government would be accomplished by the obtaining of a certain number of convictions. I should expect to hear of thirty or forty leading half-breeds or white men and leading Indians having been found guilty.

(7) It may be, and from the information which the Government has it seems probable, that the rebellion has been encouraged actively by whites, particularly of Prince Albert. Nothing in the whole duty entrusted to you is, I apprehend, more important than that we should, if possible, find out some of the men who have, with far better knowledge than the half-breeds and Indians, stirred them up to rebellion, and your special attention is asked to this point.

I am, &c.,

A. Campbell, Minister of Justice

(*Source*: *CSP* 1886, no. 43, 12)

d) Guilty Pleas – Riel's Councillors, 1885
(Beal and Wright)

Name	Sentence	Witnesses who swore affidavits*
Pierre Parenteau	7 years	A, JA, N, F, M
Pierre Henri	7 years	A, JA, N
Maxime Lépine	7 years	A, JA, J, N, F, M, P, TS
Albert Monkman	7 years	A, BA, JA, J, N, F, CN, P, TS
Phillippe Gariepie	7 years	A, J, N, S, M
Alexandre Cadieux (Cayen)	7 years	A, N, RJ, C
Baptiste Vandal	7 years	A, JA, N, P, M, GN, M, TS
Pierre Vandal	7 years	A, N, C
Jim Short	7 years	A
Maxime Dubois	7 years	A, N, GN
Philippe Garnot	7 years	A, J, F, LM
Moïse Ouellette	3 years	A, JA, J, N, F, M
Pierre Gariepie	3 years	A, JA, N, M
Alexander Fisher	3 years	A, JA, J, F, P, LM, N, W, HM, M, GN
Joseph Arcand	1 year	A, BA, N, RJ, C
Ignace Poitras, elder	1 year	A, JA, N, P, M
Ignace Poitras, younger	1 year	A, N
Moïse Parenteau	1 year	N
Alexis Lombarde	c. discharged	A, N
Emmanuel Champagne	c. discharged	A, J, N, F, M, HM, P, M
Joseph Delorme	c. discharged	A, N
Francois Tourond	c. discharged	A, K, N, G
Patrice Tourond	c. discharged	A, N, P
Joseph Pilon	c. discharged	A, K, P, GN
Baptiste Rochelieu	c. discharged	A, JA, N, P
Octave Regnier	c. discharged	
Abraham Montour	no. proc.	
Andre Nault	no. proc.	
Daniel Parenteau	no. proc.	N
André Nolin	no. proc.	
Eleazer Swain	no. proc.	
Frederick Fidler	no. proc.	

*A-Fr. Alexis André, F -Fr. Vital Fourmond, C-Fr. Louis Cochin, P-Prisoners generally, K-George Kerr, GN-George Ness, BA-Baptiste Arcand, JA-John Astley, J-Eastwood Jackson, N-Charles Nolin, RJ-Robert Jefferson, G-Goger Goulet, CN-Charles Newitt, S-Eleazer Swain, M-Thomas McKay, HM-Hillyard Mitchell, LM-Louis Marion, W-Henry Walters, TS-Thomas Sanderson

Source: 'Affidavits and Sentences,' CSP 1886, no. 52, 381–408.

NB: Some of these names were variously spelled in the documentation. There is clearly no relationship between the number of times a person was mentioned in the affidavits and his sentence. Few other patterns emerge. Fr. André attested to everyone's good reputation except that of Moïse Parenteau. Alex Fisher received the most praise. But he was the ferryman at Batoche who knew everyone and did business with everyone.

e) First Nations Convictions, 1885
(Waiser)

Defendant	Offence	Trial Venue	Conv. Date	Sentence
Tahkokan	Larceny	Battleford	June 27	2y
Natoose	Horse Stealing	Battleford	June 29	6y
Chesenus	Larceny	Battleford	June 29	6y
Mistatimawas	Assault & Larceny	Battleford	June 29	6y
Charles Pooyak	Horse Stealing	Battleford	June 29	6y
Papequositauce	Stealing Cattle	Battleford	July 22	6y
Seahkatamo	Stealing Cattle	Battleford	July 22	6y
Weasaskewen	Stealing Cattle	Battleford	July 22	6y
Big Belly	Arson	Battleford	July 22	6y
White Face	Horse Stealing	Battleford	July 22	6y
One Arrow	Treason-Felony	Regina	August 14	3y
Poundmaker	Treason-Felony	Regina	August 19	3y
A-ya-ta-ka-me-ka-pe-tung	Felony	Regina	Sept 5	3y
Aw-pis-ke-nen	Felony	Regina	Sept 5	3y
Was-pos-o-yan	Felony	Regina	Sept 5	2y
Big Bear	Treason-Felony	Regina	Sept 10	3y
Nan-e-sue	Treason-Felony	Regina	Sept 16	2y
Mic-cha-chaq-e-mish	Treason-Felony	Regina	Sept 16	2y
Kah-sah-ko-wa-tit	Treason-Felony	Regina	Sept 16	2y
Koos-top-e-quob	Treason-Felony	Regina	Sept 16	2y
Nah-pace-is	Treason-Felony	Regina	Sept 16	2y
Kah-ke-we-pah-tow	Treason-Felony	Regina	Sept 16	2y
Oos-ka-ta-task	Treason-Felony	Regina	Sept 16	2y
Ah-tim-yoo	Treason-Felony	Regina	Sept 16	2y
Ah-tom-iss-com-co-ah-wah-see	Treason-Felony	Regina	Sept 16	2y
The Hole	Treason-Felony	Regina	Sept 17	6 months
Red Eagle	Treason-Felony	Regina	Sept 17	3y
Poor Crow	Treason- Felony	Regina	Sept 17	3y
Red Bean	Treason-Felony	Regina	Sept 17	3y
Left Hand	Treason-Felony	Regina	Sept 17	3y
Wandering Spirit	Murder	Battleford	Sept 24	Death
Four Sky Thunder Toussaint	Arson	Battleford	Sept 24	14y
Calling Bull	Arson	Battleford	Sept 24	10y
Little Wolf	Arson	Battleford	Sept 24	10y
God's Otter	Horse Stealing	Battleford	Sept 24	4y
Old Man	Horse Stealing	Battleford	Sept 24	6y

Idol	Horse Stealing	Battleford	Sept 24	6y
Erect Man	Horse Stealing	Battleford	Sept 24	2y
Little Runner	Horse Stealing	Battleford	Sept 24	4y
Mountain Man	Stealing Cattle	Battleford	Sept 25	6m
Charles Ducharmes (Alias Charlebois)	Murder	Battleford	Sept 25	Death-reprieved
Dressy Man	Murder	Battleford	Sept 25	Death-reprieved
Bright Eyes	Murder	Battleford	Sept 25	20y (man-slaughter)
Louison Mongrain	Murder	Battleford	Sept 25	Death-reprieved
Round the Sky	Murder	Battleford	Oct 1	Death
Bad Arrow	Murder	Battleford	Oct 3	Death
Miserable Man	Murder	Battleford	Oct 3	Death
Itka	Murder	Battleford	Oct 5	Death
Man without Blood	Murder	Battleford	Oct 5	Death
Mus-sin-ass	Treason-Felony	Battleford	Oct 8	2y
Oo-pin-ou-way-win	Treason-Felony	Battleford	Oct 8	2y
Pee-yay-cheew	Treason-Felony	Battleford	Oct 8	2y
Iron Body	Murder	Battleford	Oct 9	Death
Little Bear	Murder	Battleford	Oct 9	Death
Wahpiah	Murder	Battleford	Oct 21	6y

Source: 'Report of the Commissioner of the North-West Mounted Police, 1885,' *CSP*, 1888, no. 8, appendix O.

NB: The list does not include several Indians who were sentenced to less than six months

4. SECURING THE DOMINION

Extracts from the Canadian Criminal Code, 1892 55–56 Vic. c.29
(*Brown and Wright*)

TITLE II OFFENCES AGAINST PUBLIC ORDER, INTERNAL AND EXTERNAL

Part IV Treason and Other Offences Against the Queen's Authority and Person

65. Treason is–
(a) the act of killing Her Majesty, or doing her any bodily harm tending to death or destruction, maim or wounding, and the act of imprisoning or restraining her; or
(b) the forming and manifesting by an overt act an intention to kill Her Majesty, or to do her any bodily harm tending to death or destruction, maim or wounding, or to imprison or to restrain her; or
(c) the act of killing the eldest son and heir apparent of Her Majesty, or the Queen consort of any King of the United Kingdom of Great Britain and Ireland; or

(d) the forming and manifesting, by an overt act, an intention to kill the eldest son and heir apparent of Her Majesty, or the Queen consort of any King of the United Kingdom of Great Britain and Ireland; or

(e) conspiring with any person to kill Her Majesty, or to do her any bodily harm tending to death or destruction, maim or wounding, or conspiring with any person to imprison or restrain her; or

(f) levying war against Her Majesty either –

(i.) with intent to depose Her Majesty from the style, honour and royal name of the Imperial Crown of the United Kingdom of Great Britain and Ireland or of any other of Her Majesty's dominions or countries;

(ii.) in order, by force or constraint, to compel Her Majesty to change her measures or counsels, or in order to intimidate or overawe both Houses or either House of Parliament of the United Kingdom or of Canada; or

(g) conspiring to levy war against Her Majesty with any such intent or for any such purpose as aforesaid; or

(h) instigating any foreigner with force to invade the said United Kingdom or Canada or any other of the dominions of Her Majesty; or

(i) assisting any public enemy at war with Her Majesty in such war by any means whatsoever; or

(j) violating, whether with her consent or not, a Queen consort, or the wife of the eldest son and heir apparent, for the time being, of the King or Queen regnant:

2. Every one who commits treason is guilty of an indictable offence and liable to suffer death.

66. In every case in which it is treason to conspire with any person for any purpose the act of so conspiring, and every overt act of any such conspiracy, is an overt act of treason.

67. Every one is guilty of an indictable offence and liable to two years' imprisonment who –

(a) becomes an accessory after the fact to treason; or

(b) knowing that any person is about to commit treason does not, with all reasonable despatch, give information thereof to a justice of the peace, or use other reasonable endeavours to prevent the commission of the same.

68. Every subject or citizen of any foreign state or country at peace with Her Majesty, who –

(a) is or continues in arms against Her Majesty within Canada; or

(b) commits any act of hostility therein; or

(c) enters Canada with intent to levy war against Her Majesty, or to commit any indictable offence therein for which any person would, in Canada, be liable to suffer death; and

Every subject of Her Majesty within Canada who –

(d) levies war against Her Majesty in company with any of the subjects or citizens of any foreign state or country at peace with Her Majesty; or

(e) enters Canada in company with any such subjects or citizens with intent to levy war against Her Majesty, or to commit any such offence therein; or

(f) with intent to aid and assist, joins himself to any person who has entered Canada with intent to levy war against Her Majesty, or to commit any such offence therein – is guilty of an indictable offence and liable to suffer death …

69. Every one is guilty of an indictable offence and liable to imprisonment for life who forms any of the intentions hereinafter mentioned, and manifests any such intention by conspiring with any person to carry it into effect, or by any other overt act, or by publishing any printing or writing; that is to say –

(a) an intention to depose Her Majesty from the style, honour and royal name of the Imperial Crown of the United Kingdom of Great Britain and Ireland, or of any other of Her Majesty's dominions or countries;

(b) an intention to levy, war against Her Majesty within any part of the said United Kingdom, or of Canada, in order by force or constraint to compel her to change her measures or counsels, or in order to put any force or constraint upon or in order to intimidate or overawe both Houses or either House of Parliament of the United Kingdom or of Canada;

(c) an intention to move or stir any foreigner or stranger with force to invade the said United Kingdom, or Canada, or any other of Her Majesty's dominions or countries under the authority of Her Majesty …

…

[Official Secrets:]

76. In the two following sections, unless the context otherwise requires –

(a) Any reference to a place belonging to Her Majesty includes a place belonging to any department of the Government of the United Kingdom, or of the Government of Canada, or of any province, whether the place is or is not actually vested in Her Majesty;

(b) Expressions referring to communications include any communication, whether in whole or in part, and whether the document, sketch, plan, model or information itself or the substance or effect thereof only be communicated;

(c) The expression 'document' includes part of a document;

(d) The expression 'model' includes design, pattern and specimen;

(e) The expression 'sketch' includes any photograph or other mode of expression of any place or thing;

(f) The expression 'office under Her Majesty' includes any office or employment in or under any department of the Government of the United Kingdom, or of the Government of Canada or of any province …

77. Every one is guilty of an indictable offence and liable to imprisonment for one year, or to a fine not exceeding one hundred dollars, or to both imprisonment and fine, who –

(a) for the purpose of wrongfully obtaining information –

i. enters or is in any part of a place in Canada belonging to Her Majesty, being a fortress, arsenal, factory, dockyard, camp, ship, office or other like place, in which part he is not entitled to be; or

ii. when lawfully or unlawfully in any such place as aforesaid either obtains any document, sketch, plan, model or knowledge of anything which he is not entitled to obtain, or takes without lawful authority any sketch or plan; or

iii. when outside any fortress, arsenal, factory, dockyard or camp in Canada, belonging to Her Majesty, takes, or attempts to take, without authority given by or on behalf of Her Majesty, any sketch or plan of that fortress, arsenal, factory, dockyard or camp; or

(b) knowingly having possession of or control over any such document, sketch, plan, model, or knowledge as has been obtained or taken by means of any act which constitutes an offence against this and the following section, at any time wilfully and without lawful authority communicates or attempts to communicate the same to any person to whom the same ought not, in the interests of the state, to be communicated at that time; or

(c) after having been entrusted in confidence by some officer under Her Majesty with any document, sketch, plan, model or information relating to any such place as aforesaid, or to the naval or military affairs of Her Majesty, wilfully, and in breach of such confidence, communicates the same when, in the interests of the state, it ought not to be communicated; or

(d) having possession of any document relating to any fortress, arsenal, factory, dockyard, camp, ship, office or other like place belonging to Her Majesty, or to the naval or military affairs of Her Majesty, in whatever manner the same has been obtained or taken, at any time wilfully communicates the same to any person to whom he knows the same ought not, in the interests of the state, to be communicated at the time:

2. Every one who commits any such offence intending to communicate to a foreign state any information, document, sketch, plan, model or knowledge obtained or taken by him, or entrusted to him as aforesaid, or communicates the same to any agent of a foreign state, is guilty of an indictable offence and liable to imprisonment for life.

78. Every one who, by means of his holding or having held an office under Her Majesty, has lawfully or unlawfully, either obtained possession of or control over any document, sketch, plan or model, or acquired any information, and at any time corruptly, or contrary to his official duty, communicates or attempts to communicate such document, sketch, plan, model or information to any person to whom the same ought not, in the interests of the state, or otherwise in the public interest, to be communicated at that time, is guilty of an indictable offence and liable –

(a) if the communication was made, or attempted to be made, to a foreign state, to imprisonment for life; and

(b) in any other case to imprisonment for one year, or to a fine not exceeding one hundred dollars, or to both imprisonment and fine.

2. This section shall apply to a person holding a contract with Her Majesty, or with any department of the Government of the United Kingdom, or of the Government of Canada, or of any province, or with the holder of any office under Her Majesty as such holder, where such contract involves an obligation of secrecy, and to any person employed by any person or body of persons holding such a contract who is under a like obligation of secrecy, as if the person holding the contract, and the person so employed, were respectively holders of an office under Her Majesty.

Part V Unlawful Assemblies, Riots, Breaches of the Peace

...

Part VI Unlawful Use and Possession of Explosive Substances and Offensive Weapons – Sale of Liquors

...

Part VII Seditious Offences

123. No one shall be deemed to have a seditious intention only because he intends in good faith –

(a) to show that Her Majesty has been misled or mistaken in her measures; or

(b) to point out errors or defects in the government or constitution of the United Kingdom, or of any part of it, or of Canada or any province thereof, or in either House of Parliament of the United Kingdom or of Canada, or in any legislature, or in the administration of justice; or to excite Her Majesty's subjects to attempt to procure, by lawful means, the alteration of any matter in the state; or

(c) to point out, in order for their removal, matters which are producing or have a tendency to produce feelings of hatred and ill-will between different classes of Her Majesty's subjects.

2. Seditious words are words expressive of a seditious intention.

3. A seditious libel is a libel expressive of a seditious intention.

4. A seditious conspiracy is an agreement between two or more persons to carry into execution a seditious intention.

124. Every one is guilty of an indictable offence and liable to two years' imprisonment who speaks any seditious words or publishes any seditious libel or is a party to any seditious conspiracy.

125. Every one is guilty of an indictable offence and liable to one year's imprisonment who, without lawful justification, publishes any libel tending to degrade, revile or expose to hatred and contempt in the estimation of the people of any foreign state, any prince or person exercising sovereign authority over any such state.

Index

(procedure, *cont.*)
  courts martial, 40–2, 43, 47
  grand jury, 13, 143
  Indian unfamiliarity with, 462–3
proclamations. *See* Pacific Railway con-
    struction
professional policing. *See* police
prohibition orders. *See* Pacific Railway
    construction
prosecutions, crown
  Fenian accused. *See* Fenian trials
  Indian trials. *See* North-West rebellion,
    1885 Indian trials
  Lépine, Ambroise. *See* Lépine, Ambroise,
    trial of
  riot prosecutions. *See* riot prosecutions
    (Quebec)
  sedition, 15
  Tenant League. *See* Tenant League
  treason prosecutions. *See* North-West
    rebellion, 1885 treason prosecutions
prostitution, 181–2
Protestants
  Orange-Catholic/Irish tension/riots,
    161, 163, 164, 167, 171, 188–9
public-order offences, 527

Quebec. *See also* riot policing; riot prosecu-
    tions
  Beauharnois Canal riot, 184
  collective violence in, forms of, 163, 173
  election violence in, 161
  Gavazzi riots, 163, 167, 182, 184
  labour violence in, 161, 163, 171, 180,
    184
  Legislative Assembly building burning,
    163
  population growth in, 161
  private violence in, 161
  Protestant-Catholic tensions in, 161, 163,
    171, 188, 189
  school tax riots, 161, 163
  state authority/monopoly over force,
    162–3
  vaccination riots in, 161, 171, 188, 189
  violence in, generally, 161–4
Quinn, Daniel, 68
Quinn, John, 53, 55, 68
Quinn, Richard, 101, 103

Rae, John, 467
Rahim, Hussain, 497–8, 500
Railway Labour Disputes Act, 264
railway strikes. *See also* labour disputes
  Alien Labour Act, 269
  Amalgamated Association of Street Rail-
    way Employees, 273
  charts re 1886–1914 strikes, 260–3
  coercive state force, use of against, 269
  community vs. public official toleration,
    259
  community solidarity displays, 259,
    270–3
  community violence, condemnations of,
    273–4
  courts, role of, 280
  dramatic scenario, 257–8
  ethnicity of strikers, 282
  fatalities, 275
  foreigners and agitators, blame on, 276
  Fort William/Port Arthur strike (1913),
    275
  generally, 20–1, 282–3
  Halifax strike (1913), 278
  Hamilton strike (1906), 275, 277, 278, 281
  Industrial Dispute Investigation Act,
    259
  injunctions, use of, 264
  London strike (1899), 276, 281
  militia, use of, 276–9
  Montreal strike (1903), 279, 281
  offences and sentences, 280–2
  police deployment, 264, 275
  police magistrates, role of, 280
  police organization commission, 266
  private police, use of, 280
  public disorder associated with, 259
  public order, calls for, 274
  Railway Labour Disputes Act, 264
  replacement workers, use of, 269, 273
  Riot Act, 265, 266
  Saint John strike (1914), 275, 277, 278
  special constables, use of, 279–80
  state conciliation efforts, 259
  street railway companies, unpopularity
    of, 271
  strikebreakers, use of, 269–70, 273, 280
  support for striker demands, 272
  Toronto strike (1886), 273, 278, 280

644   Index

2009 William Kaplan, *Canadian Maverick: The Life and Times of Ivan C. Rand*
R. Blake Brown, *A Trying Question: The Jury in Nineteenth-Century Canada*
Barry Wright and Susan Binnie, eds., *Canadian State Trials, Volume III: Political Trials and Security Measures, 1840–1914*
Robert J. Sharpe, *The Last Day, the Last Hour: The Currie Libel Trial* (paperback edition with a new preface)

2008 Constance Backhouse, *Carnal Crimes: Sexual Assault Law in Canada, 1900–1975*
Jim Phillips, R. Roy McMurtry, and John T. Saywell, eds., *Essays in the History of Canadian Law, Volume X: A Tribute to Peter N. Oliver*
Greg Taylor, *The Law of the Land: The Advent of the Torrens System in Canada*
Hamar Foster, Benjamin Berger, and A.R. Buck, eds., *The Grand Experiment: Law and Legal Culture in British Settler Societies*

2007 Robert Sharpe and Patricia McMahon, *The Persons Case: The Origins and Legacy of the Fight for Legal Personhood*
Lori Chambers, *Misconceptions: Unmarried Motherhood and the Ontario Children of Unmarried Parents Act, 1921–1969*
Jonathan Swainger, ed., *A History of the Supreme Court of Alberta*
Martin Friedland, *My Life in Crime and Other Academic Adventures*

2006 Donald Fyson, *Magistrates, Police, and People: Everyday Criminal Justice in Quebec and Lower Canada, 1764–1837*
Dale Brawn, *The Court of Queen's Bench of Manitoba, 1870–1950: A Biographical History*
R.C.B. Risk, *A History of Canadian Legal Thought: Collected Essays*, edited and introduced by G. Blaine Baker and Jim Phillips

2005 Philip Girard, *Bora Laskin: Bringing Law to Life*
Christopher English, ed., *Essays in the History of Canadian Law: Volume IX – Two Islands: Newfoundland and Prince Edward Island*
Fred Kaufman, *Searching for Justice: An Autobiography*

2004 Philip Girard, Jim Phillips, and Barry Cahill, eds., *The Supreme Court of Nova Scotia, 1754–2004: From Imperial Bastion to Provincial Oracle*
Frederick Vaughan, *Aggressive in Pursuit: The Life of Justice Emmett Hall*
John D. Honsberger, *Osgoode Hall: An Illustrated History*
Constance Backhouse and Nancy Backhouse, *The Heiress versus the Establishment: Mrs Campbell's Campaign for Legal Justice*

2003 Robert Sharpe and Kent Roach, *Brian Dickson: A Judge's Journey*
Jerry Bannister, *The Rule of the Admirals: Law, Custom, and Naval Government in Newfoundland, 1699–1832*

George Finlayson, *John J. Robinette, Peerless Mentor: An Appreciation*
Peter Oliver, *The Conventional Man: The Diaries of Ontario Chief Justice Robert A. Harrison, 1856–1878*

2002   John T. Saywell, *The Lawmakers: Judicial Power and the Shaping of Canadian Federalism*
Patrick Brode, *Courted and Abandoned: Seduction in Canadian Law*
David Murray, *Colonial Justice: Justice, Morality, and Crime in the Niagara District, 1791–1849*
F. Murray Greenwood and Barry Wright, eds., *Canadian State Trials, Volume II: Rebellion and Invasion in the Canadas, 1837–1839*

2001   Ellen Anderson, *Judging Bertha Wilson: Law as Large as Life*
Judy Fudge and Eric Tucker, *Labour before the Law: The Regulation of Workers' Collective Action in Canada, 1900–1948*
Laurel Sefton MacDowell, *Renegade Lawyer: The Life of J.L. Cohen*

2000   Barry Cahill, *'The Thousandth Man': A Biography of James McGregor Stewart*
A.B. McKillop, *The Spinster and the Prophet: Florence Deeks, H.G. Wells, and the Mystery of the Purloined Past*
Beverley Boissery and F. Murray Greenwood, *Uncertain Justice: Canadian Women and Capital Punishment*
Bruce Ziff, *Unforeseen Legacies: Reuben Wells Leonard and the Leonard Foundation Trust*

1999   Constance Backhouse, *Colour-Coded: A Legal History of Racism in Canada, 1900–1950*
G. Blaine Baker and Jim Phillips, eds., *Essays in the History of Canadian Law: Volume VIII – In Honour of R.C.B. Risk*
Richard W. Pound, *Chief Justice W.R. Jackett: By the Law of the Land*
David Vanek, *Fulfilment: Memoirs of a Criminal Court Judge*

1998   Sidney Harring, *White Man's Law: Native People in Nineteenth-Century Canadian Jurisprudence*
Peter Oliver, *'Terror to Evil-Doers': Prisons and Punishments in Nineteenth-Century Ontario*

1997   James W. St.G. Walker, *'Race,' Rights and the Law in the Supreme Court of Canada: Historical Case Studies*
Lori Chambers, *Married Women and Property Law in Victorian Ontario*
Patrick Brode, *Casual Slaughters and Accidental Judgments: Canadian War Crimes and Prosecutions, 1944–1948*
Ian Bushnell, *The Federal Court of Canada: A History, 1875–1992*

1996   Carol Wilton, ed., *Essays in the History of Canadian Law: Volume VII – Inside the Law: Canadian Law Firms in Historical Perspective*
William Kaplan, *Bad Judgment: The Case of Mr Justice Leo A. Landreville*

Murray Greenwood and Barry Wright, eds., *Canadian State Trials: Volume I – Law, Politics, and Security Measures, 1608–1837*

1995 David Williams, *Just Lawyers: Seven Portraits*

Hamar Foster and John McLaren, eds., *Essays in the History of Canadian Law: Volume VI – British Columbia and the Yukon*

W.H. Morrow, ed., *Northern Justice: The Memoirs of Mr Justice William G. Morrow*

Beverley Boissery, *A Deep Sense of Wrong: The Treason, Trials, and Transportation to New South Wales of Lower Canadian Rebels after the 1838 Rebellion*

1994 Patrick Boyer, *A Passion for Justice: The Legacy of James Chalmers McRuer*

Charles Pullen, *The Life and Times of Arthur Maloney: The Last of the Tribunes*

Jim Phillips, Tina Loo, and Susan Lewthwaite, eds., *Essays in the History of Canadian Law: Volume V – Crime and Criminal Justice*

Brian Young, *The Politics of Codification: The Lower Canadian Civil Code of 1866*

1993 Greg Marquis, *Policing Canada's Century: A History of the Canadian Association of Chiefs of Police*

Murray Greenwood, *Legacies of Fear: Law and Politics in Quebec in the Era of the French Revolution*

1992 Brendan O'Brien, *Speedy Justice: The Tragic Last Voyage of His Majesty's Vessel Speedy*

Robert Fraser, ed., *Provincial Justice: Upper Canadian Legal Portraits from the Dictionary of Canadian Biography*

1991 Constance Backhouse, *Petticoats and Prejudice: Women and Law in Nineteenth-Century Canada*

1990 Philip Girard and Jim Phillips, eds., *Essays in the History of Canadian Law: Volume III – Nova Scotia*

Carol Wilton, ed., *Essays in the History of Canadian Law: Volume IV – Beyond the Law: Lawyers and Business in Canada, 1830–1930*

1989 Desmond Brown, *The Genesis of the Canadian Criminal Code of 1892*

Patrick Brode, *The Odyssey of John Anderson*

1988 Robert Sharpe, *The Last Day, the Last Hour: The Currie Libel Trial*

John D. Arnup, *Middleton: The Beloved Judge*

1987 C. Ian Kyer and Jerome Bickenbach, *The Fiercest Debate: Cecil A. Wright, the Benchers, and Legal Education in Ontario, 1923–1957*

1986 Paul Romney, *Mr Attorney: The Attorney General for Ontario in Court, Cabinet, and Legislature, 1791–1899*

Martin Friedland, *The Case of Valentine Shortis: A True Story of Crime and Politics in Canada*

1985   James Snell and Frederick Vaughan, *The Supreme Court of Canada: History of the Institution*

1984   Patrick Brode, *Sir John Beverley Robinson: Bone and Sinew of the Compact*
        David Williams, *Duff: A Life in the Law*

1983   David H. Flaherty, ed., *Essays in the History of Canadian Law: Volume II*

1982   Marion MacRae and Anthony Adamson, *Cornerstones of Order: Courthouses and Town Halls of Ontario, 1784–1914*

1981   David H. Flaherty, ed., *Essays in the History of Canadian Law: Volume I*